DATE DUE

JY 2 '93			
MY 1 3 '94			

DEMCO 38-296

R

Fodor's

TWELFTH 12th EDITION

China

JOHN SUMMERFIELD

104G003

FODOR'S TRAVEL PUBLICATIONS, INC.
New York & London

MAR '92

DS
712
F6
1991

Fodor's China

Editor: Vernon Nahrgang
Editorial Contributor: Cliff Gaw
Drawings: Alida Beck, David Canright
Maps: Burmar, David Lindroth, Inc., Pictograph
Cover Photograph: Kubota/Magnum

Cover Design: Vignelli Associates

Special Sales

Fodor's Travel Publications are available at special discounts for bulk purchases
(100 copies or more) for sales promotions or premiums. Special editions,
including personalized covers, excerpts of existing guides, and corporate
imprints, can be created in large quantities for special needs. For more
information, write to Special Marketing, Fodor's Travel Publications, 201 East
50th Street, New York, NY 10022. Inquiries from the United Kingdom should
be sent to Fodor's Travel Publications, 20 Vauxhall Bridge Rd., London,
England SW1V 2SA.

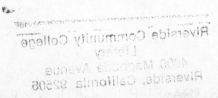
MANUFACTURED IN THE UNITED STATES OF AMERICA
10 9 8 7 6 5 4 3 2 1

CONTENTS

FOREWORD

Startling events in China in June 1989 created renewed interest around the world in this country, its people, and its government's determination to maintain a hard-line political and economic system that other nations were turning away from.

This year's edition of *Fodor's China* takes into account the events of 1989 in Tiananmen Square and elsewhere. The hotels sections for Beijing, Guangzhou, and Shanghai have been reorganized and revised extensively to incorporate new information. Essays on the Chinese people, their history, politics, art, and food are followed by thorough explorations of more than 40 major tourist centers, including the principal cities of Beijing, Guangzhou, and Shanghai.

While every care has been taken to ensure the accuracy of the information in this guide, the passage of time will always bring change, and consequently the publisher cannot accept responsibility for errors that may occur.

All prices and opening times quoted here are based on information supplied to us at press time. Hours and admission fees may change, however, and the prudent traveler will avoid inconvenience by calling ahead.

Fodor's wants to hear about your travel experiences, both pleasant and unpleasant. When a hotel or restaurant fails to live up to its billing, let us know and we will investigate the complaint and revise our entries where the facts warrant it. Send your letters to the editors of Fodor's Travel Publications, 201 E. 50th Street, New York, NY 10022.

Acknowledgment

The author wishes to give special thanks to Valerie for her contribution to the language section, and especially for her help and constant support.

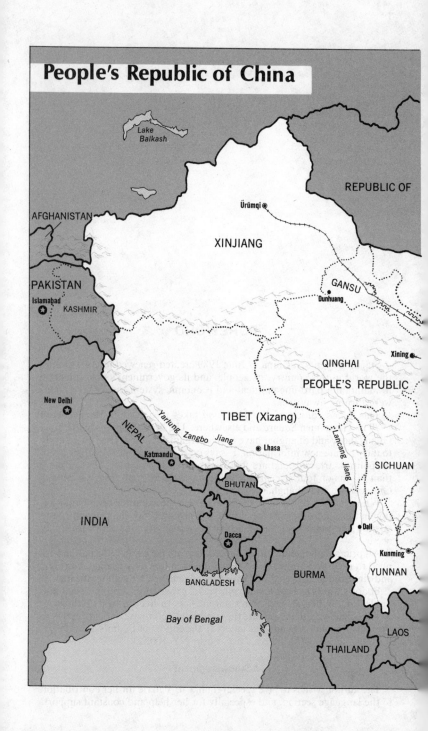

CHINA TODAY

To think of China today is to recall the hope inspired by the democracy movement known as the Beijing Spring of 1989, a movement that was savagely crushed. Although martial law in China was lifted early in 1990, the rest of the world will not forget the events of the night of June 3, 1989, and their aftermath.

The Beijing Spring movement had its origins in the late 1970s, after the "pragmatists" gained control of the Communist Party. Small but significant changes then began to appear in the Chinese way of life, changes that reflected a relaxation of control on the part of the authorities. Yet the easing of control was selective; it did not embrace political freedom. When big-character posters suggesting a "fifth modernization" went up on what came to be known as Democracy Wall in Beijing, the posters were torn down by the police and many of their authors given long jail sentences.

Never stifled, the cry for greater freedom arose again during student protests throughout China in the winter of 1986–87. Hu Yaobang, the Party secretary-general who had been sympathetic to the political reform movement, was dismissed from his post—a victim of the old guard within the Party. Resentment against the regime simmered in the academic community, with open dissent led by the astrophysicist Fang Lizhi and the journalist Liu Binyan.

In the population at large there was increasing suspicion that corruption had become entrenched in the system. Students were angered when authorities reversed an earlier decision allowing graduates to choose their own careers. Then the death in April 1989 of Hu Yaobang—considered a pioneer of reform—sparked the protest movement once more. Big-character posters appeared again on campuses, protesters took to the streets, and a sit-in began in Tiananmen Square in Beijing. When a strike was begun on some 30 campuses around the country, the democratic movement was reborn.

Within days the ranks of the protesters had swelled, as students and academics were joined by workers and bureaucrats. Hundreds of students started a hunger strike to protest the lack of political freedom in China. When Soviet President Mikhail Gorbachev arrived in Beijing in mid-May for the first meeting of the Sino-Soviet heads of state in 30 years, he was greeted as a hero by enthusiastic demonstrators numbering about 150,000 in Tiananmen alone. Days later, more than a million people thronged the center of Beijing—the biggest spontaneous demonstration China had ever seen. On May 19 the authorities responded with a declaration of martial law.

For about 10 days there was a standoff, the demonstrators on one side and the police and the military on the other. On May 30 the Goddess of Liberty, a provocative symbol of the movement's aspirations, appeared in Tiananmen. Behind the scenes, a great debate was going on within the Party, a debate that would be won by the hard-liners.

On June 2 the unarmed soldiers ordered into the city were blocked by the inhabitants of Beijing, and barricades were erected throughout the city. A handful of demonstrators on bikes were killed when a police car rammed into a crowd—the first fatalities since the demonstrations began. On June 3 the police used tear gas and clubs to disperse protesters in Tiananmen, and there were many violent confrontations. By midnight the first tanks had begun to take up positions in the inner city. In the early hours of June 4 the massacre began.

Hundreds of demonstrators were killed during the nighttime repression, and thousands more were arrested in the weeks that followed. There have been reports of hundreds of executions; terror was inflicted throughout the nation.

International condemnation came swiftly. Economic sanctions were imposed and government-to-government programs suspended, leaving the Chinese regime isolated and the economy sliding into a recession. Then, in January 1990, martial law was ended and the country began to return to normal.

One cannot doubt the durability of the Chinese nation. Countries have come and gone, empires have risen and fallen, but China lives on. It has done so for thousands of years.

Perhaps it is the Chinese perception of themselves that has given the nation its survival qualities. There is definite stability in the very symbol of the country, a square with a stroke slashed through it: the world with China at its center—*Zhongguo,* the Middle Kingdom—the place where all must eventually come, bearing tribute.

The name China is said to have come from the word "Qin," which was the name for the dynasty that ruled the first unified empire over two thousand years ago. The name was to travel to the Western world along the dusty "Silk Road," although the West was not to learn anything much about the country or its people until Marco Polo gave his accounts in the thirteenth century. His stories of this incredibly advanced civilization seemed so fantastic at the time that many believed them to be merely beautiful lies. China was then known to the West as "Cathay," from the word "Kitai," the name of a tribe with Mongol affinities that was then living in part of China.

The centuries that passed after the visits of Marco Polo saw increasing contact between East and West. By the mid-twentieth century China had become the People's Republic of China and was organized—paradoxically—on a system inspired by a Western political philosophy (Marxism). It once again became a mysterious, impenetrable land where few foreigners were allowed to enter and even fewer allowed to travel.

The ancient Chinese viewed the passage of history as a series of cycles, of light following darkness, of peace following calamity. This notion remains alive in China today, and perhaps it is this perception that helps the Chinese citizen survive in a changing world.

Consider what has happened in China since the establishment of the People's Republic in 1949. The Chinese people have witnessed a series of political campaigns: the Hundred Flowers campaign, the Great Leap Forward, the Cultural Revolution orchestrated by the Gang of Four, the Four Modernizations, and more recently Economic Readjustment. Each of them was a brainchild of the Party.

The Cultural Revolution, which began in 1966, did not end until the ousting of the "radicals" at the end of 1976. New leaders then revealed that the campaign had not only brought the economy to its knees but had led to the persecution of more than 100 million people. During the transition period at the end of the 1970s, greater liberty of expression was granted—provided that no criticism be directed at the Party, the system, or its leaders.

The 1980s saw a flowering of the arts. Painters took up new subjects. Theater companies produced new plays and revised others that had been banned for decades. Operas were shown throughout the country. Printing houses made the classic works of China and the West available to an eager public. Film studios produced new movies, while cinemas showed Chinese films that had been kept from view for years. Orchestras played a wider range of Chinese and classical Western music, and dance companies revived famous ballets.

With the drive to modernize China came more liberal policies in industry and agriculture, encouraging "more, better, faster" production. In factories, controls became less centralized, management was freed of some of the more intense restrictions, workers were spurred on by incentives, and profits were demanded of the enterprise. On the farms, the new "responsibility system" emphasized private farming and virtually eliminated the rural commune.

The 1980s also brought huge changes in tourism. Hundreds of centers were thrown open to foreign visitors, new hotels of international standard were opened at major tourist destinations, domestic and international air links were expanded, Chinese ports became regular cruise destinations for international lines, and air-conditioned land transport became the norm. Luxury facilities such as country clubs, golf courses, and revolving rooftop restaurants appeared. *Maxim de Pekin* opened its doors in Beijing.

International trade and commerce changed, too. Foreign investment in China was encouraged, foreign technology sought, and foreign advertising permitted. Special economic zones were established for foreign enterprises. Hundreds of foreign firms set up offices in Beijing, Guangzhou, and Shanghai. Billboards advertised a wide range of locally and foreign-produced consumer items. And, above all, the state attempted to streamline administration and improve efficiency in the vast bureaucracy that administers China, perhaps the hardest task of all.

The movement did not emerge again until the winter of 1986–87, this time among the student body, and again it was suppressed. The Beijing Spring of 1989 followed. The political pendulum in China has now swung toward a more repressive form of government at a time when many other communist governments have collapsed. The decision to smash the movement was preceded by a bitter power struggle within the Party, largely unobserved by the Chinese people and the world outside. What will happen in the 1990s? Will the people's desire for some measure of political freedom be extinguished? Or will freedom be won when the last of the old guard disappear?

What is the future for tourism? While the political future may remain clouded for the Chinese people, tourism in China should continue to expand. Tourism has become too important a source of hard currency for the government to abandon it, and China will continue to upgrade accommodations and travel facilities. New tourist centers will be developed, guides and hotel staff will be better trained, and greater efforts will be made to meet the travel requirements of overseas visitors. International air links should expand further, and a wider variety of package tours should become available. The majority of tourists visiting China will continue to embrace the benefits of group travel.

What can you expect to find in China? You will discover that this is a country like no other country you have visited. Although you will notice definite western influences, the nation remains fundamentally eastern in its ways. You will also find that China is still a socialist country, though it may flirt with western economic and business systems. For even though the authorities may be changing the economic ground rules, they are still directing the nation firmly along socialist lines. What you will perceive during your visit is a state under the sway of Chinese-style socialism.

When viewing Chinese society on your journey, you will probably be left with three main impressions: the changes taking place in the socialist state; the impact being made by western influences; and—underlying these—the enduring customs of the East. At a superficial level, socialism is readily evident in the lack of conspicuous private property and in the degree of control exerted over the citizenry, the major change being the new freedom to engage in business privately. The western influence is evident in the new hotels, factories, and planes and trains—indeed in the nation's basic infrastructure. The eastern influence is pervasive everywhere: in language, customs, and social behavior, all of them remnants of the traditional Chinese culture that predates the revolution and stretches back to the dawn of history.

You will certainly notice that the Chinese people are immensely curious about you, your country, and your cultural heritage. They may ask you endless questions about your way of life, but under the present circumstances they are unlikely to raise such issues as democracy and political freedom. While there may be an earnestness in the content of the questions, they will pose them in a friendly and polite manner. "Friend" (*pengyou*) and "friendship" (*youyi*) are important words to the Chinese. These are the natural antidotes to the poisonous national and personal humiliations the Chinese suffered during the foreign occupation of China, humiliations that are even today so sensitive in the Chinese psyche. So if your approach to the Chinese people is gentle, polite, and friendly—and not patronizing—then you will be welcomed everywhere, whatever your nationality.

It is obviously difficult in such a vast country to gain more than a fleeting impression of what "the real China" is like—perhaps there is no real China, perhaps it is always changing before our eyes like a chameleon. Yet a journey through China reveals a lot, even if most visitors start out with only a little knowledge. Whatever doubts may enter your mind about the way of life in China, you are not likely to leave with doubts about the Chinese people. As you travel around, you are in a fine position to observe their behavior.

You will see them working in the fields and in factories, you will see them at recreation in parks and in gardens, and you will even see them at rest, in the backs of trucks curled up on bags of flour. You will see them doing exercises, playing badminton, flying kites, practicing *taiji quan,* playing cards in the streets, reading books under streetlights, practicing musical instruments in the park, and singing by the shores of a lake. Whatever the circumstances, you will find them to be warm, kind, and polite people.

And the scenery. When you enter China you will discover a landscape carved from jade, terraced fields that look manicured, mist-covered mountains that have inspired the poets, vast rivers that can sweep all before them, dusty plains that are gray and barren, gentle lakes that soothe the eye, and grassy foothills that shelter flocks.

A note on the province of Taiwan: This offshore island is considered by the Chinese government to be a province of the People's Republic of China. When in China, it is polite to refer to the island as the Province of Taiwan. *Never* refer to it as the "Republic of China" (the name adopted by the Nationalist forces after they fled to Taiwan).

PLANNING YOUR TRIP

Travel Arrangements

The easiest and least expensive way to get to China is by joining a group tour on an all-inclusive travel-and-accommodation package. Your travel agent will be able to recommend many tour options.

Another way is to join an affinity group or friendship society and participate in a group tour. These agencies are listed in the sections that follow.

Visas allowing visitors to travel throughout China on their own are available. You then have two alternatives: you can "design" a tour, submit it to a travel agency authorized by China International Travel Service (CITS), thereby getting it approved and costed; or you can get a visa, set out for China, and "do it on your own" as a free-lance traveler.

Alternatives to consider when planning a tour are given under Suggested Tours under "Travel in China," later in this section.

Many foreign students are making use of individual travel visas. Others go to China to undertake course work, particularly language training (some courses last only six weeks), then arrange extensive travel around China.

Executives wishing to visit China for business purposes should consult the section *Doing Business in China*.

WHAT IT WILL COST. First you must decide whether you want to travel as part of a package group tour; in an individually planned package tour organized through China International Travel Service (CITS); or on your own— recommended only for the very adventurous who have plenty of time, particularly those who speak and read some Chinese.

The price of an individual "on land" package tour will be provided by China International Travel Service after you have submitted details of the exact itinerary, standard of hotel accommodations, mode of travel, domestic connections, dates of travel, and so on.

If you take an individually planned package tour through CITS, two people who are sharing hotel accommodations and the same car, driver, and guide can expect to spend about US$125–175 per day *each* during a 15-day tour of China. Obviously, this figure varies according to the standard of accommodations and the itinerary followed, but the amount is a useful rule of thumb.

The cost includes hotel accommodations, meals, car and driver, guide services at each town visited, and miscellaneous travel expenses. The figures do not include the cost of banquets, shopping, liquor, and cigarettes. If you request only half-day escorted sightseeing with private car and a guide/interpreter, you can usually reduce your per-person per-day cost considerably. If you request modest hotel accommodations, no meals, and no guided tours, then the cost should come down to about US$75–90 per person per day. However, cost reductions of this nature are available only for certain destinations on the standard tour route: e.g., Beijing, Guangzhou, Guilin, Hangzhou, Kunming, Nanjing, Shanghai, Tianjin, and Xian.

The above costs are based on what might be described as a "standard" tour for a couple spending, say, 5 days at Beijing and 10 days traveling through Nanjing, Suzhou, Shanghai, Hangzhou, Guilin, and Guangzhou.

The figures relate to individually organized travel through CITS and do not apply to visitors on package tours, or to group travel programs arranged by Chinese host organizations. Package and group tours are invariably cheaper.

Tours which include a cruise on the Yangzi River can cost twice as much as a "standard" tour, while tours that include Tibet can go as high as US$300–350 per person per day for on land costs.

The cost of a standard package tour for group travel available from a travel agent normally includes the fares to and from China, fares for on land travel, hotel charges, meals, and sightseeing. The overall cost should be listed in the tour bro-

1

chure. Sometimes fares to and from China and the total "on land costs" are shown separately. All you must do is to take account of any additional money you may need to cover the cost of personal items such as beverages, film, souvenirs, toilet articles, and sundry purchases. A package tour represents the least expensive way of comfortable travel in China, unless you undertake "free-lance" travel—a method that is not for everyone.

Cost of Freelance Travel

The cost of freelance travel depends on how much you are prepared to rough it. You can probably travel for as little as US$20 per day per person for food and lodging if you are willing to "go basic" every day. To this cost you would have to add the cost of transport within China. With plenty of time available and traveling "hard bed" or "hard seat" all the way, you could visit a dozen famous cities for a fare of US$300–450. You will need plenty of time and patience for the continual haggling you will face in order to get the cheapest bed and the cheapest seats on trains and boats. Those travelers with a low threshold of patience should not try to do China on the cheap.

Even a small knowledge of spoken and written Chinese is of help during the haggling process, for many of the railway and hotel clerks at the level you will be dealing with have little or no command of English. If you are not prepared to engage in regular bouts of bargaining, then you will not be able to travel China inexpensively, but you will certainly be able to travel for much less than someone on a package tour, be it on a group basis or individually.

If you want to travel freelance but prefer a modicum of comfort, go (on arrival) to the CITS office of each center you are visiting, and have them arrange a hotel room and your onward transportation to the next point. The CITS office will charge a fee for this and will tend to book you into standard tourist accommodations. They will not book you into a dormitory or provide train tickets at the Chinese price or in hard-seat class. CITS will also arrange your tour program in the particular city you are visiting if you ask them to do this. If you use CITS at every point on your tour, then the per-person cost can rise to US$80 per day and up.

(At press time the exchange rate was US$1 = ¥4.72.)

Cost of Rooms

Hotel accommodation charges are based on a per-room rate rather than the number of persons occupying it. Couples, or travelers sharing a room, are thus able to keep daily per capita costs of accommodation to a minimum.

Most standard rooms accommodating two guests cost about ¥200–275 per day at regular hotels, ¥475–600 and up at luxury hotels of international standard. Rooms are sometimes available at around ¥100 per day in cheaper hotels in major cities and in many provincial capitals.

Dormitory costs have been covered under "Staying in China," later in the section.

Cost of Meals

Two people dining at a leading hotel in Beijing, for example, would pay about ¥35 each for lunch, about ¥45 for dinner, when ordering the set menu.

Meal costs in Shanghai and Guangzhou are slightly more, but in the provinces a little less. Western dishes usually cost slightly more than Chinese dishes.

You should allow US$20–25 per person per day for meals while in Beijing and other major cities and about US$15–20 per day while in the provinces.

Obviously, this amount does not include the cost of banquets, where it is up to the customer to name his price. You may order a Chinese banquet ranging from ¥100 per person to ¥250 and beyond, depending on the type of food ordered and the number of courses. (For advice on ordering banquets consult the chapter *Chinese Cuisine.*)

Cost of Cars

A car and driver can be arranged by your travel guide or by calling the car-rental agency in the center you are visiting. For a standard-size car seating a maximum of 3 people, besides driver and guide, per-kilometer rate is charged. Sites are frequently a good distance from each other—some are miles outside the city or town you are visiting—so that car-hire costs are usually high.

Taxi charges vary from city to city, but are always based on the number of kilometers traveled plus a small hiring tariff. There is also a rate for waiting time but it is generally small. There is no tipping.

Cost of Entertainment

The cost of attending an evening's entertainment, such as an opera, ballet, or concert, is small—usually a few yuan at the most. To this must be added the taxi fare, including waiting time. If you are traveling in a group, all these costs are usually built into the overall cost of the tour.

Air and Rail Fares in China

Keep in mind that China is larger in area than the continental U.S. Even though you will normally spend most of your time in the northeastern and southeastern areas of China, distances can be considerable. For example, the journey from Beijing to Shanghai is about 700 miles by air; Beijing to Guangzhou is about 1,150 miles.

As the following list of fares shows, the cost of a journey from Beijing to Shanghai, to Guangzhou, and then to Hong Kong—all by air in economy class—will amount to about US$200 per person, one way.

Air Fares: Beijing to Shanghai, ¥345; Shanghai to Guangzhou, ¥362; Guangzhou to Hong Kong, ¥198; Beijing to Hong Kong direct, ¥978.

Train Fares: The train from Beijing to Guangzhou, including a sleeping berth in the deluxe car, costs about ¥716 per person. The train fare from Guangzhou to Hong Kong is ¥95 per person. The journey from Beijing to Hong Kong by train therefore costs about US$175 per person, one way—only slightly less than the airfare.

Now consider the cost of fares on what is a "standard" tour of China: Beijing–Nanjing–Suzhou–Shanghai–Hangzhou–Guilin–Guangzhou–Hong Kong:

Beijing to Nanjing: by air	¥290
Nanjing-Suzhou-Shanghai: by rail	¥95
Shanghai-Hangzhou: by air	¥67
Hangzhou-Guilin: by air	¥360
Guilin-Guangzhou: by air	¥147
Guangzhou-Hong Kong: by air	¥198

The total fare on this route would cost about US$245 per person. This amount must be increased for transfer charges between airports/railway stations and hotels. Costs can be brought down considerably if you travel "hard seat." See "Chinese Trains" for further information.

WHEN TO GO. There are no seasonal events in China that draw tourists except the festivities taking place on May 1 (Labor Day) and on October 1 (National Day). The most suitable time to visit is determined almost entirely by climatic conditions. If you have a choice in the matter, you will enjoy your tour much more by going at the right time of year.

China, occupying nearly 3.7 million square miles, is slightly larger than the United States and covers similar latitudes. There is just as much variation in climate among regions as there is within the U.S. If you are visiting for the first time, most of your travel will be in the regional divisions known as North China and South China. These divisions, along with the others shown on the map, are mainly defined by the west-to-east alignment of the more important mountain ranges and by the associated climatic patterns. The dividing line between north and south is the Yangzi River, now known in China as the Chang Jiang.

During your tour you will not range far north of Beijing or south of Guangzhou. The city almost midway between these two is Wuhan. The climate patterns of the areas around these three cities are comparable to those of certain cities in the U.S. when judged by latitude, rainfall, elevation above sea level, and temperature variations throughout the year. On this basis Beijing resembles Philadelphia, Wuhan resembles New Orleans, and Guangzhou resembles Miami. The weather between Shanghai and Guangzhou resembles that of the southeastern coastal states of the United States. However, in China, the rainfall tends to be concentrated over the summer months.

The ideal time to travel in North and South China is autumn, particularly the six weeks or so between the first week of October and mid-November. In the north, during this season, the weather is warm and dry, with the evenings pleasantly crisp. In the middle and lower Yangzi plains the weather is slightly warmer but refreshingly free of high humidity. In lower southern areas, the weather is warmer still but comfortable, with reasonable levels of humidity.

Probably the worst weather occurs midwinter and midsummer. The north of China in midwinter is bitterly cold, being dominated by the movement of dry polar and continental air masses with associated high winds. In summer, particularly during July and August, hot and oppressive weather dominates, caused by the warm, moist air streams of the monsoons from the South and Southeast. About 80 percent of the rainfall occurs between May through October, July and August being the wettest months. The middle and lower Yangzi plains are notoriously hot and humid during this period.

MAKING ADVANCE ARRANGEMENTS. China International Travel Service: The China International Travel Service, or CITS, is the official government agency responsible for "foreign friends" travel arrangements in China. It authorizes travel agents in overseas countries to offer group tours to China with pre-arranged itineraries and costs. CITS also handles arrangements for group travel to China by "affinity groups," e.g., doctors, archeologists, teachers, to name just a few examples, as well as "friendship societies." CITS has established offices overseas to assist travelers, and these are listed below.

In China, CITS branch offices will assist independent travelers and business executives make travel and hotel reservations, as well as obtain tickets for cultural events. CITS will also provide any assistance required to visitors who are on a pre-arranged group tour, although such additional assistance is usually not necessary, because CITS will normally have made all the arrangements on behalf of members before the group arrives.

A sister organization, China Travel Service (CTS), does similar things, but it is set up to help visitors of Chinese origin, e.g., Overseas Chinese, compatriots from Hong Kong and Macau. CTS tours are often conducted in Mandarin or Cantonese.However, if you are in Hong Kong, investigate the tours offered by the "foreign passenger department" of CTS. This department has a wide range of China tours, from one-day visits to nearby centers to visits lasting two to three weeks and longer. CTS-HK will also arrange a visa, normally within two to three days, or on a "same-day" basis (for an additional fee). CTS-HK offices are listed in "Getting to China," below.

China International Travel Service Overseas Offices

France	**Japan**
7 Rue Jean Goujon	1st Floor, AK Building
75008, Paris	6-1, 5 Bancho, Chiyoda-ku
	Tokyo

Hong Kong	**U.K.**
Units 601/605/606	4 Glenworth Street
6th Floor, Tower II	London NW1 5 PG
South Seas Centre, TST	Tel. 01–935–9427
75 Mody Road, Kowloon	

U.S.A.
60 East 42nd Street, Suite 465
New York, NY 10165
Tel. (212) 867–0271

China National Tourist Office
333 West Broadway, Suite 201
Glendale, CA 91204
Tel. (818) 545–7505

TOUR OPERATORS IN THE UNITED STATES. The following companies offer both individualized and package tours.

American Travel Abroad, 250 West 57th St., New York, NY 10107, tel. (212) 586–5230 or (800) 228–0877, offers nine tour packages of 2 to 15 days with optional Asian "extensions" to cities and regions of interest to the first-time visitor. The 12-day "Best of China" tour, about $2,300, includes airfare from Hong Kong to Hangzhou, Shanghai, Beijing, Xian, and Guilin; first-class accommodations, meals, transportation, and extras. Airfare to China is not included.

Pearl Cruises, 1510 S.E. 17th St., Fort Lauderdale, FL 33316, tel. (800) 426–3588 or (800) 338–1700 on the west coast, the pioneer cruise line of the Orient, has a year-round schedule of China cruises. The 18-day "China Dynasty" package includes hotel accommodations before and after the cruise, shore excursions, meals, and transportation. Fares range from $3,395 to $6,750. Airfare to China is not included.

Cameron Tours, Box 709, Alexandria, VA 22313, tel. (703) 836–3555 or (800) 648–4635, organizes special-interest China tours by bike, by rail, by plane, and on foot. Cameron will arrange package tours, partial packages, or individualized tours, depending on the traveler's own interests. The average tour costs around $3,500.

Pacific Select, 1500 Broadway, Suite 2207, New York, NY 10036, tel. (212) 575–2460 or (800) 722–4349, organizes escorted package tours. A 14–15 day tour for around $3,000 includes airfare from the west coast on United Airlines, accommodations in first-class or deluxe hotels, all meals, tours, and transportation between Beijing, Xian, Shanghai, Guilin, Guangzhou, and Hong Kong. Prices of individual packages are higher.

Chinasmith, Inc., 324 W. 42nd St., New York, NY 10036, tel. (212) 239–2410 or (800) 872–4462, follows the Silk Road on a 21-day "Great Wall Tour," with 2–3 day stopovers in nine cities. Accommodations in first-class hotels, meals, and tours are included in the $2,750 price. Airfare can also be arranged. Other tour packages include 3-day cruises on the Yangzi River.

United Vacations, Box 3633, Culver City, CA 90231, a subsidiary of United Airlines, offers 15 package tours of China ranging in length from 2 to 18 days. The "Memorable China" tour visits Shanghai, Beijing, Xian, Guilin, and Guangzhou in 11 days and gives the first-time visitor both an overview of modern China and a historical perspective. The $2,500 price includes accommodations in first-class hotels, all meals, escorted tours, and transportation by land and air between the five cities. Airfare to China is not included. All arrangements with United Vacations must be made through a travel agent.

TOUR OPERATORS IN THE UNITED KINGDOM. The following companies offer tour packages.

Bales Tours Ltd., Bales House, Barrington Rd., Dorking, Surrey RH4 3EJ (tel. 0306–76881), has seven escorted tours to China. Of particular interest is the 15-day Romantic China tour, which visits Beijing, Xian, Shanghai, and Hong Kong; prices range from £1,375 per person.

Globepost Ltd., 324 Kennington Park Road, London SE11 4PD (tel. 071–587–0303) presents a range of specialist tours that includes lotus blossom garden tours; tours by motorcycle, horseback, or train; bird-watching tours; and cooking tours. All tours are fully escorted; prices range from £599 to £2,500 per person, full board.

Kuoni Travel Ltd., Kuoni House, Dorking, Surrey RH5 4AZ (tel. 0306–885044), offers an 18-day China Highlights tour with stops at Beijing, Xian, Nanjing, Wuxi, Suzhou, Shanghai, Guilin, Guangzhou, and Hong Kong, with optional extensions to Japan, Bali, or Thailand. Prices from £1,498 per person, including all meals in China.

Thomas Cook, Box 36, Thorpe Wood, Peterborough, Cambridgeshire PE3 65B (tel. 073–333–0300), offers a 19-day escorted tour that includes a Yangtze River cruise and stays in Beijing, Wuxi, Nanjing, Shanghai, Qingdao, Dalian, Tianjin, and Hong Kong. Prices from £2,195 per person, full board in China.

Sponsoring Agencies for Affinity Travel. The U.S.–China Business Council, Suite 500, 1818 N Street N.W., Washington, D.C. 20036, tel. (202) 429–0340, a membership organization, provides information on U.S.–China trade relations for its corporate business members and potential members.

The U.S.–China Peoples' Friendship Association (USCPFA), Suite 603, 306 W. 38th Street, tel. (212) 643–1525, sponsors language tours and other group tours to China. Association members have varied backgrounds and a common interest in furthering friendly relations between the two nations. The USCPFA quarterly, *U.S.–China Review*, covers current events in culture, politics, and economics.

International Sponsoring Agencies

Australia

Australia—China Society
228 Gertrude Street
Fitzroy, Victoria 3065

Australia—China Business
Cooperation Committee
c/o Confederation of Australian
Industry
Industry House
Barton, Canberra, A.C.T.

Australia—China Chamber of
Commerce and Industry
P.O. Box 4, Wahroonga
N.S.W. 2076
Australia

Austria

Osterreichische Gesellschaft zur
Förderung freundschaftlicher
und kultureller Beziehungen zur
Volksrepublik China
A–1080 Vienna
Wichenburggasse 4/1
Tel. 43.97.93

Belgium

Association Belgique—Chine ASBL
Commission Economique
Rue du Meridian 13
1030 Brussels
Tel. 02/219.22.35
Cable: "Belchina"

Canada

Canada—China Friendship
Association
318 Dundas Street
Toronto, ONT.M5T–1G5
Canada
Tel. (416) 597–0051

Colombia

Asociación de la Amistad
Colombo—China
A.A. 17028, Bogotá

Denmark

Venskabsforbundet Danmark—Kina
Griffenfeldsgade 10, DK–220
Copenhagen
Tel. 01/35.88.11

Federal Republic of Germany

Gesellschaft für Deutsch—Chinesische
Freundschaft
Innsbrucker Strasse 3
1000 Berlin 62
Tel. 030–8545744

Gesellschaft für Deutsch—Chinesische
Freudschaft
Rotlinstrasse 13
6000 Frankfurt/Main
Tel. 069–439163

Ost—Ausschuss der Deutschen
Wirtschaft Arbeitskreis China
Gustav—Heinemann—Ufer 84–88
5000 Köln 51
Tel. 22113708417
Telex, 8882601

Ostasiatischer Verein e. V.
Neuer Jungfernstieg 21
2000 Hamburg 36
Tel. 403562557
Telex. 211728

France

Associations des Amitiés Franco—
Chinoises
51, rue de Rivoli
75001 Paris
Tel. 236–4430

Italy

Associazione Italia—Cina
Via del Seminario 87
00186 Roma

Instituto Italo-Cinese per gli Scambi
Economici e Culturi
Via degli Uffici Vicario, 35 or Via
Carducci 18
00186 Roma 20123 Milano
Tel. 679–7090

Japan

The Association for the Promotion
of International Trade, Japan
(Nihon Kokusai Boeki
Sokushin Kyokai)
c/o Nihon Building
6–2, Ohtemachi 2-chome
Chiyoda-ku
Tokyo 100
Tel. 245–1561

Japan China Cultural Exchange
Association
(Nicchu Bunka Kohryu Kyokai)
c/o Yurakucho Bldg., 10–1
Yurakucho 1-chome
Chiyoda-ku, Tokyo 100
Tel. 212–1766
Cable: NITTYU BUNKA TOKYO

Japan China Association on
Economy and Trade
(Nicchu Keizai Kyokai)
c/o Aoyama Building
2–3, Kita Aoyama 1-chome
Minato-ku, Tokyo 105

Japan China Friendship Association
(Nicchu Yukoh Kyokai)
c/o Toho Yukoh Building
4–1, Nishi-Kanda 2-chome
Chiyoda-ku
Tokyo 101
Tel. 234–4701

Mexico

Sociedad Mexicanna de Amistad con
China Popular
Dakota 74–A, Colonia Nàpoles
Mexico 03810, D.F., Mexico
Tel. 523–2943

Netherlands

Koninklijke Nederlandse Academie
voor Wetenschappen (Royal
Academy of the Sciences)
Box 19121
Kloveniers Burgwal 29
Amsterdam 100 GC
Tel. 020–222902

Vriendschapsvereniging Nederland—
China
(Friendship Association Netherlands—
China)
Box 79
3500 AB Utrecht
Tel. 030–510874

New Zealand

The New Zealand China Society
20 Swanston Street
Auckland
Tel. 32–193

Chinese Social Club
13 Commerce Street
Auckland
Tel. 34–822

Student Travel Bureau
New Zealand University Students'
Assoc.
32 Blair Street
Box 9047
Wellington 1
Tel. 856–669
Telex: NZ 3813

Norway

Vennskapsambandet Norge-Kina
St. Olosfsgate 21C, N–0165 Oslo
Tel. 11.00.57

Philippines

Association for Philippines—China
Understanding
Rm. 215, Luna Consolacion Building
Gen. Santos Street, Cubao
Quezon City
Tel. 78–85–66

Spain

Asociacion de Amistad con el Pueblo
Chino
Calle Azcona 17–4°
Madred 28028
Tel. (91) 246–6068

Sweden

Svenski-Kinesiska Vanskapsforbundet
Maria Prästagardsgatan 31
Stockholm. S-11652
Tel. 08/68.87.50
Cable: Swedschina

Svenski—Kinesiska
Vanskapsforbundet
Lund/Malmo
Box 2044
S–220 02 Lund
Tel. 046/134540

United Kingdom

The British Council
10 Spring Gardens
London, SW1A 2BN
Tel. 01–930–8466
Telex: 916522

Department of Trade and Industry
Trade Promotion with China
Branch
1 Victoria Street
London, SW1
Tel. 01–215–5252
Telex: 8811074

Great Britain/China Centre
(primarily concerned with cultural
educational, and social issues)
15 Belgrave Square
London, SWIX 8PS
Tel. 01–235–9216

The Royal Society
6 Carlton House Terrace
London, SW1Y 5AG
Tel. 01–839–5561
Telex: 917876

Sino-British Trade Council
Abford House
Wilton Road
London, SW1V 1LT
Tel. 01–828–5176

Society for Anglo-Chinese
Understanding
152 Camden High Street
London, NW1 ONE
Tel. 01–485–8236

The Universities China Committe
Regis House
43–46 King William Street
London, EC4R 9AN

Chinese Host Organizations. The nature of the group visiting China determines which Chinese organization will act as your host. For example, the host organization for political and some academic tours is the Chinese Institute of Foreign Affairs. On the other hand, if you are going to China as a member of a sports team or association you will most likely be hosted by the China Sports Association. Business-affinity groups are usually hosted by the China Council for the Promotion of International Trade, or CCPIT. If you are a business executive, then your host organization will be the particular Chinese state trading corporation responsible for the product or service that your company deals in. For example, if you are a buyer or seller of metals, then the China National Metals and Minerals Import Export Corporation will act as host during your visit.

Business visitors wishing to attend the bi-annual Chinese Export Commodities Fair held at Guangzhou must obtain an invitation from a Chinese state trading corporation. (See the *Doing Business in China* chapter.)

If you are a member of a group tour organized by a travel agency, your host will normally be one of the following: the China International Travel Service (CITS); the China Travel Service (CTS), if you are an "overseas Chinese"; or the China Youth Travel Service (CYTS).

The major host organizations in China are:

Chinese People's Institute of Foreign Affairs—The institute normally invites leading members of government, well-known public figures, prominent journalists, members of national opposition parties, and so on.

Chinese People's Association for Friendship with Foreign Countries—This association is largely responsible for cultural exchanges in the field of art, music, literature, and dance. It works directly with national friendship associations in non-Communist countries.

Overseas Chinese Travel Service—This organization handles travel arrangements for Chinese compatriots living outside China. Overseas Chinese represent the greatest proportion by far of all visitors entering China. Group and individual tours are arranged.

Chinese Scientific and Technical Association—This organization sponsors visits by scholars, academics, scientists, and so on; it is not responsible for invitations to members of the medical profession, educators, or architects (see the following organizations).

China Medical Association—This association invites members of the medical profession; it is also responsible for arranging invitations for medical groups wishing to study acupuncture.

Chinese Ministry of Education—The ministry sponsors professional staff, teachers, educators, administrators, and delegations from foreign schools and universities.

Chinese Architecture Society—This society sponsors architects and other members of the profession.

All China Sports Federation—The Federation is responsible for visits by sportsmen and athletes from foreign countries; it also sponsors international sports events in China.

All-China Women's Federation—The Federation sponsors exchanges between women's groups in China and foreign countries.

All-China Youth Federation—The Federation sponsors visits to China by foreign youth organizations, and sends delegations of China's youth abroad.

Chinese Council for the Promotion of International Trade (CCPIT)—The council is responsible for tours by foreign private-sector business groups.

There are many other organizations in China that invite and sponsor foreign individuals and groups, and only the most important ones are listed here. You should note that contact with the Chinese organization is normally through government agencies or quasi-official agencies in your own country, or through a counterpart professional or affinity group of national status.

VISAS. If you are traveling as a member of a package-tour group, then you normally do not need to attend to the matter of getting a visa. Instead, your travel agent or affinity group will take on the task, and your tour leader will be in possession of a "visaed manifest" listing your name and nationality. If you are traveling on a privately arranged tour through CITS, then each individual must obtain a visa. Application for a visa should be made to the Embassy of the People's Republic of China in your country of residence. If you are out of your country, then you may apply to a People's Republic of China embassy or consulate abroad. A list providing many of the Chinese embassy addresses around the world is given below.

Getting a Visa for Free-lance Travel

Visas for free-lance travel within China are now available through many Hong Kong travel agents and at most Chinese embassies and consulates around the world. Such a visa must be obtained by the persons concerned, without the assistance of a travel agent or sponsoring group.

The visa is valid for 90 days from date of issue *but not date of entry* (as used to be the case). You may then travel to any one of the 542 "open" cities, towns, villages, and counties in China. If you wish to visit a place that is not on the "open" list, then after arrival in China you will need to get permission to visit these other cities and towns. These destinations are then listed on your visa.

You can have your visa extended—sometimes twice—for periods varying from 2 to 4 weeks. Since you may not be able to get more than one extension, it may be best to ask for the 4-week extension.

Getting a visa for free-lance travel at a Chinese Embassy or Consulate located in your own country can sometimes be tricky, simply because guidelines for issuing such visas seem to vary greatly from one place to another. Try to get a visa for free-lance travel in your own country but, if you don't succeed, try in Hong Kong, the gateway for free-lance travel.

In Hong Kong you can obtain a visa through China Travel Service (CTS), through CITS, or through authorized travel agencies. Visas are usually granted in two to three days, or on a "same-day" basis for an additional fee. You can get a visa, then make your own travel arrangements, or you can get a visa as part of a rail package to Guangzhou. You should note that a one-day trip to Shenzhen and Macao will not present an opportunity to extend your travel further into China.

If you are traveling by train from Europe or the Soviet Union to Hong Kong, then some P.R.C. missions in Europe will grant you a transit visa valid for a 10-day period in China—and these are sometimes extendable.

Visas on Arrival at Beijing

If you are traveling by air to Beijing from a foreign country you can now arrange to get your visa at Beijing airport, but you must be sure that your passport is in order before you arrive. For example, make sure that the validity of your passport is not due to expire a few days from your date of arrival at the Chinese border. The "visa-on-arrival" has been introduced mainly to assist business visitors. If you are a tourist you should endeavor to get your visa in your home state or in Hong Kong rather than risk being turned back on arrival.

Major Chinese Embassies Around the World

Australia
247 Federal Highway
Watson, Canberra
2600
Tel. 41.24.46

Austria
A-1030 Vienna
Metternichgasse 4
Tel. 75–31–49
Telex: 13–57–94 chinba

Belgium
21 Boulevard General Jacques
1050 Brussels
Tel. 640–4210
640–4006

Canada
411–415 St. Andrew St.
Ottawa, Ontario K1N5H3
Tels:
234–4721 (Cultural)
233–5785 (Military)
234–2718 (Commercial)

Denmark
25 Oeregaards Alle
DK2900 Hellerup
Copenhagen 2900
Tel. (01) 62–58–06

Handelsafdeling (Trade Section)
Oregards Allé 12
DK–2900 Hellerup
Copenhagen 2900
Tel. (01) 61–10–13

France
11 Avenue George V
Paris 75008
Tel. 723–34–45
723–38–43
723–36–77

**Federal Republic
of Germany**
Kurfurstenalee 12
5300 Bonn 2
Tel. 0228–345051

India
50–D, Shantipath
Chanakyapuri
New Delhi 110021
Tel. 69–03–48
69–03–49

Italy
56 Via Bruxelles
Roma 00198
Tel. 884–8186 (Chancery)
865–121 (Consular & Visa)
865–475 (Commercial)

Japan
4–33, Moto-Azabu
3 Chome
Minato-ku
Tokyo 106
Tel. 403–3380

Malaysia
299 Jalan Ampang
Kuala Lumpur
Tel. 42–85–85

Mexico
Av. Rio Magdalena 172
Colonia Tizapán
01090 Mexico D.F., Mexico
Tel.548–1437

Netherlands
Adriaan Goehooplaan 7
Den Haag
Tel. 070–55.15.15

New Zealand
2–6 Glenmore Street
Kelburn
Wellington 5
Tel. 721–382

Philippines
Commercial Office & Consular Office:
2018 Roxas Boulevard
Metro Manila
Tel. 57–25–55; 58–46–36
(Commercial); 57–25–85
(Consular)

Spain
Calle Arturo Soria III
Madrid–28043
Tel. (91) 413–48–91
Telex: 22808 EMCHI-E

Switzerland
Kalcheggweg 10
Bern 3000
Tel. 44.73.33

United Kingdom
31 Portland Place
London W1N3AG
Tel. 636–5726

U.S.A.
2300 Connecticut Avenue N.W.
Washington, D.C. 20008

Tel. (202) 328–2501
Telex: 440038 PRC U1

WHAT TO TAKE. You should bring your own prescribed medicines and, perhaps, some tablets to counter possible stomach upsets and headaches. Also bring your own twin-track razor blades, favorite cosmetics, shampoo, and bath oil, particularly for Beijing where the water is hard.

Bring a screw-top glass or plastic bottle. Fill it with the boiled water found in the thermos flask in your room, and take it with you to sip during your day excursions.

Smokers may purchase most international brands at major hotels and selected stores in cities. Of the large variety of Chinese brands available, "Golden Deer" is said to come somewhat near the flavor of the American "outdoor" type of cigarette.

Local toilet paper and soap are of reasonable quality. You will probably find it wise to bring with you other standard toilet articles even though supplies of the local products are readily available.

You may bring in a camera, 8mm movie camera, or ½-inch video-recorder, plus as much film as you wish for these. Special permission is required to bring in 16mm and 35mm film equipment, as well as 1-inch video-recorders. Chinese customs have the right to examine any film before it is taken out of China, but this regulation is rarely enforced.

Although 35mm color film and black-and-white film is processed locally, results are variable, so photographers usually prefer to have exposed rolls of film processed outside of China, particularly in Hong Kong where processing is cheap. You are advised to bring a good quantity of 35mm rolls as well as movie/video film into China because you can expect to use up a great deal during your stay. However, some foreign-brand color and black-and-white film may be purchased at Friendship stores and in hotel-lobby shops.

Bring a flashlight (or buy one in China) if you are going to visit any of the Buddhist cave sites, because it will add immeasurably to your appreciation of the statues and frescoes.

Business visitors are advised to bring books for their own entertainment; there are many early evenings ahead which cannot be prolonged by the usual distractions present in other international cities. Tourists will usually be tired after each day's full program and will normally not require much reading material. International publications such as *Time* and *Newsweek* are readily available at major hotels.

Western brands of Scotch, gin, and vodka may be purchased at Friendship Stores with foreign exchange certificates, sometimes at prices lower than those in national capitals outside China. Jars of imported instant coffees are available in major cities.

Bring traveler's checks and/or cash because credit card acceptance is still not universal. Personal checks are not usually accepted. Allow five days minimum for cabled funds to arrive.

Take plenty of warm clothing in winter, when temperatures stay below freezing in North China. A hat and thick-soled shoes are essential. Take a sweater any time of the year. In summer, natural fibres are better than synthetics. Bring a light raincoat in the showery seasons and bring (or buy) a collapsible umbrella. Always bring a good pair of comfortable walking shoes, with perhaps a smarter pair for evenings. The golden rule is to dress for comfort but avoid clothing that may offend your hosts (low-cut dresses; brief shorts; g-string bikinis). For detailed information on clothing, consult the section *Staying in China*.

TIPS FOR BRITISH VISITORS. Passports and visas. You will need a valid passport (cost £15) and a visa (cost £20). Get your visa from the Embassy of the People's Republic of China, 31 Portland Place, London WIN 3AG (tel. 071–636–1835). Allow *at least* three days for your visa to be processed. Vaccinations against typhoid are recommended.

Customs. Chinese customs regulations are described below (see *Arriving in China*). Returning to Britain, you may bring home: (1) 200 cigarettes or 100 cigarillos or 50 cigars or 250 grams of tobacco; (2) two liters of table wine with additional allowances for (a) one liter of alcohol over 22% by volume (38.8° proof, most spirits), or (b) two liters of alcohol under 22% by volume; and (3) 60 milliliters of perfume and ¼ liter of toilet water, and (4) other goods up to a value of £32.

Insurance. We recommend that you take out medical insurance to cover your trip to China. It is also wise to take out insurance to cover loss of luggage (though check that this isn't already covered in an existing homeowner's policy that you may have). Trip cancelation is another wise buy. *Europ Assistance,* 252 High St., Croydon, Surrey CRO 1NF (tel. 081–680–1234), offers a good service. The *Association of British Insurers,* Aldermary House, Queen St., London EC4N 1TT (tel. 071–248–4477), will give comprehensive advice on all aspects of vacation insurance.

Getting to China

If you are traveling in a group on a package tour, your route will be known and predetermined, so you can skip this section. However, if you are traveling as an individual tourist you should consult this section carefully. You can save yourself time and money, usually both, by planning in advance. To help you, the following sections deal with the various entry and exit routes and their respective advantages. Flight and train timetables are also provided for this reason, but remember to use them as a guide—the timetables do change, and there are minor seasonal changes as well. Always consult your airline or travel agent to confirm details.

INTERNATIONAL AIR SERVICES. International air services operate between the following cities and Beijing: Addis Ababa, Athens, Bahrain, Baghdad, Bangkok, Belgrade, Bombay, Bucharest, Dubai, Frankfurt, Geneva, Hong Kong, Karachi, Kuwait, London, Manila, Melbourne, Moscow, Nagasaki, New York, Osaka, Paris, Phnom Penh, Pyongyang, Rangoon, Rawalpindi, Rome, San Francisco, Sharjah, Singapore, Sydney, Tehran, Tirana, Tokyo, and Zurich.

If you are traveling via Southeast Asia, there is a service between Bangkok and Beijing, and there are flights from major capitals in the region to Bangkok that allow you to link up with onward flights to China. You can even travel from Rangoon, Burma, to Beijing via Kunming and Xian. Hong Kong is the most popular departure point because it offers the greatest range of flight frequencies to various destinations in China.

If you are traveling from the United States, the most direct routes are via Tokyo, Hong Kong, or Manila. If you are traveling from Europe, the most direct routes are via the Middle East, the Indian-Pakistan subcontinent, or the Soviet Union.

Visitors should note that the Chinese flag carrier, Air China (formerly CAAC), may charge cancellation or no-show fees.

Most passengers entering China do so by way of Hong Kong, Tokyo, or Manila, so let's consider each of these in turn. Each has a tourist fascination of its own, and each presents interesting alternatives in terms of time, money, and connecting travel.

Tokyo to Beijing. There are flights from many other international capitals, but Tokyo is the nearest to Beijing. The fastest direct flight time is about 4 hours. Baggage collection and customs formalities at Beijing will normally take half an hour; the drive from the airport to your hotel takes about 30 minutes. Normally the door-to-door time (allowing two hours for travel and check-in at Tokyo) is about eight hours.

Manila to Beijing. An interesting alternative is to fly to China via Manila, stopping over at Hawaii or Guam en route if you feel like a break.

This itinerary has a number of advantages. You can break the long Pacific crossing into smaller segments, resting up on the way. A luxury hotel accommodation in Manila is probably the least costly in Asia and reservations are usually easy to get (in contrast to Hong Kong). And there are many daily flights between Manila and Hong Kong; flight time one hour 45 minutes.

Hong Kong to China. China is now served by scheduled flights from Hong Kong to many destinations, and numerous charter flights are available. You can fly direct to Beijing, Chengdu, Chongqing, Dalian, Fuzhou, Guangzhou, Guilin, Haikou, Hangzhou, Hefei, Kunming, Nanchang, Nanjing, Qingdao, Shanghai, Shantou, Shenyang, Wuhan, Xiamen, Xian, Zhanjiang, and Zhengzhou. Flights may be booked through CITS, CTS, travel agents, or with the airlines. Timetables vary with the season.

GETTING TO CHINA VIA HONG KONG. If you have decided to enter China via Hong Kong, you may want the assistance of **China Travel Service (Hong Kong)**

Ltd., or CTS-HK. This official "external arm" of China's tourist industry organizes tours to China and arranges tickets, hotels, and accommodations for individual travelers. CTS has also licensed a number of Hong Kong travel agents to do the same. CTS has a head office and branch in Hong Kong Central, and a branch office in Kowloon. There is also a check-in office at Kowloon railway station. The offices are located at: China Travel Service (H.K.) Ltd., CTS House, 4th floor, 78–83 Connaught Road, Central Hong Kong, tel. 853–3533, telex 85222 HCTSF HX, fax 541–9777; China Travel Building, 2nd floor, 77 Queen's Road, Central Hong Kong, tel. 525–2284, cable TRAVELBANK.

If you are staying on the Kowloon side of Hong Kong, the facilities of the branch office will be more convenient; it is at Alpha House, 27–33 Nathan Road, Kowloon, tel. 721–1331, telex 40536 CTSKL HX, fax 721–7157. Although the address of Alpha House is Nathan Road, the actual entrance is around the corner on Peking Road. The best way to locate it is to find the Hyatt Regency Hotel; almost opposite the car entrance ramp, on the other side of the street but slightly to the left, is a small entrance door to CTS.

China International Travel Service (CITS), China's official "internal arm" of the tourist industry, maintains an office on the sixth floor of Tower Two, South Seas Centre, 75 Mody Road, Kowloon, tel. 721–5317, telex 38449 CITC HX, fax 721–7154. There is a branch office of CITS at Room 1018, Swire House, 11 Chater Road, Central, Hong Kong, tel. 810–4282, telex 80325 CITS HX.

Office hours Monday to Saturday are 9 A.M.–1 P.M. and 2–5 P.M. On Sundays and public holidays rail travel inquiries should be directed to the CTS-HK office at Kowloon (Hung Hom) Station, tel. 333–0600.

When visiting these offices always take your passport and travel documents with you, otherwise they will be unable to issue your tickets.

Hong Kong to Guangzhou by Air. Air China operates an air service between Hong Kong and Guangzhou.Flights (35 minutes) depart Hong Kong daily at 9:15 A.M. (except Tuesday and Friday), 11:55 A.M., and 8:55 P.M. Departure times vary with the season.

Tickets: at CITS/CTS(HK); at Air China's general agent, CNAC, 95 Queensway, Central Hong Kong, tel. 861–0288; or at the CNAC office at Hong Kong airport, tel. 769–8571. (Ticketing queries to the CNAC offices are usually diverted to CITS/CTS.)

Hong Kong to Guangzhou by Hovercraft. The Hong Kong and Yaumati Ferry Company runs a hovercraft service between Hong Kong and Guangzhou twice daily. The hovercraft travels at speeds up to 40 mph and carries a maximum of 60 passengers. The trip is highly recommended, though it provides a blurred image of the passing scenery. Departures from Hong Kong are usually at 8:40 A.M. for Zhoutouzui Pier in Guangzhou (3 hours) and 9:45 A.M. for Whampoa Port in Guangzhou (2 hours, 30 minutes).

Check-in at China Ferry Terminal, 33 Canton Road, Kowloon, one hour before departure. Arriving passengers may take a bus to downtown Guangzhou, and taxis are also available.

For the return journey, one hovercraft departs Zhoutouzui Pier for Kowloon at 1:15 P.M., another leaves Whampoa for Kowloow at 2:45 P.M.but the times vary and it is necessary to verify them in advance. Your hotel will arrange a bus or taxi to take you to the appropriate check-in counter. Check-in time is one hour before departure.

Tickets can be purchased at CTS, CITS, and at the China Ferry Terminal.

Luggage: Passengers are allowed to carry 20 kg. to luggage free of charge provided it does not measure more than 4 cubic feet (0.11 cubic meter) in volume. One inconvenience: porter services are sometimes lacking at the embarkation points.

Hong Kong to Guangzhou by Catamaran. The fast boat journey, as distinct from the "slow boat" ferry service listed below, takes about 3 hours, 30 minutes. The catamaran-type vessel departs from the China Ferry Terminal in Kowloon at 8:15 A.M. and arrives at Zhoutouzui Pier in Guangzhou; the return trip departs Zhoutouzui at 1 P.M.

Hong Kong to Guangzhou by Ferry. You may travel to Guangzhou on the ferries M.S. *Tian Hu* and M.S. *Xing Hu,* operated by the Zhujiang Shipping Co. This service operates daily; the *Xing Hu* sailing on "even-numbered" days from Hong Kong and the *Tian Hu* on "odd-numbered" days; no service on the 31st. One vessel departs from the China Ferry Terminal in Kowloon at 9 P.M. and arrives at Zhoutouzui Pier in Guangzhou at 7 A.M.; the return also departs Zhoutouzui at 9 P.M. Both vessels are air-conditioned. Tickets are available at CTS, CITS, and travel agents.

Hong Kong to Guangzhou by Express Train. You may also travel to Guangzhou by the "through train." There are four "up" services daily, departing Kowloon at 8:15 A.M., 9 A.M., 12:25 P.M., and 2:25 P.M., all arriving two hours and 40 minutes later at Guangzhou main railway station.

There is a dining car serving meals during the journey; tea is served in your carriage. The journey on the express train is much quicker than that on the "regular" train (see details next section) and the time of departure is usually more convenient for most travelers (you get an extra half-day in Hong Kong).

The "down" trains depart Guangzhou at about 8:30 A.M., 10:20 A.M., 4:26 P.M., and 6:30 P.M. Reservations may be made up to seven days in advance at CTS, CITS, or travel agents. Tickets for "same-day departure" can be purchased at Kowloon railway station.

Hong Kong to Guangzhou by "Regular" Train. As the Kowloon Guangzhou timetables below show, there are plenty of trains going to the border (Lowu). The journey takes about 1¼–1½ hours. Note that there are no toilets on the electric trains used on this leg of the journey. You are advised to buy your tickets in advance from CITS, CTS, or a travel agent, thereby reserving your seat. This will also ensure that you make a suitable connection at the border; otherwise you may take much longer than the normal four hours to complete the journey to Guangzhou.

On the morning of your departure, go to Hong Kong's Kowloon (Hung Hom) Station to the CTS check-in office. There you will have your tickets confirmed and your luggage checked in.

On arrival at Lowu, you cross the Chinese border at Shenzhen, where you will pass through health, customs, and banking formalities, all in the hands of English-speaking officials. Five trains daily (in each direction) connect Shenzhen with Guangzhou East Station:

Shenzhen to Guangzhou

Dep. Shenzhen	Arr. Guangzhou
9.22	12.54
11.33	14.29
13.00	15.01
15.02	17.50

Guangzhou to Shenzhen

Dep. Guangzhou	Arr. Shenzhen
6.25	8.44
7.32	10.01
9.15	11.20
9.40	15.30
10.02	13.35

Macao to Guangzhou by bus. The bus journey takes 5–6 hours, but you must add to this the time taken to get to Macao from Hong Kong (½–1 hour). CTS will make the necessary arrangements. The CTS Macao office is located at 63 Rua da Praia Grande, tel. 88922 or 88812.

You may travel in the reverse direction by bus. This can be arranged by CITS Guangzhou, or by going to the long-distance bus station at Huanshi Xilu, near Guangzhou central railway station.

There is also an overnight ferry from Macao to Guangzhou and back. Tickets may be purchased at CTS Macao or through CITS Guangzhou.

Hong Kong to Beijing by Train. You may wish to take the train from Hong Kong to Beijing. You can break your journey if you make arrangements before departing from Hong Kong, or stay on the train the full 42 hours. Not for the faint-hearted, this trip—you will spend two nights on the train.

The sleeping accommodation is not too uncomfortable, and as the train is not air-conditioned (except on the section between the border and Guangzhou) the journey is not recommended in warm weather (April to August) unless you need to lose weight. There is a buffet car on board, and the food varies from fair to chewy. It is an interesting exercise to stroll along the platform during the many stops and watch the meat being loaded on board.

The toilet facilities are kept reasonably clean but are nevertheless not favored by the delicate. The most practical solution is to let your mind wander off somewhere else and forget exactly where you are. This condition is sometimes induced by the ammonia fumes anyway.

The train journey, though, will reveal a great deal about rural China, and you will see many beautiful scenes of Chinese peasant life. Another feature is the number of people you will see in the fields every time you look out the window, giving a constant reminder of China's vast population.

Hong Kong to Shanghai by Sea. If you enjoy sea travel, you might care to sail on either the *Haixing* or the *Shanghai* from Hong Kong to Shanghai. These vessels sail once a week and complete the one-way journey in 56 hours. Each is equipped with a swimming pool and a restaurant. The service is run by China Merchant Steamship Navigation Ltd. Tickets may be purchased from CTS, CITS, or travel agents. prices vary according to the standard of cabin required.

The name of the vessel *Mariposa* will evoke pleasant memories for those who once cruised in the Pacific. Now completely refitted and known as the MV *Jin Jiang,* the ship retains its old-world charm on the Hong Kong to Shanghai run twice a month. The ship's facilities include a pool, half tennis court, minigolf, a theater, and a library; its restaurant serves Continental and Chinese food, with specialties in Shanghai cuisine. Departures from Hong Kong are at noon on the 12th and 27th of the month, arrivals off Shanghai's Bund at 7:30 A.M. three days later. Departures from Shanghai are at noon on the 4th and 19th of the month, arrivals in Hong Kong at 8 A.M. three days later. Tour packages allow a return flight from Shanghai with an optional stopover in Hangzhou. Reservations can be made with Jin Jiang Travel (HK) Ltd., Room 1810, Wing On House, 71 Des Voeux Road, Central Hong Kong, tel. 868–0633, telex 81154, fax 810–4246; and at travel agents.

Hong Kong to Other Centers by Sea. The many vessels that ply the China coast range from fast catamarans to stately old steamships. The following schedules are listed by destination.

Fuzhou by ship (11 hours), MV *Li Jiang* departs Hong Kon 8 A.M. (even-numbered days), departs Fuzhou 7:30 A.M. (odd-numbered days).

Jiangmen (near Macao) by ferry (3 hours, 30 minutes), MV *Yin Zhou Hu* departs Hong Kong 1 P.M. departs Jiangmen 8:15 A.M.; MV *Peng Lai Hu* departs Hong Kong 8:10 A.M. departs Jiangmen 1:30 P.M.; MV *Wu Yi Hu* departs Hong Kong 9 A.M., departs Jiangmen 2 P.M.

Shenzhen (Shekou Port) by hovercraft (45 minutes), departs Hong Kong 8, 8:20, 9:30, 10:15 A.M., 2, 3:30, and 4:50 P.M.; departs Shenzhen 8:15, 9:15, 10:45 A.M., 2:30, 3:15, 4:25, and 5 P.M.

Taiping by ferry (2 hours, 15 minutes), MV *Liu Hua Hu* departs Hong Kong 8:45 A.M., departs Taiping 3:30 P.M.

Xiamen by ship (20 hours), MV *Jimei* departs Hong Kong 2 P.M. Tuesday and Friday, departs Xiamen 3 P.M. Monday and Thursday.

Zhaoqing by ferry, MV *Duan Zhiu Hu* (5 hours) departs Hong Kong 7:45 A.M. (even-numbered days), departs Zhaoqing 2 P.M. (odd-numbered days); MV *Xi Jiang Hu* (12 hours) departs Hong Kong 7:30 P.M. (odd-numbered days), departs Zhaoqing 7 P.M. (even-numbered days).

Zhongshan (Siqi or Shekkei) by ferry (1 hour, 45 minutes), MV *Xiu Li Hu* departs Hong Kong 7:30 A.M. and 1:30 P.M., departs Zhongshan 10:30 A.M. and 4:30 P.M.; MV *Yi Xian Hu* departs Hong Kong 8:40 A.M. and 2 P.M., departs Zhongshan 11:45 A.M. and 4:45 P.M.

HOTELS IN HONG KONG

Kowloon

Ambassador	26 Nathan Road, Tsimshatsui	tel. 366–6321
Bangkok Royal	2 Pilkem Street, Yaumatei	tel. 735–9181
Chungking	40 Nathan Road, Tsimshatsui	tel. 366–5362
Empress	17 Chatham Road, Tsimshatsui	tel. 366–0211
Grand Tower	627 Nathan Road, Mongkok	tel. 789–0011
Guangdong	18 Prat Avenue, Tsimshatsui	tel. 739–3311
Holiday Inn Golden Mile	46 Nathan Road, Tsimshatsui	tel. 369–3111
Holiday Inn Harbour View	70 Mody Road, Tsimshatsui	tel. 721–5161
Hyatt Regency	67 Nathan Road, Tsimshatsui	tel. 311–1234
Imperial	32 Nathan Road, Tsimshatsui	tel. 366–2201
International	33 Cameron Road, Tsimshatsui	tel. 366–6430
Kowloon	19 Nathan Road, Tsimshatsui	tel. 369–8698
Miramar	130 Nathan Road, Tsimshatsui	tel. 368–1111
New Astor	11 Carnarvon Road, Tsimshatsui	tel. 366–7261
New World	22 Salisbury Road, Tsimshatsui	tel. 369–4111
Nikko	72 Mody Road, Tsimshatsui	tel. 739–1111
Omni Hong Kong	3 Canton Road, Tsimshatsui	tel. 736–0088
Omni Marco Polo	Canton Road, Tsimshatsui	tel. 736–0888
Omni Prince	Canton Road, Tsimshatsui	tel. 736–1888
Peninsula	Salisbury Road, Tsimshatsui	tel. 366–6251
Ramada Inn Kowloon	73 Chatham Road, Tsimshatsui	tel. 311–1100
Ramada Renaissance	8 Peking Road, Tsimshatsui	tel. 311–3311
Regal Airport	30 Sa Po Road	tel. 718–0333
Regal Meridien	71 Mody Road, Tsimshatsui	tel. 722–1818
Regal Riverside	Tai Chung Kiu Road, Shatin	tel. 718–0333
Regent	Salisbury Road, Tsimshatsui	tel. 721–1211
Ritz	122 Austin Road	tel. 369–2282
Royal Garden	69 Mody Road, Tsimshatsui	tel. 721–5215
Shamrock	223 Nathan Road, Yaumatei	tel. 735–2271
Shangri-La	64 Mody Road, Tsimshatsui	tel. 721–2111
Sheraton Hong Kong	20 Nathan Road, Tsimshatsui	tel. 369–1111
Windsor	39 Kimberley Road, Tsimshatsui	tel. 739–5665
YMCA	Salisbury Road, Tsimshatsui	tel. 369–2211

Central Hong Kong

Asia	1A Wang Tak Street, Happy Valley	tel. 574–9922
Caravelle	84 Morrison Hill Road, Happy Valley	tel. 575–4455
China Merchants	160 Connaught Road, Western	tel. 559–6888
Emerald	152 Connaught Road, Western	tel. 546–8111
Excelsior	281 Gloucester Road, Causeway Bay	tel. 576–7365
Furama Intercontinental	1 Connaught Road, Central	tel. 525–5111
Grand Plaza	2 Kornhill Road, Quarry Bay	tel. 886–0011
Harbour	116 Gloucester Road, Wanchai	tel. 574–8211
Harbour View International House	4 Harbour Road, Wanchai	tel. 520–1111
Hilton	2 Queen's Road, Central	tel. 523–3111
Lee Gardens	Hysan Avenue, Causeway Bay	tel. 895–3311
Mandarin Oriental	5 Connaught Road, Central	tel. 522–0111
Marriott	88 Queensway, Central	tel. 810–8366
Park Lane Radisson	320 Gloucester Road, Causeway Bay	tel. 890–3355
Ramada Inn Hong Kong	61 Lockhart Road, Wanchai	tel. 861–1000
Victoria	200 Connaught Road, Central	tel. 540–7228

AIRLINES OFFICES IN HONG KONG

Air Canada, tel. 522–1001
Air China (CNAC), tel. 861–0288
Air India, tel. 522–1176
Air New Zealand, tel. 524–9041
America West, tel. 525–7081
British Airways, tel. 868–0303
British Caledonian Airlines, tel. 868–0303
Canadian Airlines, tel. 868–3123
Cathay Pacific Airways, tel. 747–7888
China Airlines, tel. 868–2299
Delta Airlines, tel. 526–5875
Dragon Airlines, tel. 810–8055
Northwest Airlines, tel. 810–4288
Pakistan International Airlines, tel. 366–4770
Qantas Airways, tel. 524–2101
Trans World Airlines, tel. 525–4189
United Air Lines, tel. 810–4888

CONSULATES IN HONG KONG

Australia, tel. 573–1881
Canada, tel. 528–2222
Eire (Republic of Ireland), tel. 367–5151
India, tel. 574–9106
Mexico, tel. 521–4365
New Zealand, tel. 526–0141
Pakistan, tel. 527–4623
United Kingdom, tel. 523–0176
United States, tel. 523–9011

Arriving in China

ENTRY FORMALITIES. A foreign visitor must undergo passport, health, customs, and currency formalities prior to entering China.

If you enter China by regular train from Hong Kong, these checks take place at the border post of Shenzhen. If you take the "through" train from Hong Kong to Guangzhou, the formalities take place on arrival. This applies also if you go by hovercraft or by boat.

If you arrive on the Trans-Siberian from Moscow, the checks are made at the border posts of either Manzhouli (Sino-Soviet border) or at Erenhot (Sino-Mongolian People's Republic border).

Passengers arriving on international flights undergo these formalities at their port of entry, e.g., Beijing, Shanghai, Guangzhou.

The first control point you will encounter in China will check your passport to insure that it is in order and that the visa entry is correct.

HEALTH DOCUMENTATION. The second control point will check your health documents. Usually there is no need for evidence of inoculations on entering China, unless you have come from or through an area where an epidemic has broken out recently. For example, if you are entering China from certain regions of India, Pakistan, Burma, Thailand, Malaysia, Indonesia, the Philippines, and some other countries you may need cholera shots. If in doubt, check with your travel agent well before you are due to set out on your journey.

If you are arriving from an African or Latin American country where yellow fever is prevalent, a valid yellow fever certificate is also needed. Typhoid shots may also be advisable in view of confirmation by the Chinese authorities that this disease has been detected, especially in some coastal areas.

If you are traveling on an assignment that will keep you in China for more than a year, you will be required to be tested for acquired immune deficiency syndrome (AIDS). Diplomats are exempt from this rule.

CUSTOMS. At the third control point you and your baggage will be subject to customs formalities. Chinese Customs authorities classify visitors in three groups when assessing duty on the goods being brought by them into the P.R.C.

The first group are foreigners who are not residents of the P.R.C. and who are traveling in China for business or tourism. These visitors are allowed to bring in two liters of liquor, 600 cigarettes (or the equivalent in tobacco products), one pint of perfume, and an unlimited amount of medicines for personal consumption. Business machines imported for temporary use are exempted from duty.

The second group are Overseas Chinese—foreign citizens of Chinese origin, foreign citizens who are residents of China, and Chinese citizens who have been abroad to visit relatives. Visitors entering China under this category are permitted to bring in a certain quantity of goods duty-free, and a limited quantity of goods subject to customs duty. The list of duty-free imports (and exports) permitted visitors under this category is available from Chinese embassies and consulates abroad, or from CTS (Hong Kong).

The third category for customs purposes comprises Hong Kong (Xianggang) and Macao (Aomen) "compatriots." Visitors from these territories make up the largest proportion by far of all travelers entering China. Subject to payment of import duties, Hong Kong-Macao compatriots above the age of 16 can bring into China one (and only one) of the following six "luxury items"; television set, watch, camera, radio, tape recorder, or electric fan. One mini-electronic calculator may be imported *per visit* upon payment of 20 percent duty.

Prohibited imports: arms and ammunition, explosives; wireless receivers and transmitters (other than a personal radio); Chinese currency, Chinese drafts and bills, stocks and bonds; live animals and birds; printed material detrimental to the politics, economy, culture, or ethics of the People's Republic of China, opium, morphia, and poisons, strong poisonous drugs; lottery tickets.

Prohibited exports: articles of historical value (see later under "Shopping"); literary works of historical value; the first four categories under prohibited imports; foreign currency, all foreign drafts and bills except those previously declared to and registered by Chinese customs on arrival.

After carrying out the inspection of a passenger's luggage, the Customs Administration may exempt goods from import duty, even though there are dutiable items in the visitor's possession.

Customs Declaration. Whatever your "category," you are required to make out a customs "baggage declaration" specifying your valuables, such as cameras, typewriter, etc. You may bring in an electronic calculator, wristwatch, pocket watch, radio, tape recorder, cassette player, camera, and movie camera and film for personal use. (Special approval is required for 16mm or 35mm movie cameras and 1-inch video recorders.) You must keep the baggage declaration for your departure.

Customs Formalities on Departure. When departing China, keep all "declared" articles readily available because customs officers are likely to want to inspect them. Do not give away any "declared" item while in China, otherwise you will have to explain why it is not in your possession and then pay duty.

"Cultural relics" may not be taken out of China unless they have been officially approved for export (usually a red seal in wax or an export certificate authorized by the Cultural Relics Administration). Make sure that for each cultural relic purchased you have a receipt stamped "Foreign Exchange Purchase."

Currency Declaration. When you make out your baggage declaration form for customs, you will be expected to declare "Chinese and foreign currencies, bills, and cheques," including traveler's checks, in the space provided on the form. Once you have declared your foreign currencies, in whatever form, you will then be able to buy "foreigners' banknotes," officially called "foreign exchange certificates" (see section under this title below), as well as Chinese bank notes (see "Money" below).

There is no limit on the amount of traveler's checks, letters of credit, and drafts that you may bring into China. Each time you change money you will be given an exchange slip or receipt recording the amount of the transaction. Do not lose your currency declaration form or any of the exchange receipts. These are required by the currency-control desk when you are leaving China. An official will compare the amount exchanged with the amount originally declared.

It is illegal to take Chinese banknotes out of China, and unwise to do so, since the RMB cannot be exchanged by banks outside. Normally you can exchange any FEC (foreign exchange certificates) that you may have in your possession on departing China, providing your currency documentation is in order.

MONEY. Chinese currency is called *Renminbi*. The expression literally means "the people's currency" and is often abbreviated to RMB. The unit of currency is the yuan, although the term *kuai* is generally used when speaking about sums of money.

All notes and coins have Western numerals, so you will find them easy to identify. The largest note is Yuan 100, written ¥100; other notes circulated are ¥50, ¥10, ¥5, ¥2, and ¥1. Smaller notes are also used: ¥0.50, ¥0.20, ¥0.10. The Yuan is composed of 100 fen. Ten fen equal 1 Jiao (known as "Mao"). There are 5-fen, 2-fen, and 1-fen coins.

Remember to take your currency declaration form (the one you filled in at the border) with you whenever you change money. Each time you will receive a currency exchange slip recording the transaction. When you leave China the amount exchanged is subtracted from the amount declared. All exchange receipts should be retained until you leave China.

Credit Cards: The Bank of China will issue cash against presentation of certain international credit cards, but only in a limited number of cities in China, although it applies a hefty commission charge. Check credit-card companies before you depart for China because additional arrangements are under negotiation. Eight credit cards are currently accepted: American Express, Visa, Master-Card, Diners Club, East Americard-Visa, Federal, Million, and JCB. Credit cards may also be used for shopping in a limited number of Friendship stores and antique shops. The Great Wall credit card has been issued by the Bank of China for use in China only.

Traveler's Checks. The Bank of China in Hong Kong now issues traveler's checks in Chinese currency and these may be cashed throughout China. Any checks left over at the conclusion of your tour may be reconverted into other currencies. Traveler's checks in major currencies such as U.S. dollars, German marks, British pounds sterling, Swiss francs, and Japanese yen are all acceptable.

Staying in China

MEETING YOUR HOSTS. Chinese Names. Chinese family names are always placed first, with the given name following, *e.g.,* Huang Hua. This is the equivalent in English of saying "Smith John." You would normally address such a person as Mr. Huang, the given name being used by a close friend or a member of the family. A wife usually retains her maiden family name. For example, the wife of Mr. Huang may be Mrs. Chen.

The given names are not merely a means of address, as in English, but also have a meaning, such as "strong and capable," "cool-headed and upright," and so on.

Chinese family names are almost always of one syllable and are therefore fairly easy to remember. Never resort to the use of nicknames when in China.

Dress. Older men and women often wear the "Mao suit," known to the Chinese as a "Zhongshan" suit (named after Sun Zhongshan, the other name for Sun Yatsen). In wintertime this suit is worn over numerous layers of warm underclothing, while in summertime the jacket is removed and a short-sleeved open-neck shirt or blouse is worn. Chinese dress is thus simple and unpretentious. This should be the rule also for visitors to China.

The normal attire for male visitors to China depends upon the function and the weather. During warm weather there is no need to wear a jacket: slacks and an open-neck shirt are quite suitable. The same attire can be worn by a business executive attending negotiations.

If you attend a formal banquet in hot weather you may prefer to wear a jacket, although you will find that these are usually taken off during the meal. For this reason safari suits are popular with visitors; they are ideal for the hot months yet convey a more formal impression.

In colder weather men will find that the most convenient attire is a jacket and tie or a suit.

The form of dress for women is also determined greatly by the weather. In the hot months standard-length simple dresses and slacks are the most practical form of clothing. In the cooler weather slacks are usually worn and are perfectly acceptable even on formal occasions. Women's attire should preferably be plain and simple. The more flamboyant Western styles may cause some embarrassment because of the attention they attract from curious onlookers. It is also a good idea to avoid plunging necklines and the excessive use of jewelry.

Both men and women should consider bringing a comfortable pair of rubber-soled walking shoes for sightseeing and visiting communes and factories.

If you are visiting China for the Guangzhou Fair only, dress is casual; the weather there during the spring and autumn is generally warm to hot. All that is required is an open-neck shirt or a blouse to be worn with slacks. Take a sweater for the evenings, especially if you are visiting during the autumn fair.

If you intend to travel to Beijing and other cities in northern China between mid-November and the end of March, you should be prepared for very cold conditions. Bring warm boots or good shoes that keep out the cold, and warm caps or hats to protect you from the chilling winds.

Punctuality. The Chinese place emphasis on punctuality, and you will be expected to arrive on time for your appointments and social functions.

If you are hosting a social function at a restaurant, you should arrive there at least a quarter of an hour in advance. Your Chinese guests will arrive exactly on time, sometimes even a few minutes early.

Greetings. When you are meeting Chinese, always bear in mind that physical contact such as back-slapping or hugging, as well as gestures of affection such as kissing on cheeks, will not usually be understood by the Chinese and may cause embarrassment. However well disposed you may feel towards your hosts, try to avoid these forms of behavior. Obviously you should always avoid any boisterousness.

A good guide is to treat your Chinese hosts in the same way they treat you: be reserved and polite. This does not mean you have to put aside your natural charm and humor or become unduly serious. Act naturally, but in a manner that is perhaps more restrained than your normal behavior in the West.

When you visit schools, factories, communes, or theatres, the local people may clap as you arrive. It is polite to clap in return, and you will quickly find that this is a very pleasant exchange.

Chinese Morality. The Chinese people have a strict code of morality, and in their society, infringements are dealt with severely. So as a visitor you should avoid any frivolous or flirtatious display of affection towards the opposite sex; it may be completely misinterpreted.

Gifts. The presentation of gifts to Chinese is a practice that requires good judgment and common sense. At high official levels it is acceptable as a gesture of friendship between nations; at lower levels of the hierarchy the practice could be seen by the authorities as a soft form of corruption. Many traders and investors have used "gifts" as a way to hasten the progress of negotiations, and some have been subject to pressure by their Chinese counterparts for Western goods. Although campaigns against corruption have been conspicuous in recent years, the practice of gift giving seems to be increasing.

The average tourist, whether traveling alone or with a group, will rarely need to present gifts. If a need does arise, standard gifts that are usually presented are framed paintings and books, particularly technical books or books depicting the flora and fauna of your own country.

You may wish to present badges or mementos to individuals, but do not press them upon the recipients if there seems to be any reluctance on their part.

COMMUNICATION. You will find that most of the staff at leading hotels will speak some English although they may not be very fluent. When you attend meetings or have appointments with Chinese organizations, interpreters will be provided, but they vary from excellent to poor.

There are certain points to keep in mind when you are working through an interpreter. Their observance will mean the difference between good communication and a lack of understanding on the Chinese side.

Keep your sentences short and simple. Pause at the end of each sentence to allow the interpreter to translate the sentence into Chinese. If you make your sentences short and pause after each one, the meaning of each sentence should be conveyed in translation to your audience. However, if you make your sentences too long or run many sentences together, the translator will tend to summarize what you have said and thereby effectively lessen the content of your communication.

You should try to speak to the point, speak slowly, and speak distinctly. Do not use slang, unusual words, or elaborate or flowery phrases; these may confuse the interpreter and lead him to make an incorrect interpretation. When you ask a question, be direct rather than skirt the issue.

When you are attending meetings on your tour or are involved in business negotiations with the staff of Chinese organizations, you may wish to take full and detailed notes. You will find that this is a practice frequently adopted by the Chinese themselves. Many China traders even bring their old notebooks with them in case they need to refer to earlier negotiations. And most keep notebooks with them at all times, ready to use at a moment's notice.

While note-taking and the keeping of notebooks is in order, the Chinese will rarely if ever allow you to make tape recordings of your business negotiations and dealings with them. Their attitude is far more flexible toward requests to record discussions at the meetings that inevitably occur when you are on tour and visiting factories, communes, and cultural organizations.

FOREIGN EXCHANGE CERTIFICATES. You will be expected to pay for most goods and services in hotels and shops by using "foreigners' banknotes," called "foreign exchange certificates." You obtain this form of banknote when exchanging traveler's checks, drafts, or foreign currencies at branches of the Bank of China.

These special banknotes are issued in denominations of 100, 50, 10, 5, 1, and 0.10 yuan. While they are equal in value to the local currency used by the Chinese, they are different in appearance. They are easily distinguishable from local money because on the reverse side is printed "Foreign Exchange Certificate."

Chinese authorities announce periodically that FECs will be phased out, but no date for this action has been set and no advice provided on what alternative will be provided, if any.

Foreigners may also still use the standard form of Chinese banknote called *Renminbi* for purchases in taxis, restaurants, and *local* shops. When changing money, you should specify the "mix" of "certificates" and local money that you require. All Chinese banknotes must be exchanged before you leave China. The authorities will convert FECs into foreign currencies when the bearer leaves China.

It is illegal to buy goods in China using a foreign currency. If you are asked by anyone to do so, resist the temptation, because such transactions are against Chinese law.

HOTELS. The Chinese International Travel Service usually arranges hotel bookings, and you will generally find that you have little choice. However, the new international-standard hotels accept direct bookings from outside China, either from individuals or travel agents, through the international hotel reservation network. Many of these hotels are booked out 2–3 months in advance in peak travel periods (April–June, September–October) and are heavily booked in other periods.

Rates. Room rates vary from city to city, but the following rates will serve as a guide. At deluxe hotels in Beijing a standard twin-bedded room starts at about ¥375 per day. At minor hotels in Beijing, a twin-bedded room costs ¥200–275 per day. Rates in provincial cities usually vary from ¥80 at modest hotels to about ¥275–375 per day at international-standard hotels. Foreigners traveling privately pay 100 percent of these room rates, while foreigners in touring parties pay 90 percent. Overseas Chinese and citizens of Hong Kong pay 90 percent of the rate when touring privately, or 70 percent when members of a touring party.

During the winter an additional 15 percent is sometimes levied for heating, and during the hot summer months a small additional charge is added if an electric fan or air-conditioning is provided. The practice of adding these charges varies from hotel to hotel.

Hotel Service Counters. The older hotels usually have a service counter on each floor as well as a general service counter on the ground floor. You may pick up your laundry at the floor service counter, order drinks and other beverages and ice, and book international telephone calls. Deluxe hotels of international standard provide all these facilities by way of room service.

Hotel staff in the older establishments are not particularly well-trained or speedy in their tasks, so you will need to demonstrate patience. They are often young boys and girls who are students undergoing language training. They are keen to please and will usually treat you with unfailing courtesy. If you adopt a friendly and pleasant approach, they will in return do all they can to help you; an aggressive attitude will probably bring negative results. They will appreciate your thanking them for any service or assistance, but never offer a tip.

Hotel staff in deluxe hotels vary in performance. Some are excellent and up to international standard; others are slow or ineffective and still require proper training.

Telephone operators have difficulty with Western names. Therefore, if you want someone to contact you, provide them with your hotel room number.

Storage at Hotels. Some hotels offer storage facilities, a service that can be particularly useful if you are on tour or returning to the same city just before departure from China.

Regular business visitors to the Guangzhou Fair often leave their stationery and equipment in storage pending their return. The maximum period of storage is usually six months. The general service counter will make arrangements for you and advise you of the charge.

Items to be stored are always inspected; no food, beverages, or explosive materials may be locked away.

DORMITORIES. Dormitory beds, although difficult to arrange, are very cheap in China: about US$3–5 per person per day. Often those Chinese hotels that possess dormitory accommodations are not allowed to offer them to foreign visitors. However, in the larger tour centers there is usually at least one hotel able to offer a dormitory bed to anyone who asks for it. In smaller Chinese cities and in small towns off the beaten track, dormitory accommodations may be difficult to find; in some places there are none available. Generally speaking you will not expect to find cheap accommodations in an establishment describing itself as a "binguan" so you should try to find a "luguan" or "fandian."

Your negotiating tactics might also be important in gaining you access to a dormitory. Often you will be told that the dormitories are completely full when in fact they are not. Sometimes you will be told that there has been a recent fire in the dormitory or that it was swept away in the last typhoon. If you are polite with the receptionist and are prepared to wait many hours, you may succeed in getting access to that full, burnt-out, or water-logged dormitory. Just tell the receptionist that you will wait until a bed becomes available and often, within half a day, you may be given a bed. But you will need to pick your target carefully because there is no point trying this in an establishment that has no dormitory accommodations. Under these circumstances your wait may be a long one indeed.

Keep in mind too that most dormitory accommodations in China are unheated in winter and uncooled in summer. Usually there are plenty of blankets available so the first need not be a problem; but the heat, humidity, and insects in an uncooled room in summer can make life pretty unbearable. Some travelers thrive in primitive conditions, others wilt. Know thyself and choose accordingly.

Once you have managed to stay in a dormitory, keep the receipts, for they will be useful when haggling at other destinations. You can then demonstrate that you have stayed in cheap accommodations elsewhere, thereby helping your case.

DINING. When in China you will have the opportunity to eat delicious Chinese meals and be exposed to a new range of taste experiences. Anyone who enjoys Chinese cuisine at home will relish the opportunity to expand his range, for there are dishes to be enjoyed in China that are not available at home. And for the few who don't enjoy Chinese cooking, don't despair: almost all the hotels serve Western-style food.

Prepaid group tours usually have meals included in the price of their tour, so visitors in this category will normally be provided with a menu that has been fixed in advance. Other visitors can go to the hotel restaurant and eat Chinese (or Western-style) food by selecting from the menu, i.e., à la carte.

You should always ask whether there is a "fixed menu" when ordering Chinese food. This is usually the most economical way of ordering Chinese dishes. The fixed menu may not always be displayed, so you need to ask. If you are not understood, ask for "feng fan," which is the Chinese expression for a fixed menu.

It would be a pity to visit China and not try a meal in one of the top restaurants outside of your hotel. To allow you to do this, we have listed suggested restaurants for the centers described later. You can go in a party of two, or organize a group of 8–10 or more. At popular restaurants you should always make a reservation. The hotel can arrange this for you.

If you decide to arrange a banquet, the hotel clerk will again help, but you will need to tell him how much you want to pay per person (excluding drinks), and whether you have any requests for special dishes. If you decide to leave the selection of dishes to the restaurant, always check their suggested menu: they may put in an expensive dish that no one will like (e.g., sea slugs). If they do, ask for another choice. Banquets must always be ordered in advance, at least 24 hours ahead.

You can also ask the hotel clerk whether the restaurant you want to visit serves a fixed menu (again, "feng fan") or will serve à la carte, for sometimes you and your party may not want to indulge in a banquet with many courses.

At restaurants located outside of hotels you will eat in private dining rooms, shut off from "the masses" who eat where it is noisy, smoky, and none too clean. You should arrive on time, for a late arrival is considered rude behavior.

The table will normally be set with chopsticks. If you prefer to use a knife and fork, ask for them. Often the table will be equipped with a lazy susan to allow each dish to be moved easily from one guest to another. If there isn't one available, use two hands when passing the dish to your neighbor, as a gesture of politeness.

If you have arranged for a group to eat à la carte (or are arranging a banquet), a good rule of thumb is to choose one dish per person, then one extra one, plus rice and/or noodles. In other words, if there are 6 in the party, order 7 dishes plus rice/noodles. In China, the dishes ordered are usually served consecutively, not all together. For this reason, it is better to order a range of dishes that complement each other.

For more guidance on dining out, consult the *Chinese Cuisine* chapter.

Formal Banquets. You may be invited to a formal or official banquet during your visit to China, and there are certain social conventions that you should know about.

You will always be met on arrival by your host and often ushered to lounge chairs where you will sit and exchange polite conversation over tea. A light bantering mood usually prevails during this period. After about five or 10 minutes your host will usher you to the table.

The host will begin the banquet by serving you food with the long chopsticks which are set before him. He will invariably make a speech a short time after the banquet commences, and you, as the guest of honor, will be expected to reply. Your reply may be made immediately or after one or two more courses are eaten.

Frequent toasts are made, the first one only after the host has made his speech. Ensuing toasts may involve the whole table or simply the Chinese sitting on either side of you. It is not considered discourteous for nondrinkers to avoid the potent *maotai* liquor and make a toast with mineral water, soft drink, beer, or wine.

If you are the guest of honor you will be expected to leave with members of your party before your hosts. You will know the meal is over when a large bowl of fruit is served. Hot towels are usually distributed at the same time so that you can wipe your face and hands.

It is polite to depart about 10 minutes after the towels have been passed and the last cups of tea served.

Evening banquets usually begin early, 6:30–7 P.M., and end early, around 8.30 P.M.

Full details of dining customs are given in the chapter *Chinese Cuisine*.

Beverages. Foreign beverages are available in China at leading hotels and Friendship stores. These include not only whiskey, gin, rum, cognac, champagne, and wines (from France, Germany, Italy, Spain, and the United States) but also Coca-Cola.

Local vodka is quite drinkable, but Chinese whiskey bears little resemblance to the real thing. Local gin is not available.

At Chinese banquets you will undoubtedly be served maotai, a potent, colorless alcohol that is fortunately used only for toasts. Most visitors manage to get used to it, but you are advised to approach it with caution. Bottles may be purchased locally, should you wish to amuse or astonish your friends when you return home. Maotai is a superb gift for the friend who "has everything."

Lao Shan, the Chinese alkaline mineral water, is of good quality and available in two forms, still and carbonated. It is often served at banquets. The label declares that it is "good for chronic affections of the urinary organs . . . gout and other troubles of the stomach."

Most brands of local beer are of good quality and inexpensive. Some are produced in breweries that were taken over from Europeans during the revolution. The most sought-after brands are Beijing and Tsing Tao, although sometimes these are not available in the provinces. Another whose quality has improved greatly in recent years is the Wu Xing-Five Star brand.

There is a limited range of local soft drinks available, mostly lemonade or orange flavor, and you can buy canned juices, such as orange, lemon, grapefruit, and tomato.

You may wish to experiment with various local wines by trying different ones with your meals. The best known red wine is Shaoxing, a rice wine that is usually served warm in small porcelain cups. The reds are fairly sweet and heavy, tending towards port, while the dry whites often have a taste reminiscent of the *retsina* wines of Greece. You may also care to sample the local champagne, a fairly sweet beverage which, if nothing else, has the advantage of being inexpensive.

Some wines are more than they seem. For example, Chiu Lu wine, according to the label, has "the efficacy of stimulating spirit, invigorating heart, producing fresh blood, strengthening stomach, and preventing vomition."

If you buy white wine at the store, ask the room attendant at your hotel to have it chilled. You can then drink it in your room or take it to your table in the restaurant.

At small provincial hotels, if you like a glass of cold beer with your meals, you should order it chilled in advance; that is, during the preceding meal; otherwise you will probably have it served warm. This is usually not a problem at the leading hotels in the major cities.

Tap water is generally not safe to drink, so you should take care only to drink (and brush your teeth with) the boiled water that is placed in the carafe in your room. There is usually also a vacuum flask of hot water in your room for tea or coffee. Remember that you can always use the hot water for general drinking purposes by pouring it out and allowing it to cool. That is why it is a good idea to carry on your daily excursions a screw-top bottle filled with water that has been boiled.

TIPPING AND BARGAINING. You may cause embarrassment, perhaps even offense, if you try to tip. However, with the greater influx of travelers, the practice is on the increase. Do your bit for tourism and don't tip.

Bargaining is practiced in China only at the "free markets," especially where there are stands selling antiques or second-hand goods. About the only other place that you can bargain is at commission shops and antique stores, where a gentle suggestion about an "adjustment" in price is not out of place. Bargaining in any other situation is rare.

LAUNDRY. Same-day laundry service is available in the larger hotels throughout China but less frequently in the provincial cities.

Generally speaking, you will find the laundry service at the cities you would normally visit to be adequate for your purpose. You may find it useful to include at least one drip-dry article, such as a shirt or blouse, to get you through periods when your stay is too short to utilize the laundry service.

Dry cleaning is available in the major cities and usually takes 24–48 hours. It is not always of a high standard.

BARBERSHOPS AND BEAUTY SALONS. Most hotels in China have a hairdressing salon of a reasonable standard. In Beijing, Shanghai, and Guangzhou the leading hotels all have both men's and women's salons. In the provinces some hotels provide hairdressing service, but quality varies.

You may take your own shampoos, conditioners, or sprays into salons for use by the hairdresser. Do not expect fashionable or elaborate stylists and cutters to be available, except in salons located within luxury hotels.

ELECTRICITY. You should bring your own hairdryer and electric razor. American visitors should also bring a small transformer (110v. to 220v.) and a few three-prong (flat, not round prong) plugs. Sometimes your hotel will supply plugs; they are also available at the Friendship stores in large cities.

Hotel rooms will normally be supplied with 220-volt 50-cycle service. Both the 220 volt (50-cycle, single phase) and 380 volt (three phase) systems are in use throughout China.

Electricity in rural areas is often in short supply, but the major cities are adequately served most of the time. However, city voltage can sometimes drop to as low as 190 volts. This variation creates no real problems for any hairdryers and electric razors brought in, but there may be a need for a stabilizer for sophisticated business equipment.

NEWSPAPERS. Many foreign newspapers and magazines are available in China at hotel lobbies and foreign bookstores, e.g., *Time, Newsweek, Asian Wall Street Journal, The New York Times.* There are Chinese publications that appear daily in English; one, the *China Daily,* has coverage of both Chinese and international events.

RADIOS. You may wish to bring a short-wave radio receiver; it is possible to receive clear transmissions from Voice of America, BBC, Radio Japan, and Radio Australia. This is probably not advisable for someone on tour, but it is a good idea for business visitors who are likely to stay in one city for a lengthy period.

TELEPHONING. Local intracity calls are free; international calls are priced according to destination and time, the minimum charge being based on a three-minute call. The clarity of international calls varies enormously: sometimes you have to shout to be heard, while at other times reception is perfectly clear. After you book a call it may take several hours to get through, but this will depend on the destination and the amount of traffic on the line.

The deluxe hotels offer direct-dial facilities to other countries on the latest push-button telephones. However, at the older hotels and in the provinces, when you wish to book a long-distance call you will normally have to go to the lobby floor and fill in the information on a small form. You must then go back to your room and wait for the connection. The operator who makes the call on your behalf will normally speak English, and demonstrate patience and courtesy. After you have been connected you should time the call yourself; the operator will not cut in to advise that the minimum period of three minutes is approaching. Usually when you have completed the call and hang up, the operator will ring you back to ask whether you have finished. It is useful at this time to ask how long the call took and what the charge will be.

If you want to know the rates for international calls, ask at your hotel. Collect calls are usually cheaper because rates in the receiving country are often less than those applied in China.

If you are expecting an international call, it will help if you telex or cable your hotel's name and your room number to your caller. The room number is most important; telephone operators often have difficulty understanding Western names, and hotel reception desks are frequently careless about guests' room numbers.

To assist you with your international calls, a table showing the time around the world is given in the following section. Remember to exercise the usual caution when conducting sensitive conversations by telephone.

POSTAL SERVICE. Surface mail, airmail, parcel post, air parcel post, and registered mail services are available at post offices. All leading hotels in major cities have a post bureau or center providing standard services.

Airmail letters take about 5–6 days between Guangzhou and New York, for example, and vice versa. Private airmail letters from Beijing to New York take about 10 days, while Chinese state-trading corporation letters take about 5–6 days. Airmail letters from New York to Beijing take about 10 days. Delivery times to and from Europe are similar.

Telex and Cable Services. Telex service is available covering most destinations. Telexes can be sent from most of the deluxe hotels or from the main post and telegraph office in the city you are visiting.

At some telex offices you may be expected to punch your tape on a tape-cutting machine. Once you have done so, go to the counter and book your "call" by filling out the telex form. You may then have to wait from anywhere between five minutes to several hours, depending on the time of day and telex traffic. When the call comes through, go to the assigned cubicle and feed in your tape. Beginners should request the assistance of one of the Chinese attendants. (Rates now vary from center to center; and also from hotel to hotel.)

Cable service is available to almost all destinations. LT (night letter), Ordinary, and Urgent rates apply. Cables may be sent during business hours from the post office situated in leading hotels or from the main telegraph office of the city you are visiting.

PHOTOGRAPHY. Use discretion when taking photographs. In principle you can photograph most things except military installations. Sometimes these may be difficult for the visitor to recognize; the authorities may regard a harmless-looking area such as a railway yard as a "military installation." By the same token, military personnel will normally object to having their photographs taken.

Exercise the same caution that you would in any foreign country when photographing individuals. Normally you should ask first. Authorities do not like visitors to photograph people or activities in a way that appears to be emphasizing poverty.

SHOPPING. You will enjoy shopping in China; there is a host of things to buy. Purchases may be made only with "foreigners' money," i.e., with your foreign exchange certificates.

You will probably find that the Friendship Store in any city you are visiting is the easiest and most convenient place to shop. It is set aside especially for the foreign visitor and usually contains the full range of Chinese products that are available for sale. However, if you have more time, you may care to visit the local department stores and local shops to see what they have to offer. A tour of local shops will reveal the wide range of products available to the Chinese family, and represents one of the best ways of mingling with the Chinese and getting a "feel" of their way of life.

Most cities you will visit will have an antiques shop, and you should ask your guide to take you there. Sometimes these are located in the Friendship Store in a special section, and sometimes they are separate. In the larger cities there are usually a number of antique stores. They display a huge range of items, from small and inexpensive stone chops to large and costly porcelains. There is an array of tiny yet reasonably priced antiques that make wonderful mementoes of your visit or admirable gifts, and possess the obvious advantage of taking up little space in your luggage. But if you see articles which are too large to carry back, you can arrange to have them exported to your home address. Remember that an antique should carry a wax seal indicating that it is authentic and is able to be exported from China. Make sure that your purchase is recorded on your currency declaration form, and keep the receipt given to you by the shop.

China has, of course, been famous for its silks for centuries, and you will find an excellent range at reasonable prices. Ladies' silk scarves make excellent gifts, as do gentlemen's silk ties. Chinese cashmere garments are of superb quality and are attractively priced. Wool garments, particularly sweaters, are also excellent values.

You will find the linen and tableware to be a good value. However, cotton sheets and towels, while inexpensive, usually feature unexciting designs. There is a superb range of basketware, caneware, pottery products, and general arts-and-crafts items, and all these are usually priced to suit your pocket. The country is, of course, the home of chinaware, and there are some excellent bargains to be had. You may find many of the styles overly ornate, but if you look carefully you will certainly find something suitable. Obviously it is preferable to have chinaware packed for export and delivered to you back home.

Leather and fur garments are popular items; the quality is good and the price low. But try on such garments carefully: sometimes the cut may not be up to standard, and use your nose to detect any unusual odors. With careful selection you can come away from China with leather or fur garments that are attractive and priced far below similar garments on sale at home.

Details of shopping facilities along with regional specialties are given in the sections devoted to the various cities.

EVENING ENTERTAINMENT. All modern hotels in China have bars, cocktail lounges, or "pubs," many of which offer music in the evenings, often played by groups. Nightclubs in the larger hotels may have a floor show, but usually they are discos, some of them with the most sophisticated sound and light equipment.

Only a handful of bars exist in China outside the international hotels, and they are not usually patronized by foreign visitors. A few discos exist outside the hotels, and they are occasionally attacked in the local press for attracting the attendance of "roadside chickens" (the Chinese expression for prostitutes). However, by Western standards, these discos are about as racy as a Cornish floral dance.

Cultural Performances. Most visitors to China like to experience cultural performances that are not normally available at home; they look for evening activities that are peculiarly Chinese in nature.

You may wish to see one of the modern variations of the famous Peking Opera in major cities. A number of stage plays have been revived and are playing to packed houses. Most are in Chinese, but there are Western plays, even Shakespearean classics, being performed.

Concerts, both Chinese and Western, and sometimes featuring repertoire from both cultures, are given regularly. Many Chinese films are showing, some with themes that were once taboo. A limited selection of American, English, and European films are screened. So too are films from Japan, Hong Kong, and India.

Most visitors like to see the Chinese acrobatic troupes and, even more colorful, the Chinese circus. You may also be invited to a Chinese sporting event in the evening: table tennis, gymnastics, or a football game.

So, between evenings of banquets and evenings of these entertainments, you will find there will be little time for writing letters, compiling notes, or simply putting your feet up. Your hotel or CITS will be pleased to arrange tickets for any of these performances.

HEALTH. Sometimes visitors to China get colds or sore throats due to the dry, dusty environment, but do not be unduly alarmed if you develop such a condition. You may also get stomach upsets at some stage, and it is therefore advisable to bring appropriate tablets with you. These minor stomach problems last only a short while and appear to be caused by too much of the unfamiliar fatty food. If you do come down with a gastric complaint and wish to maintain your schedule, you should carry a supply of the local toilet paper with you, since bathrooms are not always well-equipped. If a gastric condition persists you should ask to receive medical attention, though instances of serious stomach upsets are rare.

The golden rule for visitors to China is: "Don't drink the tap water." Hotels always provide boiled water for each guest room. Use it—even to brush your teeth. If you are going on an excursion and you tend to get thirsty, then take a small bottle of boiled water from your room to sip during the day.

In the tropical areas of South China, viral encephalitis and outbreaks of malaria can occur. These are mosquito-borne diseases and are more prevalent in rural areas. Visitors to urban areas have a lower exposure to these diseases. Nevertheless, try to avoid mosquito bites, by sleeping under mosquito nets, wearing "cover-up" clothing during the day, and applying insect repellent to bare skin. Of course, mosquitos are more active at dawn and, particularly, at dusk.

Do not be alarmed by these remarks. They are made to help you avoid ill-health during your visit to China. The actual incidence of such diseases is extremely low among the millions of visitors China receives each year.

MEDICAL SERVICES. Medical services are available in cities where tourists normally visit. An interpreter should be used to describe other than obvious, simple ailments. Your hotel will quickly arrange a visit by a doctor or escort you to a hospital should you require medical attention.

Hospitalization is rarely free of charge, but payment is expected to cover the cost of medicine and drugs. Information about hospitals is provided for all major centers.

SECURITY. China is one of the safest places in the world for personal security. You can walk almost anywhere at any time and be safe. The only security measure you need adopt is to lock the door of your hotel room when going out; and keep your pocketbook and wallet secure when outside in a crowded place.

EMERGENCIES. If you encounter an emergency situation in your hotel, the hotel staff will be your first point of contact for assistance. You will find them to be attentive, resourceful, and considerate in the face of any emergency situation you may be confronting.

If the emergency is medical, then they will either summon a doctor or nurse, or arrange for your transport to a hospital, usually by taxi—because Chinese ambulance services are not well developed.

If the emergency involves your urgent departure from China, the hotel staff will contact CITS to arrange for prompt attention to your travel requirements. They will also ensure that any international messages you need to send are given priority. However, in hotels with direct-dial international services and telex facilities, communication with the outside world presents no problems.

If you notice a fire in your hotel, contact hotel staff immediately. The same applies to any incidence involving your personal security or someone else's.

The chance of emergency events occuring to you is extremely low, and millions of visitors tour China annually without the need for emergency services. However, all the information you need has been included in this book.

NATIONAL HOLIDAYS. New Year's Day, 1 January; International Working Women's Day, 8 March; Labor Day, 1 May; Youth Day, 4 May; Children's Day, 1 June; Founding of Communist Party of China, 1 July; People's Liberation Army Day, 1 August; National Day, 1 October. Also Spring Festival (late January or early February).

LOCAL TIME. Beijing standard time applies throughout China. Therefore Beijing, Guangzhou, Shanghai, and all major cities are on the same time. China now observes daylight-saving time, which begins in April and ends in September.

Time Around the World. When it is noon in Beijing, Guangzhou, and Shanghai, the standard time in other cities of the world is:

City	Time	City	Time
Bangkok	11:00	New York	23:00*
Bombay	9:30	Osaka	13:00
Cape Town	6:00	Paris	5:00
Delhi	9:30	Rome	5:00
Geneva	5:00	San Francisco	20:00*
Hong Kong	12:00	Singapore	11:30
London	4:00	Tokyo	13:00
Manila	12:00	Vienna	5:00
Melbourne	14:00	Washington, D.C.	23:00*
Mexico City	22:00	*Wellington	16:00
Moscow	7:00		

*denotes previous day.

WEIGHTS AND MEASURES. Most of China's business is conducted in the metric system. The Chinese system of measures is limited to agricultural accounting and shopkeeping. The main units are:

1 Jin (catty)	=	1.102 lbs	=	0.5 kgs
1 Dan (picul)	=	0.492 tons	=	0.5 tonnes
1 Mou	=	0.165 acres	=	0.067 hectares

Travel in China

CHINA'S TRAVEL SERVICES. China International Travel Service (CITS) is responsible for making travel and tour arrangements for non-Chinese individuals, tour groups, and professional bodies visiting China. The organization will arrange guide services, interpreters, accommodation, transport, meals, sightseeing, and all other services required.

Once you have arrived in China your travel arrangements will normally be handled by CITS. CITS arranges transfers from trains or planes to hotel, baggage transfers, guide services, hotel bookings, and the delivery of tickets. The headquarters' address is China International Travel Service, East Changan Street, Beijing, People's Republic of China; Cable: "Luxingshe" Beijing, tel. 557558, 557496, 551379.

CITS-authorized travel agencies in your country work alongside CITS in China to achieve the necessary "ingredients" for a tour.

When in China, members of an all-inclusive package group or affinity group tour will be in daily—but indirect—contact with CITS branch offices, as the guide assigned to the group at each center will act as liaison officer. Any special requests for assistance outside that already "built in" to the tour program can be conveyed by the guide to the CITS branch office in any particular center. For example, you may have learned of a cultural event that you want to attend on a free evening. Your guide in that center should be in a position to obtain tickets, if available, through the CITS branch office. Consult the "Guide Services" section below.

By contrast, a free-lance traveler on an unprogramed tour of China, will usually be in regular contact with CITS branch offices in China, as he or she makes arrangements for the next leg of the journey (unless direct contact is made with ticket offices of regional airlines or with the rail/bus/boat companies responsible for the next connection in the journey). For this reason, CITS branch offices have been listed under "Tourist Information" in the "Practical Information" section for each center.

GUIDE SERVICES. When you travel in China as a member of a tour group, you will be assisted by a guide provided by CITS. The guide acts as your interpreter and is there to help you get the most from your visit.

Unless you are part of a VIP delegation, a new guide will take care of you in each city. The guide will see you off at the airport or railway station, and you will be met upon arrival at your next stop. Guides do not usually travel in China with you.

Guides are like people everywhere: some have sparkling personalities and some are rather dull; some try hard while others take the easy way out. Their language ability runs the full range from first-class to poor. They do possess one thing in common: unfailing politeness and courtesy. When you consider the large number of people they have to deal with each year, all asking much the same questions about the same things, you will begin to appreciate their impeccable manners even more.

The guides may represent the only opportunity you will have in China of forming a "normal" relationship with a Chinese person. And, with rare exceptions, they will win you over by their manner and their dedication to China.

If you are traveling privately under a visa that permits individual travel, you will not encounter the guide service nearly as often. While this may present some disadvantages, these are usually more than offset by the direct contact you will have with Chinese people. Such encounters can sometimes give you a rare insight into the Chinese way of life.

PASSPORTS. When you are traveling on a group tour, your escort will usually be in possession of a "visaed manifest" listing the names and nationalities of all members on the tour. Group tourists are rarely required to surrender their passports to authorities, but, of course, passports may be inspected at any time.

If you are traveling independently and wish to visit a center that is not "open" for foreign visitors, you will need to have your visa noted accordingly. Since you

MAJOR DOMESTIC AIR ROUTES

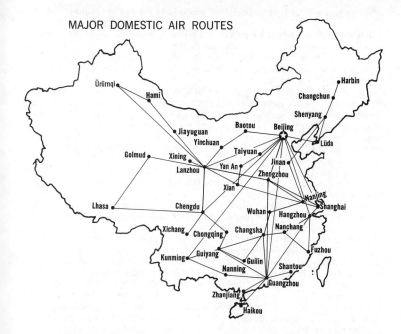

will be traveling "off limits" you may expect to have your travel documentation regularly checked by authorities, hotel clerks, ticket sellers, and so on.

Remember, without special permission you are not allowed to stop at any center that has not been declared to be open for tourism. If you ignore this advice, you may be apprehended at the railway station when you get off the train. If not, you will certainly be checked on arrival at a hotel and your presence reported to the local authorities. You may be detained, then put on a train for the nearest open city or even sent out of China. The choice will not be yours. However, it has been known for an independent traveler to turn up in a small town not listed on the travel permit and be allowed to stay. Generally speaking, taking such a course is not worth the risk.

CHINESE AIR SERVICES. Chinese domestic flights provide a host of alternatives for the traveler, as the accompanying map reveals. The network is administered by the Civil Aviation Administration of China (CAAC). Operations are in the hands of six new companies, each based on one of the former regional branches of CAAC: Air China (Beijing), China East Airline (Shanghai), China South (Guangzhou), China Southwest (Chengdu), China North (Shenyang), and China Northwest (Xian). All international flights are operated by Air China. Within China, tickets may be purchased at CITS or direct from regional airline offices. Note that the regional ticket offices in many centers still bear the old name CAAC or may appear under joint names.

CHINESE TRAINS. Train fares are almost as expensive as plane fares, unless you travel "hard seat."

Soft Seat. The top category for day travel in Chinese trains is "soft seat" in a "soft carriage." The seats are well-padded, comfortable, and may be reclined. The carriage is usually "open" in construction and kept very clean.

Soft Sleeper. You should consider this class of travel for any overnight journey. The "soft-sleeper" compartments are comfortably furnished, the seats on either side give accommodation for four, with overhead bunks of the same width providing sleeping accommodation for the two who are to sleep "up top." The floors are carpeted, and there are usually pairs of plastic sandals provided for each passenger—

although you will not squeeze into them unless you have feet as small as the Chinese.

Pillows and hand towels are provided. There is a small table under the window on which you will find a lamp with a gaudy hexagonal shade. You will also find large cups, with lids, for your tea. Under the table there is a large thermos of hot water which will be refilled by the cabin attendant. He will also provide sachets of tea ("cha") for a few fen.

You should look carefully beneath the table to locate the volume control for the radio speaker in each compartment. Every compartment contains an oscillating electric fan which, in summer months, mercifully circulates some air. For some reason, perhaps attributable to the incipient madness of your cabin attendant but more likely related to an instruction he has received on reducing maintenance on the fan's circuitry, the master switch is sometimes thrown during the night to bring your fan and all air circulation to a halt.

Dining Car. There is a dining car, and meals are usually ordered in advance. A waiter will come to your compartment with a menu to take your order and will come to get you when the meal is ready.

Beer and soft drinks are available, but more often than not are served at room temperature. Red and white Chinese wines can also be had. It is a good idea when ordering your meal to ask the waiter to put a bottle on the ice.

Hard Seat. At the other end of the comfort scale, traveling "hard seat" can save you a lot of money and the description is not as bad as you might think. The seat, padded thinly under the vinyl cover, is quite comfortable for day travel. Most Chinese travel hard seat or hard sleeper so you will find yourself among the locals.

It is important to realize that the purchase of a hard-seat ticket does not guarantee you a seat. To have a seat assigned to you for the journey you need to make a hard-seat reservation. Otherwise you will have to stand or sit in the aisles. The hard-seat sections of the train are very crowded and noisy; the light is on all night.

Hard Sleeper. If you are a budget traveler undertaking a long journey, you may want to consider paying a supplement to travel "hard sleeper." This consists of six bunks in a compartment, three on either side, each provided with a thin mattress, sheets, a pillow, and a blanket. The loudspeaker system and lights are turned off during the night so sleep is possible. To reserve a hard sleeper, go to the special counter established for this purpose or pay a supplement at the hard-bed carriage.

Tickets. Ticket offices throughout China will sell you a ticket from any location in China to any destination. However, you can only reserve a seat or a sleeping berth for your immediate journey, not for any other destinations after the first break in your journey (although these are a few exceptions to this).

You may purchase your ticket for long-distance travel and break your journey at will provided the center is fully open for visitors, or provided you have a permit to visit. If you break your journey, you must go to the ticket office to have your ticket restamped. This procedure often takes less time than purchasing a new ticket for the next leg of your journey. Even when you are arriving at your last destination, carry your ticket with you as you will always be checked when you are leaving the station.

LINER SERVICES. China has an active liner service operating between ports along the coast. Vessels from Hong Kong to various destinations have been listed in the "Getting to China" section. Vessels from other Chinese ports to destinations on the coast are listed in the "Practical Information" section for a particular center. For example, the section for Shanghai explains about vessels to Qingdao, Dalian, Tianjin, and so on.

Ferries. The ferry service along China's inland waterways is extensive. Many of the vessels are not suitable for the visitor used to standard conveniences and a modicum of comfort, but are often used by the young budget traveler. However, some vessels have been upgraded for foreign visitors while others have been specially designed for tour purposes. These will provide you with a wonderful means of traveling between centers and, at the same time, give you a close look at China's river life and countryside.

The most celebrated boat journey inside China is the trip along the Yangzi (although some visitors have expressed disappointment in this voyage). Perhaps the

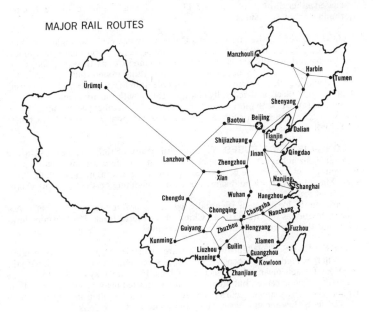

MAJOR RAIL ROUTES

best-known trip is the day excursion down the Li River from Guilin. The river systems at Guangzhou and Shanghai also provide the opportunity for excursions.

Free-lance travelers have a host of opportunities to explore, because of the greater flexibility that their tour program provides.

TAXIS. Taxis can be arranged for through the lobby desk of your hotel. If you can speak Chinese you can call a taxi yourself; consult the chapter dealing with the city you are in and you will find the number to ring. In most centers, taxis cannot be hailed in the street.

Drivers do not usually speak English, so tell the dispatcher where you want to go and whether you want the driver to wait for you. If you have a number of destinations, get the desk clerk to write down the name and address of each destination in Chinese.

Usually it is a good idea to have the taxi wait for you after you reach your destination, unless you are going to spend a considerable time there. There may be a delay of 30 minutes to an hour at certain times of the day before your next taxi will arrive. Waiting time is relatively inexpensive.

In some centers, taxis are equipped with meters. In others, the driver calculates the cost according to the mileage and waiting time and presents you with tickets representing the fare to be paid. Sometimes the fare for the same run may vary from trip to trip, but not by very much. Often the driver cannot give you change, so it pays to carry plenty of small notes and coins. Failing that, the driver will do everything possible to get change from a hotel or people in the street, but this can sometimes delay you.

TOUR BUSES. Members of organized tours are usually conveyed to sights in Chinese cities and towns in comfortable air-conditioned buses or minibuses. These are organized as part of the package and no special arrangements are necessary.

In some major centers, independent tour buses operate to leading sights, usually those on the outskirts of the city, or on day excursions to places further afield. For example, in Beijing, you can buy tickets for bus excursions to the Great Wall, Ming Tombs, Summer Palace, and Fragrant Hills, to name just a few. Tickets may be purchased either through your hotel, CITS, or at the ticket office of the bus company running these excursions.

LOCAL BUSES. After arriving at a Chinese city or town, you might like to try out the local bus or trolley-bus system. At major centers, good maps in Chinese and English are usually available from hotel counters, or at the hotel bookstore. Travel on local buses can be a cheap way of getting around, but they are often jammed with people, you may experience problems in locating the bus stop, getting off at the right place, and generally communicating with the driver and conductor.

Budget travelers with more time at their disposal than other visitors, usually persevere with local buses. A rudimentary knowledge of written and spoken Chinese eases matters considerably.

LONG-DISTANCE BUSES. Visitors with plenty of time available can travel on China's local bus service. Some of the buses are modern with air-conditioning, for example, on the service between Shenzhen and Shantou, in Guangdong Province. Many buses are old and slow, the service operating on the "stop anywhere" system en route.

Fares on the local system are usually low and appeal to the budget traveler. Another attraction is the chance to see China off the tourist track. Most visitors, however, find the service too primitive and too slow.

HIRED CARS. Chauffeur-driven cars are available for hire in major centers. Hire charges tend to be expensive, but using a car and driver is undoubtedly the most comfortable means of sightseeing in China. Hire cars may be used on one-day excursions from a center, but are not usually permitted between cities. Apart from China's sensitivity about security matters, the roads are often in a poor state or choked with slow-moving carts, many drawn by horses or donkeys.

BICYCLES. In some centers, bicycles represent an ideal way of getting around. They are cheap to hire, allow you to circulate at will, and you can cover a lot of territory. Your hotel can direct you to the nearest rental location. If it is not close by, get one of the hotel staff to write down the name and address of the place and take a taxi there. You will be expected to leave a deposit for each bicycle rented. Some places insist that you leave your passport as additional security. (Try to leave some other "document" instead, e.g., your driver's license, because your passport is too important a document to let loose into the hands of innocents.)

Check the condition of the bike thoroughly before setting off. Always lock your bike when parking it. In a few centers, theft of rented bicycles has become a problem, but generally you need not fear the loss of your deposit, provided you secure your bike each time you leave it somewhere.

ON FOOT. In many places in China, you will have the opportunity to walk around. We always indicate which cities may be explored on foot because there is no better way of getting a glimpse of the "real" China. You can walk anywhere in China without fear for your personal safety.

SUGGESTED TOURS. When visiting China as a member of a package tour group, your itinerary will have been organized in advance by the travel agency as set out in the agent's brochure. These itineraries are not usually altered unless CITS has overbooked certain centers.

If you have been invited to China by a Chinese organization, then your tour itinerary will normally have been established prior to your arrival. Nevertheless, the host organization may ask for your suggestions. Your requests for changes will usually be countered by announcements that the town you want to visit has been swept away by a flood, reduced to rubble the day before during an earthquake, or is closed for repairs. Often after a great deal of discussion, your program usually stands in its original form.

Although your host organization will go as far as possible to meet the needs and interests of the members of the group, essential places may be left out because it is "inconvenient" at the particular time you are traveling in China. There is little or nothing you can do about this except to quietly remind the guide at every possible opportunity of your wish to visit the places that have been omitted. Sometimes quiet

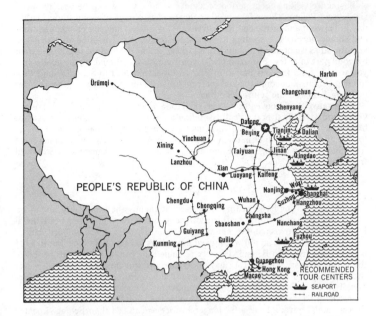

persistence pays off, and sometimes even outright criticism of the itinerary can produce results, provided this is done without showing irritation and without offending the person you are addressing.

If you have the inclination to design your own tour, the advice provided in the sections that follow will assist you. After considering the information, you should be in a position to plan your travel according to the time and money that you have available, your sightseeing requirements, the season, your capacity for endurance, and the most convenient point for arrival and departure.

Free-lance Tour

Free-lance travelers have the opportunity to range far and wide throughout China. The many hundreds of places that are "open" to foreigners and yet are not on the regular tourist beat attract them. Even places that are not officially open can be visited, provided that permission is first obtained.

Free-lance travelers usually like to mix standard destinations and unusual ones. Here is a route that is often followed by a first-time free-lance traveler to China: Hong Kong to Guangzhou, then to Wuzhou by boat, on to Yangshou or Guilin by bus, then by train to Kunming (with side trips to Lunan, Dali, Xishuangbanna) and Chengdu (stopping off at Emeishan and Leshan en route). From Chengdu the favored route is to Chongqing, then down the Yangzi by boat to Wuhan, continuing by plane to Nanjing, then rail to Shanghai, stopping off at Wuxi and Suzhou en route.

Some prefer to go straight to Xian by rail from Chengdu, then on to Luoyang and Beijing. Those with more time often go west from Xian to Turpan and Ürümqi before going to Beijing.

Tour of the Major Cities

First-time visitors to China, especially those who can spend only two weeks, might prefer to concentrate on the three major cities: **Beijing, Shanghai,** and **Guangzhou.** Details of how to get to each of these cities and what to do after arrival are provided in the sections devoted exclusively to them.

If you are visiting for a period of about 14 days, you would be wise to spend six days in Beijing, three days in Shanghai, and two days in Guangzhou, with a day in between and at the end for traveling. Obviously, these are only suggestions and should be varied according to your specific interests. The order in which you visit the cities is not important and, in any case, will be determined to a large extent by your port of entry. For example, if you fly by international carrier to Beijing, you would spend the first period in that city, then proceed to Shanghai and then to Guangzhou. You could then travel from Guangzhou to Hong Kong, and fly out of Hong Kong on the return leg home.

Alternatively, if you enter China via Hong Kong, you might care to make Guangzhou your first port of call, spending a few days there and using it as your base for excursions. You could then take the train or fly to Beijing and then go to Shanghai, taking an international flight from there to Tokyo. Or you could return from Shanghai to Beijing to take an international flight to the many cities serviced from the capital.

Tour of Ancient Capitals

Although **Beijing** has a history that goes back many thousands of years, it did not become the capital until the thirteenth century A.D., during the reign of Kubilai Khan. Marco Polo visited the capital in 1275, shortly after it was founded. Under the Ming dynasty the capital was moved for a short period to Nanjing, but in 1421 it was reestablished in Beijing. The city remained the capital for the full period of the Ching dynasty, 1644–1911, and under the governments that assumed power thereafter, except for a short period when it was moved to Nanjing under the Nationalists. On 1 October 1949 the Communist movement established the People's Republic of China and chose Beijing again as the capital.

Xian and Luoyang have a far longer history as capitals than Beijing. Located in the Wei Valley of the middle Yellow River area, they were the cradle of early Chinese civilization. Their history as capitals spans almost 2,000 years, beginning with the Zhou dynasty and ending under the Tang dynasty in 907 A.D. The cities, located as they were at the crossroads of East and West, became in time the most important influences in military, economic, and cultural affairs, in the whole of Asia.

Xian, then known as Chang An, was one of the largest cities in the world, possessing a population of more than one million (few people in Europe believed Marco Polo when he described the town). It was also capital of the kingdom in the earlier centuries.

Luoyang first became the capital of the kingdom in the eighth century B.C. (under the Zhou), and again during the later Liang (A.D. 907–923), the later Tang (A.D. 923–936) and even under the later Jin (for 11 months). At this point the capital was moved to what is present-day Kai Feng, whereupon Luoyang lost forever its rank as a capital city of China.

There is so much to see in each of these three cities that you could easily spend some weeks in each. If you are visiting for a period of 14 days, you might consider dividing your time as follows: Beijing, five days; Xian, three days; and Luoyang, three days, leaving three days for travel. If you have a particular interest in the Buddhist religion and culture, you should extend your stay in both Xian and Luoyang.

Luoyang is an overnight train journey from Beijing, as is Xian, and the two cities themselves are about eight hours apart by train. The three are connected by air service, and it is possible to fly from Beijing to either city in three hours.

Lakes and Rivers Tour

The itinerary below covers far more than simply lakes and rivers in China, but the name gives you an indication of its flavor. The itinerary is as follows: Beijing-Nanjing-Wuxi-Suzhou-Shanghai-Hangzhou-Guilin.

You would hardly countenance coming to China without visiting **Beijing,** so the tour starts in that city. You can easily get to Nanjing, the next point, by overnight train from Beijing or by direct flight of a few hours. From Nanjing onwards it is best to proceed by train. Wuxi is only a few hours away, as is Suzhou and Shanghai.

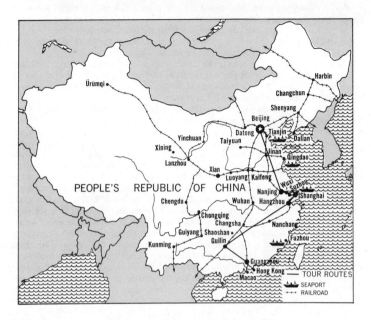

You can fly from Shanghai to Hangzhou or take the train, which provides you with a comfortable journey of only 3½ hours.

Nanjing is a pleasant, tree-filled city with a history going back 2,500 years. It served as the capital during many of the ancient dynastic periods, the last time under the early Ming, but then only for a brief period. Nanjing was also the capital during the Tai Ping rebellion and again when the Ching dynasty fell in 1911. The city was last established as the capital under the presidency of Sun Yat-sen. It is located on the famous Yangzi (Chang) River Bridge. If you arrive by train you will cross the river by way of the well-known Nanjing Bridge.

Wuxi stands on the shore of beautiful Tai Ho, or Tai Lake, China's second largest freshwater lake, and is one on China's most famous scenic spots. It is also well-known for its beautiful gardens.

Suzhou is one of the most delightful cities in China. You feel as though you have been transported back into a peaceful settlement of the Middle Ages. It is also one of the oldest existing cities, with a history spanning more than 3,000 years. It first became well-known when the King of Wu chose it for his capital in 518 B.C. It is a city of waterways and gardens, and visitors are often reminded of Venice. But in Suzhou the canals are lined by whitewashed houses with gray-tiled roofs rather than flanked by Italian Renaissance architecture.

Shanghai, once notorious, is now more famous for its vast industrial sector and for having the largest population of any city in the world. The core of the city still retains an architectural façade along the river which is Western in style; it dates from the period when European nations dominated life in China and established concessions and extraterritorial rights. Shanghai is also China's most important port. The river on which the city stands, the Huang Po, is only a short distance from the delta of the Yangzi. The site dates back to the eleventh century, when there was nothing more than a fishing village in existence; it is now the most important industrial center in the whole of China.

Hangzhou is southwest of Shanghai, about 40 minutes from that city by air and about three hours by rail. The town has a history of about 2,500 years. In the eighth century dikes were built along the river to control the flood waters, and in the tenth century the seawall was constructed to protect the town from the ravages of the ocean. Hangzhou became the capital for the Southern Song Dynasty in the twelfth century but fell under the Yuan Dynasty when the Mongols captured the town.

Marco Polo visited the city toward the end of the thirteenth century, when the population was estimated to be just under one million. He described it as the greatest in the world, where one could find any pleasure one fancied—a reputation the town was to keep for quite a long time. Even later, under the Qing, the town was considered one of the richest and largest in the whole of China.

The West Lake of Hangzhou is one of the most famous scenic spots in the country, though some would rate the Tai Ho Lake of Wuxi higher. There is no doubt, however, that Hangzhou's reputation for beauty and the fame of its lake make it one of the most sought-after tourist centers.

Guilin is located in the far south of China, about one and one fourth hours' flight from Guangzhou; by train you must take an overnight journey due to the zigzag course of the railway line. Many people feel Guilin has the most beautiful landscape in China. As far as the eye can see there are craggy, toothlike mountains rising out of plains. They appear to be floating on a vast green lake. The tops of the mountains are often covered in cloud, and there are mists that swirl down into the valleys below. The River Li flows through the town and surges around the base of the mountains on its way to join the Xi River, which eventually empties into the sea through the Pearl River delta. It is worthwhile putting aside a whole day to make the boat trip from Guilin along the River Li to view this incomparable scenery.

Visitors who wish to do the Lakes and Rivers Tour, and who have only 14 days at their disposal, should consider spending three days in Beijing, one day in Nanjing, one day in Wuxi, one day in Suzhou, two days in Shanghai, one day in Hangzhou, and two days in Guilin. This is a very tight schedule, and one or more cities might have to be cut to allow for traveling time (only three days have been allocated), which can mount up since sometimes the connections are not convenient. You could save some time by lopping a day off your stay in Beijing and, perhaps, eliminating Nanjing altogether. Another possibility would be to reduce the visit to Shanghai to one day.

Visitors who have 21 days could consider four days in Beijing, two in Nanjing, two and one half days in Wuxi, two in Suzhou, one in Shanghai, two and one half in Hangzhou, and two in Guilin, leaving four days for travel. Again, if you have to reduce your stay in these various cities to increase the time available for travel, you are advised to consider first reducing the period of your stay in Beijing and Shanghai, perhaps cutting Nanjing down to one day or eliminating it from your program altogether.

If you do not intend to leave China via Guangzhou and Hong Kong, you may have to make the difficult decision of cutting Guilin out of your tour. It is a long way south from either Shanghai or Hangzhou, especially if you have to return to Shanghai or Beijing to leave China. However, for those leaving China by Guangzhou, it would be a pity to miss seeing this scenic spot, even though many visitors feel that it has developed many of the unfortunate characteristics of an overvisited tourist destination.

Buddhist Caves Tour

If you are interested in Buddhist art you may wish to make an excursion to **Datong,** about an eight-hour train journey from Beijing. Here you will see the famous cave carvings, made about 1,500 years ago, which are masterpieces of Buddhist art. The caves were hollowed out of the cliff-face by man, the major ones in about 40 years, and they contain over 51,000 statues.

The court of that era moved to **Luoyang** in A.D. 494, and caves were constructed at Long Men. If you visit Luoyang you may make a comparison between the caves and carvings at the two sites.

The earliest known cave temples in China were hewn out at **Dunhuang** about 100 years earlier than those at Yun Gang. Unfortunately, the site in Gansu Province is time-consuming to reach.

You can see most of the sites of Datong in a day-and-a-half. A convenient way to visit is to take a late afternoon train from Beijing, arriving late that night; spend the next day-and-a-half exploring, then take the train back to Beijing after lunch, to arrive late that night.

You will see some interesting countryside on your way and catch regular glimpses of the Great Wall; the train runs near it frequently.

Leaving China

If you are a visitor to China traveling on a package tour or one that has been preplanned, then you need not bother yourself with this section. Your departure procedure will already be known. If, however, you are planning your own itinerary, then you should read this section carefully.

For many visitors, the most convenient point of departure from China is either Beijing, Shanghai, or Guangzhou.

If you intend to enter China by way of Hong Kong and then fly out to Tokyo from Shanghai, you will need to plan your tour so that you finish in the north of China. Conversely, if you intend to visit China by taking the train from Moscow to Beijing and you plan to visit southern China, then your point of departure would most likely be Guangzhou and your onward destination Hong Kong, Manila, or Bangkok.

All this may seem fairly self-evident, but you will find that a little advance planning on your part will save you a day of hanging around a departure point waiting for a connecting onward flight or vessel.

The simplest and often most convenient way out of China is by the Beijing–Tokyo flight (four to five hours) or the Beijing–Hong Kong flight (two hours 45 minutes). Of course there are many other international capitals which have a direct air link with Beijing, e.g., Manila, Paris, Zurich, Geneva, Athens, Bombay, Karachi, Teheran, and Moscow, to name the most important. However, in general there are only a few flights per week to these destinations, so you should consult your travel agent.

You should also note that it is possible to terminate your Chinese tour program in Shanghai; then you will be able to fly direct from that city to Osaka or Tokyo (about three hours), or direct to Hong Kong in one hour 50 minutes.

Departure on China's Flagship Carrier. Passengers intending to depart from China on China's national flagship carrier, Air China, should be sure they understand their obligations in the event of their canceling or failing to show up for a flight. While most international airlines are fairly flexible about such practices, Air China may apply cancellation or no-show charges. We say "may" because sometimes they do and sometimes they don't. But you need to know what might happen to you if you breach their reservation rules.

If a cancellation is made by a passenger holding an international ticket more than 24 hours before the scheduled departure time, full refund will be made. However, if a cancellation is made less than 24 hours but more than two hours before the scheduled departure time, a cancellation fee may be charged. When a cancellation is made within two hours before the scheduled departure time, the cancellation fee will be 25 percent of the ticket fare. The ticket fare here refers to the applicable one-way fare for the sector(s) not flown or to the first point of stopover exceeding six hours' flight duration.

If a passenger holding an international ticket fails to appear for departure, a no-show charge will be assessed: 25 percent of the applicable one-way fare for the sector(s) not flown or to the first point of stopover exceeding 6 hours' flight duration.

Baggage allowances on Air China flights are those that normally apply on international routes. Each international passenger paying full or half adult fare is entitled to a free baggage allowance of 30 kilos for first class and 20 kilos for economy class. In addition, each passenger may carry in his own custody a handbag, an overcoat, an umbrella or walking stick, a reasonable amount of reading material for the flight, infant's food for consumption en route, infant's carrying basket, and a fully collapsible invalid's wheelchair.

Trans-Siberian Express. If you are adventurous or simply have plenty of time, another way to leave China is on the Trans-Siberian Express traveling from Beijing to Moscow. The journey will take you about 6 days. There are two services: The Trans-Mongolian via Mongolia (capital Ulan Bator), and the Trans-Manchurian via the area of China once known as Manchuria. Erenhot is your port of departure when traveling via Mongolia; Manzhouli is the port of departure for the other route.

You will need a visa for the journey passing through Mongolia, even if you are not getting off at the capital, Ulan Bator.

A deluxe compartment accommodates two people and opens into a bathroom which houses a washbasin and a rudimentary shower. The appointments of the compartment are of a high standard, and you will have plenty of room and feel very comfortable during your journey. The carriages are well heated during winter, excessively so to some people's taste. It is perhaps better to avoid the journey during the hot summer months, when the temperature in the compartments rises to an uncomfortable level and there is a section of the journey which is very dusty.

In the "soft" compartment four people share the accommodation and there is no adjoining bathroom.

There are two trains per week, the Chinese train (no. 3) departing 7:40 A.M. every Wednesday via Ulan Bator (definitely *not* worth a stopover) and the Russian train (no. 19) via Manchuria departing 8:32 P.M. every Saturday. (Departure times vary slightly according to the season; be sure to verify them and check the time and date written or printed on your ticket.) The Chinese train has the better reputation for friendlier service and better food. Carry some canned food and biscuits for the Mongolian section, where the food can be abominable. You can continue all the way by train to Paris, Helsinki, or London if you wish.

Some visitors travel from Beijing to Irkutsk, just inside the Russian border, and fly on the Soviet domestic service to Moscow. The cost is considerably less than flying the Beijing-Moscow international route.

Chinese engineers and workers are constructing a 138–mile rail line in Xinjiang Province, from Yining to the Soviet border, where it will link up with the Soviet line to Alma Ata in Kazakhstan. The new line will open up one of the most remote areas of the world and shorten the distance of the rail journey between Beijing and Moscow by about 1,250 miles.

Recommended Reading

General. *China* (in the Time-Life *Library of Nations* series) is a good introduction for the reader new to the subject. *Ancient China* (in the Time-Life *Great Ages of Man* series) is also useful to the reader who has limited knowledge of China.

David Bonavia's *The Chinese: A Portrait* is a fine description of the customs, traditions, politics, contradictions, and lifestyles of the Chinese peoples.

Dennis and Ching Ping Bloodworth's *The Chinese Machiavelli* introduces the reader to the three millennia of cultural, political, and military influences that shape the thinking of the Chinese today.

The Travels of Marco Polo is a remarkable account of life in China in the thirteenth century, during the reign of Kublai Khan.

Michael Sullivan's *The Arts of China* is one of the best introductions to the subject.

Two excellent collections of maps are the *Tourist Atlas of China* (Cartographic Publishing House, Shanghai), a slender booklet that also has information about major tourist centers, and *China in Maps* (George Philip & Sons, London), which covers major historical events, politics, climate, geography, agriculture, and population.

The monthly *China Tourism*, published in Hong Kong, has interesting travel articles accompanied by wonderful color photographs.

Personal Accounts. Han Suyin's trilogy, *A Crippled Tree, A Mortal Flower*, and *Birdless Summer*, interprets the great tides of China's history leading to the revolution and interweaves a narrative of her own life during those times.

Maxine Hong Kingston's *The Woman Warrior* combines fact and fantasy in a superb memoir about being a woman and being Chinese.

Mark Salzman's *Iron and Silk* recounts the author's adventures in Changsha in the 1980s, where for two years he studied Chinese martial arts and taught English to medical students.

Jean Pasqualini's (Bao Ruowang) *Prisoner of Mao* describes in chilling detail twelve years in one of China's "reform through labor" camps.

Liu Binyan tells of his career as an investigative reporter, interrupted by years in internal exile, in *A Higher Kind of Loyalty*; his *"Tell the World"* (also published in 1990) analyzes the events of the Beijing Spring of 1989.

History. C. P. Fitzgerald's *The Birth of Communist China* follows developments in China from the fall of the Qing Dynasty in 1911 to the establishment of the People's Republic in 1949.

John King Fairbanks's *The United States and China* is a classic examination of the relationship between the two countries.

Edgar Snow's *Red Star over China* is the American journalist's well-known account of life with the Communist forces in China during the period that followed the Long March.

Arnold Brackman's *The Last Emperor* tells the fascinating story of the life and times of P'u Yi, the last emperor of China.

Hsu I. C. Y.'s *China Without Mao* studies the five years in China that followed the death of Mao Zedong in 1976.

Business. *China's Foreign Trade Corporations and Organizations*, published by CCPIT in China, lists all the major trade and commerce organizations and their products and services. Indispensable for the China trader.

China Handbook, published by Ta Kung Pao in Hong Kong, provides detailed information about China's economy, trade, bureaucracy, and political structure. Appears annually.

INTRODUCTION
TO CHINA

LIFE IN CHINA

Everyone knows that China is the most populous nation on earth, yet no one had a precise estimate until the results of China's massive 1982 census were released. The official figure for the population now stands at 1.09 billion, including the populations of Taiwan, Hong Kong, and Macao. Half the population is under 21 years of age. The 1 billion figure is startling in itself, but even more amazing when translated into terms of total population of the planet. Almost one person in every four is Chinese.

In the hour that it probably takes you to bathe, dress, and prepare yourself for your day's activities, China's population will have increased by 1,375 people. For every 24 hours you spend in your life, there are about 33,000 additional mouths to feed in China. In any one year, China's population increases by about 14 to 15 million people, more than enough to replace the whole population of the vast metropolis of Shanghai—or Tokyo, or New York.

Mao Zedong exhorted: "the more people the better," but Chinese planners have long adopted a different view. Since the mid-50s authorities have encouraged family planning through delayed marriages and the distribution of free contraceptives, but these policies were not effectively implemented until the early 70s, and then mainly in the cities. Beijing is seriously concerned that all the extra mouths are eating away the hard-won gains in food production. Of the 17 million babies born each year, nearly 30 percent are either third or fourth additions to the family. China's population is growing at a rate of 1.4 percent a year.

China's official goal is a population of 1.2 billion by the year 2000. This objective can be achieved only if the 65 percent of the population now under 30 agrees to limit their families to one child. A vigorous campaign has now been mounted to restrict China's natural growth rate to 11 per thousand.

The one-child family is now being rewarded with an income bonus, a greater health-care subsidy, and a better retirement pension. The family will be given priority in the allocation of housing or private vegetable plots. The only child will also receive preferential consideration for day-care enrollment and, later, in job allocation. In contrast, a family that chooses to have more than two children will be penalized by not being given ration coupons for food other than staples, and will pay 10 percent of its monthly wage as a welfare tax.

Many of the new measures are designed to encourage Chinese peasants to reduce the number of children born to each family. Earlier population programs were reasonably successful in the cities but failed to overcome the peasant couples' traditional desire to bear as many sons as possible.

There are other aspects of China's population of interest apart from size: its distribution and composition, for example.

What is often not understood outside of China is that there is a marked imbalance in the distribution of population: about 80 percent of the people live in the countryside. And when you consider that over half of the country is covered with mountains, that two-thirds of the land is arid, and that only 12 percent is arable, it is easy to understand why 90 percent of the population inhabits little more than 15 percent of the total area. There is another figure illustrating the imbalance in population distribution: half of China—comprising the "autonomous regions" of Inner Mongolia, Xinjiang, and Tibet—is home to only 4 percent of the population.

Ethnic Groups

The largest ethnic group in China is of Han Chinese origin, representing 93.3 percent of the entire population. The name comes from the Han Dynasty which ruled China between 206 B.C.–A.D. 220. The Han Chinese lived originally in the Great Yellow Plain area and in the mountain and plateau land surrounding it. As they expanded southward during the first thousand years A.D., they assimilated a great many non-Chinese cultures.

When you travel in South China, that is to say south of the Yangzi, you will notice that the southern physical type differs from the northern. The difference has arisen through the intermingling of different racial elements. Not only are the bodily characteristics and facial features different but also the temperament. The southerners tend to be more fiery and emotional than their northern brothers, and it is no coincidence that the south has been the source of a great many uprisings against authority. The modern revolutionary movements have largely originated in the south.

The remaining 6.7 percent of the population are known as the "National Minorities" and reside in regions which account for about two-thirds of China's total area. These areas are located along the frontiers. This has posed a dilemma for the Chinese leadership: How is China to grant these ethnic groups a degree of independence and autonomy and yet secure the border areas against potential territorial incursions by one or more of its 12 neighbors along a vast land frontier?

The government response has been to put aside the aspirations of ethnic groups and arrange for a large migration of Han Chinese into the national minority autonomous regions. This has been motivated not only by national security considerations, but also by the wish to control or guide these territories, to develop open lands, and to ease the pressure of population in other provinces. The movement of Han people into the autonomous regions has put pressure on national minorities in their own homelands and has sometimes led to dissent.

Peasant Life

Peasant life in China has changed dramatically. After decades of poverty, China's peasants have begun to experience a better life, as they respond eagerly to the production incentives and marketing opportunities that have accompanied the dismantling of the commune system and the elimination of mandatory state purchases of farm produce. The enormous energy that has been unlocked by these measures has created a surge in production so large that it has provided the entire population with a greater volume and increased variety of food and, at the same time, lifted the Chinese peasant out of impoverishment.

The wealth created in Chinese peasant households has meant better food, better clothing, better farm implements—but above all, better housing, as the families pour money into new farmhouses. So how do they live, these men and women who make up 80 percent of China's population?

Most of China's peasants live either in small thatch-roof farmhouses made of mud bricks or in newer tile-roof cottages made of clay bricks. The whole family lives in two or three rooms. They keep warm in winter by keeping a fuel stove lit. In the evenings, the clay or brick beds, called *kang* are heated by flues running from the stove; sometimes flues are laid down through the floor to keep the whole cottage warm. Evening light is provided by oil or kerosene lamp. Often the bedrooms have no windows, to conserve heat. Other rooms may have window frames sealed with white paper to allow light to enter and shut out drafts, yet provide ventilation. More modern cottages have glass windows. Outside, everyone keeps warm by putting on additional layers of clothing and wearing top garments of padded cotton. They wear out their clothes quickly because they work hard in them; and while the cotton cloth ration is usually not enough for the family's needs, they manage to get by. A lot of patching is done.

Family meals are simple, consisting mainly of vegetables and cereal: rice in the south and wheat and millet in the north. These staples are supplemented by pork and chicken when available. The family consumes good quantities of hot tea and sometimes plain hot water. Although there are a table and chairs for meals, there is very little other furniture apart from the beds.

Under the new incentive system laid down for agriculture, forestry, animal husbandry, fish raising, and side-line production, the family is likely to work under a contract between the household and the nearby state commerce department. The "all-around contract with the household" lays down how much land the household is to farm, and what amount of crops, pigs, poultry, eggs, etc., it should sell to the state. It also lays down how much the household must contribute in the way of agricultural tax. Any produce left over the contract is fulfilled may be consumed, stored, or sold on the open market. Compulsory purchases by the state have been abandoned, although the state sets protective prices and buys any surplus if market prices fall too low.

The working day is long and the work hard. For hundreds of years the pattern of work throughout the year has followed a regular cycle.

South of the Yangzi rice cultivation dominates farm life. In the early spring the family plows the field and removes the stubble remaining from the winter crop. Fertilizer is added to the soil and water allowed to run on to form a paddy. The rice plants that have been growing in the nursery fields are then transplanted, and thereafter the field is repeatedly weeded and cultivated. The water irrigating the field is run off as the rice plants grow and the grain matures. Harvesting and threshing take place, the harvesting usually by hand and the threshing by a primitive foot-pedaled threshing box. When harvesting is complete the fields have to be prepared for winter crops. These vary according to the location of the farm. In the south a second or a third rice crop may be planted; in the north the fields may be sown to wheat or rape.

In the north of China the peasant family spends a good deal of its time bringing water to the farmlands. When spring arrives, some of the fields are in winter fallow and must be prepared for spring planting by plowing and fertilizing. In the other fields, continual hand-irrigation and hoeing are necessary to sustain the winter wheat that is beginning to sprout. In April/May the fallowed fields are sown to other crops, particularly millet and *kaoliang*. In other areas cotton may be planted. Again, these fields must be irrigated constantly to ensure germination.

A short time later, in June or July, the winter wheat is harvested, threshed, and winnowed; the fields are then prepared for the planting of corn or soy beans. In autumn the summer crops are harvested and the fields plowed once again for the planting of winter wheat. During the cold winter months the family undertakes maintenance work around the farm and inside the farmhouse.

Urban Life

The urban dweller spends much of his life in a factory or workshop. Probably about 125 million people in China out of a work force of more than 500 million are so engaged. The worker is normally allocated a job by the central or local labor bureau, but if he is a college graduate these organizations will be aided by the Ministry of Education and the State Planning Commission. Entry into the work force is a crucial point in his life, for he can usually expect to spend the rest of his working life in that factory or office. Technical and professional staff are sometimes transferred from one place to another in the service of the same organization, but transfers between organizations are rare.

The lot of an urban worker is not easy, involving long hours, low pay, and few holidays; but the industrial worker seems to be materially better off than the peasant. He does not work as hard and he certainly lives under better conditions.

The urban worker lives in a small house or apartment with only two or three rooms, sharing a kitchen and bathing facilities with one or more other families. He will not possess many belongings; there will be a table and a few chairs, a bed for each member of the family, perhaps a wardrobe for clothes but more usually a trunk or two, and little decoration on the wall except for a print of the Chairman.

If electricity is connected, as it usually is in the big cities, there will be a bare light bulb hanging from the ceiling—but not more than 40-watt, to save electricity. In the country towns light will be provided by kerosene lamp. In the colder weather the dwelling will be heated by a small charcoal stove. Running water will sometimes be provided in city apartments, but more often than not water will be obtained from the communal taps and, in smaller country towns, from street wells.

Little in the family's life is wasted. Solid human waste is collected during the night by wagons and taken to centers for treatment before being applied to the surrounding fields. Garbage is separated so that food scraps can be collected for pig feed.

Everyone in the family who is not a student, or too old, sick, or lame is expected to work. The family will rise early, usually before sunrise, and eat a light meal of cereal and vegetables. They will often visit a nearby park to do exercises before their work hour approaches. They will then cycle or take the bus to their factory or workshop.

Output per worker appears low by most international standards because of the heavy overmanning adopted in an attempt to give everyone a job. Even so, China has admitted recently to the existence of an enormous number of unemployed people, a particularly disturbing problem among Chinese urban youth.

Other than the slow pace of work, conditions are not too favorable. In almost all except showcase factories that are shown to visitors, safety standards are low. Factories are usually not heated in winter, except in the most northerly latitudes, nor well-ventilated in summer. Noise and dust levels are apt to be high. Most of the machinery is fairly old, and there is a fair amount of shutdown for repairs.

Welfare conditions are not bad. Women workers are entitled to 56 days of pregnancy leave; there is usually a nursery at the factory; kindergartens and schools are often provided, and the bigger factories may have their own hospital unit. However, there are no ambulances, and the sick or wounded are usually conveyed to the hospital on the rear platform of a tricycle. Older folk can stay on to help out at the factory if they wish, and some do, but others who prefer to retire can do so at 60 years for men and 55 for women. On retirement 85 percent of the worker's wage is paid.

The wage scale for industrial workers has eight grades, the range from the highest to the lowest being about three to one. The scale for technicians and engineers has 16 grades, and that for government administrators 26 grades.

Wages are only part of the total remuneration. Except in the bureaucracy and social services, a sum equal to 10–12 percent of the total wage bill is available for bonuses, distributed in a variety of ways but not always according to work performance. Another 10–12 percent goes to finance pensions, sickness benefits, and housing under the workers' welfare fund. Then there are state subsidies paid to industrial workers to help them meet the increased cost of food and staples. These subsidies amount to 10–15 percent of the average *per capita* income. There are no paid vacations, workers receiving only seven public holidays each year and one day off per week.

About 7–10 percent of an average worker's wages go toward rent, water, and electricity; and about 20 percent for the two meals per day taken at the factory. After all other expenses are taken into account the worker has about 15 percent of the wages left for the purchase of clothing, or to put away for consumer items such as a bicycle, sewing machine, radio, television set, or furniture. Additional working members in the family would augment the amount saved.

Authorities in China are introducing reforms in the industrial and commercial sectors that are having enormous consequences for China's urban worker. Each factory is supposed to make its own production, price, and wage decisions. Wages are supposed to be tied to profits and individual productivity. Workers will gain or lose according to the success or failure of the enterprises in competing in the more open market. However, these reforms are meeting resistance in the factories.

While the urban worker is now fed, clothed, and housed at a bare minimum level, he finds his living standards have improved slowly over the past 30 or so years. He is far from being well provided for, yet probably realizes that he and his family are better off and have hope for improvement in the future. Life is not easy but most people are sharing the same hardships.

Education

The educational benefits of the revolution have been enormous. Before 1949 more than 80 percent of the population could neither read nor write. Now there are hundreds of millions of pupils in primary, secondary, and tertiary schools throughout the nation. Indeed, the whole country has been compared to an enormous school where every citizen spends part of his time learning and another part passing on his knowledge to someone else. Everywhere you go in China you will see people reading books and newspapers or taking notes about various subjects. Even though every word that comes from the media is controlled by the party and the state, there can be no doubting the gains made by humanity in terms of the sheer number of people who can now read and write.

The form of early child-training in China is bound up with the role of women in Chinese society. A woman is both mother and worker. She will normally work at her job till the last few weeks of pregnancy and resume duties about a month after the birth of her child. During the day the baby will be looked after in a nursery attached to the factory or commune or one near the family home. At the end of a working day the mother will bring the baby home to enjoy family life.

When the baby reaches three years of age he or she may enter kindergarten, although it is not compulsory for parents to send their children there if they have a grandparent or another member of the family able to take care of the child.

Classes are usually divided into groups according to age, the senior classes being for the six-year-olds. When you visit a kindergarten in China you will be impressed by the self-assurance of the children. They will stand up and sing or dance without the slightest trace of shyness or embarrassment, and you will certainly be captivated by their songs and dances. This is one of the few occasions in China when it is probably best not to understand Chinese; the performance may raise doubts in your mind when you learn that many of the songs are little more than political slogans.

You will also notice in your travels around China how well behaved the children are inside and outside the classrooms. Rarely will you hear a Chinese child cry; they run, play, sing, and dance, but rarely appear to be naughty in public. Their good behavior has been attributed to constant affection given in their early years, a practice that is centuries old. Yet the relationship between parent and child in public can be completely the opposite. Foreigners who have spent many years in China will tell you that they have been with Chinese guides or officials who have walked by their child in a kindergarten group without giving it the slightest acknowledgment. Indeed, this seems to be the accepted form of behavior between parents and children of school age.

Children may start primary school at the age of six, depending on whether places are available. They are subject to fairly strict discipline and regimentation. Emphasis is placed on collective activities. Primary school education now lasts for six years.

Secondary schools are usually referred to in China as middle schools. Children are usually aged about 12 when commencing middle school, which takes another six years. They will not begin to do additional work in literature, sciences, mathematics, and foreign languages. Serious political study is usually commenced at this level. There appear to be serious differences in the level of secondary education provided to city and country students. Rural areas seem to be at a disadvantage, although efforts are being made to reduce this imbalance.

Many children upon reaching the age of 13 or 14 years begin to work, but usually they attend part-time classes and undergo practical training in a trade or profession at work-study institutions called "vocational middle schools." In contrast, "general middle schools" cater to the minority who attend to their studies on a full-time basis.

The next step in the educational ladder for those fortunate enough to be selected is attendance at a tertiary institute such as a university, specialized institute, technical university, or teacher-training college. About a million students currently attend tertiary institutes.

Tertiary education has suffered from changes in policy over the last two decades. These institutions in particular occupy an exposed position in Chinese society and are subject to intense pressure resulting from the differing doctrinal viewpoints in the party. Examples of intense pressure—repression may be a better word—were conspicuous during the Cultural Revolution and in the aftermath of the Beijing Spring of 1989, when many university students were jailed and some executed for being "counter revolutionaries."

During the Cultural Revolution (1966–1976), far-reaching changes were made to China's educational system. Universities and institutes of higher learning were criticized for turning out an "elite" of technicians and bureaucrats trained to run the economy and the government but insufficiently motivated by political ideology. The radicals in the party felt that tertiary institutes should be producing Communists rather than experts. Furthermore, it was claimed that sons and daughters of bureaucrats, military officers, and party cadres were gaining entrance to universities in preference to other members of society.

As a result the Party, through the Ministry of Education and other agencies, had the system changed. Entrance examinations were abolished, student numbers were reduced, courses were shortened from five to three years, and the selection procedure for students altered. Worker-students who had completed two years of industrial work after middle school could apply for tertiary education provided they had the support of their fellow workers. Soldier-students were drawn from the People's Liberation Army and returned to the PLA on graduation. Peasant-students were drawn from the children of peasants and from those middle-school graduates who had been sent to the countryside to work on the farms.

As the number of places available relative to the number of candidates applying was small, competition was fierce. Many of the middle-school students sent from cities to work in the countryside were at a disadvantage in this system; they were likely to be passed over in favor of the sons of peasants. There was a great deal of disillusionment among city youth who had gone down to the countryside to work. They could expect to work at peasant labor for the rest of their lives once they had been passed over for university entrance. Furthermore, the selection of students for courses was made on the basis of their class background and ideological purity rather than on the basis of entrance examination results. These policies lost China millions of tertiary graduates when the nation needed them desperately.

Following the overthrow of the radicals in the Party at the end of 1976, the new leadership began to revamp the whole system once again. Middle-school graduates now enter China's universities each year without undergoing prior farm or factory work. Candidates must now pass a university entrance examination, and all vacancies at institutes of highest learning are filled on this basis. A candidate's ideological credentials, so important during the Cultural Revolution, were disregarded or given little emphasis until 1985, when they were again taken into account. Students are now able to state their preferred institute and subject majors, although they still have little or no choice regarding how or where they will be employed after graduation.

One of the most important decisions, one that had immense conse-quences about a decade later, allowed Chinese students to study abroad. Tens of thousands of young people flocked to institutes of higher learning in scores of countries, where they experienced a liberty of movement and expression that had a profound impact on their personal development. The seeds of the democracy movement had been sown. Returned to China, these young people began to press for changes not only in the education system but in the entire system that dominates China's way of life. These students formed the nucleus of the campaign for greater political freedom, a campaign that was savagely crushed at Tiananmen Square and in other cities in June 1989.

Growing numbers of foreign students now come to China to study, some for technical training but the majority to increase their understanding of the Chinese language. Some students from developing nations also study in China as part of a program to produce technicians for Third-World countries. Foreign students in China get a closer glimpse of Chinese soci-ety than almost anyone else. Many write and speak the language; some are ideologically receptive to the Marxist philosophy and the Communist system; others are drawn to the apparently simple but basic values of life in China.

Many returned students have provided an insight into student life in China. It would appear that many foreign students become disillusioned with the system after living under it for a while. They do not appear to mind the spartan living conditions, poor food, and lack of outside enter-tainment, but do object to the apparent attempt by some authorities to stifle friendships.

Some foreign students say they go through an emotional tunnel in China, beginning with initial euphoria and then passing successively through a phase of self-questioning, lurking doubt, determined goodwill, seething frustration, and ending in either passive acceptance or open re-volt. The students frequently complain that the Chinese authorities are evasive, secretive, and self-righteous. Some return to their home countries blaming themselves for taking China too seriously and for believing that it offered salvation for humanity and all its problems when, in fact, it is a country in search of solutions, just like any other.

Crime and the Law

Crime exists in China as it does in every country in the world. It exists from the petty level of theft and minor violence through murder, rape, and sabotage. All this is well-known to people who travel regularly in China. You will see the evidence too: bars on first-floor windows, broken glass cemented into the tops of walls, bicycles locked while parked. And in crowded cities there are pickpockets.

Occasionally, but very rarely, a foreigner is attacked in China by a knife- or club-wielding assailant. So rare are occurrences of this sort that only three or four are known in the past decade, and quick retribution fol-lowed—the assailants were executed. In general, foreign visitors have nothing to fear when they visit China, either materially or physically.

Visitors are sometimes victims of petty crime such as the theft of a cam-era, money, or personal items, and they have been targets for the occasion-al pickpocket on crowded streets, buses, and trains. Yet compared with most other countries, China is still relatively free from these problems.

Chinese authorities are more concerned with the rise of white-collar crime (a misnomer in the PRC): corruption, the misuse of public funds, the improper use of foreign currency, and black-marketeering—all practices that increased when restraints on the domestic economy were lifted.

China's legal system has three administering institutions: the police, the public prosecutor's office, and the courts. In criminal cases, the police are responsible for investigation, apprehension, and inquiry; the public prosecutor's office approves warrants for arrests and determines whether the evidence is sufficient for prosecution; the courts try the case and pass sentence.

A new legal code has been adopted in an attempt to introduce the rule of law in order to grant the Chinese people some measure of protection from the "rule of men." In doing so, Chinese leaders have admitted that there have been massive abuses of justice in the past. The individual now has the right to a defense, the right to be represented by a lawyer, and the right to a public trial. However, the Party retains the right to discipline its own members.

The new legal code has brought greater clarity to the question of "counter-revolutionary" crime. Under the code, a citizen cannot, in principle, be imprisoned for showing the wrong political attitude or because of class background. However, people can still be prosecuted for attempting to overthrow "the political power of the dictatorship of the proletariat and the socialist system."

Nevertheless, some observers entertain doubts about the authorities' giving up their tendency to intervene in due process of law, even though the new legislation clearly stipulates that the public prosecutor's office and the courts should administer justice independently, with no interference from individuals or organizations. Only time will tell whether the new laws will be administered fairly, independently, and impartially.

Public order in China is maintained by the Ministry of Public Security. It is subordinate to the State Council but in reality effectively controlled and directed by special committees operating within the Central Committee of the Party. By these means the Party is able to pursue citizens who do not agree with Party policies and their implementation. Such are labeled counter-revolutionaries.

Although the Ministry of Public Security is responsible for combating crime, however it may be defined, the most effective means of control is instituted at the civilian level. Families living around a courtyard are expected to form a courtyard committee; families in blocks of flats form a block committee, and there are equivalent street committees, urban block committees, suburb committees, factory committees, and so on right through the Chinese community. Delegates from these grassroots committees report to higher committees about the situation in their portion of the hierarchy and advise about any unusual behavior or counter-revolutionary tendencies. Conversely, instructions about carrying out new policy lines adopted by the Party come down from the top and permeate the structure until the family and individual unit is reached.

The network is set up to ensure a two-way flow of information and no one in Chinese society is outside the scrutiny of the members within the network. This scrutiny embraces their total life at home, at work, and at recreation. However, it must not be thought that the system is only for surveillance. It has an important community role to play relating to public health, settling local disputes and disagreements, providing community services (such as garbage disposal, sewage, water, fuel, and electricity), and community welfare in general. Operative members of the system work closely in conjunction with the national police force known as the People's Police.

The Media

Modern media systems—newspapers, magazines, radio and television—are widely developed in China and are controlled by the state under the direction of the Party. China has an important place in media history, for the first "newspaper" in the world was published in the Middle Kingdom, in the form of court circulars put out during the reign of Emperor Ming (A.D. 713–741). They predate the European counterparts by some 800 years and represent an important step in the development of public information systems.

The New China (Xinhua) News Agency publishes newspapers in China and is the major source of news for all media. The Central Broadcasting Bureau owns and operates all radio and television stations. The Publications Bureau publishes and distributes most of the books, and the Cinema Bureau produces the nation's documentary news and feature films. All these agencies work closely with the Ministry of Education to coordinate the course content in schools with news information, and with the Ministry of Culture to coordinate artistic activities and political developments.

Although the New China News Agency and the Central Broadcasting Bureau are part of the State Council apparatus, they are under the direct control of the Politburo of the Central Committee of the Party.

More than six thousand newspapers and magazines are published in China. Hundreds of under-the-counter publications known as "red-light" journals are periodically swept away by the authorities for causing "spiritual pollution." A handful of "underground" political newspapers are treated by officialdom as illegal. The explosion of the print medium in China is being fueled by the graduation each year of hundreds of journalism students.

The most important national newspaper in China is the *People's Daily* or *Renmin Ribao,* which is the official organ of the Central Committee of the Party. Since the radicals were removed from office in late 1976 it has tried to refurbish its image and produce more imaginative and less turgid prose. More photographs have been used and colored type adopted.

Another famous national newspaper is the *People's Liberation Army Daily,* which, of course, prints official news items that are of major interest to the armed forces. There are hundreds of other government-controlled newspapers distributed throughout China.

The most important periodical in China is *Seeking Truth* (formerly *Red Flag*), the official journal of the Central Committee of the Party. Distributed widely throughout the nation, its articles reflect the changes in thinking and policy that are going on inside the Politburo and are therefore eagerly studied by foreign observers.

An English-language newspaper called *China Daily* is published in China and distributed widely for local and foreign readers. English and foreign-language newspapers and magazines are on sale throughout China at major hotels.

Big-character posters (*dazibao*) are an important form of communication that became prominent in 1957–1958 during the "Hundred Flowers" campaign when the population at large were invited to comment upon or criticize the regime. They were used heavily during the Cultural Revolution by the Red Guards and their antagonists; walls of buildings were plastered with posters, most of which had been written by hand. However, when posters directed against the regime began to appear in the late 70s, the authorities jailed many of their authors and banned such posters. The posters reappeared during the democracy movement of 1989, plastered everywhere or printed by hand for distribution to the populace. Almost all of them were critical of the regime and its leaders.

Radio programs in China are extensively broadcast throughout the land. Programs are beamed from a handful of central stations, the transmission being picked up and rebroadcast by relay stations located in the provinces. Local stations in turn transmit to a network of rediffusion stations which feed programs into loudspeakers installed in communes, factories, offices, and institutions. By these means the party is able to reach everyone in the country. While the content of the broadcasts is similar in substance to that found in newspapers and periodicals, the nature and style of the presentation is different. Information programs are supplemented by music, drama, comedy, sports reports, and descriptions of official functions.

Television stations in China provide similar programs. Many Chinese feature films are shown on TV, as well as documentary programs, live drama, opera, children's programs, and news broadcasts—all produced by state film studios. The images picked up by TV sets are excellent; the transmission is based on the 625-line system, which gives fine definition.Television played an important, perhaps critical role in the democracy movement that developed in 1989. The movement gained momentum during Soviet President Mikhail Gorbachev's visit to Beijing in mid-May, the events being captured by foreign TV crews and transmitted by satellite to a fascinated world. Many of the crews stayed on and were able to report the events of early June, when the movement was crushed.

Religion and Philosophy

The four great old religions of China—Confucianism, Buddhism, Taoism, and Ancestor Worship—have been almost swept away. Nevertheless, with the exception of Taoism, remnants of the four old religions have survived. When you travel through China, you will be able to visit certain Buddhist temples, Lamaist monasteries, and former Confucian shrines. With few exceptions, they are now more like museums than centers of religious faith. They have been restored to preserve their religious art rather than to encourage the faithful, and their vigor is spent.

Their re-emergence as guiding lights to the Chinese is improbable, even though some of the priests of the old religions have been "rehabilitated" recently and there is greater tolerance shown to religious practices.

One of the characteristics of the Chinese people that has given these religions a survival quality has been the practical approach of the Chinese to the role of religion in life. For example, the great upheavals that have marked the development of various religious streams in the West did not take place in China. For thousands of years the Chinese have considered that the world is a complete entity unto itself, populated by one great human family ruled by only one sovereign, the Emperor or "Son of Heaven." Religious ideas were allowed to permeate society provided they did not upset the Chinese way of life too much.

The primitive religions adopted by the peasant before the introduction of the three great literate traditions tended to consider the observable and the supernatural world as merely separate expressions of the same phenomenon. The Chinese were therefore largely indifferent to the doctrinal conflicts presented by religions. There was little or no preoccupation with the conflicts between the deities and man: they were in a sense extensions of each other. Religious feeling was more a reflection of the harmony of nature; religious rites and practices were means of enhancing and preserving their harmony. This approach to religious philosophy probably stems from the agricultural nature of the Chinese civilization and its dependence on the regular harmony of the seasons. The Chinese have long considered that nature and the moral order were of the same substance. Natural catastrophes such as earthquakes, floods, and droughts were the result of lack of virtue in the emperor. Catastrophes were seen as portents of a change in the dynasty. After severe earthquakes in July 1976, the Communist press exhorted the population to dismiss thoughts of any connection between natural phenomena and an imminent change in leadership as ignorant superstition. That the press had to adopt such a line indicates that the belief was still widely embraced among the peasantry. The events that followed the earthquakes some months later when the radical leadership, known as the "Gang of Four," was arrested and removed from the mainstream of political life must have served only to reinforce this age-old belief.

Confucianism, more a system of thought and moral philosophy than a religion, has had considerable influence in China. The name given to the religion is the latinized form of the Chinese Kung Fu Zi, or "Master Kung." He and his disciples developed the philosophy which became a potent force for over 2,000 years. Confucius was born in the province of Shandung in 551 B.C. He was the first figure in Chinese history to develop a code of ethics, his interest being in man and society rather than nature. His philosophy rejects all forms of supernaturalism. The Confucian ethics were adopted by the scholar-official class and became the essential ideology ensuring the political unity of China. However, as it was neutral towards religion, it did not appeal to the religious instincts of the people. Even the ceremonial sacrifices made by the emperor according to Confucian tradition had few religious overtones and, when the emperor performed these ceremonies, he was never seen as a high priest. It was only in the nineteenth century that Confucianism as a religion was developed. Despite state support, it never became a popular religion. Nevertheless, it continued as the source of moral order in China.

Buddhism stems from the teaching of the Guatama Buddha (who lived in India 563–483 B.C.) and was first introduced into China in the first century A.D. The Mahayana ("Great Vehicle") school of Buddhism was adopted in China, but changed by Chinese adherents in such a way that it became in effect a new religion. The Indian Buddhist philosophies were never in the mainstream of the Chinese Buddhist tradition.

The influence of Buddhism in China has been great despite many reversals. The principal form of Buddhism in China from the fourth to the ninth centuries was "Chan" (meaning "meditative") Buddhism, which was eventually transmitted to Japan where it became known as "Zen." This school rejected theology and shunned written texts. Direct and sudden enlightenment is sought through intuitive understanding. "Non-attachment" is attained through the complete absence of thought by sitting in meditation and getting back to the original pure nature of the self. There were seven other schools of Buddhism in China, differing primarily over the question of "being" and "nonbeing," but the Chan or Zen form was the most revolutionary and purely Chinese of all.

Taoism arose from the philosophy of Lao Tzu (or Laotse) who was born about 50 years before Confucius, around 604 B.C., but like Buddhism, it did not develop in China until the first century A.D. Lao Tzu's philosophy is contained in a short book which may be translated into English as "The Way and Its Power." It is difficult to understand, being expressed in apparent contradictions and paradoxes. In a philosophical sense it is opposed to Confucianism and in a religious sense opposed to Buddhism. The work is preoccupied with the mystical side of human nature and promises immortality in return for faith. It was associated with alchemy and medicine from the earliest times, and the priestly research represents the first attempts made to study natural history.

In practice the organization of the priesthood and the rituals performed imitated Buddhism. From the Song Dynasty onward, each religion had borrowed so much from the other that they were in substance indistinguishable. Like the Buddhist religion, Taoism was almost a spent force by the 1930s, the last hereditary spiritual leader being dispossessed by the Nationalist Government in 1927. Officially this spelled the end of the Taoist religion.

Although Confucianism, Buddhism, and Taoism represent the great religious "movements" in China, the most pervasive of all Chinese religious practices was ancestor worship. It was practiced by all Chinese regardless of their other religious loyalties. Some authorities regard ancestor worship as *the* religion of China, for it was practiced in all classes of society throughout the entire country. Moreover, it has greater historical continuity than any other religion practiced in China.

Ancestor worship is a further illustration of the traditional Chinese concept that the natural and supernatural are connected and are part of the same whole. This religious practice is based on the assumption that the living can communicate with the dead. The family, by worshiping the spirits of their ancestors, can expect to be repaid by the good fortune created through the activities of the spirits in the netherworld.

Most Chinese homes once had one or more shelves set into the wall to house the wooden ancestral tablets, each inscribed with the name and title of the ancestor. On the first and the fifteenth day of the lunar month, incense would be burned and candles lit in front of the tablets. On special festive occasions food was offered, the whole family kowtowing before the tablets. The most important ceremony was the *Ching Ming,* or First Feast of the Dead at Spring Festival time. One of the ancestor's several souls remained near the grave and needed to be propitiated. One way of doing this was to burn yellow paper currency for the use of the departed ancestor. The graves were also swept and tidied up.

Ancestor worship and the attendant belief in an afterlife was once so strongly rooted in Chinese society that a condemned Chinese preferred to be strangled rather than be decapitated and appear deformed in the next life. Whether ancestor worship is dying out completely under the new regime is difficult to judge. Travelers in China report frequent evidence suggesting that some graves are still being swept.

One aspect of modern Chinese life will surely help the demise of ancestor worship. Cremations are paid for by the state; burials are at the expense of the family of the deceased.

Islam is the most important of the "foreign" religions embraced in China. It was the faith of the Turkish, Arabian, and Iranian tribes who made China their home under the Tang. The religion became prominent in the thirteenth century when the Mongols ruled China. Prior to the defeat of the Nationalist forces in 1949 there were said to be about 10–15 million Moslems in China, particularly in the provinces of Xinjiang, Inner Mongolia, Gansu, and Yunnan. Over the centuries the Moslem community never sought to identify itself with Chinese culture and religions. It was possible for Moslem sons to marry Chinese girls, but daughters were never permitted to marry out of the faith. Because of the religion's insistence that there is only one God and that Mohammed is his prophet, Islam never became popular with the Chinese.

Christianity is a minor "foreign" religion in China, the number of adherents being relatively small. It was first brought to China during the Tang Dynasty in the form of Nestorian Christianity, a sect of the Eastern Orthodox Church. There is a tablet commemorating the arrival of a Nestorian priest at Chang An (present-day Xian) in 781 on display at the Shaanxi Historical Museum at Xian. The Christian influence of this era did not last long and was eliminated entirely during the religious persecutions of the late ninth century.

Christianity did not re-establish itself until the sixteenth century following the entry of the European explorers into the Pacific regions. The Italian Mateo Ricci headed the Jesuit mission in Beijing. The influence of the Jesuits spread because the court was impressed by their knowledge of mathematics and astronomy rather than their religious convictions. But in 1742, 200 years of religious work was dissipated when a Papal edict forbade the Chinese to participate in Confucian rites and to observe ancestor worship. In reply the emperor ordered all Chinese Christians to observe these Chinese practices.

This event and other developments in Europe effectively spelled the end of Christian influence in China until the mid-nineteenth century when the Western nations opened up China and the missionaries followed the path beaten by the soldiers and traders. Missionaries were granted the right to live and travel in China, and members of the Roman Catholic and Protestant churches fanned out through the country to establish a great many Christian centers.

The Chinese authorities saw the missionaries as a dangerous arm of the "European advance" and there was a strong undercurrent of hostility directed towards the religious movement. Nevertheless, by 1910 the movement counted almost two million adherents.

With the Christian religion came other ideas from the West which stirred the revolutionary fervor of the Chinese against de facto foreign occupation. This movement eventually led, in 1911, to the overthrow of the Manchu court and the establishment of the Republic. Later, anti-Christian sentiment was nourished by the Communist movement and by some sections of the Nationalist Government. Nevertheless, on the eve of the Communist takeover in 1949, Catholic and Protestant organizations were running thousands of schools, hundreds of hospitals, and scores of universities.

Religion under Communism

When the Communists formed the People's Republic of China in 1949 there were immediate repercussions for the religious organizations. Buddhism and Taoism, already reeling under serious blows administered by the Nationalists, were hit even harder by the new regime's measures. Within a short time both religions were effectively stripped of their lands, temples, and priesthood. The major source of income—land—was removed from the organizations under the land reforms. Temples were used as public meeting places, warehouses, or granaries. Priests were turned over to "productive labor." At the peasant level, campaigns were launched to show the superstitious and antisocial nature of ancestor worship and all its associated ceremonies.

In 1952 the Chinese Buddhist Association was formed under Communist auspices and has since been used as a means of controlling Buddhists in Tibet and Inner Mongolia and, as well, to convey the impression that religious observance is allowed in China. This last stance was considered particularly important in China's relations with countries in southeast

Asia possessing Buddhist populations. In 1978 China sent a Buddhist delegation to Japan, the first of several such delegations that traveled over the following years.

Christian churches met a similar fate, but different means were used to eliminate their influence. During the period of land reform no public assemblies were allowed and in consequence all the churches in the countryside were closed and thereafter never reopened. Campaigns were launched against missionaries and members of the church conducting hospitals and clinics, and by the early 50s many had been expelled. By Christmas 1966 the few churches that remained were closed following harassment by the Red Guards of the Cultural Revolution. Church buildings were stripped and often used to house the throngs of Chinese youth roaming the countryside. For years there were only two Christian churches holding services in China: one Roman Catholic and the other Protestant, both located in Beijing and used almost exclusively by foreign diplomats residing there. About 45 of the 65 bishops remaining in China by the mid-1960s were chosen by the pro-government Catholic Patriotic Association and consecrated without the consent of the Vatican. In turn the bishops subsequently ordained several priests. In 1978 Beijing adopted a softer line, permitting many Christian churches to reopen. Tentative communications have been opened up with the Vatican and the Protestant Church. Christian services are now well-attended.

After the revolution, the Islamic religion, even though it was subject to various forms of repression, fared better than the Christian faith. There are numerous reasons. Islam is the faith of many of the ethnic minorities, particularly those in certain strategic boundary areas, and Chinese authorities saw the danger of dissent in sensitive locations. Furthermore, the faith binds together a large number of adherents, so they were better organized to resist attempts at repression. Indeed, early efforts to control the religious activities of the Moslem communities met with strong resistance. It is understood that there was armed resistance to the state's attempt to take over the land belonging to the mosques under the land reform program. However, Moslem schools, particularly those in the larger cities, appear to be under the control of the Party. The preservation of Islam in China is probably assured so long as China wishes to enhance relations with the Islamic nations.

Geography

China is a vast country, the third largest in the world after the U.S.S.R. and Canada, with an area (3.7 million square miles) slightly larger than that of the United States.

China is situated between the Siberian steppes in the north and the tropical jungles in the south. In the west there is a vast area of desert and high plateau country, and to the east a coastline, about 2,500 miles long, which gives onto large stretches of shallow water: the Yellow Sea in the north, the East China Sea in the center, and the South China Sea.

China's physical environment is dominated by its mountains. The major mountain chains are oriented west to east and tend to divide the country into separate climatic zones. The orientation has also impeded the movement of people and goods north and south and to some extent created natural regional and cultural boundaries.

The mountains dominate the way of life of the people in China in another way. The rivers formed by drainage from the mountain slopes flow from west to east and have created distinct patterns of land use along their routes. The best agricultural land lies in the fertile plains and valleys of the three major rivers of China: the Yellow River or Huang He (2,980 miles long), the Yangzi or Chang ("Long") River (3,237 miles long), and the Xi or West River (1,300 miles long). As agriculture developed, so the population grew. Even today the greater proportion of the population lives in the valleys and plains of the giant river systems and, quite naturally, the development of industrial areas there and the most important transportation networks followed.

The Yellow River, so called because of the thousands of tons of yellow loess soil that it sweeps downstream, has deposited so much silt in the lower reaches that, over the centuries, the river bed has risen as much as 15 feet above the level of the surrounding plain. It now flows within man-made levees. When the rain falls in late summer and early autumn tremendous amounts of water pour down from the upper reaches. In the past, water would burst through the dikes downstream and sweep across the countryside, inundating thousands of square miles and causing frightful devastation and loss of life. In recent years, dams have been built along the course of the river to prevent serious flooding on the plains.

The Yangzi has a much greater discharge than the Yellow River and is also longer; its flow rate is said to be the third largest in the world, after the Amazon and the Congo rivers. While it is less prone to flooding than the Yellow River, terrible floods have occasionally taken place, the worst being in 1931 when over three million people died.

The Yangzi is navigable for quite a distance along its course; coasters up to 10,000 tons can sail 630 miles upstream, as far as Wuhan.

The Xi River, while over 1,300 miles in length, has a three times greater flow than the Yellow River, caused by the heavy monsoonal rains that fall in the south. The river is joined by the North and the East rivers south of Guangzhou to form a large estuary, the main channel of which enters the sea near Hong Kong through the famous Tiger Gate Channel, known to the early European sailors as "Bocca Tigris."

Climate

The very existence of China's vast population depends upon the food grown in a relatively small area of the country. The climate is therefore crucial to the population's existence, and the weather pattern can mean the difference between an abundance of crops in good years and devastation through droughts or floods in bad years. When there is little rain, many of the fields must be watered by hand, placing a great burden on the peasant. Excessive rainfall brings the floods which still plague large areas of China despite enormous improvements through the construction of dams and dikes. China is therefore still at the mercy of the weather.

Climatically China is in the monsoon area, but it is only in the Southwest that the traditional hot and wet monsoonal climate exists. The center of the country has little rainfall and the north relatively little; the east tends to be humid and moist in contrast to the west part, which is largely hot and dry.

In winter, cold Siberian air masses build up anti-cyclone conditions over the Asian land mass, but the prevailing winds are dry and bring little rain. In the North there are clear days with low temperatures and humidities, but in the South winters are mild and the weather generally pleasant.

In summer, warm and moist air from the sea builds up over the eastern parts of China and heavy rains fall over much of the area. High temperatures and humidities prevail from north to south. It is not difficult to understand why the climate varies so greatly: China extends north and south over a distance greater than that from Maine to Puerto Rico. Nevertheless, the similarity in latitude to the United States means that temperature and rainfall throughout the year for different regions are similar in some respects to those of certain U.S. states.

Although these comparisons are indicative only, U.S. visitors will be interested to learn that the climate in Beijing resembles that in North Dakota and Kansas; the climate of Xian and Luoyang resembles that of Kentucky and Oklahoma, while the climate between Shanghai and Guangzhou resembles that of the U.S. southeastern coastal states.

There are some systematic differences between the two countries. For example, Chinese towns will invariably have lower winter temperatures than those located at a similar latitude and elevation in the U.S. Summer temperatures, on the other hand, are more or less the same.

The climate patterns for the regional divisions referred to earlier are described below:

North China: U.S. visitors will find that the climate is similar in many ways to that of Kansas and Nebraska, except that winters in the areas around Beijing bring little rain or snow. In late winter and spring there are regular dust storms carried down from the Gobi Desert and the Mongolian Plateau.

South China: The climate pattern resembles that of the Gulf Coast states, but in South China winter storms are much less frequent. Winters in the area tend to be shorter but feature overcast gray skies and fairly constant drizzle. Summer is hot and humid with a fair incidence of rain and showers. Autumn is undoubtedly the most pleasant period although some rain does fall during the season.

Northeast: The climate resembles that found in Minnesota and features long hard winters. However, tourists do not usually visit this area unless they are interested in manufacturing or industry.

Administrative Divisions

China has 23 provinces, three municipalities (Beijing, Shanghai, Tianjin), five Autonomous Regions (harboring the National Minorities), 174 prefectures, and about 2,200 counties.

The largest city is Shanghai with a population of over 12 million. About 15 other cities have a population exceeding 1 million. The cities with populations greater than two million are

Shanghai	12.1 million
Beijing	7.6 million
Chongqing	6.0 million
Tianjin	5.1 million
Shenyang	4.0 million
Chengdu	3.6 million
Wuhan	3.2 million
Guangzhou	3.1 million
Xian	2.5 million
Harbin	2.6 million
Nanjing	2.4 million
Lanzhou	2.0 million

The Economy

China has a centrally planned economy, the state controlling almost all economic activity. The three major sectors of the economy are state-operated organizations, family-run farms, and "private" businesses.

The state-operated organizations, found mainly in more urban areas, are the dominant force in the economy. These organizations operate factories, steel mills, shipyards, refineries, chemical plants, and so on, right down to tiny repair shops.

The family-run farm now dominates the rural environment, producing most of China's cash crops, farm produce, livestock, fish, and forestry products. The family is now considered to be the basic "unit of production," operating under contract within the responsibility (or incentive) system to produce a certain amount of farm products.

The "private sector" operates in city, urban, and country areas—always under the watchful eye of the state authorities—running small service and repair facilities, as well as small shops and stalls.

The current leadership has reaffirmed its commitment to socialism and an economy that is centrally planned, but one in which market forces have an important role to play. Enterprises and individuals are to be rewarded according to the quantity and quality of their work. Workers can be dismissed. Factory managers, now employed under contract, can directly hire staff, set wage levels within certain limits, and pay bonuses.

When the Communists set up their government in 1949 the immediate objective was to revive the economy following the destruction caused during the Civil War and the Sino-Japanese War which preceded it. Industrial production, never very great, had been cut in half. Nevertheless, by 1952 it had been restored to its former level. The government brought inflation under control, introduced land reforms by handing over farms to the lower and middle peasants, and established the framework for the socialization of the economy.

It was at this time that the Chinese leadership introduced central planning. The first five-year plan, drawn extensively from the Soviet model, covered the period 1953–1957 and gave priority to heavy industry. The Soviet government provided credit and sent thousands of experts to help China achieve the objectives laid down.

Although emphasis was placed on the development of heavy industry, great changes were made in the structure of the agricultural sector. Peasants were grouped first into mutual aid teams. These were household groups sharing work during peak-labor periods. Later, peasants were combined into 100–300 household groups known as "cooperatives." Later again the more tightly organized "people's communes" were formed, involving still larger groupings of households. At this point, private ownership of land was abolished and peasants were allowed to cultivate private plots only to satisfy their own family's needs.

The second five-year plan, begun in 1958 and launched as the "Great Leap Forward," was an attempt to attain enormous economic growth rates. The "Great Leap" may have been forward but was straight into an economic bog. Many of the industrial production targets in industry were reached only by sacrificing product quality. For example, large amounts of unusable steel were produced in "backyard furnaces." On top of this man-made mess natural calamities occurred. Agricultural production was hit by bad seasons, there being three bad harvests in succession. The economy was in serious trouble.

Furthermore, by 1960 the split between China and the Soviet Union, exacerbated by the differences of opinion within the Party over the plan, came into the open. The dispute led to the withdrawal of the Soviet experts. At the same time, the attempt to create new Chinese industrial centers in country areas caused agricultural work to be neglected with a resultant fall-off in food production at a time when the country needed it most. The population of some provinces faced starvation.

It was only during this serious setback to the economy that China's leaders recognized that agriculture had to prosper and expand if the economy as a whole was to develop. Agriculture was from that time onward given priority over heavy industry. During the period of economic readjustment, China's leaders mobilized the masses and sent about 30 million town dwellers to the countryside to assist agricultural production. Industry was directed to give priority to the production of goods essential for agricultural production, and instructed to improve the quality of factory output instead of concentrating upon large increases in quantity. Manufacturing costs also had to be cut.

The third five-year plan (1966–1970) was launched after a delay of three years. However, the Great Proletarian Cultural Revolution burst upon the scene in the same year and caused industrial chaos, although this time production in the agricultural sector was largely undisturbed. The Cultural Revolution placed emphasis on raising the political consciousness of the masses at the expense of production. It was considered better to be "red" than "expert." The campaign split the Party, and opposition hardened between the Mao faction which initiated the campaign and the more pragmatic faction which was branded by its opponents as "revisionist."

By 1967, industrial production had dropped by about 15 percent from the previous year. As the excesses of the Cultural Revolution did not dissipate until the end of 1967, the economic downturn continued the following year. Consequently, the targets of the third five-year plan could not be met.

The fourth five-year plan (1971–1975) again gave support to agriculture as the basis of the economy, stressed the mechanization of agriculture, and gave continuing emphasis to the development of the economic infrastructure, transport, electrification, the development of mining industries, and the expansion of the iron and steel and petrochemical sectors. The fourth plan was undoubtedly an economic success: there was reasonable growth, particularly in the industrial sector, and a major shift in emphasis toward importing technology and whole plant. China purchased 13 chemical fertilizer plants from the U.S.; two steel-finishing mills, one from western Europe and another from Japan; and a number of chemical fiber plants, industrial chemical plants, and other installations.

The fifth five-year plan, due to commence in 1976, was delayed because of the internal political struggle taking place. During that traumatic year Zhou Enlai, Zhu De, and Mao Zedong died, acting Premier Deng Xiaoping was dismissed, and the so-called "Gang of Four" vanguard of the radical movement were arrested and deposed. The turning point in China's economic management came in December 1978, when the agricultural reform policies were announced; they led to the breakup of the communes and the establishment of the "responsibility system," which linked the income of workers to productivity. The fifth five-year plan was replaced by a ten-year plan which was later scrapped as unworkable; it was replaced by a "readjustment" plan undertaken in 1979–1981.

The sixth five-year plan (1981–1985) continued the emphasis on readjustment, with agriculture and light industry being given priority over heavy industry. The new plan featured a strategic shift in resource allocation from investment to consumption, and from producer goods to consumer goods with emphasis on better living conditions rather than rapid industrial growth, with increasing account being given to market forces, greater management autonomy, and decentralization. It was highly successful.

The seventh five-year plan (1986–1990) emphasized continued growth through expansion and modernization of existing plants rather than through the development of new facilities. Investment was concentrated on harbors, railways, power stations, and coal mines. The main objective of the plan was to maintain economic stability, thereby allowing further economic reform, particularly in the crucial area of prices. By mid-plan, China's economy began to overheat, inflation rose to dangerous levels, and the introduction of market pricing was postponed. In 1988 the government embarked on an austerity program. Then came the democracy movement in 1989, followed by a severe economic showdown: Foreign credits, vital to the economy, were held back by donor governments and agencies, foreign investment slowed to a trickle, revenues from tourism dropped sharply, and China's balance of payments suffered. Late in 1989 China devalued the Renminbi. The government also restored a greater measure of central planning. By 1990 the economy had begun to slide into a recession.

Agriculture

When you travel through China you will see Chinese peasants working in the fields. Ankle-deep in water and bent low planting rice in the paddy fields, or jogging along the path by the edge of a field bearing huge loads on either end of a bamboo pole, the peasant is everywhere. He was identified by Mao Zedong early in the revolution as the vital force that would bring it to its successful conclusion: "In a very short time . . . several hundred million peasants will rise like a mighty storm, like a hurricane, a force so swift and violent that no power, however great, will be able to hold it back . . . " (*Report on the Investigation of the Peasant Movement in Hunan,* March 1927).

The recognition of the peasant as the most important element in the revolutionary force turned Marxism on its head and was the beginning of what was to become "Mao Zedong Thought." Later, when the revolution was won, Mao used the peasants again to help set up a new Communist social order before the industrial infrastructure was established.

Land reform was implemented: acres of land were taken from landlords and rich peasants by the end of 1952, and distributed to about 300 million peasants with little or no land. Because many families lacked tools and capital, mutual-aid teams were formed—comprising two to a dozen households—to share work during planting, harvesting, and at other times of the agricultural cycle when the workloads were heavy. By 1955 almost 60 percent of the Chinese peasants were incorporated into mutual-aid teams farming their family-owned plots. However, these household groupings were a long way from meeting the socialist ideals espoused by China's leadership, so moves to introduce collectives were made, involving larger groupings of 20 to 30 households. However, the most significant change was that the private ownership of land was abolished, hence the term "collectives." Only small plots for household cultivation were permitted. By 1956, 88 percent of China's peasant households were organized into collectives.

Within a few years, in 1958, full communization of agriculture was introduced during the Great Leap Forward. The collectives were combined into still larger units called people's communes. Within a few months almost all peasant households became part of the then 26,000 national communes. As before, each household was permitted to have a small private plot to grow vegetables for the family. An essential part of the reorganization involved the mobilization of rural labor during slack periods for work on vast projects in the countryside. Some projects were successful; others failed lamentably. Faced with serious management problems and three years of bad weather, the communes got into difficulties, and food production declined. Peasants, who had worked hard in the mutual-aid teams where they knew everybody and could see the fruits of their labors, put in much less effort in the larger, impersonal communes. There was no material incentive to work hard because the "work points" awarded often bore little or no relation to the quantity and quality of work. Then, after 1966, attempts were made to abolish private plots, and side-line production was declared to be "capitalistic."

Over the years the commune system developed until, in 1979, there were over 53,000 communes in existence. Early attempts by the authorities to destroy the traditional family system by organizing communal mess halls and nurseries failed, and indeed the government policy of restricting migration from rural areas to the cities has helped encourage tighter family bonds. The family (or, more usually, the extended family) lived in its own house and grew its own food on a private plot.

Again in 1979, new policies were introduced to stimulate production in the countryside. The family once again became the most important unit of production. Under the "responsibility system" or "all-around contract system," family income is linked to output. A contract is drawn up between the family and the state defining the area of the plot to be worked, and the amount of crops, forestry, fish, animals, and side-line production to be sold to the state. After the family pays its agricultural tax and makes its contribution to welfare and other social funds, whatever remains may either be kept by the household or sold to other peasants at rural fairs. Compulsory sales to the state have been abandoned. Private plots have been restored and their acreage enlarged, and there are few restrictions on the type of crop or livestock to be cultivated or raised. Families are now permitted to own draft animals, tractors, farm implements, tools, and other means of production. Farmers can now sell their services by using their tractors to plow or harvest other farmers' land. The new systems have improved the lot of the peasant and at the same time brought more supplies of food to the entire population of China.

Some idea of the magnitude of the task confronting China's peasants may be conveyed by comparing agricultural production in China and the U.S. The area of land available for agriculture in China is about two-thirds that of the U.S. but it must support a population four times larger. Each year China has about 14–15 million additional mouths to feed, so that while agricultural production has generally managed to increase year after year, consumption pursues it relentlessly.

The increases in agricultural output that have taken place in China have been achieved through the use of chemical fertilizers, flood control, eradication of pests, the introduction of double and triple cropping in certain areas, and the use of better plant and seed varieties. Irrigation is probably the most important factor of all. About 111 million acres out of a total cultivated area of 280 million acres is said to be irrigated, making China (after India) the country with the largest agricultural area under irrigation in the world.

Two-crop and three-crop rotations are now important in China and depend upon new seed varieties. These provide quick-maturing, high-yielding crops demanding increased applications of chemical fertilizers and intensive irrigation. There is some doubt in the minds of agricultural experts about how long the Chinese can maintain double and triple cropping without reducing soil-fertility structure.

Whatever the future may hold, China today produces more rice, millet, tobacco, barley, and sweet potatoes than any other country in the world. Rice is by far the most important grain crop, and rice acreage represents one-third of total agricultural acreage. China ranks second or third in the world in the production of wheat, soy beans, cotton, tea, raw silk, rape seed, sesame seed, and kaoliang. The acreage sown to wheat is second only after that sown to rice; wheat is a most important crop in China.

While China is a rice exporter, it often buys wheat on the international market. It may seem surprising that China, being the world's largest grain producer, is also a grain importer, but there are a number of explanations for this. The internal transport system is chronically overloaded, so it is economical for China to import wheat through the northern ports for consumption in the north rather than ship surplus rice from the south to the north. Furthermore, for every ton of rice exported, China can import two to four tons of wheat, depending on the international market price of these two commodities at any particular time.

For those who like numbers, the average consumption of "grain" (in Chinese terminology this includes such items as sweet potatoes and beans) is about 750 pounds per person per annum. In case you feel this is a lot, it amounts to less than 2 pounds of grain per person per day.

Industry

Shortly after the Communists took power in China, the Chinese drew up the first five-year plan (1952–1957). The plan directed that emphasis was to be placed on industrial growth, even at the expense of growth in the agricultural sector. The rationale behind this approach was based on the Russian experience that industrial growth could be fueled by the surpluses created on the farm. However, it soon became apparent that the rationale was based on a misapprehension. One simple fact was overlooked: the U.S.S.R. was a net grain exporter with a large agricultural surplus (especially in the early days); China was not. By the middle of the 1950s the Chinese leadership decided to redirect their development programs and give first priority to agriculture, second to light industry, and third to heavy industry. This approach reversed the emphasis given in the Soviet model.

Nevertheless, industry has expanded steadily over the last quarter of a century; numerous major plants producing both industrial and consumer goods have been established and industrial production has increased many times. China's heavy industry has also grown, and large quantities of iron and steel, machinery, motor vehicles, rolling stock, ships, and industrial chemicals have been produced.

Industry, however, still remains comparatively undeveloped in relation to the country's resources (see below), population, and ambitions. To make more rapid progress, China has adopted a policy of importing whole plants from Western industrial nations and Japan. Purchases of steel-finishing mills, chemical factories, synthetic fiber plants, and chemical fertilizer units have been made. Plans have also been announced for an expansion of purchases in these and other sectors.

China faces enormous problems in building up its industrial infrastructure. The transport sector is underdeveloped, the highway system being almost nonexistent, the railway network limited and often restricted by routes that are single-tracked, the ports heavily congested, and the river and canal waterway network limited to vessels of small capacity. China has made progress in remedying some of the deficiencies but still has a long way to go to reduce the braking effect imposed by this portion of the economy. China's leaders face another problem: the growth of industrialization, particularly between 1957 and 1977, was accompanied by an almost negligible rise in living standards of the people.

In the late 70s, China embarked on an ambitious program of "four modernizations," the modernization of industry, agriculture, science and technology, and defense. But soon after, a new "readjustment" program was unveiled in reaction to the ambitious "four modernizations." Output targets for heavy industry were slashed, greater emphasis was given to consumer goods instead of producer goods, and growth in light industry was pursued. More radios, television sets, cameras, bicycles, watches, sewing machines, textiles, and beer are being produced for the Chinese consumer. Stress is being laid on more efficient production, better management, better stock control, better utilization of resources, and greater "capital accumulation," a term used in China instead of the bourgeois capitalist word "profit."

Early in the 80s, the authorities introduced a "stabilization" plan to reduce excessive investment, cut the budget deficit, and enforce price controls. The greater economic stability that resulted from these measures allowed the government to introduce a program of industrial reforms designed to boost production and improve the lot of the industrial worker. So far these measures have had only mixed success.

Resources

China is one of those fortunate countries possessing abundant resources. In energy, abundant supplies of coal, oil, gas, and hydropower give Chinese planners important alternatives in a nation that is already the world's fourth largest producer and consumer of energy.

China is also one of the largest coal-producing nations. Coal provides about two-thirds of the total energy consumed in China, and total recoverable reserves are said to be in excess of 600 billion tons.

Crude-oil production is steady, and the nation is a net exporter. Production of crude is between 100 and 120 million tons per annum. China is the thirteenth largest crude-oil producer in the world and is becoming increasingly important as an oil-exporting nation. Onshore oil reserves are estimated to be slightly more than five billion tons, about the same size as U.S. onshore reserves. While there is much greater uncertainty about the level of offshore reserves, conservative estimates put them at close to another five billion tons. These vast resources will ensure that China has sufficient energy for its economic development and will continue to earn substantial amounts of foreign currency through the sale of oil to an energy-hungry world.

China also has enormous reserves of natural gas and, even today, in its early stage of development, is the tenth largest natural-gas producer in the world.

Electric power output has been expanding at more than 10 percent per annum throughout the 70s and, even though the nation's electric power-generating capacity is ninth largest in the world, shortages still persist, and industrial and consumer demand is not fully met. Output is over 500 billion kwh. On a per capita basis this puts China well down on the list; it is comparable with the per capita output in India and one or two African nations. However, China is constructing the giant Gezhouba Dam on the Yangzi which will add another 14 billion kwh to the national output, and plans to build an even bigger dam farther upstream at Three Gorges. Together, these systems will generate energy equivalent to the combustion of about 500 million tons of coal each year.

As for minerals, metals, and ores, China is one of the world's largest producers of antimony (7,000 tons per annum), tungsten (15,000–20,000 tons of concentrate per annum), tin (20,000 tons) and magnesite. The nation has large reserves of iron ore, but mostly low-grade, so that until sufficient beneficiation plants are installed, China must continue to purchase high-grade iron ore from other countries.

China has good reserves of rare earths and ferro-alloys, and minor deposits of cobalt and chromites. China each year produces about 22,000 tons of nickel, 80 tons of gold, 100 tons of silver, and 185,000 tons of lead. China is poised for take-off in aluminum consumption due to the expansion of power generation and the availability of local bauxite, currently produced at a level of 2.2 million tons per annum. Copper production is about 300,000 tons per annum; zinc production stands at about 220,000 tons a year. China's asbestos production stands at about 150,000 tons per annum, but no estimates are available on reserves.

These figures give a glimpse of a nation that has a sound future as far as basic raw materials and energy resources are concerned.

Wages

Equality in the distribution of wealth, a major goal of the Communist Party in China, was urged by Confucius about 2,000 years before Marx was born. The idea has thus been known for a long time in China, but little attempt was made to put it into practice until the Communists took power. The principle being applied at present is "from each according to his ability and to each according to work done."

Most industrial workers are paid wages according to the eight-grade wage system. The new, young worker entering the factory will commence at Grade 1 and work progressively through the grades: on attaining Grade 8, the worker will receive a salary three times higher than that of Grade 1. The exact amount of wages paid for each of the eight levels depends to a certain extent upon the work done.

Only about 2 percent of the industrial work force is paid at the eighth-grade level, while less than 25 percent of the workers receive the higher wages paid in Grades 5 to 8. When you visit China and learn what an industrial worker or your room attendant earns, remember that it can be quite misleading to compare the wage levels, expressed in foreign currency, with levels existing in other countries. Rather, the wage levels should be interpreted in terms of local purchasing power, details about which are given in the section "Urban Life in China."

Only half of the nation's estimated 125 million urban workers are on the industrial eight-grade system. The other half, comprising China's civil service, military, and service workers, are subject to a different scale. For example, technicians and engineers are subject to a 16-grade scale, while government administrators have a 26-grade scale. The ratio of the highest to lowest wage in the system for industrial workers is about three to one, but for bureaucrats is about fifteen to one.

Under the industrial reform plan introduced in 1985, workers may be paid according to the profit made by the enterprise, the output of the individual, the quality of the work performed, and the skill brought to the task. The plan aims to sweep away the practice of paying a worker irrespective of his performance (known as the "iron rice bowl"). The leadership that took charge following the purge of the radicals is treading cautiously towards better and more efficient production by improving the rewards given to workers. Wage increases are part of the new industrial campaign aimed at more efficient management, greater discipline in factories, and improved profit (called "capital accumulation" in Communist terminology).

An industrial worker works six days a week, eight hours a day, and enjoys seven public holidays a year. A worker may not have to toil as hard as his counterpart in other countries, but does spend more time on the job.

PEOPLES AND LANGUAGES

China is a multinational state. Apart from the Han, who represent about 93.3 percent of the population, there are about 54 other ethnic groups living within China. These non-Han groups, known as "National Minorities," together form a population of about 67 million people. A reminder of their presence is conveyed by the Chinese flag, which shows a large gold star, representing the Han people, in the top left-hand corner, surrounded by four smaller gold stars, representing the major National Minority areas: Xinjiang, Inner Mongolia, Tibet, and Manchuria. In the West, the word "Chinese" generally refers to all who live in China, whereas in Chinese there are two different expressions, one referring to Chinese citizens (*Zhongguo ren*) and another to the largest ethnic group, the Han (*Hanzu ren*).

While the non-Han groups may be relatively insignificant in numbers, they are of considerable importance politically. For one thing, many of them live in strategic frontier territory: over nine-tenths of China's border cuts through territory populated by non-Han people. Indeed, these minority groups are in fact "national majorities" in about 60 percent of Chinese territory. For another, many of the groups have ethnic or religious ties with groups living in countries across the border. The Chinese government's policies in the non-Han border areas suggest that the authorities view the situation more as a strategic problem than an opportunity to assist ethnic independence. Han Chinese have been sent to these outer and remote regions to settle in increasing numbers, often altering the Han-to-non-Han ratio significantly.

Han Chinese

The people traditionally known as the "Chinese" are Han, and there are probably about 937 million of them. The word "Han" comes from the

72

name given to the dynasty that ruled the greater part of what is today the eastern area of China in the period 206 B.C.–A.D. 220.

The Han originated in the Yellow River valley area of north China. As they expanded their territory they assimilated other ethnic groups, resulting in the development of a different physical type in the south from that existing in the north. For example, southern Chinese tend to be shorter and stockier than their northern counterparts.

For over 2,000 years various groups with different social characteristics have been formed within the Han population, possessing different spoken languages and living in well-defined territories. For example, within the Han group there are subgroups known as the Hokkiens, Ticchius, Kheds, and Hailams—all from different regions of China.

The Han Chinese use a number of languages, often call dialects, in the Sino-Tibetan family. These languages possess a common written form but are for the most part mutually unintelligible. The Beijing dialect of the northern language has been selected as the national language and is now taught in schools and institutions throughout China. The spoken form is known as *putonghua,* or "common language." The term "Mandarin" is often used, although technically this term refers to the northern language as a whole rather than to the reformed version used as the national language.

The other Chinese languages, spoken by tens of millions of people, are Wu, Yue (Cantonese), Xiang, Hui, Hakka, Gan, and Min. The structure and grammar of these languages are all more or less alike and the written form is the same. They are distinguished by the sounds used to express the written word and also by some differences in vocabulary.

Putonghua is said to be the speech used by more than two-thirds of the Han population, making it by far the widest-spoken language. However, the Chinese of southeast Asia mainly speak Yue and Min.

Asian languages such as Japanese, Vietnamese, and Korean have all been influenced by Chinese and there are many shared words in all these languages. The spoken forms, however, are not mutually understood. The Chinese and Japanese have little difficulty in reading each other's languages although the comprehension rate is certainly far from perfect.

Non-Han Ethnic Groups

About 90 percent of China's long border divides territories occupied by non-Han people and, while they represent only 6.7 percent of the population, they occupy just under two-thirds of the total area of China. About 10 of the 54 groups have populations larger than one million; about 25 of the groups live in the province of Yunnan.

Over thousands of years of interaction, many of the nationalities became absorbed into the Chinese culture and were eventually considered to be Han. Others, however, had customs and a way of life that did not lend themselves to assimilation. The Mongols, Tibetans, and Uygurs have historic and cultural traditions which reach back thousands of years, and they have tended to maintain their national identities.

Mongols

There are a few million Mongols living in China, mostly along the northern border areas in the Inner Mongolian Autonomous Region, Gansu Province, and Heilongjiang Province. The Mongols once ruled China. Under Genghis Khan they invaded China (thirteenth century) and first controlled the area north of the Huang He or Yellow River. Under

Kubilai Khan they took the whole of China and established their capital at Khanbalic, present-day Beijing, in 1279. Mongol power rapidly declined after Kubilai's death in 1297, and they were eventually expelled from China. They then settled north of the Great Wall in the region now divided into Inner Mongolia and the Republic of Outer Mongolia.

The inhabitants of Inner Mongolia are closely related in culture and language to the people of the Mongolian People's Republic; however, the Mongols in China still use the traditional Mongol script, whereas those living in the Mongolian People's Republic have "officially adopted" the Cyrillic alphabet. The Chinese find the Mongol language quite different from their own.

The Mongols have for centuries been nomads, depending for their livelihood on domestic animals, particularly cattle, sheep, and horses. They are a proud race possessing characteristics usually associated with nomadic existence: independence, resourcefulness, egalitarianism, and toughness. Over the centuries they have tended to be scornful of the farmer's settled way of life and his commercial instincts. There is some evidence that they have shown resistance to the recent Han Chinese movement into their traditional territories.

The Mongol religion has for a long time been Lama Buddhism, and even today many of the Mongols try to maintain their religious traditions. It is difficult to assess whether the Han Chinese have been successful in gaining adherents to the view that such religions are based on superstition and ignorance.

Tibetans

Tibet, known as Xizang in Chinese, came under Chinese control in 1950. This action was seen by the West as an invasion, but Chinese Communists view it as a liberation of the Tibetans from a feudal way of life. Tibetans live in an area of China that is larger than the area of old Tibet. There are estimated to be over three million Tibetans living principally in the Tibetan Autonomous Region, Sichuan Province, and Qinghai Province.

About 80 percent of the Tibetan population are farmers, mainly engaged in the cultivation of crops such as barley and wheat, and vegetables such as potatoes and turnips. The remaining portion of the population are nomads who herd sheep and yaks in the northern plateau regions.

Prior to 1950, all land was in principle the property of the Dalai Lama but could be worked by the landholder and peasant provided he paid taxes and fulfilled his obligations to the spiritual leader. Land could not be accumulated and had to be passed on to the eldest son upon the death of the head of the family. Other sons either entered a monastery or became tenant farmers for one of the landholders. There was another group who were laborers and did not possess any land or servants. These were not permitted to marry but nevertheless raised families outside of marriage.

The religion of the Tibetans was Lamaism, a form of Buddhism which has elements of an ancient religion involving belief in evil spirits, magic, and spirits of nature. The Dalai Lama, who was the spiritual head of Lama Buddhism, fled from Lhasa in 1959 to India, some nine years after the Communist soldiers occupied Tibet.

During the Cultural Revolution (1966–1976) severe damage was inflicted upon Tibetan religious shrines: temples were looted and razed; countless sites were destroyed. Chinese authorities are attempting to repair some of the damage. In 1987, and again in 1988, anti-Chinese demonstrations broke out in Lhasa and other centers of Tibet. They were put down severely; scores of monks were reported killed.

Uygurs

Other important ethnic societies are the Turkic groups of Xinjiang Uygur Autonomous Region. The most important peoples in the group are the Uygurs, the Kazakhs, and the Kirghiz. (There are other Turkic groups such as the Uzbeks and the Tartars.)

The Uygurs live almost entirely in Xinjiang Province and are Turkic in language and Moslem in religion. They have a strong sense of national identity and maintain relations with the rest of the Moslem world. Descendants of ancient members of the Sunni sect, they are not strict in observing Moslem religious ritual. Nevertheless, they have built a great many places of worship throughout their settlements.

Their social customs place great emphasis upon the family. Marriage and raising a family are considered to be a religious obligation, although the attitude towards the family unit is probably weaker than in most other Moslem communities elsewhere in the world. The Uygurs have a reputation as pleasure-lovers with a weakness for feasting, music, and uninhibited sexual indulgence. Living as they do in one of the most barren areas of China and largely dependent on agriculture supported by irrigation, their livelihood relies greatly upon oases and natural springs.

Kazakhs

Another Turkic group with the Moslem religion are the Kazakhs, who were of Uzbek origin and formed part of the "Golden Horde." They became a separate group after the collapse of the Mongol empire in the sixteenth century and lived as nomadic animal herders with their own territory until they came under control of the tsars in the nineteenth century. They are probably better known in the West under the related Slavic term "Cossack."

There are thought to be about half a million Kazakhs in China, living mainly in Xinjiang Province. The greater proportion of their group, about 7 or 8 million, lives in the Soviet Union in the Kazakh Soviet Socialist Republic.

Some Kazakhs have adopted agriculture but most are engaged in herding sheep, cattle, horses, goats, and camels. Being Moslems, they do not eat pork, their diet consisting mainly of beef and mutton supplemented by grain and tuber crops.

Kirghiz

A third major Turkic Moslem group is the Kirghiz; they are about 75,000 of them in China. They are mostly herders of sheep, cattle, and goats, and inhabit the mountain areas, moving from the lower slopes in winter to higher pasture lands as the snows begin to thaw. They also engage in some agriculture. They adhere to the Moslem faith but show a number of variations from the conventional practices.

Zhuang

Another important ethnic group is the Zhuang, who number about 8 or 9 million and reside largely in Guangxi Autonomous Region, although some settlements are found in Yunnan and Guangdong Provinces. They are a Thai-speaking group who have been known since the eleventh century and lived by agriculture. Although they have been assimilated to a certain extent by the Han-Chinese, they possess some characteristics which resemble those of the Miao group. They live in settlements located close to water and in dwellings raised from the ground. They grow rice in paddy fields and use water buffalo as both a beast of burden and a measure of wealth.

Very little has been documented on their religious beliefs, although it is thought that some of their rites involved sorcerers and men of magic who used small replicas of human beings in their ceremonies.

Miao and Yao

Two other well-known ethnic groups are the Miao and the Yao, who live in scattered communities, mostly in the southwest regional division. The two groups have developed different cultural variations and, being surrounded mainly by Han-Chinese for centuries, have also adopted many attributes of the Han culture. Most of the population of these groups (there are over three million Miao and about a million Yao) are found in inaccessible settlements on mountain slopes and along streams and rivers. They are agricultural people who raise crops, often on terraces carved from the mountainsides, as well as on rice paddies along the edges of the streams.

Their religion used to feature magical rites and elaborate ceremonies, sometimes involving animal sacrifice. The Miao particularly placed strong belief in supernatural beings, and any unusual events were attributed to the spirit world.

A good many of the Miao live in Guizhou Province.

Yi or Lolo

A group thought to be quite numerous, with a population between three and four million in settlements in Yunnan, Sichuan, and Guizhou Provinces, is the Yi or Lolo. The group is divided into clans which have a social organization based on caste. The dominant caste owns all property and thereby controls the lower caste, which is in effect a landless laboring group. Feuds between clans used to be prevalent. Marriage is confined within clan and within caste. Agriculture is the main form of activity, work in the fields being done only by the lower caste. Corn appears to be the major crop. The Yi believe that all objects possess spirit and that their lives are ruled by destiny. Amulets are worn to protect the wearer throughout his life. There is a large element of magic and sorcery in their religion.

Manchu

The Manchu currently number about two or three million and live predominantly in Liaoning, Heilongjiang, Jilin, and Hebei, as well as in the Inner Mongolia Autonomous Region. In the seventeenth century they came out of the northeast and conquered China, establishing an enormous empire that lasted almost 300 years (A.D. 1644–1912). But the conquerors were in turn vanquished by the culture of the conquered. Within a few generations the Manchu lost their language and almost all their traditions. Those who today claim the Manchu nationality are indistinguishable from the Han in every way except lineage.

Hui

Visitors to China often hear reference made to the Hui national minority group. The locals use this terminology loosely to refer to Chinese Moslems. The term was originally applied to the merchants who arrived in China from central Asia. A large group of the Hui, believed to number four or five million, live in the Ningxia Autonomous Region toward the upper reaches of the Yellow River, but there are also settlements in the Xinjiang Autonomous Region, in areas between Beijing and Wuhan, and in Yunnan.

The Hui, who write and speak the Chinese language, are indistinguishable from the Han. Now that greater tolerance is being shown by Chinese authorities towards religious practices, the Hui—both young and old—are congregating in large numbers at the mosques.

Minority Group Languages

There are a great many non-Chinese languages spoken in China today, mainly around the border areas and often by only relatively small ethnic populations. The most important ones can be classified into four language groups: the Altaic, the Tibeto-Burmese, the Thai, and the Miao-Yao.

The Turkic languages spoken by the Uygurs and Kazakhs in Xinjiang and the dialects spoken by the Mongols in the Inner Mongolian Autonomous Region all belong to the Altaic family of languages (named after the Altai mountain region). People who speak the Altaic languages live in a wide area encompassing Asia Minor, central Asia, and Siberia. The inhabitants of China speaking Altaic languages represent only a small proportion of the total speakers found in the area described.

The Tibeto-Burmese language group includes the Tibetan, Yi or Lolo, and Tujia tongues. The people who speak these languages live mainly in the west and southwest areas of China. The Tibetans, for example, inhabit a large area of China and are the most important ethnic group speaking Tibeto-Burmese. The other Tibeto-Burmese speakers are hill people who live by subsistence farming in the southern area of Sichuan Province and in scattered areas of Yunnan.

The Thai language group, spoken by more than 10 million people of different ethnic groups living in China, is closely related to Chinese. The Thai languages are mostly confined to the Guanxi Autonomous Region (spoken by the Zhuang minority) and the provinces of Yunnan and Guizhou. Most of these dialects possess no written form.

The languages spoken by the Miao-Yao group belong to the Sino-Tibetan family. For a long time it was thought that these two ethnic groups spoke dialects that belonged to different language families, but linguistic studies have brought evidence to light to suggest that they are in fact closely related.

Relationships between Han and Non-Han

In the earliest days the Chinese Communist Party embraced Lenin's view that national minorities had the right of self-determination and complete separation from China. However, in 1949, when the Communists came to power, they shelved these ideas and spoke only of national minorities forming "Autonomous Regions," believing that many of the minorities had to be liberated from feudalism.

It was only about a decade after the formation of the People's Republic that the existence of national minorities was linked with China's national security. The split with the Soviet Union in the early 1960s highlighted the vulnerability of certain border areas which had the same ethnic group on both sides of the border.

Questions arose about the balance of loyalties of these groups who were on either side of the border in the summer of 1962 when about 50,000 Kazakhs and some other non-Han Chinese crossed the Sino-U.S.S.R. border and settled in the Kazakh Soviet Socialist Republic, a federated state of the Soviet Union. From then on the Chinese leadership linked the existence of national minorities to the problem of guarding China's territory. The Chinese were once again confronting a problem that had plagued them for thousands of years and had led to the construction of the Great Wall: how to guard a long frontier against attack in areas where there was doubt about the loyalty of the frontier population.

These border problems led the Chinese authorities to step up their program of settling Han Chinese in traditionally non-Han areas.

In the Xinjiang Autonomous Region the proportion of Han to non-Han rose from about 5 percent to about 45 percent between 1949 and 1956. In the Inner Mongolian Autonomous Region, during the 21-year period beginning in 1947, the Chinese population increased from 75 percent of the total to about 93 percent. It is believed that in 1969 and 1970 over one million Han settlers were moved into Inner Mongolia.

The carving up of the Inner Mongolian Autonomous Region is linked to national minority loyalty and the problem of defense. In 1970 this Autonomous Region more or less covered the area settled by the Mongols. But in that year the territory was cut up, a part being given to "Han provinces" in regions where there were defense problems. There have also been reductions in the area of the Ningxia and Xinjiang Autonomous Regions. The former boundary lines of Inner Mongolia were restored in 1980.

The Chinese government since its inception has carried out a program of bringing Communist ideology to the national minorities but, at the same time, preserved those customs which do not stand in the way of achieving socialist goals. Some people feel that this is an attempt to preserve the cosmetic features of the ethnic group, such as song and dance, while doing away with its basic philosophies. Others see it as a means of preserving minority group cultures but ridding them of their feudal and superstitious elements.

The most important means of influencing the non-Han minorities, apart from the "voluntary" settlement of Han people in their areas, has been the training of selected members of the minority groups at the Institute of Nationalities in Beijing and at similar organizations in the provinces. Students are taught the national Chinese language (Putonghua), undergo instruction in political ideology, and participate in minority cultural pursuits such as song and dance. At the end of their training students go back to their own communities and normally work alongside Han cadres in attempting to influence their group's attitudes and way of life.

These efforts have had mixed success. Some members of the ethnic communities appear to have welcomed these developments, while others have rejected them and consider the returning students merely agents of the Han. There also appear to have been different reactions from different ethnic groups as a whole, some accepting the attempts to control or modify their group's behavior (e.g., the Mongols), others reacting against these efforts (e.g., the Tibetans, Uygurs, Kazakhs and Hui), sometimes violently.

The Chinese Language

The origins of Chinese writing are obscure, but it is known that even before the empire was unified under the Qin in 221 B.C. there was a common script used by great numbers of people who spoke different dialects. The attachment of different sounds in different dialects to the same written form has been a feature of Chinese cultural history and of course exists even today.

The development of the Buddhist religion in China influenced language. To convey the ideas of this religion to the people, Buddhist priests used texts approximating the spoken language, so that two modes of written expression grew up, one expressing the vernacular, the other the unspoken language of the scholar. These two forms existed side by side from the Tang Dynasty (A.D. 618–907) onwards.

The next milestone in the history of the language was the invasion of China by the Mongols. Kubilai Khan established the capital at Beijing, and it remained there for over six centuries, long after the Mongols had been swept out of China by the Ming. The establishment of the capital in the north led to the northern language or dialect being adopted by the court and scholar-officials. Thus *Guanhua,* or Mandarin, as the northern dialect came to be called, began to spread throughout the empire.

During this period literature flourished and was written in the spoken language of the north. The symbols representing the spoken form of the language (known as *Baihua*) existed alongside the system (*Wenyan*) used by the scholar-officials as an unspoken written form, until in the early years of this century the unspoken written form was dropped because of its inability to cope with the ideas being generated by the modern world, leaving *Baihua* as the only written system.

When the Communists took power in 1949 a common spoken language known as *Putonghua* was decreed to be the official language of the People's Republic of China. Putonghua is based on the northern dialect, its pronunciation is that of Beijing, and its written form is largely *Baihua.* It is used throughout schools in China and spread to all regions of the country by means of newspapers, magazines, radio, television, and films. It is the objective of the Chinese government to have Putonghua spoken in the future throughout the length and breadth of China.

Chinese Characters

There are about 50,000 Chinese characters in existence but fewer than 6,000 are in common use. Generally speaking, about 3,000 to 4,000 characters must be learned for fluent reading. These would represent a much greater number of words, since most characters can be combined with others to form words of more than one syllable.

Because the traditional characters are difficult to write, an official program to simplify them has been introduced. It was started in 1956, and since then more than 3,000 of the commonly used characters have been simplified.

The first character you should learn is the one representing the word "China." It is written as follows:

Its meaning is very clear. The part resembling a rectangle is the globe, and the slash through the middle of it indicates the "middle kingdom,"

or "the center of the world." It is a notion that has been fairly important in the Chinese way of viewing world affairs. Some would say that the notion is now more powerful than ever.

CHINESE HISTORY

The earliest references to China's ancient rulers take the form of legend rather than history, beginning with Fu Xi, who is said to have reigned in the thirty-fourth century B.C. He supposedly inspired the sacred book of ancient China, the *I Ching,* from which is derived the theory that the physical universe is subject to alternating pulses of yin and yang. This way of interpreting history, greatly influenced by the Taoists, remains deeply rooted in the Chinese psyche.

According to this tradition, history proceeds in cycles; after light comes darkness, after enlightenment comes repression—the sequence of yang and yin rolls on through eternity. Thus, suppression of the democracy movement of 1989 in China could be seen as a chapter in history that will inevitably be followed by more enlightened times.

Historical (as opposed to legendary) sources make no specific reference to any ruler in China before the Shang (1766–1122 B.C.). Their capital was near modern Anyang, and excavations have revealed evidence of a settled agricultural society possessing an elaborate class system and ruled by a sovereign who was also the "Son of Heaven" and hence the religious leader. The attainments of this society were considerable; they had also developed bronze casting to a high level of artistry.

The Shang were overthrown by the Zhou, who first of all established their capital near what is now Xian and later, around 750 B.C., fled before barbarian invaders and set up near present-day Luoyang. These two sites were to remain as capitals for the next 2,000 years, under a multitude of leaders of many dynasties.

The Zhou were originally a nomadic people. When they came to power they established a semi-feudal system. Power was centralized in the hands of the emperors in the early period of the dynasty, but later local chieftains ruled over areas that had become virtually independent kingdoms. From 770 B.C. these regional rulers carried out warfare against each other in what is known as the "Warring States" period. At the same time, these states were being attacked by barbarian invaders in the north and northwest, and huge walls were built for defense purposes.

Eventually the Prince of Qin emerged as the most powerful of all the regional leaders and overthrew the existing Zhou ruler. The new emperor, Qin Shi Huang Di, established the Qin Dynasty in 221 B.C. He was one of the most famous emperors in China's history and the first to establish a unified Chinese empire, an idea that was to be dominant for over 2,000 years and is extant in Chinese thinking even today. He also left his mark on Chinese society in other ways: 36 provinces with civil and military governors directly responsible to the emperor were created; a road system was developed; writing, coinage, weights, and measures were all standardized; the Great Wall was repaired and the large gaps in it joined up. The emperor is also notorious for persecuting the Confucian scholars and burning all but technical books. It is probable that China first became known to the West during this period through silk from the "Qin." Some authorities believe this is how the Western word "China" came into existence.

The Chinese Dynasties

When the emperor died in 210 B.C. a struggle for leadership broke out among the regional commanders, and the victor, Liu Bang, founded the Han Dynasty (206 B.C.–A.D. 220). Under the Han, Chinese territory was expanded considerably, agriculture was developed—influenced by the introduction of iron tools, allowing more efficient plowing and more effective use of irrigation—and trade was developed with central Asia. Confucian ideas were adopted again by the court, and were to remain influential for most of the next 2,000 years. Traders and soldiers of fortune who traveled the "Silk Road" brought Buddhism to China, and this religion became a potent force. The Han was one of the great dynasties of China, exhibiting considerable prosperity and stimulating the arts and literature.

Xia (Hsia)	2205–1766 B.C.	Southern and Northern	
Shang	1766–1122 B.C.	Dynasties	A.D. 420–589
Zhou (Chou)	1122–247 B.C.	Sui	A.D. 589–618
Spring and Autumn Period		Tang	A.D. 618–907
	770–476 B.C.	Five Dynasties and	
Warring States	476–221 B.C.	Ten Kingdoms	A.D. 907–960
Qin (Ch'in)	221–206 B.C.	Song (Sung)	A.D. 960–1279
Han	206 B.C.–A.D. 220	Yuan	A.D. 1279–1368
Three Kingdoms	A.D. 220–280	Ming	A.D. 1368–1644
Jin (Chin)	A.D. 265–420	Qing (Ching)	A.D. 1644–1911

When the Han fell, three kingdoms, Wei, Shu, and Wu, fought for supremacy. A short time later there were as many as 16 states vying for dominance. In 581 the Sui took control and set about unifying the empire once more. Work began on the Grand Canal linking the lower Yangzi with the middle reaches of the Yellow River.

The Sui fell, and the empire was ruled by the Tang, whose reign (618–907) was one of the most illustrious in China's history. During this period China became the most powerful state in the world and a dominant force in east Asia. The capital of the empire, located at present-day Xian, had a population of about one million, and foreign traders flocked to it. Cultural activities flourished: classical painting flowered: arts such as music, dancing, and the theater developed; magnificent ceramics were produced; the first white translucent porcelains were manufactured; Confucian ethics and the Buddhist religion expanded, and science—particularly astronomy and mapmaking—advanced. A great many Moslems from the northwest entered China under the Tang.

Toward the end of the ninth century invaders began to make raids into Chinese territory, and local insurrections also began. In 907 the dynasty collapsed, and was followed in quick succession by five others. Nevertheless, during this period paper money was introduced and a primitive printing press made. But an ominous development was also taking place: the northern barbarians were growing stronger, particularly the Khitan, who had established an empire in the northeast with their capital in what is present-day Beijing.

Then the Song (960–1280) established an empire that was to last over 300 years. The dynasty for a greater part of this period constantly faced the threat of invasion by the northern barbarians. Despite this pressure, social and artistic life developed further. Scholars were active all over the empire; many books were printed; literature and poetry flourished; painting reached its zenith; and magnificent porcelain and ceramics were produced. During this period the capital was moved to Linan, south of the Yangzi, the first time in history that the center of Chinese life had moved from the middle Yellow River region.

The Song bribed the Mongols in the northeast and other barbarians before them, to stay away, but eventually they became so attractive a prey that Genghis Khan invaded China early in the thirteenth century. By 1223 his troops controlled the area north of the Yellow River. The Song were finally vanquished in 1279 when Kubilai Khan took the whole of China and became emperor.

The Mongols and the Manchus

The Yuan Dynasty (1280–1368) established by the Mongols maintained their capital at Khanbalik, present-day Beijing. For the first time the whole of China was under foreign rule, becoming part of an enormous empire which stretched to Europe and Persia in the west, and enclosing the plains of Russia and the steppes of Siberia in the north. The "Silk Road" was reopened and trade reestablished between east and west. Foreigners arrived in large numbers and introduced new religions. Franciscan and Dominican friars came; so did Nestorian Christians, Moslems, and a trader by the name of Marco Polo. The court of Kubilai Khan was greatly interested in Western scientific developments and ideas. Trade was encouraged, the vast size of the Mongol empire under one ruler ensuring security of passage. There was also a transfer of technology westward, Chinese printing techniques and the formula for gunpowder being carried to Europe.

But the presence of foreign soldiers on Chinese soil combined with Mongol appropriation of vast areas of farmland led to widespread discontent and eventually to peasant uprisings. The revolt of the Red Turbans in the mid-fourteenth century was a decisive event in the ultimate downfall of the dynasty.

The Mongol Empire began to crumble after Kubilai's death in 1297, and once again the trade routes became unsafe. The Mongols were eventually driven from China and the Ming Dynasty (1368–1644) established, first at Nanjing and a short time later at Beijing. Agriculture was developed, new crops were introduced, power was centralized in the court, and great sea expeditions were sent to Java, Sri Lanka, and as far as the Persian Gulf and Africa.

Within a century the east coast was being ravaged by Japanese pirates and the northern frontier threatened by the Manchu. In the court real power passed into the hands of the eunuchs. There were threats of insurrection by peasants and strikes by workers. Eventually the people rebelled, forces entered Beijing, and the last Ming emperor committed suicide. The Manchus, taking advantage of the internal disorder, invaded China, took Beijing, and established the Qing Dynasty (1644–1911).

The Manchus were the second foreign culture to control China. But they adopted Chinese culture so rapidly that after a few generations very few Manchu spoke their own language. The boundaries of the empire were pushed out considerably, and great prosperity was enjoyed by the population for the first 150 years of Manchu rule. There were further developments in agriculture, more new crops were introduced (tobacco and corn), industry expanded (production of pottery and silk being particularly important), and the population grew (it tripled to 430 million over the 250 years between 1600 and 1850).

In the early part of the nineteenth century European vessels began to appear in greater numbers on the coast, and tsarist Russia was pressing on the north, having already taken Siberia. The Opium Wars (1839–1842) led to Shanghai and Nanjing being taken by the British, the opening of five ports to British trade, and British occupation of Hong Kong.

The Chinese, who did not want to trade with the European powers, were forced to import opium in order to balance trade.

The Manchu court was also threatened by the Taiping revolt (1848–1864), led by a religious fanatic who claimed he was the younger brother of Jesus Christ. He and his followers took larger areas of China and established the "Celestial Capital" in Nanjing. Their attempts to take Beijing and the weak response of the Manchu court prompted the British and French to extract further concessions from the emperor. The result was the Treaty of Peking, which opened up additional ports to foreign traders and granted extraterritorial rights and other privileges to foreign residents. The allied powers and the Manchu forces then defeated the Taiping, and Nanjing was retaken.

Later, China fought a disastrous war with Japan (1894–1895), losing Korea, Taiwan, and the Pescadores Islands. China was practically at the mercy of any foreign invader and, in this weakened state, could not have resisted the dismemberment being planned by the great powers that already had firm footholds in Chinese territory.

While these developments were taking place, secret societies were growing up inside China in reaction to Manchu rule. But with the continuing encroachment on Chinese territory by the Europeans, their venom became directed more and more toward the foreign powers. The Yi He Tuan ("Society of Righteous Fists," or "Boxers," as they were known to the Europeans) came to Beijing in 1900 and attacked the foreign quarter. The siege lasted 50 days before an expeditionary force of the seven western powers and Japan arrived and put the "Boxers" to flight. The reigning Empress-dowager also fled and the imperial palace was occupied.

All these events so weakened the court that revolutionary movements prospered and led eventually to the fall of the Qing Dynasty in 1911.

The End of Empire

When the Manchu Dynasty began to collapse toward the end of 1911, the revolutionaries set up a provisional government at Nanjing. Sun Yatsen was proclaimed first provisional president on January 1, 1912. However, it was military strongman Yuan Shikai who forced the Manchu to renounce the throne in 1912 and declare the Republic the constitutional form of state. He then became president, and Beijing was restored as the capital.

In the same year Sun Yatsen formed the Guomindang (old spelling: Kuomintang), but it was outlawed by Yuan Shikai in 1913. Yuan did all he could to establish himself as emperor, but failed. When he died in 1916 the way was opened for regional rivalries to surface, and China, now in the hands of warlords, was torn apart by military action. Even during Yuan's reign there was trouble: Japan took advantage of China's internal dissension to seize Shandong Province, putting forward "twenty-one demands" which would have effectively placed China under Japanese rule. China was forced to accept a toned-down version of the demands, and the date has since been observed as a day of national humiliation.

Yuan's supporters set up a government in Beijing with almost no support, while the Guomindang under Sun Yatsen set up a rival government in Guangzhou. The real power was held by the regional warlords.

World War One

In 1917 China entered the World War, to a certain extent motivated by the desire to recover its lost province; but when this hope was denied at the Versailles Peace Conference the nation was outraged, and demonstrations, now known as "The Fourth of May Movement," broke out in 1919. Revolutionary fervor was intense. In July 1921 the Chinese Communist Party was formed in Shanghai, with Mao Zedong as one of the founding members.

In 1924 the Guomindang, denied support by Western democracies, was reorganized by Sun Yatsen under guidance from the newly established Russian government. Individual members of the Communist Party joined the Guomindang, and a revolutionary army was created with the assistance of Russian advisers. Sun died in 1925, and the Guangzhou National Government came under the control of Chiang Kaishek.

The "northern expedition" followed, and the Nationalist forces captured province after province as they advanced, finally taking Shanghai in 1927. The right wing of the Guomindang led by Chiang Kaishek then broke with the Communist Party, rounded up members, trade unionists, and adherents of the leftist movement, and had them executed or imprisoned. Similar purges took place at other cities, and the Communists went underground, many regrouping in Jiangxi Province where they established a revolutionary base. In April 1927 the Provisional Nationalist Government was formed at Nanjing and was recognized by foreign powers in 1928. The president was Chiang Kaishek. Beijing in the north was taken, and the Guomindang was now dominant.

The Thirties

For almost a decade thereafter Chiang Kaishek tried to reestablish political unity throughout the country but faced considerable opposition. During this period Japan began to press from the north, taking Manchuria in 1931 and advancing to the outskirts of Beijing by 1933. Chiang Kaishek was more concerned with the elimination of the Communists and launched a series of "extermination" campaigns against them. By 1934 the Communists had been driven out of their main base in Jiangxi Province and began the Long March, which took them 6,000 miles through the southwest and then north to Shaanxi Province. By 1935 Mao Zedong had established himself as undisputed leader of the Chinese Communist Party.

Chiang Kaishek's attempts to annihilate the Communists while neglecting the continuing advances of Japanese forces were proving unpopular among the people and even within the ranks of his supporters. One of his own military leaders, Zhang Xueliang, arrested him in December 1936 at Xian, and he was released only after agreeing to cooperate with the Communists in a joint effort against the Japanese armies.

Within six months a full-scale Japanese invasion had begun, and by October 1938 the Japanese Army controlled all the eastern provinces from Manchuria to Guangdong. Puppet governments were established in Beijing and Nanjing. The Chinese Guomindang forces withdrew to Chongqing while the Communists held the northern line and dug in in Shaanxi Province, at the same time conducting guerrilla warfare in the occupied areas.

World War Two

By 1939 the European nations were at war, and later the United States entered the war in Europe and the Pacific. In 1945, the year the Japanese were defeated in the Pacific, their troops in China capitulated.

The Chinese Communists wished to take control of the provinces they had fought in, but the armies of Chiang Kaishek, with the aid of U.S. airlifts, took the surrender of the Japanese armies and thereby regained control of the key strategic points in Japanese-occupied territory. Although the United States attempted to reconcile the two Chinese factions, it was unsuccessful, and civil war broke out in 1946.

Using the same guerrilla tactics they had adopted against the Japanese, the Communists gained control of almost all of the north by 1948, took Beijing in January 1949, and completed their conquest of the mainland in the same year. The forces of Chiang Kaishek were completely routed and fled to Taiwan. Mao Zedong then proclaimed the establishment of the People's Republic of China on October 1, 1949.

The People's Republic of China (P.R.C.)

The first actions of the new government were directed toward restoring the economy and creating socialist institutions. The Chinese were assisted in their efforts by the Soviet Union under the Sino-Soviet Friendship Pact of February 1950. Soviet specialists poured into the country, and China procured large quantities of equipment to help set the economy back on its feet. All the assistance was provided by repayable loans. Trouble loomed on the northern border, and China entered the Korean War in October that year.

At the same time, agrarian reforms were being introduced to provide more equitable distribution of land, but were accompanied by widespread execution of the landlord and rich peasant class. Millions of people who resisted the revolution are said to have been eliminated. There were also "mass movements" against political and economic corruption.

In 1953 the first five-year plan was introduced, attempting to develop the Chinese economy by following the Soviet model, and placing emphasis on heavy industry based on agricultural surpluses. The land, given to the peasant under the land reforms, was taken back in the movement to form cooperative farms.

In 1956 the "Hundred Flowers" campaign was launched, inviting criticisms of the new society; it resulted in an outpouring of opposition that appeared to surprise the Party. Within a short time authorities silenced the critics and made reprisals against many intellectuals. The earliest signs of the Mao cult began to emerge, in contrast to the Soviet Union, where "de-Stalinization" was under way.

In 1958 the second five-year plan was launched and the industrial and rural sectors were reorganized into communes. An attempt was made to bring about enormous increases in production in industry and in agriculture under the "Great Leap Forward" program. In industry, many of the targets were reached only by sacrificing quality. In agriculture, the reorganization of the peasants coincided with a number of bad seasons, and there was a severe drop in food production. Some communities faced starvation.

Strains began to appear within the Party. Defense Minister Peng Dehuai spoke against Mao and was dismissed. Although Mao did not lose prestige, he lost direct political control. Liu Shaoqi became Chairman of the Republic in April 1959. In the same year there were border clashes between China and India over Tibet.

The Sixties

Strains began to develop between China and the U.S.S.R. and, during 1960, the Soviet technicians withdrew from China, the aid program was cancelled, and relations between the two countries worsened.

In 1962 the authorities were forced to reorganize the communes into more effective smaller units. In that year the border skirmishes with India erupted into a minor war. Two years later China surprised the world by exploding an atomic bomb, thereby joining the small number of nations possessing nuclear capability. By this time the split with the Soviet Union was out in the open and China began to criticize the U.S.S.R. for its "revisionist" policies.

In 1965 what at first appeared to be an irrelevant literary criticism turned out to be the opening shot in what became known as the "Great Proletarian Cultural Revolution." The criticism was a veiled attack by the Mao group against President Liu Shaoqi and his supporters. It has been widely interpreted as an attempt by Mao to regain complete control. In 1966 the Red Guards took over the movement and rose up throughout China. They stormed the offices of the Party and seized universities and schools, physically attacking officials and teachers. When the movement was put down by the army early in 1968, Mao was in control again. Liu Shaoqi and many prominent Party members were purged. Lin Biao was designated Mao's successor, and Jiang Qing, Mao's wife, was elevated rapidly in seniority within the Party. Industrial production suffered during the two years of turbulence but agricultural production was largely undisturbed.

In 1969 there were serious border clashes between China and the U.S.S.R. on the Ussuri River. High-level consultations between leaders of both sides failed to resolve the dispute, but the clashes subsided.

The Seventies

In 1971 Lin Biao attempted to take control of the leadership with the help of some sections of the army, but he failed and was killed in an air crash in Outer Mongolia, while he was trying to escape to the U.S.S.R. A year later President Nixon visited China and, at the conclusion of his visit, the "Shanghai Communique" was issued, the U.S. acknowledging the Chinese claim that Taiwan is an integral part of China. Later that year Japan established diplomatic relations with China. In the succeeding few years China established relations with a great many countries, but Sino-U.S. relations remained below "full recognition" status. George Bush, now president of the United States, was the first chief of the U.S. mission in Beijing.

In 1976, the year of the dragon, the most momentous events in China's history since the founding of the P.R.C. unfolded. In January, Premier Zhou Enlai died and, within a short time, a virulent campaign was launched against his likely successor, Deng Xiaoping, by the radicals of the Party. In April, Deputy Premier Deng was dismissed from all posts and the relatively unknown Hua Guofeng selected as Acting Premier.

In July, China suffered a devastating earthquake at Tangshan, near Beijing, which killed an estimated 240,000 and caused widespread damage to one of China's major industrial areas. (Natural disasters such as earthquakes have long been regarded by peasants as signs of an imminent change in leadership.) Then, in September, Chairman Mao died, and by early October the leading radicals of the Party, branded the Gang of Four, were arrested. One of them was Mao's widow, Jiang Qing. They were dismissed from the Party and, four years later, put on trial, found guilty, and given long jail sentences.

In 1977 Deng Xiaoping was reinstated to all his posts and was clearly the *de facto* head of a leadership group of moderates and pragmatists attempting to initiate economic development and reform. China began to embark on a program of "four modernizations" to upgrade the performance of industry, agriculture, science and technology, and defense.

On January 1, 1979, full diplomatic relations were established between China and the United States. In February, China invaded Vietnam, withdrawing 17 days later after both sides suffered heavy losses. During the year, civil dissent became more evident but was eventually stifled. At year's end, price controls were removed from thousands of non-staple food items. Important rural reforms were introduced.

The Eighties

In 1980 Mao Zedong was criticized for making serious mistakes in his later years, and the Sino-Soviet Friendship Treaty expired and was not renewed. Parts of northern China suffered the worst droughts in over 100 years, while central and southern China were badly flooded. The Chinese economy witnessed increasing inflation and a soaring state budget deficit. Changes in political leadership took place: Hu Yaobang was appointed Chairman and Zhao Ziyang was appointed Premier; but Vice-Chairman Deng Xiaoping remained the most powerful political figure.

In the 1980s the leadership, under the hand of Deng Xiaoping, focused on economic issues and ignored the political needs of the country, a distortion that would have tragic consequences at the end of the decade. The government pressed ahead with economic reforms, dismantling the collectives, stripping the communes of political power, altering the cumbersome state pricing mechanisms (a change that was crucial to the restructuring of the nation's economy), and beginning the delicate surgery of separating government from the operation of factories and farms in order to force organizations to operate at a profit.

Toward the end of the decade a series of political storms buffeted the leadership. They began late in 1986 with the onset of student demonstrations for democratic reform in Hefei, an outburst that spread quickly to other centers and continued the following year. In 1987 Hu Yaobang, the secretary general of the Communist Party, was forced to resign from his post, the major political casualty of the student demonstrations, and he was replaced by Zhao Ziyang. Other senior Party members were purged in what appeared to be a conservative backlash in the Party against "bourgeois liberalism," a code phrase for "Western ideas and influence." In China's southwest, anti-Chinese demonstrations broke out in Tibet, and scores of monks were killed and many imprisoned in the military crackdown that followed.

The death of Hu Yaobang, the disgraced former Party chief and reformer, in April 1989 sparked the reemgergence of the democracy movement. All over China students demonstrated for greater political freedom, and this time they gained the support of workers and intellectuals.

Before long hundreds of thousands were demonstrating in major cities. The Soviet president was cheered enthusiastically by the demonstrators during his state visit in mid-May. After he left, the Chinese authorities declared martial law. When the demonstrations continued, the military was brought in on June 3 to crush the movement.

Hundreds of demonstrators were killed and, later, thousands of citizens arrested. The outraged international community imposed sanctions on the regime. Zhou Ziyang was dismissed from the post of general secretary, the second Party chief to fall in less than two years. Martial law was ended in January 1990.

THE CHINESE
POLITICAL SYSTEM

Political power in the People's Republic of China (PRC) is distributed among three organizations: the Party, the state, and the army. The Party dictates state policy, the state executes Party policy, and the Party controls the army.

The structure of the Chinese political system involving these three major elements is shown in the diagram on the next page ("Distribution of Political Power in China"). Keep in mind that it does not fully represent the power structure in China, nor does it represent how power is supposed to be distributed according to the constitution. Rather, it conveys the reality of the situation in oversimplified form.

The Party

The Communist Party came to power in 1949 when its forces defeated the Nationalist forces in the Civil War. In the early days a membership of some four–five million was claimed. Now membership is known to be about 46 million—i.e., one out of every 25 Chinese is a Party member. While it is undoubtedly the largest Communist Party in the world, it probably has the smallest per capita membership.

The relationship between the Party and the government is clear-cut: the Party decides on policy and the government executes it. Although the government is the formal bureaucratic structure for the execution of policy, the Party exercises control and leadership of the country. Key positions in the government are held by Party members. The Party also has organizations which parallel those of the government, extending from the top to the bottom. The Party has key members in all the national institutions

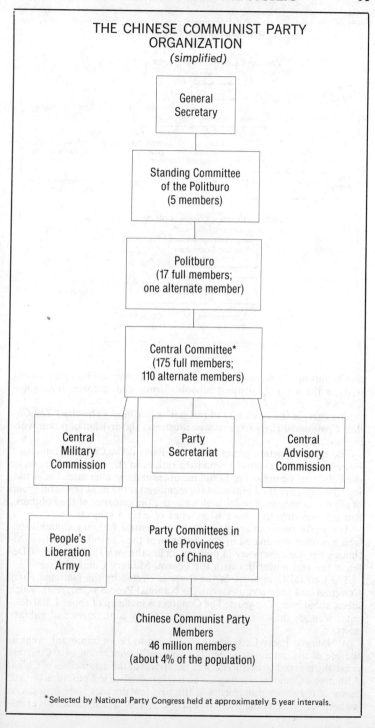

THE CHINESE COMMUNIST PARTY ORGANIZATION
(simplified)

General Secretary

Standing Committee of the Politburo (5 members)

Politburo (17 full members; one alternate member)

Central Committee* (175 full members; 110 alternate members)

Central Military Commission

Party Secretariat

Central Advisory Commission

People's Liberation Army

Party Committees in the Provinces of China

Chinese Communist Party Members 46 million members (about 4% of the population)

*Selected by National Party Congress held at approximately 5 year intervals.

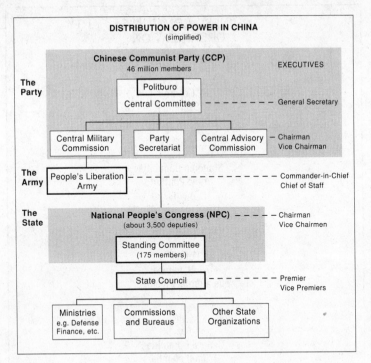

DISTRIBUTION OF POWER IN CHINA
(simplified)

The Party

Chinese Communist Party (CCP)
46 million members

EXECUTIVES

Politburo

Central Committee — — — — — — — General Secretary

Central Military Commission | Party Secretariat | Central Advisory Commission — Chairman / Vice Chairman

The Army

People's Liberation Army — — — — — — — — — — — Commander-in-Chief / Chief of Staff

The State

National People's Congress (NPC) — — — Chairman / Vice Chairmen
(about 3,500 deputies)

Standing Committee
(175 members)

State Council — — — — — — — Premier / Vice Premiers

Ministries e.g. Defense Finance, etc. | Commissions and Bureaus | Other State Organizations

and by this means controls them. In addition, Party members play leading roles in the army, ministries, schools, farms, and factories throughout China.

The Party is the repository of real power in China. (The chart *The Chinese Communist Party Organization* illustrates the division of power within the Party.)

The most important group within the Party is the Central Committee. Power within the Central Committee resides in the Political Bureau, or the Politburo, composed of 17 full members and one alternate. The Standing Committee of the Politburo (five members) is the most powerful group of all; it is in charge of policy-making under the guidance of the Politburo, and it issues directives on a wide range of crucial subjects.

The Party runs the army through the Central Military Commission, which is often dominated by the executive of the Central Committee. Although the state has a say in military affairs through the Minister of Defense, the real power lies with the Central Military Commission.

The Central Committee of the Party is elected by the National Party Congress (not to be confused with the National People's Congress), which meets about every five years. The Congress is made up of about 1,500 delegates who are drawn from the provincial Party committees and military units.

A National Party Congress is considered to be an important event in the life of a Communist state. The successful conclusion of a Congress is usually marked by celebrations in the streets of the major cities of China. Although a Congress meeting has an important place in Communist ritual, many of the major movements of the past few decades were introduced without reference to the National Party Congress. The conspicuous examples are the Great Leap Forward launched in 1958 and the Great Proletarian Cultural Revolution launched in 1966. There were no meetings of the Party Congress at all between 1965 and 1974, but since then meetings have been held more regularly.

The Army

Effective control of the military is in the hands of the Party through the Central Military Commission. Whoever heads this Commission usually becomes the Commander-in-Chief of the Armed Forces.

Considerable emphasis is placed on political training in the armed forces. In Communist ideology the army is seen as a body of peasants and workers who are assigned the role of national defense. The military often cooperate in helping civilians with harvesting, flood control, and land reclamation. Such cooperation maintains the army's popularity and helps identify the People's Liberation Army (PLA) with the masses.

China's military numbers three million, soldiers being conscripted at the age of 18 for service varying from three to six years. Only about ten percent of those available for service are inducted. The land army represents about two-thirds of the total number of soldiers in uniform.

The Chinese soldier, being largely drawn from the ranks of the peasant class, is usually in excellent physical condition, having been brought up in tough spartan conditions. During his stay in the army he can expect to work and train hard and live in austere surroundings. However, he is provided with an excellent diet and good quality clothing. Regular doses of intense political indoctrination ensure his commitment to the cause.

In 1965 the system of ranks in the PLA was abolished, and there were supposed to be no officers. In reality there was a hierarchy of leadership even though the leaders did not wear insignia to distinguish themselves. Rank and insignia have since been reintroduced.

By comparison with most armies of the world, the Chinese army is ill-equipped. There is little between the foot soldier and the nuclear missile. A great range of military hardware appears to be lacking, and existing weaponry is outdated. Naval vessels are old and slow. According to defense experts, China's air force, thought to be one of the largest in the world with over 5,000 planes, would not survive in the sky against modern squadrons. The weapon imbalance may be corrected under the "four modernizations" program.

In a country where capital resources are thin, any increased expenditure on the armed forces will be at the expense of the economy in general. China currently spends about 6–8 percent of the gross national product on defense, according to foreign military experts.

The State

The State Council acts as the executive of the National People's Congress (NPC). It is headed by a premier, supported by vice-premiers who are usually senior members of the Politburo of the Party. The State Council and its Standing Committee coordinate the work of the government ministries, commissions and bureaus, such as the Planning Commission and other state organizations responsible for tourism, broadcasting, news, publications, and so on. The members of the State Council are appointed by the NPC on the recommendation of the Party Central Committee and are in theory responsible to the NPC. However, there is no day-to-day control exercised by the NPC over the State Council. The distribution of

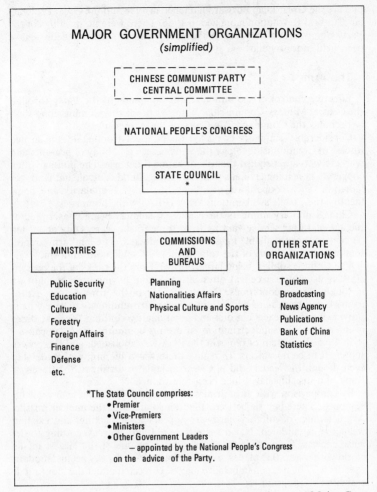

MAJOR GOVERNMENT ORGANIZATIONS
(simplified)

CHINESE COMMUNIST PARTY
CENTRAL COMMITTEE

NATIONAL PEOPLE'S CONGRESS

STATE COUNCIL
*

MINISTRIES	COMMISSIONS AND BUREAUS	OTHER STATE ORGANIZATIONS
Public Security	Planning	Tourism
Education	Nationalities Affairs	Broadcasting
Culture	Physical Culture and Sports	News Agency
Forestry		Publications
Foreign Affairs		Bank of China
Finance		Statistics
Defense		
etc.		

*The State Council comprises:
- Premier
- Vice-Premiers
- Ministers
- Other Government Leaders
  - appointed by the National People's Congress
on the advice of the Party.

political power within the state is illustrated in the diagram "Major Government Organizations."

The headquarters of the State Council are located at Zhongnanhai in Beijing in buildings located on the edge of a lake inside a walled compound. The entrance is a beautifully preserved gate (known as the "China Gate") slightly west of Qianmen Gate on Chang An Avenue. You may drive past but not enter; it is guarded by PLA men, and inside the gate is an inscription by Chairman Mao embossed in gold.

The NPC is described by the Chinese authorities as "the highest organ of state power" while "local people's congresses at various levels are the local organs of state power." However, in reality, it has less power than the State Council.

The NPC is composed of deputies elected by the people's congresses of the 30 provinces and municipalities directly under Central Government control, by the people's congress of each autonomous region, and by members of the PLA. There are currently 3,500 NPC deputies. The main action in the NPC takes place in the Standing Committee, comprising 175 members.

Deputies to people's congress are elected for five years in communes, towns, municipalities, and so on, by citizens 18 years and older. Elections are by secret ballot "after democratic consultation." The "grass roots" people's congresses then elect the deputies to the people's congress at the next highest level, a process that is repeated until the supreme body, the NPC, is elected.

Despite changes to electoral procedures and the introduction of new state organs of power, the major functions of people's congresses are still to endorse and enforce the policy decisions made within the Party. Although the NPC is described in the Constitution as "the only legislative authority in the country," it is nevertheless "under the leadership of the Communist Party of China" and, in reality, exercises no significant power. The membership of the Party executive and the NPC overlap considerably, most of the leading NPC vice-chairmen being members of the Central Committee of the Party. In practice the role of the NPC is little more than a rubber stamp for decisions taken by the Party.

The NPC is not an active body and its decisions, being merely confirmations of policies adopted elsewhere, are merely token ones. To help preserve the appearance of popular participation in government, the activities of the NCP are given considerable importance in the Chinese press. In reality, the convening of the NPC is of significance almost only as an indication that agreement has been reached in the Central Committee of the Party over policies to be followed. The headquarters of the NPC are in the Great Hall of the People.

Relatively new institutions are the local people's governments, introduced in 1980 to replace the "revolutionary committees" which fell out of favor when the Cultural Revolution was over. The local people's governments carry out the decisions of the people's congresses at the corresponding level and the orders of the state administration at the higher levels.

Under the latest constitution, the head of state is elected by the NPC. The maximum term of office allowed is two consecutive five-year periods.

Government Organizations

The implementation of Party and state policy is carried out by government ministries and agencies. The major government agencies are listed below.

Chinese Ministries, Commissions, and Agencies

Ministry of Aeronautics and
  Astronautics
Ministry of Agriculture
Ministry of Chemical Industry
Ministry of Civil Affairs
Ministry of Commerce
Ministry of Communications
Ministry of Construction
Ministry of Culture
Ministry of Education
Ministry of Energy
State Family Planning Commission
Ministry of Finance
Ministry of Foreign Affairs

Ministry of Foreign Economic
  Relations and Trade
Ministry of Forestry
Ministry of Geology and Minerals
Ministry of Justice
Ministry of Labor
Ministry of Light Industry
Ministry of Machine Building and
  Electronics Industries
Ministry of Materials
Ministry of Metallurgical Industry
Ministry of National Defense
State Nationalities Affairs
  Commission

Ministry of Ordinance Industry
People's Bank of China
Ministry of Personnel
State Physical Culture and Sports
  Commission
State Planning Commission
Ministry of Posts and
  Telecommunications
Ministry of Public Health
Ministry of Public Security
Ministry of Radio and Television
Ministry of Railways
State Commission for
  Restructuring the Economic
  System
State Scientific and Technological
  Commission
Ministry of Space Industry
Ministry of State Security
Ministry of Textile Industry

Ministry of Water Resources

Special Agencies

Auditing Administration
Commission of Science, Technology,
  and Industry for National Defense
Bank of China
China International Trust and
  Investment Corporation
People's Insurance Company
Xinhua News Agency
Central Broadcasting
  Administration
General Administration of Civil
  Aviation
China Travel & Tourism
  Administration Bureau
Academy of Science
Academy of Social Science

All these report to the State Council and receive policy instructions from the Council.

The Courts

The People's Courts are the institutions of the state exercising judicial authority. There are four levels: the Supreme People's Court, the Higher People's Courts, the Immediate People's Courts, and the Basic People's Courts. The People's Procuratorates are the organs of state supervising the administration of justice in China. These are found at three levels: Supreme, Local, and Special.

The separation of power between the state and the judiciary that is standard in most western industrial democracies is not evident in China. Chinese courts are not able to challenge Party edicts in any way.

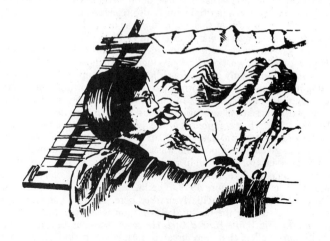

CREATIVE CHINA

All forms of artistic expression throughout the ages in all civilizations have tended to reflect the social system of the times. The art that emerged in China after the revolution in 1949 was no exception. Communist leaders, repudiating the view that art has intrinsic value, branded supporters of this idea as bourgeois and decadent. They believed that literature and art should serve the people and the revolution. Artists—whether they believed this or not—were forced to comply.

In old China the scholars or intellectual class were the effective rulers, and they dominated the life of the workers, peasants, and soldiers entirely. After the revolution the proletariat became the ruling class and the intelligentsia one of the targets of the revolution. The Party, the vanguard of the revolution, decided to destroy traditional art forms which showed bourgeois or elitist tendencies, at the same time bringing down the intellectual class associated with them.

Even though most of the ancient arts were declared decadent, the Communist government, fortunately, attempted to preserve them. However, the Red Guards caused irreparable damage to some of China's great art heritage during the turmoil of the Cultural Revolution.

The "party line" dominated artistic creation. It encouraged certain forms of art but suppressed others. For example, poster and peasant art flourished, woodcut illustrations were encouraged, contemporary theater expanded significantly, and new music and dance given support.

Artists and artisans were organized into associations, thereby raising the status of the artist to a certain extent but at the same time placing them directly under control of the Party and the government apparatus.

Music and dance received the greatest impetus from the revolution; they were recognized to be a colorful and direct means of conveying messages to the masses. So too were drama, opera, and cinema.

Most of the traditional music of China was rejected by the new regime. Modern Chinese music—that is, music developed between 1911 and 1949 and essentially Western in origin—was also rejected on the grounds of its middle-class origins. Nevertheless, most of the music acceptable to the regime after the revolution was Western in style.

Orchestral music, never prominent in old China, was used extensively to support well-known theatrical productions such as *The East Is Red, Sister Chiang,* and many others. So-called "socialist music" was also used to support group-singing performances and ballet, both of which served to convey revolutionary themes to the masses. Symphony orchestras had to play works based on revolutionary and socialist themes.

Dance, which was a component of theater before the revolution, became an art form of its own. Dancing, particularly by regional and ethnic troupes, was given full support and was well received throughout the country. Professional troupes brought regional and minority dance to city and country audiences alike. Particular attention was given to ballet, virtually nonexistent in China before 1949. The influence of the West, especially the Soviet Union, was particularly marked here. The best known new ballets to emerge during the Cultural Revolution were *Red Detachment of Women* and *The White-Haired Girl.* However, these and other "model" revolutionary ballets that were created during this period are no longer shown.

The famous Peking operas of former years were not performed after 1949, although a few "reworked" versions were later permitted, demonstrating a style so altered as to be almost unrecognizable. In their place a new form of opera was installed, Western in style and using song and dialogue to tell the story, the best known of these being *The Lantern, Taking Tiger Mountain by Strategy, Raid on the White Tiger Regiment,* and *On the Docks.* Now, the traditional form of the Peking opera has reemerged along with other regional variations.

In comparison with the development that has taken place in opera, spoken drama was slow to develop. Dramatists were encouraged to create new plays when the Great Leap Forward was launched in 1958, and within a short time a good number were produced, all of them with strong revolutionary themes. Mobile theater teams were introduced to bring the revolutionary drama to the masses. Drama presentations are often seen in city parks, especially during national holidays, as well as in formal theaters. Professional companies also tour the country. Although many plays written in the 50s and 60s were suppressed during the Cultural Revolution, these were revived in the late 70s and are playing to enthusiastic audiences. Plays by new authors are also being produced.

Film production was seized upon by the Party to promote the revolutionary cause. The industry, begun in China before the Sino-Japanese conflict, has grown steadily. Projection teams were established to tour the countryside and show films to the largely peasant population. Most films had the fairly predictable theme of class warfare showing how revolutionaries finally overcame the ruling clique against great odds, applied vengeance, and restored justice. However, since 1976, many films featuring human interest themes have been made.

Painting and graphic art were also used in China to bring revolutionary ideals to the masses. In the past calligraphy and painting were the domain of the scholar. The old brush technique of painting was permitted, provided subject matter did not smack of "individualism," i.e., glorifying the ego. The calligraphy of the leadership was particularly revered, and examples were to be seen everywhere in China. The title of the *People's Daily* was printed in Mao's calligraphy.

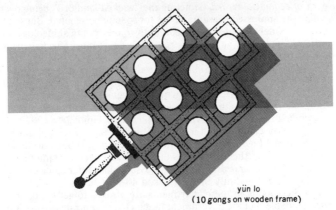

yün lo
(10 gongs on wooden frame)

Many painters used to be employed to create images resembling poster art in the West. The themes were often thought up by committee and the artist instructed to change the emphasis according to committee direction during the evolution of the painting. Beaming Chinese and National Minority citizens working hard at socialist reconstruction was a standard theme. Another favorite was a group of workers, peasants, and soldiers and National Minority groups showering adulation on the leadership. Artists are still employed to draw cartoon-style images supported by written dialogue to convey ideology to the masses. They also create the well-known New Year's pictures as well as wall posters.

However, in recent years art exhibitions have been held which, while still giving emphasis to acceptable socialist themes, have broken new ground by showing unusual landscapes, still-lifes, portraits, and even nudes. Chinese art schools, closed down during the mid-60s, have now re-opened and are accepting students.

Modern literature played its role in the revolution, but the poetry, novels, and plays produced before 1949 were with few exceptions not acceptable to the new regime. They were considered bourgeois and tainted by individualism.

Writers were encouraged to work on farms and in factories to understand the life of the peasant and worker and to create literature about it. Writers were expected to illustrate the ideals and policies of the Party and the Government and to help educate the people, revealing to them correct thoughts and deeds. Most of the pre-revolutionary works were suppressed or rewritten to conform to the new ideology.

Many writers preferred to engage in literary criticism rather than undertake new work and face the likelihood of the work and themselves being attacked and severely criticized. Criticism in this sense relates to the political ideology of the work and is not concerned with the form or style. However, even literary criticism had its own problems, as many critics found in 1966 when they themselves were criticized and purged for faulty interpretations.

Lu Xun's works are still highly regarded, although many new authors have emerged and are gaining popular acclaim as well as literary recognition. Many of the ancient classical works, such as *Dream of the Red Chamber* (or *The Story of the Stone*) and *Romance of the Three Kingdoms* have been revived and are very popular.

Sculpture had to restrict itself to themes conveying socialist realism. Some of the sculptures were lifelike presentations of dramatic situations out of the new literature. A typical example is the group of figures shown in *Rent Collection Courtyard,* depicting the "wicked landlord" being over-thrown by the oppressed peasants he has for so long persecuted. But sculpture was not widely adopted as a medium to convey political ideology and revolutionary fervor to the masses, probably because more effective means were available.

Architecture fared badly. Shortly after the revolution the government began the construction of a number of modern buildings. Some were in modified traditional style, usually with gray cement walls and a glazed tile roof; others were featureless square blocks, often with a large tower on top, copied from plans provided by the Soviet Union.

Since the early 1960s, when the Chinese and the Soviets fell out, numer-ous modern buildings, completely functional and without adornment, have been erected in the major cities of China. Workers' accommodation has been built in the same drab style, comprising block after block of apart-ments, their interiors dimly lit with naked 40-watt bulbs.

The workers living in these apartments are pleased to get them; and it is understandable that the government prefers to concentrate on providing housing for their hard-pressed population rather than devote attention to the aesthetic effects of their building programs.

However, one depressing feature all too evident in Chinese buildings is the lack of care and maintenance given to them after they are put up, a surprising situation in view of the large amount of manpower available.

Arts and the Cultural Revolution

It is significant that a work of literature was used to launch the Great Proletarian Cultural Revolution that threw China into turmoil. The open-ing shot was fired by one of the now infamous "Gang of Four," Yao Wen-yuan, who made an attack on a historical opera entitled *Hai Rui's Dismissal from Office,* written in 1961 by Wu Han, former historian and professor and then Deputy Mayor of Beijing. The criticism was leveled at the ideology of the play itself and at an author who was a high Party official. He and a few other literary figures were purged, and the events eventually led to the explosion of the Cultural Revolution in 1966.

Many intellectuals in literature and the arts were purged and their works repudiated and suppressed. Some artists were physically hounded by the Red Guards, and a number committed suicide. Some were even killed by their young tormentors.

Chairman Mao's wife, Jiang Qing, emerged as a driving force in the at-tack on culture and eventually established herself as the leading figure in the Chinese cultural climate from the mid-60s until her downfall in 1976. Numerous works of writers, musicians, singers, and others were de-nounced as counter-revolutionary, capitalistic, and bourgeois. Even the composer of *The East Is Red* was denounced as a counter-revolutionary. There are many other examples of artists who believed they were fulfilling the revolutionary role demanded by the Party and who fell from grace when the cultural policies changed.

Now that the radicals who pursued the new policies in art and other fields have themselves fallen, relaxation has taken place. Obviously, how-ever, creative minds are very cautious lest the winds of fortune turn against them once more. Those forms of socialist art that were popular before the Cultural Revolution have emerged once again. The old artists—those that survived—have been rehabilitated.

Some of the popular operas, plays, and films that were well known prior to the Cultural Revolution are now being shown. Also, new works in the performing arts, music, art, and literature are being brought out. Foreign

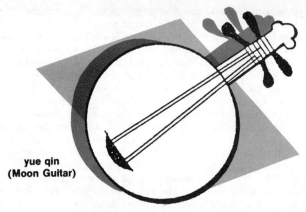

**yue qin
(Moon Guitar)**

orchestras play in China regularly now, and Western classical music concerts, ballets, and plays are once more being presented to the public.

Evolution of the Arts in China

About 3,000 years ago in China two cultures appear to have existed, both of them making and using pottery featuring designs stamped into the surface. The two were the Yang Shao ("Painted Pottery") culture and the Long Shan ("Black Pottery") cultures.

The Yang Shao culture, called after the village in Henan where the site was excavated, features gray and red pottery with black or red designs, mainly geometric, painted onto a burnished surface. The Long Shan culture developed later than the Yang Shao and showed considerable advancement in the art; objects were wheel-turned, the walls of the vessels were thinner, and more complicated geometric designs were used. Polished blackware was a feature of this culture. The shape of the vessels inspired the form of the earliest bronze vessels developed under the Shang.

The Shang Dynasty, which reigned for almost six and a half centuries (1766–1122 B.C.), saw the development of bronze art in China. Bronze vessels were rarities before then, being used mostly by kings and royal families. While we are appalled to learn that servants were buried alive in the royal tombs along with their sovereigns, we are grateful that the bronze ware was treated in a similar fashion. Excavations have recovered magnificent specimens.

New pottery techniques were developed during this period. Glazes were used and with new clays white pottery was produced for the first time. Jade carving was well developed, nephrite being used exclusively. Marble sculpture featured animal and human shapes, some approaching life-size.

When the Zhou (1122–247 B.C.) conquered the Shang, the court customs of the vanquished were adopted and art forms remained the same. It was not until the period of the Spring and Autumn Annals (770–476 B.C.) that stylistic changes began to appear. In bronzes, dragon handles and shapes became more elongated and interwoven in long strips, eventually losing their animal form. The jawless animal faces (Tao Tie), a particular feature of Shang bronzes, disappeared. Objects made of iron appeared, and the techniques for the manufacture of bronze mirrors were developed.

During the Warring States era (476–221 B.C.), a period of great upheaval through large areas of China, changes in the styling continued. Designs in bronze ware reveal elegance and imagination.

Lacquer ware was made for the first time. It was discovered that lacquer could be obtained by refining the juice of a tree grown in certain regions of China. Layer after layer of lacquer was then applied to a wooden article, and when it was built up sufficiently, the surface was carved, inlaid, or painted. This art form is still widely used in China today.

In 221 B.C. Qin Shi Huang Di defeated his military opponents and unified China under a central authority for the first time. Excavations near his mausoleum in Shaanxi Province have unearthed many life-size figures of warriors and horses in terracotta (see "Excursions from Xian"). However, there were no innovations in art during this short (15-year) period.

The peasant Liu Bang overthrew the Qin and established the Han Dynasty (206 B.C.–A.D. 220), one of the most illustrious in Chinese history. He set up its capital at Chang An (near present-day Xian), ushering in a period known as the Western Han. Later the court moved to Luoyang, beginning a period known as the Eastern Han. By this time the custom of entombing servants and animals with the dead emperor had almost entirely disappeared, and instead figurines made of pottery, wood, or metal were used. For this reason the tomb finds from the Han era have yielded a great deal of information about the mode of dress and way of life of the court of the day.

The paintings and sculpture of the dynasty are magnificent. Few silk paintings have survived, but those that have reveal a meticulous and delicate design. Perhaps the most famous examples of painting, sculpture, lacquer ware, and carving so far excavated have been taken from the Western Han tomb of Mawangdui in Changsha. The objects found there are on display at the Changsha Museum and are described in the chapter devoted to that city.

Pottery continued to develop under the Han, and craftsmen were making prototypes of the porcelain ware that was to follow later. By the end of the Han era prototypes of celadon ware were also being produced.

Magnificent bronze figurines, notably of chariots and horses, were also made during this period, as recent excavations in Gansu revealed. The most outstanding set features a procession of court officials, soldiers, and armed horsemen.

During the dynasties that followed the Han, art was influenced by Buddhism. This religion spread slowly throughout China, introduced by priests and adherents coming in from the dusty caravan routes connecting India and Persia. The religion first took hold on the outskirts of the empire where travelers first came in contact with the Chinese. Later it spread throughout China.

Carvings of the Buddha were made in the rock walls of caves dug into the hillsides on the outskirts of the empire. Wall paintings depicted the life of the Buddha. The famous paintings of this period still intact are to be found in the caves at Dunhuang in Gansu Province. These were made in the fourth century at a settlement that was then a border post for the army and foreign traders. Over the ensuing centuries rock shrines were carved out in hundreds of sites throughout China, but the most famous ones remaining today, besides Dunhuang, are Yun Gang outside Datong and Long Men outside Luoyang.

At about the same time, the first celadon ware was being produced in Zhejiang Province in the third century. Potters had tried for centuries to produce a substance resembling jade, and had at last succeeded. They were also producing white porcelain on a large scale in north China, laying the foundation for the manufacture of the magnificent white porcelain of the Tang and Song Dynasties.

Under the Tang (A.D. 618–907) Chinese civilization flowered and China became the most powerful nation in Asia. The curved-shaft plow, a significant technological development in that age, allowed the expansion of grain production and fast growth in population. The capital of the Tang, Chang An (now Xian), with a population of over a million, was the largest city in the world and possessed a vast colony of foreign traders.

During this period blockprinting was developed and the production of ceramics and textiles and paper advanced further. Celadon ware and white porcelain reached a high level of perfection. The famous tricolor glazes were introduced and the magnificent Tang animal porcelains created. Superb stone carvings were produced, particularly the bas-relief and haut-relief carvings of animals used to adorn the walls of palaces. Other art forms flourished. Painters, musicians, poets, and calligraphers created a remarkable range of artistic work. The period was a golden age for art.

Artistic traditions were maintained under the Song (960–1279). Pottery attained a remarkable level of perfection: there were technical improvements in clays, glazes, and design, faster wheel speeds, and more advanced firing methods.

Under the Song, the porcelain capital was Jingdezhen in the north of Jiangxi Province. Abundant deposits of kaolin, the white, fine-textured clay used in porcelain production, were located there in a hill east of the city. It is even today China's most important porcelain center. Other famous centers were Ding Zhou (Hebei Province) and Ruzhou (Henan Province).

Painting and calligraphy were well developed under the Song. An early form of theater appeared, the actors playing their parts on a square stage with railings all around. The performance of dramas on a stage had not been known before this time, although during the Tang period song, ballads, and dance were popular forms of court entertainment.

When the Song fell to the Mongols, China was subjugated for the first time by a foreign invader. Although the Yuan Dynasty (1279–1368) did not stimulate the development of art during its short existence, it reopened trade, and the renewed contact with foreign countries led to the importation of cobalt blue from Persia and the development of the first blue-and-white porcelains that were to become so famous in succeeding dynasties. Underglazed red porcelains were also developed featuring elaborate patterns—floral designs, dragons, and phoenix. Jingdezhen produced large quantities of fine blue-and-white porcelain, and specimens from those kilns were exported as far as India and Persia.

Only a few artists and scholars joined the alien court, the others preferring to flee to South China away from the invader. An important group of landscape painters established themselves in the south, the most notable of whom are Ni Zan, Huang Gong Wang, Wang Meng, and Wu Zhen. One who stayed was Shao Neng Fu, a landscape painter and calligrapher. He was also well known for his paintings of horses.

During the Ming period (1368–1644) art flourished, especially during the region of the third emperor, Yong Le, who provided opportunity for artists and artisans to produce creative works destined to embellish the palaces, pavilions, and gardens he established in and around Beijing.

Craftsmen produced the finest carved lacquer ware that has ever been seen and fine lacquered furniture. Artisans developed cloisonné enamel ware and created objects in precious metals in styles that have rarely been surpassed.

Superb porcelains were made, especially in blue-and-white designs, the most notable pieces being produced during the Xuan De period, 1426–1435. Other magnificent pieces were made at the end of the Ming period featuring landscapes and literary scenes rather than the dragon and floral motifs used for hundreds of years. Many of these pieces found their way to Europe and inspired the designers in pottery centers there to produce "Chinese styles." The "five-color" pieces were developed, using an underglaze including enamel, the precursor of the *famille verte* creations of the Qing Dynasty era.

Painting and calligraphy continued to develop under the Ming, the best known being Shen Zhou, founder of the Suzhou school; his pupil Wen Zheng Ming, and Dai Jin, whose work often depicted ordinary people engaged in daily activities.

When the Manchu invaded China and established the second period of foreign rule under the Qing Dynasty (1644–1911), the early emperors restored the damage that had been done during the invasion and had new palaces, gardens, and pavilions built. Under the Qing vast libraries were established, an encouragement to scholars, and the court painters were able to continue their traditional work. Some painters retired to Buddhist monasteries, notably Shi Tao (whose work is now exhibited in the Shanghai Museum), while others such as Bada Shan Ren and Hong Ren, actually became Buddhist monks. Others, like the "four masters named Wang," concerned themselves with different art forms.

Midway through the reign of the Qing many of the fine arts took a decided turn toward overextravagance and exaggerated decoration. The *famille verte* enamels were developed and were followed by the *famille rose,* many of the pieces featuring excessive decoration and the use of discordant colors, particularly in those pieces destined for the West.

The fall of the Manchu court in 1911 and the formation of the Republic ushered in a period of turmoil in China that was confusing for artists and stultified their development. Painting was probably the only art form that underwent some evolution. Perhaps the most famous artist of the period was Qi Bai Shi (1863–1957), whose paintings of flowers and animals, particularly shrimps and fish, were highly admired. Another was Ren Bo Nian. Some painters continued along the traditional path (Zhao Ji Qian, Yao Meng Fu, Ni Mo Geng), while others introduced foreign influences into their work, particularly those who had studied in the West and Japan (Zhen Shi Zheng, Gao Jian Fu, and Xu Bei Hong).

Poetry

For thousands of years the Chinese people have been imbued with the traditions of poetry. The earliest Chinese poems are to be found in one of the Confucian classics, *Book of Poetry,* otherwise known as the *Classic of Songs (Shi Jing).* The poems were then sung to the accompaniment of musical instruments. This rich source of material formed one of the two mainstreams of Chinese classical poetry, the other being *Li Sao,* the work of Qu Yuan, who lived in the fourth century B.C. These major works were the main inspiration for poets throughout the ages, particularly under the Tang, the Song, and the Yuan.

The poetic tradition in China has not perished. Many of the well-known leaders of China write poetry. Sometimes one will convey his thoughts to another by a poem and, in time, receive a poem in reply. It is this poetic form that has survived the revolution in the same way that calligraphy has. Indeed, the two are often inextricably bound together.

Although poetry is the main literary force in China, historical writings, the novel, and the short story also have an important place.

Historical Writings

One of the earliest historical works is the *Spring and Autumn Annals,* which relates the history of the Kingdom of Lu over the period 722–481 B.C. It forms part of the Confucian Canon which was developed over many centuries. Another work, again of Confucian origin, is the *Classic of Documents* or *Shu Jing,* dealing with the legendary kings of ancient China.

The first history of China, the *Historical Records* or *Shi Ji,* was written by a scholar, Si Ma Qian, who is regarded as one of China's finest writers. The work was compiled from original documents held in the imperial archives and libraries of Emperor Wu, one of the rulers of the Han Dynasty. From these sources a general history of China from the earliest known kingdoms until the events of the author's own era were recorded. Thereafter the work dominated historical literary efforts for nearly 20 centuries. The official historical works that followed also adopted the form laid down by Si Ma Qian. There now exists a continuous and uniform history of China from the Han to the end of the Ming which owes its style to this great historian.

Novels and Short Stories

Novels and short stories first appeared under the Six Dynasties. Both forms used material drawn from history and were largely written records of oral tales and anecdotes. The Buddhist and Taoist religions made great advances during this period, and their influence on the people and their tendency to stress the mind and the unity of the physical and supernatural world greatly influenced the tales of the era. These tales of mystery and imagination had developed by the seventh to the tenth centuries into a distinct literary form. It was also during this period, especially under the Tang, that prose in the form of novels developed. Although the themes were largely fantasies with elements of the supernatural, some stories had a romantic vein. Occasionally the writings used the supernatural theme as a cover for attacks on the social and political conditions of the day.

Under the Song, a period famous for its poetry, painting, and pottery, the first novels written in the vernacular appeared. It was an age of storytellers who enthralled audiences in market squares and in village streets all over China. They were often accompanied by musical instruments, gongs, and drums. Their stories were laced with poetry and song, and they used notes written in everyday language to help them during their performances. The storytellers were so popular and their art so widespread that their notes were copied and their stories expanded, a development which led eventually to the emergence of the spoken-word novel.

The greatest novels to emerge in later centuries were the *Romance of the Three Kingdoms* (a great favorite of Chairman Mao when he was a youth), and the *Water Margin,* otherwise known as *All Men Are Brothers,* or *Outlaws of the Marsh* (used by the radical group in the Party in 1975 to attack Confucianism and a number of Party leaders). Other famous works include *Xi You Ji,* or *Record of a Journey West, Dream of the Red Chamber,* or *The Story of the Stone,* and one of the great social satires in Chinese literature, *Ru Lin Wai Shi,* written in the eighteenth century.

Chinese writers concerned themselves more with narrative, the flow of events, and dramatic invention than with the development of their characters. Their works, largely because of their popular origins, were considered outside the mainstream of the country's literature. It was only when the empire fell and modern China began to emerge that the novel and short story took their rightful place as important art forms.

The downfall of traditional society in China in the early twentieth century brought to an end most literary efforts in traditional form. Before that, traditional literary education had been the substance of the power of the scholar-officials. Their means of ascending to power crumbled away when the examination system for traditional literary knowledge was abolished in 1904.

New ideas in democratic and scientific thought, largely from the West, had found the old literary language based on the ancient classics lacking. By the 1920s the written vernacular was adopted by law throughout China and taught in all schools. During this period the impact of foreign literature was considerable. The best-known writer of the period was Lu Xun, who is revered in China; but other first-class writers such as Mao Dun, Lao She, Cáo Yu, and Ba Jin created fine works of literature.

For a few years after the revolution in 1949, writers were encouraged to create new works. Then followed a backlash against the critics of the regime after the "Hundred Flowers" campaign of the mid-50s. Many writers were persecuted, some being sent to do manual labor in the "re-education" programs. Then, almost 10 years later, even greater suppression followed during the Cultural Revolution. Many more writers were criticized and humiliated, their works being suppressed.

Only in the late 70s was the repression relaxed and the authors "rehabilitated." Many of China's well-known works of literature were reprinted. Classics that were revered throughout China reappeared and were seized upon by a book-hungry public. Even the classic works of western and Russian writers were reprinted: Shakespeare, Dickens, Ibsen, Balzac, Flaubert, Hugo, Chekhov, Gogol, Turgenev, Tolstoy, and Pushkin being the most notable among them.

Novels and short stories by new Chinese writers are now appearing and being eagerly read. It is yet too early to tell whether these "new flowers" of literature will fade as quickly as they blossomed or will endure to become classics of the age.

Drama

Chinese drama has a long history; its origins are lost in antiquity. The earliest known theater appeared under the Song in the form of a square stage enclosed by railings. It is thought that theater was in existence before this period, as suggested by bas-relief carvings in Han tombs depicting play-acting. The courts of the Han gathered together groups of jugglers, acrobats, clowns, musicians, dancers, and singers, but it is doubtful if the tradition of presenting a full story enacted in dramatic form existed in those times. More likely these entertainers performed brief sketches to amuse the court.

Drama really began to flourish after the Mongol armies took China and the Yuan Dynasty (A.D. 1280–1368) was established. Then music, song, and dance were interwoven into well-developed plots, the actors—both men and women—giving performances in fixed theaters. In the old Yuan operas only the leading actor who portrayed the hero was permitted to sing parts of his role. Chinese theater became a complete art form in itself, incorporating visual and sound effects and using all forms of the lively arts.

From this time on, among the most popular forms of theatrical entertainment were the puppet show and shadow play. These drew for their themes on Chinese historical events, tales from former ages, and folk stories. Again, these shows used music and song to augment the action.

Since the nineteenth century the theater has been dominated by a form called Peking Opera featuring colorful costumes, elaborate make-up, stylized gestures, and dialogue spoken in the northern dialect (Mandarin). A Peking Opera is full of sound and color. The most famous Yuan operas are *Romance of the Western Chamber* and *The Lute;* the best-known Ming opera is the *Peony Pavilion;* the outstanding opera from the Qing is *Peach Blossom Fan.*

Although Peking Opera survived in China during the twentieth century up until the revolution, after 1949 it was changed so much that it was scarcely recognizable.

When the protagonists of the Cultural Revolution were removed from power in the late 70s, the revolutionary operas, which represented the model for all new theater presentations of this sort, were relegated to obscurity. Revivals of the famous Peking operas were produced, but because of the rambling plot and excessive length of some of them (some used to take an entire day to perform), abridged versions or excerpts are usually shown. Other operatic forms from Shanghai, Suzhou, and Guangzhou are also being produced.

Western visitors are sometimes offended by the screeching falsetto of the singers, the loud clacking of the clappers, the strident shriek of the fiddle (hu-qin), and the noisy banging of drums and cymbals. At first the noise may defy comprehension, but eventually the role of the strange little orchestra of eight to 10 pieces usually begins to emerge. The sounds in a Peking opera are as new and strange to most Westerners as the sounds of rock or Stravinski are to most Chinese.

Since the Cultural Revolution ended, new stage dramas and many revivals have been produced. It is ironic that Wu Han's *The Dismissal of Hai Rui* is playing once again, for the opening shot of the Cultural Revolution began with a criticism of this play and its author.

Calligraphy and Painting

Of the fine arts, calligraphy deserves special emphasis; the Chinese used to consider it the highest art form. The first great calligraphers lived in the period of the third through sixth centuries A.D. and their traditions were carried on right down to the Qing. Using a brush of animal hair dipped into ink made of soot from special woods mixed with resin, the calligrapher formed Chinese characters on paper with spontaneity and vigor. He brought life to the characters with elegant brushwork, an accomplishment that combined art and scholarship.

Training in calligraphy would begin soon after a child began to read and write. In the days of the imperial court it was a prerequisite for success in the examinations held to choose the scholar-officials. Even after the abolition of the system of examinations for scholar-officials in 1904, calligraphy continued to be widely practiced. Today in modern China you will see examples of the calligraphy of Mao Zedong, Zhou Enlai, and other leaders; it is perhaps the only art form that survived relatively unscathed following the revolution. The message conveyed is of course revolutionary, but the approach to creating art using Chinese characters is still basically the same.

Chinese painting grew up alongside calligraphy, the same brushes and inks being used on the same types of paper and silk. Before paper was invented in China, about A.D. 105, and before silk became less of a luxury, Chinese painting was mostly done on walls. The oldest frescoes still in existence are to be found in the Dun Huang Buddhist caves in Gansu Province. As the art of papermaking became more widespread, artists began to paint more and more on scrolls, in the early stages concentrating on Buddhist themes.

Under the Tang (A.D. 618–907) painters turned to a particular form of landscape painting known as *shan-shui,* of "mountain and water," in what was essentially a visual presentation of the relationship between nature and man. A Chinese painting was a philosophical exercise attempting to examine the meaning of nature and man's place in the scheme of things. There was no attempt to reproduce nature in visual form and no pursuit of the composition of light or the technical aspects of perspective. Colors, if used at all, were applied sparingly, and tonal qualities were conveyed by altering the intensity of the ink. The artist's brushwork was the means by which he conveyed his personal style. Chinese painters never painted directly from scenery but always from memory. The final result was a reflection of the psyche of the artist and his character. Greatness in a painting could only come from the greatness of the man. All the qualities revealed in a fine painting were those that existed in the artist.

Music

Music has always meant more to the Chinese than relaxation and the pleasure of listening. They believe that music has a philosophical relevance to life and is an essential part of the harmonious relationship between man, nature, and the spirit. Traditional Chinese music probably had its origin in ancient religious rites performed in temples and the courts of ancient kings.

A number of Chinese instruments have been unearthed that have no counterpart today, but many are precursors of the instruments used in traditional music now. Although the range of instruments in China is limited, the varieties within the different types are considerable.

Percussion instruments exist in great variety and are made from quite different materials. Bells, gongs, drums, and cymbals have been used for thousands of years in religious ceremonies and were adapted to popular music in very early days. Wind instruments are made of wood or bamboo and range from flutes to mouth organs.

Excavations have revealed that musical instruments were in use more than 3,500 years ago, while historical records suggest that the egg-shaped ocarina was invented in even earlier times. The predecessor of the yu, or pitch pipes, dates from about 3000 B.C. The qin, or lute, was also in existence at about the same time and was certainly well known during the Zhou dynasty period (1122–770 B.C.) when it had been developed to produce the refined and subdued sounds that characterize this well-known instrument.

Stringed instruments have always played an important part in Chinese music. The most familiar instruments are the pipa, somewhat like a mandolin, the er hu, or two-string violin, and the si hu which has four strings, the last two being played with a bow. The other stringed instrument which is most important in Chinese music is the qin referred to earlier. In ancient times, the rounded top end of the instrument represented heaven while the square bottom end represented earth. This philosophical relationship between music, musical instruments, man, the earth, and heaven was later reflected in the Confucian school where music corresponded to what is "heaven" in man and common to all human beings, while "rites" corresponded to the "earth" in man and the differences between men.

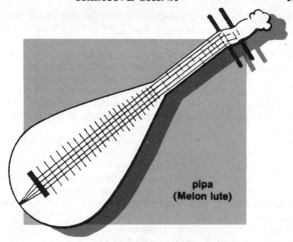

pipa
(Melon lute)

Music and rites, that is "heaven" and "earth," became an inseparable part of Confucian and court ceremonies. Indeed, classical music was eventually thought of as a means of regulating the state and perfecting the individual.

Man's reverence for music and its role in Chinese society led to a classical work on the subject by Ma Yong, a disciple of Confucius. His work became the standard reference material on the application and theory of music for more than 2,000 years and were an essential part of the teaching of classical music in China's schools, where more than half the teaching time was devoted to this subject. It was the solemn duty of every young man of artistic bent to undertake a nine-year course in classical music so that he could participate in the emperor's ceremonies, the court pageants, and the religious rites. The ceremonies at court sometimes involved many hundred of musicians, singers, and dancers performing for days on end.

The upheavals that heralded the end of the Zhou dynasty also heralded for a time the demise of ancient classical music. However, traditions were restored again during the Han dynasty (206 B.C.–A.D. 220), and during this period Chinese musical traditions began to make their way to Korea, Japan, Mongolia, and Vietnam. Later, Chinese music was itself influenced by the introduction of instruments from foreign countries, particularly India. Indeed, the introduction around 140 B.C. of the Indian sitar marks a significant turning point in Chinese music.

Following the downfall of the Han dynasty, the development of music again went into a decline for about 400 years, only to be revived again during the Tang (A.D. 618–907). During this era, music flourished again and classical techniques were revived. The common people, as distinct from the aristocracy and the court, began to take up musical instruments so that the traditions of music became more pervasive. It was also during this period that the oldest known musical notation was developed. Until then music had been traditionally learned by ear. However, the best-known form of musical notation came later: it was adopted around the tenth and eleventh centuries and has, except for a few modifications, been used until the present day.

The Ming dynasty (1368–1644) saw the restoration of classical music as a complement to state ceremonies, rituals, and functions. Yet probably the most significant development under the Ming was the emergence of Chinese opera, a forerunner of the Peking and Cantonese operas of today.

In the northern opera, the leading player is the only participant who sings, the supporting cast speaking all their lines; in the southern opera all members of the cast participate in the singing.

Toward the end of the Ming dynasty classical music again went into decline, but was revived again under the Qing (1644–1911), the foreign Manchu invaders wishing to preserve the old forms of art in China. The se (a 25-stringed instrument resembling a zither) and the qin (which had all but disappeared), were reintroduced. A considerable number of scholarly works on music and musical instruments were published during the period.

Western musical notation was introduced during the nineteenth century, but it was only after the downfall of the Qing that Western music really became popular in China, being played in concerts and on radio to an increasingly large audience. However, in 1949, when the Communists came to power, Western-style music along with traditional Chinese music was rejected as either feudal, middle class, or imperialistic. Nevertheless, most of the music composed under the Communists adopted Western forms and was written for musical instruments of the West. Many of the compositions were of martial tradition with lyrics attempting to inspire the people of China to rouse themselves in support of the revolution and socialism.

During the decade 1966–1976, many Chinese musicians were purged and their works destroyed, following the attacks made on intellectuals, artists and others in the period known as the Cultural Revolution. Late in the 1970s, the mild cultural thaw that occurred in China affected music as it did all other forms of art. Many of the old and famous Peking operas were produced, as were the traditional opera forms of Shanghai, Suzhou, and Guangzhou. Even foreign operas were put on. Chinese symphony orchestras are once again playing music by Western composers; leading musicians and conductors from foreign countries have been invited to China on cultural exchange programs; and Chinese orchestras and opera troupes are now touring foreign countries to perform before international audiences.

Architecture

Traditional Chinese architecture considers the building to be an integral part of the surrounding countryside, not an entity in itself. It is regarded as a monument, not simply a place to be used. Harmony should be created between the different buildings, and between the group of buildings and the surrounding environment.

Buildings were invariably laid out on a North-South axis, the courtyards between the major buildings being flanked by smaller pavilions. Buildings were usually one-storied with particular emphasis given to the roof, following the traditions largely established under the Tang and the Song.

While the structure of the roof is the same throughout China, the shape varies. In the South, it is more exaggerated, with greater curvature near the extremities. In the North, the roof is more austere and the curvature subdued. A notable feature of Chinese roofs are the glazed figurines (*kuilongzi*), usually made of terracotta. The tiles on important buildings were, by tradition, always glazed, mostly in yellow or blue. Ordinary buildings had roofs with unglazed tiles, mostly gray. The Chinese roof is generally supported by wooden columns, not by the walls. The columns have no capitals because the roof is placed directly on them.

The layout of towns tended to follow the principles adopted for the layout of buildings, the whole town being considered a monument. Great emphasis was placed on the arrangement of buildings along the north-south axis, and it was this feature, rather than the central square, which marks the layout of Chinese towns. Usually the town itself had a wall or double wall constructed around it containing numerous gates, each with a tower on top. These gates and the drum and bell towers were traditional features of the larger Chinese settlements.

China is noted for its pagodas, buildings erected to mark the site of a holy place or to house the Buddhist holy books, or *sutras*. Most of the pagodas surviving today are constructed of brick. The oldest is in Henan on the grounds of the Song Yue Temple, and was constructed about A.D. 523. A great many brick and wood pagodas exist in China today, some restored and some in derelict state. None of them is used for religious observance now.

Under the Qing, a religious building called a *dagoba* became popular; a famous example is the White Dagoba in Bei Hai Park at Beijing. The architectural style for the dagoba originated in India.

Chinese scholars have been fortunate in being able to study ancient architectural forms from the funerary objects retrieved from the tombs of emperors and members of the court. Many of these objects were fashioned to represent the buildings of the day and provide a vivid record of China's architectural past.

Wood carvings in temples also characterized the architecture of ages past. A particularly fine example is found in the Lower Hua Yan Monastery at Datong.

Architecture was also important in the construction of tombs for the emperors. The layout of the chamber to house the corpse followed the same tradition from the Han era onwards. The site of the tomb was chosen after a study had been made of the disposition of wind and water according to the laws of *feng shui*. The chamber was usually dug into the ground, filled in after the corpse had been put into place, and protected by a huge mound or tumulus. Many false passages and traps were made to deceive or kill tomb robbers. Archeologists and historians can be grateful for the success of many of these devices; the opening up of tombs has led to a greater understanding of Chinese history and past ways of life.

Gardens have long played an important part in Chinese architecture and are considered a natural extension of the rooms of a building. Above all, Chinese gardens convey a sense of mystery; no one vantage point gives an idea of the whole. The garden usually comprises different sections linked by small passageways, zigzag paths, small bridges, and covered ways. A Chinese garden is often likened to a traditional landscape painting, and indeed the elements of *shan shui* (mountain, water) are closely linked to this art form. Different styles of garden exist, varying according to location and the types of vegetation and rock available in the region. The gardens of Guangzhou, for example, in the far south of China are different from those of Suzhou in the middle region of the country, and both differ from the gardens of the north.

Chinese gardens, once the preserve of the ruling class and the rich, have now been made available to the ordinary man and woman. The citizens of China flock to these havens and make full use of the facilities. There is probably more spontaneity among the general Chinese public in the gardens and parks of a town than you can perceive anywhere else.

Sculpture

Ancient Chinese sculpture developed as a tomb art, to reproduce objects and figures representing the worldly possessions of the deceased, essential for happiness in the spirit world. However, sculpture did not really become

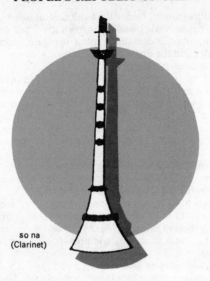

so na
(Clarinet)

important until the Buddhist religion began to spread through China, having been brought into the country by the merchants arriving by caravan along the "Silk Road." As it spread, caves were dug out of the hillside and statues representing the Buddha and events in his life were carved from the rockface. Hundreds of these rock shrines were created, but the most famous still in existence are located at Dunhuang in Gansu Province, Yun Gang in Shaaxi Province, and Long Men in Henan Province.

Carving was always considered a minor art form, created through the collective efforts of artisans rather than by the individual work of artists. After the Tang Dynasty fell, sculptural art gradually declined and never really emerged again as a major form in Chinese art.

Folk Art

Folk art has a long tradition in China and reflects the mores, beliefs, and aspirations of the people in the same way that poetry, calligraphy, and painting reflected the life of the intellectuals.

Folk art activities include dollmaking, weaving, rattan and bamboo work, pottery, painting, and making paper cutouts. These activities were once carried out by peasant women who remained indoors because they were too old to work in the fields, were sick or pregnant. Even today, when there are slack periods during the agricultural cycle, the entire family participates in folk art and handicrafts.

CHINESE CUISINE

Most people have tried Chinese dishes of some sort at Chinese restaurants in their own country, for Chinese cuisine is known the world around. However, you are indeed fortunate if you can visit China and try some of the exquisite dishes in the home of this art. You will almost certainly detect a difference in quality, substance, and style in the food prepared in China compared with the food served at many Chinese restaurants abroad. That is not to say that fine Chinese restaurants do not exist beyond the borders of China; there are many, but to the gastronome and amateur alike, eating Chinese food in China is like eating French food in France: you are at the heart of things.

Most visitors appreciate that Chinese cooking has traditions which go further back in history than those of French cuisine, and understand that it is an art which grew out of a highly developed civilization. While Chinese cooking uses almost all of the meat, poultry, fish, and vegetables known to the Western palate, it has also embraced other foodstuffs which, to Western taste, may appear rare or even repugnant.

As Marco Polo put it: "They eat all sorts of flesh, including that of dogs and other brute beasts and animals of every kind which Christians would not touch for anything in the world." The Cantonese, for example, are said to make use of "anything with four legs excluding tables," and cook dog, cat, snake, bear, monkey, and birds' nests in various forms. However, if your tastes are not adventurous, do not be put off by these unusual dishes; they are not in the mainstream of Chinese cooking. There is any amount of other food prepared in ways that will delight your palate.

In contrast to the subtlety and delicacy of Chinese food itself, the surroundings are often simple, even austere. In Beijing there are few restaurants outside of the major hotels possessing any visual appeal but Guangzhou is different. Some of the restaurants there are set in the most beautiful grounds featuring groves of bamboo, stands of tropical trees, decorative gardens, goldfish ponds, and small pavilions.

Styles of Chinese Cooking

One of the highlights of your visit to China will be the opportunity to savor the exquisite regional dishes of China. The main styles of Chinese cooking are Cantonese, Northern or Pekinese, Shanghainese, Sichuan, Fukienese, and Chaozhou.

Cantonese Style

The Cantonese style of cooking is probably the most familiar to the Western palate, for the greater number of Chinese restaurants established outside China are of this type. The name for this school of cuisine comes from the old name for the southern city now known as Guangzhou. Features of this style are the great variety of dishes and the beauty of their presentation. Steam and water are used in preparation more than frying, and the great abundance of fresh vegetables in the region are cooked for the shortest time possible to maintain their natural crispness. The dishes have a slight tendency to be sweet and spices are used with moderation.

The banquet usually begins with a cold plate made up of a variety of meats and vegetables in the form of an animal such as a peacock, phoenix, butterfly, or fish. Not only are different foods used for color effect; they are positioned according to the texture they give to the visual form. To appreciate the artistry of this dish it is worthwhile standing up after it is placed on the table in order to see it in better perspective. Photographers delight in the subject matter. When you finally get down to eating the dish you will note that the contents comprise a variety of foodstuffs such as chopped liver, minced quail eggs, smoke-cured ham, prawn slices wrapped in translucent rice flour, cold wine chicken slices, to name but a few.

Main dishes are roasted goose, fresh straw mushrooms bathed in a sauce of white shredded crabmeat, large prawns sauteed in ginger and scallion sauce, rice birds served on a bed of green vegetables, chicken slices with sharksfin (a most elegant and sought-after rarity), wintermelon soup, beef cooked in oyster sauce, boned fish, turtle, eel, and white chicken. There are also many dishes based on snake, baby seal, dog, cat, and the famous but now very rare delicacy, bear's paws.

Desserts on the menu usually comprise four or five different sweet cakes made individually from such materials as water chestnut jelly, walnut cream, and almond cream—all served either hot or cold. Fresh fruits usually follow the desserts.

Typical of Cantonese cooking is the *dim sum* which is generally served for lunch. This course consists of a variety of little dumplings and meats chosen by the guests from a cart brought to the table; there are roast pork buns, shrimp toasts, chopped pork formed into flowers, spring rolls, little ribs in black-bean sauce, watercress, and steamed beef balls, to name a few.

As Guangzhou is in the south of China in a high-rainfall crop area it is not surprising that white rice is the usual accompaniment to the meal.

Northern Style

Northern or Pekinese cooking tends to be oilier and the dishes more salty and spicy. Grains other than rice tend to be used, and there are countless varieties of "breads" in the form of dumplings, buns, and noodles.

The northern cooking style has evolved from four distinct backgrounds. The methods of cooking indigenous to Hebei Province, which surrounds Beijing, and Shandong Province, which is contiguous, have been a major influence. Another has been the style of cooking found in the lower Yangzi River area, and yet another comes from one province in the central west, Sichuan. A fourth influence has been the Moslem cooking of Inner Mongolia and Xinjiang, which features barbecuing, deep boiling, roasting, and the use of rich seasonings and sauces. And finally there is the cuisine of the Old Imperial Palace which, by virtue of the origin of the last dynasty, brought the influence of Manchurian cooking to China and with it the tendency to highly refined and rare dishes.

All these cooking styles make extensive use of local vegetables such as garlic, ginger, leeks, tomatoes, scallions (spring onions), bean sauces and pastes, cucumber, and particularly the famous northern white cabbage; for meats: duck, pork, chicken, and seafoods, particularly prawns. The Chinese Moslem influence was largely responsible for the introduction of beef, lamb, and duck into the northern repertoire.

Although restaurants in Beijing may be found serving food dominated by one of the four influences, by far the greatest number represent either the Hebei/Shandong style or the Moslem-Chinese influence. The relatively small impact that the magnificent Cantonese style of cooking has had in the north often leads southerners to describe northern cooking as "provincial." This description is hardly fitting; yet it is difficult to find many restaurants in Beijing which cater to the taste of those who prefer the cuisine of the Lower Yangzi and central west, while restaurants preparing Cantonese food are rarer still.

Many visitors to China are surprised to learn that the northern style has been so influenced by Chinese-Moslem cooking. Yet this population is quite extensive and lives even now in a belt of land stretching westward from Beijing through Inner Mongolia to the far western border of the Soviet Union. These nomads had extensive herds and flocks and brought to northern cooking many lamb and beef dishes, particularly Mongolian hot pot and also the famous Peking roast duck.

Shanghai Style

The Shanghai school of cooking is dominated by the *Sooche* influence, which is based on the cuisine in and around Nanjing, Suzhou, Hangzhou, and, of course, Shanghai itself.

Shanghai food tends to be heavier than Cantonese and usually takes slightly longer to prepare, this lengthier preparation for vegetables and meats rendering them softer so that they tend to absorb more of the sauces. Much of the food is fried and there is greater use of sesame oil and vinegar. Spices like garlic, ginger, and small (but very hot) red peppers are used; the seasonings tend to be sweeter with more sugar and dark soy used in their preparation. Noodles are favored, although rice is eaten more in this region than wheat. The rich variety of vegetables available in the region ensures their widespread use in many of the dishes.

Shanghai's position on the coast and the existence of a large fishing fleet there supplies the city with a rich variety of seafood. Prawns, crab, and salt-water fish therefore feature in this style of cooking, and these seafoods are supplemented by freshwater fish, particularly carp, and the famous hairy crab. Of course there is an abundance of chicken, duck, and pork available for meat dishes.

One of the favored ways of preparing dishes in the region is the "red-cook" method, where chunks of meat are cooked for a long time in sugar, soy, ginger, and mixed spices. The other is the well-known sweet-and-sour method of preparing food, particularly carp, a favorite dish from the Hangzhou area. Another style is to cook a whole chicken or big fish-head in a glazed ceramic pot with vegetables prepared in their own juices.

Sichuan Style

Sichuan (and Hunan) cooking is characterized by the use of many spices and liberal application of pimiento and hot red peppers. Noodles are a very popular basis for the meal, and the hot form of this dish is known throughout China as Sichuan noodles. Hot bean curd, usually heavily spiced, is also another staple of the Sichuan menu.

Some of the better known dishes are minced bean curd in pepperground pork, sauteed eggplant slices, and sliced meats, poultry, and seafoods cooked in an essence described as "fish-flavored." This essence derives its flavor from a combination of garlic, vinegar, ginger, and chili, and has nothing at all to do with fish. You will sometimes see dishes of this sort described as "pork with fishy flavor" or "prawns with fishy flavor," but they are more suitably translated as "Sichuan pork" or "Sichuan prawns." Another favorite dish is hot spicy chicken with peanut sauce, hot prawns with peanuts, and cold noodles in red pepper and sesame oil.

The Chinese feel that spices are necessary in hotter, damper climates to stimulate the appetite, and this is one of the explanations given for the development of the particularly hot cuisine of Sichuan and Hunan.

Fujien Style

Fujien cooking is another style that is popular in China. It is similar to the Cantonese style except that more of the dishes are fried rather than steamed, not too much oil is used, and the dishes are not too spicy. Some tend to be sweet and feature coconut and pineapple.

Chaozhou Style

The Chaozhou style is also well known: almost every dish comes with a different sauce, and so food prepared in this way is favored by those who like to dip. There are a number of Chaozhou restaurants in Guangzhou. The food tends to be salty and the dishes are usually eaten not with ordinary rice but with a kind of rice soup. Most of the dishes are fried.

A favorite dish is sliced goose fried in goose blood, the morsels being dipped into a sauce of white vinegar and chopped garlic. Salted pickled vegetables are an important part of the menu. Another feature is the variety of strong tea served at the beginning and end of each meal, standard tea being served as the main refreshment during the banquet.

Three Senses and Five Tastes

In Chinese gastronomy three senses must be satisfied: smell, sight, and taste. To begin with a dish should not have a strong aroma dominating the other dishes. Certainly any unpleasant smells would not be tolerated.

In addition, a dish must be of an appearance and composition that is pleasing to the eye, and there should be a balance not only of colors but of different textures. As for taste, there are five considered necessary: salty, sweet, sour, hot, and acidic. And "balance" is not confined to taste alone: the texture of food in the mouth should vary, so that a banquet should contain dry and sticky dishes as well as crisp and juicy ones. Usually a crisp dish is followed by a smooth one, and the salt dish followed by a sweet one, and so on.

Famous Chinese Dishes

There are many Chinese dishes that are well known throughout the world and even though they may not have been tasted by a great many, people have heard of them. For example, one of the great dishes is **Birds' Nest Soup,** which is made from the mucus from the salivary glands of the small salangane. The mucus is collected by boiling the nests of these birds. It is a soup with a most subtle flavor.

Shark's Fin is another rare and famous dish and, because the fins are purchased dried, requires a long and careful preparation, after which only about half is usable. The shark's fin is usually braised in three changes of chicken stock before it can be served. In preparing shark's fin soup, half a catty is required for 12 servings. Only the loose shark's fin is used, and this is prepared with shredded chicken, crabmeat, or pork in chicken stock. The finest and most costly shark's fin soup is a clear one to which no starch is added. To allow guests to savor the delicate soups made from shark's fin, they are served at the beginning of a banquet, a rare exception to the Chinese practice of serving soup at the end.

Another world-famous dish is **Peking Roast Duck,** one of northern China's famous specialties. It is prepared from a 3–4-month-old white Peking duck; after cleaning, the duck is plugged and half filled with water; it is then placed in the oven so that while the water steams the inside of the duck, the outside is roasted over a fire made from wood of the jujube, pear, or apricot tree. The duck is cooked for about three-quarters of an hour and is basted with its own fat.

The whole duck is usually brought to the table by the chef and then taken away to be cut into thin slices which are eaten wrapped in thin crepes or in rolls covered with sesame seed. The slices of duck are usually dipped into a thin brown sauce, chopped leeks, cucumber, and scallion.

In the famous **Mongolian Hot Pot,** thinly sliced strips of lamb are cooked in boiling water contained in a special vessel attached to a brazier. The lamb strips are picked up with chopsticks and placed in the boiling water, then taken out a few minutes later, when cooked, to be dipped in one or more of the sauces that are set out for each guest, such as soy, shrimp, pimiento, wine, chive, bean-curd, or sesame-seed sauce. To end the meal a soup is prepared using vegetables, noodles, and bean curd which are added to the boiling stock in the brazier.

Sea Cucumbers are also well known to foreign visitors, perhaps more for the distaste they arouse than the delight they bring to the palate. However, to the Chinese these small sea creatures represent one of the finest gastronomic experiences possible. They are often served with abalone or fish maw, so if you do not like the thought of swallowing the sea slugs themselves, concentrate on the other portion of the dish.

Another famous dish consists of **"Hundred-Year-Old Eggs."** These, despite common belief, are not over 100 years old but have been slowly cooked by chemical reaction brought about by immersing them in a lime bath.

Snake is a highly fancied dish in the south of China but is rarely eaten in the north; it is usually in the form of stews or soups and has a flavor somewhat like chicken. **Bear's Paws** are another famous dish but are becoming extremely rare; some gastronomes consider them the rarest delicacy of all.

Fruit is almost always served at a Chinese banquet, usually at the end but not always so; and aside from local fruits, such as mandarin oranges, kumquats, etc., there are strawberries, grapes, chestnuts, and figs to be ordered, as well as tropical fruit such as pineapples, mangoes, and papaya. You should also try the delicately flavored lichees, well known in China and abroad, and also longans, which come exclusively from the southern provinces. The persimmon is also highly favored by the inhabitants and is picked in the late autumn. Azerolas are usually eaten in a form similar to toffee apples.

There are other well-known dishes, and these are described in the section devoted to recommended menus for specific restaurants.

Dining Customs

Banquets

Banquets are a feature of almost every visitor's stay in China, and you will no doubt find yourself eating unfamiliar food and downing many toasts.

If you do not like a dish and it is served onto your plate, accept the food graciously and simply leave it untouched. Your plate will soon be whisked away and an empty one provided for the next course. If you do not drink alcohol or do not like the potent *mao tai,* you will not cause offense by toasting with another beverage. Wine is probably more acceptable for this purpose than mineral water, soft drink, or beer, but the most important thing is to honor the spirit of the toast in some way or other.

Chopsticks are normally used in China, but you should not hesitate to ask for a knife and fork if you are embarrassed about your ability to eat with the Chinese implements. However, your hosts will show infinite patience with your attempts to master the use of chopsticks, and you will be surprised at how quickly you will progress.

Chopsticks are made from a variety of materials ranging from plain wood, lacquered wood, bamboo, and ebony to ivory. They have been used in China for thousands of years and were in existence long before the ladies and gentlemen of the courts of Europe gave up eating with their fingers and took to the knife and fork.

Not surprisingly, the use of chopsticks has had its effect on the preparation of the food: each course has to be cut up into pieces beforehand. As a result, the original food is sometimes unrecognizable and the natural flavor augmented or even masked by piquant sauces.

The meal is begun when the host takes up the pair of serving chopsticks before him and places food on the plates of the guests sitting on either side. If you are the host, it is not good etiquette or hygienic to use your own chopsticks to place food on other guests' plates (although it was once standard practice).

The seating arrangements at a Chinese banquet follows custom: the host sits opposite the entrance door and the guests will be seated to his right and left according to precedence. Alternatively, the guest of honor will be placed opposite the door leading into the room with the other guests to the right and left of him or her in order of precedence, the host taking the last place. The first method seems to be the one usually adopted in China now. (Incidentally, the custom of seating the guest of honor facing the door is to reassure him that he will not be murdered from behind during the banquet. This was apparently a standard way of disposing of a rival in ancient times.)

On formal occasions and at official functions, speeches and toasts are invariably made. If you are sharing a banquet with members of your tour group, or the occasion is a relaxed get-together, then you won't be bothering about any speeches and your only toast will probably be a simple "here's cheers."

The first speech on a formal occasion is always made by the host. The guest of honor may either reply immediately or wait for one or two courses before responding. If you are a guest, you may raise your glass to drink to the health of your host or those guests sitting around you, but a toast involving the full table is normally made only after the opening speech. Toasts are made right through the banquet, usually by raising a glass of *mao tai* or other beverage to the person sitting next to you, to those sitting around you, or to the whole table. Sometimes the toast can be simply a quiet exchange with your neighbor, and sometimes you may rise and clink the glasses of all the guests at the table, in which case they will rise and do likewise.

Where there is more than one table of guests at a banquet, the host, at the conclusion of his opening speech, may proceed to the next table, clink the glass of each of the foreign guests, drink a toast, refill, and then move on to the next table to repeat the sequence, finally coming back to the head table to toast the guests there. If you are a guest of honor at a banquet where this procedure is followed, it is courteous at the end of your response to adopt a similar procedure, this time toasting in turn all the Chinese guests at the other tables, proceeding one table at a time and leaving your own table until last.

You will know when the meal is over, for banquets as a rule end with fruit served either at the table where you are sitting or at small tables set before the armchairs where you were first received. Hot towels are usually distributed at this point so that you can wipe your face and hands.

It is polite to depart about 10 minutes after the towels have been passed and the last cups of tea have been drunk. The guest of honor makes the first move to depart from a banquet and all the other guests are expected to leave at the same time. Normally, at restaurants located outside hotels, dinners begin early (6:30–7 P.M.) and end early (8:30 P.M.). Lingering is not appreciated.

Tour Group Banquets

Tour groups traveling in China often arrange informal banquets in addition to those that are included in their package. If you have been satisfied with the attention you have received from your guides in that particular center, it would be a nice gesture to invite them to the banquet as guests of the group. If they decline your invitation, do not persist. On most occasions, however, they will be pleased to share a meal with you and your group.

Banquets in Hotel Restaurants

If you want to arrange a banquet for a small or large group at your hotel, you should contact the particular restaurant ahead of time. You will be asked how much per person you want to spend (excluding beverages), the number of guests, and whether you have any preferences concerning the courses to be served. Most hotel-restaurants make it easy for guests by having a range of banquet menus available at set prices. After selecting one of these, all you have to do is set the date and time.

Banquets in Other Restaurants

If you wish to arrange a banquet for a group of people in a restaurant located outside of a hotel, then you will still need to enlist the aid of your hotel. Some hotels have a form that you will be asked to fill out, specifying the restaurant and other details. Otherwise ask someone on the lobby floor to call the restaurant that you have chosen.

In either case, you will be expected to indicate the price that you wish to pay per person (excluding beverages), the number of guests, and whether you have any preference concerning the courses to be served. If you do not wish to specify particular dishes, the restaurant will attempt to provide a suitably balanced meal within the price limit set.

Bookings should be made at least a day in advance to ensure the best service, but some restaurants will provide excellent meals even if advance notice is not given. Popular restaurants may need as much as 3 to 4 days' notice for a banquet.

Most banquets start about 6:30–7 P.M. and usually take about two hours to complete. It is the custom to leave the restaurant about 10 minutes after you have finished eating. Most restaurants expect to close by 8:30 P.M.

Return Formal and Business Banquets

Visiting delegations are sometimes given a welcome banquet by their Chinese hosts. It is polite to offer and arrange a return banquet. It is usually sufficient to extend an invitation orally. Once it is accepted you should make arrangements as far in advance as possible.

Similarly, visiting business executives, either alone or as part of a company delegation, usually return the hospitality of their hosts by arranging a return banquet before departing from China.

Dining Out in Guangzhou

Few visitors to China will be unfamiliar with food cooked Cantonese-style, simply because the large proportion of Chinese restaurants established around the world serve food that is Cantonese, or strongly influenced by this school of cooking. Visitors thus have the chance to eat at the home of Cantonese cuisine—Guangzhou—and compare indigenous Cantonese cooking with that they know at home.

You will note that we used the words "Canton" and "Cantonese" in this section. These have been adopted because they have become internationally accepted in relation to Chinese cuisine. And the word "Canton," despite its association in the Chinese mind with foreign exploitation and national humiliation, can be freely used in China, although when speaking of subjects other than cooking it is probably more polite to use the name "Guangzhou."

During your visit to China you will also be in a position to compare the food prepared in the two great gastronomic centers of the nation: Guangzhou and Beijing.

Dining out in Guangzhou is altogether different from dining out in

Beijing. For one thing, the style of cooking is different; for another, the setting and decor of some of the restaurants in Guangzhou are magnificent, in contrast to the austerity of Beijing's restaurants.

The description of the dishes is more poetic in Guangzhou. How could anyone be more subtle than a chef who describes a dish as "Dragon and Tiger" when he is referring to snake and civet cat? Or "Snake Crossing the Mountain Peaks" for a soup containing meat from the boa constrictor? Or "Fragrant Meat" when referring to dog?

Such dishes are exceptions, not in the mainstream of Cantonese cooking; but the poetry extends to dishes which will find favor with the Western visitor's palate. For example, "A Hundred Flowers Floating on the Lake" is a consommé in which poached quail eggs, decorated to resemble flowers, float on the surface; "Jade Trees" are green vegetables.

Another notable difference is the emphasis given to the appearance of the food. This is nowhere more noticeable than in the presentation of cold hors d'oeuvres, where the foodstuffs will be arranged to form a bird, butterfly, or flower. They will be distributed to provide not only an appropriate color but the right textural appearance as well. Stand up and take a good look at this when it is served. You will often feel it is too attractive to break up for serving.

Keep your eyes open when the other dishes are served. You will often notice the decorative touch that has been deftly applied; a fine example is the filigree carving on the top of the melon used as the bowl in presenting the famous winter-melon soup. There is a host of other examples.

The Top Ten Restaurants of Guangzhou

In the pages that follow, we list the "top ten" restaurants of Guangzhou. You will not usually have time to try them all, but any one of them will prepare a meal or banquet that you will long remember. Also listed are three speciality restaurants: snake, vegetarian, and game.

Nan Yuan. The Nan Yuan, or South Garden Restaurant, is a good 15 minutes' taxi ride from the city center but well worth the effort. You arrive to find a glade hidden behind a white wall topped with green glazed tiles. Inside is one of the most beautifully landscaped greeneries you will ever see: bamboo groves, camphor trees, flowering vines, and colorful orchids set amid ponds and running brooks. There are small dining pavilions with finely worked colored glass windows, deep blues and whites predominating. The setting is perfect for serving the exquisite food prepared by the chefs of this restaurant.

A specialty is the Assorted Cold Platter served to commence the meal. A variety of meats, poultry, seafoods, and vegetables are put together to represent a butterfly or peacock, for example. The dish is typical of the Cantonese approach to cooking: food should have visual appeal as well as satisfying the taste buds. Another speciality is Mao-tai Chicken; this dish, as the name suggests, has a pungent flavor derived from the famous and potent Chinese liquor in which it is cooked.

The Nan Yuan is at 120 Qianjin Lu (tel. 550532, 448380, 551576).

Bei Yuan. The Bei Yuan, or North Garden Restaurant, is in an old teahouse surrounded by ornamental pools connected by paths and framed by stands of tropical plants and fine gardens.

A specialty of the restaurant is the famous Shark's Fin Soup with Shredded Chicken. Shark's fin is a delicacy in China, and in this dish it is combined with shredded chicken to form a subtly flavored broth. Usually a small bowl of pink-colored vinegar is placed alongside your plate; you should add a little to your shark's fin to bring out the subtlety of the flavors.

Another specialty, Shao Xing Chicken, is cooked whole in the Hua Diao brand of Shao Xing red wine. It is served sliced, and it possesses a special fragrance and subtle sweetness.

Another excellent dish is Chopped Crab Balls. The crabmeat is finely chopped and compressed, then deep-fried. It is served with the small piece of claw protruding.

The Bei Yuan is at 320 Dongfeng Road (tel. 332471, 332466).

Ban Xi. From the outside, this fine restaurant resembles a vast private residence. Inside, the dining rooms are situated in rambling teahouses spread around a small lake. One section of the restaurant is even located on a floating houseboat. You should take the opportunity of strolling around this landscaped garden restaurant, following the zigzag paths up and down, over bridges, across ornamental lakes, alongside bamboo groves, and through stands of tropical foliage. The center piece is a three-story teahouse with upswept eaves, traditional Chinese roof, and decorated window glass in deep blues and white.

Although the restaurant caters for a vast number of guests, the atmosphere is dominated by the beauty of the surroundings. However, as you would expect from one of Guangzhou's finest restaurants, the dishes prepared and served there match the images that greet the visitor. Nor is the comfort of guests forgotten: there is a section which has been modernized and includes air-conditioning, a facility visitors appreciate in the hotter, more humid months. But since this section was more recently built you will be sacrificing old-world charm for modern comfort.

A banquet at this restaurant often begins with cold hors d'oeuvres arranged, for example, in the shape of a bird or butterfly. The Scallop and Crab Soup is prepared with shredded dry scallops, a Chinese delicacy, and shredded crabmeat in a chicken stock, cooked with herbs and mixed with eggwhite.

Another specialty is Quail Eggs on a Bed of Green Vegetables. Quail eggs are a Guangzhou specialty. They are served hard-boiled after having been cooked with shrimp roe. The sauce is also derived from shrimp roe. The color, smooth texture, and taste of the quail eggs contrast with the flavor of young green vegetables.

The Ban Xi is at 151 Xiang Yang Road 1 (tel. 885655, 888706, 889318).

Guangzhou. The Guangzhou restaurant is set in a rambling old teahouse with many staircases and terraces. Foreign visitors dine upstairs, where there is a maze of landings with individual dining salons located on the various terraces. It is a noisy, animated place with the central courtyard overlooked by verandas on each floor. When you look down from your own veranda you will see room after room of diners and hear the chatter, laughter, and clink of plates rising from the floors below.

Depending on the season you should try to begin your banquet with a soup that is a Cantonese specialty. Eight Treasures in Winter-Melon Soup is served in a hollowed-out melon. The top of the melon is carved in a filigree effect, and the translucent melon meat contrasts with the dark green of the skin, giving the effect of a magnificent jade carving. The first course is the soup itself with the eight delicacies, which include game, chicken, ham, mushrooms. For the second course the flesh of the melon is scooped away.

Another seasonal dish that is enormously popular is an hors d'oeuvres platter of whole boiled shrimp. A specialty of the restaurant, the prawns are cooked within their shells and are eaten with sauce dips of different flavors.

Braised Meats of Chicken and Frogs' Legs are a speciality of the restaurant. The meats are served off the bone, cut into very thin slices, and presented in layers on a bed of jade-green vegetables. A fine sauce is poured over the meat to create a subtle difference in flavor.

In Webbed Feet of Duck Stuffed with Shrimp, chopped shrimp is placed on cooked skin from the feet of the duck and molded to resemble a flower. When this attractive and tasty dish is served it resembles a platter of small flowers. Roast Sliced Goose is a famous Cantonese specialty. It is moist, succulent, and not oily; the skin is crisp, and the overall flavor is sweet. This is goose at its best.

The Guangzhou is at 2 Xiuli 2-Road, at the intersection with Wenchang Road (tel. 887136, 887840).

Dongfang. The private dining rooms of the Dongfang Hotel prepare superb meals. Roast Suckling Pig is a specialty of this restaurant. The whole pig is cooked on a spit and the skin glazed with honey, plum, and soy. Then the skin is separated from the fatty layer beneath, cut into small squares, and put back in place on the carcass. The pig is then served whole on a platter. The skin is eaten by dipping each square into plum sauce and then wrapping it with some scallion in a crepe-like pastry. When the skin has been eaten, the remainder of the pig is removed to be cut up, then returned as a separate dish.

Shark's Fin with Eggs, or "Cassia Flower with Eggs," is another specialty. Shark's fin, usually served in a soup, is prepared here with eggs. The dish is both delicious and visually appealing: the meat is translucent in contrast to the eggs, which are fluffy yellow.

Salt-baked Chicken is a well-known Cantonese dish, wrapped in clay and baked in salt. The dish is served with the skin and meat cut into slices. The name stems from the old days when beggars, who had no pots, cooked chicken in the earth.

Floating Flower Soup is a consommé in which poached quail eggs, decorated to resemble flowers, float on the surface. This is another example of a dish which is both a visual delight and a fine gastronomic experience.

The Dongfang private dining rooms are to be found in the Dongfang Hotel, 120 Liuhua Road (tel. 669900).

Datong. The Datong Restaurant is on the top floor of the building on the Bund (now known as Yan Jiang Road). On entering the building you will be taken to the restaurant in an elevator, and on the top floor you will walk down an aisle past the "masses" section of the restaurant, then down a flight of stairs to an open terrace. There you will find dining rooms for foreign visitors.

There is a fine view of the Pearl River from the terrace and you will see the busy river traffic. In the evening you will feel a cool and refreshing breeze from the river, a welcome relief from the heat and humidity present at certain times of the year.

There are also a fountain and fish pond with a small stone bridge crossing to one of the dining rooms. Altogether it is a pleasant, elegant, small restaurant with exceptionally good food.

Cantonese cooking is renowned for its *dim sum,* which literally means "touch the heart." These bite-sized morsels of exquisitely prepared dumplings are a favorite in teahouses in China. The salty dim sum are usually served at the beginning of the meal and the sweet ones at the end after the *jiao zi,* a meat-filled dumpling.

A specialty of this restaurant is Peacock Chicken. The braised chicken is cut up and presented in the form of a peacock with its fan opened. It is served with vegetables and ham.

Another specialty is Straw Mushrooms on Crab. For this fine dish, the restaurant picks the plumpest, juiciest mushrooms, sautés them with spices, and serves them on a snow-white bed of shredded crabmeat with a cream sauce. It is a delicious and almost sensual dish; regrettably, it is seasonal.

The Datong Restaurant is on the top floors of the building situated at 63 Yanjiang Road, on the downtown riverfront (tel. 885365, 888988, 885933).

Yu Yuan. The Yu Yuan, located in a fairly new building, has an attractive modern entrance opening into a center courtyard that features a rock garden and fish pond surrounded by tropical foliage. Foreign visitors dine in the upstairs dining rooms, which are fairly noisy but have a festive atmosphere about them.

A specialty of the restaurant is Squab Slices with Silver Bean Sprouts. The squab meat is cooked off the bone, sauteed, and served on a bed of bean sprouts which have had the pointed head and tail portion clipped off so that the remaining slender portion resembles a "silver needle." The meat is tender and the flavor subtle. There is an excellent contrast in the softness of the meat and the crispness of the bean sprouts.

Peking Roast Duck is not a specialty of Guangzhou, but if you missed this dish in Beijing or want to try it again, then go to the Yu Yuan. When the dish is prepared, the chef will follow tradition and bring the platter to the table to show the guests. Then he will carve the crisp skin from the meat, cutting it into small squares. You may then take a few pieces of skin with your chopsticks and dip them into the rich brown sauce provided, add some chopped scallion, and wrap the garnished skin in thin crepes or pancakes. The stuffed pancake is usually eaten with the fingers. After the skin has been eaten, the carcass containing the meat of the duck is taken away and carved up by the chef, then served for eating either in the small pancakes or without embellishment.

The Yu Yuan is at 90 Liwan Nan Road (tel. 888552, 888369, 886838).

Dongjiang. This restaurant in the center of Guangzhou serves excellent food in simple surroundings. Foreign visitors eat upstairs in the first-floor dining room where most tables are separated from each other by screens. There are only a few tables located in private dining cubicles.

Braised Duck stuffed with eight delicacies and glutinous rice is a specialty of the restaurant. It is a richly flavored and succulent dish. Guangzhou is more famous for its goose dishes, and the duck dish at this restaurant is a rather unusual exception.

Other delightful dishes are Stuffed Giant Prawns Served with Roast Squab and Crab Pieces in Black Bean Sauce (in season); both may be eaten with the fingers.

The Dongjiang is at 41 Zhongshan Si Road (tel. 335568, 335343).

Dongshan. The restaurant is about 15 to 20 minutes by taxi from the center of the city. On arrival you will see two large trees outside the restaurant in a street that is cobblestoned and dimly lit; it is faintly reminiscent of the old sections of Paris. You walk up stone steps to the entrance and will be ushered to the second floor where there are dining rooms for foreign visitors.

A fine way to begin your banquet is with the Assorted Cold Platter, which has a superb visual arrangement. The meats, poultry, and vegetables are laid out to represent a bird or butterfly. The foodstuffs are also placed on the plate to convey a realistic texture to the animal or flower represented.

The Whole-Fried Squirrel Fish is unusual in the way it is served. It is prepared for deep frying by cutting the surface of the skin to form a diamond pattern. During the cooking process the surface forms small cubes which separate from each other. The texture is firm but the juices are retained inside the cubes. It is a most unusual way to prepare fish, and you are recommended to try this dish.

The Seal Stewed with Mushrooms may present difficulties for Western visitors. The taste is somewhat similar to chicken but with a slightly firmer texture.

The Dongshan is at Dongshan, 1 Guigang Malu (tel. 770556, 776108, 770078).

Shahe. This restaurant is located in an old building without distinctive features, other than the many flights of steep stairs you will have to climb. The dining rooms for foreign visitors are located around the small terrace, where you may sit at a ceramic table and take tea before eating. The rooms themselves are not particularly attractive but are quiet.

The name of the restaurant is derived from *ho fan,* the Cantonese name for flat rice noodles. These are the specialty of the restaurant and are served at the end of the banquet. There are four or five different types served with different toppings. You will never taste noodles anywhere in the world quite like these; they are reputedly made using only water from the springs of nearby White Cloud Mountain. Many believe this restaurant has brought the art of preparing noodles to a peak of perfection. Certainly many Cantonese Chinese who live outside China make a pilgrimage to this restaurant when they return to their homeland just to taste the magnificent noodles. No better recommendation can be made.

The normal range of Cantonese dishes, prepared to an excellent standard, is available at this restaurant as a forerunner to the noodles course. The tea prepared here is reputed to be brewed also in White Cloud Mountain spring water.

The Shahe is at 79 Xianlie Dong Road, Shahe (tel. 775639, 777239, 770956).

"Hideaway" Restaurants

Sometimes you wish to escape and be alone for a while. Here are five out-of-the-way restaurants that will require a little time and effort in searching them out, but once you have found them, you will appreciate their particular "hidden away" character.

The Bei Xiu restaurant is a delightful little spot, but don't think you can "escape" by going to this restaurant during the Guangzhou Fair; instead try the Liu Hua, where the chefs specialize in seafood; the Jingji, a pleasant little place that is convenient to dining after you have explored Sha Mian Island; the Taiping, where you'll get an abundance of food; or the Dong He, a luncheon restaurant that is better known for its setting than for the food.

Bei Xiu. The Bei Xiu, or Northern Beauty Restaurant, is close to the China Hotel (about 3 minutes' walk) and is therefore popular with fairgoers. If you are going to the restaurant from the hotel, turn right on leaving the exit gate and walk to the main road (Liberation Road) about 150 yards away. Follow the road to the right for about 200 yards; you will recognize the restaurant by the large number of bicycles parked nearby, hence the name "The Bicycle Restaurant" given it by the China traders.

Go up the stairs to the top landing on your left. You may eat either in the large dining room or on the terrace. The terrace is particularly attractive, though noisy, during the warmer weather; in the evening colored lights in the surrounding trees are turned on, and the effect may provide you with a fleeting memory of a small Mediterranean restaurant. Across the road there is an open-air cinema and you can glance across and catch glimpses of the Chinese movie being shown. The interior salon is furnished with dark wooden chairs and tables, and the atmosphere is cool and somber; there are large overhead fans to keep the air circulating.

The restaurant is well known for its Sunday brunch, which features an excellent variety of dishes at a most reasonable price.

The Bei Xiu is at 899 Liberation Road.

Liu Hua. The Liu Hua Restaurant (tel. 668800; 664095 ext. 21) is located in the park of the same name situated on the western side of the Dong Fang Hotel. If you enter the park by the corner entrance opposite the Dong Fang, take the path that runs to the left along the edge of the lake; turn right following the shoreline and you will come to a gateway. Go through the gateway and along the path to the two-story building ahead, and go to the top story of the building where foreign guests eat.

The dining room is noisy, but you will have a pleasant view through the full-length window of the tropical foliage that grows in abundance around the restaurant. It specializes in fish, mostly fresh-water types, and seafood, especially prawns, squid, and shrimp. Pork and beef dishes are also available. Try the *Wanyu*, which is a fresh-water fish caught in the nearby lake; it is a specialty of the house. The Fish Balls with Sesame Seeds are also excellent.

Jingji. The Jingji, or "Economy" Restaurant, is a tiny place situated on Sha Mian, an island that once was a foreign enclave. The restaurant is a pleasant place to visit for lunch or dinner after you have spent a short time exploring the island.

When arriving from the city center, you will cross the small bridge at the eastern end of the island. Then continue straight ahead for about 300 or 400 yards until you come to a cross street called Sixth Street; turn right into this street, and about 20 yards down on the right-hand side you will see the restaurant entrance. There is a large camphor tree just outside.

The section for foreigners is upstairs in two small rooms, each accommodating two tables and overlooking a small courtyard with a tree growing in the center. You might easily imagine that you are in New Orleans, and while there are no Cajun dishes served, you can order Western food.

A specialty of the restaurant is Rice Birds Stuffed with Liver Sausage, a dish that is seasonal. These tiny birds are caught in the rice fields in nets during the autumn. After preparation they are cooked whole and sometimes stuffed with a type of liver sausage and are eaten whole, the bones being softened during the cooking process.

They are a delicacy in South China and represent for most foreign visitors a new gastronomic experience. If in doubt, try a small plateful for your first order.

The Jingji is at 8 Er Ma Road, Shamian (tel. 888784, 887790).

Taiping. The Taiping, situated in one of the busiest sections of the city, was once a restaurant in the Lam Brothers chain, which operated in Guangzhou, Hong Kong, and Macao prior to World War II.

The section for foreign visitors is on the third floor, and there are numerous steep flights of stairs to climb before reaching the upper landing. The dining hall is not subdivided into smaller banquet rooms. The tables at the rear are pleasantly situated near the windows and are cooler; you look out over miniature trees which decorate the window sills and down onto the tops of tall trees growing in the nearby park.

The restaurant is suitable for banquets and for couples who may wish to dine alone, although it certainly lacks privacy.

Some of the better dishes are: Crispy-Skin Roast Goose; Fish Fillet with Plum Sauce; Carp Baked with Ginger and Scallion; Whole Chicken Baked in Oyster Sauce; Braised Garnished Duck; Braised Crab with Ginger and Onion; and Mushrooms Stuffed with Shrimp.

The Taiping is at 344 Beijing Bei Road (tel. 335529, 331147).

Dong He. The Dong He, or East River Restaurant, is in Dongshan He (East Mountain River) Park, located in a modern building on the edge of the lake. The restaurant serves meals only at lunchtime and closes at 2 P.M.

You enter the grounds of the restaurant through an elliptical moongate set in a white wall. Inside there is a large ornamental pool set into the floor and a tall stand of bamboo growing through the cutaway ceiling. The restaurant opens onto a patio where there are gardens and shade trees, and from the patio there are steps leading to the edge of the lake.

While the setting is both modern and pleasant, you can expect to find chrome chairs with vinyl covers and see a plastic tablecloth laid out before you, a disappointing contrast with the natural beauty outside.

The food is basic and rather similar to that served in one of the "masses" restaurants. There is no menu, so you must be guided by the waiter. Some English is spoken.

Specialty Restaurants

Snake Restaurant. The Snake restaurant, or She Can (pronounced "Shur Tzan") Guan, is enormously popular with the locals. When you arrive at the restaurant you will be confronted at the entrance by a window filled with writhing snakes. There are hundreds of them, including the deadly cobra. As you stand watching this bed of coiled venom, the snakes will ignore you, but tap on the window and they will flick their tongues at you. It is not the most inviting welcome you will receive at a Chinese restaurant, but it's probably the most unusual one.

As you walk up a few flights of stairs to the foreign visitors' section, you will note that the restaurant is packed with diners eating the various snake specialties.

When you are seated at your table, and before you begin your meal, you should, if your taste is so inclined, order snake bile. You can also ask to see the bile sac removed from a snake while you sit at your table, an operation you will not see in many other places in the world. One of the snake men from the restaurant will arrive with a basket of snakes and squat down beside you. He will take a snake from the basket, place one foot gently on its head and the other gently on its tail, and feel along about one-third of the length of the snake from the tail end until he finds the bile sac under the skin. You may, if you wish, also try to locate it by running your thumb along the snake's underside.

Once the bile sac is located, the snake man slices into the skin, using a thin blade, and with a quick movement of the fingers squeezes the bile sac from the body and severs it. He then places the bile sac on a small saucer and returns the snake, seemingly undisturbed by this 30-second operation, to the snake basket, selecting another one for the next bile sac extraction.

The snake man repeats this operation as often as necessary to remove a sufficient number of bile sacs for the attendant guests. The bile is squeezed from the sac and is served mixed with mao tai in a small glass. The beverage has the reputation, probably unfounded, of being good for the heart and for virility. It is also expensive.

You may ask to see the snake you are about to consume skinned before your eyes. This operation is not for the faint-hearted, but it has the advantage of being over in about 20 seconds. As far as can be determined there is no advantage for the snake.

The snake man takes the snake destined for your table from the basket, puts its head gently under his foot, and, holding the snake up by the tail, runs a thin blade the full length of its body. He then severs the head and pulls the skin from the snake's body, leaving a writhing, headless and skinless carcass. It is not the most pleasant way to begin a meal, and you will probably have visions of the operation while you are eating. Of course, you may prefer to dispense with the whole performance and concentrate on the delicacies on the menu.

A specialty of the restaurant is Chicken Soup with Three Kinds of Snake. This is a tasty broth with the meat of three deadly snakes mixed with chicken meat and flavored with spices. Obviously, the venom is removed from the snake prior to cooking; otherwise there would be few people remaining who could testify to the existence of the restaurant. It is traditional when serving this dish to garnish each individual bowl with petals from the chrysanthemum flower.

Another specialty is Clear Broth of Big Mountain Snake, which is made from the meat of one or more of the large snakes, particularly the boa constrictor, that live in the south of China. This is a delicately flavored broth and slightly sweet. You may also like to try the Dragon and Tiger Stew. The real name of this dish is the "Struggle of the Dragon and the Tiger," referring to a well-known Chinese myth concerning these two animals. The "dragon" is in fact snake and the "tiger" is civet cat, prepared together in a thick soup which is almost like a stew. It is a famous dish in Guangzhou.

The Snake is at 41 Jianglan Road (tel. 883811, 883424, 882517).

Vegetarian Fragrance Restaurant. Vegetarians on a tour of Guangzhou will be delighted to find this fine restaurant where, of course, there are no meat dishes. The dining rooms for foreign visitors are upstairs. The decor of this restaurant is in bamboo: the tables, chairs, and even the walls are made of this attractive wood.

All the dishes served at the restaurant are derived from vegetables, yet they are sometimes presented on the serving platter in the form of a fish or a steak. On these occasions, herbs are used to simulate the taste of a particular meat. For example, the cold platter called the Dish of Six Treasures, which is usually served at the beginning of the meal, features vegetables which are cooked and prepared to provide the appearance, texture, and taste of various meats such as duck, chicken, sausage, and meat balls. The Snow Mushroom Consommé is a soup made from the woodear, a flower-like fungus which is translucent and almost silver. It is a rare delicacy, and in the consommé has an exquisite flavor.

The Vegetarian Fragrance is at 167 Zhongshan Liu Road (tel. 886836).

Wild Game Restaurant. The restaurant, called Ye Wei Xiang in Chinese, is at 247 Beijing Road (tel. 330337, 330997). The restaurant is crowded and noisy, but it is the place to eat if you want to try the game of Guangdong region. Some of the dishes served in the restaurant are derived from the salamander, pangolin, snake, turtle, and civet cat.

One non-game dish that is a speciality of the restaurant is Fish Balls in Jade Vegetables. The meat from the fish is chopped up with water chestnut and other delicacies. The dish when served resembles a platter of small round flowers, the bed of green vegetables representing the leaves.

The dish for the adventurous is Fragrant Dogmeat Stew, which is cooked in an unglazed earthenware pot with soy sauce, ginger, wine, and various spices. The dish tastes very much like stewed beef but is more fragrant. The color of the meat is brownish-red through absorption of the wine and soy. Traditionally chefs prepare this dish only from young black dogs.

Dining Out in Beijing

The capital offers the visitor wonderful opportunities to become acquainted with one of the highly developed aspects of its civilization: the exquisite preparation of food. When you visit Beijing you will carry away memories of sumptuous banquets where the dishes are nothing short of magnificent.

Not unexpectedly, the restaurants of Beijing specialize mainly in the northern or Pekinese style of cooking. This style has evolved over the centuries: from the Moslem Chinese, from the traditions of the Lower Yangzi River area, and from the cuisine developed in the Old Imperial Palace of the Qing Dynasty.

Northern or Pekinese cooking tends to be oilier (e.g., Peking roast duck) and the dishes saltier and spicier than other styles. The northern style alone uses lamb, a characteristic borrowed from Moslem-Chinese cooking. Wheat and other grains in the form of dumplings, noodles, and buns are standard fare at northern Chinese meals. Moslem-Chinese restaurants invariably feature roasting, barbecuing, and deep-boiling techniques.

Outside the leading hotels, there are only a handful of restaurants in Beijing devoted to eastern, central-western, and southern cooking and you will be hard put to find a Cantonese restaurant worthy of the name. Most restaurants with banquet rooms cook in the Hebei, Shandong, or Moslem-Chinese styles.

The restaurants of Beijing located away from hotels are noted for their austere surroundings, lack of decoration, and subdued ambiance. There are two exceptions: the Fang Shan in Bei Hai Park and the Sichuan Restaurant. Both have magnificent decors.

Of course, there are several thousand "masses" restaurants in Peking which are patronized by the locals and, having no private rooms, cannot cope with a large number of foreign guests with what would be considered appropriate courtesy. If you wish to visit a "masses" restaurant you will need to speak Chinese or have someone in your party who does, and there should not be more than four or five people in your group, or it will be difficult for the restaurant to seat you without causing too much fuss or inconvenience to the other patrons.

Generally speaking, the food served at the "masses" restaurants is simple but quite nutritious. However, you should be warned that their hygiene is probably suspect by the standards of the West.

Listed on the pages that follow are descriptions of the "top ten" restaurants of Beijing. They cover most of the regional styles of China and offer you a wonderful opportunity to eat the best that the nation has to offer. You will note that the restaurants specializing in Peking Duck have not made the top ten, not because they are not fine restaurants, but simply because their range is limited. The Peking Duck restaurants are reviewed in the "Practical Information for Beijing" section.

The Top Ten Restaurants of Beijing

Feng Ze Yuan. This restaurant specializes in the dishes of Shandong Province and North China. Although it is one of the top restaurants in Beijing and therefore one of the foremost Chinese restaurants in the world, its decor lacks distinction. If you are a gourmet, or even someone who simply likes Chinese food, you should take the opportunity to indulge yourself here. If you order many of the rare and exquisite delicacies you can expect to pay accordingly.

A specialty of the restaurant is Chicken Puffs with Shark's Fin. This dish consists of chopped white chicken meat with whipped egg white cooked with shark's fin in chicken stock. Another special dish is the *Hong-shao Yu,* a fish cooked in a dark soy sauce. The fish is served in the rich brown sauce, the ingredients being mainly ginger, chili pepper, sugar, and scallion.

The Feng Ze Yuan is at 83 Zhushikou Street, one block west of the intersection with Qianmen Street (tel. 332828).

Sichuan Restaurant. The Sichuan Restaurant (pronounced "sss-chewarn") vies with the Fang Shan and the Ze Yuan as the most prestigious restaurant in all of Beijing. It certainly has one of the best settings of any restaurant in the capital, with its fine courtyards and contrasting red-and-gold decor, befitting the style and opulence of its (reputed) former owner, Yuan Shihkai, the general who tried unsuccessfully to become emperor in the earlier years of the century.

The name of the restaurant stems from the well-known central province. The former name, Cheng Du, is the capital of that province. The area is famous throughout China for its hot and spicy food, but, in keeping with Chinese gastronomy, there is always in a banquet menu a fine balance of different foods providing both contrast and interest to the palate.

Try the Sichuan prawns, which are the famous large prawns sautéed in soy sauce and vinegar, garlic, ginger, and chili. Not unexpectedly, this is a hot, spicy dish. Another specialty of the restaurant is Shark's Fin with Chicken and Bamboo Shoots. Try also the Chicken with Peanuts.

The Sichuan is at 51 West Rong Xian Lane, south of the intersection of Xidan Bei Street and Chang An Boulevard (tel. 336356).

Fang Shan. This fine restaurant specializes in the cuisine of the Qing Imperial Court. Located on Qiong Hua Island in Bei Hai Lake (tel. 751024, 442573), it is the most beautiful restaurant in Beijing and highly sought after as a place for banquets.

Enter Bei Hai Lake and Park by the southeast gate (main entrance). Turn to the right and cross the bridge to the island. Take the path to the right and follow it along the shoreline. You will pass the Bridge of Perfect Wisdom on your right and finally enter the "covered way," similar to the one at the Summer Palace. Note the beautifully painted cross-members and ceiling.

As the corridor curves to the left you will notice the Pavilion of the Five Dragons on the opposite shore. The corridor separates a group of fan-shaped buildings from the lake and then opens up into an ancient pavilion which is now the restaurant.

There are so many wonderful dishes served at this restaurant that it is difficult to make recommendations. However, try the Stewed Three Whites, a form of soup containing bamboo shoots, fish maw, mushrooms, and their juices. Spicy Whole Fish is prepared from fish freshly caught in the Bei Hai Lake outside the restaurant. Minced Pork Stuffed in Sesame Buns may sound commonplace, but it is a delicious dish of minced pork, flavored with herbs. The minced meat is stuffed into sesame buns. The Cold Dessert in this menu consists of small red-and-white bean paste cakes, favorites of the last Dowager Empress. One of the better known and delicious hot desserts is Almond Cream Soup, prepared with freshly ground almonds.

Two remarkable dishes of this restaurant are the rare and famous Camel's Hump and Bear's Paws.

Note: This restaurant must be booked at least 4 to 5 days in advance for dinner as it is used extensively by the Chinese ministries and corporations for entertaining foreign guests. If you wish to dine at Fang Shan, you should reserve a table as soon as possible after you arrive in Beijing.

Cui Hua Lou. This restaurant was formerly known as the Shoudu, which means "capital." It is certainly one of the finest restaurants in Beijing specializing in Shandong-style cuisine. One specialty is the Chicken with Bamboo Shoots, which is something like a soup and suitable for eating with rice. The dish is made from shredded chicken breasts, shredded bamboo shoots, salt, ginger, and sherry. Other ingredients are egg white and flour. The chicken is cooked for only a very short time, and the result is a dish which is light and simple.

The Vegetables in Hot and Sour Sauce is another well-known dish. The sauce is made from chicken broth by adding salt, pepper, sherry, vinegar, coriander, sesame oil, and spring onions.

Another specialty of the restaurant is Grilled Shark's Fin. This dish is rare in China; shark's fin is usually served shredded, not in the form of whole pieces. It is, therefore, expensive.

The restaurant prepares a delightful dessert in the form of Almond Bean Curd with Mixed Fruit. Visitors from overseas who are familiar with Chinese food may have had this at their favorite Chinese restaurant, but it will have been prepared with almond-flavored gelatin instead of the freshly ground almond paste used in this first-class restaurant. Consequently the flavor and texture are richer.

The Cui Hua Lou is at 60 Wangfujing, about halfway between the Beijing Hotel and the National Art Gallery (tel. 554581, 552594).

Jin Yang. The Jin Yang specializes in dishes from Shanxi Province. Although this province is not in the forefront of the various schools of Chinese cooking, the restaurant nevertheless produces some excellent dishes. The Deep-Fried Prawns are highly favored at Beijing restaurants, and perhaps nowhere are they done better than at the Jin Yang. The giant prawns are heated in a pan with onion, ginger, garlic, and salted beans, stir-fried rapidly, and allowed to simmer until the sauce has almost dried. The prawns are then turned in molten lard a few times before serving.

The Diced Chicken Sautéed with Hot Pepper is another well-known dish, providing cubes of chicken slightly scorched on the outside but juicy and tender inside, served in a hot and spicy sauce.

The Jin Yang is at 241 Zhu Shi Kou Road, about a block north of the Qianmen Hotel (tel. 334361, 331669, 332120).

Huai Yang Fan Zhuang. This restaurant's name is formed by combining the words for the Huai River and the city of Yangzhou, near Shanghai. The food tends to be rich, and many of the dishes use seafood or fish and eels from the coastal waterways.

A specialty is Three Whites, otherwise known as Triple-White in Thick Wine Sauce, made by stir-frying chicken breast slices, then placing them over fish slices in the pan and frying them quickly on either side. Bamboo shoots, chicken broth, salt, ginger, wine sauce, and sugar are added to complete this dish.

The restaurant is at 217 Xidan Bei Road (tel. 660521).

Kang Le. The Kang Le specializes in dishes from Yunnan Province, in the South of China. One of the restaurant's renowned dishes—which is not derived from the South—is Crossing-the-Bridge Noodles. The name comes from the days of the Imperial Court, when the noodles were dropped into the pot of boiling water just as the chef reached the bridge to the Imperial City. By the time the pot arrived at the Emperor's table, the noodles were perfectly prepared for his immediate consumption. Kang

Le's Jade Spinach Soufflé has a superb, velvety texture and is also appealing to the eye.

The Kang Le is at 259 Andingmen Nei Road, on the intersection with Gulou Dong Road, about 3 blocks east of the Drum Tower (tel. 443884).

Tong He Ju. This restaurant specializes in Shandong-style cuisine. One renowned dish is Asparagus with Dried Abalone. Dried abalone is an expensive delicacy in China, and when combined with asparagus forms a dish with subtle flavor and contrasting textures.

Another well-known dish at this restaurant is the curiously named Three Non-Stick, or Triple None Stuck. It is an egg dish which derives its name from the fact that it sticks neither to the teeth, the spoon, nor the chopsticks.

The Abalone and Asparagus Tips dish is prepared from dried, whole abalone, mixed with asparagus tips in a cream sauce. This dish, one of the finest on the restaurant's menu, has a delicate flavor and an interesting contrast in textures. Fried Duck Livers with Sesame Seeds are made with plump fried livers, rolled in sesame seeds. This dish has a pleasant, nutty flavor. The Winter Melon with Preserved Shrimp is different from the carved winter melon soup described elsewhere. This particular dish comprises chunks of winter melon served with preserved shrimps.

The Tong He Ju is at 3 Xisi Nan Road, at the intersection of Fuchengmennai Road, almost opposite the Guangji Temple (tel. 666357).

Zhenjiang. This restaurant specializes in food from Jiangsu Province and the Shanghai region. In these regions the "red cook" method of preparing food is well known. For example, the Red Cook Oxtail is prepared by cooking an oxtail slowly in dark soy, ginger, wine, and brown sugar. The meat is cooked until it is ready to slide from the bone. The name of this process derives from the color given to the meats cooked in this way. Another dish worthy of note is Golden Coin Prawns. The prawns are flattened and fried and when served have the appearance of golden coins. You will note that as the origin of the cuisine moves further south, the dishes become more decorative and the names more descriptive.

Another specialty of the restaurant is Chicken Puffs with Shark's Fin, described under the Feng Ze Yuan Restaurant. The Lamb Shaslik is excellent even though it is not a specialty of the region. It is well worth trying, particularly if you do not have an opportunity to visit one of the restaurants specializing in Moslem food.

The Zhenjiang is at the intersection of West Chang An Boulevard and Xidan Road (tel. 662115, 662289).

Lili Restaurant. This restaurant specializes in the hot spicy food of Sichuan Province. Best dishes are: Hot Bean Curd or Noodles; Sichuan Prawns; Chili-Pork with Peanuts; and excellent dumplings.

The Lili is at 30 Qianmen Road (tel. 752310).

DOING BUSINESS
IN CHINA

DOING BUSINESS IN CHINA

Merchants and others come here on business in great numbers... because it affords a profitable market.

—Marco Polo, *The Travels*

At the dawn of the 1990s the Chinese economy continued to slide into a recession. The deterioration brought about by the government austerity program was made worse by the imposition of international economic sanctions following the brutal repression of the democratic reform movement. The economy was also hurt by a drastic reduction in tourist revenues.

The economic slowdown presents a stark contrast to the booming conditions of the eighties, when business took off under the stimulus of market reforms and China roused itself from the deep narcosis induced in earlier decades by huge doses of ideology. Production roared ahead, overloading the old system and making the economic framework creak; trade soared and international transactions boomed, straining the nation's rudimentary commercial network.

These conditions brought new opportunities for foreign trade and investment. They also brought new commerce and investment laws—some of them timely, many of them late, most of them confusing—and with the new laws came a bewildering array of new corporations designed to open China economically to the world.

One major effect on foreign trade and investment in the 1980s was decentralization. The leadership showed ambivalence, first plunging ahead, then drawing back, then moving ahead again, and finally showing uncertainty when faced with the problems of inflation, bureaucratic confusion, corruption, and shortages of raw materials. At the end of the 1980s the government was turning back to central control and planning.

The reversals and swings in government regulation are confusing to the foreign investor and trader, and they can be costly as well. Many companies are concerned about the stability of a China whose leaders seem incapable of allowing even a modest degree of political freedom. Although the Chinese government has adopted a "business as usual" attitude, many foreign companies have made a "wait and see" response. Meanwhile, the changes taking place in Eastern Europe pose not only a political threat to China but a business threat as well. The 1990s could prove to be a quiet decade for business in China.

Negotiations

A business visit to China can be pleasant, but if you are a newcomer it can be a trying experience. You may feel isolated in a strange environment where discussions are protracted, the weather is enervating, and conditions are unsettling. Your negotiations appear to be moving at the speed of continental drift, and the negotiators across the table seem to be paying a frustrating degree of attention to trivial details. You begin to think of the deals you could be closing elsewhere, the work piling up in your office, the great expense of the visit, and the weekends you are missing at home.

Your competitors are here, and the Chinese are beginning to play them off against you. It took you an hour to get a telex sent, three hours to make an international call. Your office must be sending its replies by carrier pigeon. Now that you are ready to make a counteroffer, you can't get a quick appointment with the Chinese corporation handling the product. You'll threaten to leave. Yet everyone else seems to be making deals but you. Then you think maybe you'd better stay. But how long will it take? Another week? Ten days?

Mental pressures such as these build up rapidly in China. You are probably under the constraints of a travel schedule to other countries or appointments back home. The Chinese negotiators seem to be under no time constraints at all. In certain respects it can be the lack of results at meetings in China that is getting to you. So try to remain constantly alert during negotiations. Pay close attention to every detail of the contract. The Chinese tend to interpret contracts strictly, so make sure that you gain inclusion of important conditions and definitions, even though these may be considered "as read" in most international contract negotiations.

Relax. Talk to some old China hands. They'll tell you that the only way to handle the situation is to "go with the flow." You may even find that visiting China will change your whole lifestyle.

China Trade Services

Some firms cannot afford the expenditure of money and time to initiate and then maintain a business relationship with China. One alternative to consider, even though it may not bring the same results as a well-planned and thorough attempt to win a contract made by you or an executive of your company, is to employ the services of a specialist China trader to deal on your firm's behalf. Such a specialist will undertake work for a fee or will act as agent, usually for a percentage of sales. Consult your national chamber of commerce or federal trade agency to determine the names of persons or companies who act for third parties. Another alternative is to employ a Hong Kong company (see below).

Always interview such firms carefully. Find out about their track record. Ask whom they have represented in the past. Ask the firm's permission to contact existing or previous clients. Study the financial basis of the proposed remuneration or fee. Then you will be in a position to decide which firm will best represent your company and promote the sale of its products or services.

Recent Developments

Significant changes have taken place in China's economic and trade policies; the nation is undergoing a period of economic readjustment, featuring a shift in resource allocation in favor of the consumer, increased emphasis being given to market forces, greater management autonomy and decentralization. Programs for the importation of foreign technology, equipment, foreign capital, and management skills are in full swing.

China has entered into joint development arrangements with foreign firms in the form of "compensation agreements" and "contract manufacturing." In a compensation agreement, a foreign firm sets up a factory in China and the firm's capital outlay is repaid in an annual processing fee, in goods produced, or in periodic cash payments—or a combination of all three. In contract manufacturing the foreign firm does not supply a factory but does provide the raw materials or essential components, and pays a processing fee to the Chinese manufacturing or assembly plant.

China encourages joint-venture operations allowing foreign firms to make direct investments. A special corporation has been established at national level to handle negotiations: the China International Trust and Investment Corporation. It has many counterparts at provincial level. Their establishment represents a significant policy change by the Chinese.

Science and technology has been given great emphasis in China. Many science and technology agreements have been signed with foreign governments, paving the way for increased inflow of information from abroad, leading to a vast increase in foreign firms being invited to China to give technical seminars.

China has set up enormous lines of buyers' credit through commercial bank loans, foreign government export credit agencies, deposits made in foreign banks of the Bank of China, and through loans and direct foreign investment arranged by provincial Chinese agencies or corporations. Some lines of credit were frozen after the democracy movement was crushed in 1989.

A range of new institutions has been created to control the nature and extent of China's economic relations with foreign companies. New legislation has been created to deal with the complexities of international trade and foreign investment in China. Many foreign companies have established offices in China.

All these recent developments are important for anyone engaging in business with China or contemplating doing so. Information about these new developments is given in the sections that follow.

China's Modernization Drive

China's seventh five-year plan (1986–1990) calls for the nation's gross national product (GNP) to grow at an average of 7.5 percent annually through 1990. The government will concentrate foreign investment and loans in developing the energy, transport, and communications sectors of the economy. Vast amounts of capital will be channeled into industrial and resource development to provide more adequate infrastructure such as electric power, petroleum, port and harbor construction, electronics, and machine-building. Greater emphasis will be placed on increasing the

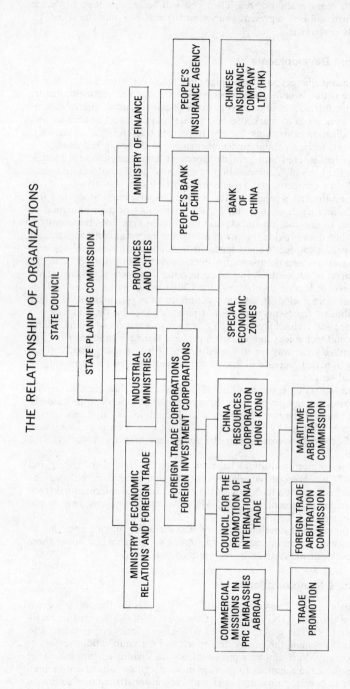

THE RELATIONSHIP OF ORGANIZATIONS

STATE COUNCIL

STATE PLANNING COMMISSION

MINISTRY OF ECONOMIC RELATIONS AND FOREIGN TRADE

INDUSTRIAL MINISTRIES

PROVINCES AND CITIES

MINISTRY OF FINANCE

FOREIGN TRADE CORPORATIONS
FOREIGN INVESTMENT CORPORATIONS

SPECIAL ECONOMIC ZONES

PEOPLE'S BANK OF CHINA

PEOPLE'S INSURANCE AGENCY

COMMERCIAL MISSIONS IN PRC EMBASSIES ABROAD

COUNCIL FOR THE PROMOTION OF INTERNATIONAL TRADE

CHINA RESOURCES CORPORATION HONG KONG

BANK OF CHINA

CHINESE INSURANCE COMPANY LTD (HK)

TRADE PROMOTION

FOREIGN TRADE ARBITRATION COMMISSION

MARITIME ARBITRATION COMMISSION

production of goods for export. The development of the tourist industry will continue at an accelerated pace.

Obviously, the greater proportion of this massive development will be funded within China. However, China will need to make huge purchases of foreign technology, services, machinery, capital equipment, and basic raw materials if it is to implement the plan.

The plan is a remarkable document. It sets China on a course which varies considerably from the direction traditionally taken by socialist nations. It calls for a more extensive reduction in party and central power than has ever been attempted elsewhere. It aims to separate party and government functions, then remove government from business.

Beijing is attempting a significant reduction in government control over the nation's economic enterprises. By 1990, according to the plan, managers will be expected to have assumed full responsibility for their enterprise's performance, and enterprises will have become entirely responsible for their own profit and loss.

China's Business Structure

It is useful for the China trader to understand the connection between the various organizations dealing with trade, commercial, and related matters. The chart *The Relationship of Organizations* illustrates this.

China's overall business plan is established by important economic policy-making organizations such as the State Planning Commission, assisted by China's government ministries and financial institutions. In recent years there have been significant changes in China's foreign-trade infrastructure and the organizations that conduct trade.

The decentralization of China's foreign trade and the creation of a new and more complex infrastructure means that foreign firms wishing to do business with China are often faced with a bewildering array of choices.

Much of China's foreign trade is carried out by Foreign Trade Corporations (FTCs) under the supervision of the Ministry of Foreign Economic Relations and Trade (MOFERT). This ministry may be considered the most important single trade organization in China. However, you should note three important developments: the first is the emergence of import and export corporations established by many of China's industrial ministries; the second is the emergence of major municipal and provincial trade and investment organizations; the third is the establishment of trading companies by factories and individuals.

Most of the FTCs supervised by MOFERT are organized to trade according to commodity or product. However, China's industrial ministries have also established trading corporations and have taken a more active role in China's foreign trade, particularly for products and services in industrial sectors such as petrochemicals, transportation, and shipbuilding. Some agricultural products are also affected.

All these corporations have the authority to initiate and coordinate contacts between foreigners and enterprises or industrial plants. They also arrange and conduct technical and commercial negotiations with foreign firms.

Furthermore, the three Chinese municipalities—Beijing, Shanghai, and Tianjin—as well as a number of provinces, have been given autonomy to pursue economic ventures with foreign companies. These municipalities and provinces have established "local" FTCs to act as the principal point of contact for the foreign firms. These local FTCs usually oversee the local branches of the national FTCs.

The municipalities and provinces have also established investment and trust corporations responsible for attracting foreign investment and securing financing for joint ventures and compensation-trade agreements. They provide services similar to the national body charged with attracting foreign investment and finance, the China International Trust and Investment Corporation (CITIC). However, they are able to act independently of CITIC although they do work closely with it. Details concerning the activities of CITIC are provided in a separate section.

China's business infrastructure is still evolving and there are regular changes in emphasis. Authorities in Beijing know that they must "free up" the rigid bureaucratic system by decentralizing decision-making. However, such devolution conflicts with their wish to maintain adequate control of their vast economic system and, at the same time, ensure coordination of national policy at all levels.

China's Business Organizations

Foreign firms wishing to do business with China are well advised to consult or purchase a small handbook entitled *China's Foreign Trade Corporations and Organizations* compiled by the Department of Public Relations of the China Council for the Promotion of International Trade (CCPIT). It lists all the major corporations and organizations that engage in business with foreign firms. It provides details of the type of goods, commodities, and services traded and will quickly allow the foreign firm to locate the right corporation. It is available by writing to the CCPIT (see details below).

We have also provided a list of major corporations along with a brief description of their activities later in this chapter. The more detailed list provided by the CCPIT should be consulted if you are in any doubt.

Hong Kong is an important center for many of China's FTCs. Some of the corporations have set up a branch office there. Others operate through a separately established company known as the China Resources Corporation (see "The Hong Kong Connection" later in this chapter).

Some of China's FTCs have set up branches in foreign countries to facilitate business. You should check whether these branches have been established in your country because direct contact with an FTC branch will enable you to initiate negotiations with a Chinese business organization prior to visiting China.

A list of those corporations that have established branches in the U.S. is provided at the end of the chapter. Business executives from other countries should consult their Ministry of Trade or Commerce, or their national Chamber of Commerce for the address of any locally established Chinese FTCs.

Chinese Embassies and Consulates

The most immediate point of contact with China is through the Commercial Office of the Embassy of the P.R.C. in your country of residence or through the Chinese Consulates in major cities. The Chinese Embassy and Consulates possess a staff of commercial officers available for discussions with representatives of firms in the host country. A list of the P.R.C. Embassies established in various centers around the world is provided in an earlier section of this guidebook (see "Facts at Your Fingertips").

Some of the embassy and consular staff members represent China's FTCs and, although they do not get involved in contract negotiations, they can offer advice on preparing proposals for the parent corporation in China and can also assist you in developing business with China.

China Council for the Promotion of International Trade

Every business executive should know about the CCPIT. Although the Chinese Government describes CCPIT as representing the "non-government sector," it in fact works closely with MOFERT, other Chinese ministries, the FTCs, and financial institutions such as the Bank of China. Outside of China it is well known for its organization of China's exhibitions in foreign countries. It is also responsible for arranging foreign exhibits in China.

Two important commissions within the CCPIT are the Foreign Economic and Trade Arbitration Commission and the Maritime Arbitration Commission, both of which arbitrate commercial and shipping disputes between foreign companies and Chinese organizations. CCPIT also has a Legal Affairs Office which assists the drafting of new Chinese laws on foreign trade and acts as adviser to FTCs on international legal questions. The address of the CCPIT is 4 Fuxingmenwai Street, Beijing, People's Republic of China (tel. 867229; cable COMTRADE Beijing; telex 22315 CCPIT CN).

CCPIT also distributes literature to Chinese "end-users." When appropriate, CCPIT will also distribute samples of new foreign products. This unit of the CCPIT is important for any foreign firm making its first approach to the Chinese market. Contact may be made at the Center for Introducing Literature and Samples of New Products, CCPIT, Box 1420, Beijing, People's Republic of China.

China International Trust and Investment Corporation

Another important organization at the national level in China is CITIC. Its role is to facilitate foreign investment in China and to introduce advanced technology and equipment to be used in running joint ventures. CITIC accepts venture capital and can arrange suitable joint-venture partners for foreign participants. Through its subsidiary merchant bank, China Investment and Finance Corporation (CIFC), CITIC issues bonds and assumes financial management of China's overseas investments.

CITIC has a Hong Kong branch office which operates with a considerable degree of independence; it also has offices in the U.S. and several European countries, as well as Japan. The U.S. branch of CITIC is listed at the end of this chapter. Should you wish to contact CITIC directly, you may do so at this address: CITIC Building, 19 Jianguomenwai, Beijing (tel. 5002255; cable 0207 Beijing; telex 22305 CITIC CN).

Regional Development

China has introduced a system of economic zones, "open cities," and "open coastal areas" to facilitate foreign investment in China and to encourage the inflow of capital, technology, and managerial skills.

There are five "Special" Economic Zones or SEZs. The SEZs are located at Shenzhen, Zhuhai, and Shantou (all in Guangdong Province), Xiamen, and Hainan Island. The zones have not proved to be the success that Chinese economic planners had hoped, so the earlier ambitious growth targets have been replaced by ones that are more realistic.

In addition, 14 coastal cities of China have been granted economic decision-making power allowing them to offer incentives similar to those offered by the SEZs. The 14 coastal cities are, from north to south: Dalian in Liaoning Province; Qinhuangdao in Hebei Province; Tianji; Yantao, and Qingdao in Shandong Province; Lianyungang and Nantong in Jiangsu Province; Shanghai; Ningbo and Wenzhou in Zhejiang Province; Fuzhou in Fujian Province; Guangzhou and Zhanjiang in Guangdong Province; and Beihai in the Guangxi Autonomous Region.

You should note that economic development in these cities is not expected to proceed at the same rate as that planned for the SEZs. Indeed, the initial plan for the development of 10 of the 14 cities has been cut back following the mixed success of the SEZs. Of the 14, development will be directed mainly towards Shanghai, Guangzhou, Tianjin, and Dalian.

The "open coastal areas" represent another variation of China's development plans for foreign investment. These areas embrace large portions of the delta regions around Guangzhou (the Pearl River or Zhujiang area) and Shanghai (the Yangzi or Changjiang area) as well as regions on the Dalian peninsula and the Yantai peninsula, both of which jut out into the Bo Hai sea. There is also another "open area" in the Xiamen region.

China's rush to bring in foreign capital and technology is not directed only toward the coastal provinces. Those provinces located in China's vast interior are trying to encourage foreign investment too. But while a number of them are rich in resources and can provide special incentives, they tend to lack the industrial infrastructure, transportation links, and the power generation and communication facilities provided by their coastal counterparts.

The varied nature of these different centers for regional development can be confusing. The important point to keep in mind is the reason for their establishment: to attract foreign investment. The regional development centers therefore encourage investment proposals from foreign firms seeking to establish a wholly owned subsidiary, to engage in a joint venture with a Chinese partner, or simply to invest capital.

The development of these special centers has evolved in fits and starts. So if you are approaching the negotiation phase, be alert for any policy changes that may have an influence on your dealings with the Chinese authorities.

Special Economic Zones (SEZs)

For more information on the special economic zones the foreign investor should contact:

Shenzhen Economic Zone Development Co., 2/F Luohu Building, Jianshe Road, Shenzhen, People's Republic of China.

Shekou Development Company, Nanshan, Shekou Industrial Area, Shenzhen SEZ, Guangdong Province, People's Republic of China.

Zhuhai Development Co., Zhuhai SEZ, Shuiwantou, Guangdong Province, People's Republic of China.

Shantou SEZ Administrative Office, 4/F Foreign Trade Building, Yingchun Lu, Shantou, Guangdong Province, People's Republic of China.

Xiamen SEZ Development Corporation, 105 Xian Jie, Fujian Province, People's Republic of China.

Note that Shekou is an "industrial zone" within the Shenzhen special economic zone.

Investment Incentives

Some of the incentives offered to investors in the regional development centers are: an income tax rate of 15 percent compared with 33 percent elsewhere in China; tax holidays or reductions in tax for large capital investments; reduction or elimination of import and export taxes; simpler visa procedures; the right of enterprises to hire and fire staff under a contract system; the right to repatriate after-tax profits; sale of up to 30 percent of certain products within China; no restrictions on sales within China of certain "high-tech" products; and preferential land-use leases and fees.

Keep in mind that these incentives may vary between cities, zones, and areas, and may even vary according to the interpretation placed on them by a particular negotiating team handling the investment proposal.

Selling in China

Initially, the Chinese authorities insisted that all foreign joint ventures be export-oriented. Under strong pressure from foreign investors, Beijing agreed that products from joint manufacturing ventures could be sold in China, provided advanced technology is used in the factories producing the goods, or provided the goods are classified as "import-replacement."

Bureaucratic Decision Making

The decision-making process within the Chinese bureaucracy places considerable emphasis on achieving a consensus among all the interested parties. A deal may often be discussed at national, provincial, and local levels before a consensus is achieved.

The Chinese "end-user" is the key to the foreign firm's success. The end-user must first be convinced of the usefulness of the product or service. The operations of an end-user, say, a factory, may be monitored by one of the Chinese industrial corporations. Moreover, the end-user may draw upon the advice and recommendations of one or more internal advisory groups, associated research institutions, or scientific societies. So when you are engaged in negotiations or technical discussions the agenda is usually detailed and long, simply because of the large number of "technical" people from different agencies that need to be consulted by the end-user.

Once the technical phase is over, the end-user will then have to convince a number of Chinese planning and coordinating agencies that the purchase from the foreign firm is consistent with China's overall economic and import needs. The factory would have to demonstrate that no domestic substitute is available and that the proposed purchase is commercially sound.

If the factory plans a large-scale purchase, then the potential contract must be approved by the State Planning Commission. If it is a large-scale joint venture, then the potential contract would need to be reviewed by MOFERT. If the factory is purchasing technology or is about to engage in manufacture-under-license, then the contract may need to be reviewed by CITIC or other agencies to determine that the terms of the deal are consistent with China's overall policy on the acquisition of technology.

Even after the commercial and technical details of the contract have been concluded, the factory—if it does not possess its own foreign exchange—must apply to purchase hard currency from the Bank of China or arrange for a loan from the Bank, usually through one of the Chinese corporations.

At present much of China's foreign trade is channelled through the Chinese FTC. The FTCs are mainly concerned with the commercial terms of any contract for, as purchasing agents, they rely on technical advice from the actual end-user. However, the current trend is to "free up" the system and allow end-users to negotiate directly with foreign firms.

So when you are in China negotiating a deal and the discussions appear to stall, it is probably because the pro-forma contract is being passed up or down (or sideways) along the decision-making line-of-command for advice or approval. Awareness of the way bureaucratic decisions are made in China should help you to understand why negotiations can be broken off for one or two days for no apparent reason.

Business Invitations to China

You may visit China on business only after your company has received an invitation from one of the Chinese FTCs. Your company will rarely if ever be invited unless it has first approached the corporation dealing with your product or service.

Researching the Market

The first step you must take is to "research" the P.R.C. market to determine whether there is a need for your goods and services in China or, if you are an importer, whether China produces and exports the particular product that your firm handles. A good way to start is to contact the federal agency in your country dealing in foreign trade and commerce, because it can provide a wealth of advice and information.

From these sources, you can receive first-hand advice on the product or service that interests you, obtain documentation on how to approach the China market, get statistical data, and be able to consult the organization's reference library for more detailed information. To begin, you may wish to consult the *Economic Yearbook* and the *Statistical Yearbook* published by the Chinese authorities. These provide excellent general background material on industry and trade in China.

In the United States the prime source of information on trade with China is the U.S. Department of Commerce. Contact details are provided below.

In other countries, the prime source is usually the Ministry of Trade, Industry, or Commerce, as well as the local Chamber of Commerce.

U.S. Department of Commerce

U.S. business executives may contact the U.S. Department of Commerce at this address: China Desk, Room 2317, 14th and Constitution Avenues NW, Washington, DC 20030 (tel. 202–377–3583 or 202–377–4681).

There are many district offices of the U.S. Department of Commerce located around the United States, so you might begin by contacting the one in your city to determine what information is available locally. If the nearest district office cannot help, then the "China Desk" in Washington should be able to assist you.

Identifying the FTC

The next step you must take is to identify the FTC in China dealing with your product or service. You can do this by consulting the list below,

"Locating the Right Corporation." This list provides a series of product/service categories and (against each category) a "key word."

Use the key word to enter the table provided later in the business section listing Chinese FTCs. You will then find the title, address, telephone number, telex number, and cable address of the corporation that you need to contact.

A more detailed list of these corporations is provided in *China's Foreign Trade Corporations and Organizations,* published by the Department of Public Relations of the CCPIT.

Locating the Right Corporation

If you are new to the China trade, you may have trouble locating the corporation handling your company's product range or service. The following table will help you. Run your eye down the column "Product/Service" until you find a category that appears to cover the goods or services that interest you. Make a note of the "key word." Then consult the list entitled "China's Major Foreign Trade Corporations" located at the end of this chapter. Against each "key word" you will find a product coverage for each corporation, full address, cable/telex codes, and telephone number.

Product/Service	**Key Word**
Aero-Products/Ships/Vehicles	XINSHIDAI
Agricultural Machinery	AGRIMEX
Aircraft and Parts	CATIC
Animal Byproducts	CHINATUHSU
Arts and Crafts	ARTCHINA
Automobiles and Parts	AUTIMPEX
Banking	CHUNGKUO
Books/Periodicals	PUBLIMEX
Cereals/Oils/Foodstuffs	CEROILFOOD
Chartering (see also "Shipping")	SINOCHART
Chemicals/Petroleum Products	SINOCHEM
Coal	CHINACOAL
Coal Handling in Ports/Railways	JENDEV
Coal Production Development	COALDEV
Complete Plant (exported from China)	COMPLANT
Consultants/Technical Services	CONSULTEC
Crop Seeds/Vegetables/Fruits	CHINASEED
Electronics Equipment	CHINELECTRON
Engineering: Tech/Commercial Deals	MACHINTERCORP
Films	CHINAFILM
Housing (Prefab.) and Equipment	NEWBUILD
Instruments	INSTRIMPEX
Insurance: Ocean Marine/Land Cargo	PICC
Investment	CITIC
Light Industrial Products	INDUSTRY
Livestock	BSIEC
Machinery	MACHIMPEX
Machinery & Equipment (exported from China)	EQUIMPEX
Machinery: Precision for Aircraft/Ships	PMIEC
Metals & Minerals	MINMETALS
Mining & Metallurgical Projects/Equipment	CHINAMET

Nonferrous Metals	NONFERMET
Nuclear Instruments/Equipment	CNEIC
Offshore Oil Exploration	CNOOC
Packaging (of Chinese exports)	CHINAPACK
Petroleum Exploration and Development	PETCORP
Postage Stamps	CHINASTAMP
Publications/Posters (exported from China)	GUOJI
Scientific Instruments	CHINSCICAD
Shipbuilding	SHIPBUILD
Shipping (see also "Chartering")	COSCO
	PENAVICO
Silk	CHINASILK
Space Industry Products/Processes	CHINAWALL
Sporting Goods/Sewing Machines/Cosmetics	CLETC
Technology, Factories (imported into China)	TECHIMPORT
Textiles	CHINATEX
Trade Promotion/Trademarks/Patents	COMTRADE
Transportation (within China)	SINOTRANS

Consult the section "China's Major Foreign Trade Corporations" at the end of this chapter for the address of the corporation handling particular products.

Appointments

After you have done the preliminary research, make an appointment with the Commercial Counselor of the Embassy of the P.R.C. in the capital city of your country. (Most P.R.C. embassies are listed in "Planning Your Trip.") If you do not live near your nation's capital, check to see if there is a Consulate in your home city and, if so, seek its help. Chinese Consulates-General located in the U.S. are listed below.

Also check to see if one or more of China's FTCs have a branch office located in your country. If so, make an appointment to see an officer of that branch. These branch offices bring you closer to the China market. U.S. branches of China's major business corporations have been listed at the end of this chapter.

Chinese Missions in the United States

Contact details for the Chinese Embassy and the Chinese Consulates-General established in the U.S. are given below. Address your written inquiries to the Commercial Office.

Chicago: Consulate-General, People's
                  Republic of China
                  104 South Michigan Ave.
                  Chicago, IL 60603
                  Tel. (312) 346–0287

Houston: Consulate-General, People's Republic of
                  China
                  3417 Montrose
                  Houston, TX 77006
                  Tel. (713) 524–0778

Los Angeles: Consulate-General, People's

Republic of China
501 Shatto Place, Suite 300
Los Angeles, CA 90020
Tel. (213) 380–2507

New York: Consulate-General, People's Republic of
                       China
                       520 12th Ave.
                       New York, NY 10036
                       Tel. (212) 279–1270

San Francisco: Consulate-General, People's Republic of
                       China
                       1450 Laguna St.
                       San Francisco, CA 94115
                       Tel. (415) 573–4885

Washington: Embassy of the People's Republic of China
                       2300 Connecticut Ave., NW
                       Washington, DC 20008
                       Tel. (202) 382–2526

Contacting the FTC in China

After you have discussed your trade and/or investment requirements
with officials in locally established Chinese missions and offices, you
should write to the corporation headquarters in China dealing with the
product or service that your company handles.

Alternatively, you might approach one of the regional branches of the
FTC in China. In following this course, you will usually need the advice
of the Commercial Office of the Embassy or Consulate, or of the staff of
the locally based FTC. If in any doubt you are well advised to contact
the main office of the FTC first, perhaps sending a copy of your correspondence to the regional branch of the FTC in China.

Embassies and Consulates in China

You should also seek the advice of the commercial officers located in
your nation's embassy and consulates in China. They have direct access
to officials in the ministries and corporations that you are seeking to deal
with and so can be most helpful to your efforts to develop or expand trade.

Consider sending them a copy of your letters and telexes directed to
the Chinese FTC or other business organizations with whom you may be
dealing. Then, if you have not heard from the FTC or wish to clarify some
points, you can write or cable the commercial staff to seek follow-up action.

Your government department or ministry dealing with trade, commerce, or industry can provide the address and other communication details necessary to contact your countries missions in China. The U.S. missions in China are listed below.

When sending telex messages to China do not reveal sensitive or critical
information likely to affect the outcome of negotiations. Such information
should be conveyed by other means.

U.S. Embassies and Consulates in China

U.S. business executives can get assistance from the U.S. missions in China at the following locations:

Embassy of the United States of America
Commercial Office   Tel. 5321831 ext. 480
3 Xiushui Beijie   Telex: 22701 AMEMBCCN
Beijing, People's Republic of China

United States Consulate-General
1469 Huaihai Zhong Road   Tel. 379880
Shanghai, People's Republic of China   Telex: 33383 USCGCN

United States Consulate-General
Dong Fang Hotel   Tel. 669900
Guangzhou, People's Republic   Telex: 44439 GZDFHCN
   of China

United States Consulate-General
40 Lane 4, Section 5   Tel. 290000
Sanjing St., Heping District   Telex: 80011 AMCSCN
Box 45, Shenyang
People's Republic of China

United States Consulate-General
Jinjiang Hotel   Tel. 51912 or 52791
36 Renmin Nan Road
Chengdu, People's Republic
   of China

National Organizations

You should also check other public and private national organizations that are involved in contact with China. Each nation usually possesses one or a number of such organizations.

Two important business organizations in the U.S. are:

U.S.-China Business Council
1818 N Street NW
Washington, DC 20036
Tel. (202) 828–8300

**The National Academy of Sciences' Committee on Scholarly
   Communication with the People's Republic of China**
2100 Pennsylvania Avenue NW, Suite 200
Washington, DC 20037
Tel. (202) 334–2718

There are many other organizations similarly involved, and you should acquaint yourself with them.

The Hong Kong Connection

Another means of making contact with Chinese FTCs and similar organizations is by getting in touch with their branch offices in Hong Kong. Many Chinese FTCs have set up operations there. This method is particularly useful if you travel regularly in the Southeast Asian region and visit Hong Kong frequently.

You should obtain a list of the Hong Kong-based branches of FTCs from the nearest Embassy or Consulate of the P.R.C. in your country or from the federal government agency in your country overseeing trade and technical exchanges with the P.R.C.

Some of the corporations use the China Resources Corporation (CRC) in Hong Kong to act on their behalf. FTCs adopting this practice are: Chemicals; Metals and Minerals; Machinery; and Textiles. Foreign traders visiting Hong Kong often deal directly with the CRC as an alternative to visiting centers in China. However, it all depends on the nature of the deal and the extent of the relationship existing between the trader and the corporation.

Contact with the CRC may be made as follows: China Resources Corporation, China Resources Building, 18th Floor, 26 Harbour Road, Wanchai, Hong Kong (tel. 5–8317111; telex 73277 CIREC HX, cable CIRECO, Hong Kong).

When you are in Hong Kong you might also like to seek the assistance of the commercial officers based in your country's diplomatic mission. Located on China's doorstep, these officers can be a valuable source of information about trade with China. They can also brief you on the most recent developments in China's trade and investment policy.

For U.S. business executives visiting Hong Kong, the contact point is: Commercial Office, U.S. Consulate-General, 26 Garden Road, Central Hong Kong (tel. 239011; telex 63141 USDOC HX: mailing address: Box 30, FPT, San Francisco, CA 96659–0002).

Hong Kong Middlemen

There are also firms set up in Hong Kong which act as middlemen in trade and investment between foreign countries and China. Although Chinese officials state that they prefer to deal directly with the foreign supplier, the increasing decentralization of decision-making in China has led to a role for Hong Kong middlemen.

Before you appoint one of them to act as your representative for negotiations or for dealings with China make careful inquiries. Check on the firm's background, experience, and commercial reputation. Ask the firm to provide the names of companies that it represents or has represented in the past. Check the Hong Kong firm's performance with these companies. Many middlemen companies established in Hong Kong are known as "briefcase companies," simply because that is their only asset.

Product Information

If you are an exporter, the usual and most effective approach is to send at least 20 copies of your firm's catalogs and descriptive literature, each with a covering letter, to the Beijing headquarters of the appropriate corporation. A list of the corporations, their product responsibility, their addresses and cable codes, is included at the end of this chapter under "China's Major Foreign Trade Corporations." If your company's products are handled by more than one corporation, you should send 20 copies of your proposal, including attachments to each one.

You may also wish to send product literature to the following organizations in Beijing: China Center for Introducing Literature and Samples of New Foreign Products, Box 1420, Beijing, People's Republic of China; or to the Department of Documentation Service, Institute of Scientific and Technical Information, Box 615, Beijing, People's Republic of China.

The Covering Letter

It is often helpful to have your covering letter translated into Chinese as this will improve the chance that your letter and package of product literature will reach the right corporation and end-users. Translations of the major points in your proposal may be helpful also, but is not absolutely necessary.

If the Chinese show interest in your initial proposal it may be advisable to translate some of the technical documentation—but to do so in advance of their signifying interest would be wasteful. In selecting a translation agency check to ensure that they can provide written translations in the simplified form of Chinese characters now in use in the P.R.C. Also check that they are familiar with the technical terminology relevant to your product or service.

While the PRC is now more relaxed about reference to Taiwan, you are well advised to avoid such expressions as "the Republic of China" or "Nationalist China." Similarly, do not refer to Hong Kong as the "Crown Colony." And avoid using terms such as "Red China," "Mainland China," and "Communist China."

Translation services are available in most countries, especially in the capital. Your local department of commerce, ministry of trade, or chamber of commerce should be able to provide the names of suitable translation services. The CCPIT in Beijing also undertakes translations of technical information for a fee.

If you are dealing with a translation service in your own country, you might also like to check with firms that have used the service to find out whether they were satisfied with the work done. A good translation agency will normally be pleased to refer you to satisfied clients.

Keep information up-to-date with new literature as available, but do not send samples until requested unless they are vital to your initial approach. Fairly detailed proposals should be submitted when first making contact, but keep them straightforward and precise. Send a copy of all correspondence to your country's Commercial Counsellor in Beijing, and another set to the Commercial Counsellor of the Embassy of the P.R.C. in your nation's capital city. You can then follow up through them if necessary. Should there be a branch office of the FTC in your country, send a copy of your correspondence to that office as well.

Response from China

You will need to be patient. The trading corporations handle China's trade with more than 100 countries and deal in tens of thousands of products. Consequently initial inquiries can take some time to process. If their reply says that "there is no requirement at the present time," it does not necessarily mean a lack of interest in the product. All it means is that the purchase of such products is not part of the current year's import plan. It is important therefore that companies keep the trading corporations informed of the latest details of their products.

Invitation to China

Once contact has been made, or even on your initial approach, you should request an invitation to visit China to discuss your proposed business. Provide full details about your company, how long it has been in business, its commercial and trading experience, the range of products it deals with, specific product interests in China, proposed duration of your visit, and the number of executives requiring entry. In general, be over-generous with information rather than skimpy.

First-timers often find the recommendation of certain governmental and nongovernmental bodies to be of assistance. For U.S. businesspeople the U.S.–China Business Council—a non-profit, private association of American China traders—may prove useful in this regard.

If the Chinese are interested in the products you have for sale, or feel that you are a potential customer, they will issue your firm an invitation to visit China. The company may be invited to Beijing, Shanghai, or other appropriate center of trade. Alternatively, your company may be invited to attend the Chinese Export Commodities Fair. The Guangzhou or "Canton Fair," as it is widely known, is held twice every year: April 15–May 5 and October 15–November 5.

Export companies should take into account China's interest in, and emphasis on, two-way trade and, where possible, should include in their approach the possibility of purchasing materials from China, particularly since the Fair emphasizes Chinese exports. It is advisable for a company to send executives who have the authority to make on-the-spot decisions as well as to sign contracts in the company's name. As a rule, Chinese respond better to higher-level personnel. Occasional visits to China by the firm's top executives are also appreciated and enhances the standing of the company with the Chinese officials.

Technical Seminars

You should also consider other means of making contact with the Chinese authorities. One of the most effective means of introducing your firm directly to your Chinese counterpart and end-user is the technical seminar. It is accomplished by making arrangements to visit China to make a technical presentation of your firm's products and services. This can be arranged through the CCPIT, but technical seminars are also arranged by China's industrial ministries and corporations, and also by scientific and professional organizations.

Fairs

China's import and export commodity fairs present another means of making direct contact with China's foreign trade corporations and end-users. You should consult the federal government agency in your country responsible for trade with China to obtain a list of the import and export commodity fairs. Your country may even be cosponsoring a fair in China for a particular range of commodities or services. In such a case there would be an opportunity for your firm to make technical presentations to selected groups of officials from Chinese corporations, ministries, and end-users.

Delegations

You should also always check to find out whether there are any delegations from your country visiting China. One of them might provide the opportunity to open up negotiations on your company's products or services. You could then try to become a member of the delegation. Alternatively, there may be a Chinese delegation visiting your country in which case you can then arrange to be included in their program and thereby hold direct discussions with the officials in the delegation.

If you company is large enough, it may be possible to arrange for a specific delegation from China to visit the company for commercial and technical discussions. If you invite a Chinese delegation to visit your firm in the U.S., make sure both sides are clear about the financial obligations involved. Such direct invitations to Chinese delegations are often to the account of the foreign firm, but this is negotiable. The important point is to clarify the matter in advance.

You should also check other public and private organizations that arrange visits by Chinese technical and commercial delegations. Each nation usually possesses one or a number of such organizations. In the U.S., for example, the most important organizations for this purpose are the U.S.–China Business Council and the National Academy of Sciences' Committee on Scholarly Communication with the People's Republic of China. There are many other organizations similarly involved and you should acquaint yourself with them.

Visas for Business Executives

Once an invitation has been received by a firm, the executive designated by the company as their delegate should apply for an entry visa at the Embassy or Consulate of the People's Republic of China in the country where the invited firm is located. This is done by presenting the original invitation extended by the state trading corporation or the Fair (photocopy is unacceptable) along with a letter certifying your representative's status. An application form for each executive intending to visit China must also be completed and submitted with two passport-type photographs.

If the applicants are unable to apply for entry visas to the Embassy or Consulate in the country where the invited firm is located, they can obtain their visa through the CTS in Hong Kong or on arrival in Beijing. Obviously an executive arriving at either center must have a valid passport as well as the invitation from one of the FTCs or from an organization authorized to issue such invitations.

Exporting to China

Once your firm has an invitation to visit China you need to consider carefully which executives should form the delegation. Two key personnel should be included: the first should be one who has the authority to make on-the-spot decisions; the second should be a person (or persons) able to provide detailed answers to technical questions about the company's product or service. If you do not include both types of people in your negotiating team, you may unnecessarily prolong the negotiations, increase the number of visits that your firm will have to make to China, and even jeopardize the chance of negotiating a successful contract.

If the above personnel do not also possess the appropriate financial expertise, do not understand letter-of-credit (L/C) sales, and are not able to negotiate the financial aspects of the deal, then an additional member must be added to the team.

Separate sections have been provided on the problems that can be associated with Chinese L/Cs and also on the financing of sales to China (see "Payments" and "Financing Exports to China" sections, below). In particular, you should note that Chinese L/Cs made out for foreign exporters are usually "advised" and not "confirmed." If a foreign exporter allows the advising bank to act as collecting agent, it means that credit is extended to the Chinese buyer by a period of about 20 to 30 days, the time taken for the advising bank to negotiate with the Bank of China. If the foreign exporter requires immediate payment, he can sell his L/C to the advising bank at a discount. Most banks will discount the L/C only with recourse to the exporter, although sometimes it is possible to arrange a discounted payment against a L/C without recourse.

When developing a financial package keep in mind that China has access to inexpensive buyer's credits available from various national export/import banks (known by different names in different countries). Usually the Bank of China is offered a financing package which is a mixture provided by the national Export/Import Bank and a group of commercial banks, the buyer providing 15 percent of the total purchase cost. Short-term credit is available for Chinese purchases from major U.S. and European banks able to tap the Eurodollar market and provide short-term Eurodollars at the London Inter-Bank offering rate (LIBOR). Medium-term Euro-dollar loans are also available.

Many U.S. and European banks can also offer short-term credit at less than LIBOR market rates, so you should make inquiries with your bank prior to negotiating the contract in China. Although the Chinese authority importing the products from your company will usually be expected to pay 15 percent of the total contract price, some of them will be interested in a 100 percent finance package, so you should explore this aspect during negotiations.

Your position regarding patents, trademarks, and copyrights should be taken into account when selling to China. China is a signatory to the Paris Convention for the Protection of International Property (effective March 19, 1985) so your firm's products are now protected by the usual international arrangements regarding industrial property. However, it would be prudent to make inquiries about your protection during negotiations. Additional information on the protection of industrial property is given in a section that follows.

One other aspect that needs your close attention in negotiating sales to China is the method of operation of the P.R.C. inspection and arbitration facilities. Chinese importers invariably hold foreign exporters to the letter of the agreement, concerning the quality and technical characteristics of the goods being imported. The standard purchase contract that a foreign firm signs with a Chinese FTC usually includes a clause which provides a guarantee period extended to 18 months or more from the date of arrival of the cargo. Goods and commodities are usually inspected in minute detail by officers of the Commodities Inspection Bureau on arrival of the goods in China.

You should attempt to deliver the goods to China exactly as described in the contract. Some firms have had shipments rejected because they have supplied a later model than that specified in the contract. Such equipment has been rejected even though the manufacturer was supplying it in good faith and giving the Chinese a "better deal."

If disputes do arise, on quality aspects or any other reasons connected with the contract, the Chinese will try to settle a dispute in a friendly and amicable way, avoiding litigation over the contract if possible. Where negotiations fail to settle the dispute, it is usually arbitrated by the Foreign Trade Arbitration Commission in Beijing. However, in more recent times Chinese importers have been willing to specify a third-country arbitration organization.

Importing from China

If your company has an invitation to visit China to undertake negotiations for the purchase of goods and commodities, then you will need to pay close attention to some aspects of trade with China that differ from those with other countries.

For example, the standard Chinese export contracts call for the purchaser to open a "confirmed, irrevocable, transferable, and divisible" L/C. This is usually payable at sight to the Bank of China. Usually the L/C has to reach the seller about 30 days before date of shipment (or even for a longer period). The L/C must usually remain valid 15 days after the expiration of the shipment period.

There are usually clauses in the contract requiring the L/C to allow for transshipment and/or partial shipment. All these clauses tend to increase the period of time covered by the L/C, thereby increasing the financial exposure of the foreign importer.

The Chinese exporter requires that the L/Cs be "confirmed" so that the foreign importer has little protection over delivery. Furthermore, because the standard clause in Chinese export contracts designate the Chinese inspection of goods to be final, the foreign importer is at a considerable disadvantage when receiving goods considered to be defective or otherwise not up to quality. Chinese exports are subject to inspection by the Chinese Commodities Inspection Bureau (CCIB). When the foreign importer is dissatisfied with the quality of goods received, the Chinese FTCs involved usually try to avoid making a cash payment, offering instead a concession on future orders.

Problems over the delivery of Chinese exports remain a regular source of irritation to foreign importers. The Chinese inland transportation system and ports are choked with goods, so there are often delays in delivery. Such delays are often made worse by the Chinese practice of transshipment. The delivery problem is particularly difficult for firms ordering products which are fashionable or seasonal.

When shipment delays occur, the foreign importer is faced with the additional expense of extending the L/C. The Chinese exporter rarely shows sympathy by agreeing to make up the difference for this expense. All you can do is ask the Chinese exporters to make payment against documents, thereby eliminating the need to extend an L/C. At times they have been known to agree.

Negotiation Hints

Whether you are negotiating at Beijing, the fair, or at any other center, you should try to observe the following procedures.

Obtain the business cards of the Chinese traders with whom you are negotiating. The first name in Chinese is equivalent to our surname, but remember that names like "Chang" and "Wang" are as common as our "Smith" and "Jones" and are often shared by a multitude of people in the corporation. You should if possible secure their given names. In addition, find out their product responsibilities.

Talk slowly, enunciate clearly, and avoid slang and sarcasm. Use the time employed by the translator in interpreting your remarks to prepare your thoughts. Be concise, and give your counterpart time to speak.

Avoid any display of anger. Be flexible whenever possible. However, do not hesitate to take a firm but quiet stand; the Chinese respect an astute negotiator.

Always remember that strict adherence to the contract is the expected norm. Yet, in the building of a long-term business relationship with a corporation, it is the extracontractual behavior that is important in your being considered eventually as an "old friend of China."

You should also be cautious when spelling out assurances about product performance. The Chinese sometimes may buy only a section of a processing line, preferring to substitute for the remainder more labor-intensive methods, and such substitution may affect the performance of the entire system.

Keep these points in mind when negotiating, and you will make it easier for you and your team members to draw the meetings to a successful conclusion.

Letters of Intent

Sometimes negotiations end not with a contract legally binding on both sides but with a "letter of intent" or similar document. When that happens, proceed with due caution. The Chinese authorities do not usually like publicity about a possible business venture before a contract is signed. In contrast, businesses in the industrial West like to draw attention to any successes, even preliminary agreements. The difference in attitude here is a good example of cultural conflict at the commercial level.

The best course to follow is to get an agreement in writing from your Chinese counterparts regarding preliminary publicity (by either side) or to keep the matter confidential until the contract is signed. To do otherwise may jeopardize all that has been accomplished; preliminary announcements or publicity have sometimes led to a cancellation of further talks by the Chinese. Conversely, the Chinese have been known to leak news of a pending deal in order to extract concessions at later negotiating sessions.

Negotiation Phases

You should bear in mind that there are usually two phases in contract negotiations in China. The first phase is technical; the second commercial. The Chinese carefully assess the technical qualities of the product or process being offered and technical competence of the foreign firm making the offer. They often use this phase of the discussions of negotiations to obtain detailed information of the "state of the art" of the particular technology under review.

The Chinese negotiators will usually push the foreign firm to the limits of its preparedness to divulge proprietary information. You should not hesitate to indicate to your Chinese negotiators just how far you are prepared to go in divulging such information. Such an attitude is no bar to the negotiations continuing.

It is usually in the technical phase of the negotiations that the Chinese negotiators show a frustrating attention to detail. It is to your advantage to provide as much information as possible and, at the same time, show patience. Although the commercial phase is yet to begin, commercial matters may be raised during the technical phase, such as information about price and delivery.

When the commercial phase begins, the pace of negotiations usually picks up. One of the problems facing a foreign negotiating team is that the commercial members of the team may be idle during the technical phase and the technical people idle during the commercial phase and frustration may build up in the individuals in your team.

Because it is difficult to predict just when the technical phase will end and the commercial one will begin, or when negotiations may shift suddenly from one to the other phase and back again, both technical and commercial personnel should attend all the meetings. And of course, the negotiations may be broken off for a few days at a time while the Chinese team clarifies certain questions with superiors or with the end-user.

All this can be very confusing to the new "China hand" but is accepted and well understood by those who have been doing business with China for a longer period. You should try to conceal any impatience you may be feeling. Revealing your frustrations will have no effect on the speed of the negotiations and indeed show the Chinese that they hold the psychological advantage. This may indicate, for example, that you will be more willing as time drags on to make concessions in order to conclude the business quickly.

Compensation Trade

Compensation trade is also known as "counter-trade" and is usually adopted by countries with insufficient foreign-exchange reserves for planned expansion of production and trade. In its simplest form, imports of machinery and equipment are paid for with the goods produced.

As China does not have sufficient foreign currency available to purchase the plant, machinery, equipment, and technology necessary for industrial modernization, the government has encouraged compensation trade with developed industrial countries. The following example serves to illustrate the scheme.

A foreign company importing, say, knitwear from China agrees to install high-speed knitting machines in one or more of the Chinese factories and provide a technical service covering the installation and use of the machines, quality control, packaging, and so on. The foreign firm then receives the knitwear at a discounted cost for a number of years until the total amount received amortizes the cost of machinery and technical service. There are a great many variations of this example.

The contracts between the parties usually begin with a statement of letter of intent concerning the project. There are three essential contractual elements in the previous example: the foreign company negotiates a machinery export contract; either party or both will undertake to supply materials for the project under a materials supply contract; and the company to receive the goods produced negotiates a merchandise import contract.

There are usually other secondary contracts or agreements associated with such a deal, such as a contract to cover the technical-assistance portion of the project, a contract on trademark and labeling, and so on.

Price

You should keep in mind that the export price of Chinese products may bear no relationship to the domestic cost of production and is determined mainly by the Chinese corporation's perception of the world market price.

Therefore, importers should show no hesitation about pointing out the availability of similar goods at better prices.

In general, Chinese exports are sold C and F, or CIF, and imports purchased FOB. However, there are numerous exceptions to this generalization.

Availability

Buyers of Chinese products are often apportioned goods because the demand exceeds supply. The quantity of goods made available to a specific buyer depends on the buyer's nationality, the ultimate market destination of the product, and the length and warmth of the business relationship enjoyed by the buyer.

Contracts

Sales and purchases are usually concluded by contract. Terms and conditions depend upon the product and vary from corporation to corporation, but reference to major conditions is usually fairly standard. However, Chinese organizations have become more flexible when negotiating many clauses in contracts. Obviously, the foreign trader should try to ensure that his own terms and conditions are embodied in the contract. Consider almost every aspect of a contract negotiable, but yet be prepared to receive fairly stiff objections during contract negotiations.

The Chinese have acquired an excellent reputation for meeting their contractual obligations and in return expect a foreign trader to honor the contract, even when it may prove extremely difficult to do so. Examples of standard contracts for both sales and purchases are provided at the end of this section.

Contracts are in Chinese and English, and each is equally valid. If you are an importer, you should take great care over packaging and labeling requirements for goods destined for your home country; failure to comply with your home-market regulations may prevent the goods from being imported. As the Chinese may not wish to acknowledge the specific regulations of a foreign government, you may not be able to make direct reference to them in your contract. The only alternative is to insert clauses that embody the substance of the requirements.

The China trader's uncertainty about the Chinese legal system and confusion about China's position in relation to international trade law often give him a sense of insecurity and frustration. Since most contracts between corporations and traders are executed in China, the agreement is subject to Chinese law. Fortunately, China has a very simple law of contract, and you should not be too concerned about being fairly treated.

While China adopts international trade devices such as bills of lading, letters of credit, marine insurance, and so on, there can be differences of interpretation applied to such well-known terms as FOB, for example. The interpretation among the Chinese is known to vary from "FOB warehouse," "free on wharf," and "under ship's hook" to "FOR." This variation is not uncommon to older nations. The point is, to avoid costly claims later you should get clarification in the contract of what standard terms actually mean.

Payments

Contracts often call for payment by irrevocable letter of credit (ILC). When a Chinese corporation or agency purchases goods, the Bank of

China (BOC) issues a L/C. When a foreign company purchases goods, the firm's bank issues an ILC.

In selling to China, an exporter should be aware of the peculiar nature of China's L/Cs. The Bank of China (BOC) is not a member of the International Chamber of Commerce and is not legally bound to conform to ICC practices. Nevertheless, the BOC usually follows the international code in L/C payments, except for "confirmation."

The Bank of China's L/Cs are merely "advised." The advising (foreign) bank may therefore only agree to act as a collecting agent for the exporter, forwarding documents to Beijing for negotiation. As the collection takes about 20 days, the exporter in effect extends credit for this additional period.

On the other hand, an exporter can arrange immediate payment through his bank by discounting the draft, although this is often arranged on the understanding that the bank has recourse to the exporter, should problems in collection arise.

Although the BOC does not issue confirmed L/Cs, it expects companies that purchase Chinese goods to arrange confirmed L/Cs. This can be done through any bank enjoying a full correspondent relationship with the BOC.

Companies experienced in dealing with China often arrange for the validity of an L/C to extend 15 days beyond the anticipated expiration date stated in the contract. Such a precaution while costly, is usually less expensive than arranging a second L/C providing the equivalent extension.

The BOC has established an extensive network of correspondent banks throughout the world, mainly in nations where China trades. In the United States the list is extensive. Check with your own bank or with the U.S. Department of Commerce. Major U.S. banks maintain representative offices in China but are not yet authorized to undertake financial transactions, their role being one of liaison only.

Shipping

China's FTCs normally buy FOB and sell CIF, so shipping for both imports and exports is usually handled by China Ocean Shipping Company (COSCO), China's national carrier. COSCO is part of the Ministry of Communications. Despite the attempt by China to move all imports and exports in Chinese vessels, COSCO does not own enough ships or have enough vessels under charter to carry all the FTCs' cargoes. So a proportion of China trade continues to be carried on ships flying flags of third countries.

The China National Chartering Corporation (SINOCHART) is used by Chinese FTCs and other Chinese and foreign business organizations in chartering vessels and booking shipping vessels for Chinese import and export cargoes. SINOCHART reports to the MOFERT.

Another agency involved in shipping is the China Ocean Shipping Agency, or PENAVICO. It handles the agency business for vessels calling in Chinese ports and is responsible for booking passenger and cargo space on Chinese and foreign vessels; it also arranges cargo consolidation and transshipment. The PENAVICO agency also charters, leases, or purchases ships when required by the Ministry of Communications, to whom it reports.

Customs Clearance in China

Customs clearance for import and export cargoes is arranged by the China National Foreign Trade Transportation Corporation (SINO-TRANS), an agency that reports to the MOFERT. The SINOTRANS corporation acts as the authorized agent for clearing/delivering goods in transit through China's ports, airports, and border posts, arranges for marine and other insurance where necessary, and will act on behalf of cargo owners initiating insurance claims. The SINOTRANS corporation is also responsible for the domestic transportation of Chinese imports and exports.

Insurance

Some contracts specify the People's Insurance Company of China (PICC) as insurer. P.R.C. exports are usually covered for 110 percent of the CIF invoice value of the goods. Damage claims should be submitted within 30 days after arrival of the shipment. If the PICC is not specified, the trader is free to arrange his own insurance. American International Group, Inc. is the only insurance company in the U.S. and Canada to represent the PICC on claims and related matters, i.e., surveys.

Patents

China's patent law, introduced in 1985, specifies that foreign patents relating to technical inventions will be protected for 15 years, industrial designs for 5 years, and minor inventions also for 5 years. The protection may be extended for an additional three years if required. Patent applications are handled by the P.R.C. Patent Office, which has branch offices throughout Chinese provinces. Inventions or processes will only be granted a patent if they possess novelty, inventiveness, and practical application. The negotiation of these matters is handled by the Patent Registration Agency, CCPIT, Fuxingmenwai Dajie, Beijing; cable COMTRADE, Beijing; telex 22315 CCPIT CN.

Trademarks

China's trademark law conforms in many respects to international trademark practices, although China has not acceded to the International Trademark Convention. While the authority responsible for trademarks is the General Administrative Bureau for Industry and Commerce under the State Council, registration arrangements are handled by the Trademark Registration Agency of the CCPIT, Beijing.

Trademarks which are registered in China by foreign persons or organizations are valid for a period of 10 years and renewable for another 10-year period. Application forms and information on trademark applications may be obtained from the agency referred to above.

Copyright

China has not yet acceded to the Universal Copyright Convention (UCC), so any company entering the book market there will be on uncertain ground. In China, as in most other communist states, the author has no rights over the publication and distribution of his work. If China joins the UCC, foreigners will be given rights similar to those of Chinese citizens. These rights would appear to convey little or no advantage. It is therefore uncertain whether the establishment of copyright relations with China will mean that royalties and profits from foreign works published and/or distributed in China will be guaranteed. Perhaps the only way for a foreigner to obtain copyright royalties is to negotiate a contract prior to publication or distribution in China.

Advertising

Foreign companies may advertise in China in newspapers, magazines, billboards, and television. However, there are restrictions on the nature of the ads, the products that may be advertised, and the media allowed. Companies interested in advertising their products in China should contact one of the international ad agencies handling media accounts in China, or make direct contact with the China National Foreign Trade Advertising Association, 2 Chang An Street E., Beijing (tel. 553031, ext. 397), which represents both national and provincial level organizations.

Generally speaking, Mandarin is used for broadcast media and, without exception, the simplified form of the Chinese written characters is used in the print and outdoor media. Media advertising is new to China. It has to be kept simple and straightforward because it tends to be interpreted literally by the population. "Hard sell" techniques are not appropriate in China; rather there should be an attempt to inform and educate the Chinese consumer.

All foreign companies wishing to advertise in China must first register with MOFERT's Import and Export Bureau, 2 Chang An Road E., Beijing. Chinese regulations on advertising are directed toward ensuring that the contents of advertisements are clear and truthful, and that they conform to the state's economic and broadcast-policy provisions.

Two periodicals that have been used successfully by foreign advertisers in contacting Chinese end-users are the monthly *International Trade News* (issued by the International Reader Research Institute of MOFERT) and the bimonthly *Trade and Technology* (issued by the China Trade Consultation and Technical Services Institute also of MOFERT).

Video-tape can be used to promote new products and techniques to "decision-makers" in Chinese state trading corporations and ministries through the Chinese Science and Technology Commission.

All advertisers are counseled to seek expert advice in their approach to the Chinese market.

Companies wishing to promote technology, methods, and "know-how" might consider the opportunities presented by advertising through China's Science Press publications. Science Press publishes 57 journals in fields such as electronics, computer science, physics, chemistry, mathematics, automation, and agriculture, to name a few.

Foreign Investment

The most important organization facilitating foreign investment in China is the China International Trust and Investment Corporation (CITIC; see above for contact details). CITIC assists foreign and Chinese enterprises to find appropriate partners for both equity and contractual joint ventures; negotiates the establishment of 100 percent foreign-owned enterprises; assists the negotiation of compensation trade agreements; serves as China's principal channel for investment funds originating from Overseas Chinese and foreigners; and acts as agent for China in the purchase of advanced foreign technology and equipment.

A foreign company, wishing to explore joint-venture possibilities, should find a "Chinese participant" through CITIC or one of the government ministries, agencies, or trade corporations. The company must then negotiate an agreement with the prospective joint-venture partner. The time taken to reach an agreement will normally be long, unless the foreign company happens to possess technology vital to China's industry.

Under China's modernization plan, investment priorities are well established. China seeks foreign investment in the broad sectors of energy, transport, telecommunications, and tourism; its objective is to modernize production in these sectors and to expand and improve the nation's infrastructure.

Foreign investors face formidable hurdles: China's legal system is undeveloped, inaccessible, and difficult to understand. Accountancy and financial control are poorly developed. The nation's complex pricing system makes planning difficult. Labor is relatively inefficient and subject to Party intervention. Management control over business operations is often inadequate.

China's planners are aware of these difficulties and are attempting to reduce their effect. The need to provide a secure legal framework for foreign investors was addressed in changes to the PRC Constitution in 1982, yet many of the commercial laws that followed were ad hoc and confusing. However, by 1987 the enactment of the General Principles of Civil Law helped define the status of both domestic and foreign enterprises and identified their civil obligations and rights. More legal work remains to be done before foreign investors will consider China as a nation with secure investment prospects.

Joint-Venture Law

The law on joint ventures states that a foreign company's contribution to registered capital must not be less than 25 percent, but no maximum proportion is laid down. Top officials have confirmed that the foreign proportion can be higher than 50 percent and that the duration of the joint venture may be longer than 20 years. However, each project will be considered on an individual basis, and no general principles can be cited at this stage.

The foreign company may appoint directors to the governing board of the venture, and may also appoint executives to participate in day-to-day management. The Chinese side appoints the chairman of the board, while the foreign partner may appoint one or two vice-chairmen. Management functions are not assigned to either party in the legislation, nor are rights of hiring and firing clearly spelled out.

Repatriation of profits and other funds is permitted. Joint ventures equipped with the latest technology are subjected to a reduction in or exemption from income tax for the first two to three profit-making years. Incentives are provided for the reinvestment of profits in China.

These points touch on just a few issues raised by the new law. Foreign firms seeking to take up joint-venture opportunities in China will need to pay attention to a host of uncertainties, not the least of which relate to the definition of "profit" and "truly advanced technology."

Potential investors will want to determine whether the "investment climate" is favorable and will remain so. So far, the Chinese have established some of the basic legal framework necessary to allow foreign investment to establish itself and grow. Yet China's existing legislation falls short of the investment standards applicable in many target nations around the world. China's legislators are trying to bring the PRC into line with the rules that govern international commerce, but progress has been slow. When adequate legislation is in place and investors more confident that the rules will be interpreted consistently, joint-venture programs are bound to increase.

Financing Exports to China

Suppliers' Credit. The extension of credit by foreign exporters has become an important part of a sales contract, so the credit facilities offered may be critical to the success of any negotiations.

China has made use of foreign financing from the early 1970s, when the government—through its FTCs—bought whole plants and equipment on deferred-payment terms. Suppliers obtained credit, usually under their own countries' export-incentive schemes, and passed on the costs of financing in the form of higher prices in the contract. Most of the Japanese plants sold to China during the early 1970s were financed this way, utilizing five-year credits granted by the Japanese Exim Bank against Bank of China guarantees.

The credit package now offered by a supplier to China depends on the size of the transaction and the borrowing term. Exporters to China can usually arrange short-term credit through U.S. and European banks able to tap the Eurodollar market, or from those banks' domestic funds and through bankers' acceptances. However, China's medium-to-long-term credit demands for multimillion-dollar projects are more likely to utilize direct buyer credits of the large, syndicated loan type.

Buyer Credits. Buyer credits are available to Chinese government import agencies from a range of foreign government export-credit agencies, most of which are variations of the Exim Bank. The essential ingredients for this form of credit are: long maturities, fixed interest rates, and maximum subsidization of interest rates.

Buyer credits enable Chinese corporations and agencies to finance up to 85 percent of the purchase price through international commercial banks by utilizing the suppliers' national export-agency guarantee. The other 15 percent is in the form of a cash payment, but this too can be financed by the buyer at ruling international interest rates through standard bank procedures. The lines of credit so far established by China are substantial.

Chinese Lines of Credit. To enable medium- to long-term financing of multimillion- and billion-dollar projects to take place, China has established huge lines of credit with quasi-governmental agencies, private banks, and banking consortia. The most important credit lines so far granted are by: COFACE of France, ECGD of the U.K., EDC of Canada, Exim Bank of Japan, and Mediocredito of Italy.

Contract Differences

There are a number of important differences in import and export contracts, all of which tend to favor the Chinese.

For example, there is usually no penalty clause for delay in delivery by Chinese sellers, for the simple reason that the Chinese are often late making delivery. When a corporation completes a contract with a foreign trader, the matter of delivery is then handed over to the COSCO for shipping to the ultimate destination. China's internal transport system is chronically overloaded and her ports heavily congested (although improvements are being made), so delivery deadlines are often not met.

Another difference relates to L/Cs. Foreign buyers usually have to open L/Cs much earlier than Chinese buyers. Foreign buyers often have to give immediate notice of completion of loading, while Chinese buyers are apt to be given more time.

Foreign buyers are required to have their L/Cs confirmed; Chinese L/Cs are usually not confirmed.

Contract Disputes

Chinese contracts all specify that any dispute resulting from disagreement about the performance of either party under terms of the contract should be settled by consultation, friendly negotiation, and agreement between the parties.

Only in rare instances do negotiations fail to bring an agreement and, where this occurs, the Chinese usually insist that the issue then be considered by the Foreign Trade Arbitration Commission of the CCPIT in Beijing. This tribunal has decided only a handful of cases, although there have been a few instances where proceedings were begun and then settled out of court.

There have been very few arbitration cases considered outside China except where they were related to maritime matters. In maritime disputes the Chinese usually follow the accepted international practice. Maritime disputes with China are handled by Maritime Arbitration Commission of the CCPIT.

Any party requiring arbitration should apply in writing to one of the two commissions referred to above. The application should list:

(a) the name and address of the claimant and the party on whom the claim is being made;

(b) details of the claim and supporting evidence;

(c) the name of the arbitrator representing the claimant or, in the absence of a nominee, a request to the Director of the Arbitration Commission for the appointment of an arbitrator.

All relevant documents should be forwarded. Make sure that you keep photocopies of everything sent.

A deposit to cover the estimated cost of the arbitration is required on application. The cost of foreign trade arbitration is usually 1/2 percent of the disputed amount, and 1 percent for maritime arbitration. The successful party is entitled to a refund of the deposit.

The claimant may appear in person or be represented by a Chinese citizen or citizen of another nation.

Customs Tariff in China

China has a two-column tariff system. Goods imported into the P.R.C. from countries which have established official commercial agreements with China granting reciprocal most-favored-nation (MFN) treatment, are subject to the minimum rate. Other countries are subject to the general rate, which in some instances is double the minimum rate. The U.S. and China have granted each other MFN treatment.

The value of imports for the calculation of duty payable is the CIF value at the port of importation in China. Customs assess this value as the total landed cost of the import, including export duty, packing charges, and other miscellaneous charges involved in the transfer of the goods to the Chinese port. The Customs follow the normal commercial practice of requiring documentation providing the information necessary for duty assessment.

The tariff schedule lists over 1,800 items, classified according to 17 categories and 89 sections. However, tariffs need not concern companies exporting to China; these are settled within the system and therefore do not need to be taken into account when pricing exports.

Business Cards

Exchanging business cards is a routine practice in China. If you wish to make a good impression, have the reverse side of your card printed in Chinese. Printing can be done quite cheaply in Hong Kong. At the trade fair it can be arranged through your hotel, but it may take a few days.

CHINESE EXPORT COMMODITIES FAIR

The Chinese Export Commodities Fair, also known as the Canton Fair or Guangzhou Fair, is held twice a year, April 15–30 and October 15–30. Each fair is attended by tens of thousands of business executives.

The fairground is located at the Guangzhou Foreign Trade Center off Renmin Road between the Guangzhou Railway Station and the Dong Fang Hotel. The fair buildings and open areas provide over a million square feet of display and office space for China's state trading corporations. About 40,000 different items produced in China are displayed and most are available for sale. However, some goods are not traded at the fair, as more and more buyers now travel to China outside the fair period to deal directly with provincial organizations, or attend "mini-fairs" held away from Guangzhou.

As the name suggests, the fair is set up essentially to assist China's export drive. Consequently Chinese state trading corporations have shown a reluctance to negotiate import contracts, although there are some exceptions.

The fair has evolved considerably since it was first held in 1956. In those early days just over a thousand businessmen attended, and a few were from Western industrial countries and Japan. Over the years, the number of products exhibited and the number of traders seeking invitations grew rapidly, the venue being changed three times to cope with the rapid expansion. Now held twice a year at the Trade Center, the fair serves mainly the needs of foreign importers of light industrial products and craftware.

If you are a business executive going to the Guangzhou Fair you should read the *Guangzhou* chapter, which provides information about climate, clothing, travel to Guangzhou, currency control, customs, and so on.

The *Guangzhou* section also covers the leading hotels, their facilities, what to see, restaurants, shopping, and sightseeing.

Fair Administration (CECFEO)

The Gaungzhou Fair is organized and administered by the Fair Executive Office based permanently in Guangzhou. The address is CECFEO, Guangzhou Foreign Trade Center, 117 Liuhua Lu, Guangzhou (cable: 0070 CECFA, tel. 677000, telex 44465 FAIR CN).

When the fair is in progress CECFEO operates a liaison office at major hotels.

Flight Reservations

During the fair there are sometimes delays in obtaining reservations at the CITS office, and you may wish to move quickly. If so, you can deal direct with CAAC/China South Airline by going to their office at 181 Huanshi Road, off Liuhua Square, adjacent to the railway station.

Alternatively, you may first call the CAAC/China South Airline office at the following numbers in Guangzhou:

International Passenger Service   661803

Domestic Passenger Service	662123, ext. 904
Cargo Service (international)	661381, ext. 32
Cargo Delivery Service	662917
Guangzhou Airport (Baiyun)	332878

If you go to the CAAC/China South Airline office, you will have to take your passport in order to purchase air tickets.

Rail Reservations

You must purchase your train tickets and make reservations through CITS, whose main office (tel. 677856) is located at 179 Huanshi Road, not far from the entrance of the main railway station. During the fair, CITS sets up office in some major hotels, one of them the Dong Fang Hotel (tel. 662427 or 669900 ext. 2366). Other hotels provide a travel service for guests; inquire at the lobby desk.

Train Services

Domestic and international train services link cities and towns in China, and major cities with capitals in other countries. CITS will make any necessary reservations. Information about Chinese trains and train fares is given under "Travel in China" in the *Planning Your Trip* section.

Boat and Hovercraft Services

CITS also arranges reservations and tickets for boat and hovercraft services; see the Practical Information section for Guangzhou (below) and "Getting to China" for details.

Guangzhou Branch Offices of Major State Trading Organizations

The address and telephone number of each of the main state trading organizations located in Guangzou are given below. During the fair, each organization maintains an office at the Guangzhou Foreign Trade Center.

Animal By-products	Shamian Nan Road	Tel. 886018
Arts and Crafts	2 Qiaoguang Road	Tel. 334208
Cereals and Oils	2 Qiaoguang Road	Tel. 334154
Chemicals	61 Yanjiang Xi Road	Tel. 885531
Foodstuffs	59 Yanjiang Xi Road	Tel. 861220
Light Industrial	87 Changdi Road	Tel. 337522
Machinery	61 Yanjiang Xi Road	Tel. 885531
Metals and Minerals	77 Dongfeng Dong Road	Tel. 776875
Native Produce	486 Liu'ersan Road	Tel. 889215
Textiles	63 Wenming Road	Tel. 331750

CHINA'S MAJOR FOREIGN TRADE
CORPORATIONS

The headquarters of the major FTCs are listed in alphabetical order according to the "key word" or cable code of each agency/corporation. These are often used by China traders when speaking of an organization rather than the more cumbersome Organization name.

Agency/Corporation Head Office	Telephone	Product Interest
AGRIMEX China National Agricultural Machinery Import and Export Corporation (CAMC) Sanlihe Beijing Cable: AGRIMEX Telex: 866361	838361 866252	Coordinates and administers China's import and export of agricultural machinery and equipment.
ARTCHINA China National Arts & Crafts Import & Export Corp. 82 Donganmen Street Beijing Cable: ARTCHINA Beijing Telex: 22155 CNART CN	558831	Pottery and procelain, human hair, pearls, precious stones and jewelry, ivory and jade carvings, lacquerware, plaited articles, furniture, artwork handicrafts and other handicrafts for everyday use.
AUTIMPEX China National Automotive Industry Import and Export Corporation c/o Ministry of Machine Building 12 Fuxingmenwai Street Beijing Telex: 22341 CMIC CN	362561	Imports automobile spare parts, accessories, raw materials, and special equipment. Imports of samples of motor vehicles and motorcycles. Exports motor vehicles, motorcycles, accessories, and production equipment.
BSEIC China National Breeding Stock Import and Export Corporation Heping Li Beijing Cable: CNABSIEC, Beijing	464344	Imports and exports breeding cattle, sheep, pigs, horses, donkeys, camels, rabbits, poultry, bees, dogs, forage grass seeds, and animal feedstuffs.

Agency/Corporation *Head Office*	*Telephone*	*Product Interest*
CATIC China National Aero Technology Import and Export Corporation 67 Jiaodaokou Nan Dajie Box 1671 Beijing Cable: CAID Beijing Telex: 22318 AEROT CN	442444	Deals in aircraft, aero-engines, aircraft meters, accessories, and electrical appliances, aircraft parts, testing instruments and equipment, measuring and cutting tools, parachutes.

CEROILFOOD
China National Oils and Foodstuffs
  Import and Export Corp.
82 Donganmen Street
Beijing
Cable: CEROILFOOD Beijing
Telex: 22281 CEROFCN
      22111 CEROFCN
	558831
	ext. 221
		Cereals, edible vegetable and animal oils and fats, vegetable and animal oils and fats for industrial use, oil seeds, seeds, oil cakes, feeding stuffs, salt, edible livestock and poultry, meat and meat products, eggs and egg products, fresh fruit and fruit products, aquatic and marine products, canned goods of various kinds, sugar and sweets, wines, liquors, spirits of various kinds, dairy products, vegetables and condiments, bean flour noodles, grain products, canned goods, nuts, and dried vegetables.

CHINACOAL China National Coal Import and Export Corporation (CNCIEC) 16 Heping Bei Lu Andingmenwai Beijing Cable: CNCDC Beijing Telex: 22494 CNCDC CN	461228 550520	Coal import and exports; develops technical cooperation with foreign countries.
CHINAFILM China Film Distribution and Exhibition Corp. 25 Xinwai Street Beijing Cable: CHINAFILM Telex: 22195 FILM CN	2015533	The corporation is the sole importer of foreign films and exporter of Chinese films.
CHINAMET China National Metallurgical Import and Export Corporation 46 Dongsixi Dajie Beijing Cable: 2250 Beijing Telex: 22461 MIEC CN	550197	Imports metallurgical and mining equipment, accessories, spare parts, meters, and instruments.

Agency/Corporation Head Office	Telephone	Product Interest
CHINAPACK China Packaging Import and Export Corporation 28 Donghu Lane, Andingmenwai Beijing Cable: CHINAPACK (Beijing) Telex: 221490 CPACK CN	462124	This organization is responsible for the packaging of China's exports.
CHINASEED China National Seed Corporation 16 Donghuan Road N. Beijing Cable: 4429 Beijing	593619	Imports and exports crop seeds, saplings, roots, bulbs, cuttings and sprouts of grain crops, cotton, oilbearing crops, vegetables, hemp, flax, jute, tea, melons, fruits.
CHINASILK China Silk Corporation 82 Donganmen Street Beijing Cable: CHINASILK Telex: 22280 CNTEX CN	558831	Exports silk yarns, tops, piecegoods, and fabrics. Negotiates contracts, compensation trade, and processing materials for silk.
CHINASTAMP China Stamp Export Company 82 Donganmen Street Beijing Cable: CHINASTAMP Beijing	557144	Exports Chinese postage stamps to collectors around the world.
CHINATEX China National Textiles Import and Export Corp. 82 Donganmen Street Beijing Cable: CHINATEX Beijing Telex: 22280 CNTEX CN	558831	Cotton, cotton yarns, raw silk, wool tops, rayon fibers, synthetic and man-made fibers, cotton piece-goods, woolen piece-goods, blended fabrics, garments, knitted goods, cotton and woolen manufactured goods, readymade silk articles.
CHINATUHSU China National Native Produce and Animal By-Products Import and Export Corp. 82 Donganmen Street Beijing Cable: CHINATUHSU Beijing Telex: 22283 TUHSU CN	554124	Tea, coffee, cocoa, tobacco, bast fiber, resin, feedings stuffs, timber, forest products, spices, essential oils, patent medicines, medicinal herbs and other native medicinal products, bristles, horse tails, feathers, down, feathers for decorative use, rabbit hair, wool, cashmere, camel hair, casings, hides, leathers, fur products, carpets, down products, live animals.

Agency/Corporation Head Office	Telephone	Product Interest
CHINAWALL China Great Wall Industrial Corporation 1 Hongqiao Dong Dajie Congwenmenwai (Box 847) Beijing Cable: GWIC Beijing Telex: 22484 CPMC CN; 22337 BEDC CN	893155 985325	Designs, manufactures, and exports special-purpose machinery, electronics instruments, cyrogenic and automatic control techniques; deals in joint-venture contracts with foreign firms for technical designs; provides technical services.
CHINELECTRON China National Electronics Import and Export Corporation 49 Fuxing Road Beijing Cable: DZJSJCK Beijing Telex: 22475 CEIEC CN	810910 811188	Responsible for foreign trade in electronics equipment, product components, plant, and technology.
CHINSCICAD Oriental Scientific Instruments Import and Export Corporation c/o Chinese Academy of Sciences Sanlihe Beijing Cable: 2233 Beijing Telex: 22474 ASHICN	866119 868361	Exports scientific instruments manufactured by factories affiliated with the Chinese Academy of Sciences; imports technology and equipment on behalf of Academy of Science.
CHUNGKUO The Bank of China 410 Fuchengmennei Ave. Beijing Cable: HOCHUNGKUO Beijing Telex: 22254 BCHO CN	665325	China's most important bank dealing in foreign trade, foreign exchange, and foreign finance.
CITIC China International Trust and Investment Corporation 2 Qianmen Dong Dajie, 14th floor Box 9021 Beijing Cable: CITIC, Beijing Telex: 22305 CITIC CN	550905 558841	Coordinates use of foreign investment and technology; arranges foreign investment; introduces advanced technology and equipment through foreign investments.
CLETC China Light Industrial Foreign Economic and Technical Corporation 22 B. Fuwai Dajie Beijing Cable: LIGHTIND OR 6535 Beijing Telex: 22465 LIMEX CN	894743 895369 890751	Responsible for trade in sporting goods, bicycles, sewing machines, cosmetics, and light industrial machinery. Has authority to negotiate joint ventures, cooperative agreements, feasibility studies, processing and assembly work.

Agency/Corporation *Head Office*	*Telephone*	*Product Interest*

CNEIC

| China Nuclear Energy Industry Corporation
21 Lishi Road S.
Beijing
Cable: CNEIC Beijing
Telex: 22349 SSTCC CN | 866415 | Imports and exports special instruments and equipment for study and use in China's nuclear energy industry. |

CNOOC

| China National Offshore Oil Corporation
29–31 Changan Dong
Beijing
Cable: CNOOC Beijing
Telex: 2261 CNOOC CN | 555225 | Responsible for cooperation with foreign companies in exploiting oil reserves in China's offshore continental shelf. |

COALDEV

| China National Coal Development Corporation
16 Heping Bei Lu
Andingmenwai
P.O. Box 1409
Beijing
Cable: CNCDC Beijing
Telex: 22494 CNCDC CN | 461223
463759 | Compensation trade, joint ventures, and technical cooperation in coal production to develop China's coal resources. |

COMPLANT

| China National Complete Plant Export Corporation
28 Donghu Lane, Andingmenwai
Beijing
Cable: COMPLANT, Beijing
Telex: 225559 COMPT CN | 445678 | The corporation is responsible for the export of complete plants under the economic and technical cooperation agreements concluded at government level. |

COMTRADE

| China Council for the Promotion of International Trade
Fuxingmenwai Dajie
Beijing
Cable: COMTRADE, Beijing
Telex: 22315 CCPIT CN | 867229 | The council promotes business contracts between Chinese agencies and foreign business organizations and companies; arranges exhibitions in China and abroad; facilitates technical exchanges between China and foreign countries; and supervises the operations of the Arbitration Commission. |

CONSULTEC

| China Trade Consultation and Technical Service Corporation
2 Changan Street E.
Beijing
Cable: CONSULTEC Beijing
Telex: 22506 CTSUL CN | 462912
553031
ext.561 | Provides trade and marketing information in China; market research and investigation; introduces trade partners; provides translation and publicaton of technical literature. |

Agency/Corporation Head Office	Telephone	Product Interest
COSCO China Ocean Shipping Company 6 Dong Chang An Street Beijing Cable: COSCO Beijing Telex: 22264 CPC PK CN	555431 551518	This company is engaged in the chartering of vessels, booking of shipping space, transshipment of cargo, and cargo and passenger services.
EQUIMPEX China National Machinery and Equipment Export Corporation 16 Fuxingmenwai Street Beijing Cable: EQUIMPEX Beijing Telex: 22186 EQUIP CN	368541	Exports Chinese machine tools, heavy-duty machinery, vehicles, production-line equipment, motors.
GUOJI Shudian, Box 399 Beijing Cable: GUOJI Beijing	891178 891203	This organization is responsible for the exportation of: publications printed in Chinese and foreign languages; newspapers and periodicals in Chinese and foreign languages; posters; portraits; postcards; long playing records; folk papercuts; responsible also for the importation of material printed in foreign languages.
INDUSTRY China National Light Industrial Products Import and Export Corp. 82 Donganmen Street Beijing Cable: INDUSTRY Beijing Telex: 22282 LIGHT CN	556749 558831 554343	Paper, general merchandise, stationary, musical instruments, sporting goods, toys, building materials and electrical appliances, fish nets, net yarns, leather shoes, leather products, television, photographic equipment.
INSTRIMPEX Chinese National Instruments Import and Export Corp. Er Li Gou, Xijiao Beijing Cable: INSTRIMPEX Beijing Telex: 22242 CIIEC CN	8317733	Computers, communications equipment, radio equipment, electronics, optical instruments, nuclear equipment.
JENDEV China Southwest Joint Energy Development Corporation 16 Heping Road, N. Beijing Cable: CNCDC Beijing Telex: 22494 CNCDC CN	446671 ext. 763 or 776	Responsible for exploitation and export of coal and improvement of railways and harbors in southwest China. Authorized to sign contracts, joint ventures, foreign exchange loans, and other forms of cooperation.

MACHIMPEX

China National Machinery Import and Export Corp.	891243 890931	Machine tools, presses, hammers, shears, forging machines, diesel engines, gasoline engines, steam turbines, boilers, mining machinery, metallurgical machinery, compressors and pumps, hoists, winches and cranes, transport machinery (motor vehicles) and parts thereof, vessels, etc., agricultural machinery and implements, printing machines, knitting machines, building machinery, machinery for other light industries, ball and roller bearings, tungsten carbide, electric machinery and equipment.
Er Li Gou, Xijiao	891974	
Beijing		
Cable: MACHIMPEX Beijing		
Telex: 22242 CMIEC CN		

MACHINTERCORP

China Machine-Building International Corporation	867890 865281	Center for technical and commercial cooperation with foreign concerns including technical transfer to and from China; contracting for complete engineering design; procurement and importation of complete plants; cooperative manufacturing and compensation trade; joint investment.
12 Fuxingmenwai Street	362561	
Beijing		
Cable: MACHINTERCORP Beijing		
Telex: 22341 CMIC CN		

MINMETALS

China National Metals and Minerals Import and Export Corp.	890931	Steel plates, sheets and pipes, steel sections, steel tubes, special steel, railway materials, metallic products, pig iron, ferro-alloys, nonferrous metals, precious rare metals, ferrous mineral ores, nonferrous mineral ores, nonmetallic minerals and products thereof, coal, cement, hardware.
Er Li Goi, Xijiao		
Beijing		
Cable: MINMETALS Beijing		
Telex: 22241 MIMET CN		

NEWBUILD

China National New Building Materials Corporation	891260	Sets up factories to produce prefabricated housing; imports advanced equipment and technology; exports building materials and equipment.
Zizhuyuan Road, Xijiao		
Beijing		
Cable: 4554 Beijing		

Agency/Corporation Head Office	Telephone	Product Interest

NONFERMET

China Nonferrous Metals Industrial Corporation
46 Dong Sixi Dajie
Beijing
Telex: 22461 MIEC CN

550197
557431

Coordinates plans for production, mine construction, and import/export trade of China's nonferrous metals.

PENAVICO

China Ocean Shipping Agency
6 Dong Chang An Street
Beijing
Cable: PENAVICO Beijing
Telex: 22264 CPC PK CN

553424

This organization undertakes agency business for international oceangoing ships engaged in passenger and/or cargo services calling at Chinese coastal ports.

PETCORP

Petroleum Corporation of People's Republic of China
Box 766
Liiupukang
Beijing
Cable: 3112 Beijing
Telex: 22312 PCPRC CN

444313

Responsible for the development of China's oil industry; has two subsidaries: China National Oil and Gas Exploration and Development Corporation; and China Petroleum Processing Corporation.

PICC

People's Insurance Company of China
Box 2149
Beijing
Cable: 42001 Beijing
Telex: 22102 PICC CN

335150

This company underwrites ocean marine and hull insurance, aviation insurance, cargo land transportation insurance.

PMIEC

China Precision Machinery Import and Export Corporation
2 Yuetan Bei Xiojie
Beijing
Cable: CPMIEC Beijing
Telex: 22484 CPMC CN

895012
896364

Imports and exports various kinds of precision machinery, instruments and meters for space navigation, aircraft and ships; trades in electronic, electrical, optical, and chemical products.

PUBLIMEX

China National Publications Import and Export Corp.
Chaoyangmennei, Box 88
Beijing
Cable: PUBLIM Beijing
Telex: 22313 CPC CN

440731

The corporation is mainly involved with the trade in foreign books, newspapers, periodicals, documents, and other materials.

SHIPBUILDING

China State Shipbuilding Corporation (CSSC)
5 Yuetan Beijie
Beijing
Cable: 0038 Beijing
Telex: 22335 CSSC CN

890971

Responsible for planning and supervision of the shipbuilding industry; conducts trade through its subordinate China Shipbuilding Trade Company Ltd. (CSTC).

Agency/Corporation Head Office	Telephone	Product Interest

SINOCHART

China National Chartering Corp.
Er Li Gou, Xijiao
Beijing
Cable: ZHONGZU Beijing
Telex: 22265
22153
22154 TRANS CN

890931
893566

Chartering of vessels and booking of shipping space required for Chinese import and export cargoes. Also, similar business on behalf of principals located abroad. Canvassing cargoes for shipowners.

SINOCHEM

China National Chemicals Import and Export Corp.
Er Li Gou, Xijiao
Beijing
Cable: SINOCHEM Beijing
Telex: 22243 CHEMI CN

899881

Rubber, rubber tires, and other rubber products, petroleum and petroleum products, chemical fertilizers, insecticides, fungicides, pharmaceuticals, medical apparatus, chemical raw materials, dyestuffs and pigments.

SINOTRANS

China National Foreign Trade Transportation Corp.
Er Li Gou, Xijiao
Beijing
Cable: SINOTRANS Beijing
ZHONGWAIYUN Beijing
Telex: 22867 TRANS CN

831773

Arranges customs clearance and delivery of import/export cargoes by land, sea, and air or by post. May act as authorized agents clearing and delivering goods in transit through Chinese ports. Arranges marine and other insurance, and institutes claims on behalf of cargo owners on request.

TECHIMPORT

China National Technical Import Corp.
Er Li Gou, Xijiao
Beijing
Cable: TECHIMPORT Beijing
Telex: 22244 CNTIC CN

892116
890931

This corporation is concerned primarily with the importation of complete industrial plants and industrial technology generally.

XINSHIDAI

Xinshidai Company of China
Box 511
Beijing
Telex: 22338 XSDCO CN

664714

Imports and exports aeroproducts, electronics, ships, vehicles, some general and precision machinery; contracts to provide technical and engineering as well as skilled labor services; enters into joint ventures with foreign firms.

U.S. BRANCHES OF CHINA'S MAJOR
BUSINESS CORPORATIONS

Bank of China
415 Madison Ave.
New York, NY 10017
Tel. (212) 935–3101

China National Arts & Crafts
I/E Corp.
(Beijing Branch)
1133 Ave. of the Americas
New York, NY 10026
Tel. (212) 398–1748

China National Metals &
Mineral I/E Corp.
1 Bridge Plaza
Fort Lee, NJ 07024
Tel. (201) 461–3750

China National Oils & Food-
stuffs I/E Corp.
250 West 34th St.
New York, NY 10019
Tel. (212) 947–2466

China National Technical
Import Corp.
3911 Bradley Lane
Chevy Chase, MD 20015
Tel. (301) 654–6996

China National Textiles
I/E Corp.
Tel. (212) 719–3251
209 West 40th St.
New York, NY 10018

China National Tourist Office
60 East 42nd St.
New York, NY 10165
Tel. (212) 867–0271
and
333 West Broadway
Suite 201
Glendale, CA 91204
Tel. (818) 545–7505

China Ocean Shipping Co., Inc.
22 Battery St.
Suite 700
San Francisco, CA 94111
Telex: 278–658
Tel. (415) 867–7392

China United Trading Corp-
oration
1 Penn Plaza
Suite 1915
New York, NY 10119
Tel. (212) 947–3140
(MOFERT's U.S.
Representative)

Civil Aviation Administration of
China (CAAC)
45 East 49th St.
New York, NY 10017
Tel. (212) 371–9898
and
51 Grant Ave.
San Francisco, CA 94108
Tel. (415) 392–2156
and
2500 Wilshire Blvd.
Suite 100
Los Angeles, CA 90057
Tel. (213) 297–1444

EXPLORING CHINA

BEIJING

Beijing has been in existence as a settlement for more than 3,000 years, capital of the nation over many centuries, and for almost 700 years the center of power under the Mongols, the Ming, the Manchu, and now the Communists. Today it is the political, cultural, and administrative center of a resurgent China, home of eight million citizens, headquarters of the Communist Party, and seat of government.

Visitors to Beijing are often surprised at how little remains of the past empires. Other great capitals of the world, most of them in existence for a much shorter period than Beijing, often possess a grandeur and style that reflect their illustrious past. But in China relatively few historic buildings have survived the wars that have swept across the nation for centuries. Beijing, along with other important cities in China, has been sacked, looted, and burned innumerable times by countless armies. As a result, most of the old buildings that remain are from recent dynasties.

Beijing's heart is Tiananmen Square, 34 acres in area, the largest square in the world. After the Revolution ended in 1949, it was made the center for organized mass demonstrations and a place where the leaders review parades on important national days. (Visitors may arrange to view the square from the leaders' podium.) It was here in May 1989 that hundreds of thousands of Chinese citizens demonstrated for greater political freedom and some small measure of democracy. It was here, too, early on June 4, that the military crushed the movement, leaving a death toll in the hundreds.

Beijing's artery is Chang An Boulevard, running east-west through the heart of the city. It is flanked on either side by modern buildings conveying no hint of Old China. Yet within a block or two you will come across tracts of tiny gray houses, the skyline broken here and there by a factory or a block of apartments.

Beijing is a city of bicycles: there are millions of them. As the vast population cycles its way to and from work, the city is alive with the metallic ring of bicycle bells. The crowds are orderly and good natured, and harmony seems to prevail. You may walk in the streets with perfect safety, although you may draw curious stares from the Chinese citizens around you.

Beijing was once a walled city. There was a wall around the Forbidden City, one around the Imperial City, another around what was known as the Tartar City, and yet another around the southern portion known as the Chinese City. Most of the walls are gone now, having fallen into ruin over the years or been demolished by the new regime to make way for roads. Most of the old gates are gone, too, but you will get an impression of their grandeur when you see the famous Tiananmen Gate and the beautifully restored Qian Men Gate, each standing at opposite ends of the Square of Heavenly Peace. In your travels you will occasionally catch a glimpse of a part of the old wall or one of the few remaining towers still standing, a reminder of the past splendor of Beijing.

You could spend days exploring the old Forbidden City; for more than 500 years it was the center of imperial power in China. Then there is the magnificent Temple of Heaven, the most famous in all China and an architectural wonder, Bei Hai Lake with its dagoba-capped island, and the woods of Coal Hill Park.

The most exciting excursion of all is to the Great Wall, the only man-made structure said to be visible from outer space. Its construction was a remarkable achievement and a monument to the threat that China has faced for thousands of years: invasion from the north. When you visit the Great Wall you will be seeing an object that has inspired the curiosity of people around the world for ages.

Then there are the majestic Ming Tombs, some restored but most splintering into ruin in a gentle area of hills and mountains not far from the Great Wall.

A visit to Beijing is not restricted to sightseeing. You will have the opportunity to indulge yourself in the capital of Chinese cuisine. Beijing's restaurants are world renowned, and they will prepare sumptuous banquets that you will long remember. Then there are evening entertainments such as Chinese operas, Chinese and Western theater, music and dance, concerts, the ballet, the circus, acrobatic troupes, and sporting events.

Your memory of Beijing will be colored by the seasons. In winter the days are cold but sunny; in spring the city is transformed by green foliage; in summer the air is filled with hazy light and warmth; and in autumn the streets are paved with golden leaves. There is something here for you whatever time you visit the "Northern Capital."

History

The first recorded settlement in the area of Beijing was the city of Ji, which is known to have been in existence in the twelfth century B.C. The settlement was also the capital of the Kingdom of Yen (723–221 B.C.), before it was destroyed by Qin Shi Huang Di, the first emperor of unified China.

A town known as Yu Chou developed in the time of the Tang Dynasty (618–907) but was destroyed in 986 by the Liao. A city was then established on the site by the invaders; they called it Nan Jing, or "Southern Capital," to distinguish it from their northern capital in Manchuria. In the eleventh century it was renamed Yen Jing.

The Liao were in turn defeated by the Jin in 1135 and the name of the town was once again changed, this time to Chung Du.

The Mongols under the leadership of Kubilai Khan defeated the Jin in 1264 and built a new city on a site slightly to the north. They called it Da Du, or "Great Capital," also known as Khanbalic.

The Yuan Dynasty was swept out by the Ming in 1368 and the site became known as Bei Ping, or "Northern Peace," the capital being established farther south at Nanjing. The third emperor of the Ming, Yong Le, moved the capital back to the north in 1403 and rebuilt the city, naming it Beijing, or "Northern Capital." When the Manchu armies drove out the Ming the city was retained as the capital, and it remained so until the dynasty fell in 1911. The capital was then moved to Nanjing but was reestablished in Beijing a few months later.

In 1928 the Nationalist Government established the capital in Nanjing once again, and Beijing reassumed its provincial role, adopting the name of Bei Ping. However, it lost its status for only two decades, becoming the capital again after the Communists took the city on January 31, 1949. The Constitution of the People's Republic of China declares that the capital of the nation is Beijing.

EXPLORING BEIJING

Tiananmen Square

Tiananmen Square is the center of Beijing. It is a vast place, an enormous square by any standard in the world. The square derives its name from the imposing gate and tower on the north side, which give entry to the Imperial City and the Old Forbidden City within. The wide, tree-lined Chang An Jie, or Avenue of Perpetual Peace, runs east–west past the square, parallel to the old walls of the Imperial City. Against the old walls permanent stands have been built to enable the nation's leaders to review parades and preside over the enormous rallies that take place in the square. When Chairman Mao died, over a million people gathered in the square to pay homage.

If you stand for a moment with your back to the Tiananmen Gate and the Forbidden City, you will see the Great Hall of the People on the right or western side of the square, the Museum of Chinese Revolution and Museum of Chinese History on the left or eastern side, the Monument to the People's Heroes straight ahead or south, and the Mao Zedong Memorial Hall behind it. These are all described below.

Tiananmen Gate

Tiananmen, or the "Gate of Heavenly Peace," bounds the northern end of the square. Built in A.D. 1651 and standing 110 feet high, it has five passages leading through it and is surmounted by a wooden tower with a double roof of glazed tile. Five marble bridges lead over the moat to each of the gateways.

Formerly the five passages were closed and used only on ceremonial occasions. Only the emperor could pass through the central passageway. Before leaving on a journey he would make a sacrifice before the gate. At other times imperial edicts were lowered, in a gilded box shaped like a phoenix, into the hands of officials kneeling below. The practice gave rise to the expression "the Imperial Orders given by the Gilded Phoenix." The edict was then taken to the Ministry of Rites, where copies were made for dispatch to the far corners of the empire.

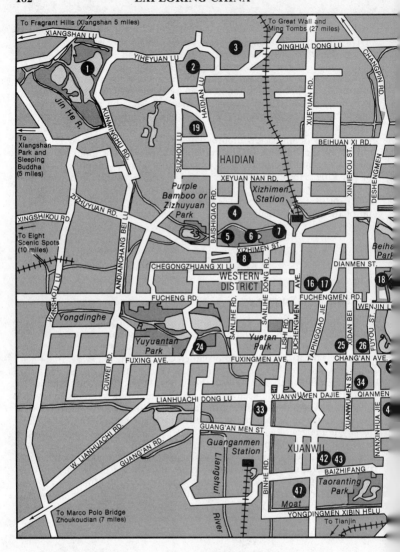

Points of Interest

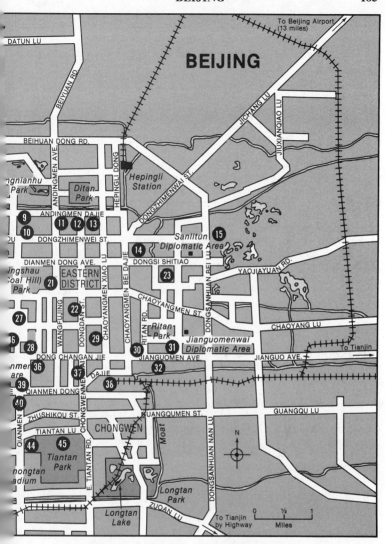

The gate is famous in modern history too, for it was here, on October 1st, 1949, that Mao Zedong proclaimed the establishment of the People's Republic of China.

The nation's leaders appear here to review the enormous parade that takes place on China's national day.

Monument to the People's Heroes

Looking south to the square from the gate, you will see a tall granite obelisk standing on a two-tiered marble terrace with balustrades: it is the Monument to the People's Heroes. The gilded inscription on the north face is in Chairman Mao's calligraphy and reads: "The People's Heroes Are Immortal." The base of the obelisk is decorated with bas-relief carvings depicting major events of the revolution.

The monument also has its place in modern history. In 1976 during the Qing Ming Festival, when the Chinese honor their dead, people laid thousands of wreaths on and around the monument in memory of Premier Zhou Enlai, who had died in the previous January. The authorities began to remove the wreaths soon after they were placed there, an act that was regarded as an insult to Zhou Enlai and politically motivated. People began to struggle with those removing the wreaths. A riot began, cars were overturned, a building burned, and thousands were arrested. The Tiananmen Incident is now known in China as the "April Fifth Movement Against the Gang of Four."

Great Hall of the People

The Great Hall of the People flanks the western side of the square; if you stand with your back to Tiananmen Gate it is on the right hand side of the square. The National People's Congress, China's parliament, sits here when it is in session. The Great Hall, an immense building covering an area of 561,800 square feet, was erected in just over 10 months, although the interior took additional time to complete. It has numerous conference rooms, banquet halls, and reception areas, many of vast size: the major conference hall accommodates 10,000 people and the huge banqueting hall can seat 5,000. Open all day Tuesdays and Wednesdays, and in the morning only on Saturdays.

The Great Hall possesses a restaurant (tel. 335484) that is open to visitors for banquets by prior arrangement. The entrance to the restaurant is on the north side of the building on Chang An Jie.

Museum of the Chinese Revolution

The Museum of the Chinese Revolution is housed in the left wing of the building that flanks the eastern side of the square. It covers the revolutionary history of China from the onset of the Opium Wars (1839–1842) until the founding of the People's Republic of China in 1949. A description in English is available at the entrance. Open daily, 9 A.M.–12:30 P.M. and 2–5 P.M.

Museum of Chinese History

The Museum of Chinese History is housed in the right wing of the building that flanks the eastern side of the square. The exhibits cover the development of man—from a Marxist perspective—from primitive society, through slave, feudal, and capitalist societies, to the era of the socialist society. You will need a guide who reads Chinese and speaks English, as the exhibits are described in Chinese text only. Open daily, 9 A.M.–noon and 2–5 P.M.

Mao Zedong Memorial Hall

Immediately behind the Monument to the People's Heroes is the Chairman Mao Zedong Memorial Hall. It occupies about 200,000 square feet of floor space, stands just over 100 feet high, the twin-roof being supported by 44 granite pillars. A wide stairway leads up to the entrance, over which appears the inscription, in Chairman Hua Guofeng's calligraphy, "Chairman Mao Memorial Hall."

The hall was completed in November 1977. For a time it was closed while the Party debated Mao's place in history; in 1983 it reopened as a museum with exhibits on the lives of Mao, Zhou Enlai, Zhu De—the leader of the Long March with Mao—and Liu Shaoqi, the former president of China whom Mao had imprisoned.

As you enter the first auditorium you will be confronted by an enormous seated figure of Mao sculptured in white marble. Light falling on the statue creates an ethereal effect, and the figure appears to be translucent and floating. The backdrop is an enormous landscape painted by Huang Yangyu, a well-known Chinese artist. The scene extends into the distance as if observed from a great height, perhaps to remind the visitor of Mao's revolutionary vision.

You then pass to the next auditorium where the body of Chairman Mao, draped with the red flag of the Communist Party of China, is preserved in a crystal coffin.

Prospective visitors simply join the lines of people waiting outside the entrance. Handbags and cameras may not be carried inside; they should be left at one of the many small kiosks outside the mausoleum before you join the queue. Dignified dress and behavior is expected. Photography is not permitted.

Qian Men Gate

At the southern extremity of the square stands the Qian Men Gate. This is one of the few remaining gates of the Imperial City Wall constructed under the Ming emperor Yong Le (1403–1425). In those days the top of the wall, wide enough to allow the passage of a man on horseback, was protected by towers placed at regular intervals around the perimeter. All the original nine gates in the wall were protected in a similar way. A traveler arriving at the wall of the old city would pass through the first gate into an elliptical courtyard within the walls and would cross this to pass through the inner gate into the city itself. This double-gate system was of great value in repulsing enemy attacks: if the first gate was breached, the attackers would still find themselves outside the city wall and could be fired upon from the tower over the inner gate.

The original gates allowed goods and commodities to be brought into the city. One gate was used to transport grain, another wood, another coal. One of the western gates was used by carters bringing spring water to the emperor's table from the Fragrant Hills outside Beijing; it was always transported at night to arrive cool. One gate, aptly named An Ding Men or "Gate of Certain Peace," was used to carry away nightsoil, which was then treated near the Altar of the Earth outside the city before being used as fertilizer. One of the two northern gates, the Gate of Virtue and Victory, was used by the imperial army when embarking on a campaign.

In imperial days the use of the central Qian Men Gate was reserved for the emperor only, the smaller side gate being used for other purposes. The emperor would pass through the gate in great pomp and splendor on what was probably the most important day of the year: a visit to the Temple of Heaven at the winter solstice, when he would "speak with the heavens."

A great deal of restoration work has been done on the Qian Men Gate and pavilions and they are currently in beautiful condition. The pavilions date only from the early part of this century when they were rebuilt after the fires of the Boxer Rebellion in 1900.

Zhongnanhai

You will often see the entrance to Zhongnanhai as you pass up and down Chang An Boulevard on your way to various places around the city. The entrance is half a mile west of the Tiananmen Gate. It is easy to recognize. There is a red screen with calligraphy in gold, a flagpole on which flies the red flag, and two military guards.

Inside the gate are the two lakes that give the place its name: Zhonghai or ("central sea") and Nanhai or ("southern sea"). Around the lake are the buildings that house important Party Committees such as the Central Committee and the Military Commission. Some of the highest-ranking Party members have residence there. (Mao Zedong and Zhou Enlai used to live in Zhongnanhai.) For obvious reasons, foreign visitors are rarely allowed to enter and, if they are, it is always after special arrangements have been made through the appropriate authorities.

The Forbidden City

When the Ming drove out the Mongols, Beijing was razed and the capital established in Nanjing. Thirty-five years later in 1430 Yong Le, the third Ming emperor, decided to re-establish the capital at Beijing. He also decided to rebuild palaces on the site previously occupied by the Mongols,

THE FORBIDDEN CITY—KEY

Entry through Tiananmen Gate (A) from Chang An Blvd., then through Tuan Men (B) to:

The First Courtyards
(1) Meridian Gate (Wu Men)
(2) Gate of Supreme Harmony

The Three Ceremonial Palaces
(3) Hall of Supreme Harmony
(4) Hall of Perfect Harmony
(5) Hall of the Preservation of Harmony
(6) Gate of Heavenly Purity

The Three Private Palaces
(7) Palace of Heavenly Purity
(8) Hall of Union
(9) Palace of Earthly Tranquility

Imperial Garden and Outer Gates
(10) Imperial Garden
(11) Pavilion of Imperial Peace
(12) Shun Zhen Gate
(13) Gate of Divine Pride

Northwest Sector
(14) Palace of Culture of the Mind
(15) Hall for Practicing Tai Ji Quan

(16) Hall of Official Meetings
(17) Palace of Eternal Spring
(18) Hall of Assistance to Officials
(19) Hall of Longevity
(20) Palace of Accumulated Elegance

Northeast Sector
(21) Palace of Abstinence
(22) Hall of Sincerity and Solemnity
(23) Hall of Charity
(24) Hall for Carrying Out Imperial Orders
(25) Hall of Eternal Peace
(26) Hall of Time
(27) Imperial Study
(28) Clock Museum (former Hall of Ancestors)
(29) Nine Dragon Screen
(30) Palace of Peace and Longevity
(31) Qian Long Garden
(32) Hall for Cultivating Character
(33) Hall of Happiness and Longevity
(34) Pavilion of Peace and Harmony

Southeast Sector
(35) Arrow Pavilion
(36) Hall of Culture (Old Imperial Library)

Southwest Sector
(37) Hall of Military Prowess
(38) Garden of Peace and Tranquility

THE FORBIDDEN CITY
(Entry courtyards not drawn to scale)

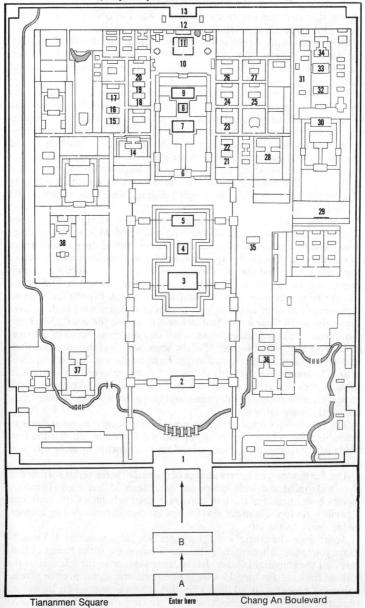

Tiananmen Square   Enter here   Chang An Boulevard

and a vast construction program was undertaken over a period of 14 years, commencing in 1407. Hundreds of thousands of workers were engaged on the project, and materials, particularly stone and timber, were brought from all parts of China.

The palaces within the walls became known as Zi Jin Cheng, or the Purple Forbidden City, the color being associated with the North Star, considered a sign that the emperor's residence was the cosmic center of the world. Its other name is Gu Gong, or Imperial Palace.

Only occasionally would an emperor venture forth from the Forbidden City, and no one was allowed to enter without permission. The Forbidden City with its formidable walls was enclosed within the Imperial City, and that again was enclosed within the walls of Beijing itself.

Twenty-four emperors of the last imperial dynasties, the Ming and the Qing, ruled from the Forbidden City. Each was considered to be the "Son of Heaven." China remained under their absolute rule for almost five centuries, until the last dynasty fell in 1911. From the Dragon Throne commands were made that were carried to the far corners of the empire and obeyed without question. A sign of the ruler's absolute authority is conveyed by the edict which states that no buildings would be constructed in Beijing which might overlook the Forbidden City's walls. It was only after the last emperor fell that larger buildings were constructed in and around the city.

Over the centuries many new palaces were built within the Forbidden City walls and the others refurbished and renovated. Most of the buildings now standing are from the eighteenth century. Inside the secluded Inner Palace the emperors lived in splendor, amidst fabulous treasure and wealth from the empire and abroad, surrounded by a court comprising the empress, concubines, princes, eunuchs, court favorites, priests, and ministers. Lavish living was a feature of their daily existence. Five to 6,000 cooks were needed to cater to them. Vast hoards of treasure were built up over the centuries to decorate the palaces and to amuse the court. When the last dynasty fell the palaces began to fall into disrepair. Some of the treasures were sold off by former officials, some were lost in numerous fires, and large quantities were looted by the Japanese during the Sino-Japanese War. Thousands of crateloads of treasure were removed by Chiang Kaishek's forces to Taiwan on the eve of the Communist takeover in 1949. However, some treasures still remain and give a notion of the former splendor of the imperial courts.

The Forbidden City and its palaces are slowly being renovated and considerable progress has been made. A visit will convince you that the Forbidden City is one of the most marvelous monuments to architecture in the world today.

The Forbidden City covers an area of about 250 acres and is surrounded by a wide moat and walls which are more than 35 feet high. There are towers built at each of the four corners of the Forbidden City, each with a pavilion on top. There are also four gates, each surmounted by a tower, giving entry to the city.

Apart from the central core of palaces (see plan: numbers 3–5 and 7–9) on your right, after entering through Tiananmen, is the Palace of Culture and the Imperial Library. In the southwest, or to the left, stands the former Imperial Printing House. In the northeast sector are the private palaces of Emperor Qian Long (1736–96), who was responsible for having the city almost entirely rebuilt, and the private palaces of Empress Ci Xi and the former apartments of the concubines. In the northwest sector are the former private apartments of the emperors and empresses. In the descriptions that follow we will confine ourselves mainly to the central core of palaces.

The Forbidden City has now been turned into a museum that contains a magnificent collection of Chinese bronzes, porcelain, paintings, jade, and other treasures. Here you will be able to see the famous jade suit and the "flying" horse (provided they are not out of the country on exhibition). The Forbidden City is open Tuesday–Sunday, 8:30 A.M.–4:30 P.M. Tickets are sold until 3:30 P.M., but entry is not permitted after that time. Cassette tape rentals in ten languages provide guided tours by such celebrities as Peter Ustinov (in English), Ugo Tognazzi (Italian), and Fernando Rey (Spanish).

The First Courtyards

The central feature of the Forbidden City is the area harboring the six Imperial Palaces (three ceremonial and three private) set one behind the other along a north-south axis (numbers 3–5 and 7–9 on the plan). To reach the "central core" you must pass through the entrance tunnel of the **Tiananmen Gate,** then walk down a long roadway which leads to another gate called the **Tuan Men.** After passing this gate you will walk down an even longer corridor towards Wu Men, or the Meridian Gate, which gives entry to the grounds of the Inner Palaces.

The **Meridian Gate** (1) is the largest in the Forbidden City; it was built in 1420 and restored in 1647 and 1801. The five pavilions surmounting the gate are known as the "Five Phoenixes." It is from here that the emperor presided over military parades and ceremonies. Each year he would also announce the new calendar from the gate.

After you pass through the gateway you will come into a paved courtyard with the **Golden Water Stream,** Jin Shui He, traversing it in a gentle arc from east to west. You cross the stream by one of the five marble bridges believed to be symbols of the five virtues. Ahead stands the large **Gate of Supreme Harmony** (2), or Tai He Men. It is a two-roofed structure with orange glazed tiles and is seven bays wide. The building rests on a single tier surrounded by white marble balustrade; three sets of stairs lead to the terrace, the central one featuring a bas-relief carving in marble and used only by the emperor himself. Note the magnificent bronze lions guarding the entrance on either side, the bronze incense burners, and the model pavilion carved out of white marble and mounted on a small pedestal to the right of the stairways.

You are now about to enter the heart of the Forbidden City.

Three Ceremonial Palaces

After you pass through the gate you will enter an even larger courtyard, and in the distance before you, resting on a three-tiered terrace each surrounded by a white marble balustrade, is the **Hall of Supreme Harmony** (3), or Tai He Dian. As you walk towards it, note the three flights of stairs leading to the upper terrace: the middle one features a carved marble ramp over which the emperor was carried. There are many bronze incense burners flanking the stairways and, on the terrace, pairs of bronze storks and tortoises on either side. On the western side of the terrace there is a marble model of a pavilion housing a bronze grain measure; on the eastern side stands a sundial; these symbolize imperial justice and righteousness. Also note the two enormous bronze cauldrons with finely cast handles.

Inside the hall the central columns are gilded and carved with a dragon motif. There is a fine coffered ceiling. The emperor's throne stands on a raised platform surrounded by incense burners, screens, and other treasures. The emperor used the hall on great occasions to mark such events as the New Year, the nomination of military leaders, the publication of lists of scholars who had successfully passed the imperial examinations, the celebration of the winter solstice, and so on. All these ceremonies were performed amidst pomp and splendor.

Immediately behind this hall stands the **Hall of Perfect Harmony** (4), or Zhong He Dian, a small, square-shaped pavilion with a single roof; there are traditional Chinese windows on all sides. Inside there is a raised throne, a sedan chair on either side, and a fine array of incense burners, room heaters, and decorative treasures; the ceiling is beautifully crafted. Here the emperor would come to make final preparations before presiding over the ceremonies in the Hall of Supreme Harmony.

The next palace is the **Hall of the Preservation of Harmony** (5), or Bao He Dian. It is a two-roofed pavilion, seven bays wide, housing a large throne. The emperor used to preside over ceremonies here: receiving the scholars who had passed the court examinations and, under the Qing, hosting enormous banquets in honor of foreign emissaries and ambassadors.

Three sets of stairs lead to the front of the throne, and two sets lead to the side. Note the four incense burners standing before the throne and the two gilt lamps. The hall is now often used to house exhibits of some of China's art treasures, the most recent being the collection of bronze figurines, chariots, and horses taken from the eastern Han tomb in Wuwei (Gansu Province) in 1969. There is also a permanent exhibition of Chinese art objects inside the hall.

You now descend the steps from the three-tiered terrace into a courtyard and walk toward the **Gate of Heavenly Purity** (6), or Qian Qing Men. It has three sets of stairs, the middle one with the traditional carved marble ramp, guarded by two gilt lions; on either side stand five giant bronze cauldrons. This gateway leads to the three private palaces or apartments, as distinct from the first three, which were used for ceremonial purposes.

Three Private Palaces

After passing through the gateway you will enter another courtyard where a wide path lined with a white marble balustrade leads to the **Palace of Heavenly Purity** (7), or Qian Qing Gong. Note the four large bronze incense burners on the terrace. The palace has a two-tiered roof featuring fine sets of figurines on the roof line corners. Note the inscription in Chinese and Mongolian on the framed plaque between the eaves of the roof; also the bronze grain measure to the left and the sundial to the right (again symbols of imperial justice and righteousness); and the bronze cranes and tortoises standing on either side of the terrace (symbols of immortality). Walk to the end of the terrace and you will see, at either end, a gilded model pavilion standing on a white three-tiered stone terrace. The purpose of these models is not understood. The palace once contained the emperor's bedroom, but later, under the Qing, it was used by the emperor as an audience room and for receptions. Four incense burners stand before the throne; there are three sets of stairs mounting the throne dais in front and two on the sides. Note the candle holders in the form of storks and the very ornate dragon screen behind the throne. There are huge framed mirrors to the right and left of the throne. Note also the cupboard on the left with the fine woodwork. The carved ceiling is magnificent.

Behind this hall is the **Hall of Union** (8), or Jiao Tai Dian, a single-roofed square pavilion with inscription over the entrance doorway in Chinese and Mongolian. Within there is a small throne surrounded on all sides by caskets with covers on, housing the imperial seals. Overhead is a fine ceiling with a recessed portion featuring a coiled gilt dragon. The two giant clocks, one mechanical, the other a water clock, that used to be housed in this pavilion now adorn the vestibule of the Clock Museum (28).

To the rear of this hall is the **Palace of Earthly Tranquility** (9), or Kun Ning Gong. This palace was variously used as a residence for the empresses under the Ming, a venue for the sacrifices to the God of the Kitchen, and a nuptial chamber for the last Qing emperor and his bride.

Imperial Garden and Outer Gates

By descending the stairs of the terrace at the rear and passing through the **Gate of Earthly Tranquility,** or Kun Ning Man, you can enter the **Imperial Garden** (10), or Yu Hua Yuan. This is a quiet place where you may wish to sit for a while and take a rest after your long walk. There are a number of fine old trees in the gardens; particularly noteworthy are the two intertwined around each other and known locally as the "love trees." On leaving the garden you pass through the **Shun Zhen Gate** (12), and walk toward the massive outer **Gate of Divine Pride** (13). You have now completed your tour of the Inner Palaces of the Forbidden City.

Other Palaces

You will find that it takes a few hours to stroll through the Inner Palaces and surrounding courtyards, but, should you wish to continue, there are many other palaces to see. If you are too tired you could arrange to come back on another day. Most people do not have enough time and find the tour of the Inner Palaces to be sufficient.

The outer palaces are not described in this book, but the following list is indicative of what you should cover if you wish to take a more extensive tour of the Forbidden City. As there are sometimes special exhibitions held in the outer halls and pavilions.

In the northwest sector: the **Palace of Culture of the Mind** (14), or Yang Xin Dian, and the **Six Western Palaces** (15–20).

In the northeast sector: the **Palace of Abstinence** (21), or Zhai Gong; the **Six Eastern Palaces;** the **Clock Museum** (28); the **Palace of Peace and Longevity** (30), or Ning Shou Gong, and the Annexes. The passageway to the Palace of Peace and Longevity features a magnificent **Nine Dragon Screen** (29) which rivals the one in Bei Hai Park and is definitely worth seeing.

In the southeast sector: the **Hall of Culture** (36), or Wen Hua Dian, where the Imperial Library was housed.

Temple of Heaven

The Temple of Heaven is the most famous temple in China and should be given high priority during your visit. The name Temple of Heaven, or Tian Tan, refers to a group of ceremonial buildings inside a walled park in southeast Beijing. They were built in the fifteenth century, restored in the eighteenth century under Qian Long, and in this century under the present government.

The most important building in the grounds is the **Hall of Prayer for Good Harvests** (sometimes known as the **Temple of Annual Prayer**), or Qi Nian Dian, where the emperor would go each year to spend the night fasting and in prayer. The temple is set on a triple marble terrace, each

TEMPLE OF HEAVEN

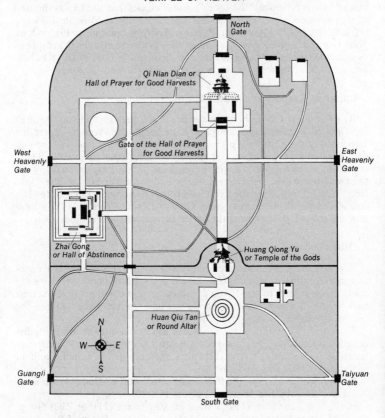

North Gate

Qi Nian Dian or
Hall of Prayer for Good Harvests

Gate of the Hall of Prayer
for Good Harvests

West Heavenly Gate

East Heavenly Gate

Zhai Gong
or Hall of Abstinence

Huang Qiong Yu
or Temple of the Gods

Huan Qiu Tan
or Round Altar

N
W   E
S

Guangli Gate

Taiyuan Gate

South Gate

with a balustrade. The terraces are intersected by eight flights of stairs, the major one set with a carved ramp of white marble. The temple is round with three roofs of glazed blue tiles, the top roof being surmounted by a gilded ball. The temple is 123 feet high and (apart from the roof tiles) is constructed entirely of wood without any nails being used. The absence of nails makes the temple one of the architectural wonders of the world. The exterior of the building is lavishly decorated in red, blue, and green with elaborate gilt overlay. The temple has but one door which opens to the south. Inside there are 24 wooden columns arranged in a double circle around four central ones. All of these are made from the trunks of trees brought from the south of China. The four central columns are said to represent the four seasons of the year, the outer circle of 12 the months of the year, and the inner circle of 12 the hours of the day (according to the old Chinese calendar). All these columns support an elaborate system of pillars that hold up the three roofs, an arrangement that has attracted the admiration of architects throughout the ages.

The temple is flanked on either side by two blue-roofed pavilions with exterior walls decorated in red and gold. These pavilions have an elegance that blends perfectly with the style of the temple itself. Opposite the temple is the **Gate of the Hall of Prayer for Good Harvests,** or Qi Nian Men. You pass through this double gate and walk along a wide pathway through another gate to a round-walled enclosure housing the **Temple of the Gods,** or Huang Qiong Yu. It is a small circular temple built entirely of wood, with a conical blue-tiled roof capped with a gilt ball; it dates from 1530. Here you can amuse yourself by standing close to the inside of the circular wall and whispering a message. Listen and your voice will come back along the wall from the opposite direction. There are also the San Yin Shi, or Three Echo Stones, from which you can create unusual acoustic effects (ask your guide to demonstrate).

A little farther south of this temple is the **Round Altar,** or Huan Qiu Tan. It is here that the emperor would come to make a sacrifice to heaven. The ceremony was accompanied by the chanting of priests, burning of incense, banging of gongs, and the performance of ritual music. This ceremony was one of the most important of the year, the Chinese believing that the very destiny of the whole nation depended upon this mysterious rite. The Round Altar comprises three terraces in tiers one above the other, each surrounded by a white marble balustrade with 360 pillars. The terraces were thought to represent man, earth, and heaven.

When the "Son of Heaven" went from the Forbidden City to the grounds of the Temple of Heaven to perform ceremonies throughout the year, all windows and gates along the way had to be closed, no noise was permitted, and no foreigner allowed to set eyes on the procession. Only the emperor himself, the princes of the court, priests, officials, musicians, and soldiers guarding the procession were allowed to take part.

The Great Wall

The Chinese name for the Great Wall is Wan Li Chang Cheng, or "the Long Wall of Ten Thousand Li." The first sections were built as early as the fifth century B.C. when a number of Chinese states in the north were fighting against each other and occasionally against the northern "barbarian." It was not until the unification of the empire under Qin Shi Huang Di in 221 B.C. that the various sections of the Wall were linked up. It is said that more than 300,000 men worked for 10 years to complete it. The wall had a pounded earth interior with stone facing walls and stone roadway along the top. It was built wide enough to allow a brace of five horses to gallop between the battlements and was thus used to convey soldiers, arms, and food with great speed to various parts of the northern frontier.

From the sixth century to the fourteenth the wall was abandoned and fell into disuse, but after the Mongols took China and were repulsed eventually by the Ming in 1368, the emperor decided to rebuild the wall. The rebuilding and restoration continued until the sixteenth century. However, when the Manchu armies captured China and the Qing Dynasty ruled (1644–1911), the wall was again abandoned and fell into ruin. It has been restored at various places, and you may now visit the passes nearest Beijing at **Badaling** (40 miles from the capital) or at **Mutianyu** (50 miles).

You may travel by tour bus or car to Badaling or go by train. You should set aside a full day for the car journey, leaving at about 8–8:30 A.M. in the morning so that you will have time to take in the Ming Tombs on the return journey in the afternoon. This program would normally get you back to your hotel around 4 P.M. If you go by car you should stop at the old gate (at **Juyong Pass**) which lies to the right-hand side of the road at a point where you begin to climb the foothills. The gate is built of white marble, and inside are bas-relief carvings of Buddhist themes with inscriptions in Chinese, Mongol, Sanskrit, Tibetan, Uighur, and Tangut. The carvings are thought to date from the fourteenth century and are rare examples. A Sunday visit will mean coping with traffic jams and hordes of people, but an early morning (7 A.M.) visit any day will just about give you the place to yourself.

You may also visit the Badaling section of the Great Wall by train. The special tourist train (T1) departs the main Beijing Station between 7:30 A.M. and 8 A.M. daily except Wednesday; the trip takes about 2 hours 15 minutes. For the return journey you take the T1 departing 12:36 P.M., arriving Beijing at 3:15 P.M. Tour groups usually stop at Nankou on the return journey to connect with coaches going to the Ming Tombs.

Helicopter tours can be arranged through CITS at the Lido and Majestic hotels, returning around 2 P.M. (after a stop at the Ming Tombs).

Anyone wishing to visit the pass of the Great Wall at Mutianyu will have to hire a car or rough it on the local bus. Bus tickets must be purchased the day before at the Dongzhimen Long Distance Bus Company ticket office (reached by subway, at the fifth stop, or station 6, on the Circle Line). Buses depart at 7:10 A.M. daily; the last bus returns to Beijing at 4 P.M.

This section of the wall, steeper in parts than at Badaling, is 1½ miles long and has 22 watchtowers. The area is thick with trees, and the view from the highest elevation of the wall is superb. There are fewer people about because the location is less accessible than Badaling. There is a restaurant.

Whatever way you travel to the Great Wall, always wear comfortable shoes with nonslip soles. The climb is steep in parts and sometimes the stones are slippery. If you are going in cooler weather wear plenty of warm clothes; the wind that comes through the mountain in that region will cut right through you.

Everybody who visits Beijing wants to see the Great Wall and for a good reason: it is one of the wonders of the world. As you stand on the top tower and look at the wall snaking its way across the tops of the mountains, close your eyes for a moment. See in your mind's eye the ancient armies locked in combat, and hear the whistle of arrows and the clang of striking swords.

The Ming Tombs

For almost 3,000 years Chinese rulers have had tombs built on the outskirts of their capital. The Zhou emperors appear to be the first who adopted this practice—at least, no earlier tombs have been found—and the tradition was maintained throughout the ages down to the Qing.

The earliest Ming Tomb, located outside Nanjing, is that of Hong Wu, the founder of the Ming Dynasty. The second Ming emperor reigned only for four years before he was overthrown by Yong Le in 1403, who then moved the capital to Beijing. During the third emperor's reign the site for his tomb was selected outside Beijing using the age-old method of geomancy, which takes into account the disposition of wind and water (*feng shui*) at the site. The foothills and mountains protect the corpse of the emperor from the evil spirits carried by the northern wind, and the lower sloping ground was ideal for the gentle flow of water before the tomb.

When you visit the area you will be impressed by the beauty of the location and the tranquility of the surroundings. It is now a favorite picnic spot for foreign residents in Beijing, and if you go there on a weekend you will find many families sitting on the grass under the old pine trees that dot the grounds.

The Chinese name for the area is Shi San Ling, or "the Thirteen Tombs"; 13 of the 16 Ming emperors are buried there. Only two of the sites have been restored, and of these, only one has been excavated. Both are worth visiting, but you may not have time if you are going to the Great Wall and the Ming Tombs the same day. If you are not pressed for time, you can visit both comfortably and even ask your guide to take you to some of the other tombs scattered in the hills. They are suffering extreme deterioration, with splintered timbers, grass growing on the roofs, tiles spilled throughout the area, statues broken, and pillars overturned. Budget travelers may want to take a local bus (no. 5 or 44) from Beijing to Deshengmen, then no. 345 to Changping, then no. 314 to the Tombs.

The site where the tomb buildings have been renovated and the tomb itself excavated is Ding Ling, which is the tomb of the fourteenth emperor, Wan Li (1573–1620). One site that has not been excavated but where the buildings have been renovated is the tomb of the third Ming emperor, Yong Le (1403–1424), the first emperor to be buried in the area. Both sites will be described; but first, details of the famous route leading to the tomb area will be given.

The "Sacred Way"

As you begin to approach the site by car, the first sign of the tomb area is a white marble portico with five gateways located off the road to the right. It was once the entry point of the Sacred Way. Note the fine bas-relief carvings forming the base of the pillars. The portico was built in 1540.

A little further on you will come to the **Dagong Gate,** a massive edifice about 120 feet high. There are three gateways: the two on either side were used by the living rulers, and the central gateway was used only to carry the corpse of the dead emperor into the sacred area. This huge gateway was once part of a wall which enclosed the area. No one was allowed to enter under pain of death, except of course the officials and attendants who resided there permanently, nor was anyone allowed to enter on horseback.

After passing down the avenue a short way you will come to a twin-roofed pavilion with a single archway in each side leading to an open inner chamber housing a stele. This is the **Stele Pavilion,** or Pei Ting. The stele is about 30 feet high and stands on the back of a giant tortoise about 6 feet high. There is an inscription on one face of the stele by the fourth Ming emperor and on the other by the fourth Qing emperor, the famous Qian Long. Outside at each of the four corners of the building stands a large marble column with a dragon carved in bas-relief and a mythical beast perched on top.

A few hundred yards further the famous **Avenue of Animals** begins. Stone animals had first been placed before tombs during the reign of the Han (206 B.C.–A.D. 220), and the custom was adopted by the rulers of all the dynasties that followed. At the Ming Tomb site there is a row of animals on either side of the road, one pair being spaced equidistant from the next pair along the route. There are six animals represented in all: a lion, a mythical animal called the *xie chi,* a camel, an elephant, another mythical beast called a *qi lin,* and a horse. Each animal is shown in a standing and a kneeling position. In all, there are 12 statues on each side of the road, a total of 24.

In accordance with the traditions of geomancy, the Sacred Way turns slightly to the right, and reveals a row of six statues of mandarins dating from the fifteenth century on either side of the road. First there are two military mandarins with swords, next two civilian mandarins holding tablets, and finally two retired mandarins. The exact significance of the statues is not clear, but they are thought to have been erected in order to serve the dead emperor and his wives in the next world.

Beyond the Avenue of Animals stands **Lingxing or Longfeng (Dragon-Phoenix) Gate,** with three archways. The road passes on either side of it toward the sites of the 13 tombs.

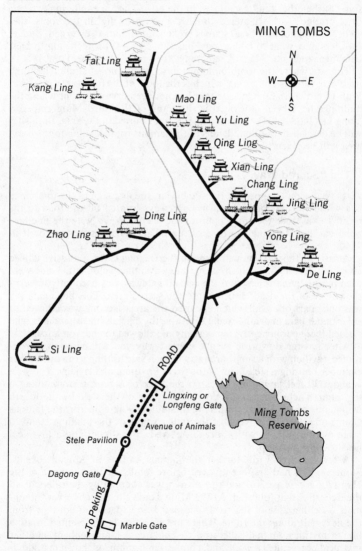

MING TOMBS

Tai Ling
Kang Ling
Mao Ling
Yu Ling
Qing Ling
Xian Ling
Chang Ling
Jing Ling
Ding Ling
Zhao Ling
Yong Ling
De Ling
Si Ling
ROAD
Lingxing or Longfeng Gate
Avenue of Animals
Ming Tombs Reservoir
Stele Pavilion
Dagong Gate
To Peking
Marble Gate

Tomb of Emperor Wan Li (Ding Ling)

You will first come to a small bridge with a balustrade leading to an unmarked stele standing on the back of a stone tortoise. The road then leads to an entrance gate with three arched doorways set in the wall. This is the entrance to the Ding Ling, or Tomb of Emperor Wan Li (1573–1620). *Ding* was the burial name of Wan Li and *Ling* means "tomb."

After entering the sacred area you walk along a wide path toward a terrace which is intersected on either side by a red-colored wall surmounted by glazed yellow tiles. All that remains of the building that once stood on the terrace are the bases of a number of stone columns. There are three stairways leading from the terrace to a courtyard with many old trees growing on either side. Ahead there are three stairways, the middle one with a bas-relief slab ramp, leading up to a terrace which was the foundation of a building known as the **Ling En Dian,** a place where sacrifices were made. The bases of 20 columns are all that remain of this building.

You then continue along the path and pass through a gateway leading to a large square tower **(Fang Cheng)** surmounted by a pavilion housing a stele. The tower forms part of the wall that encircles the tumulus. At the foot of the tower there is a stone altar with two stone vessels standing on either side of a larger sacrificial vessel. To the right and left are two small buildings housing a museum of the site.

Steps at the side of the tower lead up to the chamber housing the stele. The tablet rests on a tiered base carved out of marble.

To enter the excavated tomb you must go down the three flights of stairs set into the tumulus. The first chamber is modern and of no particular interest, but the marble gateway leading from it to the next chamber contained two six-inch-thick marble doors which are now on display behind glass. Note the "locking stone" standing against the wall; this fitted into a slot in the floor and would slide down to lock the door from the inside once it had been closed. Another pair of stone doors lead to the central chamber where there are three altars standing in a row, the first two being those of the empresses and the third that of the emperor. The vessel which stands on a pedestal in front of the altars was filled with oil at the time of burial to provide an "eternal" flame. Behind this lamp are five pedestals used to support ritual vessels (these are missing); behind them is a throne with a finely carved dragon on the back. Marble pedestals stand on either side of each altar.

Another doorway leads into the last chamber, which is larger than the others and features a stone base where the coffins of the emperor and the empresses were placed. Copies of the treasure chest are in position on the dais.

Two side chambers lead off the central one, each containing a dais, but they were found to be empty when the excavations were made.

Two small museums are located on either side of the pathway leading toward the exit.

Tomb of Emperor Yong Le (Chang Ling)

Yong Le was the first Ming emperor to be buried in the sacred area (1424). His remains along with those of his wife lie within the huge unexcavated tumulus. "Chang" was the burial name of Yong Le.

Entry to the sacred area is through three huge doorways set into a vast gate which is part of the wall enclosing the grounds and tomb. Inside, to the right of the courtyard, is a twin-roofed pavilion enclosing a Qing stele mounted on a mythical scaled beast that looks like an overfed dragon. There is a fine coffered ceiling.

At the end of the first courtyard stands the **Gate of Eminent Favors,** or Ling En Men, with three doorways and a single roof of yellow glazed tiles. As you pass down the stairway on the other side of the gate, note the center ramp in white marble with figures in bas-relief: a coiled dragon, clouds encircling mountains, horses in fields. Note also to the right and left the model pavilion with a wall of glazed tiles; the low roof presents an ideal opportunity to photograph the roof figurines.

At the end of the long courtyard with large pine trees dotted on either side stands the **Hall of Eminent Favors,** or Ling En Dian, a twin-roofed building on a three-tiered white marble terrace with balustrades all around. Three sets of stairs lead up to the building, the central stairway with a marble ramp depicting the same motif as before but in a slightly different design. Inside the hall, 32 giant columns made from single tree trunks (from South China) supported the roof by means of enormous cross beams. There is a fine coffered ceiling. On the opposite side of the hall there is a screen wall hiding the exit from view.

When you leave this building note the two magnificent pine trees to the left of the path. Immediately ahead is another gate with three doorways leading to a final large courtyard. The path leads through a small portico past some beautiful trees on either side to a sacrificial altar with five ritual vessels. Behind is the **Square Tower,** or Fang Cheng, with the **Ming Lou Pavilion** on top. There is a tunnel sloping upwards through the Square Tower leading to the pavilion housing the stele and the tumulus. The tumulus has not been excavated, and its probable contents have aroused the curiosity of archaeologists around the world.

Summer Palace (Yiheyuan)

The Summer Palace is a fine place to go to relax. There is a large lake where you can hire a rowboat in the summer or skate in winter. There is also an excellent restaurant, the **Ting Li Guan,** or Pavilion for Listening to Orioles Sing. If you feel energetic, you can climb the many stairs to the top of the man-made Hill of Longevity. Or you can just sit under the shade of a tree. The Summer Palace is only 45 minutes' comfortable drive by tour bus from the heart of Beijing. (Budget travelers should take bus no. 32 from the zoo.)

The first palace known to have existed on the site was built in the twelfth century. At that stage the lake was not very extensive; it was considerably enlarged under the Yuan in the fourteenth century. Other temples and pavilions were built there under the Ming, and the site was developed enormously under Emperor Qian Long (1736–1796) of the Qing.

The area became known as the Summer Palace because all the court stayed there during summer to avoid the heat of Beijing. The palaces and pavilions were burned down by the Anglo-French allied force in 1860, and the place fell into ruins. In 1888, Empress Dowager Ci Xi (or Tzu Hsi) had it rebuilt with large sums of money earmarked for expanding the Chinese navy. The **marble boat** constructed during her reign, which now sits on the edge of the lake, therefore has certain ironic significance. It was the Empress Dowager who renamed the area the Yi He Yuan. The palace was seriously damaged again in 1900 during the Boxer Rebellion but was restored once again in 1903. Three-quarters of the 660 acres that make up the area is occupied by **Lake Kun Ming,** the remaining quarter being taken up by **Longevity Hill** and the foreshores.

The major attractions (in approximate order when walking from the eastern entrance around the northern foreshore) are the **Eastern Palaces Gate,** or Dong Gon Men, the **Benevolence and Longevity Palace,** or Ren

Shou Dian, the **Palace of Virtue and Harmony,** or De He Yuan, the **Jade Waves Palace** or Yu Lan Tang, the **Palace of Joy and Longevity,** or Le Shou Tang, the **Palace of Orderly Clouds,** of Pia Yun Dian.

Still proceeding along the foreshore you will come to one of the most interesting features of the Summer Palace—a covered way with beams painted to depict historical and fictional events and landscapes of Hangzhou. This leads past the Ting Li Guan Restaurant, located in a pavilion on the right, and goes on to the "stone boat."

Returning along the covered way to the Palace of Orderly Clouds you may, if you have time, climb the many sets of stairs to see the **Bronze Pavilion,** or Tong Ting, the **Pavilion of Precious Clouds,** or Bao Yun Ge, and the **Hall of the Sea of Wisdom,** or Zhi Hui Hai.

By returning to the northern shore and following the shoreline as it turns south you will be able to walk to the elegant arched bridge which leads out to a small islet called the **Temple of the Dragon King.** Just before reaching the bridge you will pass the **Bronze Ox** protected by a stone balustrade.

The Summer Palace is open daily, 6 A.M.–5.30 P.M.

Ruins of Yuan Ming Yuan

If you have sufficient time, you may visit the ruins of the **Old Summer Palace,** located only a few miles from the existing Summer Palace. Nothing much remains now except a few blocks of stone and broken marble that once belonged to the European palaces constructed under Qian Long between 1740 and 1747.

The Old Summer Palace, or Yuan Ming Yuan, was once a sumptuous and magnificent pleasure ground for the court. Hundreds of palaces dotted the area. Superb landscaping was created; exotic flowers and trees adorned the slopes, huge pleasure-boats plied the lakes and streams. The emperor's apartments were adorned with art treasures of an astonishing richness.

The British and French troops took the area in 1860, set aside the most valuable objects for Queen Victoria and Napoleon III, looted the remainder, and set fire to all the palaces. Although an attempt was made to restore them about 20 years later, it was unsuccessful, and they fell completely into ruin.

The area is a favorite picnic spot for foreign residents. It is also a pleasant place to spend a quiet hour.

Bei Hai Lake and Park

Bei Hai Lake is one of three imperial lakes in the center of Beijing and perhaps the most attractive of all. The shores of the lake have been made into a fine park, beautifully landscaped and dotted with temples and pavilions. There is an island close to the southeast shore on top of which is a famous landmark in Beijing: the **White Dagoba,** or Bai Ta.

Historical records show that a pleasure palace had been built there by the Liao over a thousand years ago and that the first lake on the site was dug out under the Jin some time in the twelfth century. When the Mongols took China, Kubilai Khan decided to live on the island in the lake.

Over the centuries the park and lake went through periods of restoration followed by periods of neglect, right up until the present day. The lake was deepened in 1951 and the marble bridge separating the north and middle lake constructed in 1956. The park was closed after the Cultural Revolution in 1966 and reopened again only in March 1978.

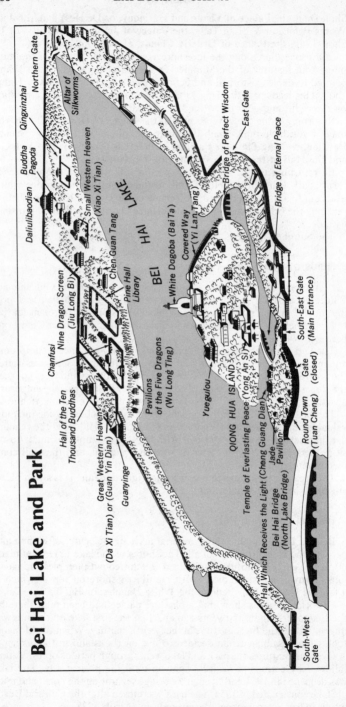

Bei Hai Lake and Park

Northern Gate

Qingxinzhai

Altar of Silkworms

Buddha Pagoda

Small Western Heaven (Xiao Xi Tian)

Daliulibaodian

Chen Guan Tang

Nine Dragon Screen (Jiu Long Bi)

Pine Hall

Library

Chanfusi

Pavilions of the Five Dragons (Wu Long Ting)

Hall of the Ten Thousand Buddhas

Great Western Heaven (Da Xi Tian) or (Guan Yin Dian)

Guanyinge

BEI HAI LAKE

White Dagoba (Bai Ta)

Covered Way (Yi Lan Tang)

Bridge of Perfect Wisdom

East Gate

Bridge of Eternal Peace

South-East Gate (Main Entrance)

Gate (closed)

Round Town (Tuan Cheng)

Yuegulou

QIONG HUA ISLAND

Temple of Everlasting Peace (Yong An Si)

Hall Which Receives the Light (Cheng Guang Dian)

Jade Pavilion

Bei Hai Bridge (North Lake Bridge)

South-West Gate

If you go in by the southeast gate, which is the main entrance, you will note the large curved wall on your left. This is the **Round Town,** or Tuan Cheng, which was once an island in the lake. The walls of the Tower, built in 1417, protected the residence of Kubilai Khan. Although parts of the wall date from the fifteenth century, the buildings within date from the middle of the eighteenth. The most important building is the **Hall Which Receives the Light,** or Cheng Guang Dian, but there is a smaller building worth visiting called the **Jade Pavilion.** It was built in 1745 to house a black jade bowl (said to measure more than 15 feet in circumference) given in 1265 to Kubilai Khan.

From the Round Town you may cross to **Qiong Hua Island** by an arched marble bridge which curves gently to the right, the path passing under an archway with three gateways toward the **Temple of Everlasting Peace,** or Yong An Si. You can walk through the grounds of the temple to the **White Dagoba.** Both the temple and the dagoba were built in 1651 by Emperor Shun Zhi to commemorate the first visit of the Dalai Lama to Beijing. The view of the surrounding lake and of Beijing itself is outstanding.

On the northern side of the island you can walk under a beautifully restored **"covered way"** past numerous pavilions on the shoreline. The **Fangshan Restaurant** is located at the mid-point of the covered way in a building called the **Hall of the Rippling Waves.** You may leave the island by crossing the **Bridge of Perfect Wisdom.**

As you approach the northern tip of the lake you turn sharply to the left towards the **Small Western Heaven,** or Xiao Xi Tian, which was built under Emperor Qian Long (1736–1796). Behind it stands the **Buddha Pagoda Pavilion.** To the west lies the **Nine Dragon Screen,** or Jiu Long Bi, one of the most famous monuments in Beijing. It is a wall covered with glazed tiles depicting nine dragons playing in the waves. It is interesting to compare this with one located inside the Forbidden City (and with the other famous screen at Datong).

Further to the west on the shore of the lake are the attractive **Pavilions of the Five Dragons,** or Wu Long Ting, built in memory of five brothers who were famous scholars in the second century B.C.

Still further west and against the far wall of the park are the buildings known as **Great West Heaven** (Da Xi Tian, or Guan Yin Dian), first erected under Emperor Kang Xi (1662–1723). From here you can stroll along the western edge of the lake to the southwest gate.

Bei Hai Park is open daily, 7:30 A.M.–4 P.M. You can get there on bus no. 103 from the Wangfujing Street stop (around the corner from the Beijing Hotel).

Jing Shan, or Coal Hill Park

Jing Shan Park, otherwise known as Coal Hill or Mei Shan, is due north of the Forbidden City. It is simple to locate and easily recognized by the symmetrical layout of the five pavilions on the hill, the largest one being at the top.

The main entrance gate is through the southern wall directly opposite the Gate of Divine Pride (Shen Wu Men) of the Forbidden City. On entering you will see before you the **Beautiful View Tower,** or Qi Wang Lou. The path leads up the hillside to the top of the central hill where the **Pavilion of Ten Thousand Springs,** or Wan Chun Ting, stands. Here you may take in the magnificent panorama of Beijing.

The park was used by the court from the thirteenth century onwards. Under the Ming, five hills were constructed, supposedly by using earth taken from the moat around the Imperial City. In the time of the Qing, Qian Long (1736–1796) had pavilions built, trees planted, and the park stocked with animals. The park fell into disuse in the nineteenth and twentieth centuries but has recently been restored. It was closed during the Cultural Revolution and only reopened in 1978.

There are two stories connected with the park. One claims that an emperor had coal buried under the central hill, hence the name often given to the park. The other alleges that the last Ming emperor hanged himself there in 1644. The first story is uncorroborated by evidence; the second may be true, there being some historic documents that tend to confirm the event.

Drum Tower

The Drum Tower, or **Gu Lou,** is one of the oldest buildings in Beijing. It is due north of Coal Hill at the northern end of Dianmen Street and lies on a north-south axis, passing through the Forbidden City and Tiananmen Square. The present building is over 700 years old, having been erected under the Ming in 1420. It was restored under the Qing. The site marks what was once the center of the old Mongol capital **Da Du,** founded in the thirteenth century.

The tower has a solid brick base intersected in the north-south direction by three passageways and in a east-west direction by one passageway. Above the base is a pavilion with a balcony and a triple roof.

Drums used to be beaten from the tower at sunset every day.

Bell Tower

The Bell Tower is due north of the Drum Tower. It was first constructed under the Ming and was later burned down. The present building, comprising a base (with straighter sides than the Drum Tower) and an upper story with a double roof of gray tiles, was constructed under the reign of Qian Long (1736–1796). The upper story is traversed by three passageways from each side. It once housed a giant iron bell that has since been removed.

There is a legend that the virgin daughter of the bellmaker threw herself into the molten iron before the bell was cast. Her father was able to grab only her shoe as she plunged into the vat, and legend has it that the bell when struck made a soft sound resembling the sound of the Chinese word for shoe *(xie).*

Lama Temple (Yong He Gong)

The temple lies at the northern end of Dongsi Street in the northeastern sector of Beijing, near Andingmen. Known in Chinese as the **Palace of Peace and Harmony,** or Yong He Gong, it was at one time the palace of the prince who later became emperor. According to the custom of the time, it was then declared forbidden ground, but nine years after his son, Qian Long, ascended the throne (1745), it was made into a lamasery devoted to the cult of the living lama.

The monastery housed many hundreds of Tibetan lamas and disciples who studied there. Sacred Tibetan texts were chanted from the walls each day, and on certain occasions the famous Devil Dance was performed. A doll made of dough and stuffed with artificial blood was torn to pieces during the ritual by the priests. In the earliest forms of the ritual human sacrifices were made.

The first courtyard leads toward the **Hall of the Celestial Guardians,** or Tianwangdian; here there is a statue of the Maitreya Buddha flanked by his celestial guardians. The defender of Buddhism, Weituo, faces north behind the screen. In the second courtyard there is a large stone pond supporting a bronze representation of Xumi Mountain, which, according to Buddhist doctrine is the "king of mountains" and the center of the world. The founder of Buddhism, Sakyamuni, lives at the peak in paradise, represented by the altar at the top of the bronze.

In the galleries on either side are many figures of Congkaba (in yellow cap), the founder of this particular lamaist sect. On the northern end of the courtyard stands the **Hall of Eternal Harmony,** or Yong He Dian, housing statues of the buddha surrounded by disciples, called *Buohan.*

After the third courtyard stands the **Hall of Eternal Protection,** or Yong You Dian; then beyond the fourth courtyard is the **Hall of the Wheel of Dharma** (i.e., Law), or Fa Lun Dian. In this last pavilion there is a 10-meter-high bronze image of Congkaba sitting cross-legged on a raised pedestal, hands clasped together. Both the Dalai and Panchan lamas were his disciples. The tiny statue of the buddha seated in front of the large figure is the most venerated of all those in the lamasery. The frescoes on the walls of this temple illustrate the life of the sect's founder.

In the gallery off the fourth courtyard, in the **Hall of the Mi Sect,** some of the erotic statues are to be found, e.g., the Duola warrior attendant possessing a human body but with a beast's head who is copulating with a beautiful woman.

At the far end of the fifth courtyard stands the **Pavilion of Ten Thousand Happinesses,** or Wanfuge, a triple-roof structure housing the giant standing image of the Maitreya Buddha in his Tibetan form. It was carved out of a single piece of white sandalwood, stands 18 meters high, and has a girth of 3 meters.

The **Yonghe Gong** is just a few minutes' drive from the Jianguo, Sheraton Great Wall, and Huadu Hotels. Public buses no. 116 (most direct), 44, or 13 will also get you there. Open Tuesday–Sunday, 9 A.M.–4:30 P.M.

Temple of the White Dagoba

The first pagoda built on the site was erected in the eleventh century. Kubilai Khan had it opened up in 1272 and hundreds of relics were found. It was then restored and a Lamaist Temple built in front of it. The temple was rebuilt under the Ming and restored under the early Qing. When repairs were made in 1978, archaeologists found several boxes containing over 20 relics: a small buddha made of pure gold encrusted with 44 gems; a small glazed Goddess of Mercy; a gilded bronze box containing 33 fragments of Buddhist relics; a monk's cap and kasaya (made of appliquéd brocade); and a Tripitaka sutra in the handwriting of Emperor Qian Long (offered to the temple in 1753). According to buddhist practice, all dagobas had three treasures hidden within to keep away evil spirits: a statue, the scriptures, and a monk's kasaya and cap. All these objects are on display in the White Dagoba (Baidasi).

The Dagoba is located in the northwest sector of Beijing on the northern side of Fu Cheng Men, down a little lane that must be traversed on foot.

Great Bell Temple

Located not far from the corner of Baishiqiao Road and the North Circular Road, the temple, **Da Zhong Si** in Chinese, houses an enormous bell. The bell was cast by Yao Guangxiao under orders from the Ming emperor,

Yong Le (reigned 1403–1424). It weighs 46.5 tons, measures 22 feet high, 10 feet across, and 8 inches at the thickest part of its wall. There are 17 Buddhist sutras inscribed on its sides, written in 220,000 characters by the Ming calligrapher Shen Du. There are complete passages of the Diamond and Lotus sutras inscribed.

The bell was cast in a pit, scores of furnaces being used to pour the molten bronze through a great many clay troughs branching off in a multitude of directions. The bell had to be cast in one pouring and is testimony to the superb skill of the Ming craftsmen. However, the bell lay in its pit for 170 years before another Ming emperor, Shen Zong, had it moved to the Temple of Longevity in 1577. When the temple collapsed in 1743, the bell was moved to its present site, then called Jue Sheng Si. From then on the temple became known by its present name.

A number of bells cast under the Song, Yuan, Ming, and Qing dynasties—a period spanning almost a thousand years—are on display in a courtyard of the temple grounds. Although the bell is more than 570 years old, it gives a full sonorous vibration when struck, and can be heard, it is said, over 25 miles away. The bell resonates for over a minute when struck.

Yellow Temple

The remains of the **Huang Si,** as it is called in Chinese, have been restored. The temple, situated southeast of the intersection of Beihuan and Changping roads—you will identify it by the gold-and-white dagoba—has existed on the site since the Liao. In the seventeenth century, part of the temple was made into a residence for visiting Panchen Lamas from Tibet. When one of them died in residence in the reign of Qian Long (1736–1796), the emperor had a white marble mausoleum built to house the remains of the visiting dignitary.

White Cloud Temple

The White Cloud Temple, or **Baiyunguan,** is a Taoist temple that was founded during the eighth century. It is the largest Taoist temple still functioning in China, and is the center of the Taoist faith in North China. The halls of the temple were rebuilt in the Ming and enlarged under the Qing. Taoist monks are in residence.

The temple is located in the western sector of Beijing. The easiest way to find it is to head south from the Yanjing Hotel along the street that stands opposite it on Chang An Boulevard. The temple is on the left about 150 yards down the street. Open Tuesdays and Fridays: visiting hours are 9 A.M.–10 P.M.

Tianning Temple Pagoda

A few blocks southeast of the White Cloud Temple stands the Tianning Temple Pagoda. The temple no longer exists and the pagoda, surrounded by factories, is in poor condition.

You can reach the pagoda by continuing south from the White Cloud Temple, turning left into Xuanwumen Avenue West, then right into North Binhe Road.

Temple of the Five Pagodas

The Temple of the Five Pagodas, or **Wu Ta Si,** is not easy to find; it is tucked away behind the zoo in the middle of a field on the outskirts of Beijing. To get to the temple you should head north along the Bai Shi Qiao Road, which passes between the Zi Zhu Yuan (Purple Bamboo) Park on the left-hand side and the Beijing Zoo on the right. About half a mile along this road you will cross a stream. The dirt track which follows the stream to the east leads to the temple. The temple is not Chinese in style at all, but Indian; it was constructed in 1473 from a model of an Indian Buddhist temple presented to the Ming court of Yong Le. The five pagodas arising from the base are more like obelisks with numerous horizontal platforms diminishing in width towards the apex.

Fayuan Temple

The Fayuan Si houses some of the rarest Buddhist antiquities in China, including over 100,000 rare Buddhist texts. Located on Nanheng Jie in the southwest of Beijing near the Niujie Mosque, the temple was first built in A.D. 696 although the extant buildings date from the Ming and Qing. The temple is the center of the Buddhist Academy of Beijing and prints texts for the Buddhist Association of China. The architecture and interior design of the Fayuan pavilions exemplify the difference in style between a Buddhist and Taoist temple (an example of the latter being the White Cloud Temple described earlier).

Guangji Temple

The Guangji Si is the headquarters of the Buddhist Association of China. The temple is on the northern side of Fucheng Men Nei Street, just to the west of the intersection with Xisi Street, or about a half mile east of the well-known landmark, the White Dagoba Temple.

Access to the temple is not easy, but there are plans to open part of it to the public. The temple is reputed to house some magnificent Buddhist statues and a large library of rare Buddhist texts.

Jietai Temple

The Jietai Si is outside the city, to the southwest, and is usually visited as part of the excursion to the Tanzhe Temple (see below). First built in A.D. 622, this Buddhist temple has one of the three extant initiation platforms in China. There are a few pavilions of interest, as well as various stupa dating from the Liao (916–1125) and Yuan (1279–1368).

Tanzhe Temple

Tanzhe Si is the oldest temple in Beijing Municipality. Founded in the third century under the Jin (265–316), but modified under the Liao, Tang, Ming, and Qing, the temple derives its name from the nearby *tan* (pool) and *zhe* (a species of tree) growing on the hillsides. The temple is located about 2 hours' drive from Beijing, and there is a daily bus excursion to the site.

Beijing's Local Flavor

There are many places not far from your hotel that convey an idea of local life. These streets are dusty, noisy, and full of people, bicycles, tripeds, and carts. They are not tourist places but simply areas of Beijing where the locals are going about their daily business.

If there has been any conscious selection in the areas described below it relates to shopping: in all these locations you can shop as the Chinese do, in small stores crammed full of merchandise.

One of the busiest quarters in Beijing is the area around **Qian Men Street,** which runs directly south from the Qian Men Gate at the southern edge of Tiananmen Square. Here you can mix with the crowds, visit the busy Chinese shops, and wander down the tiny *hutung* or lanes which crisscross the back areas.

You are also close to **Liu Li Chang,** which is an interesting area to visit for those who enjoy browsing in antiques shops.

Another region to visit for local flavor is the area around **Chongwen Menwai,** which cuts across Chang An Jie a few blocks east of the Beijing Hotel. Both the north and south sides of the street are interesting. If you take the south side you can stop in at the "Theater Shop" to hunt for antiques. When walking south from Chang An Jie it is on the left-hand side (no. 12), only a short distance from the intersection.

Then of course there is **Wang Fu Jing,** which runs adjacent to the Beijing Hotel in a north-south direction. It is easy to locate: on leaving the Beijing Hotel, head east on Chang An and take the first left turn.

Grand View Garden

Grand View Garden, or Daguanyuan, and the **Gongwufa Palace** allow a glimpse of what life was like a few hundred years ago in Beijing for a rich family with connections at court. The name comes from the Qing novel *Dream of a Red Chamber* written in the eighteenth century by Cao Xueqin. The garden was part of the family residence. The Grand View Chamber was the bedroom of the tragic heroine who was a concubine of the emperor.

The setting—with its pavilions, ponds, rockeries, and courtyards—is exquisite. Attendants representing characters in the novel and dressed in Qing costumes are a feature of the place. The gardens and palace are located off Liu Yin Street, near the Shishahai Lake. You can reach the site by Bus 59 south from the Qianmen bus station or by taxi; the journey time is about 15 minutes. If you miss the Grand View Garden in Beijing, do not despair. There is another replica just outside Shanghai.

Fragrant Hills (Xiang Shan)

The Fragrant Hills area is one of the most delightful spots outside Beijing and a visit there makes a pleasant excursion. It is located in the northwest of Beijing, past the Summer Palace, and can be reached comfortably in an hour by car. You may walk (and climb the last part) to the highest peak, or take a 20-minute ride on the chair lift. There is an excellent restaurant at the Xiang Shan Hotel (tel. 285491) as well as a coffee shop, and the small restaurant in the park (tel. 819242) is open every day.

When you are traveling to the Fragrant Hills, you will pass by some interesting sites, some of which are accessible to visitors. Leaving Beijing, you take the road to the Summer Palace, follow the east wall to the **Jade**

Fountain with its two pagodas, then continue northwest. Soon after you will note the red-and-yellow roof of Ming Emperor Jing Tai's **Stele Tower** on the north side of the road. Keep going northwest until you come to the crossroads. Turn right and follow the road leading north. The south road leads to **Badachu**, or the Eight Great Sites, where there are eight old temples in a military zone that is not accessible to visitors. Soon after you will come to the **Temple of the Reclining Buddha**, or Wofosi.

The **Wofosi** stands behind a three-arched portico; you reach it by following the stone path lined on either side by ancient cypress trees. The temple was founded under the Tang, but was enlarged and rebuilt several times during the centuries that followed. There used to be two reclining buddhas in the temple, both of which were smashed during the Cultural Revolution. Although probably a copy of the one cast in 1331, the statue is still centuries old and, at 54 tons, the largest bronze statue in China. It is flanked by twelve disciples. Inexpensive but rudimentary accommodations are available at the temple.

Return to the main road and proceed in the same direction, then turn right toward the hills. Soon you will come to a village; at the end of the village square take the right fork and follow it until you reach the **Temple of Azure Clouds**, or Biyunsi.

The **Biyunsi** was built in 1366, later fell into decline, and was thereafter restored under the Ming. The Qing Emperor, Qian Long, had the diamond throne pagoda built in 1792; this edifice—consisting of a terrace, a tall pagoda at the center, and six stupas around the perimeter—is still standing. However, of the pavilions only two now house statues of the Buddha: the Hall of the Maitreya (Coming) Buddha, featuring a fine seated statue, and the Hall of the Five Hundred Luohan (to the left after passing through the Hall of the Five Pusas). Sun Yatsen's body lay in the Biyunsi after he died, but was transferred to the mausoleum in Nanjing in 1929.

To reach the park of the Fragrant Hills, return to the village square and take the road leading up the hill to the right. The park, known as **Xiang Shan Park**, has a long history. The area was frequently used by the emperors of succeeding dynasties, many of whom used to hunt there. Emperor Qian Long (1736–1796) of the Qing had it developed into one of the most beautiful parks in China. Many pavilions were built, pagodas and temples erected, a wall constructed around the park, and game reintroduced. During the nineteenth and twentieth centuries the park fell into disuse, and it was considerably damaged in 1860 by the Anglo-French forces and again in 1900 during the Boxer Rebellion. Some restoration work has been undertaken in the last few decades, and the park and its buildings are in much better condition.

You may care to wander along the paths amid the pine forests and, if you are really energetic, climb to the top of the mountain at the back by following the path along the northern (upper) wall. Only the fit should undertake this climb; the path is broken and gets steep towards the top. Many prefer to take the cable-lift. You may want to visit the **Luminous Temple**, or Zhao Miao, the former Panchen Lama's residence, built in 1780. It is easily recognized by its Tibetan style and the five porticoes standing before it.

Slightly above and to the west of the temple is the seven-story **Pagoda of the Luminous Temple**, faced with glazed tiles with bronze bells hanging from the corner of each roof. You can get a good view into the Luminous Temple from the pagoda.

Close by but further to the north is the **Pavilion of Introspection**, which is not of great architectural interest.

In the southeast corner of the park you will find the remains of the **Xiang Shan Temple.** Only the terraces are left, but they will convey an idea of the immense size of this temple.

Ancient Observatory

The Ancient Observatory, or **Guguanxiangtai,** is a landmark in the city. You will see it on the right-hand side of the road when you are traveling between the Beijing Hotel and the Friendship store. It is a rather stark, fortlike building with an array of astronomical instruments on the balcony. Kubilai Khan's observatory was built on the site, but the building you see today is modern. However, the instruments on the balcony (sextant, quadrant, and celestial globe) attract the attention of visitors.

There are interesting historical references to the Observatory. First constructed in 1296, under Kubilai Khan, it then marked the southeast corner of the city walls protecting the capital. It was built because Kubilai wanted to draw up a new calendar, the one that existed then being inaccurate. Centuries later, the astronomers of the day were replaced by Jesuit missionaries from Europe, who were more advanced in the science of heavenly bodies. In 1674, the ruling Qing emperor had Father Verbiest build a set of five astronomical instruments to complement the one sent as a gift to the emperor by Louis XIV. These were removed by the Germans after the Allied Powers intervention in 1900 during the Boxer Rebellion. They were returned in 1919 and are presumably the instruments now standing on the Observatory terrace. Open Tuesday–Sunday, 9–11 A.M. and 1–4 P.M.

Marco Polo Bridge

If you like old bridges you will want to see the Marco Polo Bridge, or **Luguoqiao,** which spans the river Yong Ding southwest of Beijing. The bridge has been given its name because it was described by Marco Polo when he visited China in the thirteenth century. He thought it was one of the most beautiful bridges he had ever seen. It was first constructed in 1192 and restored in the fifteenth century and again at the end of the seventeenth. It is 770 feet long and has 11 arches and many stone columns along the parapets at either side. There are two stone elephants at either end. The bridge holds a place in modern history for what became known as the "Marco Polo Bridge Incident" in 1937, which led to full-scale resistance against the Japanese in the Sino-Japanese War. Located about 10 miles to the southwest of Beijing, it is often visited on the way to Zhoutoudian where the bones of the "Beijing Man" were found (see "Excursions from Beijing," below).

Christian Churches

Although Christianity came to China for the first time through Nestorian Christian priests as early as the ninth century, it did not really take root until the thirteenth century under the Yuan. The Franciscan and Jesuit missions from Rome were the first to establish themselves with any degree of permanence in Beijing. Over the centuries that followed, the Christian religion was subject to widely differing attitudes by the reigning sovereign. During some periods it was encouraged, during others treated with suspicion, and from time to time it was driven out.

The **Eastern Church,** or Dong Tang, located in Wang Fu Jing, was built on the site of the house occupied by the well-known Jesuit Father Adam Schall. After he died in 1666 part of the house was converted into a small church, and after the Jesuits were suppressed the Lazarists of Portugal used it. They were expelled under the reign of Jia Qing (1796–1821), but the site was returned to them after the Anglo-French military conquest in 1860. The second Dong Tang was then built but was in turn destroyed during the Boxer Rebellion in 1900.

The present building is used as a primary school during the week, but is open for church services on Sunday morning.

The next longest-established church still in existence is the **Northern Cathedral,** or Bei Tang, located a few blocks west of Bei Hai. The edifice is still standing but the two spires are gone. It is now being used as a school. You can get a good glimpse of this old church through the gateway leading into the grounds. This is the third Bei Tang; it was consecrated in 1889 and restored after the Boxer Rebellion in 1900. The first Bei Tang was built at the end of the seventeenth century but destroyed in 1827. The second was built on the ruins of the first after 1860 and destroyed in 1911. The third is located on a different site from the first two, having been moved by imperial edict that it cast an "unlucky shadow" over the palaces in the Zhongnanhai.

The **Southern Cathedral,** or Nan Tang, erected in 1703, was built on the site of the house where the well-known missionary Matteo Ricci lived. The building standing today is the fourth Nan Tang, the other three having been destroyed during the various rebellions that took place over two and a half centuries that followed its consecration.

The Catholic Bishop of Beijing, Michael Fu Tieshan, who was ordained in 1979, celebrates mass at the Nan Tang. This church has become the main place of worship for Catholics in Beijing. The mass is said in Latin, a rarity in the world. On special religious occasions such as Christmas and Easter an exceptionally good Chinese choir sings the choral portion of the mass. Religious services are attended by Chinese, as well as foreigners, following the relaxation of controls by the authorities after the Cultural Revolution ended. The Southern Cathedral is located on Xuan Wu Men Street, a few blocks south of West Chang An Jie. Mass is said on Sunday at 9 A.M.

The **Rice Market Church,** or Mishitang, located just one block north of Chang An Boulevard in a lane off Dongdan Street, is now considered the center of the Protestant faith in China. The church was built in 1915 and takes its name from a rice market that was once located on the site. Services are held on Saturday at 7 P.M. and Sunday at 9 A.M.

The other church used for Protestant services, the **Xisi Protestant Church,** is located in Xisi Nan Dajie, about a mile west of Bei Hai Park. It too is used by the foreign residents in Beijing and practicing Chinese Protestants, the numbers of whom have increased considerably since freedom of religious belief has been permitted by the authorities.

Islamic Mosque

If you have never been to an Islamic temple you could visit the Niu Jie Mosque. The site is almost a thousand years old, the first mosque having been built there in A.D. 996 to serve the Moslem community. Many Chinese Moslems still live in the area around the mosque. The exterior of the mosque is in Chinese style, but the interior reflects the mosque's Arabic origins. As a courtesy, non-Islamic visitors should call (tel. 557824) to arrange a specific time to visit. The mosque is located in the southwestern sector of Beijing at 13 Nanheng Jie, just south of Guang An Men Dajie. Open 8 A.M.–10 P.M.

Museums

Beijing has a number of fine museums. With a full program, you may find it difficult to visit more than one or perhaps two at most.

The finest collection of objects in Beijing—perhaps in all of China—is housed at the **Gugong Museum** (or the Forbidden City Museum). You will visit the museum on your tour of the "inner palaces" of the Forbidden City. The Hall of the Preservation of Harmony (or Bao He Dian) there has a permanent exhibition of works of art and archeological finds. Many of the outer palaces of the Forbidden City have been converted into museums, some with permanent exhibitions. If you have a particular interest in the imperial art treasures you should ask your guide for advice on which palace museums to visit and which exhibitions are currently open. You could spend days, if not weeks, going through these museums. Open Tuesday–Sunday 8:30 A.M.–3:30 P.M.

The museum at the **Cultural Palace of the Nationalities** is worth a visit if you are interested in China's national minorities or are going to minority regions during your tour and want to learn something about particular groups in a specific area. There is also a library, restaurant, and a gift shop (recommended) featuring minority arts and crafts items. Part of the Cultural Palace has been converted into a hotel. It is located about one and a half miles west of the Forbidden City on Chang An Boulevard, and is easy to recognize with its 13-story tower and blue-green tiled roof. Open 9 A.M.–5 P.M. daily.

The **Capital Museum** is housed in the second largest Confucian Temple in China—only the temple in Qufu where Confucius was born is larger. It has a forest of steles in the courtyard, and exhibits of stone drums, weapons, and armor in the museum. The temple was once used as an examination hall for scholars wishing to enter the civil service of the imperial court. The temple is located in Yonghegong Street East, almost opposite the Lama Temple in northeast Beijing. Open 9 A.M.–4 P.M. daily.

The **Museum of Chinese History,** located in the right wing of the large building flanking the eastern side of Tiananmen Square, has a fine collection of exhibits. The periods of history are divided into three: primitive society, covering the Paleolithic era down to 4000 B.C.; slave society, 2100–475 B.C.; and feudal society, which in the eyes of the Chinese lasted from 475 B.C. through to the mid-twentieth century. You should be aware that many of the exhibits are copies of originals or restorations made from historic drawings or plans. Nevertheless, there are a great many valuable objects on display and the collection as a whole conveys a good impression of the evolution of history over a period spanning half a million years. Open 9 A.M.–noon, 2–5 P.M. daily.

The **Museum of the Revolution** occupies the left wing of the building flanking the eastern side of Tiananmen and is adjacent to the Museum of History. This museum covers a period from 1840 to the 1960s. There are three major sections: the first covers the revolutionary period between 1840 and 1911; the second covers revolutionary events between 1911 and 1949; and the third covers the revolutionary period between 1949 to the 1960s. Open 9 A.M.–12:30 P.M., 2–5 P.M. daily.

The **Lu Xun Museum** will interest visitors who are students of modern Chinese literature. It is devoted, of course, to the most admired revolutionary writer in China, Lu Xun (1881–1936). The museum, located west of the Xisi intersection, stands to the east of the house Lu Xun lived in for a time. Open 8:30–11 A.M., 1:30–4 P.M. Closed on Sundays.

The **Military Museum** has exhibits devoted to the history of the People's Liberation Army (PLA), from its formation in 1927 until the present day. There is a section on the Long March and excellent photographs of China's leaders in the early days of the revolution.

The museum is on Fuxing Road, and may be reached by heading west for about three and a half miles along Chang An Boulevard from the center of Beijing. It is on the right-hand side of the road and the Junshibowuguan subway stop is right outside. Open 8.30 A.M.–5 P.M.

Galleries

If you are interested in what is happening in the visual and graphic arts in China, you might care to visit the **National Art Gallery** located in Chaoyang Men Street. It is located almost due north of the Beijing Hotel and can be reached from there by walking along the Wang Fu Jing in a northerly direction for about 10 minutes until you reach the major crossroads. It stands near the northwestern corner, and its "Sino-Soviet modern" style of architecture is unmistakable. Closed Mondays. Hours are 9 A.M. to 5 P.M.

The **Xu Beihong Gallery** has an exhibit of the paintings of the famous Chinese artist Xu Beihong. This small gallery is at 53 Xinjiekou Bei Dajie, to the northwest of Bei Hai Lake.

Libraries

The **National Library** has a large collection of texts, some 14 million in all, as well as a remarkable collection of rare books. About a third of the total collection is in languages other than Chinese. Scholars and librarians who want to visit the library should first make arrangements through CITS. The library is located in new premises near the Friendship Hotel. Open Sunday–Friday, 8 A.M.–8 P.M.

The **Capital Library,** or Shudian, is housed in the old Qing pavilions that were once the Imperial College. The Piyong Pavilion is handsomely decorated; it was here that the emperor would talk each year to his kneeling subjects about Confucian ethics. The site dates from 1306 and was once the highest seat of Confucian learning in all of China. The library houses collections of rare books and ancient stone tablets.

Sun Yatsen Park

Beijing has some fine parks to explore, these often providing a welcome relief from the hectic pace of a busy tour program. Although some are located on the outskirts of Beijing, there are many quite near the central hotels. The main entrance to Sun Yatsen Park, or **Zhong Shan Gong Yuan,** is through a gateway about a hundred yards or so west of Tiananmen Gate. There is also another entrance on the left of the Meridian Gate to the Forbidden City. Open 8 A.M.–9 P.M.

When you enter the main gate you will pass under a white marble *pai lou* which has three passageways. Follow the path as it turns left and take the first turn to your right towards the gateway in the wall. Note the beautiful cypress trees, many of which are thought to be over a thousand years old; note also the small pavilion with the single glazed tile roof in orange.

After you pass through the gateway you will see a fan-shaped modern theater with large columns to your right, built in a design completely out of character with the rest of the buildings in the park. Ahead of you is the **Altar of the Earth and Harvests.** The Altar is surrounded by a small square wall faced with orange tiles to the south, blue tiles to the east, black to the north, and yellow to the west. The passageway through each wall passes under a *pai lou*. Inside the walls there are three square-shaped tiers leading to the top surface which is the altar. Step up the three tiers and you will see that the top surface is hard-packed earth divided into five areas, represented by earth of different colors: red to the south, yellow in the middle, black to the north, white to the west, and green to the east. This earth was originally carried to the Altar from the all corners of the empire and symbolized the principle that the "Son of Heaven" owned everything on earth.

The emperor came twice a year to make sacrifices to the gods so that sowing would be successful and the crop bountiful. North of the altar stand two pavilions: the **Hall of Prayer** and the **Hall of Halberds.**

There are numerous other interesting corners of this park, the most popular area lying in the southwest and featuring attractively decorated covered walks. There is also a hothouse which provides welcome warmth in the freezing winter months.

People's Cultural Park

Known as **Renmin Wen Hua Gong** to the Chinese, the site of this park is the "twin" of the Sun Yatsen Park, lying on the eastern side of the Tiananmen Gate. Again, the main access is through a gateway in the wall a few hundred yards or so east of Tiananmen or by a gateway to the right of the Meridian Gate to the Forbidden City.

Inside the entrance there are magnificent cypress trees surrounding a large paved area. Cross the courtyard towards the gate with three enormous studded doorways. Pass through the gate and cross one of the bridges spanning the small stream. The steps then lead through the **Da Ji Men Gate** to another courtyard. Beyond, a large pavilion known as the **Qian Dian** stands on a three-tiered terrace. It has the traditional twin roofs of orange tiles. The gargoyles at the corners of the building are particularly well carved. The central marble ramp of the stairways to the top of the terrace has a design motif of horses, lions, and dragons. Inside there are 10 huge central columns of timber supporting a roof which has a fine coffered ceiling. The building was used for ceremonies associated with the Tablets of the Ancestors.

The **Zhong Dian,** or Middle Hall, which is to the north of the first building, was used to store the tablets when they were not being used in the ceremonies. A third hall stands on a separate terrace north of the Middle Hall.

Cultural events and movies are held in the park on weekends and holidays. There is boating in summer and skating in winter. Open 8 A.M.–9 P.M.

Other Parks

If you are a park-lover you will want to continue your explorations, and you should next see the **Temple of the Sun Park,** or Ritan Gong Yuan, only a few hundred yards from the International Club. Although it has not yet been fully restored, there are some interesting old pavilions, one of which has been converted into a restaurant (closed Friday) where perhaps the best *jiaozi* in Beijing are served. You can also visit the site of what was once an altar to the sun. This site is surrounded by a circular wall, but inside nothing is left of the original altar.

Another park worth visiting is the **Purple Bamboo Park,** or Zi Zhu Yuan, adjacent to the zoo in the northwestern sector of Beijing. It has fine walks, a lovely lake, and attractive scenery. The **Joyous Pavilion Park,** or Tao Ran Ting, located slightly west of the southern end of Qian Men Street and not far from the Temple of Heaven, also features a lake and a number of pavilions.

"Beijing Man" Site

Visitors with an interest in archeology may wish to make an excursion to the prehistoric site at **Zhou Kou Dian** where bones of the "Beijing Man" were excavated in 1929. The excavation was most important in the development of theories relating to the origin of man. Studies have shown that the fragments of human bone are about 500,000 years old. The site is located about 30 miles southwest of Beijing. Apart from the excavation site there is a small museum. Unless you are interested in archeological digs, give this excursion a low priority. CITS organizes excursions by bus to the site.

Other Places of Interest

For those who are inexhaustible or have special interests, there is even more to see and do. For example, you may care to take a ride on the **Beijing Subway.** Work on the subway commenced in 1965 and the first line, completed in 1969, has 17 stations along 15 miles of track. The second line, a 10-mile section that forms a loop around the city, was completed in 1987. The subway is open 5 A.M.–11 P.M. You will be impressed by its cleanliness.

The **Dazalan Underground Shelter** is popular with visitors. Dazalan is a narrow side street running west from Qianmen Street, where thousands of locals throng the old shopping center. There is an enormous air-raid shelter beneath the street; it is almost two miles long and big enough to accommodate about 10,000 people. Authorities estimate that this number could be cleared from the surrounding streets in just six minutes through the 90 entrances.

Another attraction is the **Beijing Zoo,** located in the northwest sector of the city not far from the Exhibition Center. It has an interesting display of animals, but undoubtedly the most popular are the pandas, which are to be found not far from the entrance. If you would rather eat and watch the animals than watch the animals eating, you can do so at the Russian Restaurant, which has large windows overlooking the zoo. There is no truth to the rumor that meat served there comes from zoo residents that die of old age.

For those interested in astronomy, a trip to the **Beijing Planetarium** will prove interesting. It is located on San Lihe Road across the street from the Beijing Zoo and near the Capital Gymnasium.

Visitors who are members of the teaching profession may be interested in touring **Beijing University** (known as Bei Da), the **Qinghua University,** or the **Beijing Languages Institute.** If you or a member of your group wishes to make a visit, you should raise the subject with your guide as early as possible.

Requests to visit jails or courts are occasionally granted, so there is no harm in asking.

BEIJING ENVIRONS

0   miles   25

0   km   25

Baihe

H E B E I

Yanqing

Badaling 3330 ft.

Gouya Cliff

■ *Ming Tombs*

Guanting Res.

Juyong Pass

Changping

BEIJING

Mt. Miaofeng

Yiheyuan (Summer Pala

Xiangshan

Mentougou

Mt. Baihua 6532 ft.

Tanzhe Temple

Jietai Temple

Beijing

Marco Polo Bridge

Daxing

Yunshui Cave at Mt. Shangfang

Shidu

Zhoukoudian

Yunju Temple

Zhouxian

Juma R.

Beijuma R.

Yong

Western Qing Tombs

Yixian

H E B E I

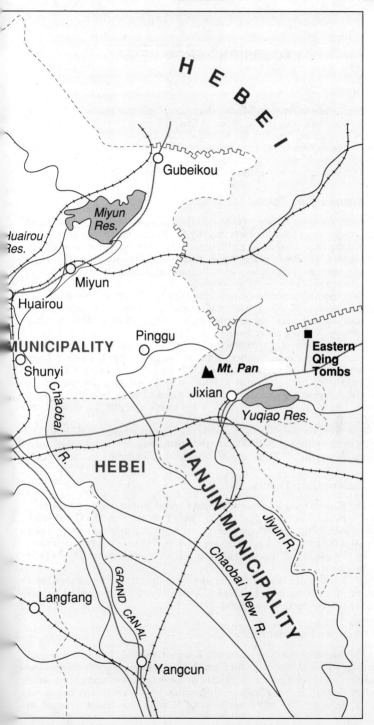

H E B E I

Gubeikou

Miyun Res.

Huairou Res.

Miyun

Huairou

MUNICIPALITY

Shunyi

Pinggu

▲ *Mt. Pan*

Jixian

Eastern Qing Tombs

Yuqiao Res.

Chaobai

R.

HEBEI

TIANJIN MUNICIPALITY

Jiyun R.

GRAND CANAL

Chaobai New R.

Langfang

Yangcun

EXCURSIONS FROM BEIJING

Yunshui Cave

The Yunshui Cave is at Mount Shangfang, located southwest of Beijing. It is about half way to the Western Qing Tombs (see below) and a few miles beyond the "Beijing Man" site at Zhoukoudian. The cave has easy pathways, is well lit, and possesses some interesting rock formations. A visit to the cave can be a pleasant diversion while on an excursion to another destination, but is hardly worth a visit for itself alone.

Western Qing Tombs

When the Qing Dynasty (1644–1911) overthrew the Ming, they sought an area far away from that site used by the Ming emperors to bury members of their royal family. Practitioners of feng-shui (wind-water) were sent out to find a suitable place: where there was adequate protection from wind-borne evil spirits, and where there was also a stream trickling across the landscape.

Two major sites were located and became the Qing burial grounds: one to the east near Jixian where the Eastern Qing Tombs (see below) were established; and one to the southwest near Yixian where the Western Qing Tombs, or Xi Ling, were built.

There are four major tombs, being the burial chambers of emperors, empresses, and senior members of the aristocracy. They are Chang Ling, Chong Ling, Mu Ling, and Tai Ling. Chong Ling, the tomb of Emperor Guangxu, has been excavated. He died in 1908. Although he was not the last of the Qing line, his was the last imperial tomb to be built in China. Work began on the tomb in 1915, a few years after the fall of the Qing Dynasty.

The Western Qing Tombs are about 70 miles southwest of Beijing. The road to the tombs goes to Yixian, then turns west for about seven miles to reach the site. CITS arranges one-day bus excursions to the tombs.

Eastern Qing Tombs

The Eastern Qing Tombs are located 63 miles east of Beijing (about midway between Jixian and Zunhua), in Hebei Province near the Great Wall. The tombs of the famous Qing emperors Kangxi and Qianlong are there; so too is the tomb of Empress Dowager Ci Xi. The area has been described in more detail in the "Excursions from Tianjin" section under *Tianjin* later in this book.

CITS arranges a one-day bus excursion to the tombs, the journey there taking about three and a half hours. About three hours is spent at the site before the bus returns to Beijing.

Chengde Imperial Resort

The second of the Qing emperors, Kangxi (1662–1723), decided to construct a palace for his court far from Beijing. He then ruled from the Forbidden City, from a palace that had been constructed under the Ming—the rulers that his dynasty had overthrown in 1644. A site was chosen at Chengde, some 155 miles northeast of Beijing. Construction began in

1703, the palaces being built in a style that avoided the upswept eaves and decorated woodwork so prominent under the Ming. Work was not completed at the resort until 1790.

During May through October Chengde became the summer residence of successive Qing emperors. The entire court stayed with the emperor, as well as his ministers and officials, so that he could run the affairs of state.

The **Imperial Summer Villa**—as it became known—was ringed by a wall nearly seven miles long. Outside the walls, 11 temples were built between 1713 and 1780. These became known as the Outer Temples, and the sites of seven remain today. The design of the temples reflects Manchu, Mongolian, Tibetan, and Han architectural styles.

Inside the walls of the Imperial Summer Villa there are two areas: the palace area and the scenic area.

You enter the palace area through the **Lizheng Gate** to get to the Front Palace, with its seven courtyards, each linked to the other. The halls now form a museum. From the palace grounds you come to the lake, bounded by the wall on the western shores, and by parks and hills on the other shores. There are 72 scenic spots inside the walls.

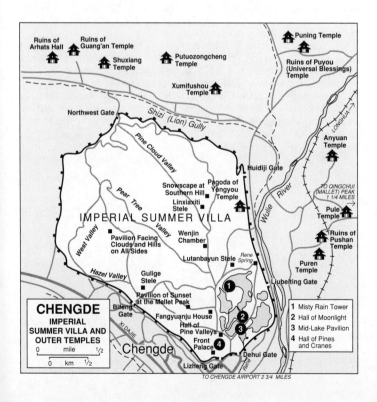

CHENGDE
IMPERIAL
SUMMER VILLA AND
OUTER TEMPLES

1 Misty Rain Tower
2 Hall of Moonlight
3 Mid-Lake Pavilion
4 Hall of Pines and Cranes

The outer temples form an arc in the hills sweeping from northwest to due east. One of the most interesting is **Putuozongcheng,** built in 1767–1771 to resemble the Potala Palace in Lhasa. In the East Hall there are the erotic statues representing part of the religious ceremony practiced by the Lamaist Red Hat sect. The temple was built to celebrate Emperor Qian Long's sixtieth birthday.

To the east stands the **Xumifushou Temple** which blends Han Chinese and Tibetan architecture. Built in 1780, it is modeled on the Zhanxilhunbu Monastery in Xigaze, Tibet, the seat of the Panchen Lama. There is a "glazed" pagoda on the grounds. The temple was built to commemorate Emperor Qian Long's seventieth birthday.

To the northeast stands the **Puning Temple,** built in 1755, and housing a 73-foot high statue of the Guanyin with 42 arms, there being an eye in each hand.

The **Anyuan Temple** is to the south. Built in 1764 to resemble the Guerzha Temple at Ili in Xinjiang Province, only one hall remains. South of it stands the **Pule Temple,** a twin-roofed round temple that displays similarities to the main hall of the Temple of Heaven in Beijing. It has a fine coffered ceiling, and a round Buddhist altar called the Mandala.

Two temples were in ruins and have been restored. The **Puren Temple** stands due east of the Summer Villa. Built in 1713 and the oldest of all the temples, its style is Han Chinese. The other is the **Shuxiang Temple,** built in 1774, after the style of the temple of the same name at Mount Wutai, in Shanxi Province.

CITS arranges charter-flight excursions to Chengde (40 minutes). There is also a train service from Beijing (fast train 5 hours; slow train 7 hours). Train 325 departs Beijing at 7:17 A.M. and arrives Chengde at 12:12 P.M.; and train 551 departs 10 A.M. and arrives 5:16 P.M.

You can stop over at the Chengde Hotel in Nanyingzi Road, at the Xinhua Hotel nearby, or at the Mountain Villa Hotel near the main entrance to the Imperial Summer Villa. Tour groups usually stay at the latter.

PRACTICAL INFORMATION FOR BEIJING

FACTS AND FIGURES. Beijing lies at about the same latitude as Philadelphia, Indianapolis, and Denver. It is about 1,400 miles by air from Tokyo, about 4 hours actual flying time on the fastest direct service. Time difference is one hour. Other distances: 698 miles northwest of Shanghai by air, 2 hours' direct flight; 915 miles northwest of Shanghai by rail, 26 hours' train journey; 1,150 miles north of Guangzhou by air, 34–35 hours' train journey.

Beijing is 165 feet above sea level.

The table shows the temperatures in Beijing throughout the year.

Beijing Temperature Range (°F)

	High	Average	Low
January	50	22	−9
February	58	27	−2
March	71	38	7
April	87	55	26
May	94	66	38
June	101	74	51
July	103	77	60
August	100	75	53
September	89	66	39
October	83	53	27
November	73	38	0
December	55	26	−3

LOCAL TIME. Beijing standard time applies throughout the whole of China. When it is noon in Beijing, it is 9 P.M. the previous day in San Francisco and midnight (12 hours earlier) in New York. Time differences between Beijing and most major international cities are provided in the table in *Planning Your Trip* at the beginning of the book.

WHEN TO GO. The best times of the year to visit Beijing are late spring or early summer (May to mid-June) and autumn (late August to early November).

Winter is dry and cold with short days and infrequent light snowfalls. There are biting winds which deposit a fine yellow silt-dust from the northern plateau and desert regions onto the city. The relative humidity drops considerably and you will receive a zap of static electricity every time you touch a metal object. Even kisses are subject to these electrostatic forces unless the participants are cautious enough to ground themselves beforehand. Thus for many reasons a winter visit to Beijing is not recommended. Of course, a winter visit is better than no visit at all.

Spring arrives in April, but after a week or so of warmer weather which brings out tiny green leaf-buds on the trees, dust storms sweep out of Central Asia. Fortunately these unpleasant winds usually stop by mid-May. You will also note that the average temperature rises from about 38°F. to 55°F. from March to April and from 55°F. to 66°F. from April to May.

Summer begins at the end of May or early June and, as the season progresses, temperatures and humidity build up, reaching a peak in July and August. Coinciding with the spells of oppressive heat when temperatures occasionally exceed 100°F. there are periods of heavy rainfall. Insignificant until June, most of Beijing's 25-inch per annum rainfall is concentrated in June and July, and there are often sudden thunderstorms, usually in the late afternoon.

Autumn is a delightful period in Beijing, by far the best season of all, and usually extends from early September through mid-November. The days are pleasantly warm, the humidity at optimum levels, and the evenings possess a faint refreshing coolness. The forest of trees growing in the city gradually turn to gold until, in mid-

November, the temperatures begin to drop suddenly, the winter winds begin to reassert their authority, and the leaves are torn violently from the trees.

HOW TO GET THERE. International Air. There are direct flights to Beijing from many cities around the world—see the *Planning Your Trip* section. The nearest international airport is Hong Kong, 2 hours 50 minutes away by jet.

Domestic Air. Beijing is connected to 35 provincial centers by air services, and the network is expanding continuously. You should have no difficulty in finding a service to Beijing from major provincial centers, but keep in mind that flights to the capital are heavily booked, particularly during the tourist season. Make your onward reservations as early as possible before your anticipated date of departure to Beijing.

International Train. The other way to enter China is by rail, from Hong Kong or via the U.S.S.R. The journey from Hong Kong to Beijing, though a long one, is an interesting experience. It takes about 36 hours, with 2 nights on the train. Passengers in soft-sleeper class are accommodated in sleeping compartments for up to four people.

Domestic Train. Many travelers choose to arrive in southern China then make their way from there to the capital by train. There are an enormous number of possibilities to consider. Journey times to Beijing from major centers are the same as the reverse-journey times provided under "Leaving Beijing" at the end of this section. For train travel in general, consult the section devoted to trains in *Planning Your Trip*. It is preferable to avoid long train journeys in summer; many of the trains operating in China lack air-conditioning. Check with your guide or at your hotel.

Another alternative is to travel from Hong Kong to Guangzhou by boat, hovercraft, or bus, and then take a domestic flight to Beijing.

Other Options. The various travel alternatives, their advantages and disadvantages, are outlined in *Planning Your Trip*, and you are advised to read that section carefully before making travel commitments.

HOTELS. Beijing hotels are classified here according to the prices of the rooms. *Deluxe* hotels, the most expensive, all meet international standards; *moderate* hotels, at the middle price range, may or may not be first-class properties; *economy* hotels are for the budget traveler, some of them offering dormitory accommodations. Many older hotels have added new wings, allowing them to provide accommodations ranging from *deluxe* to *economy* within the same establishment.

Deluxe Hotels

Anglers' Rest. The Anglers' Rest is a prestigious state guest house known in Beijing as the Diaoyutai. You are unlikely to be accommodated at this elegant and sumptuous guest house unless you are on a private tour, are a member of an important delegation, or have excellent connections in China. Until the 1980s the Anglers' Rest was used exclusively for visits by heads of state or by top-level international delegations. The rooms are enormous, the service impeccable, the grounds beautifully landscaped, and the lawns manicured. Double rooms from US$350, suites from US$750. 2 Fucheng Road, Sanlihe. Tel. 866152, 868831. Telex 22798 DYTGH CN.

Beijing Hotel. The hotel comprises four wings: the 17-story east wing completed in 1974, used exclusively by foreign guests, although rarely by tour groups; the middle wing, once the old French "Hotel de Pekin"; the west wing, built in the 50s in Soviet style, but refurbished to accommodate foreign guests and tour groups; and the new wing opened in 1987. The latter, located opposite the west wing, is known as the Guibinlou or "Distinguished Guests Building." Rooms are spacious, many with a balcony, and many overlook Chang An Boulevard, providing a panorama of the city. The rooms at the western end overlook the Forbidden City and Tiananmen Square (room numbers ending in 36, 37, 38, 39, 43, 44). The hotel has restaurants, bank, post and telegraph office, arts and crafts shop, food shop, hairstyling salons, cashmere garment shop, an antiques shop, and an airlines ticket office. The main dining room provides a Chinese and Western menu and caters to nonresident visitors as well as hotel guests. On the second floor you will also find a Japanese restaurant and private banquet rooms. In the lobby of the west wing there is a Sichuan-style restaurant. There is a bar-coffee shop in the east wing. Double rooms from

US$65 plus 10 percent service. 33 East Chang An Avenue. Tel. 513–7766. Telex 222755 BHCRD CN. Cable 6531. Fax 513–7703.

Beijing International (or Guoji). Located opposite Beijing's main railway station and just a few blocks away from Tiananmen Square, the Beijing International is a 29-story luxury hotel offering accommodations in 1,047 rooms, each equipped with color TV, refrigerator, direct-dial telephones, room-controlled air-conditioning, and 24-hour room service. The hotel has 11 restaurants including a revolving roof-top restaurant offering a superb view over the city; numerous bars, shops, and lounges; an indoor swimming pool; tennis courts; health club; sauna; bowling; and a billiards room. There is also a shopping arcade, a ballroom capable of accommodating a thousand guests, and 20 banquet and meeting rooms. Business services are available. There is a post office, bank, and travel service. Double rooms from US$95 plus 10 percent service. 9 Jianguomenwai Avenue. Tel. 512–6688. Telex 211121 BIH CN. Fax 512–9972.

Capital Hotel. Located south of the Beijing Hotel, the Capital offers luxury accommodations in 320 rooms in the heart of Beijing. All rooms have air-conditioning, color television, refrigerator, direct-dial telephone facilities, and 24-hour room service. Twelve restaurants and banquet rooms providing either Chinese, Japanese, or Western-style meals; guests may also dine in the coffee shop. The hotel offers tennis facilities, swimming pool, bowling, a health club, and a billiards room; post office, bank, telex, typing service are available; 120 office suites are offered on three floors. Underground parking for 100 cars. Double rooms from US$110, suites from US$180, plus 10 percent service. 20 Dongjiaomin Lane. Tel. 512–9988. Telex 222650 CHB CN. Cable 8288. Fax 512–0309.

Changfugong Hotel. Its name a combination of the characters for the Great Wall and Mount Fuji, this Japanese-run hotel was scheduled to open in spring 1990. The centrally located 24-story building offers 512 air-conditioned rooms, each with IDD, color TV, minibar, and executive desk. Hotel facilities include Chinese and Japanese restaurants, banquet hall, coffee shop, and grill bar; a business center; indoor pool, tennis court, gym, and sauna; a shopping arcade and parking. The lightness and quality of the interior decoration more than make up for the austere and functional exterior. Double rooms for US$120 plus 10 percent service. Jianguomenwai Dajie. Tel. 512–5555. Telex 210342. Fax 512–5346.

China World Hotel. The 21-story hotel, part of the huge China World Trade Center complex, offers 465 double rooms, 222 king-size rooms, and 56 suites, each with color TV, console-controlled central air-conditioning, minibar and refrigerator, tea and coffee maker, and hair dryer. Two floors are reserved for executive accommodations with "Club 21" lounge and business center. The ultramodern convention hall accommodates 2,000 and is supplemented by 29 meeting and function rooms and a banquet hall for up to 1,100. There is a limousine service for guests and parking for 1,200 cars. The three restaurants are Chinese, Japanese, and Continental; the hotel has a coffee shop, a lobby bar, a disco, and a shopping arcade. Recreational facilities include a fitness center, gymnasium, two heated indoor pools, four squash courts, two indoor tennis courts, and a 12-lane bowling alley. Double rooms from US$120, suites from US$275, plus 10 percent service. 1 Jianguomenwai Avenue. Tel. 500–5258, 900–5106. Telex 211206 CWH CN. Fax 500–5258.

Dragon Spring Hotel. Located far from the center of Beijing (45 minutes by car) but in a splendid setting in the Western Hills, this new hotel with its traditional Chinese architecture offers excellent accommodations in 225 rooms. Double rooms from US$70 plus 10 percent service. Shui Zha Road North, Mentougou. Tel 301–4366, 877–3366. Telex 222292 DSHBJ CN. Fax 301–4377.

Exhibition Center Hotel. Located in the northwest of the city near the Exhibition Center, the hotel has 260 air-conditioned rooms, each with IDD telephone, color TV, and refrigerator. One of two Chinese restaurants specializes in Shandong-style dishes, the other in Chao Zhou cuisine. Other facilities include a lobby bar, pub, billiards room, beauty salon, barber shop, and a business center. The garden-style setting, near a lake, allows bicyling, jogging, and strolling. Double rooms from US$85 plus 10 percent service. 135 Xizhimenwai. Tel 831–6633. Telex 222395 BECH CN. Fax 802–1450.

Holiday Inn Lido. Situated 20 minutes from Beijing International Airport and 15 minutes from the center of Beijing, the Lido Hotel possesses 1,000 guest rooms and suites and boasts the facilities expected of this international hotel chain. All guest rooms are air-conditioned, with private bathrooms, color televisions, radios, self-dial telephones, refrigerators, and mini-bars. Guest facilities include the Patio lobby restaurant, Gallery cocktail lounge, Marco Polo restaurant, indoor swimming pool, health club, sauna, tennis courts, disco, and a 12-lane bowling alley. Business center; residential apartments; separate building with office accommodations. Shuttle bus. Double rooms from US$80, suites from US$115, plus 10 percent service. Jichang Road, Jiang Tai Road. Tel. 500–6688. Telex 22618 LIDOH CN. Cable 8333. Fax 500–6237.

Jianguo Hotel. This seven-story, 445-room hotel, located a block and a half from the Friendship store, is one of the best in Beijing. It has modern facilities in keeping with international standards, e.g., all rooms have individual air-conditioning, stocked refrigerator, touch-dial telephone. There are coffee shops; bars; pool; disco. The restaurants are located on the top three floors: Justine's Grill Room (Western cuisine); Four Seasons Restaurant (Guangdong cuisine). Charlie's Cocktail Lounge is a popular place. The hotel has an indoor heated swimming pool. A number of foreign companies, particularly banks, have their offices in the hotel. Double rooms from US$95 plus 10 percent service. 5 Jianguomenwai Avenue. Tel. 500–2233. Cable 6677. Telex 22439 JGHBJ CN. Fax 500–2871.

Jinglun Hotel. The Jinglun, or the Beijing Toronto, is situated just 10 minutes from Tiananmen Square and very close to the Beijing Friendship store. A 12-story hotel with 659 guest rooms, the Jinglun offers air-conditioned rooms, direct-dial telephone, color TV, radio, refrigerator, and mini-bar. Public facilities include the Dynasty restaurant (European style) on the first floor, Tao Li Chinese restaurant on the second floor, Serena Coffee Shop, Noble's Bar, a number of private banquet and meeting rooms, indoor swimming pool, sauna, parking facilities, hairdressing salons, beauty shop, and shopping arcade. Double rooms from US$95 plus 10 percent service. 3 Jianguomenwai Avenue. Tel. 500–2266. Cable 5650. Telex 210012 JLH CN. Fax 500–2022.

Kunlun (formerly the Majestic). This 30-story hotel stands opposite the Sheraton Great Wall and offers luxurious accommodations of equivalent standard. It has 853 air-conditioned rooms and 74 office suites (floors 3 and 4) equipped with touch-dial telephone, refrigerator, mini-bar, and the range of facilities expected of an international standard hotel. There are numerous restaurants, including a revolving rooftop restaurant decorated in French classical style. The hotel possesses a nightclub, disco, ballroom, and shopping arcade. Facilities for recreation include a swimming pool, tennis courts, a health club, and exercise rooms. Helicopter tours to the Great Wall and the Ming Tombs may be taken, guests departing directly from the hotel's roof-top heliport. Double rooms from US$115 plus 10 percent service. 2 Xinyuan Road South, Chaoyang. Tel. 500–3388. Telex 210328 BJKLH CN. Cable 2745. Fax 500–3228.

Palace Hotel. Superbly situated at the center of Beijing, the 15-story Palace Hotel offers 580 guest rooms of luxury standard. All rooms are equipped with controlled air-conditioning, color TV, refrigerator, direct-dial telephone, and are provided with 24-hour room service. More than a dozen restaurants/banquet rooms provide Chinese, Japanese, and French menus, and there are several bars and a coffee shop. Telex, typing, photocopying, and translation facilities are available, and the Palace Club on the 12th and 13th floors provides exclusive business services. Parking available underground for 250 cars. Limousine service uses Rolls Royce, Mercedes Benz, and Toyota, and the hotel has a fleet of radio-controlled taxis for guest use. Double rooms from US$125 plus 10 percent service. 5A Yongan Road West. Tel. 512–8899. Telex 222696 PALBJ CN. Cable Palacehotel. Fax 512–9050.

Shangri-La International. Next to the Purple Bamboo Park in northwestern Beijing, the Shangri-La offers deluxe accommodations in 786 rooms and 40 suites, each equipped with individual air-conditioning, color TV, in-house movies, refrigerator, and minibar. There are two wings: the main building and the west wing. A large restaurant serves Cantonese specialties, another serves Continental dishes; a coffee shop, lobby lounge, bars, and a discotheque. The Grand Ballroom can accommodate 1,000 people; and there are 13 smaller function rooms. Recreational facilities include a heated pool, gymnasium, sauna, steam rooms, solarium, and massage rooms. The business center offers secretarial, translation, and interpreting services, as well as the standard range of office facilities. The office-residential tower has guest rooms, each with fully equipped office adjoining. The hotel is conveniently located near the building that houses many of China's foreign trade corporations. Double rooms from US$110 plus 10 percent service. 29 Zizhuyuan Road. Tel. 831–2211. Telex 222231 SHABJ CN. Cable 1123. Fax 802–1471.

Sheraton Great Wall. The Chang Cheng, or Great Wall Hotel, comprising three square-shouldered, glass-encased wings, provides luxurious accommodations throughout its 1,004 rooms. Situated near the Agricultural Exhibition Center, the Chang Cheng has an atrium six stories high, a cocktail lounge on the top floor, a French restaurant, Chinese restaurants serving Cantonese, Huai, Yang, and Sichuan-style food, a 24-hour coffee shop, a poolside terrace, a nightclub, a ballroom capable of seating 1,200 people, and a theater. There are tennis courts, a gymnasium, a heated indoor swimming pool, and a business center. The hotel is about a 20-minute drive from the center of Beijing, and about 35 minutes from the airport. Double rooms from US$115 plus 10 percent service. 6A North Donghuan Road. Tel. 500–5566. Telex 22002 GWHBJ CN. Fax 500–1938.

Tianping Lee Gardens. The two identical tinted-glass towers of this new hotel in the commercial district were scheduled to open in summer 1990. In the lobby area are a three-story atrium, an illuminated fountain, maroon marble floors, glass-walled elevators, and live music. The 428 air-conditioned rooms have color satellite TV, IDD telephone, minibar, and refrigerator. Continental fare is available in the dining room, Cantonese cuisine in the restaurant, and there's a coffee shop, an English pub, and a lounge. The business center has four function rooms; a meeting room seats 350. The Lawyer's Club has law library, offices, meeting rooms, and pub. Additional facilities include an indoor pool, sauna, gym, shops, and a clinic. Double rooms from US$100, suites from US$180, plus 10 percent service. 38 Jianguomenwai Avenue. Tel. 513–8855.

Traders Hotel. This new 298-room hotel in the China World Trade Center complex is just north of the China World Hotel. Its rooms have air-conditioning, minibar, IDD telephone, color TV—and there's an executive center. Dining facilities include Chinese and Western restaurants, bar, and lounge. Double rooms from US$120 plus 10 percent service. 1 Jiangoumenwai Avenue. Tel. 505–2277. Telex 211206 CWH CN. Fax 500–5258.

Xiangshan Hotel. Known as the Fragrant Hills Hotel because of its location on the slopes west of Beijing, this superb hotel was designed by the Chinese-American architect I. M. Pei. There is a magnificent atrium; swimming pool; health club with sauna; 313 rooms, all with modern facilities. The hotel suffers the disadvantage of being some distance from the center of Beijing; however this is balanced by the peaceful countryside and the easier access to the major sites located to the northwest and northeast of Beijing. Double rooms from ¥ 350, suites from ¥ 550, plus 10 percent service. Xiangshan Park. Tel. 256–5544. Telex 222202 FHH CN. Cable 7391.

Moderate Hotels

Bamboo Garden (Tingsonglou). This tiny hotel, known also as the Zhu Yuan, with 35 single rooms and 4 suites, is hidden down a narrow hutung just near the Drum Tower. Rooms are small, air-conditioned, and equipped with color television. The hotel site was once the residence of a high official in the Qing Dynasty, and was used in the 70s by Kang Sheng, one of the high-ranking officials who was later imprisoned with the "Gang of Four." Double rooms from ¥ 120. 24 Xiaoshiqiao, Jiugulou Street. Tel. 444661. Telex 22023 BBGH CN. Cable 3428.

Dong Fang. The new 17-story wing of this hotel offers 250 rooms and 25 suites, each with air-conditioning and color TV. The renovated old wing offers 70 rooms of a lower standard. Facilities include a coffee shop, tea house, bar, disco, Chinese- and Western-style restaurants, exercise room, and sauna. Limited business services are available. The hotel is conveniently situated close to the shopping area Liulichang, and a comfortable walk south of the Qianmen Gate that borders Tiananmen Square. Double rooms from Y 225. 11 Wanming Road. Tel. 331431. Telex 222385 DFH CN. Cable 1432.

Friendship Hotel, or Youyi Binguan, a gray-brick building with a traditional green-tiled Chinese roof, is located in the northwestern district of Beijing, 25–45 minutes by car from the center. The hotel was originally built in the early 50s to accommodate the thousands of Soviet technicians who were sent to provide technical assistance to China. An attraction of this hotel is its outdoor swimming pool, open from June through September, and tennis courts. The dance hall is sometimes used as a disco. Post office, foreign exchange counter, shops, hairdressers, billiards, and table-tennis are available. The main disadvantage of the hotel is its distance from the city. However, the hotel runs a shuttle bus service to the center of Beijing. Double rooms from ¥ 225, suites from ¥ 525. 3 Baishi Qiao Road, Haidian. Tel. 890621. Telex 222362 FHBJ CN. Cable 2222. Fax 831–4661.

Huadu Hotel. The Huadu is located in the Sanlitun Embassy area. The hotel consists of six five-story buildings set in large and well laid-out grounds. The 522 rooms are air-conditioned, possess televisions, radios, and telephones. There are Chinese and Western restaurants, a bank, hairdressing salon, beauty parlor, and a bar. Double rooms from ¥ 175, suites from ¥ 350. 8 Xinyuan Nan Lu. Tel. 500–1166. Telex 22028 HUADU CN. Cable 5431. Fax 500–1615.

Minzu (Nationalities) Hotel. The yellow-brick building off West Chang An Avenue is about seven minutes from Tiananmen Square and the center of Beijing. Two ground-floor restaurants serve Chinese food (to the right of the entrance) and Western food (left of entrance). There are shops, a post office, bank, hairdressing salons, and a billiards room. Double rooms from ¥ 275, suites from ¥ 250. 51 Fuxingmen-nei Avenue. Tel. 601–4466. Telex 22990 MZHTL CN. Cable 8541.

Peace (Heping) Hotel. The Peace Hotel has one of the best locations in Beijing, situated just off Wangfujing, the city's main shopping street. The hotel provides first-class accommodations in the new 18-story tower, where there are 335 rooms equipped with air-conditioning, color TV, refrigerator, and direct-dial telephone. Standard restaurant and bar facilities are available. Business visitors can make use of the special facilities provided: telex; secretarial assistance; translation service. Double rooms from ¥ 275. 3 Jinyu Hutong, Wangfujing. Tel. 512–8833. Telex 222855 PHB CN. Cable 5131. Fax 512–6863.

Xiyuan or West Garden Hotel. Formerly the Shoudu (or Capital) Hotel, the 27-story hotel is located in the northwest of the city at the Erligou "business district" (near some of the major Chinese Foreign Trade Corporations). It offers excellent accommodations in its 750 rooms, as well as a revolving rooftop restaurant and bar that features music and dancing. There is an indoor swimming pool, health club, sauna, and massage room. Double rooms from ¥ 300. 5 Erligou, Xijiao. Tel. 831–3388. Telex 22831 XYH CN. Cable 8766.

Yanjing Hotel. The 20-story Yanjing Hotel is located just outside the Fuxingmen Gate. The hotel comprises four buildings providing accommodations for 1,200 guests in 437 standard rooms, 19 deluxe rooms, and 59 suites; there are 19 meeting rooms. The standard service facilities are provided: restaurants, post office, exchange counter, shops, hairdressing salons, massage parlors, a luggage storeroom. All rooms are air-conditioned (not sufficiently) and have color TV. Double rooms from ¥ 175, suites from ¥ 375. 19 Fuxingmenwai. Tel. 868721. Telex 20028 YZHTL CN. Cable 1500.

Zhaolong Hotel. The 22-story Zhaolong Hotel is smaller than most of its modern competitors, offering 270 rooms equipped with air-conditioning, refrigerator, and closed-circuit TV. There is a coffee shop, bar, nine dining rooms, and a shopping arcade. The hotel possesses a swimming pool and sauna. Double rooms from ¥ 345, suites from ¥ 650. 2 Gongti Road North, Chaoyang. Tel. 500–2299. Telex 210079 ZLH CN. Cable 4559.

Economy Hotels

Beiwei Hotel. 13 Xijing Road. Tel. 338631. Cable 3362.

Dadu Hotel. Chegong Zhuang Avenue. Tel. 890981. Telex 222447 DDH CN.

Huizhong Hotel. 120 Zhushikou Avenue West. Tel. 301–2255. Cable 3592.

Jimen Hotel. Xueyuan Road, Haidian. Tel. 201–2211. Telex 222325 JMH CN. Cable 5636.

Jingfeng Guest House. 71 Fengtai Road, Fengtai. Tel. 372411.

Lusongyuan Guest House. 22 Banchang Lane. Tel. 440436.

Quinghauyuan Guest House. 45 Chengfu Road, Haidian. Tel. 256–2420.

Shao Yuan Lou Guest House. Beijing University. Tel. 282471.

Tiantan Tiyu Binguan. 10 Tiyuguan Road West. Tel. 752831. Telex 222283 CIST CN. Cable 3128.

Wanshou Guest House. 12A Wanshou Road. Tel. 812901.

Xizhimen Hotel. Beixiaguan, Haidian. Tel. 802–2744, 802–1155. Cable 4379.

Ziyu Hotel. 5 Huayuan Cun, Fucheng Road. Tel. 890191. Telex 22078 ZIYU CN.

RESTAURANTS. For detailed information on China's cuisine and dining customs, and complete descriptions of Beijing's best restaurants and their specialties, consult the *Chinese Cuisine* chapter of this book.

The Top Ten Restaurants of Beijing. The following list ranks the best restaurants located outside the major hotels. Gourmets agree that the finest food in Beijing is served in the Feng Ze Yuan, the Fang Shan in Bei Hai Park, and the Sichuan Restaurant. The other seven restaurants are listed in no particular order.

Address	*Restaurant*	*Style*	*Tel.*
Feng Ze Yuan 83 Zhushikou St. (West)	Garden of Abundance and Color (or "Horn of Plenty")	Northern Chinese Shandong	332828
Fang Shan Bei Hai Park	Dining on a Boat Restaurant	Northern Chinese and Imperial Court	442573 751024
Sichuan 51 West Rong Xian Lane	Sichuan Province Restaurant	Central/Western (Hot, spicy)	336356
Cui Hua Lou 60 Wangfujing	Capital Restaurant	Northern Chinese (Shandong)	554581 552594
Jin Yang 241 Zhushikou St. (West)	Sunny Shanxi Restaurant	Northern Chinese (Shanxi)	334361 331669 332120
Huai Yang Fan Zhuang 217 Xi Dan Bei Dajie	Huai Yang Style Restaurant	Eastern Chinese (Jiangsu; Zhejiang)	660521
Kang Le 259 An Ding Men Nei Dajie	Happiness and Enjoyment Restaurant	Southern Border (Yunnan)	443884
Tong He Ju 3 Xi Si Nan Dajie	Peace and Harmony Restaurant	Northern Chinese (Shandong)	666357
Zhenjiang Xidan & Chang'an Av.	City of Zhenjiang Restaurant	Eastern Chinese (Jiangsu; Shanghai)	662115 662289
Lili 30 Qianmen Rd.	Sichuan	Central/Western (Hot, spicy)	752310

Peking Roast Duck Restaurants. Everyone visiting Beijing wishes to try Peking roast duck, a dish with a reputation throughout the world. In a sense it is a misnomer to call it a dish because, at the famous roast duck restaurants in Beijing, it is served as a series of dishes, most parts of the duck being consumed. Of course, other dishes are served between the duck courses to add variety to the banquet. It is possible to order Peking roast duck as only one or two courses. Indeed some visitors prefer to take this approach.

Peking Roast Duck is one of Northern China's famous specialties. Prepared from a 3-to-4-month-old white Peking duck, the carcass is plugged, half filled with water, then roasted in the oven. Only wood of the ju-jube, pear tree, or apricot tree is used. While the outside of the duck is roasted and brought to a golden brown by basting, the inside of the bird is steamed by the evaporating water. The duck is roasted and steamed for about three quarters of an hour. When ready for serving, the whole duck is usually carried to the table on a platter, the chef often making an appearance to display his culinary creation. The duck is then returned to the kitchen, where the skin is cut in small squares. Then the pieces are served to the guests. The slices of golden skin are eaten by wrapping them inside thin crepes or in sesame rolls, dipped in a sauce of chopped leeks, cucumbers, and scallions. The Duck Bone Soup always follows the Peking Roast Duck dish. It has the appearance of a cream soup, but the texture of a consommé. Savor this soup slowly; it is a fine creation ending the duck portion of the banquet.

A number of top restaurants in Beijing specialize in roast duck. The best known is the Peking Roast Duck Restaurant (Beijing Kao Ya Dian), known to residents of the city as the "Sick Duck" because the restaurant is located off Wangfujing in a small lane leading to the Capital Hospital. This endearing name easily distinguishes it from the duck restaurant located in Qian Men, known as the "Big Duck."

The "Big Duck" is really a sister restaurant of the Peking Duck Restaurant; it is more brightly lit and less subdued in atmosphere and therefore less liked by some. There is no difference, however, in the quality of the food served.

Then there is the "Super Duck" restaurant, so called because of its size. It is the largest Peking Duck restaurant in the world. Located in a seven-story building, its 41 dining halls of various sizes can seat 2,500. Some foreign residents refer to it as "McDonald Duck."

Of course you can eat the Peking Duck listed on the menus in the major hotels, but perhaps the best restaurants serving Peking Duck outside the hotels—yet not specialists in preparing these dishes—are the **Donglaishun** (tel. 550069) at 16 Donghuamen and the **Hongbinlou** (tel. 656404) near the city post office at 82 Chang An Avenue West.

"Sick Duck" Beijing Kaoyadian, 13 Shuaifuyuan, tel. 553310.

"Big Duck" Beijing Kaoyadian, 32 Qianmen Street, tel. 751379.

"Super Duck" Beijing Kaoyadian, Xinhua Nan Street, tel. 334422

"Hideaway" Restaurants. One problem a group visitor to China faces is how to get away from organized activity for a while and simply be alone. For this reason we list a few "hideaway" restaurants where two people can easily slip away for a quiet meal. They are:

Kou Rou Ji, or "Season for Roasting" Restaurant, 14 Qianhai Dongyan, tel. 445921.

Dong Lai Shun, or "Favorable East Wind" Restaurant (formerly the Min Zu Fan Zhuang, or "Nationality" Restaurant), 16 Donghuamen (North entrance of Dong Feng Market off Wang Fu Jing), tel. 550069.

Ri Tan Gong Yuan, or "Temple of the Sun Park" Restaurant, Ri Tan Park, tel. 592648.

The **Kou Rou Ji** is a delightful little place, quiet, unpretentious, and the only spot in Beijing where you can dine on a balcony overlooking a lake. It is surrounded by small Chinese houses set in tiny lanes, and in the evenings you can see the Chinese sitting indoors under a dim light, gathered around a table eating, playing cards, or reading. It is rare to get so close. You will hear the chatter of the people below and children playing or singing well-known Chinese songs.

The restaurant cannot compare with those on the top ten list but nevertheless serves an excellent meal. You must book in advance, and a recommended banquet menu has been provided. It prepares food in Mongolian style and in winter features barbecues and roasted meats. You will probably need a minimum of four in your party.

The **Dong Lai Shun** is only a 10-minute walk from the Beijing Hotel and therefore very convenient for many visitors. One advantage is that you can sometimes book a table on short notice, but probably 6 P.M. would be the latest you could hope to arrange a dinner. This restaurant cooks in Mongolian style, and some residents feel that it provides the best Mongolian hot pot in all of Beijing. The Peking Duck is excellent too. A booking for two people can be made, so it is ideal for those seeking a little privacy.

The **Temple of the Sun Park** restaurant is situated in the Ri Tan Park, about 250 yards from the Beijing Friendship Store. You cannot enter the park by taxi, so on arriving at the main entrance go down the main walk, then follow the red wall of the old sacrificial ground as it curves to the right. About 100 yards along the path by the wall you will see to your right an entrance leading into a walled courtyard. Inside are two well-restored traditional Chinese pavilions, one of which houses the restaurant.

The restaurant is excessively lit, but the food though simple is good. Some residents feel that the *jiao zi* (something like dumplings) are the best in Beijing; the sautéed pepper shrimp are also worth trying. It also serves hot dogs. The restaurant is unusual in that you cannot book dishes ahead or reserve a table. It is closed on Fridays.

Mongolian Style Restaurants. Two of the restaurants serving food cooked in the Mongolian style have been reviewed in the previous section. They are:
Dong Lai Shun, or "Favorable East Wind Restaurant" (formerly the Minzu Fan Zhuang or "Nationalities Restaurant"), 16 Jinyu Hutung, tel. 550069.
Kou Rou Ji, 14 Qianhai Dongyan ("Season for Roasting Restaurant"), tel. 445921.
An interesting restaurant specializing in Mongolian food is the **Palace of National Minorities** Restaurant, located in the institute of the same name on Fuxingmen Avenue, tel. 660544. Because all the food must be ordered in advance, enlist the aid of your hotel staff or guide if you cannot speak Chinese. A good, standard menu is: cold hors d'oeuvres, shaslik, Mongolian hot pot, sesame buns, jiaozi, noodles, fruits (particularly honey melon, or "hami gua," in season). All the lamb dishes are excellent.

Period Restaurants. The **Fang Shan** in Beihai Park offers dishes cooked in the style of the Qing Dynasty imperial cuisine and served by waiters in imperial costumes. Should you wish to eat Shandong-style but be waited on by attendants wearing Qing court dress, then visit the lovely garden restaurant **Yan Yu Lou** in the grounds of the Yanxiang Hotel (tel. 500–6666) at 2 Jiangtai Road, Dongzhimen-wai.

Pork Restaurants. **Sha Guo Ju,** 60 Xisinandajie, tel. 661126. Known as the "Restaurant of the Ceramic Cooking Pots," it is famous for its pork dishes, the only meat served. It is also the oldest restaurant in Beijing, being in existence for over 300 years.

Restaurants Outside Beijing. The **Ting Li Guan** (tel. 283955) is located inside the grounds of the Summer Palace on the northern shore of the lake and at the foot of the man-made Hill of Longevity. The name means "Pavilion for Listening to Orioles Sing," and the restaurant is housed in a number of magnificently restored Chinese pavilions with traditional glazed-tile roofs and ornately decorated columns and interior walls.
The restaurant is excellent and expensive; specialties are fish from the Summer Palace Lake, prawns, and deep-fried jiaozi.
You should reserve in advance; it is a long way from Beijing (three-quarters of an hour by car), and if you take a chance you may find the restaurant booked up.
The **Fragrant Hills Restaurant** (tel. 256–5544) sits amid the pine-clad hills west of Beijing. It is a favorite place for Beijing foreign residents, who like to get away from the city on weekends and stroll among the beautiful hills. The more energetic who climb the peak often order their meal on the way up so that it will be ready upon their return. The restaurant probably has the best spring rolls in Beijing. You should book in advance on weekends.

Restaurants Serving Western Food. Perhaps you do not care for Chinese food, or maybe you have already eaten a great deal of it on your tour and are looking forward to a Western meal. All of the new hotels of international standard have Western dining rooms and coffee shops. However, should you prefer to try Western food prepared elsewhere, one of the following may suit.
Windows (tel. 500–3335 or 500–2255 ext. 2828) in the CITIC Building at 19 Jianguomenwai, is very popular with the foreign community residing in Beijing. The food is excellent but priced accordingly, although the buffet at lunchtime is quite reasonable. The complete name is "Windows on the World."
Maxim's, 2 Qianmen Dong Avenue, tel. 754003. A "branch" of the famous Paris restaurant. Good food, but very expensive. Dancing. Also has a "happy hour."
Kentucky Fried Chicken on Qianmen Street opposite the Mao Mausoleum—one of five outlets in the city—will provide solace for those facing withdrawal symptoms

from fast food. The restaurant seats 500 and is patronised by foreigners and Chinese alike. There are many portraits of Comrade Sanders.

Xin Qiao Hotel, Fan Di Lu, tel. 557731, ext. 620. You can dine here in the evenings by candlelight; superb views of the city from the sixth floor.

"Moscow Restaurant," Exhibition Hall, or Beijing Exhibition Center Restaurant, tel. 894454. Good steaks; Russian-style food may be ordered, hence the name. Caviar (red and black) particularly good. Overlooks the zoo on Xizhimenwai Street.

International Club, 11 Ritan Lu, Jianguomenwai (closed Mondays), tel. 521084. Steakhouse, pub restaurant, and Chinese restaurant. Best dishes are chicken à la Kiev, prawn fritters, pork skewers, prawns in butter sauce, cheese soufflé, chocolate soufflé (very sweet).

"Masses" Restaurants. "Masses" restaurants are where the Chinese people eat. They are usually small, crowded, and limited in their menu, so be prepared for simple fare. There are no menus written in English so you will have to point at the dishes being served to others, unless you have a Chinese speaker in the party.

"Masses" restaurants are not for everyone. For one thing their hygiene is suspect; chopsticks and bowls are sometimes greasy and poorly washed, and the cement floors are often littered with scraps, gristle, small bones. In some areas you run the risk of exposing yourself to hepatitis and tuberculosis. The ones listed below are better than most and will provide you with a glimpse of how the ordinary person eats.

Yanjing Restaurant. Located at 19 Fuxingmen Avenue, adjacent to the western wing of the Yanjing Hotel, this restaurant has supposedly become the rendezvous of some "well-connected" Chinese youth. The restaurant is distinguished from other "masses" restaurants by its clean floors, white tablecloths, curtains, and background music. Best dishes: sweet and sour fish; chicken with peanuts.

Dongfeng Market Restaurant. Located on Jinyu Hutung (Goldfish Alley), off Wangfujing. More typical of the "masses" style, the Dongfeng (East Wind) has the rare distinction of being open 24 hours a day (downstairs section only). Lots of spices and oil are used in preparing the dishes—perhaps too much for the Western palate. The plate of cold meat cuts is worth trying; so is the hot bean curd (mala doufu).

Shanxi Noodle Restaurant. Located at 16 Donganmen Road, at the northern end of Wangfujing, the Shanxi Xiaomianguan, as it is called in Chinese, serves good noodles in Shanxi style.

Duyichu Shaomai Restaurant. Serves bamboo steamers of Cantonese-style dumplings (or shaomai) stuffed with pork, shrimp, and delicacies. The restaurant is located at 36 Qianmen Road, near the Big Duck Restaurant.

Emei Restaurant is at the intersection of Lishi Road and Yuetan North Street, near the Temple of the Moon Park. This place serves hot and spicy Sichuan dishes.

TOURIST INFORMATION. CITS is located at various offices around Beijing (see *Useful Addresses and Telephone Numbers* at the end of this chapter). Most of the deluxe hotels maintain a travel office for the benefit of hotel guests.

Air China also has offices in the capital. These, and the PSB office, are listed in "Useful Addresses and Telephone Numbers," below.

HOW TO GET AROUND. Normally your transport arrangements in Beijing will be handled by CITS. If you are in a group you may be assigned a minibus or coach, depending on the size of the group. Those traveling in China on their own must make their own transport arrangements.

Bicycle. Undoubtedly the best way of getting around is by bicycle. When the weather is good there is no better way of seeing the city. You can cycle down the narrow *hutungs* (lanes), peek into the Chinese courtyards, and see the Beijing that most visitors miss. You will need the map in this guidebook to help you find your way. Alternatively, a map of Beijing in English is available at the bookstalls of major hotels.

You can hire a bike at the Jianguomenwai Bicycle Repair Shop (6 A.M.–6 P.M.: tel. 592391) around the corner from the Friendship Store; the Xidan Bicycle Repair Shop (tel. 654005) at Xuanwumennei Dajie; Dongsi Bicycle Rental (tel. 441056), 247B Dongsi Nandajie; and the Dongsi Shitiao Bicycle Rental (tel. 443613). A 24-hour repair service is available at Xidan Liaoyuan Bicycle Repair Shop (tel.

667928), Xidan Beidajie. Normally you will be expected to leave a deposit and your passport or I.D. card as security. Avoid leaving your passport if possible.

On Foot. The next best way to see the nearby streets of Beijing is on foot. You can wander at will in the vicinity of your hotel, take a bus or use the subway and then stroll around. Again, you can use the map in this guidebook, but you should obtain a map of bus routes from your hotel if you are going to travel further afield.

Public Transport. You may care to get out on your own and use the public transport system in Beijing: the buses, trolley cars, and subway. Fares are very cheap, but be warned—public transport is usually very crowded.

Subway. The subway, open 5 A.M.–11 P.M., is clean, quiet, and not too crowded during off-peak periods. Platform signs are in Pinyin. The two routes are the Circle Line (opened Dec. 1987) and the East-West Line.

The **Circle Line** begins at Beijing Railway Station (Beijingzhan). First stop is **Jianguomen** (Friendship Store, International Club, Jianguo Hotel); fifth stop is **Yonghegong** (Lama Temple, Capital Museum); seventh stop is **Gulou** (Bell Tower, Drum Tower); ninth stop is **Xizhimen** (Zoo, North Railway Station, Exhibition Center); eleventh stop is **Fuchengmen** (Luxun Museum, Temple of White Dagoba); twelfth stop is **Fuxingmen,** where the Circle Line links with **Nan Lishilu** station of the East-West Line (no direct connection and a five-minute walk).

The **East-West Line** has 17 stops along its 11 miles. If you begin at **Beijingzhan** in the southwest of the city, the first stop is **Chongwenmen.** Get off here if you want to explore the Old Legation Area or you are going to the Xinqiao Hotel. The old Dong Tang Church is also in this region. The next stops are: **Qianmen** (Qianmen Gate, Mao Mausoleum, Tian An Men Square, Forbidden City); **Xinhuajie** (Liulichang, old shopping area); **Xuanwumen** (Nan Tang Church); **Changchunjie** (Niujie Mosque; Fayuan Temple); **Nan Lishilu** (CCPIT, and Broadcasting Building); **Muxidi** (Yanjing Hotel; Temple of the White Clouds; Tianning Temple Pagoda); and **Junshibowuguan** (Military Museum).

Taxi. Another alternative is to hire a taxi through the lobby desk of your hotel. The line for English-speaking dispatchers of the major fleet, Shoudou (Capital) Taxi Company is 557461. Other services: Beijing Taxi Company (tel. 782561); Beijing Travel Service (tel. 755246); and Beijing Auto Service (tel. 594290). Ask how long you can expect to wait before your taxi will arrive. A wait of 15–30 minutes is not unusual. Taxis are distinguished by a roof marker and red license plate. The fare depends on the distance traveled, the size and model of the car, and the disposition of the driver. Cheating on fares is on the increase.

If you are going shopping or attending a business appointment, have your taxi wait for you. Waiting time is inexpensive and you will save yourself the inconvenience of getting another and avoid a long wait. If you get stuck somewhere without transport you should either telephone a taxi company or call your hotel and ask them to send a taxi. Taxis may be hailed on the street.

If you ask your hotel desk to arrange a taxi to take you on an excursion to, say, the Great Wall, check the price by calling the Capital Taxi Company. Some hotels seem to be adding a hefty surcharge so you might be able to arrange a lower price by dealing directly with the cab company. Try to carry small notes; the drivers are usually short of change. Do not tip the driver.

Minibus. These can be flagged down anywhere along the route and passengers can get off wherever they like. Minibuses operate from 8 A.M. to 5 P.M. at 5–10 minute intervals. The four major routes are: no. 1, Beijing Railway Station to Bei Hai Park via Dongdan, Wangfujing, and the Forbidden City; no. 2, Beijing Railway Station, along Chang An Boulevard, then to the Zoo; no. 3, Beijing Railway Station to Yongdingmen Station; no. 4, Zoo to the Summer Palace (following the route of bus 332). Fares are cheap: 50 fen for up to three stops; ¥ 1 for up to six stops; ¥ 1.50 beyond.

Car Rental. You can arrange to hire a car and driver on a daily or weekly basis. There are a number of rental services: CITS, tel. 512–1122; National, tel. 331349 in Beijing; Beijing Car Company, tel. 594441; or the Capital Car Company, tel. 863661. Bookings for all cars can be made prior to your departure through National's reservation system by calling (in U.S.) 800–227–7368. To hire the Chinese-made "Red Flag" limo call 863664.

Bus Rental. National also hire buses and minibuses with drivers. In the U.S. arrangements can be made by calling 800–227–7268. In Beijing chauffeured buses or minibuses can be hired by calling 331349; Capital Car company also hires minibuses and coaches: tel. 863661.

Tour Buses. You can take inexpensive tour buses to outlying sites in Beijing from across the street from the Chongwenmen Hotel or outside the Qianmen subway station. The major routes are: Great Wall and Ming Tombs daily, departing 7 A.M.; and to Xiangshan (Fragrant Hills), Temple of Azure Clouds (Biyunsi), Sleeping Buddha Temple (Wofosi), and the Summer Palace daily, departing 8 A.M. Note that the Sunday bus goes to a place called the "Eight Great Sights" instead of the Summer Palace. Bus tours also go to the East Qing Tombs (see "Excursions from Tianjin") on Tuesdays, Thursdays, and Sundays; and to the Tanzhe and Jietai Temples on Wednesdays, Fridays, and Sundays.

There are other tours to: Marco Polo Bridge and Zhoukoudian (Site of Beijing Man); Miyun Reservoir; Chengde Imperial Palaces; and Beidaihe.

Tickets may be purchased at the blue ticket office opposite the Chongwenmen Hotel (northwest side of the intersection) or, for Chinese speakers, at 4 Qianmen Dong Av., on the eastern side of the roundabout (small sign showing the Great Wall). For information, tel. 755414 or 755246. The departure times given above will vary, so always check when receiving your tickets. Try to arrive early at the bus terminus on the day of your excursion.

Three-Wheeled Pedicabs. These are fun to use and are very cheap. You can hire them (with driver) at various locations such as the Beijing Railway Station, Chongwenmen Hotel, south of the Qianmen Gate, and in Wangfujing. Set the price with the driver before you get in.

HEALTH. The main health hazards in Beijing are the drinking water and dust.

Never drink water from the faucet. Use instead the boiled water that is provided in your room by the hotel, even for cleaning your teeth. If you are going out all day on an excursion, take some of this boiled water in a container to sip when you are thirsty.

Beijing is dusty in spring, when the winds bring in fine particles from the Gobi Desert. During this season, sore throats can be prevalent. In winter, colds are common among the local populace and you will often see them wearing surgical-type masks to prevent colds spreading. You should therefore bring your vitamin C tablets (if they work for you) or whatever you use to protect yourself from the common cold.

Do not be alarmed by the above comments. Beijing is probably no better or worse from a health point of view than your own town, and by following a few simple precautions you will ensure that your holiday is not marred by illness. Obviously, you should avoid eating food from street stalls, unless it is fruit that can be peeled immediately before eating.

MEDICAL SERVICES. The main hospital treating foreigners is the **Beijing Medical College Hospital** (tel. 553731 ext. 251 or 274; emergencies, 214). Outpatients are treated at 1 Dong Shuaifuyuan Hutong, in a lane running between Wanfujing and Dongdan streets, only a short walk from the Beijing Hotel. Dental emergencies also treated. Inpatients are treated in the new wing nearby, off Dongdan Street.

The outpatient clinic is open each morning from 8 A.M. to 11:30 A.M. from Monday to Saturday. It is also open from 2 P.M. to 4:30 P.M. on Mondays, Thursdays, and Fridays. On passing through the entrance gates, go up the stairs to the right and enter the building immediately ahead of you. English is spoken.

Emergency cases are, of course, accepted at any time. There is no ambulance service available, unless you wish to follow the practice of the locals and have yourself pedaled to the hospital lying on the back of a three-wheeled cart. But the hotel staff will be more than sympathetic to your distress and arrange a car to take you to the hospital without delay. There is an ambulance service (tel. 555678) to the *Beijing Friendship Hospital* (tel. 331631 or 338671).

Dental services are provided at a dental hospital by arrangement through your hotel.

The **Vaccination Center** (tel. 461857) is located at Ho Ping Li North Street.

SECURITY. There are few security problems in Beijing. It is one of the safest capital cities you can visit anywhere in the world. The only precaution you should take is to lock your hotel door when leaving during the day. Also make sure that you keep your pocketbook, wallet, or purse secure when you are walking in the streets or are on crowded public transport, because pickpockets appear to be operating in some areas of the city.

CHURCH SERVICES. Several Christian churches hold services on Sunday morning, and a Moslem mosque has services on Friday.

The two Protestant churches are the **Rice Market Church** off Dongdan Street, with services at 7 P.M. Sat. and 9 A.M. Sun., and the **Xisi,** on the street of the same name. The Roman Catholic Cathedral, the **Nantang** on Xuan Wu Men Street, conducts mass at 9 A.M. Sun.

The **Niu Jie Mosque,** 13 Nanheng Jie, is open 8 A.M.–10 P.M.

WHAT TO SEE. You could spend weeks exploring Beijing and still not see everything. The old Forbidden City, home of the Ming and Qing emperors, would take days to explore thoroughly. Then there are excursions to the Ming Tombs and the Great Wall, explorations of the Summer Palace, and visits to the Temple of Heaven, Bei Hai, Coal Hill, and a host of other places.

You are fortunate if you have a few weeks to spend in Beijing or can return regularly to seek out its treasures. Most visitors have only a week at most, and sometimes less, to explore the city and its surroundings, and they face problems arranging a program to include all the places of interest. To help you get the most out of your visit, these places have been grouped under "major sites," which really should not be missed: a "selection" of temples, towers, and pagodas; places which best convey the "atmosphere" of present-day Beijing; parks and museums; and finally a miscellaneous group for visitors with special interests or sufficient time to explore in full.

A five-day tour program for Beijing has been drawn up which will allow you to take in the most important places of interest over the first three days. These are places that all visitors usually want to see. The remaining two days have been set aside to allow you to make a choice, according to your particular interests, from the various categories. For instance, you may prefer to spend the last two days antique-hunting and visiting the sites of the old Christian churches. Or you may wish to visit Beijing's parks and museums. The program allows you to see the most important places and, at the same time, pursue your particular interests.

Five-Day Program

Day 1: Morning: Tiananmen Square; there you will see the Tiananmen Gate, the Great Hall of the People, the Mausoleum of Mao Zedong, the Qian Men Gate, the Forbidden City.

        Lunch: Hotel or at the Great Hall of the People Restaurant.

        Afternoon: Temple of Heaven.

Day 2: Full Day: The Great Wall of China, Ming Tombs.

Day 3: Morning: Summer Palace Lake.

        Lunch: "Ting Li Guan" Restaurant at the Summer Palace.

        Afternoon: Bei Hai Park, Jingshan (Coal Hill) Park, or shopping.

You are advised to make a luncheon reservation at the Ting Li Guan (see *Restaurants Outside Beijing*) before departure, preferably the day before. You may order a banquet or simply reserve a number of places and eat à la carte. Have your guide or hotel clerk telephone 283955.

Days 4 and 5: Program to be drawn up according to your own particular interests. Consult the following list. The Places of Major Interest have already been incorporated into the first three days of the 5-day program, so choose from the other categories. These do not list all the sights in that particular group, only the most interesting ones. The *Exploring Beijing* section gives details of all the places of interest.

Don't forget that you will probably have an hour or two to spare on some days, e.g., on Day 2 you will normally get back to your hotel at 5 P.M. If you are tired you can take a short nap, then slip down to the Friendship Store (open every day;

closes 9:30 P.M.—check at your hotel for seasonal variations) or elsewhere to begin your bargain hunting.

Places of Major Interest

Tiananmen Square and Surroundings
Imperial Palaces of the Old Forbidden City
Temple of Heaven
Great Wall
Ming Tombs
Summer Palace
Bei Hai Lake and Park
Jingshan (or Coal Hill) Park

Selected Temples and Pagodas

Lama Temple
Great Bell Temple
Drum Tower
Bell Tower
Temple of the Five Pagodas

Beijing Atmosphere

(Note: Visits to these places can be combined with shopping expeditions. But you should wander into the side streets to get the "feel" of life in Beijing.)

Qian Men Street and Dazalan
Wang Fu Jing
Liu Li Chang
Chongwenmen
Dongdan Covered Market

Fragrant Hills

A delightful place where there are pleasant walks amid the pines, where the remains of old temples are to be found, and where the energetic can scale the nearby mountain peaks. You may also have lunch at the Xiangshan or Fragrant Hills Hotel (tel. 256–5544). To be on the safe side have your hotel telephone for a reservation before you set out.

Selected Parks

Zhongshan Park
People's Cultural Park

Museums

Imperial Palace Museum (Gugong)
Cultural Palace of Nationalities Museum

Galleries

Xu Beihong Gallery
National Art Gallery

Other Selected Places of Interest

Grand View Garden and Gongwufa Palace
Beijing Zoo

Planetarium
Old Observatory
Marco Polo Bridge

MUSEUMS. The most important museum in Beijing is the Gugong or **Imperial Palace Museum** in the Forbidden City. An interesting and small place is the **Cultural Palace of Nationalities Museum,** where there are displays devoted to China's national minority groups. The **Capital Museum** has some interesting objects on display, but is more noteworthy for its buildings, which were once part of the second largest Confucian Temple in China.

Visitors interested in Chinese literature might like to visit the **Lu Xun Museum,** while those interested in history would not wish to miss the **Museum of Chinese History** on Tiananmen Square. If your interest in history extends to the Communist Revolution, then you would want to visit the **Museum of the Revolution** and the **Military Museum.**

All of these museums are covered in more detail in the "Exploring Beijing" section.

RECREATION. Many of Beijing's deluxe hotels provide sports and recreation facilities for their guests; these facilities are listed in the "hotels" section, above. Recreational facilities are also available at the **International Club** (tel. 522144; closed Mondays). There is no entrance fee or regular subscription required. Much of the existing club is being torn down and will be replaced by modern facilities.

There are outdoor and indoor tennis courts open all year round; charges are higher when the overhead lights are used. The courts provide welcome exercise in winter and are open daily (except Mondays) from 9 A.M. until 9 P.M., with no break during lunch hours.

Badminton facilities are available; to make arrangements you should call the Club in advance.

Golfers can arrange games through the Beijing International Golf Club (tel. 338731, ext. 4021), about 22 miles (35 km) north of Beijing, near the Ming Tombs.

Cultural Palace of Nationalities (tel. 653231; closed Mondays) offers club facilities (ext. 455) for visitors such as a bowling alley, table tennis, bar, restaurant, banquet rooms, ballroom (tel. 667268) sometimes used as a disco, a Friendship Store (tel. 662923) featuring products made by the national minority groups in China, an exhibition hall, and a library. Colorful singing and dancing shows are put on regularly by the national minority groups.

Ming Tombs Resort. There is a resort in the area of the Ming Tombs, featuring an 18-hole golf course, hotels, and an amusement park. Check with your hotel or CITS.

Miyun Reservoir Resort. There is an amusement park north of Miyun town, to the northeast of Beijing, on the shores of the Miyun Reservoir. The scenery is attractive in the region. A 1-day excursion there will also allow you to travel a few miles north of the lake to **Gubeikou,** where a section of the Great Wall still stands. (Much of it was torn down by the military for building materials but, years later, they were instructed to rebuild the damaged portions of the wall.)

SHOPPING. You will best savor the atmosphere of Beijing by taking a walk in any of the main shopping areas. You will then become part of the bustling crowds of Chinese on the streets and in the shops, and will see the variety of goods available—both local and imported—and all on sale (as distinct from many of the goods in Soviet shop windows).

When you go to a counter, the locals will watch with curiosity as you buy. Give them a smile and you'll get one back. A small crowd may gather, but it's all part of the fun. Curious children will probably follow you around for a while. Smile and say "Hello" in Chinese, *Nin hao,* and they will usually draw back shyly and melt into the crowd.

There are a number of large shopping areas in central Beijing that you will find interesting. They are:

Wangfujing, old Morrison Street.

Dongdan and **Chong Wen Men Dajie,** parallel to Wang Fu Jing and one block east of the Beijing Hotel, but running south from Chang'an Avenue.

Qian Men, directly south of the Qian Men Gate; and **Dazalan.**

Xi Dan, go west along Chang An from the Beijing Hotel and turn right just after the PTT Building.

Liu Li Chang, southwest of Qian Men. To reach the area, head west on Chang An Avenue from the Beijing Hotel and turn left (south) into Xinhua Nan Dajie; within a few hundred yards you will come to a white-stone pedestrian overpass. Liu Li Chang lies on either side of the overpass.

Friendship Store. The easiest way to shop is to visit the Friendship Store, but it does not convey a Chinese atmosphere. It is located on Chang An Jie near the International Club, and stocks a substantial range of goods: food (caviar is excellent), wine, clothing, leather coats, furs, silks, jade, jewelry, porcelain, scrolls, antiques, carpets, and giftware. There is also a tailor shop (slow); dry-cleaning service; and watch repair shop.

The store is open every day of the year from 9 A.M. (meat and vegetable section from 8:30 A.M.) to 9:30 P.M. daily; times vary slightly from winter to summer. There is a bank attached to the store where visitors may cash traveler's checks. Open 9 A.M.–7 P.M. Tel. 593531.

Department Stores More interesting to visit but far more crowded and time-consuming are the two large department stores in Wang Fu Jing: the **Beijing Department Store,** actually Beijing Bai Huo Da Lou, literally "Beijing Hundred Products Big Store," which is set back from the streetfront, and the **Dong Feng (East Wind)** covered market. They are opposite each other on Wang Fu Jing. Both are open 9 A.M.–8 P.M. The **Xidan Emporium,** 120 North Xidan Road, east of the Xidan intersection, is a more modern store.

Handicrafts stores. The handicrafts store, at 200 Wang Fu Jing, is worth a visit. The store is located on the right-hand side when proceeding north along Wang Fu Jing from the Beijing Hotel. The first floor sells pottery, paper-cuts, calligraphy, and art supplies. The second floor sells linens, bamboo and cane articles, and cloisonné ware. You can also buy Chinese batik, but it is expensive compared with other Asian batik and usually not as good. It is probably the best place in Beijing to buy linens; and artists will find a excellent range of good quality and inexpensive art supplies available. A good selection of linen ware and tablecloths is also available across the street at 265 Wang Fu Jing.

Another place for arts and craft items is the **Marco Polo Shop** (tel. 754940) outside the west gate of the Temple of Heaven.

Fur Shop. Just beyond the Handicrafts Store in Wang Fu Jing, again on the eastern (right-hand) side when proceeding north, you will find the Jianhua Fur Shop (192 Wang Fu Jing). It is a tiny shop and the only sign you will see is in Chinese, so keep a look out for a window with a few pelts in it. Advice on buying is given in a later section under "Furs."

Theater Shops. The theater shops sell a wide range of antiques, objets d'art, and old theatrical gowns. You will find many Chinese, Japanese, and European antiques, carriage clocks, monogrammed silverware, candelabra, crystal, porcelain, and metalware. There are also plenty of Mongolian "hot pots," brass bedwarmers, furniture locks, wooden boxes, and metal dishes. One section sells antique and reproduction Chinese furniture, and another a variety of second-hand furs, some made up into rugs and others in their natural shape. The main theater shop, known also as the **Beijing Huaxia Arts and Crafts Shop** (tel. 555331, ext. 207; and 551529), is at 249 Dongsi Nan Street. There is a branch (tel. 551819) at 293 Wangfujing Street. Another theater shop is at 130 Qianmen.

Dongsi Market is really two stores connected to each other to form a large Chinese emporium. The goods on display are the same as those found in the Beijing Department Store and the East Wind (Dong Feng) Market.

To go there you walk north along Wang Fu Jing from the Beijing Hotel. You will pass the Tianlun Dynasty Hotel, the Holiday Inn Crowne Plaza, and the Sara Hotel on your right. Take the next turn to the right, and about 50 yards ahead to your left you will see a small lane leading northward to the entrance.

"Free" Markets. They don't actually give away goods here, the name simply refers to those markets not controlled by the state, where locals can set up their own stalls. The one most convenient for visitors is in the Dongsi Market described above; there is another at the northeast of the Temple of Heaven, and there are others. Many of these markets remain open until 10 P.M. or later.

Antiques

You should always check with the vendor that the antique you are about to purchase can be taken out of China. If so, retain the invoice and make sure that the red wax seal on the item remains intact.

The **Beijing Antiques Bazaar** stocks a wide range of antiques in silver, gold, bronze, and ceramics, as well as furniture, rugs, embroidery, and arts and crafts. The 40 shops are run by private dealers, the bazaar is state-controlled. Bargaining is recommended. It's located off the west side of the southern section of the Eastern Third Ring Road. **Liu Li Chang.** Another excellent place to buy antiques in Beijing is at Liu Li Chang, literally "Glazed Tile Works Street," which, about a thousand years ago, was part of the eastern section of the capital. After the Ming established the capital at Beijing, numerous tile works were established there. At the beginning of the Qing (mid-seventeenth century) small shopkeepers moved into the area, particularly booksellers, and before long the area became a meeting place for scholars. Printers and antique shops were soon established. When the area was destroyed at the end of the Qing, only the narrow winding lanes around Liu Li Chang survived. The place has been renovated in old Qing style.

The best and most expensive antique shops are located at 70 and 80 Liu Li Chang. They sell a range of antiques: porcelain, jade, snuff bottles, old cloisonné ware, metalware, and wood carvings.

The scroll shop at 63 Liu Li Chang sells traditional-style original paintings and old calligraphy. It is here that you can look for an original by Qi Baishi, provided you have a spare $10,000 or so.

At 136 Liu Li Chang there is a small shop selling copies of Han, Tang, and Song Dynasty ceramics. There are some beautiful pieces: small figurines, large ceramic horses, camels, pigs, and dogs—all in antique finish and excellently reproduced.

There you may also buy rubbings of bas-relief carvings from tombs, temples, and caves located at various sites in China. Some of the rubbings are from carvings that are over 2,000 years old. They make excellent gifts—they are flat, light, easy to pack, and, more to the point for the impoverished traveler, quite inexpensive. Buy a few for yourself and have them mounted when you go home. They will serve as an elegant and pleasing memento of your visit to China.

Rong Bao Zhai, or Studio of Glorious Treasures, located at 19 Liu Li Chang (a little to the west across in Hu Fang Lu), sells watercolors, modern prints and scrolls. It trains craftsmen in wood blockprinting and reproduction of watercolor paintings. Their work is exceptionally good. Lanterns, lamp shades, and some modern pictures may be bought at 92 Liu Li Chang.

Commission Shops. There are a few of these scattered around Beijing and, while they deal in second-hand goods rather than antiques, collectors often go there in the hope of finding something rare that has been overlooked. The shops are popular with the foreign residents of Beijing.

The ones closest to the Beijing Hotel are at 113 Dongdan North Street and at 119 Qianmen Street. There are others at 12 Chongwenmennei, just north of the Xinqiao Hotel, and 128 Dianmenwai, near the Drum Tower. Good antique furniture (and repairs) are available at 30 Dongsi Beidajie.

Jade and Jewelry

There is a great variety of fine jade available in Beijing, as well as a huge range of ordinary-quality jade. Some experts say that you can purchase jade cheaper in other countries in Asia but that the risk of being deceived by fraudulent articles is quite high.

The advantage of buying in China is the feeling of security that comes from knowing that you get exactly what you pay for. Therefore, many visitors who do not understand the perplexities of the jade market are often happy to buy jade in Beijing, even though a similar article might be available outside China at a reduced price.

For the uninitiated, a visit to the Friendship Store jade counter represents the best starting point.

There is also a wonderful selection of jewelry available, ranging in price from a few yuan up to thousands, in an infinite variety of styles. These are small items easy to pack and therefore represent sensible gift purchases for the overloaded traveler.

Chops

Chops are used in China to stamp a crest, insignia, or name on documents. They are made from a variety of stone materials ranging from onyx to jade. You can buy antique chops with someone else's name in Chinese characters or, if you wish, have your own name or insignia carved into a new set.

If you buy a pair you can have your name in Chinese characters on one and in your own language on the other. Apart from the cost of the chop itself, there is a charge per letter, depending on the size of the chop.

There are chop shops at 78 West Liu Li Chang, 35 South Xinhua Street, and at 261 Wang Fu Jing. All these shops sell the red ink traditionally used. Some residents claim that the best ink is obtained at the Beijing Department Store.

If you are uncertain about your name in Chinese, ask to consult the books there giving Chinese equivalents for English names. Before selecting a chop you should also consult the book at the store which shows the various styles of lettering that can be engraved onto the base.

Furs

Beijing is a good place to buy furs; there is an excellent variety of pelts available, such as sable, mink, fox, and rabbit. These are all available made up into coats and hats as well as in their natural state. Mink is a good buy; the quality is not bad, and the price is certainly less than for Siberian mink. However, you will get what you pay for.

A great variety of such skins as sheep, goat, and wolf are available in natural form or made up into rugs.

Suede articles of sheepskin and pigskin are an excellent buy; the workmanship can be first-class and the price most reasonable. However, be sure to try on a number of garments to get the right fit; despite good workmanship, an occasional ill-shaped garment seems to slip through. Chinese styles tend to lag behind those of other suede centers, so you will have to be content with fairly standard styles.

When buying, use your nose. Some skins are imperfectly cured and give off a distinct odor which the buyer, concentrating on cut and color, sometimes fails to detect. On your return home you may look smart in your coat but find yourself curiously alone on the street.

Furs, pelts, skins, and a few garments are available on the second floor of the Friendship Store and at no. 192 Wang Fu Jing.

U.S. Customs prohibits the importation of furs and pelts from endangered species. Check before departing.

Carpets

Chinese carpets are world renowned, and a fine variety is available at two locations in Beijing—on the third floor of the Friendship Store and at 208 Qian Men. Carpets, rugs, and mats are available in classical styles and in the traditional designs of the autonomous regions of China such as Xinjiang, Inner Mongolia, and Tibet. Antique finishes are available.

In general, carpets are high priced, but the connoisseur may be able to find some bargains.

ENTERTAINMENT. There's a lot to do in the evenings in Beijing, whether you want to see something in traditional Chinese form—a Peking Opera, for example—or attend a symphony featuring a Western composer. There are plays, choral groups, minority dance performances, and the circus. Beijing is now on the international artistic circuit, so you may even see one of the outstanding foreign cultural events while you are there. The best way to find out what is on is to buy a copy of the English-language newspaper *China Daily*. Your hotel or CITS can arrange tickets. If you want to take a chance, just go to the event and see if you can get one of the handful of seats that are often held for surprise visits by Chinese VIPs.

LEAVING BEIJING. If you are traveling China on your own, you should pay early attention to your departure arrangements because some reservations require many days' notice. CITS (tel. 512–2256) can help independent travelers with most ongoing arrangements. This particular CITS office may be found in Room 1302 at the Chongwenmen Hotel, 2 Chongwenmen. The office is open 8:30 –11 A.M. 1:30–4:30 P.M.; and on Sunday 9–11 A.M. and 2–4 P.M. CITS also has offices at the Great Wall Sheraton (tel. 500–5566), Huadu (tel. 500–1166), and Lido Holiday Inn (tel. 500–6688).

By train. Reservations and ticketing for international train journeys (e.g., to the Soviet Union, the People's Republic of Mongolia) should be done at the CITS office, in the Chongwenmen Hotel. Bookings for domestic train departures should be arranged directly with the Chinese railways ticket office at Room 103 of the main Beijing Railway Station. Book as early as possible, especially for sleeper accommodations.

After passing through the main entrance, walk to the rear of the lobby, then go left into the waiting room for international passengers. There you will see the English sign for this office. Seats can be reserved 6–10 days in advance and purchased up to 5 days in advance. In Beijing, reservations and tickets can only be arranged for the next destination, not for a number of centers en route. (You will probably need a student I.D. card and plenty of luck to score a hard-seat ticket at Chinese prices). "Same day" tickets are available at this office; "next day" tickets are available after 7 P.M. Always arrive at Beijing Station at least 15 minutes before your train leaves because you may find that it takes at least this long to get to the departure platform.

In planning your trip it is useful to know the duration of train journeys. The following destinations are ranked according to the time taken on the fastest train available. Journey times are given immediately after each destination.

Tianjin 1¼ hrs, Shijiazhuang 3¼, Jinan 6¼, Datong 7¼, Zhengzhou 8½, Taiyuan 9, Shenyang 9¼, Hohhot 12¼, Changchun 13½, Nanjing 15¼, Wuhan 16¼, Harbin 16¼, Qingdao 17½, Xian 18½, Dalian 18¼, Shanghai 19¼, Hangzhou 23¼, and Guangzhou 33½ hours.

By plane. Tickets and reservations on international flights can be obtained at the Air China/CAAC office, 117 Dongsi Xi Dajie. For international flights on other airlines, you may first wish to telephone the carrier. The telephone numbers and addresses of other international carriers are given under "Useful Addresses and Telephone Numbers."

Tickets and reservations on domestic flights can be obtained at the Air China/CAAC office,117Dongsi Xi Dajie; at CITS offices in hotels; and at the China Swan International Tours office on the ground floor of the Beijing Hotel. Many hotels have booking offices for the new domestic carriers such as China United Airlines and Shanghai Airlines, both of which serve provincial capitals.

The earliest reservations/tickets available for some domestic destinations will be 4–5 days after you get to the ticket counter. Such delays are a common occurrence on busy domestic routes.

At the airport, remember that there is a departure tax, paid after you go through Customs. There is a bank that you can use before Customs, and another one after you have passed Customs. However, the lines at both can be very long, so try to carry the exact amount required.

By boat. You cannot, of course, leave Beijing by boat, but you can make advance reservations through CITS at the Chongwenmen Hotel for your onward journey from (say) Shanghai to Hong Kong. Taking this step may save you time in Shanghai.

USEFUL ADDRESSES AND TELEPHONE NUMBERS

Emergency Numbers

Beijing Union Hospital: Clinic ("Dongmen") Dongdan Bei Dajie, tel. 553731, ext. 251, 274, 276; Emergency Cases ("Ximen") 1 Shaifuyuan Hutong, tel. 553731, ext. 214
Fire Brigade: tel. 09
Police: emergency tel. 110

Communications

International Telephone Calls: 115
Long distance calls within China, English speaking: 553536
Long distance calls within China; Chinese-speaking: 113 or 173
Post and Telecommunications Building (PTT), Changan Xidajie, tel. 666215.
Taxis: Shoudou (Capital) Taxi Company, tel. 557461
Public Security Bureau (Foreigners Section), 85 Beichizi (8:30–11:30 A.M. and 1–5 P.M. daily; 8:30–11:30 A.M. Saturday; closed Sunday

Travel Arrangements

Air China/CAAC 117 Dongsi Xi Dajie.
　　　　　　　　Domestic passenger services: tel. 401–4441.
　　　　　　　　International passenger services: tel. 401–2221.
　　　　　　　　Domestic cargo services: tel. 473008.
　　　　　　　　International cargo services: tel. 473228.
China International Travel Service (CITS), Headquarters. 6 Changan Dong Dajie, tel. 512–1122; North American Department, tel. 512–2138.
CITS, Beijing Branch. Chongwenmen Hotel, 2 Chongwenmen Dong Dajie, tel. 512–2256, telex 20052 CITSB CN, fax 512–2447.
China Travel Service (CTS). 8 Dongjiaominxing, tel. 553491.
Hotel Information Desk. Beijing Main Railway Station, tel. 516–7766.
Beijing Hotel Company. Qianmenwai, tel. 550681.

Airlines

Aeroflot, Jianguomenwai 5–53, tel. 523581
Air France, Jianguomenwai 12–71, tel. 523894
Air Romania, Rumanian Embassy, tel. 523552
British Airways, Jianguomenwai 12–61, tel. 523768
Air China/CAAC, tel. 553245 (domestic reservations); 117 Dongsi Xi Dajie, tel. 556720 (international reservations)
Cathay Pacific, tel. 500–3339 or 500–2233 ext. 152
Ethiopian Air, Jianguomenwai 12–32, tel. 523285
Iran Air, Jianguomenwai 12–63, tel. 523249 or 523843
Japan Air Lines, Jianguomenwai 12–23, tel. 523457 or 523374
Lufthansa Airlines, Sheraton Great Wall Hotel, tel. 501616
Pakistan Airlines, Jianguomenwai 12–43, tel. 523274
Philippine Airlines, Jianguomenwai 12–53, tel. 523992
Qantas, Jinglun Hotel, tel. 500–2487
Singapore Airlines, tel. 523274 or 523989
Swiss Air, Jianguomenwai 12–33, tel. 523284
Thai International, Jianguomenwai 12–31, tel. 523174
United Airlines, Beijing Capital Airport, tel. 525015, 500–1985, or 595261
Yugoslav Airlines, Jianguomenwai 2–2–162, tel. 523486

Embassies

Australia, tel. 522331

Canada, 521475
New Zealand, tel. 522731
United Kingdom, tel. 521961
United States, tel. 523831 or 521161

Other

International Club, 21 Jianguomenwai, tel. 522144
Friendship Store, Jianguomenwai, tel. 593531
Bank of China, Xijiaominxiang 17, tel. 338521

GUANGZHOU

Guangzhou, capital of the province of Guangdong, is a pleasant city of tropical parks and long streets flanked by cool, shady arcades. It is an important industrial center, and its port, Whampoa, is South China's major foreign trade port.

In the early days of this century Guangzhou, like Shanghai, had a notorious reputation. Most of the city comprised a vast sprawl of makeshift shacks threaded by tiny lanes and serviced by open sewers. The poor—and they were the greater part of the population—lived in dreadful hovels, surrounded by putrid canals. Malnutrition and disease were widespread.

A modernization campaign got under way in the 1920s and large sections of the town were pulled down; in about 18 months almost 25 miles of streets, pavements, and sewers were put down. The layout of the existing city largely reflects the major work program undertaken during this period, although there have been considerable improvements in public amenities since the Communists came to power in 1949.

The city is located on a bend of the Pearl River, or Zhu Jiang, a major waterway of the region. It is bisected to form an eastern and western sector by the broad Liberation Avenue, or Jiefang Li; it is also bisected by an east-west road called Sun Yatsen Avenue, or Zhong Shan Lu. The inhabitants thus find it convenient to describe the location of places in Guangzhou by sector. Most of the main streets run gently downhill from north to south and end at the river's edge. This serves as a useful directional aid when you are wandering in the city. However, not all the streets end at the river's edge.

The history of the city has long been associated with trade routes which pass through the province, making it a center for foreign commerce for over 2,000 years. Although the origins of the town are not clearly known, the first settlement is believed to have been established in the third century B.C. It is recorded that merchants from Rome visited the town during the

Han Dynasty (206 B.C.–A.D. 220). Historical records also show that a large Moslem colony existed as early as the seventh century A.D.; a mosque had been established and contacts with the Middle East had developed. Recognition of the settlement's growing trading importance was given in A.D. 714 when one of the Tang emperors established officials there to oversee foreign trade, in effect formally establishing the first official trading port in China.

In the tenth century the city was recognized as the capital of the autonomous dynasty of the Southern Han when it was known as Xing Wang Su. In those days the city maintained and developed contacts with Persian, Hindu, and Arab traders.

The first European influence dates from 1514 when the Portuguese Embassy arrived. Sea links with China were important, for the "Silk Road" across Asia was no longer a safe caravan route. In 1557 the Portuguese obtained permission from the Ming to settle on an island which they called Macao, some 70 miles downstream from Guangzhou. Then came the Spanish and the Dutch. The next to appear in the China Seas were the British, but they did not establish themselves to any great extent until the early eighteenth century, preferring to concentrate their efforts in India.

By 1715 the British East India Company had become the most important firm trading with China, but like other companies it was severely limited by the "Eight Regulations" which imposed strict sanctions on the conduct of all trade and restricted the movement of merchants. To keep foreigners out, one Chinese regulation stipulated that vessels could anchor only at Whampoa, some 13 miles below the town center, to load and unload. By the early nineteenth century England had emerged as the most powerful nation in the Western world, and to underpin its growing influence in the Far East the British government "offered" a treaty regulating trade with China, an offer that was not considered acceptable by the Chinese court. The differences between the British government and the Chinese court set the scene for the conflict that was to break out.

By this time British trade with China involved the exchange of various English products for Chinese tea and silk. The balance of trade in China's favor was made up by payments of silver by the English. From 1800 onward opium from India was offered as a substitute for silver, the original owners of the opium being the British East India Company, although it was sold to China by another organization. As opium imports into China were forbidden, it had to be smuggled in. Eventually the illicit traffic increased to such an extent that its value equaled that of legitimate imports into China.

The conflict between the Chinese authorities who attempted to put down the illicit trade, the Chinese and British merchants who were profiting handsomely from the business, and the government of Britain, which was trying to force concessions from the Chinese government in an effort to open up trade even further, led eventually to the Opium Wars, which began in 1839. At the conclusion of the Second Opium War of the mid-1850s, foreign merchants who had returned to find their warehouses and factories burned decided, with the backing of their governments, to establish a foreign enclave. An island was created from a partially submerged sandbank in the Pearl River in the heart of Guangzhou, and by 1861 over 40 acres of land had been released for this purpose. Thus from the 1860s to 1949, with a short wartime intermission in 1941–46, foreign domination of Guangzhou came from Sha Mian.

Along with Western intrusion came revolutionary ideas, and by the early 1900s Guangzhou was a center of revolutionary activity. The sparks of the new ideas were fanned by widespread Chinese resentment of the power and influence possessed by foreigners operating in China. These new ideas eventually led to the overthrow of the Qing Dynasty by the revolutionary forces of Sun Yatsen in 1911. Much later, Mao Zedong and other leading Communists furthered the revolutionary reputation of Guangzhou by establishing the National Peasant Movement there during 1925 and 1926. Dedicated revolutionaries were trained to spread the Communist ideology throughout China.

Guangzhou was occupied by the Japanese at the end of 1938 during the Sino-Japanese war, and the city was once again under foreign control until the Japanese army withdrew at the conclusion of World War II. In the ensuing war between the Communists and the Nationalists, Guangzhou remained in the hands of the Nationalists until October 1949, when Communist armies took the city.

Now Guangzhou is a thriving, bustling center, one of China's bright economic stars, preeminent among the 14 coastal "open cities," and linked closely with neighboring Hong Kong. Overseas Chinese money and foreign investment is pouring in, fueled by the creation of three Special Economic Zones in Guangdong Province. Guangzhou is now setting the pace for economic development in China.

EXPLORING GUANGZHOU

Pearl River Boat Trip

If you are fascinated by river life and boats, you should take this trip along the Zhu Jiang, or Pearl River. The ferry departs from no. 1 Pier on Yanjiang Road, just east of the People's (Renmin) Bridge (the bridge that crosses the Pearl River near Sha Mian Island).

First the ferry steers along the Pearl River in an easterly direction, passes under Haizhu Bridge, and continues until reaching Zhongshan University (on the right or south bank of the river). At this point, the ferry turns back, passes under the Haizhu Bridge again, then under the People's Bridge, and turns south just as the White Swan Hotel comes abeam on the starboard (right-hand) side. The ferry then sails along this arm of the Pearl until reaching the shipyards, then heads back.

There are sailings each day at noon and 6:30 P.M. A meal is served on board during the two-hour cruise. The ferry carries 170 passengers. Your hotel or CITS can arrange tickets. Information is also available from the ticket office at the pier; tel. 664713.

Sha Mian Island

For the Western visitor Sha Mian Island is one of the most interesting places in Guangzhou. The island, originally an uninhabited sandbank, was established by building retaining walls and embankments; it is linked to the river bank by two small bridges. To the Chinese resident, however, the island recalls the period of foreign interference and exploitation and, particularly, the forced introduction of opium into China by foreign merchants.

In the mid-1850s, after the Second Opium War, the foreign merchants found their warehouses and factories burned and, rather than try to rebuild them again in the city, they decided to establish a foreign enclave on the reclaimed area of Sha Mian, which literally means "sand face." This aim was accomplished with a portion of the indemnity payments made by the Chinese for the damage caused. By 1861, 44 acres of land had been reclaimed, and embankments, paths, wide roads, and bridges were built. The British had the concession for the western four-fifths and the French the remaining one-fifth at the eastern end. The British Consulate was in the main street, while the French Consulate was at the eastern tip of the island. Magnificent villas were erected along the water's edge.

Chinese were not allowed on the island without permission, and the bridges were closed at night by iron gates.

In the early 1860s a Protestant church was built in the British concession and in the 1880s a small Catholic church was built in the French concession. The broad avenues were planted with a variety of trees, gardens were laid out, and tennis courts, a sailing club, and a football field were established.

Eventually the offices of several western banks were set up, as well as the hotel of distinction called The Victoria. By 1911 over 300 foreigners were resident on the island: British, French, Americans, Dutch, Italians, Germans, Japanese, and Portuguese.

In the 1920s Guangzhou was the center of Chinese revolutionary activities, and the presence of the foreign enclave on the island was a continual reminder of foreign domination of China. The first boilover of indignation took place in 1925 when a crowd massed on the embankment opposite the French concession. Foreign troops on the Sha Mian side opened fire with machine guns and killed 60 or 70 people. The crowd then attacked the island and incurred further losses. One resident of the island was killed.

The event became known as the Sha Kee Incident and led to a great number of anti-foreign demonstrations throughout China and a boycott of the island. As a result the residents of the island had to bring in provisions upriver from Hong Kong until the restrictions were finally lifted.

Life became quiet on the island after the turbulent early 20s, and even when the Japanese took Guangzhou at the end of 1938 there were few changes, although some residents left for Hong Kong. However, when Pearl Harbor was attacked in 1941, the foreign residents of Sha Mian were interned by the Japanese at Shanghai. After the war many residents went back to the island under the assumption that business would return to normal. But by October 1949 the Communist forces were in control, and by December 1950 all foreign assets were frozen and the few remaining foreigners left Sha Mian for good.

When you visit the island you can see the grand old buildings. In contrast to the White Swan nearby, they are dilapidated; the paint is peeling, pieces of masonry are falling out of the walls, the gardens are unkept. Many of the old buildings were torn down to make way for the new hotel; nevertheless you will enjoy strolling around and looking at those colonial relics that remain. Be sure you make a detour to the riverside embankment, where you can walk under the shade of the huge banyan trees, watch the multitude of river craft, or simply observe the Chinese schoolchildren practicing their sports and learning gymnastics.

Tomb of Emperor Wen

Hundreds of ancient objects have been recovered from Emperor Wen's tomb, and a museum has been constructed on the site to display the rare finds. Emperor Wen was the second ruler of Nanyue during the Western Han Dynasty (206 B.C.–A.D. 24). In those days the emperor's servants were buried with him, as evidenced by the skeletal remains found in the tomb. Among the 2,000-year-old objects found are rare bronzes, vessels of pre-

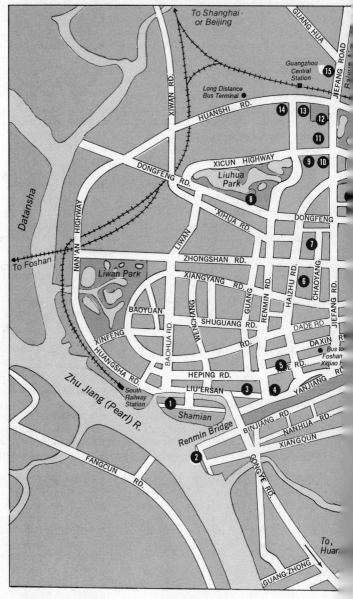

Points of Interest

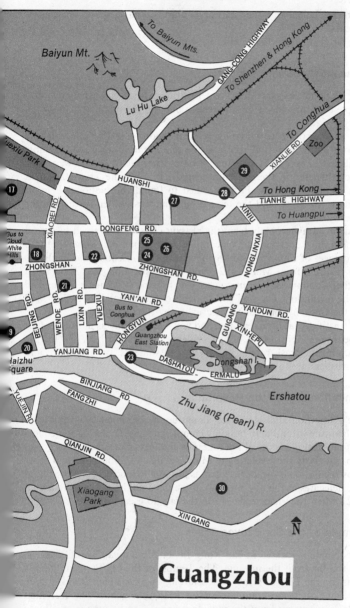

Guangzhou

cious metal, jade, ivory, gold and silver objects, weapons, and musical instruments.

The site is on Xianggang Hill, west of Yue Xiu Park.

Peasant Movement Institute

The National Peasant Movement Institute is housed in what was once a temple of Confucius at 42 Zhongshan Silu, on the northern side of the road.

The exterior of the temple is in excellent condition, and you should take care to note the beautiful roof and the fine examples of glazed-ceramic animals on the roof lines. The temple dates from the Ming and was originally constructed in the sixteenth century. In 1923 the Third Congress of the Chinese Congress Party decided to found the National Peasant Movement Institute, and the temple building was chosen as the site for this new institution.

Students, drawn mainly from the peasant class, were trained to spread the Communist doctrine and, on completion of their studies, went out into the provinces of China to lead the movement. Mao Zedong was in charge of the Institute from March 1926, and he worked alongside Zhou Enlai and other Communist revolutionaries who became well known during and after the revolution. The staff and students of the school dispersed in 1927 when the Canton Commune was crushed by the Guomindang.

The Institute has been restored, and you will see replicas in Mao's office and bedroom, dormitories of the students, the dining hall, the lecture rooms, and the wash rooms, complete with students' towels, mugs, and toothbrushes.

Exhibition Hall of the Revolution

The Exhibition Hall is located alongside the National Peasant Movement Institute in a modern building completed in 1960. It houses a collection of interesting historical photographs and texts concerning the revolution, particularly those relating to Mao Zedong and Zhou Enlai and other famous revolutionary leaders. There is also a fine model of the boat used by the delegates at the first meeting of the Communist Party at Shanghai in 1921 when they had to flee from the city to escape the police.

Temple of the Six Banyan Trees

The temple is located in Liu Rong Jie, or Six Banyan Trees Street. It is not too far from the mosque. The Temple of the Six Banyan Trees is famous for the Flower (Huata) or Liurong Pagoda which stands beside it and is one of the most familiar landmarks in Guangzhou. The decorated pagoda is deceiving: from the outside it appears to be nine stories high; inside it has 17 floors. Octagonal in shape, the pagoda stands 180 feet high.

The temple is believed to have been founded in A.D. 479 and the original pagoda in A.D. 537. The pagoda was burned down in 1098. The famous poet Su Dong Po once visited the temple and admired the six banyan trees. But they are no longer there. His reference to them in a poem well known in China has given the temple its name. Buddhists worship at the temple, so please respect their rituals.

Guangxiao Temple

Guangxiao Si is the oldest Buddhist temple in Guangzhou. Founded in A.D. 397, it grew over the centuries to be the largest Buddhist temple in South China.

In the seventh century, Hui Neng, the founder of the southern sect of Buddhism was a novice at the temple. (There is a statue of him in the temple.) The temple was destroyed on numerous occasions over the centuries and the extant buildings are of recent date. However, the two miniature pagodas that flank the entrance are over a thousand years old. Part of the temple houses the Guangdong Antiques Store. Exhibitions are held in the main hall.

The temple stands to the west of the Temple of the Six Banyan Trees and east of the intersection of Xihua and Renmin roads (tel. 885606).

Zhen Family Temple

The temple has had a varied history. Built in the 1890s by the patriarch of the Zhen clan as a Confucian school and as a place for worshiping the family's ancestors, it was closed after the revolution in 1949, later used as an army office (so preserving it from the depredations of the cultural revolutionaries), and is now the Guangdong Folk Arts and Crafts Center.

The interior is richly decorated, typical of the ornate style of Confucian temples of the late Qing. While the family memorial tablets have disappeared, the family shrine and altar are still intact.

Craft items are on sale at the temple, which is located on a street that runs from Liwan Road towards Zhongshan–7 Road (tel. 885259).

Wuxian Temple

The Wuxian Guan, or "Five Celestial Beings Temple," is supposedly where five supernatural beings were first sighted. They were the beings that appeared some millennia ago wearing colorful robes, each riding through the air on a male goat. Each goat carried a stem of rice in his mouth, to symbolize that the region would forever be free of famine. The Taoist temple was later erected on the site.

Although the site has a long history, the temple buildings are of recent origin. There is a large bell, cast under the Ming, weighing about five tons. The courtyard of the temple has a rock with an indentation said to be caused by the foot of one of the celestial beings.

The temple is tucked away in a laneway that runs off Xianyang–4 Road (which itself runs east–west between Renmin and Jiefang roads).

The Huaisheng Mosque

The Huaisheng Mosque is located at 56 Guangta Lu (south of Zhong Shan Lu) and is reputed to be the longest-established mosque in China.

Iron gates bar the entrance, but inside the archway high up on the right-hand side is a button which the visitor should press to gain entry. You will be ushered through a small pavilion into a courtyard surrounded by white walls and enclosing a number of shade trees. On the far side is the Prayer Room with modern Arabic script on the walls. Towering over the site is the 120-foot-high minaret. The original mosque is said to have been established in A.D. 627 by an uncle of Mohammed, but the present buildings are of recent construction and have little architectural interest.

The minaret is a gray cement-rendered building with an inner staircase leading up to the traditional balcony near the top; there are 153 steps. From the balcony there is an excellent view of some of the major sites of Guangzhou: to the north is the Pagoda of the Six Banyan Trees; beyond the pagoda is the concrete tower of the Yue Xiu, and beyond, the radio tower on the hill in the Yue Xiu Park; just below the radio tower you will note a blue-tiled roof which belongs to the Sun Yatsen monument (actually a theater capable of seating over 5,000 people); to the right of that in the Northeast is the 33-story Bai Yun Hotel.

If you walk around the balcony and look to the south, you will see the twin spires of the old Roman Catholic Cathedral. Nearby is the Guangzhou Binguan (hotel) located next to the Exhibition Building, which used to house the Guangzhou Fair exhibits before new facilities were built opposite the Dong Fang Hotel. Closer in, you will be able to observe the roof of the old Confucian Temple, which became the first Peasant Movement Institute established in China; very close to the minaret is the big bell tower.

The balcony also allows you to observe the buildings in the grounds of the mosque, and there is a good view of the courtyard of the temple and the school, which is used for the education of the Moslem-Chinese children.

A small tower rises from the balcony; about 30 feet high, it is accessible by an internal spiral staircase and reveals a definite lean.

Mausoleum of the Seventy-Two Martyrs

The Mausoleum of the Seventy-two Martyrs is on Yellow Flower Hill (Huanghuagang) in a park about a mile from the center of Guangzhou. It commemorates those killed in an unsuccessful uprising against the Qing Dynasty on April 27, 1911. The monument, a curious mixture of architectural styles both eastern and western, was built in 1918 from funds subscribed mostly by overseas Chinese. You will see replicas of the Statue of Liberty, a Versailles pavilion, and an Egyptian obelisk.

The mausoleum is located off Xian Lie Road, about midway between the Garden Hotel and the zoo.

Monument to the Guangzhou Uprising

The Monument to the Martyrs of the Guangzhou Uprising, located off Zhongshan Road, commemorates the heroism of those revolutionaries slain in the unsuccessful Communist uprising of December 11, 1927. The monument is set in a park possessing artificial lakes, footbridges, and pavilions. Rowboats may be hired. A special feature is the two slabs inscribed with the calligraphy of Zhou Enlai in memory of the 5,700 who died at the hands of the Guomindang during the fighting.

Sun Yatsen Memorial Hall

The memorial hall to commemorate one of China's great patriots, Sun Yatsen, was built in 1929–1931 from donations provided by local and overseas Chinese. The octagonal hall is 155 feet high and can seat almost 5,000 people. A bronze statue of Dr. Sun stands on a marble obelisk outside the memorial hall. The mansion of the Governor of Guangdong Province, later used by Dr. Sun as his Guangdong residence when he became the first president of the Republic of China in 1912, once stood at the site.

Sacred Heart Cathedral

The twin spires of the Roman Catholic Sacred Heart Cathedral are visible from many vantage points in the city. The best view of it is from the terrace of the Renmin (People's) Mansion. The cathedral, built in Gothic style after a design created by the French architect Guillemin, was consecrated in 1863; the main structure is 80 feet high, the spires attaining 160 feet. It was closed in 1966, reopened in 1979, and restored. It is known to the Chinese as Shishi or "Stone House."

The Cathedral is located near the river, on Yide Road. Mass is celebrated at 6 A.M. during the week; 6 A.M., 7.30 A.M., and 8.30 A.M. on Sunday. Tel. 883724.

Qingping Market

This colorful market, open all day (6 A.M. to 6 P.M.), is only a 15-minute stroll from the White Swan Hotel. Crowded, noisy, and not too clean, it will give you a glimpse of Chinese buying and selling basic produce. There is a huge section devoted to herbs and spices, plenty of unusual "dried animals" such as lizards, snakes, even starfish, and a livestock market that may sadden you. Pigs, pigeons, roosters, dogs, cats, snakes, pangolin, and even monkeys are for sale—all in a live or half-live state, waiting to be bought and slaughtered for human consumption. Many animals are also hung in carcass form.

At the river end of the market is a section dealing with antiques, such as ceramics, porcelains, scrolls, old coins, reproductions, and bric-a-brac.

The market is just beyond the bridge linking Sha Mian Island with Liuersan Road. From the north side of the island, cross the bridge and continue straight ahead for about 50 yards. (When seeking out the market, do not mistake the small footbridge at the eastern end of Sha Mian Island for the bridge above.)

Yue Xiu Park

Guangzhou's best-known park is Yue Xiu, located a few minutes' walk to the east from the Dong Fang Hotel. The five-story tower on a hilltop in the park is known as the **Zhen Hai Lou,** or "Tower Overlooking the Sea." The tower dates from the fourteenth century—the Ming Dynasty period—and is the oldest building in Guangzhou; indeed, it is one of the oldest buildings you will see in China. As its name suggests, it was a watchtower guarding the city against invasion. It is now a museum housing porcelain treasures and objects d'art dating from the Han period to the present day (see *Museums*).

There is a lake where you may hire rowboats, several Olympic-size swimming pools, steep hills providing the energetic visitor with excellent walks under a prolific growth of trees, a number of lookout points over the city, and at certain times of the year magnificent flower displays.

The **Statue of the Five Goats** stands just north of the tower. The statue, as does the Wuxian Temple commemorates the mythical origins of the city. The story goes that five celestial beings appeared out of the air, each riding a goat. Each goat carried a stem of rice in its mouth, symbolizing that the area would forever be free of famine.

Other Parks

A delightful park is the **Liuhua Gongyuan,** or "Park of the Stream of Flowers," on the westerly side of the Dong Fang. It has a number of lakes, pleasant paths along the lakeside, covered walks, and arched stone bridges. The Liu Hua Restaurant here is suitable for a quiet lunch (see *Chinese Cuisine*). The park is a great favorite with joggers.

Another park worth visiting is **Dongshan Gongyuan,** or "East Mountain Park," located a fair way from the city center on the western side. As you enter, you are confronted with rows of palm trees, giving the impression of a tropical rather than a temperate garden. There are many lakes in the park, and you may hire canoes to paddle around the shores and under the many humpback bridges. A zigzag bridge passes across one of the smaller lakes.

Of particular appeal is the promontory housing the Dong Hu Restaurant. You pass through an elliptical moongate set in a white wall capped by orange glazed tiles. The restaurant is to your left, but continue straight ahead to the small pavilion. It is a place to sit and contemplate; the only sounds you will hear are the cries of children, the squeak of rollicks, and the rattle of wind-blown leaves.

In contrast, Cultural Park is an active center of entertainment for the locals, especially in the evenings. You can watch cultural performances in the outdoor theaters, observe the youth of Guangzhou speeding around the roller-skating rink, take a ride on fairground-type rotary amusements, peer at the fish in the aquarium, visit one of the seven exhibition halls, or quietly sip *cha* in one of the teahouses. It is an interesting place to watch the people in a setting where they tend to be off guard. The entrance to the park is on Liuersan Road.

Gardens

Perhaps the most pleasant garden in the city of Guangzhou is the **Orchid Garden,** especially for those who want to get away from it all. Only a few minutes' walk from the Dong Fang Hotel and located off a small lane opposite the entrance to Yue Xiu Park, it is a peaceful haven despite its proximity to the noisy traffic of Liberation Road. The thick stands of bamboo, the groves of rare trees, and the lush tropical foliage filter out the hum of traffic, leaving you free to wander in quiet solitude or to sit peacefully on the veranda of the teahouse feeding the golden carp. There is a gazebo at the far end of the garden overlooking a lily-choked pond. Look carefully at the opposite shore and you will see hidden in the foliage a small stone pagoda. Open daily, 7:30–11:30 A.M. and 1:30–5 P.M. Closed Wednesday.

In the Orchid Garden there is a small gateway that leads to the **Tomb of Waggas,** who founded the Huaisheng Mosque in A.D. 627. There are other graves of the Islamic faithful, as well as a stone arch.

If you are interested in miniature trees and miniature landscapes, then you should visit Xiyuan, or **"West Garden,"** where there are thousands of examples of this art form. The garden is in a walled-off section of Liuhua Park, at the western end. The entrance is on Dongfeng–1 Road.

Old Guangdong University

The university site now houses the **Lu Xun Museum** and the **Guangdong Provincial Museum.** It is located north of Wen Ming Lu Street not far from the Provincial Revolutionary Museum.

The original university was established in 1924 by Dr. Sun Yatsen, and in 1926 the name was changed to the Zhong Shan University in his honor. Lu Xun, one of China's foremost revolutionary writers, became head of the Literary Department of the university in 1927 and worked and lived in the Bell Tower Building, which is now a museum devoted to his works. Many meetings of the Guangzhou branch of the Chinese Communist Party were held in the Bell Tower Building during the revolutionary period. The museum was established in 1958.

Zhong Shan University

Zhong Shan is one of the oldest and largest universities in Guangzhou. Visitors to the Guangzhou Fair will usually have an opportunity to go there when the regular soccer matches take place on Sundays at the university's outdoor stadium. The university provides a range of courses, the best known of which are in liberal arts, natural science, and medicine.

Guangzhou Zoo

Guangzhou Zoo is probably the best zoo in China; it boasts such animals as the panda and the golden monkey. The zoo is open from 8 A.M. to 5:30 P.M. There is a restaurant and a place selling snacks.

Observatory

Guangzhou has a fine observatory, and it is sometimes possible to visit it, particularly if you are in a delegation with a special interest in astronomy or other scientific subjects. Ask CITS.

Guangzhou Trade Fair

The Chinese Export Commodities Fair, or Guangzhou Trade Fair, is held twice a year, April 15–May 5 and October 15–November 5, at the Guangzhou Foreign Trade Center. China conducts a great deal of its foreign trade—now estimated at about 15 percent of the total—at the fair. Each fair is attended by thousands of international traders.

The fairground is located between the Guangzhou railway station and the Dong Fang Hotel. Many of China's vast range of products and commodities are on display, and over 40,000 different items are available for sale (see *Doing Business in China*).

EXCURSIONS FROM GUANGZHOU

If you have traveled to Guangzhou by train, you cannot have failed to notice the scenery of Guangdong Province. It is one of the most beautiful provinces in China, and you should try to make time available for an excursion to some of the areas located in the countryside.

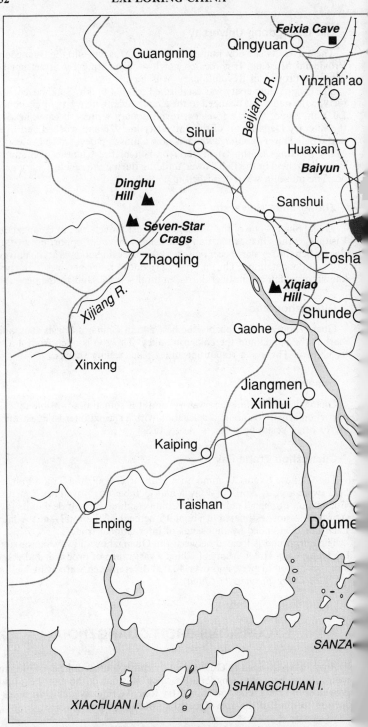

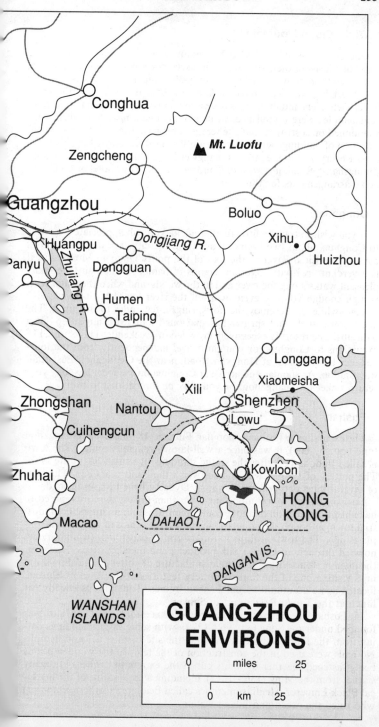

Conghua

Zengcheng

▲ *Mt. Luofu*

Guangzhou

Boluo

Xihu •

Huizhou

Huangpu

Dongjiang R.

Panyu

Dongguan

Zhujiang R.

Humen

Taiping

Longgang

Xiaomeisha

Zhongshan

Xili •

Shenzhen

Nantou

Lowu

Cuihengcun

Zhuhai

Kowloon

HONG KONG

Macao

DAHAO I.

DANGAN IS.

WANSHAN ISLANDS

GUANGZHOU ENVIRONS

0   miles   25

0   km   25

White Cloud Mountain

One favorite is White Cloud Mountain, or Bai Yun Shan, about nine miles northeast of the city. You should set aside a half-day for this excursion, even though the bus trip takes only 30 minutes. The peak is just over 1,400 feet high and commands a fine view over the town and the Pearl River Delta. The mountain was once a religious center, and many magnificent temples were established on its slopes. These have long since been abandoned or destroyed, but the temple sites have been used for the construction of buildings which serve mainly as health resorts. Express buses depart every 15 minutes from Guangwei Lu, a small street that runs off Zhongshan-5 Road, just west of Children's Park. Your hotel or CITS can make arrangements for this tour.

Conghua

If you wish to travel a little further afield, you will appreciate a journey to Conghua, about two hours by bus from the city. Located on the west bank of the Liuxi River at the foot of the pretty Qingyun Mountains, it is a verdant area with luxuriant stands of bamboo. You can take many pleasant walks along the river and in the woods, and when the water level is high enough you can even swim off the river bank. Most people visit to rest awhile and to enjoy the hot springs a few miles to the north. The guest house at the hot springs has spacious rooms with huge step-down bathtubs. The resort is excessively crowded on weekends. There are CITS excursions to Conghua, or you can travel independently from the long-distance bus terminal at Hongyun Road, near the Guangzhou East Railway Station. As soon as you arrive at Conghua on the local bus, buy your return ticket to Guangzhou, or you may be forced to stop over.

Foshan

The excursion to Foshan is popular. Situated 18 miles from Guangzhou (one hour by bus), it was once a well-known religious center. The town is called Buddha Hill after the statue standing on a small hill in the town. The pottery of Foshan was known over a thousand years ago. The sites of several kilns dating from the Song Dynasty have been excavated.

Foshan, once a more important town than Guangzhou, is reputed to have had a population of about one million. It is still an important industrial town, although the population is now only a third of what it was centuries ago. The town is famous for its crafts: papercuts, (which are renowned throughout China), silk products, and metal castings. However, the main craft activity is still the manufacture of pottery. You should not miss visiting one of the famous pottery factories at the town of **Shiwan**, located some 20 minutes from Foshan by bus. Tour groups usually eat lunch at the Taodu Restaurant in Shiwan.

In Foshan the interesting Temple of Ancestors, or Zu Miao, was founded under the Song (A.D. 960–1279), with some extant buildings dating from the fourteenth century, when the site became a Taoist temple. No nails were used in the construction of the temple, the wooden beams being fastened together by joints cut in the extremities. There are many statues from the Ming (1368–1644), including a large statue of the mythical Black Emperor, Heidi (sometimes called Beidi, or Northern Emperor) who ruled the ocean and inland waters.

One-day tours to Foshan are organized by CITS. Independent travelers can get to Foshan from the bus station in Guangzhou located west of the intersection of Jiefang Nan and Daxin roads, about a block north of the Sacred Heart Cathedral.

Seven Star Crags

The Seven Star Crags near Zhaoqing is about 60 miles west of Guangzhou, and the drive takes about 3–4 hours one way. You will pass through some fine scenery on the way and be rewarded on arrival with magnificent mountain views. The landscape resembles a miniature Guilin, and photographers delight in the mist-shrouded mountains and rivers.

Sights in the town of Zhaoqing are the Chongxi Pagoda, the Plum Monastery, and the Yuejiang Tower.

Dinghushan

Dinghushan, about 12 miles east of Zhaoqing, is renowned for its beautiful mountain scenery. It is a popular resort for the locals and therefore crowded, especially during summer. The two famous temples are the Tang Dynasty White Cloud (Baiyuan) Temple and the Ming Dynasty Auspicious Cloud (Qingyun) Temple, formerly the Lotus (Lianhua) Nunnery.

Guangzhou to Hainan Island

An interesting excursion for those who like to get off the beaten track is the bus trip to Hainan Island in the far south of Guangdong Province. The first stop is at Foshan (see above) and the next at Xiqiaoshan.

Xiqiaoshan is a delightful scenic spot about 42 miles south of Guangzhou. Here there are 72 peaks, many caves, and over a score of waterfalls. On the crater lake, Tianhu, dragon-boat races are held each year, a tradition that is several centuries old. The market town of Guanshan stands at the foot of Xiqiaoshan.

Jiangmen is a pretty river town about 75 miles south of Guangzhou. The Cha An Temple has been restored. It is also known as the Sixth Master Temple, after the sixth successor of the founder of the Cha'an or Zen sect of Buddhism. Donghu Park is a pleasant place for a stroll.

Nature lovers should visit the bird sanctuary on **Xinhui Island** in the Tianmu River, some 15 minutes south of Jiangmen. Thousands of egrets nest there. The best time to visit is at dusk. Other scenic attractions there are the Guifeng Mountains, Yuhu Lake, and the Tiancheng Lake. Nearby, on the hill overlooking **Chakang** village stands the Lingyun Pagoda.

The bus then passes through Kaiping, Enping, Yangjiang, and Zhigong, before arriving in Dianbai county.

In **Dianbai,** there are Qing Dynasty-style viewing pavilions at Bohe and Shuidong, built to allow visitors to see the "Green Wall" (a wind-break) that follows the coast of the South China Sea. There is a beach in Shuidong below Tiger Head Hill, and scuba-diving facilities opposite at Chicken Island.

The bus goes on to Maoming and Zhanjiang, the first a petrochemical town, the second a deep-water supply port for the South China Sea oil fields.

Zhanjiang, 280 miles southeast of Guangzhou, is on nearly the same latitude as Hanoi in Vietnam, some 300 miles to the west. It is one of China's "14 open coastal cities." About one and a half miles out of the town there is a beach, diving center, and amusement park at the Tachun

Island holiday village. Huguang, about 13 miles from Zhanjiang, is a well-known scenic spot. The Huguang Village Resort, located on the shore of the crater lake, features a hotel, holiday village, and a golf course. The Lengyan Temple and the White Robe Nunnery stand nearby.

To get to Hainan Island from Zhanjiang, you must either take the ferry to Haikou, a journey of some 80 nautical miles; or a bus to Hai An at the southern tip of Leizhou Peninsular, then a ferry to Haikou; or a half-hour flight to Haikou.

Hainan Island

Hainan Island may be reached by a 65–minute flight from Guangzhou or by a combination of bus and ferry from there (see above). From Hong Kong there is a flight and a ferry service to Haikou.

Haikou offers very little to the visitor. About the only sights of interest are the market, the flotilla of junks on the river in the northern part of the town, the Hai Rui Tomb, and the temple dedicated to the "five banished officials."

Tours of east Hainan by minibus or car may be arranged by CITS. (The west of Hainan is inaccessible for security reasons, there being many Chinese naval bases along the coast.) The four-day, five-night excursion takes in **Wenchang** (famous for its chicken dish), **Qionghai, Xinglong** (where many overseas Chinese and refugees from the Sino-Vietnam war have settled), **Lingshui,** and the port of **Sanya,** which is "Heaven's Limit."

Sanya, also known as **Yaxian,** is not the southern extremity of China—this accolade being given to an island further south in the South China Sea. The tourist resort in Sanya, **Luhuitou,** has new hotels, a golf course, and game-fishing facilities. The beaches there are tranquil and unspoiled.

The tour usually returns by the central route through Hainan, passing through **Baoting,** the administrative center of the Li and Miao minority groups, and Tongzhi (where there are Miao villages). The southern half of Hainan Island is the autonomous region of the Li and Miao minorities. There is also a visit en route to Wuzhi Shan, or Five-Fingered Mountain.

Guangzhou to Macao

A bus excursion from Guangzhou to the border town of Gongbei leads also to Macao.

The first county of note is **Panyu,** a name that was first used for the settlement that became the city of Guangzhou. The name is derived from a combination of **Panshan** and **Yushan,** two hills where the Qin Dynasty established a city in 214 B.C. The attractions of Panyu are Lotus Hill and the Yuyuan Garden.

Shunde is the next stop and there are fine scenic spots in the region. Of particular interest is the Qinghai Garden at Daliang town, one of the four most famous gardens in Guangdong Province.

Xiaolan is worth a stop when the chrysanthemums are in bloom, as there are flower displays and fairs that delight the visitor.

Further south lies **Zhongshan County,** an area well known for its hot springs. Guests may stay at the Zhongshan Hot Springs Resort (tennis, swimming, fishing) or at the Zhongshan Hot Springs Golf Club, where the 18-hole course was designed by Arnold Palmer. One-and two-day golf excursions are available from Hong Kong; golfers are picked up at their hotels by limo and sped by jetfoil to Zhuhai port, a one-hour journey.

Siqi, known officially as Zhongshan, is the administrative center of the county; it has an amusement center. **Cuiheng Village** is well known because the former residence of Sun Yatsen is located there.

From Cuiheng Village the road leads to **Zhuhai,** a municipality earmarked for rapid development under the Special Economic Zone (SEZ) program. The municipality boasts more than 80 hotels, many with excellent facilities, and a resort with a full range of convention facilities as well as a race track. The shopping center has architecture inspired by Beijing's Imperial Palaces.

Zhuhai is connected to Hong Kong by ferry from Jiuzhou Port, and by helicopter. The authorities are planning an international airport.

Gongbei is the border town in Zhuhai Municipality that fronts Macao. It offers nothing but commercial and residential high rises. There is a bus service from Gongbei to Macao.

Shenzhen

Shenzhen Municipality, on the east side of the Pearl River delta, is the "twin" of the Zhuhai Municipality on the southwest side. It too has a region that has been set aside as a SEZ.

The new superhighway connects Guangzhou and Shenzhen. It may also be reached from Hong Kong (one-day excursion) by ferry, by bus, or by a train/bus combination. The port for Shenzhen is Shekou, to the west of Shenzhen town. An international airport is on the drawing board.

Shenzhen is being developed both as a resort and commercial/light industrial center. Many new hotels have been built and resort facilities established. There is a convention center, a golf course, camping at Shenzhen Reservoir, and an amusement park.

The **Splendid China** theme park—well worth a visit—has miniature (scale of 1:15) replicas of the 74 greatest sites in China, including the Great Wall, the Ming Tombs, the Forbidden City, the Temple of Heaven, the Potala Palace, West Lake in Hangzhou, the Yangzi Gorges, Guilin's Karst mountains, the Stone Forest of Yunnan, and the terra-cotta army of Xian. Splendid China also has a life-size Old Suzhou Shopping Street, a Food Street serving a variety of regional cuisines, and a Botanical Garden.

A resort nearby at Xiaomeisha (Suimuisha) has a golf course, tennis courts, beach, sailing, and windsurfing. Guests go directly to the resort from Hong Kong by boat.

Shekou

Shekou is about 20 miles west of the town of Shenzhen and is the major port for the Shenzhen SEZ. Shekou is also being developed as a resort area. The amusement park is very popular with Hong Kong residents. Unusual accommodations are available on a large ship berthed at the port, the old *Minghua* that once carried cruise passengers to China. Shekou may be reached from Hong Kong by ferry, and by hovercraft in just 40 minutes. Day excursions are available from Hong Kong.

Shenzhen to Shantou

Slow local buses make this journey, but most visitors prefer the airconditioned buses specially introduced for this excursion. CITS (tel. 2151, 2149) located at the railway station in Shenzhen will arrange tickets; or try the CTS office next to the Overseas Chinese Hotel. Buses depart at noon each day.

Huizhou is some 50 miles north of Shenzhen. The area is blessed with beautiful mountains and lakes, the most renowned being West Lake, which is in fact five lakes connected by six bridges. The Song Dynasty poet Su Dongpo lived in Huizhou for a time. A memorial hall has been built in his honor; the tomb of his beloved concubine Zhaoyun is nearby.

Sizhou Pagoda on Mount Gushan provides a fine view of the region, especially of the wide Dongjiang (East River). There are hot springs in the region, and a scenic spot called the Nine Dragon Pool. Mount Luofu has a number of pavilions—the most interesting being the Taoist Chongxu Temple. The Herb Washing Pond and the "Place for Making Gehong Elixir" are both of interest.

Haifeng is about midway between Shenzhen and Shantou. The town is known for the Fangfan ("Square Dining") Pavilion, where Wen Tianxing, a Song prime minister, was captured while he and his troops were having a meal. About 25 miles further east, in the coastal town of **Lufeng,** the Fuxinglei Pagoda is of interest. The beach near Mount Guanyin will give you a glimpse of what life is like for the fishermen in this region.

On the way to **Chaoyang,** a county on the coast further north, you will pass the Lingshan Temple (first built under the Tang), the Wenguan Pagoda, and Gourd Hill. Your destination, Shantou, is just across the river.

Shantou

The port city of Shantou, formerly Swatou, is the second largest city in Guangdong Province. Located on the mouth of the Rong River, Shantou has been rescued from obscurity by being earmarked for accelerated development as a SEZ. There are two municipalities: Chaozhou and Shantou, the region often being called Chaoshan.

The Shantou region is populated by people who have distinct cultural differences and speak the Hakka and Chaozhou dialects, although Cantonese and Mandarin are also spoken. An estimated four million people from the region live abroad, with over a million living in Hong Kong alone, the others being distributed mainly throughout Southeast Asia.

Shantou existed simply as a fishing village until 1855, when Britain gained concessions there. Consequently, there are very few historic or cultural sights of interest to the visitor. Apart from Mayu Island at the entrance of Shantou Harbor, which is being developed as a beach resort, there is only the Jiaoshi scenic spot on the south bank of the Rong River, and Zhongshan Park.

There are many ways to reach Shantou. Apart from the bus journey from Shenzhen, there are buses from Guangzhou, Hong Kong, and Xiamen. There are also flights from Hong Kong and Xiamen and ferries from Guangzhou and Hong Kong.

Chaozhou

The town of Chaozhou borders on Shantou to the north and, unlike its neighbor, has a history that spans more than 2,000 years. Under the Tang, disgraced or "relegated" officials were exiled to Chaozhou. It is one of the so-called four famous ancient towns of China.

The Kaiyuan Temple was built in A.D. 738 under the Tang; it has some fine statues. Of particular interest are the Buddhist texts given to the temple by Qing Emperor Qianlong. Other attractions are the Phoenix Pagoda overlooking the river, West Lake Park, the Xiangzi Bridge, and the Wengong Temple built under the Han.

Chaozhou is well known in Chinese cuisine for a style of cooking that, while similar in many ways to Cantonese, is characterized by the use of sauce-dips of many flavors.

PRACTICAL INFORMATION FOR GUANGZHOU

Note: All telephone numbers in Guangzhou have six digits. If you are calling a telephone number listed with only five digits, repeat the first digit when dialing.

FACTS AND FIGURES. At 23° 07′N 113° 15′E, Guangzhou is at approximately the same latitude as Havana, Cuba.

It is 1,150 miles south of Beijing by air: 2¼ hours' direct flight; 1,440 miles south of Beijing by rail, 34–35 hours' train journey; 965 miles southwest of Shanghai by air, 2 hours' direct flight; 1,135 miles southwest of Shanghai by rail, 35 hours' train journey.

Guangzhou is 50 feet above sea level.

The table shows the weather pattern in Guangzhou during the year.

Guangzhou Temperature Range and Average Rainfall

	Temperature High (°F)	Temperature Low (°F)	Number of Days with Rainfall	Monthly Rainfall (in inches)
January	65	49	7	0.9
April	77	65	15	6.8
July	91	77	16	8.1
October	85	67	6	3.4

WHEN TO GO. Guangzhou is in a subtropical weather belt. In summer it is hot and humid, the rainfall heavy, with numerous thunderstorms. No pronounced winter season exists; although occasional days can be very cold, generally winter is mild and pleasant. In spring the weather starts to get warmer and the humidity higher; the rainy season begins in April and continues through September, about 80 percent of the yearly average of 64 inches falling in these six months. Autumn is a delightful season with warm days, low humidity, and infrequent rainfall.

The province is frequently affected by typhoons in August and September. Northerly breezes prevail October through February; southerly winds are more evident in the other months.

The most pleasant time to visit Guangzhou is October through March.

WHAT TO WEAR. Light and informal clothing is suitable in Guangzhou. Men do not need a jacket or tie; women are most comfortable in cotton dresses or lightweight slacks. In the winter months the temperature may drop suddenly, and it is useful to have a sweater handy.

In the rainy season (April–May) an umbrella is essential, but, if you have failed to bring one, you can purchase another very cheaply at the hotel shop or in the department store.

HOW TO GET THERE. The *Planning Your Trip* section discusses the major international routes to China and specifically covers travel between Hong Kong (the nearest international entry point) and Guangzhou. Note that Guangzhou now has two main railway stations, Guangzhou Central and Guangzhou East. If you are traveling from Hong Kong to Guangzhou on the "regular" train, stopping at Shenzhen en route, you will arrive at Guangzhou East Station.

HOTELS. Guangzhou has excess hotel capacity except during the periods of the Guangzhou Fair (April 15–30 and October 15–30), when all hotels are heavily booked and much higher rates apply.

Bai Yun Hotel. The Bai Yun (White Cloud), a 33-story hotel with 720 rooms, all air-conditioned, is in the northeast section of the city. While a little isolated, it is quiet and peaceful. There is an inner courtyard just off the entrance lobby which is most attractive, huge natural rocks supporting three large trees have been retained, and a waterfall runs over the rocks into a deep rock pool. Many tour groups stay at the Bai Yun, and business travelers find that the commercial services are efficiently run. There is a Western food restaurant on the ground floor and one serving Chinese food on the first floor. When the hotel is near-full there are often long waits for the elevators; and the air-conditioning system often becomes overtaxed. Double rooms from ¥ 135 plus 15 percent service. 367 Huanshi Road East. Tel. 333998. Telex 44698. Cable 0682.

Central Hotel. A part of the International Exhibition Center, the six-story Central provides standard accommodations in 234 guest rooms. A business center, 45 offices for rent, three restaurants (one of them fast-food), a shopping arcade, and an outdoor swimming pool. Double rooms from US$55 plus 15 percent service. 33 Ji Chang Lu, Sanyuanli. Tel. 678331. Telex 44664 GICSO CN. Fax 678331 ext. 1802.

China Hotel. This huge hotel with over 1,200 rooms and suites is situated opposite the Guangzhou Trade Fair, not far from Guangzhou Railway Station. All rooms have color TV, refrigerators, direct-dial telephones. There is a 24-hour room service, as well as a same-day laundry and dry-cleaning service. The hotel facilities include three lounges, five restaurants offering excellent Chinese and Western food, and a "food street" with stalls featuring a variety of authentic Chinese cuisines. Private banquets from 12 to 1,200 can be accommodated. The business center provides secretarial services, interpreters, a cable office, and telex facilities. There is also a beauty salon, gymnasium, sauna, massage service, bank, medical clinic, florist, post office, Friendship store, and 9-lane bowling alley. Outdoor facilities include the best outdoor swimming pool in the city, as well as a tennis court. Mercedes Benz limos may be hired. Double rooms from US$80, suites from US$150, plus 15 percent service. Liu Hua Lu. Tel. 666888. Telex 44888 CHLGZ CN. Fax 677014.

Dong Fang Hotel. Once the foremost hotel in Guangzhou, the Dong Fang has in recent years been eclipsed by newer establishments. Consisting of an old wing with 400 rooms and three new 11-story wings with 700 rooms, the hotel surrounds a small park with well-laid-out gardens and pond in the inner courtyard. It is centrally located, just a short walk from the main railway station and opposite the entrance to the Guangzhou Fair grounds. The old wing, renovated in 1979, has air-conditioned rooms with color TV, refrigerator, and direct-dial telephone. Some rooms have balconies. Many guests prefer the renovated rooms in the old wing to the modern yet more austere rooms in the new wing. Hotel amenities include a sauna, billiards room, electronic games center, beauty salon, flower shop, art gallery, photography center, shopping arcade (on the ground floor of the old wing), book store, bank, post office, cable and telex room, and medical clinic. There are many Chinese and Western restaurants, coffee shops, and bars located throughout the four wings of the hotel; also a disco. Double rooms from US$50, plus 15 percent service. 120 Liu Hua Road. Tel. 669900. Telex 44439 GZDFH CN. Cable 4221. Fax 662775.

Garden Hotel. This luxury hotel, conveniently located at the corner of Huanshi Road East and Jianshi Road Six, is set in two acres of lush gardens, only a five-minute drive from the railway station and the ferry terminals on the Pearl River. Chauffeur-driven limousines are available for transport to and from all transport terminals. Hotel facilities include eight restaurants and bars, five spacious seminar rooms, and a multi-purpose hall seating up to 1,400 people. The business center is extensive. On the spacious podium roof are squash courts, pools, a health club, and Chinese garden. The hotel offers 1,146 rooms of luxury standard. Double rooms from US$75 plus 15 percent service. 368 Huanshi Dong Lu. Tel. 338989. Telex 44788 GDHTL CN. Cable 4735. Fax 350467.

Holiday Inn City Center. A 24-story hotel offering first-class accommodations in 431 rooms, the Holiday Inn adjoins a large exhibition center and has three restaurants, a coffee shop, a business center, convention facilities, a health club, a swimming pool, a shopping arcade, and a cinema seating 800. Double rooms from US$75 plus 15 percent service. Huanshi Dong Lu. Tel. 766999. Telex 441045 HICCG CN. Fax 753126.

Jiangnan. On the south bank of the Pearl River, opposite the city center, the 28-story Jiangnan, with 480 rooms, has less expensive accommodations than those of similar quality hotels across the river. Rooms have air-conditioning, minibar, IDD telephone, color TV. Dining facilities include French and Cantonese restaurants, coffee shop, and a garden eatery. Pool, health club, and disco were scheduled to open in 1990. The hotel is about five minutes by car from the city's Hong Kong hovercraft dock. Double rooms from US$55 plus 15 percent service. 348 Jiangnan Da Road. Tel. 418888. Telex 441032 NOVGZ CN. Cable 7546. Fax 429645.

Ocean Hotel. Three miles from Baiyun airport, the Ocean has 11 floors of offices and 10 floors with 190 guest rooms; maritime decor, three restaurants, and a business center. Double rooms from $US50 plus 15 percent service. 412 Huanshi Road. Tel. 765988. Telex 44638 GOHOL CN. Cable 6054. Fax 765475.

White Swan Hotel. Located on Shamian Island overlooking the Pearl River, the White Swan Hotel provides five-star international standard accommodations. Rooms are air-conditioned, carpeted, and have IDD telephone service to Hong Kong, refrigerator, color TV, and night-table console. The 28-story hotel has four room categories: deluxe double suites, three-room suites, garden rooms, standard rooms. The Tower has 887 rooms; the five-story Riverside Garden Building has 17 apartments. Facilities include swimming pool; gym; sauna; beauty parlors; shopping arcade; dance floor; bars; disco; and 600-seat conference hall. There are 2 business centers equipped with translators, typists, telex, and cable facilities. The hotel staff is well trained. Dining facilities are extensive, and include three Chinese restaurants, a Western restaurant, a Japanese restaurant, a coffee shop, and a teahouse. The hotel is about a 30-minute drive from the airport and a 15-minute drive from the train station. Guests arriving by train can make use of the reception desk maintained at the station and take advantage of the free shuttle bus provided by the hotel. Double rooms from US$60, suites from US$150, plus 15 percent service. 1 South Street, Shamian Island. Tel. 886968. Telex 44688 WSH CN. Cable 8888. Fax 861188.

Other Hotels. The hotels listed above are the top quality establishments of Guangzhou. Among other establishments offering reasonable accommodations are the **Cathay** (tel. 765787); the **Dongshan,** a 500-room hotel (tel. 773722); the **Guangquan,** with hot springs baths (tel. 661334); the **Guangdong Guest House,** set in spacious grounds (tel. 332950); the **Guangzhou Hotel,** in the center of town (tel. 338668); the **Liu Hua,** opposite the main railway station (tel. 668800); the **Nanhu** or **South Lake,** set in superb rural scenery but lacking in amenities (tel. 776367); and the **Renmin Mansion,** overlooking the Pearl River (tel. 661445).

RESTAURANTS. The restaurants of Guangzhou serve magnificent meals and banquets, and you should take the opportunity of dining in at least one of them in this major gastronomic center of China. You might also like to visit **Food Street** in the China Hotel and **Laiwan Market** in the Garden Hotel. The following, in alphabetical order, are the "top ten" restaurants located outside hotels (except for the Dong Fang. A description of each restaurant and its specialities is given in the chapter *Chinese Cuisine.*

The Top Ten Restaurants of Guangzhou

Name and Address	Translation	Telephone
Ban Xi 151 Xiang Yang Rd. 1	Small Brook (literally "Half Stream") Restaurant	885655, 888706, 889318
Bei Yuan 318 Dengfeng Beilu	North Garden Restaurant	332471, 332466, 333365
Datong 63 Yanjiang Rd.	Great Harmony	885365, 888988, 885933
Dong Fang 120 Liuhua Road	Easterly Restaurant	669900
Dongjiang 337 Zhongshan Si Lu	East River Restaurant	335568, 335343
Dongshan	East Mountain Restaurant	770556,

Name and Address	*Translation*	*Telephone*
Dongshan, 1 Guigang Malu		776108
Guangzhou 2 Xiuli 2-Road	Guangzhou Restaurant	887136, 887840
Nan Yuan 120 Qianjin Lu	South Garden Restaurant	550532, 448380, 550542
Shahe 79 Xianlie Dong Rd., Shahe	River Sands Restaurant	775639, 777239, 770956
Yu Yuan 90 Liwan Nanlu	Happy Garden Restaurant	888552, 888369, 886838

Three Banquets in Guangzhou. If your time is short you may not have time to try many of the Guangzhou restaurants. Here, then, is a recommendation for a "three-banquet" stay in the city. Gourmets should remember that a banquet can be prepared for lunch as well as for dinner. The restaurants have been chosen on the basis of their preparing the best food available in Guangzhou in magnificent surroundings. They are: **Nan Yuan** (South Garden Restaurant), 151 Xiang Yang Rd. 1, tel. 550532, 550542; **Ban Xi**, tel. 885655; **Bei Yuan** (North Garden Restaurant), 318 Dengfeng Beilu, tel. 332471.

TOURIST INFORMATION. CITS (tel. 677856) is located at 179 Huanshi Road, to the right when facing the entrance to Guangzhou's main railway station. There are branch offices at major hotels to service guests staying at those establishments, e.g., in Room 2366 in the old wing of the Dong Fang Hotel (tel. 662427). Open daily 8:30–11:30 A.M. and 2–5 P.M.

Air China and **South China Airlines** (tel. 661803) is at 181 Huanshi Road, also to the right when facing the main railway station, and next door to CITS. For local flights, tel. 662123 ext. 904.

PSB (tel. 331060, 330003) is located at 863 Jiefang Bei Road, around the corner and south from the Dong Fang Hotel. It is opposite the road that leads to the Zhenhai Tower. Open daily 8 A.M.–12 noon and 2:30–5:30 P.M.

HOW TO GET AROUND. By taxi. Taxis are normally available outside your hotel. The fare charged depends not only on distance covered plus waiting time, but also on the type of taxi, e.g., 4-passenger or 5-passenger vehicle. The dispatcher at most hotels will speak English and will send the taxi to the destination you require. However, some hotels do not have a dispatcher, in which case taxis must be arranged for at the reception desk. Taxis can be hailed in the street.

Always carry small notes and change; your driver will often not be able to change large notes. If you forget, you will be delayed while your driver tries to get change from a nearby shop or pedestrian. You may ask the driver for a receipt if you wish. Never offer a tip.

Public transport. Guangzhou also has an efficient system of public buses and trolley buses. They look a bit dilapidated, they are crowded, and their wooden seats are not exactly inviting, but they do (sometimes) get you where you want to go. An English-language map of bus routes is available at your hotel. This form of transport is recommended for adventurous people who are not in a hurry and who can overcome the language barrier. Keep in mind that traffic often moves slowly.

On foot. Taking a stroll in Guangzhou is a good way to get a feel of the Chinese way of life in a big city. If you have a sense of adventure, wander where you like, at any hour; you will be perfectly safe. The large avenues are lined with banyan trees, the smaller streets flanked by cool arcades where shops spill their wares out onto the footpath. The streets are crowded, so don't try to hurry. There are myriads of small lanes to explore where you will find small factories turning out their merchandise side by side with herbal tea shops and covered markets bulging ·with grains, spices, and vegetables.

Take a stroll along the river's edge in the center of the city, along what used to be called "the Bund," and watch the great variety of river craft go by. If you wish to walk in well-established areas, try the parks and gardens or the zoo.

An unusual stroll for the early riser is to the Qingping Market opposite the north bank of Sha Mian Island. There you will find a vast array of produce and a fascinating display of meat, poultry, seafood, spices, as well as a variety of live animals. The market opens around 6 A.M. and closes at 6 P.M.

By bicycle. If you are game to take on Guangzhou's traffic, you can hire a bicycle at a small place opposite the White Swan Hotel on Sha Mian Island.

RADIO AND TELEVISION. For those visitors who speak Cantonese, the People's Broadcasting Station in Guangzhou broadcasts on 1060 kilocycles Mondays through Sundays from 5 A.M. to midnight. Programs in the national language are broadcast on another unit of the Guangzhou People's Broadcasting Station.

If you have brought your radio you will be able to pick up AM and FM broadcasts beamed from Hong Kong, as well as overseas services of the Voice of America and the BBC.

Guangzhou has a television station, and you can easily pick up the broadcasts on the set in your room. However, most visitors prefer to tune in to the Hong Kong broadcasts, which are in English as well as in Cantonese.

HEALTH. There are no real health problems associated with a visit to Guangzhou. Sometimes the change in diet may bring minor stomach upsets, but these can be controlled readily by the usual remedies. However, be careful not to drink water from the faucet, even in your hotel. Instead, use the boiled water provided in your room, even to clean your teeth. If you are going out on a tour, take a small container of the boiled water to sip during the day.

MEDICAL SERVICES. If you do fall ill and require medical attention, your hotel will assist you to the **First People's Hospital of Guangzhou,** telephone 886421, or the **First Hospital of Guangzhou Medical College** (Foreigners' Outpatient Clinic), telephone 770371. The Dong Fang Hotel's medical room for foreigners is open 8 A.M.–10 P.M.

SECURITY. Guangzhou, like other cities in China, is safe. You can walk around anywhere without fear. However, in crowded places, be careful to keep your valuables out of sight and in an inaccessible place because there are pickpockets about. Keep your hotel door locked when absent from your hotel.

WHAT TO SEE. The major event of the year is the **Guangzhou Fair,** held every year April 15–30 and October 15–30. A walk through the display areas of the fair is a good way to gain an appreciation of the variety and quality of the products from China's agriculture and industry. Many working models of China's commune systems and oil-producing installations are on display, and many films depict China's agriculture and industry.

Sha Mian has a great appeal to the visitor. It is an island made from a sandbank situated near the Renmin Bridge and was established from 1861 as a foreign enclave, mainly British and French. Today the buildings remain, though in shabby condition, but it is pleasant to stroll down the wide boulevards and tree-shaded walks. The White Swan Hotel is located there. Opposite the north bank of the island is the colorful **Qingping Market.**

The most interesting of the museums in Guangzhou is the **Guangzhou Museum,** located in the "Tower Overlooking the Sea" on top of the hill in Yue Xiu Park (see *Museums*).

The **National Peasant Movement Institute** is considered to be the Chinese Communist Party's first ideological training school. Mao Zedong and Zhou Enlai both worked here. The Institute, housed in a fine Ming Confucian temple, was converted into dormitories, dining halls, and libraries used by the peasants who were training at the Institute and later sent out into the countryside to spread Communist ideology.

The only pagoda in the center of the city is the **Decorated Pagoda,** located inside the grounds of the **Temple of the Six Banyan Trees.** The best view of the pagoda is obtained from the minaret of the **Huaisheng Mosque** about half a mile away. The minaret stands in the grounds housing what it said to be the oldest mosque in China, although the existing buildings are modern and of little architectural interest. However, the minaret does offer perhaps the most interesting bird's-eye view of the city because it is central to most of the major sites.

The **Sun Yatsen Monument** is a fine-looking, elegant building with a blue glazed-tile roof. It was built in 1925 after the Chinese revolutionary's death. There is a statue of him in the garden. The building now houses a theater which can seat more than 5,000 people. Another monument, dedicated to those members of the Canton Commune who were killed by the Guomindang in 1927, is the **Mausoleum of the Martyrs of Guangzhou Uprising.** It is a vast tumulus surrounded by a marble wall and containing the remains of the victims.

Guangzhou has something to offer temple lovers: the **Buddhist Guangxiao Temple,** the **Confucian Zhen Family Temple,** and the **Taoist Wuxian Temple.** For burial chambers, visit the **Tomb of Emperor Wen** with its wonderful array of ancient objects; and the old **Tomb of Waggas,** the Islamic monk who founded the Huaisheng Mosque.

Above all, Guangzhou is a city of parks and gardens, and you will see there some of the finest in all China. It is pleasant around the artificial lakes and amidst the flower gardens of such well-known parks as **Yue Xiu,** the **Liu Hua,** and the **Dong Shan Park.** Perhaps the most delightful of all is the **Orchid Garden,** which is one of the most tranquil havens you could hope to find in the middle of any city in the world. If your interest turns to miniature trees and landscapes, do not miss the **Xiyuan Garden,** where there are thousands of examples on display.

The **Cultural Park** is an interesting place to visit, for here you will see the Chinese enjoying themselves in a carnival-ground atmosphere. In particular it is pleasant to watch boys and girls roller skating. In the evenings there are outdoor theaters providing entertainment with the performance of songs, dances, and revolutionary opera.

Other interesting places to visit are the **Old Guangdong University,** the **Sun Yatsen University** located across the river from the city, and the **Observatory.**

The best panorama of the whole city is provided from the lookout point of **Bai Yun Mountain,** about 30 minutes' bus ride away from the center of Guangzhou. In contrast, the best "close-up" view of the city is obtained by going on the 2-hour boat ride along the city reaches of the Pearl River.

MUSEUMS. The **Guangzhou Museum** is located in a five-story pavilion on a hilltop in Yue Xue Park known as the Zhen Hai Lou, or "Tower Overlooking the Sea." The tower dates from the fourteenth century Ming Dynasty period and is the oldest building in Guangzhou. It was rebuilt as a lookout post in 1686. It is a rectangular building with a roof separating each story and an exterior painted dark red. The upper roof line has been beautifully restored and there are fine examples of roof figurines on the eaves. On the upper floor a balcony overlooks the city. You also look down onto a stadium which has been cut out of the hillside and is reminiscent of a Roman amphitheater. The balcony is a pleasant place to rest and take tea.

The first section of the museum has maps and models of Guangzhou, prehistoric tools, fine Han Dynasty tomb figurines excavated near Guangzhou, bronze bells, lacquer ware, bronzes, textile fragments, particularly silk, coins, wooden tomb figures, an iron sword, iron spades, and sets of weights.

From the Sui and Tang periods there are further fine examples of tomb figurines, some of Western merchants; "tribute" of silver ingot; gold and silver coins from Persia; pottery found in Guangzhou; a model of the Guang Xiao Temple (it is said that the town of Guangzhou did not exist when this temple was founded in the fourth century).

From the Song and Yuan periods there are an example of Su Dong Po's calligraphy from the Temple of Six Banyan Trees; rubbings from a tablet indicating that a merchant from the South Seas had given money for a Taoist Temple to be restored; good examples of pottery; engraved bricks; a compass; a model of the Temple of the Six Banyan Trees Pagoda.

The museum is closed Monday.

Guandong Provincial Museum is housed in a building next to the Lu Xun Museum and located in the old Guangdong University, north of Wen Ming Lu Street. It is open 8 A.M.–noon and 2–8 P.M.; tel. 332195.

Outside the entrance is a large iron cannon used during the Opium Wars and alongside it a huge lump of iron used to case cannons in Foshan. The cannon dates from 1843.

Inside the museum, the first items on display are old fossils and bones that have been unearthed around Guangzhou and in the province. There are also exhibits of weapons, spearheads, and agricultural implements, and some rare pottery fragments.

There is a fine collection of bronzes from the Western Zhou period; a particularly fine example of a *huang* with an animal-head spout and the lid and handle in animal shape; a bell from the Spring and Autumn period; a set of bells used as a musical instrument. From the Warring States period: swords, axe heads, and spearheads. From the Han: an iron sword, Foshan clay miniatures of peasants in the fields, ceramic models of miniature houses with people inside, a ceramic model boat with sailors on board, a set of ceramic musicians, and a fine collection of glazed pottery. From the Southern Han: glazed pottery and some interesting examples with crackled glaze finish. From the Tang: two large urns; from the Yuan: a bronze block used for printing money.

From the Ming: coins embedded in coral and found in the South China Sea; blue-and-white porcelain, particularly bowls and cups; celadon dishes; jade carvings; stone chops; and cotton fabrics and skirts.

From the Qing: blue-and-white porcelain urns; tricolor pots; very fine examples of terracotta figurines along with proportionately sized stove, beds, desk, chair, gong, sedar chair, and umbrella.

Lu Xun Museum is located at the Old Guangdong University site where Lu Xun once taught. The exhibits are housed in a building which is immediately before the drive leading from the entrance gates. The museum is open 8 A.M.–noon and 2–8 P.M.

The museum features many excellent photographs of China's revered revolutionary writer and of the towns in which he lived. He was born in Shao Xing (home of China's famous red wine) in Zhejiang Province, and in 1891 went to Nanjing to receive his early education. In 1902, when he was 21 years old, he went to Japan to study for a short period, but most of the time between 1919–1926 was spent in Beijing and Amoy. He went to Guangzhou in 1927 to become head of the Literary Department and lived in the Bell Tower building, now the museum devoted to his life and works. Fine photographs depict the turbulent political situation in the province in 1927. Many exhibits are associated with Lu Xun's stay in Shanghai and his activities there between 1927 and 1936, the year of his death.

RECREATION. Joggers will find their Chinese counterparts pounding the tracks of Liu Hua and Yue Xiu parks in the early morning. The scenery is tropical, and you will run by the edge of lakes and ponds.

Tennis courts are available at the China, Garden, and White Swan hotels; **squash** courts at the Garden Hotel.

A **golf and country club** at Luhu Park, not far from downtown Guangzhou, with golf, swimming, and tennis facilities for members and guests, was scheduled to open at the end of 1990. A helicopter service between Hong Kong/Macao and the club is planned.

SHOPPING. Visitors attending the Guangzhou autumn and spring fairs should make full use of the retail shops in the fairgrounds: there are stores selling down products, silks, textiles, embroidery, fur coats, leather jackets, fur products; there is also a general retail store selling items such as wine, teas, and confectionery. A bookstore stocks a wide range of scrolls, art books, paper cutouts, and general literature. Another store sells parkas, ski wear, duvet comforters, and sleeping bags.

Visitors to Guangzhou outside the fair period will probably first choose to visit the **Friendship Store** set aside for foreign visitors. It is located in the four-story building to the left of the Bai Yun Hotel. There you may purchase a wide range of goods; foodstuffs, wines, teas, candy, dried fruits, knitted goods, silks, cottons, brocades, handkerchiefs, scarves, umbrellas. You can also buy suitcases and other luggage items at the store—a useful thing to keep in mind, since you are liable to purchase many items during your travels in China and will probably need additional tote bags. Also on display are shirts, blouses, pajamas, and toys.

You may purchase scrolls, lacquer ware, cloisonné ware, pottery, and porcelain, and you will find a fine range of jewelry. These items are most suitable as gifts; they vary from inexpensive to high-priced, but their main convenience stems from their lightness in weight and small size, always an important consideration for the traveler. One section of the store sells a range of imported cosmetics, wines, spirits, cigarettes, and groceries. There is even a supermarket which stocks imported coffee, powdered milk, insecticides, sanitary napkins, shampoos, deodorants, and many other foreign-brand products. Prices are high. Address: 369 Huanshi Dong. Tel. 776296.

At the **People's Department Store**, or **Nan Fang Da Sha**, 49 Yanjiang Road (tel. 886022), you will find hats, shoes, clothing, textiles, sporting goods, bicycles, spare parts, radios, TV sets, towels and linens, to name just a few items. It is well worth going into this store and browsing around, particularly to watch the Chinese shopping. There is an excellent and inexpensive optical service: imported frames are available at low prices but prescribed lenses take about a week. A branch of the Friendship Store is also located within the People's Department Store.

Local Products

To browse in the small shops specializing in locally made products, take a taxi to the intersection of Beijing Road and Zhong Shan Road. In the streets forming this intersection you will find stores selling everything from safety pins to color TV sets. In this busy thoroughfare there are shops selling herbs, pharmaceuticals, rattan ware, basket ware, stone chops, stationery, birth-control pills (no prescription needed), books, wall posters, second-hand clothes, household items, brooms, ropes, paints, and brushes. The streets are bustling and noisy; there is a great deal of traffic and incessant honking of horns. The crowd spills out on to the roadway, since there is rarely enough room on the footpaths to make one's way. The **Guangzhou Department Store**, 4 Zhong Shan Wu Road (tel. 334152), is a good place to begin your shopping.

Antiques

If you are shopping for antiques, you should visit the **Guangzhou Antique Shop** at 146 Wende Road (tel. 331241 or 334229). Here you will find a good range of antiques and reproductions, but the strong emphasis is on pottery and porcelain ware. There is a limited range of scrolls; also old and new jade, rather unusual natural stone chops, and Qing reproductions of ancient bronze ware.

Another good place for antiques is the **Guangdong Antique Company**, 696 Renmin Road North, between the Dong Fang Hotel and the railway station (tel. 678800, 678608, or 662819). Still another is the **Guangzhou Antiques Warehouse**, 575 Hongshu Bei Road (tel. 887600), which does business with dealers prepared to spend large amounts (minimum about US$2,000).

The **Qingping Market** off Liuersan Road, opposite the north bank of Sha Mian Island, has antique stalls, but the range is limited and you will find lots of reproductions and bric-a-brac.

Documentation: Every antique sold should have a red seal affixed. You should ensure that your purchase is recorded on your currency declaration form or you will not be able to take the antique out of China.

Tailors

If you are spending quite a few days in Guangzhou and have time to spare, you may like to visit a busy and interesting shopping area in **Xiu Li Er Road.** Fairgoers often make use of the services of two tailor shops located there; their work is good and inexpensive. One is the **Guangzhou Tailor Shop** and the other the **Nan Fang Tailor Shop.** You will need to be staying in Guangzhou for at least 5–10 days to make use of their services. The Guangzhou shop does the usual range of tailoring, while the Nan Fang does shirts and blouses only. It is customary to bring an item that the shop can copy; they do not usually measure clients, and when they do the results are often disappointing. There is a large street market for clothes at Guanlu, but prices are better in Hong Kong.

ENTERTAINMENT. There are plenty of evening cultural events in Guangzhou to keep you more than occupied. In the traditional arts, there are performances of the regional variety of Chinese opera, concerts featuring Chinese classic pieces, and of course superb shows of acrobats, magicians, and conjurers. TV programs in English, beamed from Hong Kong, can be picked up on your hotel set.

LEAVING GUANGZHOU. Guangzhou often represents a visitor's first port of call in China, so details about getting away are useful, particularly to the independent traveler. We will also consider getting back to Hong Kong, as Guangzhou is sometimes the last port of call after a tour of China has been accomplished. (Full details about return journeys to Hong Kong are provided in the *Planning Your Trip* section.)

By plane. Guangzhou has a large number of services to major destinations in China. Make your onward bookings with CITS, China South Airlines, or Air China as early as possible as routes bearing heavy passenger traffic are usually booked out for days ahead.

The city airport, Baiyun or White Cloud, is about 20 minutes from the city center by bus or taxi. Passenger buses depart from the Air China/China South airline office at the main railway station about every half-hour.

By train. Guangzhou's main railway station is invariably jammed with people. Porters can be aggressive and may snatch bags out of your hands. Hang on to your bags if you want to carry them yourself. If you do hire a porter, settle on a price first; and do not let him out of your sight. Train tickets may be purchased at CITS near the main station.

The fastest express train to Beijing takes 33–34 hours; to Shanghai about 33 hours; and to Guilin 24 hours (although there are better alternatives to the latter "dog-leg" journey by train). There are services to many other destinations.

Taxis take only 5–15 minutes to reach the main station, depending on the location of your hotel, but you should allow plenty of time because congested traffic can make the journey much longer than expected, especially from downtown hotels.

By boat. The ferry and hovercraft terminal to Hong Kong and Macao is located at Zhoutouzui Pier, on the south side of the Pearl River and opposite Sha Mian Island. There are also ferry departures for Haikou (Hainan Island).

Boats departing for Zhaoqing, Wuzhou, and Jiangmen leave from Dashatou Pier at Yangjian Lu, located on the east side of the city.

By bus. The long-distance bus terminal is at Huanshi Xilu, just west of the main railway station for Macao, Shantou, Zhangjiang, Wuzhou, Zhaoqing, and Jiangmen.

USEFUL ADDRESSES AND TELEPHONE NUMBERS

International calls:
information 115
Calls within China:
long-distance 116
information 114
China International Travel Service (CITS)
Dong/Fang .... 669900 ext. 2366
Main Office, 179 Huanshi Road 677856
China Travel Service (CTS)
2 Qiaoguang Road, Haizu Square 336888
Public Security Bureau (Foreigners' Section)
863 Jiefang Road North 331326

Air Services

Air China and **China South Airlines,** (General Administration of Civil Aviation China), 181 Huanshi Road (next to main railway station): International Passenger Service, tel. 661803. Domestic Passenger Service, tel. 662123, ext. 904. Cargo Service, tel. 661381, ext. 31. Baiyun Airport, tel. 678901.

Banks

Bank of China: Guangzhou Branch, 137 Chang Ti. Cable: Chungkuo Guangzhou. Telex: 44074 BKCA CN, 44075 BKCA CN. Tel. 220543.

Bookstores

Foreign Language Bookstore, Beijing Road. Tel. 332734.
Xinhua Bookstore, 276, 280, and 296 Beijing Road. Tel. 330873.

Chinese Export Commodities Fair
(see also *Doing Business in China* section)

Foreign Trade Center and Exhibition Hall, 117 Liuhua Road. Tel. 330849.
Executive Office, Haizhu Square. Tel. 223800. Cable: CECFA or 0700 Guangzhou.

Consulates

United States, Dong Fang Hotel, 120 Liu Hua Road. Tel. 669900, ext. 1000.
Japan, Dong Fang Hotel, Room 2785, 120 Liu Hua Road. Tel. 661195; 669900.

Department Stores and Shops

Friendship Store, 369 E. Huanshi Road. Tel. 776296.
Jiang Nan Native Produce Store, 399 Zhongshan Road IV. Tel. 331207.
Nan Fang Department Store, 49 Yanjiang Road I. Tel. 886022
Guangzhou Antique Shop, 146 Wendebei Road. Tel. 331241, 334229.
Guanghzou Antique Warehouse, 575 Hongshu Bei Road. Tel. 887600.

Hospitals and Clinics

The First People's Municipal Hospital, 602 Ren Min Road (North): tel. 333090.
Foreign Guest Medical Clinic, Dong Fang Hotel (8 A.M.–10 P.M.). Tel. 669900.
The Second People's Municipal Hospital, 63 Xinfeng Road: Emergency ward,
tel. 886711.
The Chinese Medicine Hospital, 16 Zhuji Road. Tel. 886111.
The Hospital attached to *Guangzhou Municipal Medical College,* 151 Yanjiang
Road. Tel. 220518.

Parks

Guangzhou Cultural Park, Xiti Ermalu. Tel. 887232.
Guangzhou Zoo, Xianlie Road. Opening Hours: 7.30 A.M.–5.30 P.M. (Ticket
counter closes at 4.30 P.M.). Tel. 775574.
Li Wan Park, Xiangyang Road. Tel. 887880.
Liu Hua Park, Xicun Highway. Tel. 335238.
People's Park, Zhongshan Road V. Tel. 334843.
Dongshan Lake Park, Dashatou. Tel. 775672.
Yue Xiu Park, Jiefang Road. Tel. 330876.

Photo Studios

Kun Lun Photo Shop, Renmin Road (South). Tel. 225636.
Yang Fang Photo Shop, Zhongshan Road V. Tel. 331206.

Post and Telecommunications

Guangzhou Cable Bureau, 96 Renmin Road North. Tel. 420508.
Guangzhou Post Office, Yanjiang Road I. Tel. 886615.
Guangzhou Telecommunications Bureau, Liu Hua Square. Tel. 777623, 775190.

Rail Services

Guangzhou Railway Station, Liuhua Square. Information, tel. 661900. Reservations and tickets, tel. 662868.

Theaters

Friendship (Youji), People's Road North. Tel. 333402.
Red Flag (Hongqi), 250 Zhongshan Road IV. Tel. 334073.
Nanfang, 88 Jiaoyu Nan Road South. Tel. 330195.
People's (Renmin), 292 Damalu, Changti. Tel. 222917.

Theater-Cinemas

Guangming, Nanhua Road Central 116. Tel. 551436.
Yan An, Yan'an San Road. Tel. 778801.
Xianjin, 441 Xiuli Yi Road. Tel. 885679.

SHANGHAI

Shanghai's history and way of life are dominated by the river—not the nearby Yangzi, as many visitors suppose, but the Huangpu River, a wide stretch of brown water bearing a variety of craft ranging from oceangoing vessels to single-oared sampans. Shanghai, which means "up from the sea," overlooks a bend in this river where sailing craft and power vessels navigate the difficult waters side by side.

Even the city's local name stems from a river: it is known to the Chinese as "Hu," from the word *hudu,* a name given in an old legend to Suzhou Creek. This creek runs through the city and empties into the Huangpu.

Shanghai is one of three municipalities, along with Beijing and Tianjin, directly under central government control. It harbors China's major port, which extends a total of 35 miles along the bank of the Huangpu. The river waterway is about 200 yards wide and nine yards deep, and it is navigable all year for oceangoing vessels up to 10,000 tons.

Along the river's edge is a boulevard called the Bund—at least, that was its name before 1949—with wide paths and narrow gardens, a cool place during the sweltering heat of summer. Locals go there in the early morning hours to do their *taiji quan* exercises, practice their musical instruments, or sing. Make the effort to rise early and join them; and if you have left your violin behind or are not feeling too energetic, simply lean against the river wall and let the sea air envelop you. Close your eyes and listen to the sound of the sirens and horns beating across the water through the early morning mist.

Flanking the Bund are the old European-style buildings that were once the international banks and trading companies. When you look carefully you can still see the old names chipped into the stonework or written in faded paint on the plaster. These buildings now house the Chinese municipal officials, trade negotiators, customs officers, and bankers. In the middle of the Bund stands the Heping (Peace) Hotel, an elegant old building with a pointed bronze-green roof that was once owned by the well-known Sassoon family of England and called the Cathay Hotel.

Now turn back to the river and take a good look at the river craft. In few places in the world will you see old blunt-nosed steamers side by side with sailing junks tacking against the tide, and ferries with hundreds of passengers jammed between decks passing strings of barges laden with coal. And certainly nowhere else can you see such old vessels still in commission. Some are museum pieces with shiny white paintwork, while others are rust-buckets ready to slide into the river when the plates finally corrode through. And the sampans are everywhere, with entire families manning the single *yuloh* oar when the tide is strong.

From the park you can see the main shopping street, Nanjing Road, which runs into the Bund quite near the Peace Hotel. Take a stroll there: it is the shopping area which is the most western in style in the whole of China. You will notice there are plenty of shop windows—a feature absent in most of the shopping centers in other Chinese cities—and there is a semblance of window decoration to promote the goods on display. The street is packed with people, and the scene will remind you at once that Shanghai, with more than 12 million inhabitants, is the most heavily populated urban area in the world. About six to seven million people live in the city proper, in an area as small as 55 square miles.

At first sight Shanghai's appearance is reminiscent of old Europe, punctuated here and there by new glass-walled towers that house luxury hotels and office accommodations. However, most of the city is comprised of structures typical of many Chinese industrial cities: low buildings housing offices, shops, and busy markets. As you proceed further from the center you will come across large industrial areas with factories surrounded by workers' apartment buildings.

Eventually you will come into the area of intensively cultivated agricultural communes supplying fresh vegetables, grains, pork, and other food to the city. The fields are irrigated by canals drawing off water from the network of rivers, creeks, and waterways forming the Yangzi delta. Further to the west are low hills, but you can rarely see them clearly through haze caused by industrial pollution.

The polluted atmosphere of Shanghai is a reminder that the municipality is China's most important industrial base and premier center of trade and industry. Over the years, Chinese planners have developed Shanghai's light and heavy industry ventures to provide a more balanced local economy, so that the major production sectors are now iron and steel, shipbuilding, chemicals, motor vehicles, heavy machinery, tires, oil refining, petrochemicals, paper, electrical equipment, glassware, and textiles.

Many production centers are located in industrial estates in outlying areas with associated housing developments, shopping centers, hospitals, and schools. One of the most publicized centers is Minxing, about 15 miles south of the city. Another is Pengpu, about three miles north of the Shanghai urban center. The Chinese proudly show visitors these "showcase" centers.

The visitor will soon appreciate that Shanghai, because of its industrial and commercial strength, is the most prosperous city in China. You will certainly note that the women are better dressed than elsewhere and are more clothes-conscious, wearing smarter jackets and more colorful floral skirts here than anywhere else in China. Young couples hold hands in daylight, a practice rare in China, and even walk arm in arm along the Bund in the evenings. All this may appear tame to the Western observer, but it is considered quite permissive behavior in most areas of China.

The residents of the city are known for their business acumen. China traders will confirm that their dealings in Shanghai are usually handled more efficiently and effectively than in any other city in China, and that the state trading corporation officials there "understand what business is all about." No doubt this native ability has been developed throughout Shanghai's long participation in international trade and commerce.

Shanghai has the rare combination of a violent and colorful past and a stable industrial present. It is the largest metropolis on the Asian mainland and one of the largest in the world. It holds a fascination which stems from its one-time international notoriety and its current place in modern Chinese history as a revolutionary city. When you have been to Shanghai you can boast of having visited one of the most populous, polluted, and famous cities in the world.

History

In A.D. 751 there was a small fishing village at the site which—over the next 300 years—grew into a town, and then by 1292 became Shanghai County. Even so, the town was undeveloped under the Yuan (1280–1368), Hangzhou being far more important in that period, and it was not until the seventeenth and eighteenth centuries that trade and commerce began to expand to any large extent. During this period Shanghai became an important cotton-processing center with a population in excess of 200,000 people.

During the Opium War, Shanghai fell to the English fleet in 1842 and, following the Treaty of Nanjing, was opened to foreign trade. The English dominated commerce in the region, but American and European traders were also active. All claimed rights to territories where their nationals were subject to the jurisdiction of the Consul and not the Chinese ruler.

Shanghai was threatened by the Taiping armies in 1853 and from insurrection within. Both movements were eventually put down by the combined forces of the Manchu court and the European powers.

By the middle of the second half of the nineteenth century, foreigners dominated Shanghai, controlling banks, customs, trading houses, shipping, and industry. Yet incredible poverty and squalor existed in areas shut away from the magnificent mansions and grounds of the rich. A reaction to this intolerable situation developed among the Chinese working class and intellectuals. In 1921 the Chinese Communist Party was founded in Shanghai, Mao Zedong being one of the founding members. Some years later there were armed uprisings by the working class in coordination with the Guomindang northern expedition. However, the rivalries within the Guomindang broke into the open in Shanghai when Chiang Kaishek put down the Communists and Trade Unionists in a bloody massacre.

During the Sino-Japanese war (1937–1945) Shanghai was occupied by the invaders. After they were expelled, civil war broke out between the Nationalists and the Communists. By 1949 the Communist armies had crossed the Yangzi and the country was in their hands. In Shanghai, as in the rest of the country, the state took control. Private property and businesses were nationalized and the remains of the previous order swept away. Very few foreigners stayed behind to witness the changes. An industrialization campaign was undertaken and heavy industry developed—shipbuilding, iron and steel, heavy machinery. At the same time, light industry was stimulated, particularly the production of pharmaceuticals, electrical equipment, machine tools, chemicals, and tires.

Shanghai's port facilities were developed, with the result that today Shanghai is one of the top ten cargo-handling ports in the world and

China's most important industrial, commercial, and trading center. About half of all Chinese exports now pass through the port.

EXPLORING SHANGHAI

The facade of riverside Shanghai has changed little since the Communists began to govern the country in 1949. The same buildings are there; but their use is different. The banks flanking the Bund now house Chinese officials, part of the old British Consulate is the Seamen's Club and Friendship Store, the racetrack has become a park, the golf course a zoo, and the palatial villas of the rich have been transformed into "children's palaces," schools, playgrounds, nurseries, and hospitals. The once notorious "Blood Alley" is now a quiet shopping street.

Huangpu Park

In every city there is usually a corner where you can feel the pulse of city life and detect the spirit of the place. In Shanghai you do this in Huangpu Park.

It is a long, slender park that curves along the lower reaches of the Suzhou Creek and then turns south as it follows the embankment of the Huangpu River, from whence it gets its name. In the early morning it is here that you will see the city rise: witness the legion prepare for the day by performing the slow and graceful *taiji quan* body-and-breathing exercises. Later you will see them relaxing, taking children for a stroll, and reading. When evening falls, you will see people strolling hand in hand or just sitting in the cool evening air, some reading under the park lights, others practicing musical instruments.

Day or night, you can rest your elbows on the embankment wall and watch the maneuvering of the river traffic, a blending of sail and power that is almost unparalleled in the world.

The Bund

The Bund is the old European name given to the road that runs alongside the park. The Chinese know it as Zhongshan Road, or "Waitan." Along this road are many of the organizations that drive Shanghai. Many of them are located in buildings that once belonged to the "foreign concessions." The best way to identify them is to stroll through Huangpu Park and occasionally lean your back against the sea-wall to study the buildings across the road.

Probably the first building you will notice is the **Peace Hotel** with its pointed green tower. Once the most palatial hotel in the East, as its former name, Cathay Hotel, suggests, it is almost a museum piece of the dignified but old-fashioned architecture that can now be found only in cities like Vienna, Paris, and some of the East European capitals.

Next to it, to your right, is the **Bank of China,** almost exactly the same height but without the tower. The four other buildings about half the height of the Bank and also to your right were formerly old banks and trading companies; they now house the Chinese state trading corporations which are solely responsible for the import and export of goods and commodities to and from all foreign countries.

About one-third of a mile to the left stands the **Customs Building,** with a tower more than 100 feet high housing an enormous clock that once chimed bars from the composition "East Is Red." Next to it stands a lower but wider building with a small dome; this is the **Shanghai Municipal Committee Headquarters,** which houses the cadres responsible for administrating the municipality and which was "under siege" during the Cultural Revolution. It was formerly the powerful British-owned Hong Kong and Shanghai Bank.

Nanjing Road

While the Bund is Shanghai's most interesting street, Nanjing Road is its busiest. Here you will find the city's shopping area extending for some miles, a multitude of shops on each side of the tree-lined boulevard, separated here and there by restaurants, cinemas, and theaters.

Nanjing Road leads to People's Park (see below) and, to the south of it, **People's Square.** As you continue further west along Nanjing Road you will pass, on your right, the hotel known variously as the International, Park, or Guoji, and further on to your right, the **Shanghai Art Gallery.** In the next block you will see Shanghai's television tower, and on the right side near the next intersection, the **Antiques and Curios Shop** (a branch of the Friendship Store).

You will notice that the main streets running north and south are named after the provinces of China, while those running east and west, like Nanjing Road, are named after major Chinese cities.

People's Park

People's Park is of historic interest because it was the Shanghai Race Course in the days when foreigners ran the city. The Communists saw it as a part of the decadent foreign influence and converted it into a park for the people. The park is well kept, has a vast expanse of lawn, and possesses a great many trees to protect you from the summer heat. To the west of the park is the **Shanghai Municipal Library,** built in the 1850s and once the club house for members of the track.

The Shanghai Exhibition Center

The Exhibition Center (tel. 256–3037), about six blocks west of the People's Square at 1000 Yan An Zhonglu Road, is housed in a large hall built in the severe architectural style of the Soviet Union. This building, surmounted by a high spire, was formerly known as the Sino-Soviet People's Friendship Building, before the two countries suffered strains in their relationship. Trade displays and exhibitions are held regularly. A permanent exhibition of Chinese industrial products, mostly made in Shanghai, is held in the building and is of interest to business executives and visitors wishing to learn about developments in the Chinese economy. You will probably be surprised at the range and quality of goods produced by China's industries. Many items are for sale. A good restaurant on the top floor of the central building serves Cantonese-style food. Exhibition Center hours are 8:30 A.M.–noon and 2–5 P.M.; closed Monday.

Children's Palaces

The best-known of the children's palaces in Shanghai, and the one usually shown to visitors, is located at 64 Yan An Road. In these institutions,

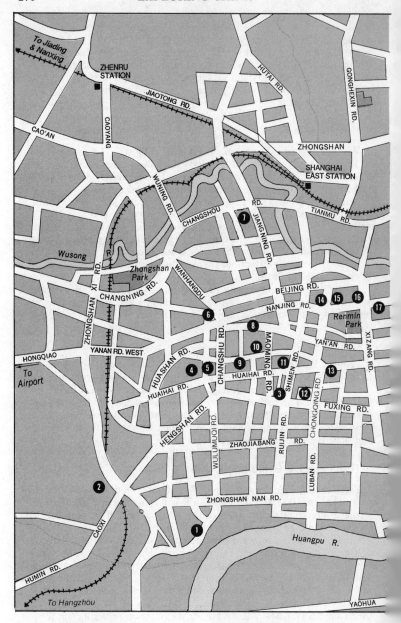

Points of Interest

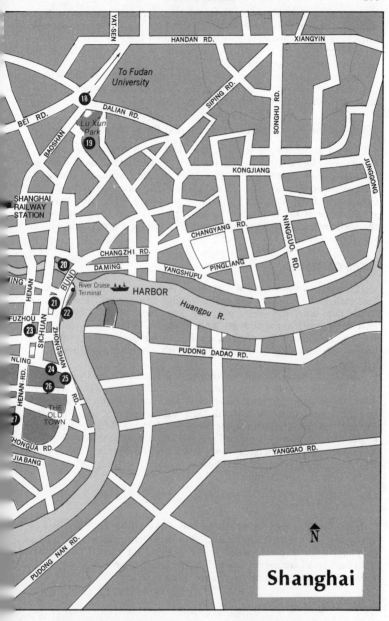

Shanghai

once the palatial homes of Shanghai millionaires, children come to learn dancing, singing, music, painting, and handicrafts, or else they exercise, listen to teachers, or simply play. From all sides you will hear the chatter of children enjoying themselves, the shuffle of feet in dance steps, the strains of musical instruments.

Children may attend these institutes outside their normal school hours to obtain extracurricular training in music, dance, art, gymnastics, etc., under the guidance of highly trained tutors.

Site of the First Chinese Communist Party Meeting

Located at 76 Xingye Road in the old French Concession area and about three blocks east of the Fuxing Park, the site has become a museum. Now beautifully restored, this gray brick building with four doorways, each with an overhead arch, was the site of the first meeting of the Chinese Communist Party founded in Shanghai on July 1, 1921. You may also see a replica of the beautifully panelled pleasure boat that was used by the participants, including Mao Zedong, to flee the secret police who invaded the meeting.

The Old Town

The Old Town is a maze of narrow alleys that was the center of Shanghai centuries ago. In the time of the "foreign concessions," few strangers would dare enter this dangerous slum area. Now the cobblestone lanes have been repaired, the cottages whitewashed, and the whole place made safe for the curious visitor. You are free to wander at will, explore the back alleys, and shop at the old market. It's easy to get lost but easy to get help.

The Old Town is not difficult to find: it is almost circled by Zhonghua Road. Trolley bus no. 11 circumnavigates the Old Town. There are many ways to get to the old area, but here is one. From Huangpu Park, walk one block west to Sichuan Road, then walk south (i.e., away from the Peace Hotel) for about seven blocks. Cross Renmin Road and continue south; turn left into Fuyou Road and you will come to the Wu Xing Ting Teahouse and Yu Yuan (see below). You are now in the Old Town. (When it is time to leave, remember that bus no. 16 goes from the Yu Yuan Bazaar to the Jade Buddha Temple.)

Yu Yuan Bazaar

In the northeastern sector of the Old Town is the Yu Yuan Bazaar, where about a hundred shops sell traditional goods and handicrafts. You may find it fun to poke around in the shops to see what the locals buy. There are small restaurants, as well as the famous Lao Fandian (see *Restaurants*), where you may enjoy a delicious lunch.

Wu Xing Ting

Wu Xing Ting, or Five-Star Pavilion, is a teahouse in the Old Town. It sits in the middle of an ornamental lake and is connected to the street by a zigzag bridge. The locale was once used as a symbol of Shanghai on pottery, ceramic ware, dinner sets, and curios. It probably conjures up in the Western mind the idea of what old China was supposed to be like.

The teahouse is quite old and was restored in 1965. A gate opposite leads to Yu Yuan.

The Yu Yuan

The Yu Yuan, or "Yu the Mandarin's Garden" is characteristic of the architectural style of the Ming and Qing dynasties. Its visual beauty captures the essence of landscape art of the period, creating the impression of maximum space in a small area.

The Yu Yuan was built during the years 1559–1577 for Pan Yunduan, a landlord and official of the Ming Dynasty. The garden, reminiscent of those in Suzhou, features more than 30 halls and pavilions. It is divided into three parts, each separated by a white brick wall the top of which forms an undulating gray dragon. Each part of the park, although divided, has a balance and harmony creating a unity of expression.

One of the pavilions, the **Hall for Heralding Spring,** has a place in revolutionary history. It was the headquarters of the **Society of Small Swords** that rose against authority in 1853 and held part of Shanghai by force, before eventually fleeing to Zhejiang (Chekiang) to join the Tai Ping Rebellion. Chen Ahlin, one of the important leaders of the Society, used it as a command post.

From this time onward the garden was neglected; eventually, in 1956, it was restored. It is very popular with the local Chinese and thus has the disadvantage of being crowded; you may have the feeling of being on an anthill as you make your way up and down the narrow paths and through the narrow passages. Open 8–10 A.M. and 2–5 P.M.; visitors may stay through the lunch hours.

Temple to the Town Gods

The temple, or Cheng Huang Miao, is only a short distance from the Yu Yuan. Once every city and large town possessed a temple devoted to the town gods, but very few have survived throughout China. This is a rare exception. Note the fine roof figurine of Guan Gong, a famous Chinese warrior.

Garden of the Purple Clouds

This garden lies at the back of the Temple of the Town Gods; its full title is "Garden of the Purple Clouds of Autumn," known in Chinese as Qiu Xia Pu, but also known as the Back Garden (Hou Yuan). The garden was originally laid out during the Ming Dynasty, later became part of a rich merchant's estate, then finally, in 1726, was made an addition to the temple. There is an ornamental lake in the park along with pavilions and some artificial hills.

The Long Hua Temple Pagoda

The Long Hua Temple, known in Chinese as the Long Hua Si, is located in the southwest corner of the city, two blocks south of Zhongshan Nan Road. Here you can see the only pagoda standing in Shanghai; it has seven stories, each with a wooden balcony. The temple buildings date from the Qing Dynasty and consist of four halls with statues of the Buddha, the Celestial Guardians, and the Celestia Defenders. The surroundings are renowned for the peach blossoms in the spring.

The pagoda was first erected during the Three Kingdoms period in about A.D. 247 and was destroyed by fire in 880. It was rebuilt in 977. The present structure is of much later date. The pagoda is of brick, with the

The Yu Yuan
or Yu the Mandarin's Garden

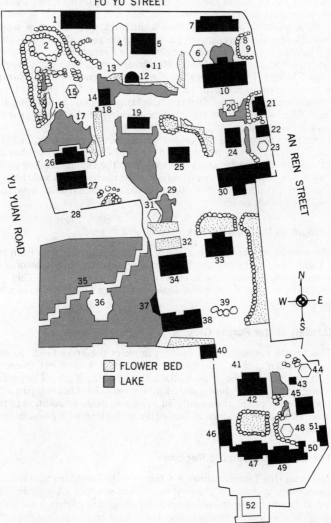

FU YU STREET

YU YUAN ROAD

AN REN STREET

FLOWER BED

LAKE

N
W—E
S

exterior balconies constructed of wood. The pagoda began to develop a lean, but maintenance work has corrected this and the foundations have since been stabilized.

The temple itself has the traditionally upswept eaves and fine supporting brackets which are a feature of southern Chinese architecture. One of the temples has a fine example of a painted-wood ceiling and a cupola. Buddhist monks still practice at the temple. There is a huge free-market outside the temple walls.

Temple of Serenity

The Temple of Serenity, known in Chinese as the Jing An Si, is one block north of West Nanjing Road and Jingan Park. Before the Revolution, the temple (Buddhist) was one of the richest in Shanghai, being headed by an abbot (Khi Vehdu) who had a rich wife, seven concubines, and a White Russian bodyguard. The buildings are from the late period of the Qing Dynasty but are not particularly noteworthy, and a visit to this site should be given lower priority.

Temple of the Jade Buddha

The Jade Buddha Temple, or Yufo Si, is located at 170 Anyuan Road in the northwest of the city. The pavilions are of recent date (1911, 1918), and recently restored. The temple is famous for the white jade Buddha seated in the far pavilion and originally brought from Burma by a Chinese monk in 1881. There is also a fine jade statue of the Buddha in a reclining position.

In the first pavilion there is an eight-foot-high statue of the protector of Buddhist scriptures, flanked on each side by the Buddhist kings: the Northern King with an umbrella; the Southern King with a sword; the Eastern King with a stringed instrument; and the Western King with a snake.

In the next pavilion, three gilded statues of the Buddha are flanked by many smaller figures. There is a Guanyin behind the Buddhas. The Jade Buddha is on the second floor of this building, surrounded by 7,000 books of sacred Buddhist texts more than two centuries old. (You must take off

---

THE YU YUAN—Key

1) Hall for Gathering Grace
2) Arbor for Viewing the River
3) Large Artificial Hill
4) Resembling a Boat
5) Tower of Ten Thousand Flowers
6) Bower of the Ancient Well
7) Treasury Tower
8) Poplar Tree
9) Garden for Learning Horticulture
10) Hall for Heralding Spring
11) Gingko Tree
12) Hall of Double Convenience
13) Double Corridor
14) Pavilion of Fishes' Pleasure
15) Arbor for Appreciating Grace
16) Bridge of Three Turns
17) Angling Terrace
18) Old Purple Rattan
19) Pavilion of Nine Lions
20) Arena for Dance and Song
21) Tower of Happiness
22) Hall for Obtaining Tranquility
23) Arbor for Listening to the Orioles
24) Hall of Graciousness
25) Tower of Elation

26) Hall of Mountain Reverence
27) Hall of Three Corn Ears
28) Entrance
29) Bridge of Three Turns
30) Office
31) Pavilion for Enlightnment by the Torrent
32) Miniature Landscape
33) Hall of Jade's Splendor
34) Tower for Appreciating the Moon
35) Nine Arc Bridge
36) Lake Pontoon
37) Pavilion for Paying Reverence to Weaving
38) Book Tower
39) Elegant Jade Carving
40) Retail Shop
41) Inner Garden
42) Temple of Tranquility
43) Fairyland of Happiness
44) Phoenix Pavilion
45) Temple of Permission
46) Tower for Observing Waves
47) Tower of Returning Cloud
48) Emerald Pavilion
49) Tower of Lasting Clearness
50) Pleasure Boat
51) Sky of Another World
52) Stage for Theatrical Performance

your shoes on entering this room.) The next pavilion houses the Reclining Buddha. Photography is not permitted. There is a vegetarian restaurant, and a store selling religious items, both run by the monks. The temple is open daily, 8 A.M.–noon and 1–5 P.M.; it is not accessible to non-Buddhists on a few special days (such as Chinese New Year).

St. Ignatius's Catholic Cathedral

Shanghai's St. Ignatius's Catholic Cathedral (or Xijiahui) with its two Romanesque towers is at 158 Puxi Lu, off Caoxi Bei Road. Built in 1906 by the French, the cathedral can seat 2,500 worshipers; there are 19 altars. Mass is conducted on Sunday and holy days.

Shanghai Acrobatic Theater

Located at 400 Nanjing Road West, this amphitheater hosts wonderful performances of Chinese acrobatic art. If you want to see some of the best acrobatics performed in the world, go to this theater. Closed Tuesday. Tel. 256–4051 or 256–4704. Tickets through CITS or at theater.

Xijiao Park and Zoo

This park is the largest in Shanghai and houses the zoo, which is a well-known attraction of the city. There are hundreds of species of animal on display: tigers from the Northeast; leopards and elephants from Yunnan; crocodiles from the Yangzi; and giant pandas. Both the zoo and the park abound with pleasant gardens and stands of trees. There is also a roller-skating rink. The park is open 7 A.M.–5 P.M. daily.

Fu Xing Park

The Fu Xing Park, built in 1909, also possesses a small zoo. It is located not far from the center of the city, quite near the site where the First National Congress of the Communist Party of China was held. It is usually crowded with the residents of Shanghai and visitors from the Chinese provinces, strolling beneath the massive foliage of the shade trees.

Botanical Gardens

The Shanghai Botanical Gardens are southwest of the city off Longwu Road, a short distance by car or bus from the Longhua Temple and Pagoda. Covering more than 170 acres, with numerous gardens, some with miniature trees over a hundred years old. The area is open daily, 8:30 A.M.–4 P.M.

Tomb of Song Qingling

Song Qingling was the wife of Dr. Sun Yatsen, the man who dedicated his life to China's independence and eventually became President of the Republic for a short time in 1912. As a young woman Song Qingling scandalized her family by eloping with Sun Yatsen when he was already married. (In one of those ironies of history, her sister married Chiang Kaishek, and the sisters became bitter political rivals.)

Song Qingling became an ardent champion of China's causes and after 1949 stayed behind when many others fled the revolution. In recognition of her services to the nation over succeeding decades, she was eventually given the title Honorary Chairperson of the People's Republic. She died in 1981.

Song Qingling's tomb is on the western outskirts of the city at Wanguo Cemetery; it may be visited conveniently on the way to the Shanghai Zoo.

Arts and Crafts Research Institute

The Arts and Crafts Research Institute is in the old French Concession area at 79 Fenyang Road, near Huaihai Zhong Road, in the same street as the Conservatory of Music. Housed in an old French mansion with sweeping staircases, the institute brings together the best artisans of Shanghai, who devote their time to developing new techniques in over 15 specialities of handicraft work. The developments are then passed on to Shanghai handicraft factories and introduced into production. The artisans also provide advice to handicraft factories throughout China. Visits to the institute may be arranged through CITS.

Hongqiao New Town

Hongqiao New Town is located on the western edge of Shanghai, midway between the airport and the center of Shanghai. When completed the new town will become the center for foreign residents of Shanghai, comprising blocks of apartments with recreational facilities, such as tennis courts, swimming pools, and gardens. There is a trade center with conference facilities, an exhibition hall, blocks of offices and hotels, and a theater. The Consulates-General of various nations will be moved from downtown Shanghai to the new facilities. Of the 165 acres site, 70 acres are being developed for buildings. The new town is about four miles from downtown.

EXCURSIONS FROM SHANGHAI

Along the Huangpu River

This is a fine boat excursion for those who wish to see Shanghai from the vantage point of the river, and get a closer look at the busy river life. The boat leaves from the center of Shanghai, heads west along the river until Fuxingdao, when it turns north. Then it proceeds to the mouth of the river, known as Wusong Kou, where the Huangpu River empties into the Yangzi, or Chang River, as it is often called in China. The boat then returns by the same route. On the way back a show is put on by acrobats, jugglers, and magicians to the delight of the passengers. The 35-mile journey takes three and one-half hours.

The boat departs from the pier at Huangpu Park, just north of the Peace Hotel, at 8.30 A.M. and again at 1.15 P.M.; an evening trip of 90 minutes departs at 7 P.M. In winter, there is only an afternoon sailing. Tickets are available through CITS or at the pier.

Sonjiang

Sonjiang is about 25 miles southwest of Shanghai, and about half-way to the northern border of Zhejiang Province. The main sight is the 160-foot high five-sided **Huzhou Pagoda,** built in 1079. You may climb to the ninth landing. There are Buddhist paintings on the third landing. The pagoda has a lean that is slightly greater than that of the famous Leaning Tower of Pisa, Italy.

Outside of what was once the Temple of the Town Gods stands a **Ming Screen.** Built in 1370 to keep evil spirits from entering the temple, it is covered with glazed tiles and depicts a mythical monster who tried to eat the sun. There are various other pavilions of recent origin in the park surrounding the site.

Outside of the west gate of the town is a place known as **Zuibai Ci Garden,** which means "the garden containing the pool of the drunken poet Li Bai." No one knows whether the famous poet actually fell into the pool in a drunken state or simply became inebriated on the foreshores, but the name stands. The garden was first laid out in 1652. There is a small museum, an interesting stone engraving, and some pavilions of recent date.

Jiading

Jiading, 27 miles northwest of Shanghai, is on the new highway linking the two cities. On this bus excursion, you will first go to Nanxiang and visit the **Guyi Garden.** (Nanxiang is famous in the region for its steamed dumplings.)

In Jiading itself, you can see a **Song Dynasty Pagoda,** and the **Quixiapu Garden** that was first laid out in 1566 and rebuilt at various times over the centuries. The garden is of classical Ming style.

Northwest of the city stands the **Temple of Confucius,** first constructed under the Song in 1219. Even though one-third of the original buildings no longer exists, it still remains one of the largest temples of its type in South China. There is a small museum in the grounds.

Dingshan Lake

Dingshan Lake is a large body of water—occupying approximately the same area as the city of Shanghai—about 40 miles west of the capital. Its western foreshores form the boundary line between Shanghai Municipality and Zhejiang Province.

On this one-day bus excursion you pass through **Qingpu**—with its **Wanshou Pagoda**—about 20 miles west of Shanghai. About eight miles further on you may visit the **Guanwang Pagoda** near the eastern foreshore of Dingshan Lake. **Puji Bridge** lies seven miles to the west.

About 250 acres of the lake's foreshores are being developed into a recreation resort for locals and visitors. The architecture of the pavilions has the traditional upswept eaves of South China.

Of major interest is the 25-acre development known as the **Grand View Garden,** or Daguanyuan, a reproduction of the pavilions, gardens, ponds, and bridges featured in the classic novel *Dream of the Red Chamber.* A visit here is a trip back into the China of centuries ago.

On the return journey, you may stop at the quaint town of **Zhujiajiao,** midway between the lake and Qingpu. Here you will see old white cottages lining the ancient canals of the town.

PRACTICAL INFORMATION FOR SHANGHAI

FACTS AND FIGURES. Shanghai lies at approximately the same latitude as Jacksonville, Florida. Distances: 698 miles southeast of Beijing by air, 1¼ hours' direct flight; 915 miles southeast of Beijing by rail, 26 hours' train journey; 745 miles northeast of Guangzhou by air, 2 hours' direct flight; 1,130 miles northeast of Guangzhou by rail, 35 hours by train.

Elevation: 50 feet above sea level.

The table shows the weather pattern in Shanghai during the year.

Shanghai Temperature Range and Average Rainfall

	Temperature High (°F)	Temperature Low (°F)	Number of Days with Rainfall	Monthly Rainfall (in inches)
January	47	32	10	1.9
April	67	49	13	3.6
July	91	75	11	5.8
October	75	56	9	2.9

WHEN TO GO. Although Shanghai's climate is subtropical, it does have a distinct change of seasons. Spring weather is usually warm but unsettled. Summer is hot and humid, with the highest incidence of rainy days of all the seasons. Autumn is the best season for visiting: warm and relatively dry. Winter, the longest season, is cold, but although the temperatures often go below freezing, snow is unusual.

HOW TO GET THERE. By plane. You can travel direct to Shanghai by international flights. There are daily flights from Hong Kong (2 hours 10 minutes); there are services from San Francisco, Los Angeles, New York, Tokyo, Osaka, Nagasaki, Fukuoka, Shajah, Paris, Vancouver, and Toronto. If you cannot get a direct flight to Shanghai, there are many domestic flights from most large Chinese cities. Flight time is 1¼ hours from Beijing; 2 hours from Guangzhou (Canton).

By train. Shanghai is connected to China's major rail network and has a regular passenger service to and from most important centers: 26 hours from Beijing; 36 hours from Guangzhou. Shanghai's main railway station, at 1 Kangji Road, is an air-conditioned facility located about 1¼ miles from the old terminus. The new station has a shopping center, bus terminus for nine lines, three taxi stands, and a subway station ready for the sheduled metro.

By boat. Boats leave daily from Chongqing and Wuhan. The journey takes 3 days from Wuhan, 5 days from Chongqing. Boat services reach Shanghai from Hong Kong, (56 hours), Fuzhou, Wenzhou (21 hours), Ningbo (12 hours), Dalian (36 hours), and Qingdao (26 hours).

Travel Warning. Delays in securing travel reservations to and from Shanghai during the peak tourist seasons make it important that you obtain onward bookings well in advance.

HOTELS. Shanghai's hotels offer accommodations ranging from the ultramodern to the old and elegant, from the small and luxurious to the large and austere. Independent travelers are warned that there has been a shortage of budget-priced hotel rooms in Shanghai in spite of the many new hotels that have opened in recent years. With all the construction under way in 1990, the city should have a surfeit of hotel accommodations by the end of 1991.

Cypress Hotel. The Cypress, or Longbai Fandian, with 191 rooms, stands on the site of the former Shanghai Golf Club, near Hongqiao Airport, about 30 minutes from the Bund by car. Its Bamboo Room, a Chinese restaurant, features Sichuan food; the Silk Road restaurant has a Western-style menu. Double rooms from

US$75, suites from US$105, plus 10 percent service. 2419 Hongqiao Road. Tel. 432–9388. Telex 33288 CYH CN. Cable 9921. Fax 432–9323.

Garden Hotel. The prestigious 33-story Garden, which incorporates the gracious old Jinjiang Club in its structure, has rooms and suites with luxury appointments and soft indirect lighting. Dining facilities include Chinese, Japanese, and Continental restaurants and a coffee shop. The health club has a 25-meter heated pool. A business center, a shopping arcade, a beauty parlor, and a travel agent are all on the premises. Double rooms from US$130, suites from US$300, plus 10 percent service. 58 Maoming Road South. Tel. 433–1111, 433–1234. Telex 30157 GHSH CN. Fax 433–8866.

Jinjiang Hotel. This distinguished establishment, for decades one of Shanghai's leading hotels, has often accommodated visiting heads of state and other dignitaries. It was here, in the modern building flanking the courtyard, that Premier Zhou Enlai and U.S. President Richard Nixon negotiated the 1972 Shanghai Communiqué that opened the way for the restoration of relations between China and the United States. Now completely modernized, the four hotel buildings set in manicured grounds contain 720 carefully decorated rooms, each with air-conditioning, IDD telephone, closed circuit TV, and refrigerator. The Jinjiang has a high reputation for fine food, with eleven restaurants offering specialties from Sichuan, Guangzhou, and Yangzhou as well as Japanese and European cuisine. The ground-floor bar is popular with the Shanghai expatriate community. Double rooms from US$65 plus 10 percent service. 59 Maoming Road South. Tel. 258–2582, 253–4242. Telex 33380 GRJJH CN. Cable 7777. Fax 258–2582.

Jinjiang Tower. This 43-story hotel in the heart of the old French quarter is 9 miles from the airport and 2 ½ miles from the railway station. Its 728 rooms, all air-conditioned, have IDD telephone, color TV, and minibar. Six restaurants serve international cuisines—Sichuan, Fujian, and European—and the revolving restaurant on the 42nd and 43rd floors offers breathtaking views over the city. Facilities include a business center, first-class convention facilities, banquet hall, function rooms, landscaped sky-deck. Airline ticket offices, foreign exchange bureau, post and telecommunications office, shops, beauty salon, and underground parking are available here. Double rooms from US$85 plus 10 percent service. 161 Changle Road. Tel. 258–2582. Telex 30040 JJFSC CN. Cable 7777. Fax 258–2582.

Nikko Longbai. An elegant 11-story hotel in the new foreign and diplomatic zone, 5 minutes by car from Shanghai international airport and 35 minutes from the city center, the Longbai has 419 modern rooms and suites, each with individual climate control, IDD telephone, color TV, minibar, and refrigerator. Business center. Three restaurants serve Cantonese, Japanese, and European cuisines, and there's a coffee shop, several bars, a disco, and a shopping arcade. Recreation facilities include a swimming pool, four tennis courts with night lighting, a fitness center, sauna, and massage service. The hotel has a business center, and shuttle bus service to downtown and the airport is available. Double rooms from US$90, suites from US$160, plus 10 percent service. 2451 Hongqiao Road. Tel. 259–3636. Telex 30138 NHISH CN. Cable 9923. Fax 259–3012.

Park Hotel. Formerly the International Hotel, the imposing 24-story Park overlooks the Renmin (People's) Park, about a mile from the Bund. Well-known once for its fashionable daily tea dance and famous chefs, the Park was where Mao Zedong stayed on his visits to Shanghai. Today the hotel is best known for its excellent restaurant. Double rooms from US$65 plus 10 percent service. 170 Nanjing Road West. Tel. 327–5225. Cable 1445. Fax 327–6958.

Portnam Hotel. The tallest building in Shanghai, the 50-story Portnam, located in the Shanghai Center, dominates the city skyline. Its 700 rooms offer deluxe accommodations, each with climate control, 2 IDD telephones, and color TV. Three floors house an executive club for business travelers. Three restaurants serve Shanghainese, Japanese, and European cuisines; a tea garden is open 24 hours; and there are several bars and an elegant lounge. Other facilities include conference rooms, a 24-hour business center, shopping complex, courts for tennis, squash, and racquetball, a putting green, and an indoor/outdoor pool. Double rooms from US$115 plus 10 percent service. 1376 Nanjing Road West. Tel. 279–8888. Telex 33272 CPTCS CN. Fax 279–8999.

Shanghai International Airport Hotel. This functional building has 300 air-conditioned rooms on eight floors, each room with IDD telephone, color TV, and minibar. One restaurant has a Japanese menu, the other offers Chinese and Western-style food. A lounge, a bar, a shopping arcade, a business center, foreign exchange desk, and airlines ticket counter are available to guests. A shuttle bus reaches the airport (¼ mile) and downtown (45 minutes, depending on traffic). Double rooms from US$95 plus 10 percent service. 2550 Hongqiao Road. Tel. 251–8888, 251–8866. Telex 30033 SIANA CN. Cable 9918. Fax 251–8393, 251–8260.

Shanghai Hilton International. Located about 25 minutes from the airport and 15 minutes from downtown by taxi, the Shanghai Hilton offers 800 luxuriously appointed rooms and 41 suites on 40 floors. Floors 36 through 38 provide executive accommodations. Rooms are equipped with individually controlled air-conditioning, refrigerator, minibar, IDD telephone, color TV, and in-house movie service. Recreational facilities include a heated indoor pool, gymnasium, saunas, an outdoor tennis court, two squash courts, billiards, and table tennis. There are three Chinese restaurants, one restaurant serving Western and Japanese-style dishes, a roof-top bar, and lounges in the lobby and by the pool. The Executive Business Center provides office, secretarial, and translation services for business visitors. Underground parking for more than 300 cars. Double rooms from US$125 plus 10 percent service. 250 Huashan Road. Tel. 255–0000. Telex 33612 HILTL CN. Cable Hiltels. Fax 255–3848.

Shanghai JC Mandarin. This stylish addition to the ranks of Shanghai's deluxe hotels, scheduled to open in summer 1990, is conveniently located next to the Exhibition Center and opposite the Portnam. The 600 large, tastefully furnished rooms have IDD telephone, color TV, minibar, climate control, and full-length mirror; bathrooms have hair dryer, scales, and telephone extension. Amenities of the executive floor (23rd and 24th levels) include butler, lounge, breakfast, and cocktail hour. A Chinese restaurant prepares Cantonese food, a brasserie has a Western menu, and there's a pub, a bar, a disco, and a business center. Two tennis courts, two squash courts, an indoor pool, and a fitness center serve recreational needs. The hotel maintains an airport desk and a limo service. Double rooms from US$135, suites from US$250, plus 10 percent service. 1225 Nanjing Road West. Tel. 433–5550. Telex 33346 SJCM CN. Fax 433–5405.

Sheraton Hua Ting. The Hua Ting, with 1,008 rooms behind a curved and stepped facade, was the first hotel to be operated in Shanghai by an international group. Located about 30 minutes from the airport (a courtesy car is available) yet close to downtown, the Sheraton boasts two lounges, a disco, and five restaurants offering Chinese, Japanese, and Western cuisine. (The hotel's most prestigious Chinese restaurant is on the 25th floor.) Guest rooms have air-conditioning, color TV, refrigerator, and stylish decor. The banquet hall accommodates 800, and there are 20 smaller function rooms. A pool, tennis court, and health club provide recreational opportunities. Double rooms from US$100 plus 10 percent service. 1200 Cao Xi Bei Lu. Tel. 439–6000, 439–1000. Telex 33589 SHHTH CN. Cable 0703. Fax 255–0830, 255–0719.

Yangtze New World. Situated in the Shanghai Economic and Technical Development Zone, about midway between the airport and downtown, this impressive new hotel has 577 rooms, each with climate control, IDD telephone, color TV, and minibar; nonsmoking floors; four floors of exclusive business accomodations; and a business center. Dining facilities include three Chinese restaurants, a Western-style restaurant, and a coffee shop. For recreation there is the swimming pool, a health club, a gym, and in the evening a discotheque. Other facilities are a shopping arcade, medical clinic, luggage storage room, airport counter, limousine service, and parking for 134 cars. Double rooms from US$100 plus 10 percent service. Yanan Road, Hongqiao. Tel. 259–5227. Fax 251–7851.

Other Hotels. The hotels listed above are the top quality establishments of Shanghai. Among other establishments offering reasonable accommodations are the **Heping (Peace) Hotel** on the Bund, an old landmark that has deteriorated (tel. 321–1244); **Jingan Guest House** at 370 Huashan Road, with excellent food and service and an outdoor café (tel. 256–3050 or 255–1888); **Shanghai Hotel** on Wulumuqi Bei Road, offering 600 air-conditioned rooms with modern amenities (tel. 431–2312 or 255–2678); and **Shanghai Mansions** at 20 Suzhou North Road, with 17 stories, 254 rooms, and breathtaking views (tel. 324–6260). Budget accommodations can be found at the **Huaqiao Hotel,** 104 Nanjing Road (tel. 327–6226), and the **Pujiang Hotel** at 15 Huangpu Road (tel. 324–6388).

RESTAURANTS. Shanghai's hundreds of restaurants prepare dishes in all the styles of cuisine found in China. The best banquet restaurants are located in the hotels, particularly in the deluxe hotels, both new and old. One such restaurant worthy of a special visit is the **Fangshan Tang** on the third floor of the Dahua Hotel, 914 Yanan Road (tel. 252–3079), where the waitresses dress in Qing dynasty costume and serve food prepared in Qing imperial style.

For an evening event out of the ordinary, you might host a banquet for up to 25 guests in the **Yu Yuan**, where the banquet hall must be reserved well in advance, preferably with the assistance of your hotel. Such a banquet will be expensive.

Yangzhou Restaurant. 308 Nanjing Dong Road, tel. 322–2777. Superb Shanghai cooking, particularly seafood. Book early; there is only one private dining room and it is one of the most popular restaurants in Shanghai. Try the wild duck.

Xin Ya Restaurant. 719 Nanjing Road, tel. 322–4393. A famous old restaurant providing good regional dishes, but specializing in Canton cooking. The ground floor is a cake and pastry shop, the restaurant being located on the second and third floors. Some of the old waiters worked there before the Revolution and speak good English. Service is excellent.

Red House Western Food Restaurant. 37 Shaanxi Road (South), tel. 256–5748. Here the influence is distinctly French. Standard favorites such as cocktail de crevettes, tournedos, and even crepes suzettes and Grand Marnier soufflé. The maître d'hôtel is fluent in English and French. Formerly known as "Chez Louis," called the "Hongfangzi" in Chinese. Prices are high. Located only a few minutes' walk from the Jinjiang Hotel.

Dahongyun. 556 Fuzhou Road, tel. 322–4459 or 322–3176. Wuxi dishes; the crab is especially good.

Meixin. 314 Shaanxi Road South, tel. 437–3991. Cantonese; the fried rice is superb.

Moslem. 710 Fuzhou Road, tel. 322–4273. Moslem-style dishes.

Leo (Old) Shanghai. 242 Fuyou Road, tel 328–9850. Shanghai and Jiangsu cuisine.

Sichuan. 457 Nanjing Road, tel. 322–1965. Spicy Sichuan-style cooking.

Chengdu. 795 Huaihai Road, tel. 437–6412. Features spicy dishes.

The Ruijin Building in the old French Concession Area of Shanghai has a host of restaurants: The **Ruijin Palace** on the 27th floor prepares Cantonese dishes, especially dim sum; the adjacent **Cellar in the Sky** offers cocktails and fifties jazz groups; on the third floor, the elegant **Jade Gardens** is popular for business lunches and evening banquets; on the fourth floor, the **Champagne Room** serves Western cuisine.

Banquet Suggestions. You can eat superbly at the leading hotels, either à la carte or at a banquet. Should you wish to get together with your friends or repay the hospitality of your Chinese hosts, you can arrange a dinner or luncheon by ordering a banquet menu. For guidance see the chapter *Chinese Cuisine.* Alternatively, leave the choice entirely to the chef. All you need do is advise the hotel desk of the day, time, number of persons attending, and the cost per head (does not include drinks), usually 24 hours in advance.

Snacks. Shanghainese delight in snacking at the hundreds of small restaurants specializing in these sweet and savory delicacies. Join them and try the steamed dumplings filled with minced pork; fried beef dumplings; steamed rice dough stuffed with delicacies; eight-jeweled rice; and sesame cakes.

Pastry, Cake, and Ice Cream. Some visitors to China get a craving for cream cakes and ice cream sundaes and, in Shanghai, you can find these in abundance.

If you would like to try the cakes and pastry that the locals eat—the people of Shanghai are well known in China for their "sweet tooth"—then you should go to one of the following shops: the **Donghai,** 145 Nanjing Road East, near the corner of the third block from the Bund, on the left-hand side; the **Deda,** 359 Sichuan Zhong Lu; the **Kaige** at 569 and 1001 Nanjing Road—formerly **Kiesling** and **Bader.** These are all well known, but if you can't find them, go into any of the multitude of cake and pastry shops.

TOURIST INFORMATION. Each of the new international-standard hotels has a travel office to serve guests. **CITS** is at 66 Nanjing Road East, about 30 yards from the northern exit of the Peace Hotel at 33 Zhongshan Road East (tel. 432–

4960, 321–7200); and at 66 Nanjing Road East. CITS also has an office at the airport (tel. 432–9327), at the railway station (tel. 324–0319), and at the Peace Hotel (tel. 321–1244) for independent travelers.

Air China (tel. 253–2255 for international bookings and **China East Airlines** (tel. 253–5953) for domestic bookings are at 789 Yan An Zhong Road, not far from the Shanghai Exhibition Center. Hours: 8:30 A.M.–12 noon and 1–5 P.M.

PSB (tel. 521–5380) is at 210 Hankou Road, near the bus stop for route 49, between Henan and Jiangxi roads. Open 8:30 A.M.–12 noon and 1:30–5:30 P.M.

HOW TO GET AROUND. From the airport. There is a shuttle-bus from the airport to the CAAC office in the city center, but few taxis on arrival to take you to your hotel. You will normally find it more convenient (but expensive) to take a taxi all the way from the airport. Many hotels provide shuttle bus service to and from the airport.

Railway station. The best way to get to your hotel from the railway station is by taxi. Taxis have a meter, and you should always insist that the driver turn it on.

Ship's terminal. Again, either taxis or the 3-wheeler bikes are the alternatives (that is, if you are not assigned to go on one of the buses organized for travelers on a package tour).

Sights. Some of the sites of Shanghai are best seen on foot, but many others are spread around the city so—if you are not on an organized tour—you will need to travel by taxi or (if you can read Chinese) by bus or trolley-bus. Bus maps may be purchased at your hotel. Buses are very crowded at almost all times. Taxis and 3-wheeled cabs can be arranged by your hotel; have the destination or directions written in Chinese. Set the price before departing.

HEALTH. The major precaution to take is to avoid drinking water from the faucet. Drink only water that has been boiled. Hotels always provide containers of boiled water in guest rooms. Use this even when cleaning your teeth. If you are going out for a long day's sightseeing in hot weather, take some water in a bottle or plastic container to sip during the day.

Avoid eating cooked food from street stalls, as their hygiene is suspect. There is usually no problem with fruit that must be peeled before eating.

MEDICAL SERVICES. If you are not feeling well, advise your hotel desk immediately. They will arrange for you to go to a clinic in a hospital or, should you be too ill to travel, for a doctor to come to your hotel room.

Shanghai has good medical facilities. The hospital normally used by foreign visitors is **Shanghai No. 1 People's Hospital,** 190 Beisuzhou Lu, tel. 324–0100. The outpatient clinic is at 410 Beisuzhou Lu (same tel.). A range of Western drugs and medicines is available at **Shanghai No. 8 Drugstore;** 951 Huaihai Zhonglu.

Hospital, medical, and pharmaceutical services are not provided free of charge.

SECURITY. You can walk around Shanghai without fear—quite extraordinary for a city of this size. However, occasional petty theft does occur, so keep your room locked. To avoid pickpockets in crowded places, keep your wallet, pocketbook, and money in a safe place on your person.

WHAT TO SEE. The **Bund,** now Zhonghan Road, still remains one of the great streets of the world. You will get a good view of the Bund from the top floors of the Shanghai Mansions and also from the Heping (Peace) Hotel. Stroll along the sea wall of the Bund and wander through its well-laid parks and gardens.

In the Old Town you will find the famous teahouse **Wu Xing Ting,** Yu the Mandarin's Garden (**Yu Yuan**), the **Yu Yuan Bazaar,** and **Temple of the Town Gods.**

Nanjing Road is the main shopping street. The **Shanghai Museum** and the **Museum of Natural Sciences** are located nearby and are worth a visit. Business executives may wish to visit the **Shanghai Exhibition Center** in Yan An Road and see the vast array of products made in the area.

The **People's Recreation Hall** (Da Shi Jie) and the **Children's Palaces** are of interest; so too are the **People's Park** and **People's Square** occupying the area of the former racetrack.

Those interested in old Chinese culture may care to visit the Buddhist **Long Hua Temple,** the **Jingansi Monastery,** and the recently restored **Yufosi Monastery,** which houses 2 jade statues of Buddha.

More recent historical sights include the old **French Concession Quarter, Lu Xun's Tomb and Museum,** the old American area, and the Japanese Concession in the Hong Kou district.

MUSEUMS. The **Shanghai Museum** at 16 South Henan Road (tel. 328–0160) possesses a valuable collection of historical and artistic objects displayed to show the evolution of art in China. There are four floors, covering the period from the Shang Dynasty down to the Qing. There is a fine collection of bronzes from the Shang and Zhou civilizations, a large 3-legged cauldron (ding); several pieces of rare Shang pottery. There are also interesting examples of wooden tomb figurines from the Warring States period as well as a fine collection of bronze lances and swords. Two life-size terra-cotta warriors and a horse are on display from the famous Qin Shi Huang Di burial chambers of Xian. It is worth a visit to the museum just to see these archeological treasures.

There is an interesting display of Han Dynasty clay tomb figurines featuring examples of a pigsty, a granary, guards armed with crossbows, some very fine carvings of ducks, horses, and dogs, as well as figures of workers with spades and soldiers with swords.

There are also some excellent pieces of sculpture from the era when Buddhism was widely adopted in China, particularly some original pieces from Dun Huang, one of the three famous centers where Buddhist cave carvings are located. There are some fine examples of the "3 colors" Tang pottery, as well as Shanxi celadon ware from the Sung period; paintings and porcelains from the Yuan Dynasty; paintings; porcelains, cloisonné ware, embroideries, and lacquer ware from the Ming. There is a similar range of art objects from the Qing period.

The museum features arts-and-crafts products from different provinces in China. These are items that have been created since 1949. Open daily, 9:30–11:30 A.M. and 1:30–5 P.M.

Lu Xun Museum: Lu Xun is the most respected and revered modern author in China. When he died in 1936 he was buried in a cemetery in the western town. In 1956 his ashes were removed and taken to the (then) Hong Kou Park, now known as the Lu Xun Memorial Park. It is located in the north of the city on Baoshan Road. There is a statue of Lu Xun seated on a pedestal in front of the tomb bearing his remains. Delightful flower beds are arranged around the pedestal. The Lu Xun Museum was opened in 1951 in the house where the writer spent the final few years of his life, but in 1956 the museum was transferred to the present site.

In the museum you will find exhibits of his letters, manuscripts, photographs depicting his wife, family, and friends. There are original copies of correspondence with famous writers, particularly George Bernard Shaw. There are also valuable copies of Lu Xun's printed works, along with woodcuts illustrating the books; the texts of lectures, particularly relating to mass education and the reform of Chinese characters, and collections of his revolutionary writings. Museum closed Sundays, Tuesday and Thursday mornings. Visiting hours 8:30 A.M.–noon and 2–4:30 P.M. Tomb open daily, 8 A.M.–7 P.M.

Sun Yatsen Museum: This small museum is located in the southwest of the city and was the house in which Dr. Sun Yatsen resided when in Shanghai. He died in 1925, and the 2-story building is now a museum dedicated to his life.

Museum of Natural History: The museum provides an excellent display of regional fauna and flora. There are also well-preserved human corpses on display, one about 3,200 years old. Museum closed Tuesdays and Saturday mornings; hours 8:30–10:30 A.M. and 1–3:30 P.M.

RECREATION. All of the deluxe hotels recently constructed in Shanghai have recreation facilities that are available to nonguests for a fee.

SHOPPING. Nanjing Road, running west from the Peace Hotel on the Bund, is the best place to shop. Here you will find stores selling the complete range of goods available to the Chinese consumer. Even though you do not speak Chinese, you can go into these shops, look around, and buy the merchandise. You will find that the excellent linen, tableware, cotton sheets, and towels (designs usually poor) are good buys. Basketware, pottery products, and other arts-and-crafts items are worth examining.

The silks produced in the region, especially from Hangzhou, Suzhou, and Shanghai itself, are superb and make wonderful gifts. One of the best places to buy silk fabric is the **Shanghai Silk Shop** (tel. 322–4830) at 592 Nanjing Dong Road.

Shanghai stores also stock excellent quality silk scarves and ties, cashmere and wool sweaters, and handbags, wallets, and jewelry. Shanghai is an important printing center, and you can buy fine writing paper, notebooks, diaries, greeting cards, and calendars.

The largest store in the city is the **Shanghai No. 1 Department Store** (tel. 322–3344) at 830 Nanjing Road East; and the second largest is the **Shanghai No. 10 Department Store** (tel. 322–4466) at 635 Nanjing Road East. Nearby is the **Overseas Chinese Store** (tel. 322–5424) at 627 Nanjing Road East. The **Shanghai Exhibition Center** (tel. 256–3037) at 1000 Yanan Zhonglu Road has many Chinese products for sale.

Handicrafts

Shanghai offers an excellent array of handicraft items available through several outlets (besides the ones already mentioned above). The **Shanghai Arts and Crafts Store** (tel. 253–8206, 253–1796) at 190–208 Nanjing Road West, next to the Park Hotel, is a good place to start. A sister organization, **Shanghai Arts and Crafts Shops** at 751 Nanjing Road, also offers a good selection. Another place worth checking is the **Jewelry and Jade Store** at 438 Nanjing Road East.

Antiques

The best place to get an idea of the range of goods available and the price levels prevailing is the **Antiques and Curios Branch Store** (tel. 253–8092, 253–2605) at 694 Nanjing West Road. It is a branch of the Friendship Store. Also try the **Shanghai Antiques Store** (tel. 321–2292, 321–6529) at 194–226 Guangdong Road. If you are seeking top-of-the-range calligraphy and paintings, visit **Duoyunxian** (tel. 322–3410) at 422 Nanjing Road East, just one shop down from the Jewelry and Jade Store.

The shop with the most interesting collection is the **Chuan Xin Shop,** 1297 Huai Hai Road Central. It has a good range of porcelain, ceramics, old wooden boxes, copper ware, music boxes, pewter ware, lacquer ware, and old jewelry.

The **Shaanxi Shop** in 557 Yanan Zhong Road (tel. 256–5489) has a large collection of Chinese and Western ceramics and porcelain ware, silverware, jewelry, furs, and clocks.

ENTERTAINMENT. One of the great entertainments offered in Shanghai are the performances by acrobats, magicians, conjurers, and animal trainers at the **Shanghai Acrobatic Theater** (tel. 256–4704; 265–4051), 400 Nanjing Road West. These shows of rare skill never fail to delight the audience. Tickets may be arranged through CITS or your hotel. Theater closed on Tuesdays.

Also check with your hotel to find out whether there are any other evening events that might appeal to you. Shanghai has a host of theaters as well as a concert hall, so there is usually a performance of some sort held every evening.

Each spring, the **Shanghai Music Festival** is held in the city. The dates vary each year, so check with your hotel or CITS. During the festival you will have the opportunity to attend many daytime and evening performances of music, song, and dance by hundreds of talented artists.

Other items of interest are the **Shanghai Marathon** run in March, and the **Mid-Autumn Festival** in October when "moon cakes" abound.

A few privately operated bars have opened in the old French Concession Area near the Hilton International; they have names such as **Manhattan, Fifth Avenue,** and **Coco's,** and they play tapes of Western and Chinese pop music.

BUSINESS CENTER. The ultramodern **Shanghai Center,** features a large exhibition hall, 280,000 sq. ft. of office space, retail facilities, theater/conference hall, and 472 apartments. Located opposite the Exhibition Center, it has become the locus of business activities in downtown Shanghai.

LEAVING SHANGHAI. Travelers departing Shanghai have an enormous range of alternatives to consider.

International air. Shanghai has international flights to Hong Kong (2 hours, 10 mins.), Los Angeles, Nagasaki, New York, Osaka, San Francisco, Paris, Toronto, Vancouver, Sharjah, Fukuoka, and Tokyo. Reservations can be made through Air China or CITS, and information provided by the appropriate national carriers located in Shanghai (see later section on Useful Addresses and Telephone Numbers.)

There is a shuttle-bus to Hongqiao airport from the Air China office at 789 Yan An Zhonglu (near the intersection with Shaanxi Road). Journey time is 30–45 minutes.

Domestic air. Shanghai has a domestic flight service to 29 regional centers, so the city is an excellent point of departure for visitors traveling on to other destinations within China. CITS or China East Airline can arrange reservations and ticketing. Because flights are heavily booked, it's important to make reservations as early as possible.

Train. Many train travelers head northwest from Shanghai along the well-known Suzhou-Wuxi-Zhenjiang-Nanjing trail. Others head southwest to Hangzhou. Either way there are plenty of train services covering these destinations.

Travel times for these destinations are: Suzhou 1¼ hours; Wuxi 1¼ hours; Zhenjiang 3½ hours; Nanjing 4 hours; Hangzhou 3 hours.

Traveling times for long distance destinations are: Zhengzhou 15¼ hours and Xian 26 hours; Nanchang 16½ hours and Zhuzhou (south of Changsha) 24 hours; Beijing 19¼ hours; and Guangzhou 33 hours.

Trains for all the above destinations depart from Shanghai Main Station in the north of Shanghai at 1 Kangji Road. Tickets may be purchased in advance at the railway office at 230 Beijing Road, or at four other locations around the city.

Ferry. The term "ferry" has been used here to distinguish those vessels that ply the inland waterways from those that undertake coastal voyages (see "Ship" below). The term does not convey any indication of the size of the respective vessels. Some of the ferries are quite large, others small. Generally the larger the ferry the better the facilities.

Of major interest to travelers are those ferries that go up the Yangzi from Shanghai. The **Shanghai-Wuhan** section of the river does not compare in scenery with the "Three Gorges" section seen by those who undertake the downstream journey from Chongqing, but is interesting nevertheless. There are two services daily: one by the slow ferry, the other by fast ferry.

The slow ferry takes 66–67 hours to make the 700-mile journey upstream to **Wuhan,** making 12 stops along the way. The river ports visited are: Nantong, Zhenhai, Ma Anshan, Wuhu, Tongling, Chizhou, Anqing, Huayang, Jiujiang, Wuxue, Huangshi, and finally Wuhan. The fast ferry takes 51–52 hours to make the journey and stops only at 6 river ports. From Wuhan there is a slow ferry that goes further upstream to **Chongqing,** taking 101 hours to do the 850-mile journey.

The ferry to Wuhan departs Shanghai from the **Shiliupu Dock,** just off Zhongshan Road and east of the Old Town. Same-day tickets are available at the ticket office (tel. 328–2070) on the dock; advance ticket purchases are made at General Navigation Company ticket office (tel. 326–1261) at 222 Renmin Road.

Ship. Shanghai offers many services to Chinese ports along the coast. The frequency varies from daily to weekly, depending on destination.

The major ports served south of Shanghai are: **Ningpo** 12 hours; **Wenzhou** 21 hours; and **Fuzhou** 34 hours. Major ports served north of Shanghai are: **Qingdao** 26 hours; **Dalian** 36 hours; and **Tianjin** 48 hours.

Vessels for southern destinations leave from **Shiliupu Dock,** off Zhongshan Road and east of the Old Town. Vessels for northern destinations leave from the **Gongping Road Dock,** off Daming Road and east of the Shanghai Mansions.

Same-day tickets for these vessels may be purchased at the above departure docks; advance tickets at the General Navigation Company ticket office (tel. 326–1261), 222 Renmin Road.

To Hong Kong by Ship. From Shanghai there is a departure every five days to Hong Kong on the *Shanghai* or the *Haixing.* The 850-mile journey takes 56 hours. Many visitors find the Shanghai-Hong Kong route a fine way to end their travels in China.

The vessels depart from the **Waihong International Passenger Terminal,** five minutes from the Shanghai Mansions and just off East Daming Road. Tickets may be purchased from the China Ocean Shipping Agency ticket office (tel. 321–6327), 255 Jiangxi Zhong Road.

USEFUL ADDRESSES AND TELEPHONE NUMBERS

Telephone Services

International telephone calls: Information, tel. 112.
Domestic long-distance calls: Information, tel. 114.

Travel Services

CITS, 66 Nanjing Road East. Tel. 321–6229.
    Peace Hotel (for independent travelers.) Tel. 321–1244.
    Airport. Tel. 432–9327.
    Railway Station. Tel. 324–0319.
CTS, 104 Nanjing West Road. Tel. 322–6226.
Air China and **China East Airlines,** 789 Yan An Zhong Road.
    International reservations. Tel. 253–2255.
    Domestic reservations. Tel. 253–5953.
    Airport—Flight info. desk. Tel. 253–7664.
PSB, 210 Hankou Road. Tel. 321–1997.
Huangpo River Tourism Service. Tel. 321–1098.
Shanghai Tourism Corporation, 14 Zhongshan Road. Tel. 321–9341.

Consulates

Australian Consulate, 17 Fuxing Road West. Tel. 437–4580, 256–3050.
Belgian Consulate, 305 Jingan Guest House, Room 303. Tel. 253–8882.
British Consulate, 244 Yongfu Road. Tel. 437–4569.
French Consulate, 1431 Huaihai Zhong Road. Tel. 437–7414.
German (FRG) Consulate, 181 Yongfu Road. Tel. 437–9953.
Italian Consulate, 127 Wuyi Road. Tel. 252–4373.
Japanese Consulate, 1517 Huaihai Road. Tel. 437–2073.
Polish Consulate, 618 Jianguo Xi Road. Tel. 437–0952.
U.S. Consulate, 1469 Huaihui Road. Tel. 437–8511, 437–9880, 437–3103.

Airlines

Cathay Pacific, Jinjiang Hotel, Room 123. Tel. 437–7899.
Japan Airlines, 1202 Huaihai Road. Tel. 437–8467.
Northwest Airlines, Jinjiang Hotel, North Bldg., Room 127 Tel. 437–7387.
Singapore Airlines, Jinjiang Hotel, West Bldg., Room 1341. Tel. 437–7602.
United Airlines, Hilton International Hotel, 250 Huashan Road. Tel. 255–3333.

Business

Bank of China, 23 Zhongshan Road. Tel. 321–5666.
Chartered Bank, 185 Yuanmingyuan Road. Tel. 321–8253.
HK and Shanghai Bank, 185 Yuanmingyuan Road. Tel. 321–8383.
Bank of America, Union Building, Room 1802, 100 Yanan East Road. Tel. 328–9661.
CCPIT, 33 Zhongshan Road East. Tel. 323–3575.
China National Import & Export Corporations:
    Animal By-Prod., 23 Zhongshan Road. East Tel. 321–5630.
    Arts and Crafts, 16 Zhongshan East Road. Tel. 321–2100.
    Cereals and Oils, 11 Hangkou Road. Tel. 321–9760.
    Foodstuffs, 26 Zhongshan East Road. Tel. 321–6233.
    Chemicals, 27 Zhongshan Road East. Tel. 321–1540.
    Transportation, 74 Dianchi Road. Tel. 321–3103.

Light Industrial, 128 Huqin Road. Tel. 321–6858.
Machinery, 27 Zhongshan Road East. Tel. 321–5066.
Metals and Minerals, 27 Zhongshan Road East. Tel. 321–1220.
Textiles (Garments), 27 Zhongshan Road East. Tel. 321–8500.
Textiles (Silks), 17 Zhongshan Road East. Tel. 321–5770.

OTHER MAJOR TOURIST CENTERS

Highlight Destinations for Extended Travel

Geographic Regions

China may be divided arbitrarily into eight major regional divisions along the lines shown in the map. These divisions arise from the general west-east alignment of the mountains and major river systems, creating certain differences in climate patterns, land use, and cultural development.

The arbitrary division between North and South China roughly follows the geographic demarcation established by the Qinling Mountain chain, which runs well south of the Yellow River and just north of the Yangzi. Shanghai, which lies almost on this arbitrary division line, is considered to be in "the South," a description that is confusing to the visitor since it is near the midpoint of the eastern seaboard and looks to be far from what might normally be considered a southern region.

The greater proportion of a visitor's time in China is normally spent in the North and South regions. As adequate hotel facilities are provided in more remote areas, more visitors are traveling to the Northeast, Northwest, Southwest, Xinjiang, Inner Mongolia, and even to Tibet.

The Xinjiang area is the home of peoples who were included in the Chinese state relatively late in history. Many of them are Moslems, yet they comprise different ethnic groups such as the Uighur Turks, the Kazaks, and the Kirghiz.

Tibet was "liberated" by the Communists in 1950 and now gives its name to the southern and western areas of China. These highlands, al-

295

though occupying more than a quarter of the total area of China, support less than 1 percent of the entire population.

In the Southwest the influence of the Han Chinese is much less pronounced, the mountainous, semitropical environment largely cutting off the indigenous groups from outside influences. The biggest ethnic-minority group in China is located in this region: the Zhuang—a Thai-speaking community numbering about seven million. They live principally in the Guang Xi Autonomous Region. The Miao is another non-Han group living in the Southwest; they number about three million and live mainly in the mountainous areas. Other ethnic groups in the area are the Yao, the Yi or Lolo, numbering over three million, and the Bouyei, numbering over a million.

The Northeast encompasses what was once Manchuria. The Manchus, who ruled China for almost 300 years until their dynasty fell in 1911, have now been almost completely assimilated and have lost their national identity. In contrast, the Koreans in the region (who number over a million) have maintained their group identity.

Finding Your Way Around

The centers other than Beijing, Guangzhou, and Shanghai appear in alphabetical order in the pages that follow. All are cities or towns, with two exceptions: Inner Mongolia and Tibet.

If you cannot locate the center by quickly flipping through the pages, then go to the index at the rear of this book. The town or village you're looking for may be listed as an "excursion from" another center.

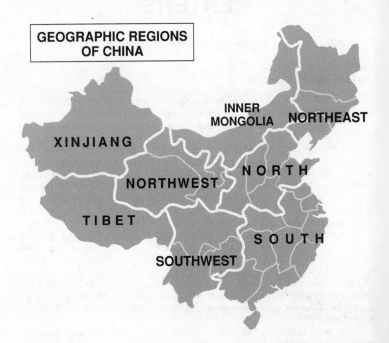

GEOGRAPHIC REGIONS OF CHINA

XINJIANG

INNER MONGOLIA

NORTHEAST

NORTH

NORTHWEST

TIBET

SOUTH

SOUTHWEST

BEIDAIHE

Hebei Province

North China

Until the beginning of the century, Beidaihe was simply a small fishing village. Then foreign diplomats, businessmen, and missionaries began building villas and bungalows there. Before long, the village became a well-known beach resort, where people went to escape the summer heat of Beijing and Tianjin. After the People's Republic was founded, the large villas and bungalows were converted to rest homes for Chinese cadres and workers. In later years, a number of the bungalows were made available in the summer months to foreign diplomats. Today, some of the larger guest houses are available to foreign visitors.

EXPLORING BEIDAIHE

There is little to do in Beidaihe but swim, bathe, and rest. Indeed, one of the most exciting events in the small town is the unfolding of a purple flower that blossoms in the evening for two hours once a year. Diplomats and their gardeners spend tense evenings in a small room, watching over every tremor of this fragile green plant. Applause and celebration greet the blossom's arrival.

Apart from blossom watching, there are pleasant walks to be made—some along the many beaches that line the coast, others amid cool pine forests lining the water's edge. Or you may simply choose to sit on one of the many small promontories and ponder. Tiger Rock, at the right-hand end of the prettiest beach in the region, is a favorite spot for "ponderers." You can also visit Lotus Rock Park and the Temple of Guanyin nearby.

EXCURSIONS FROM BEIDAIHE

One excursion worth taking is to Shanhaiguan, located about 25 miles north of Beidaihe. On the way you will pass the unattractive town of Qinhuangdao, an important all-weather port.

In Shanhaiguan, the Sheraton Old Dragon Head Resort, under constuction on the beachfront where the eastern extremity of the Great Wall meets the sea, is one of the best places in China to explore the wall, and guests will be able to walk or jog along a 7-mile section of it.

PRACTICAL INFORMATION FOR BEIDAIHE

FACTS AND FIGURES. Beidaihe, located on the coast of the Bo Hai Gulf due east of Beijing, is about five hours' train journey from the capital.

WHEN TO GO. Being a seaside resort, Beidaihe is best visited May through September.

HOW TO GET THERE. Beidaihe is usually taken as an excursion from Beijing or Tianjin. There are seven trains to and from Beidaihe daily. There are also flights from Beijing to nearby Shanhaiguan (22 miles to the north) which take 50 minutes.

HOTELS. All accommodations are either in guest houses or bungalows. The leading guest houses are: the **Dongshan,** or East Hill (tel. 2028, office, or 2528, service desk); the **Xishan** or West Hill (tel. 2018, office, or 2678, service desk); the **Zhonghaitan,** or Mid-Seashore Guest House (tel. 2445, office, 2398, service desk); the **Haibin Fandian** (tel. 2355) near the Bank of China and the **Jinshan Hotel.** The largest guest house is known affectionately to foreign residents of Beijing as "Diplomatic Asylum."

RESTAURANTS. A restaurant famous because of its past is the former Kiesling and Bader, which still features a number of European dishes on the menu and provides cutlery engraved with the names of the former European owners. The style is austere but the ambiance pleasant. The **Beidaihe Travel and Tourism Club** (tel. 2355), formerly the International Club, runs a restaurant of reasonable standard. Try their crabe gratiné. Another establishment, the **Beihai Restaurant,** specializes in seafood.

TOURIST INFORMATION. You can organize tours at the **CITS** office (tel. 2355) located near the gates of the Zhonghaitan Guest House.

HOW TO GET AROUND. Public buses operate between Beidaihe and the beach every half-hour between 6 A.M. and 6.30 P.M. You may hire cars or buses from the **Beidaihe Beach Tourism Corporation** (tel. 2748). Your hotel can arrange the hire of bicycles. Sailboats and sailboards may be hired at the beach. Beidaihe is an ideal place to explore on foot, although the elderly should note that there are lots of steps between the beach and the town.

WHAT TO SEE. The most interesting site is the **Guanyin Temple,** first built in 1911 and restored in 1979 after suffering heavy damage at the hands of the Red Guards during the Cultural Revolution. The temple is located about a mile from the West Hill Guest House.

MUSEUMS. The small oceanic and marine museum is worth visiting. Your hotel or CITS can make arrangements.

SHOPPING. A few shops sell handicraft items. The best buys are hand-embroidered articles, such as tablecloths, napkins, and handkerchiefs. Raffia and basketware are of good quality and reasonably priced.

If you hanker for Western-style pastry, there is a good cake shop and a candy store.

ENTERTAINMENT. The guest houses often show films in the evenings. You can also arrange to have lessons in *taiji quan* exercises, cooking, and massage. The Beidaihe Beach Club in the Xishan Guest House has dance areas, but you should bring your own cassette tapes.

USEFUL ADDRESSES AND TELEPHONE NUMBERS

CITS—Haibin Guest House, tel. 2355.
Car Hire—Beidaihe Beach Tourist Corp., tel. 2748.

CHANGCHUN

Jilin Province
Northeast China

Changchun, meaning "eternal spring" in Chinese, is the capital of Jilin Province. Located in the center of the northeast plain, Changchun was first settled more than 1,000 years ago. However, the town did not develop until the Russians pushed through the Trans-Siberian railway to the banks of the Yitong River at the turn of this century. The town grew enormously in the 1930s after it was made the capital of the Japanese puppet state, Manchukuo, during Japan's military occupation of the area (1933–1945). Wide avenues were constructed, tall buildings erected—most with prominent watchtowers—and electricity lines were laid underground for strategic reasons.

The town was developed further after the revolution. China's first automobile factory was built, factories were set up to produce railway cars, electric motors, machine tools, textiles, and processed foodstuffs. Major feature films were produced at the Changchun film studios. Jilin University is prominent in China in many special fields, and the town's research institutes have a good reputation in China.

EXPLORING CHANGCHUN

The town is not old, many of the buildings dating from the 1930s; as a consequence, there are no historical sites or ancient monuments in Changchun. Nevertheless, there are some places of interest for visitors. For scenery, you might care to visit Laodong Park, where you will find many pines and willows, pavilions, lotus ponds, and small bridges. There are other parks of lesser interest: Nanhu or Southlake Park, People's (Renmin) Park, and Shengli Park. You can arrange a visit to the Jilin University, the Chinese Academy of Science, and the Geological Institute. If you are interested in how cars and trucks are made, then you can visit the vast factory in the town set up in the 1950s for this purpose. If film-making is of interest, you can arrange to visit the well-known Changchun Movie Studio.

EXCURSIONS FROM CHANGCHUN

Xinlicheng Reservoir

A most pleasant excursion is one to Xinlicheng Reservoir. Situated on the upper reaches of the Yitong River, about 12 miles upstream (i.e., south) from Changchun, the reservoir is surrounded by scenic forests. There are orchards and deer farms in the vicinity.

Jilin

Jilin—renowned for the "three treasures of the northeast": ginseng, sable furs, and antler horn—is located due east of Changchun on a tributary of the Songhua River. It has beautiful surroundings: the northern reaches of man-made lake Songhua Hu flow through the town and, nearby, the Songhua River runs through thick stands of forest. Willows line its banks. In winter, they become encrusted with ice crystals, formed when the warm water from the nearby powerstation vaporizes, then freezes. As a result, the winter scenery along the river is famous throughout China.

Another place of great beauty is Beishan Park to the northwest of the town. Occupying 320 acres and with a fine man-made lake, the park possesses many pavilions. A bridge known as the Phoenix Harness, crosses the lake. Skiing and ice-skating are very popular in and around Jilin in winter.

PRACTICAL INFORMATION FOR CHANGCHUN

FACTS AND FIGURES. Changchun, the capital of Jilin Province, has a population of over 1.5 million people. Located in the far northeast of China on the Yitong River, it is about 520 miles to the north of Beijing, a journey of about 1½ hours by air and 17–18½ hours by rail. Changchun is on the same rail route as Tianjin and Shenyang.

WHEN TO GO. Avoid winter, as it is bitterly cold. Summer (mid-June through August) and fall (September and October) are the best seasons to visit. The summer months are the wettest but the rainfall is rarely excessive.

HOW TO GET THERE. The most convenient way from Beijing is by air (1½ hours) but the journey takes about 2½ hours if you make a stopover in Shenyang. The train journey from Beijing is a long one, as the route loops southeast through Tianjin until the coast is reached before turning northeast toward Shenyang, and on to Changchun. The journey takes 17–18½ hours, depending on which of the seven daily train services you choose. Perhaps the most convenient service for sightseeing is the 12:59 P.M. express from Beijing arriving Changchun at 6 A.M. the following day. The train allows 5 hours of scenery and you will see, before summer nightfall, the eastern extremity of the Great Wall, near Shanhaiguan, where it dips into the sea.

HOTELS. The most modern hotel is the **Changbaishan Guest House** (tel. 53551) at 12 Xinmin Street. Visitors also stay at the **Chunyi Hotel**, 2 Stalin Boulevard (tel. 38495), just opposite the Changchun railway station. The rooms are pleasant, well furnished, and framed with large windows. The dining room serves first-rate meals. Another place to stay is the **Changchun Guest House,** 10 Xinhua Road (tel. 22661), close to Renmin or People's Square in the very center of town. Visitors sometimes stay at the **Nanhu Guest House** (tel. 53571), in Nanhu Park near the lake.

RESTAURANTS. The best restaurants are in the Changbaishan Guest House and the Chunyi Hotel; they specialize in northern Chinese cuisine. The food at the Changchun Hotel restaurant is also of reasonable standard. For those who speak Chinese, there are "masses" restaurants to try.

Local specialities include deer-antler soup (a thick broth made from ham, chicken, prawns, and sea-cucumber), bear's paw (a rare delicacy), and the awful-sounding frog-oil soup (supposedly a tonic).

TOURIST INFORMATION. The CITS office (tel. 52401) is in the Changbaishan Guest House at 12 Xinmin Street; CAAC/China North Airline (tel. 39772) is at 2 Liaoning Road.

HOW TO GET AROUND. CITS will arrange a car or minibus and driver, or book you on excursions. If you arrive by train, trolley-bus no. 62 passes the Changbaishan Guest House.

WHAT TO SEE. There are no ancient monuments or sites in Changchun. The town is usually visited by people with an interest in industry, trade, or technical institutes. Changchun is renowned throughout China for its automobile and truck factory, producing the Hongqi (Red Flag) cars and the Jiefang (Liberation) trucks. You may also be able to arrange a visit to the Changchun Movie Studio where many of China's movies have been filmed.

Jilin University is also of interest to many visitors, as are the Changchun Branch of the Chinese Academy of Science and the Geological Institute. There are some pleasant parks, the largest being Nanhu, or South Lake Park. Another is the Renmin, or People's Park, in the center of town, and a third is Shengli Park, a short walk from the railway station. Laodong Park off Jilin Road, on the eastern side of the Yitong River, is probably the most interesting and scenic.

MUSEUMS. The only museum worthy of a visit is the **Jilin Provincial Museum.**

SHOPPING. The main shopping area is in Changchun Street, but the most convenient place to shop is at the department store located near Shengli Park. The region is known for its "three treasures": ginseng (ginger), sable furs, and antler horn. Local manufactures include carpets, embroidery, deer-leather products, and woodcarvings.

USEFUL ADDRESSES AND TELEPHONE NUMBERS

Chunyi Hotel, 2 Stalin Boulevard. Tel. 38495.
Changchun Guest House, 128 Changchun Road. Tel. 22661.
Changbaishan Guest House, 12 Xinmin Road. Tel. 53551.
Nanhu Guest House, 128 Changchun Lu. Tel. 53571.

CHANGSHA

Hunan Province
South China

Changsha, the capital of Hunan Province, has a population approaching one million living in a municipality of about 100 square miles. Located on the lower reaches of the Xiang Jiang River, a major tributary of the Yangzi, the city has a history of over 3,000 years and has been a leading trade center for more than 2,000. It is also an important port, and you will see a graceful procession of long, narrow flat-sailed boats as well as modern barges plying the river with grains, timber, coal, and a variety of industrial materials. The riverfront has changed little during the last quarter of a century, and the old warehouses, boatyards, and processing plants are still being used.

The town was opened to foreign traders in 1904. Europeans and Americans quickly moved into the area to establish businesses and warehouses. Colleges and religious missions were set up soon after. These merchant activities were boosted in 1918 when the town was linked by rail to Hankow and then Beijing, the development spurring an increase in production from the light-industrial sector, particularly in food products, textiles, paper, lacquer ware, jewelry, and furniture. Changsha then became an important port for the export of agricultural products grown in the province, such as rice, tea, cotton, tobacco, hemp, and timber. The development of industry was greatly assisted by the later rail link to Guangzhou.

The city was partially destroyed during the Sino-Japanese war (1937–1945), but the rebuilding program was not established until the end of the Civil War (1949) and the assumption of power by the Communist movement. From then on the economy of the province, and that of Changsha itself, began to expand, even though based almost entirely on agriculture. This is not surprising, for the alluvial lowlands surrounding Changsha are among the most productive in China. Hunan supplies about 15 percent of the country's rice crop, but tea, soy bean, wheat, corn, cotton, peanuts, tobacco, sugar cane, and sweet potatoes are also grown in abundance in the province.

In the 1960s the economy entered another expansionary phase leading to diversification in light industry and the establishment of small-to medium-sized factories producing electronic, chemical, metalworking, and machinery products. As a result Changsha now occupies an area several times larger than it did a decade or more ago, so that the old town with its ramshackle houses and narrow streets has been surrounded by new buildings and factories of modern but utilitarian appearance.

The south of the old city is the newest and fastest-growing section, and a visitor finds the usual combination of factories and adjoining workers' apartments spilling out into the adjacent rice fields. Heavy-industry plants have been built south and southeast of the rail line, while in the north the swampy low-lying land has been drained and is now used for industrial storage; there are also new government buildings and a school located in this area. It is to these areas that the visitor is usually taken for an inspection of some of the city's showcase factories.

Changsha city is divided into two unequal parts by the River Xiang and is connected by a highway bridge passing across Orange Island in the middle of the river. About four-fifths of the city is on the east bank, and this area encompasses most of the city's industry, all of its railroad facilities, and the center of provincial administration. The built-up area on the west bank, representing the other one-fifth of the area, houses most of the city's educational facilities and, indeed, has functioned as Hunan's cultural center since the tenth century. These educational and cultural organizations are clustered at the foot of Yuelu Shan Hill, which is at the tail end of the Nanyue Range with its well-known 72 peaks. It is a particularly attractive site overlooked by peaks and surrounded by woodlands.

In New China, Changsha and Hunan Province have become famous as Mao Zedong country. He was born in Shaoshan just 53 miles from the city, spent his adolescent schooldays in Changsha, and used it as a base to spread his revolutionary ideas. Many of the sites associated with his early education and political activities have been restored or rebuilt, and these attract a vast number of tourists from China and overseas.

Perhaps the most interesting highlight of a visit to Changsha is a visit to the museum housing the well-preserved 2,000-year-old corpse of a woman removed from the tomb dug up in 1972. The corpse is in a remarkable state of preservation; but of greater fascination are the funerary objects that were taken from the coffin and represent one of the great finds in Chinese archeology. Perhaps even more important were documents printed on silk providing information about the life and times of the people who lived under the Han Dynasty in Hunan more than 2,000 years ago.

EXPLORING CHANGSHA

Clear Water Pool

The Former Meeting Place of the Hunan Communist Party Committee is at a site known as Clear Water Pool, or Qing Shui Tang. The original pool became overgrown and eventually disappeared but has since been restored.

The entrance to the grounds is through heavy iron gates. Immediately ahead, on a 15-foot pedestal, is a 40-foot white marble statue of Mao Zedong dressed in a long overcoat and standing with one arm raised. Just behind it is the Clear Water Pool.

A little way beyond the pool at the bottom of a hill stands a restored house typical of those in Hunan Province: the outside wall of the court is clearly new, but the house itself is the original. Mao occupied it for about 18 months from autumn 1921 before moving to Shanghai.

You enter into a small courtyard and face the entrance door set in dark-stained wooden walls. On either side of the door there are the traditional zigzag patterns set into the window frames. The first room is a vestibule with dark wood paneling. There is a portrait of Mao as a young man, apparently taken when he was living in the house. The second room is the bedroom, with a traditional Hunan bed—a type of four-poster with a covered top. On the wall is a portrait of Mao's wife, Yang Kaihui, with her two children. The photograph, taken in 1925, shows Mao's sons, Mao Anying, who died while fighting for the Chinese in North Korea in 1950, and Mao Anching, who is reportedly still alive.

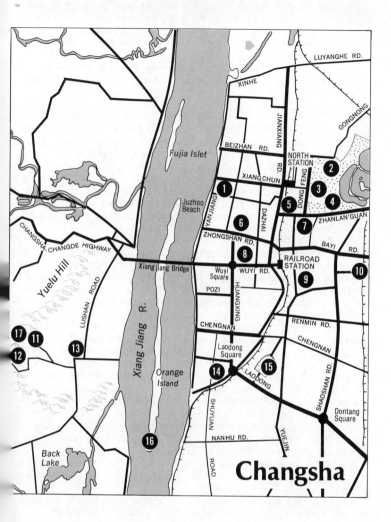

Points of Interest

Aiwan Pavilion **11**
CAAC **9**
Changsha Railway Station **10**
Department Store on
  Zhongshan Rd. **6**
Hunan Exhibition Hall **5**
Hunan Guesthouse **4**
Hunan University **13**
Lushun Temple **17**

Mao Zedong's Old School **14**
Monument and Memorial Park
  to Martyrs **3**
Provincial Museum **2**
Qingshuitang **7**
Renmin Stadium **15**
Juzi on Orange Island **16**
Workers' Cultural Palace **1**
Xiangjiang Guesthouse **8**
Yunlu Palace **12**

The next room is the bedroom that was occupied by Yang Kaihui's mother. Then there is an outside kitchen with a small iron stove, a dining room with a small table, a meeting room, and another bedroom used for guests. All the rooms have dark-paneled walls from floor to ceiling. The furniture is not the original.

There is a modern hall near the house with an exhibition devoted to the events surrounding the creation of the Party Committee in Hunan.

The Old Normal School

The original buildings of the Normal School were destroyed in 1938 when a large part of Changsha was burned down during the war against the Japanese. The Nationalists later established a hospital on the site. In 1949, after the Communists came to power, the existing buildings were again used as a school. Between February 1968 and May 1969 new buildings similar to those that were on the site when Mao attended the school were carefully reconstructed. The school is now known as Hunan No. 1 Teachers Training School and used for students training to become primary-school teachers.

Mao Zedong studied at the school to become a teacher from spring 1913 and graduated in 1918. He then went to Beijing, following Yang Kaihui, the girl he eventually married. He came back in autumn 1920 to work as a teacher at the school and stayed until 1921, when he left to attend the First General Assembly of the Party at Shanghai, returning soon afterwards to teach again before leaving for good a short time later.

The school is made up of a number of attractive buildings, very well maintained, and of a pleasant and harmonious style. There are lots of inner courtyards, arches, and columns, and the buildings are painted slate-gray, the columns being in white. The original school was established in 1912; Mao was supposedly one of the first students to enroll. Some of the rooms and desks (not originals) used by Mao in the original building have been roped off to form a small museum within the school. There are photographs of Mao and his classmates, reproductions of his schoolbooks, reproductions of the books he read with penciled margin notes, copies of articles he wrote, copies of old newspapers featuring important international events of the period, and sections of newspapers reporting the success of the Communist Revolution in Russia.

The visitor may also see the old well, which is the only original part of the school site now intact; the small pavilion covering it is a fairly recent addition.

Across a small lane in another section which, again, has been rebuilt recently are the rooms used by Mao to give evening classes. Apparently over 100 workers became students, but the classes terminated six months later when Mao left the school for the last time.

EXCURSIONS FROM CHANGSHA

The Three Han Tombs of Mawangdui

The burial mounds of Mawangdui, in an eastern suburb of Changsha, date back about 2,100 years. They were excavated in early 1972. One contained the female corpse of the official To Hou. It is known as the Number One Tomb. The Number Two Tomb was occupied by her husband, who is believed to have died in 186 B.C. Since the tomb had been robbed, the corpse had rotted and many of the funerary objects had been removed. Number Three appears to have contained their son who had died in 168 B.C.

The eastern mound in which the Number One Han Tomb was found was 65 feet high and about 165–200 feet in diameter at the base. It was constructed of pounded earth. The grave inside the mound faced north and measured 6–10 feet wide. When the mound was opened it was found that there were four steps downward from the top which terminated in a funnel-shaped wall; this led down to the grave chamber about 50 feet below. In the chamber three coffins were found, placed one inside the other, the outer coffin being covered with 26 bamboo mats. The inner surface of the coffins had been lacquered and the outside surfaces painted to depict various scenes. Many show mythical animals in various activities: fighting, hunting, playing musical instruments. There are also scenes featuring ornate geometric designs.

The inner coffin was 6½ feet wide, and 2 feet high. Inside was found an extremely well-preserved female corpse with face upward and head lying towards the north. The corpse, measuring 5 feet in height, was clad in more than 20 garments; nine silk ribbons had been fastened to it from head to foot, and a silk robe was used as a final cover. Medical examination of the corpse revealed that the muscles were still resilient and the color of the arteries the same as normally found in a fresh corpse. The soft tissue was in an extremely well-preserved state. It is estimated that the woman died when she was 50 years old.

This remarkable preservation was due to the charcoal and white-peat layers used to cover the coffins, which kept out the moisture and oxygen that cause rapid deterioration of human tissue.

Thousands of burial objects were removed from the tomb and the coffins, and they make the excavation one of the most important in China's archeological history. They were mainly items of silk, lacquer ware, bamboo ware, porcelain, and foodstuffs.

Of the silk products, most of the varieties known to have been produced during the Han Dynasty were found in the tombs. The objects include woven, embroidered, and pleated silks; various kinds of clothing including skirts and robes; gloves, shoes, and socks. Some of the silk is lightweight and similar to the finest varieties produced today; e.g., one piece 50 inches wide by 75 inches long weighs only one and three-quarter ounces. The most precious silk object of all was found covering the inner coffin. It is a masterpiece of ancient Chinese silk painting and depicts scenes from heaven, earth, and hell. Some sections illustrate the daily life of the time, while others relate to mythology.

Among the beautiful examples of lacquer ware that were excavated, some dishes still contained portions of food—lotus root, chicken bones, beef steaks, pieces of chicken, and fish. Most of the lacquer ware is in magnificent condition.

Important sets of wooden figurines were also unearthed, ranging in size from 2 to 13 inches. The most notable was a group of musicians.

An interesting set of bamboo books was unearthed. Many centuries before paper was invented, the Han used strips of bamboo, and the ones taken from the tomb contain an inventory of the articles buried. Archeologists have thus been able to confirm everything was still there.

Many bamboo baskets of various sizes were found, containing either clothes or foodstuffs. The food baskets contained beef, pork, fish, rabbit, chicken, game, and dog meat. In others there were beans, fruits such as dates, pears, and strawberries, a variety of vegetables, and eggs; also medicinal herbs, including cinnamon and thyme.

Other objects include pieces of pottery, a stringed instrument about 45 inches long and not known today, sets of flutes, a bronze mirror, bamboo fans, mats, and a seal (chop). Agricultural seeds such as rice, wheat, and various vegetable seeds were also unearthed.

A question that has puzzled Chinese archeologists is the absence of gold, silver, and precious gems. The only metal items found were the bronze mirror and a tin bell. Some experts have pointed out that there was a fashionable trend toward frugality at the beginning of the Han period; but the explanation is somewhat doubtful in view of the magnificent fabrics enclosed in the coffins. So far it remains a mystery. More information is provided in the "Museums" section.

PRACTICAL INFORMATION FOR CHANGSHA

FACTS AND FIGURES. Changsha is at approximately the same latitude as Orlando, Florida. Distances: 815 miles south of Beijing by air, about 3¼ hours' direct flight; 995 miles south of Beijing by rail, about 22 hours' journey; 315 miles north of Canton by air, about 1¼ hours' flight; 445 miles north of Canton by rail, about 14¼ hours' journey.

Elevation: 195 feet above sea level.

The table shows the weather pattern in Changsha during the year.

Changsha Temperature Range and Average Rainfall

	Temperature High (°F)	Temperature Low (°F)	Number of Days with Rainfall	Monthly Rainfall (in inches)
January	44	35	13	2.0
April	70	55	15	5.8
July	94	78	7	4.8
October	75	60	10	3.0

WHEN TO GO. Changsha is located in a humid, subtropical area, and its climate is somewhat similar to that of the southeastern portion of the United States.

The most pleasant time of year to visit is autumn, when the weather is warm but the humidity is not uncomfortable; there are frequent periods of pleasant, dry weather.

As indicated in the table, winters are cold in the city, January and February temperatures usually ranging from the mid-30s to the mid- and upper 40s. There are occasional cold snaps which depress the temperature into the 20s. Snowfalls are spasmodic, slight, and short.

Spring probably brings the least pleasant weather of all: light rainfall persists for days at a time and the skies are usually overcast. About half the annual rainfall of 52 inches is recorded between March and June. Higher temperatures and humidity begin in April, making the weather from this period onward very uncomfortable for travel.

The rain tapers off in the summer months and the weather becomes clearer, but this change is accompanied by steeply rising temperatures which regularly attain the low 90s and even, from time to time, exceed 100° F. The temperatures at night rarely drop below 75° F.

HOW TO GET THERE. Your visit to Changsha would normally form part of an itinerary beginning in Beijing, Shanghai, or Guangzhou; there are direct air services from these three cities. Visitors often visit Changsha on their way from one of the northern capitals to Guilin in the South, because some planes from Beijing and Shanghai make a stop there en route.

Changsha is also located on the major North-South rail route linking Beijing and Guangzhou, and is thus conveniently located for visitors who are traveling by train. The overnight journey from Beijing takes about 22 hours. If you are traveling on from Changsha to Guangzhou, you must take another overnight train journey lasting about 14–15 hours. The city is also well serviced by trains from other major centers.

The fastest flight time to Changsha from Guangzhou is about 1 hour 45 minutes, from Guilin 1 hour 25 minutes, Huangzhou 2 hours 10 minutes, Kunming 2 hours 25 minutes, Shanghai 2 hours, Wuhan 1 hour, and from Xian 2 hours.

HOTELS. A major hotel for foreign guests is the **Xiangjiang Guest House** (tel. 26261) at 267 Zhongshan Road, in the heart of Changsha's business center. There is an old and new wing; rooms are air-conditioned and are equipped with television. Both Chinese and Western food is available.

The newest hotel is the **Hunan Lotus** (tel. 26246) on Wuyi Dong Road, near the railway station; it has 313 air-conditioned rooms, a Chinese and Western restaurant, shops, and a conference hall. The **Rongyuan Guest House** (tel. 267294, 267801) at Hongyu Lake has pleasant parklike grounds, simply furnished rooms, and comfortable amenities, but is not conveniently located.

The **Changsha Hotel** (tel. 25029) at 116 Wuyi Road, is in the center of the city not far from May First Square. It is also close to the Changsha East railway station. Other hotels accommodating foreign guests are the **May First Hotel** at 101 Wuyi Road and the **Yueyang Guest House** (tel. 23011), with 270 air-conditioned rooms and three restaurants.

RESTAURANTS. Hunan cuisine is characterized by one feature that it shares with Sichuan—the use of liberal quantities of chili pepper. The Hunanese have advanced this method one step further: they produce meats that are smoked with chili, e.g., smoked chicken and smoked pork. These dishes are worth trying. If you like hot, spicy food, then you may well find the dishes served in the hotel dining rooms too mild. If so, try one of these restaurants: **Youyicun** (tel. 24257), 225 Zhongshan Road; the **Changsha Restaurant** (tel. 25029), 116 Wuyi Dong Road; **Changdao** (tel. 26211), West Wuyi Road; **Huogongdian** (tel. 23591), 145 Pozi Street. The province is renowned for its oranges and kumquats, so try these for dessert.

TOURIST INFORMATION. CITS (tel. 22250 or 27356), at 130 Sanxing Jie, is difficult to find. From the Xiangjiang, walk south (left) to Wuyi Lu Road, then head west (right) toward the river. After a few blocks, turn south (left) one block after Daqing Lu. Enter the gateway into the courtyard and take the stairs leading from the first doorway on the left.

CTS (tel. 98132) is in the Hunan Lotus Hotel located at Wuyi Dong Road.

CAAC (tel. 23820) located in a small building at 5 Wuyi Dong Road. From the new railway station walk down Wuyi Road. The office is only a few hundred yards away on the left-hand side.

HOW TO GET AROUND. Sites in Changsha are spread out so you will need to take advantage of CITS tours and excursions. If you arrive by train, you can take bus no. 1 from the new railway station to the Xiangjiang Guest House.

WHAT TO SEE. Undoubtedly the main attraction in Changsha itself is the exhibition featuring the recently exhumed and widely publicized 2,000-year-old-female corpse taken from a tomb only a few miles outside of Changsha. Apart from the remarkably well-preserved corpse itself, there is a magnificent collection of funerary objects. These art treasures date back about 2,100 years to the Han period. They were excavated in 1972 and may be seen in the Hunan Provincial Museum.

Other interesting places to visit in Changsha are the Hunan No. 1 Teachers' Training School, which stands on the site of the school attended by Mao (1913–1918) and whose buildings are faithful reproductions of the school as it originally existed, and the First Office of the Hunan Communist Party Committee, which met at a small house beside a pond known as Clear Water Pool. There a small museum records the early work of the Communist movement in Hunan.

You may also wish to visit Orange Island in the middle of the Xiang Jiang, which cuts the city of Changsha in two. It is an excellent place to watch the rivercraft go by. It was from the southern tip of the island that Mao would frequently swim the river in his student days in Changsha.

Yue Lu Hill is a beautiful wooded area with a path leading to the peak; on the way you will pass an old temple. Clustered at the base of this hill are Hunan University and Hunan Teachers' College.

A well-landscaped area on the other side of the river is the Monument to the Martyrs Park. You will find pleasant lakes and numerous pavilions in the park, and on top of the small hill is a monument to the Martyrs of the Revolution.

The principal excursion from Changsha is to Shaoshan, the birthplace of Mao Zedong. The village is located about 53 miles from Changsha and takes about two hours by bus or 3½ hours by train (departs 7:35 A.M.). The journey takes you through delightful rural areas and you will see fertile rice paddies and extensive tea plantations. Full details are provided under the section devoted to Shaoshan.)

MUSEUMS. The **Hunan Provincial Museum,** 3 Dongfeng Road (tel. 23866), houses the exhibition devoted to the Han Tomb excavations at Mawangdui.

An object of great interest is the well-preserved female corpse, over 2,000 years old, taken from the No. 1 Tomb. Medical tests have shown that the tissues and organs are in remarkable condition, the state of preservation of the body due to coffins having been encased in thick layers of charcoal and white peat. The body was found wrapped in more than 20 layers of silk. It is wearing decorative hair which is not its own. The corpse measures 5 feet in height and weighs about 75 pounds.

Medical examination has shown that the subject had suffered from tuberculosis and had a heart condition and a gallstone problem. Doctors believe the woman died after eating a large quantity of watermelon; 138 watermelon seeds were found in her intestines. She apparently died at the age of 50 following a gallstone attack immediately after her feast of watermelon.

The **Hunan Ceramics Museum** in Zhanglanguan Road (tel. 25898) mainly features porcelains and ceramics found and made in the province. There are about 3,000 items on display. The **Museum of Traditional Chinese Painting** is located in the same building. Both are open 8–11 A.M.; and 2.30–5.30 P.M. Items are sold in the museum shop.

SHOPPING. There are many small specialist shops in the center of the city. The **Hunan Antiques Shop** (tel. 25277) is in the Hunan Provincial Museum, Dongfeng Road. You may also shop at the **Arts and Crafts Store** (tel. 22253), 92 Wuyi Road; the **Shaoshan Road Shop** (tel. 24588, 26681), Shaoshan Road; a branch of the **Friendship Store** (tel. 26261) in the Xiangliang Hotel, Zhongshan Road; the **Overseas Chinese Store** (tel. 26539); and the **Zhongshan Road Department Store** (tel. 24621), 213 Zhongshan Road.

Changsha embroidery is well known throughout China, porcelain and pottery produced locally represent good value, and there is the usual range of handicraft items. You should visit the tea counter if you like this beverage; tea is grown extensively in the province and the local variety is well known throughout China. Down products such as eiderdowns, ski jackets, and vests are of excellent quality and reasonably priced.

ENTERTAINMENT. Changsha is famous in China for its shadow-puppet shows and marionette theater. Consult your hotel service desk or CITS for information about shows put on by the **Hunan Provincial Puppet Troupe.**

USEFUL ADDRESSES AND TELEPHONE NUMBERS

CITS—Hunan Lotus Hotel (tel. 98132).
CAAC—5 Wuyi Dong Road (tel. 23820).
PSB—Daqing Street (tel. 24898, 26241).
Taxis—Xiangjiang Hotel (tel. 26261, ext. 390).

CHENGDU

Sichuan Province

Southwest China

Chengdu, the capital of the enormous heart-shaped province in the center of China, is more than 2,000 years old. It was once one of the most beautiful towns in China, but "modernization" has left its mark. The old walls and towers have been torn down, and a number of modern streets have been bulldozed through the center of town. However, the modern streets quickly give way to small side streets and lanes where there are old wooden houses, busy marketplaces, stalls, restaurants, and food shops.

Sichuan, one of the most important provinces in China, means "four rivers," and is so named because of the rivers that flow from the north of the province into the Yangzi in the south. The Yangzi, or Changjiang as it is now known, flows through the province close to the southeastern border. Most of the western border of the province is delineated by the Yangzi, also known in that area as the Jinsha Jiang, or River of Golden Sand.

Marco Polo visited Chengdu in the thirteenth century, a short time after the region had been ravaged by the Mongol hordes of the Great Khan. Although his account tells us little of the town, it does provide some interesting comments on the region. He related that the province and its surrounding areas were inhabited by lions, bears, and other wild beasts. Travelers who slept outdoors used to place green sugar cane on their campfires. The noise of the cane continuously bursting open frightened off predatory animals.

The customs of the inhabitants, said Marco Polo, were even more interesting: "When it happens that men from a foreign land are passing through this country and have pitched their tents and made a camp, the matrons from neighboring villages and hamlets bring their daughters to these camps, to the number of twenty or forty, and beg the travellers to take them and lie with them. So these choose the girls who please them best, and the others return home disconsolate.

" . . . it is the custom for every man to give the woman with whom he has lain some trinket or token so that she can show, when she comes to marry, that she has had a lover. In this way custom requires every girl to wear more than a score of such tokens hung round her neck to show that she . . . is the most highly esteemed and the most acceptable as a wife; for they say that she is the most favoured by the gods." Marco Polo concludes: "Obviously the country is a fine one to visit for a lad from sixteen to twenty-four."

The province has always been dominated by the Yangzi, and Marco Polo commented on this: "On its banks are innumerable cities and towns, and the amount of shipping it carries . . . upstream and down, is so inconceivable that no one in the world who had not seen it with his own eyes could possibly credit it. Its width is such that it is more like a sea than a river."

311

For thousands of years, the Yangzi has provided the main access to Sichuan from the eastern provinces. Rivercraft were pulled upstream in the fast-flowing portions of the river by teams of coolies. They hauled their loads on long bamboo ropes from the river's edge, or from steep paths cut into the cliffside. The journey downstream, through the gorges, was once a fearsome dash through boiling, rock-strewn waters. Today, the waters have been somewhat tamed, and the river is navigable for 1,800 miles, from Yibin to the sea. Other forms of transport are now available: the province is traversed from north to the south by the major rail link from Beijing; and there are air services from the capital and provincial cities.

Sichuan is the richest agricultural province in China, with fertile soils and plentiful rainfall. For long periods of the year, clouds cover the sun. Mists sweep down the mountains onto the plains, and the fields are wet and green. Rich yields of rice, wheat, corn, barley, fruit, potatoes, sugar cane, cotton, tobacco, jute, and tea are harvested.

In contrast to the fertile plains of the east, the west of Sichuan province is not nearly as productive. The area is dominated by foothills that rise steeply to mountains almost 25,000 feet high. In the old days, the mountains had to be crossed on foot when following the path from Chengdu to Lhasa in Tibet. Even now, the road follows these old footways. Although barley and wheat are grown in the region, agriculture has mainly given way to forestry and livestock raising.

In western Sichuan there are a number of minority groups. The Tibetans are the most numerous, but there are also large settlements of Yi or Lolo.

Although industrial developments in Sichuan Province have not kept pace with those of other provinces, it is still an important region for the production of oil, natural gas, coal, iron ore, and rock salt.

EXPLORING CHENGDU

Du Fu's Cottage

Du Fu was a famous Tang Dynasty poet whose poetry is still revered in China. He came to Chengdu and built a cottage overlooking the Huanhua stream in A.D. 759. Du Fu spent four years at the cottage and wrote more than 240 poems there. The site later became a garden and, in the Northern Song Dynasty (960–1126), a temple was built in the grounds. The replica of Du Fu's cottage that now stands in the 40-acre garden is part of a group of buildings that date from the late Qing. Some of his poems, paintings, and calligraphy are on display. Open daily 7:30 A.M.–6 P.M.

Temple of Marquis Wu

The Temple of Marquis Wu stands in the southwestern sector of Chengdu, in Nanjiao Park. It was built originally in the sixth century to commemorate the exploits of Zhuge Liang (A.D. 181–234), a prime minister and famous strategist of the Three Kingdoms period.

In the temple grounds there are two main pavilions: one dedicated to Zhuge Liang or Marquis Wu; the other to Liu Bei, the Emperor of the Kingdom of Shu. The emperor's tomb may be found by following a small pathway from the Liu Temple.

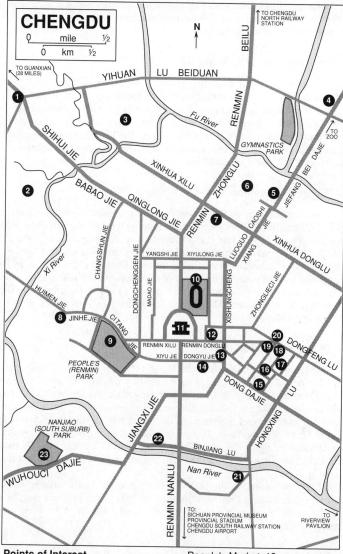

CHENGDU

Points of Interest

Acrobat Theater **18**

Advance Train-ticket Office **14**

Arts & Crafts Store **17**

Bamboo Weaving Factory **4**

CAAC **19**

Chengdu Bus Terminal **21**

Dongfeng Hotel **20**

Friendship Store **15**

Jinjiang Hotel & CITS **22**

Lacquerware Factory **8**

People's Market **13**

People's Stadium **10**

Public Security Bureau **7**

Sichuan Embroidery Factory **5**

Sichuan Exibition Center **11**

Telecommunications Building **12**

Temple of Marquis Wu **23**

Tomb of Wang Jiang **2**

Wenshu Monastery **6**

Xicheng Stadium **3**

Ximen Bus Terminal **1**

In the pavilions there are 28 statues of Shu ministers and generals, about 40 stone tablets, and over 30 inscribed plaques. There are a teahouse and a tiny antique store in the park.

Tomb of Emperor Wang Jian

Sometimes referred to as the Yongling Mausoleum, the burial mound of Wang Jian (A.D. 847–918), Emperor of the Kingdom of Shu, it located to the northwest of Chengdu. It is 49 feet high with a diameter of 265 feet. The burial chamber is 77 feet long and constructed of red sandstone. The platform for the coffin is supported by half-length male figures; three sides of the platform feature carvings of musicians. Visiting hours 9 A.M.– noon and 2–5 P.M. Closed Monday.

Riverview Pavilion

The Wangjianglou or Riverview Pavilion is located in the southeast sector of Chengdu in a park of the same name. Overlooking the Fuhe River, a tributary of the Jinjiang, it is a four-story wooden structure dating from the Xing. The pavilion provides a fine view of the river and the surrounding parklands. The park is where the famous Tang Dynasty poet, Xue Tao, supposedly drew water to make paper for her poems. The garden has been planted with over 120 varieties of bamboo to commemorate Xue Tao's devotion to the species. There are a few other pavilions in the park that are worth visiting.

Divine Light Monastery

The Baoguang, or Divine Light Monastery, stands some 10 miles north of Chengdu. This famous Buddhist monastery was first built in the Eastern Han Dynasty (A.D. 25–220), but was destroyed during the Ming. The monastery was rebuilt in 1670 by Emperor Kangxi of the Qing. The pagoda in the grounds is said to date from the Tang, has 13 stories, and is 98 feet high. There are five halls, 16 courtyards, and many objects of historical or cultural interest, e.g., the White Buddha from Burma; the Thousand Buddha Tablet carved in the fifth century; and an 18-foot-high stupa made from granite.

Of special interest is the Hall of Five Hundred Ahats housing rows of life-size clay statues that were molded in 1851. Two of these statues are of the emperors Kangxi and Qianlong, easily identified by their royal robes. Open daily 8 A.M.–6 P.M.

Wenshu Monastery

The Wenshu, or God of Wisdom Monastery, located near the south bank of the river in the northern sector of Chengdu, was founded under the Tang, although the present buildings date from 1691. You can reach the temple by traveling north through Chengdu along Zhonglu and turning right before reaching the Wanfu Bridge.

Apart from objects of historic and cultural value (many of which are housed in pavilions that are not open to visitors), the monastery is interesting because of the large numbers of the Buddhist faithful that pray at the temple. Weekends are particularly crowded. There is a small museum in the grounds displaying calligraphy and paintings. Open daily 8 A.M.–8 P.M.

Cultural Park

If you are in Chengdu during February or March, you should go to the Cultural Park to see the **Flower Festival** that begins on the fifteenth day of the second lunar month each year. Apart from the magnificent display of flowers and shrubs, there are all sorts of cultural events to entertain the local populace including theater, song-and-dance performances, and opera. The park, located in the western sector of Chengdu not far from Du Fu's cottage, is the site of the Qingyang Palace, a large Taoist monastery established during the late Han period. The buildings that remain date from the late Qing. The park is open daily 7 A.M.–6 P.M.

Zoo

The largest group of giant pandas in captivity in the world will be found at the Chengdu Zoo. The nearly extinct golden-haired monkey is another of the hundreds of animals housed in the zoo. Open daily 8 A.M.–6 P.M.

EXCURSIONS FROM CHENGDU

The fine excursion opportunities in Chengdu are presented here according to their distance from the capital. Details are given first for the Dujiang Dam and the Qingcheng Mountains because they are only about 35–40 miles to the northwest of Chengdu. Then to the south lie Meishan, Leshan, and Mount Emei. The other centers covered are a long way from Chengdu and would normally be visited on the way to another province.

Dujiang Dam

At Guanxian, about 30 miles to the northwest of Chengdu, the Min River splits into four tributaries, two of which flow on either side of Chengdu. The Dujiang Dam diverts the waters into irrigation canals.

Over the centuries, a series of water systems have been developed at Guanxian, the first as far back as 250 B.C. The water has been diverted from the Min to the nearby plains, creating one of the most productive agricultural areas in the whole of China.

There are models at the dam site that illustrate the water systems, as well as inscriptions commemorating the scholar Li Bing and his son who began the work of diverting the waters over 22 centuries ago.

Temple of the Two Kings

A half-hour drive away from the dam stands the Erwangsi or Two Kings' Temple, built in honor of Li Bing and his son who were both awarded the title of "king" (wang) after their deaths. Nearby is a Taoist temple, the Fulongguan, commanding a superb view of the river valley.

Qingcheng Mountain

Qingcheng or Green City Mountain is 45 miles northwest of Chengdu and only a short distance from Guanxian (and the Dujiang Irrigation Project). The site is considered a cradle of the Taoist religion because Zhan Daoling, the founder of the religion, once taught there. The cliffs, topped by lush vegetation, resemble city walls and hence give the mountain its name.

More than 30 buildings remain of the original 70 or more religious sites, the most interesting of which is the **Heavenly Teacher Cave** (Tianshi). There is a pavilion at an elevation of 5,245 feet on the summit of the mountain named the **Holy Lantern Pavilion** (Shengdeng) after the lantern which is lit each night. A short drive from Green City Mountain leads you to **Jian Fu Temple** close to Gueicheng, or **Ghost City Mountain.** The scenery is spectacular in this region.

Meishan

When you travel south from Chengdu to visit Mount Emei and Leshan, you will pass through the county of Meishan. Located 55 miles from the provincial capital, Meishan is noted for a shrine devoted to three members of the Su family. It was once the residence of Su Xun and his two sons, all three famous in literature during the Northern Song (960–1127). Their home was converted to a temple during the Ming (although the existing buildings date from the late Qing). While there are hundreds of objects on display, the shrine is mainly of interest to those with a knowledge or an understanding of Chinese literature.

Leshan

Leshan, a town built on a rocky promontory overlooking the confluence of the Min, Qingyi, and Dadu rivers, is 105 miles south of Chengdu. The

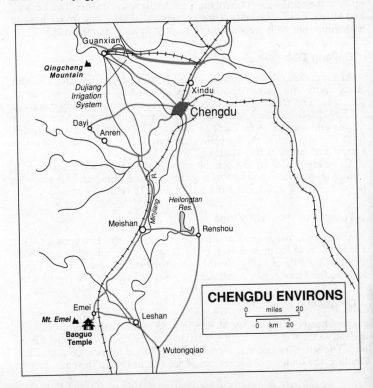

town is over 1,300 years old, and some impression of its antiquity may be obtained by visiting the old section of town with its cobbled streets and colorful old houses.

The main reason for travel to Leshan is to visit the **Temple of the Great Buddha,** and see the colossal statue of the Buddha, supposedly the largest in the world. It was cut into the face of a sandstone cliff by a team of workers under the supervision of a Buddhist monk called Haitong. Work began in A.D. 713, and the project took 90 years to complete.

The Buddha is 234 feet high, with shoulders that are 92 feet wide; the head is 48 feet high, while each of the ears is 23 feet long. Records suggest that the Buddha was carved to protect boatmen from drowning in the swift currents in the river below. The Great Buddha or Da Fu Temple itself is located above the right shoulder of the statue.

To visit the site you take a ferry which departs every 40 minutes from Leshan pier. The ferry passes the Great Buddha and stops at **Wuyou Temple,** which dates from the Tang Dynasty. There is a small museum there and some good views of the surroundings. From there it is a 15-minute walk to the Great Buddha Temple. Alternatively there is a bus tour from Leshan organized by CITS. There are also excursion tours from Chengdu by boat and by bus. Organized by CITS, these usually involve an overnight stay at Leshan.

Foreign guests usually stay at the Jiazhou Hotel or at the Jiu Ri Feng Hotel in Leshan city. Hotels used by Chinese visitors are the Dongfeng and the Jiading.

Mount Emei

At Mount Emei, or High Eyebrow Mountain, highest of the four sacred Buddhist mountains, there were once 70 temples and monasteries that sheltered thousands of Buddhist monks. Pilgrims spent days climbing to the top of Mount Emei to offer prayers to the Buddha. A number of temples still remain, and you can see them on your way to the summit. The cable car (40 passengers) reaches the summit in five minutes. An alternative is to take a three-hour bus journey to **Jieyin Peak** (8,660 feet), hike one hour to **Golden Peak** (10,090 feet), then hike another hour to **Wanfo** or **Ten Thousand Buddha Summit** (10,167 feet). Some visitors like to stay overnight at one of the temple guest houses, even though the accommodations are rudimentary.

The strong can undertake the hike up the mountain from **Wanniansi** (3,346 feet) in two days and the descent in one day. The climb is tiring, the path difficult to follow in places and dangerous in some sections, so climbers should consider taking a guide. In winter, climbers will need spikes to traverse the icy sections; spikes may be rented at the base of the mountain.

At the summit you may see the sun rise over the famous Ocean of Clouds. Late in the afternoon, around 3:00 or 4:00, you may also be fortunate enough to see the Precious Light of Buddha formed by the diffraction of light passing through moisture particles in the atmosphere.

Mount Emei takes time to reach. You can either travel 125 miles south from Chengdu by road—a four-hour journey—or take a boat down the Min River to Leshan, then travel the remaining 25 miles by car. Alternatively, you can take the daily tourist train, departing Chengdu 6:45 A.M. and arriving at the foot of Mount Emei at 9:50 A.M.; the train departs at 3:22 P.M. and arrives Chengdu 6:20 P.M. CITS arranges bus, train, and boat trips to Mount Emei.

However you arrive, you will invariably end up at the temple area of **Baoguosi** (elevation 1,805 feet), and you will usually be lodged at the Hongzhushan (Red Candle Mountain) Hotel. May through October is the best time to visit. Even in the hot mid-summer months, Mount Emei is cool. In winter, only the sure-footed would visit, because the paths can get icy.

Thousand Buddha Cliff

If you are traveling from Chengdu to Xian by rail and are interested in Buddhist cave sculptures, you might care to stop at Guangyuan. It is located about 175 miles north of Chengdu in the north of the province, only 30 miles from the Shaanxi border. Not far from the town is the Thousand Buddha Cliff, or Qian Fo Yan, where there are Buddhist sculptures comparable with those at Yungang (see Datong) and Long Men (see Luoyang). The carvings were begun in the early part of the eighth century, but of the 17,000 statues, only a few hundred remain.

Also near the town are the remains of the Temple of Imperial Favor, or Huang Ze Si. There are six caves and about 30 niches, thought to date from the Tang or the Five Dynasties period.

Other Excursions

Two nature reserves are worth visiting, but they are in remote areas of Sichuan. One that is well known to naturalists is the **Wolong Nature Reserve,** some 86 miles from Chengdu. The reserve has a few hundred pandas living in their natural state, and is a center of research for this delightful but endangered species. The reserve can be visited only with special permission and there is no hotel, only a hostel.

The other reserve is at **Jiuzhaigou,** due north of Chengdu near a town called Nanping, right on the border of Gansu Province. This area has beautiful forests and lakes, but it is isolated and difficult to reach.

PRACTICAL INFORMATION FOR CHENGDU

Travel Warning. Pickpockets, bag-snatchers, and petty thieves have been active in Chengdu. You may also be subject to cheating on taxi fares and restaurant bills. If you have a problem, you may report the incident to the foreigners' section of the Public Security Bureau (tel. 26577); your hotel should assist you in this matter.

FACTS AND FIGURES. Chengdu, the capital of Sichuan Province, is about 950 miles southwest of Beijing and about 175 miles northwest of Chongqing. Some 1.4 million people live in the city proper, while about 4 million inhabit the large urban area of almost 2,500 square miles.

WHEN TO GO. The best time to visit is early autumn (September) or late spring (May).

In summer, the temperature is hot and the rainfall high. Try to avoid July and August, because two-thirds of the year's rainfall occurs then.

In winter the temperature is mild. From mid-autumn (October) to early spring (April), a mist usually covers the plains.

HOW TO GET THERE. You can fly to Chengdu direct from Beijing in 2¼ hours by jet. There are also flights from Xian (1½ hours), from Shanghai (2½ hours), and from Lhasa (2 to 2¾ hours).

If you are traveling from Guangzhou you can take a 2-hour flight to Chengdu via Guiyang (in Guizhou Province). There are also flights from Kunming (1½ hours) and regular daily services from Chongqing (1 hour). There are nonstop package-tour charter flights from Hong Kong, covering the sights of Chengdu and the excursions to Mount Emei, Leshan, and Dazu.

Travel by train is recommended only if you have plenty of time, as Chengdu is a long way from Beijing, Shanghai, and Guangzhou. If you are traveling to Chengdu from Xian, Kunming, or Guiyang, the train journey is inconvenient; you can wait for days to get a reservation and then find the trains hopelessly overcrowded. Even budget travelers usually prefer to fly.

HOTELS. The newest hotel is the **Minshan** (tel 60247), a 21-story building with 337 rooms, three restaurants, two bars, and a disco, located at 17 Renmin Nan Road, Section 2. The new 15-story **Chengdu** (tel. 42312) on the corner of Dongfeng and Sanduan roads offers good accommodations in 258 rooms, each equipped with telephone, refrigerator, and TV. Many guests stay at the **Jinjiang Hotel** (tel. 24481), 36 Renmin Nan Road, where the accommodations in the 457 rooms have been modernized. Then there is the **Dongfeng Hotel** (tel. 27012), 31 Zongfu Street; the **Shaanxi Huiguan** (tel. 22687) at 36 Shaanxi Street; the **Wanjiang**, 42 Xia Sha He Bai; the villa-style **Jinniu** or Golden Ox (tel. 24214), located in the western suburbs about 3 miles from the city center; and the small **Rongcheng Hotel** (tel. 28496) at 130 Shaanxi Street in the middle of the city.

RESTAURANTS. Although Sichuan is well known for its hot, peppery food, it is more famous among the cognoscenti for its refined cuisine using wild herbs and the petals of flowers. Dishes such as duck cooked with medicinal herbs, soft-fried lotus flowers, and chicken shreds with orchid petals are remarkable for their subtlety, and are a contrast to dishes well known outside China, such as spicy bean curd and Sichuan noodles. Other well-known regional dishes are Sichuan pork (often described as "pork with a fishy flavor"), spicy chicken with peanut sauce, and cold noodles with red pepper. Incidentally, the fishy flavor of some Sichuan dishes comes from an essence prepared by mixing chili, ginger, garlic, vinegar, and local spices. It is not derived from seafood. All these dishes can be ordered at your hotel dining room. However, you may care to dine out, so try the famous **Furong (Lotus) Restaurant** (tel. 24004) at 27 Renmin Nan Road and within walking distance of the Jinjiang Hotel. Other restaurants that you could visit: the **Chengdu** (tel. 27301) at 642 Shengli Zhong Road; the **Rongcheng** (tel. 24647) on Renmin Xi Road; the **Yuehua** (tel. 26665) on Chunxi Road; and the **Wangjianglou** (tel. 27552) near the pavilion on Wangjiang Road. The Jinjiang Guest House serves noodles until 10:30 P.M. The **Huaxi Restaurant,** located in a bomb shelter east of the Jinjiang, is a "masses" restaurant that is different.

TOURIST INFORMATION. CITS (tel. 29474, 25042) is in the Jinjiang Hotel at 180 Renmin Nan Road.

CAAC/China Suthwest Airlines (tel. 23038, 23087) is opposite the Jinjiang at 15 Renmin Nanlu Erduan.

PSB (tel. 26577 or 22951) is in Xinhua Dong Road, east of the intersection of Renmin Zhong Road.

HOW TO GET AROUND. Try to explore the back streets on foot. Otherwise you can rent a bicycle and get around to many of the closer sites. Bicycles may be hired at 2 locations. The first rental shop is just north of the Jinjiang Hotel, on the left-hand side of Renmin Nan Road. It is open 8 A.M.–10 P.M. To reach the second place, continue north but turn left into Jiefeng Road. You will see the rental sign in English on the left-hand side at no. 31–33, about 100 yards from the corner. Open 7 A.M.–6 P.M.

Bus tours are organized by CITS; so are the 1-day or 2-day bus or local excursions to outlying sites. Chengdu is one of the few cities in China where there are passenger pedicabs, pedaled by former rickshaw-men. Public bus 16 is useful: it runs between the north and south railway stations.

WHAT TO SEE. Almost everyone enjoys strolling around the narrow streets of the old part of the town, where traditional-style wooden houses, reminiscent of

Tudor cottages, lean against each other. You will also enjoy a walk around the area that was once the Imperial City. Southwest of the town is the **Wuhou Temple,** dedicated to Zhu Geliang, one of the heroes of the novel *The Romance of the Three Kingdoms.* On the outskirts of the western sector of Chengdu stands **Du Fu's Cottage** where the famous Tang Dynasty poet once lived. To the northwest of the town lies the **Tomb of Wang Jian,** a soldier of fortune who became a prince and was given the title of "emperor" after his death. Then there is the **Riverview Pavilion,** near the East Nine-Arch Bridge, which provides a good view over the Jinjiang River. Try to visit the **Wenshu Monastery,** near the Fu River, off Renmin Bei Road, with its beautiful Buddhist temple.

MUSEUMS. Chengdu's most important museum is the **Sichuan Province Museum** (tel. 22158) on Renmin Nan Road, south of the Jinjiang Hotel and across the river. There are 2 floors: the first features items of historical interest up to the time of the revolution in 1949; the second concentrates on post-revolutionary history. There are some 2,000 items on display. Open 8–11 A.M. and 2–6 P.M. daily except Monday.

The **Sichuan Exhibition Center,** located in the very center of the city and just south of Renmin Zhong Road, sometimes features special exhibitions; check with your hotel or CITS for information.

PARKS. Wangjianglou Park, with its Pavilion for Viewing the River, is over 30 acres in area, has interesting groves of bamboo (about 100 different varieties), quiet places to rest, and pleasant walks. The Well of Xie Tao commemorates a famous singer from the Tang era (618–907).

Cultural Park, located in the far-western sector of the city, is famous for the Taoist temple, Ching Yang, and the arts and flowers festival in February–March.

SHOPPING. Chengdu is a good place to buy embroidery, brocades, rattan ware, necklaces, and bracelets. Chengdu's lacquer ware has been famous for thousands of years: examples were recovered from the Han tomb at Mawangdui (see *Changsha* section), dating back over 2,100 years. There are also old market places where you can buy local products, such as ceramics, pottery, bamboo ware, woven-straw items, and national-minority items such as sashes, tunics, hats, boots, knives, braid, and jewelry. Tibetan handicrafts, such as silver jewelry, may be purchased. There are several shopping streets flanked by old shops constructed of bamboo. The old salt market in the central part of town in Jiefang Road, and the old Chunsi Road area, now known as Fandi Road, in the northern quarter, have a few interesting shops.

Apart from the **Friendship Store** (tel. 7067) in Shengli Zhong Road, you may care to visit the **Antique Shop** (tel. 2787), Nanjiao Park; the **Arts and Crafts Shop** (tel. 6817), Chunxi Road; the **Fine Arts Company** (tel. 4184), Shengli Xi Road; the **Gold and Silver Articles Factory** (tel. 4820), Huanhuaxi; the **Lacquer-ware Factory** (tel. 6781), Shengli Xi Road; the **Bamboo Articles Factory** (tel. 92421), Jiefang Bei Road; the **Sichuan Brocade Factory** (tel. 2370), Qingyanggong; and the **Sichuan Embroidery Factory** (tel. 7347), Wenshuyuan Street.

ENTERTAINMENT. If you like Chinese opera—or want to experience it for the first time—you may have an opportunity in Chengdu. The city is home to the opera troupe that specializes in Sichuan Opera, which has a tradition that is centuries old.

If you are in Chengdu during February and March, make sure that you visit Cultural Park for the Flower Festival, because there are presentations of opera, theater, song and dance, and acrobatics.

LEAVING CHENGDU. The advance train ticket office is on Shengli Shilu. Walk south from the Sichuan Exhibition Center along Renmin Nan Road turn left into Shengli Shi Road. The office is on the right-hand side. Obviously, CITS can arrange train tickets, but for a fee.

From Chengdu's north railway station you can catch trains to Mount Emei, (3 hours, 5 min.), Leshan (4 hours), Chongqing (11–12 hours), Xian (20–21 hours), Kunming (21–25 hours), and to many other destinations.

USEFUL ADDRESSES AND TELEPHONE NUMBERS

CITS—Jinjiang Hotel (tel. 29474, 25042).
CAAC/China Southwest Airlines—Opposite the Jinjiang Hotel (tel. 23038, 23087).
PSB—Xinhua Dong Road (tel. 22951, 29551).
Taxis—Jinjiang Hotel (tel. 22305).
U.S. Consulate—Jinjiang Hotel (tel. 51912 or 52791).

CHONGQING

Sichuan Province

Southwest China

Chongqing, well known as the capital of China during World War II, stands on a magnificent site—a high promontory overlooking the confluence of the Yangzi and Jialing rivers. From the pine-clad hills surrounding the town, mists sweep down and cloak the rickety wooden houses clinging to the steep hillsides. Narrow flights of steps descend to the treacherous river.

Most of the old walls of the town are gone and "modernization" has taken place. In the central districts, new buildings have been erected. The few temples, ancient monuments, and places of architectural interest have disappeared, most of them destroyed by Japanese bombs between 1938 and 1941.

Some foreign visitors to Chongqing take the ferry excursion from the town to Wuhan, a three-day journey downstream or all the way to Shanghai, a five-day journey. However, tourists can also get a feel of "ancient China" by visiting some of the old areas of Chongqing.

For information on Sichuan Province itself, consult the section on Chengdu, the provincial capital.

EXPLORING CHONGQING

Loquat Hill

Loquat hill, or Pipashan as it is known to the Chinese, is the highest point of central Chongqing, being 920 feet above sea level. It is a good place to start your exploration of the city and surrounding areas because it provides a fine view of the entire city. During the day the park and the tearooms are crowded with locals escaping the bustle of the city. Foreign visitors are often taken to the vantage point in the evening to see the expanse of city lights, and the lights of the vessels plying the rivers below.

Cable Car

Another fine view is from the cable car that crosses the Jialing River from the south bank to the north and back again. The cable car leaves the Chongqing side from Cangbai Road and crosses to the Jinsha Jie station on the other side of the river. As you look down you will see the busy docks of Chaotianmen where the waters of the Jialing River join those of the Yangzi on their long journey through central China to the Yellow Sea.

Chaotianmen Docks

Here you will see junks, barges, and busy river craft and catch some of the color of old Chongqing. To reach the docks you walk down long flights of stairs. Along the way you will pass the old houses clinging to the hillsides. This is a fine place for photographs.

Red Crag Village

The main interest in Hongyancun, or Red Crag Village, is the former residence of Zhou Enlai who lived in Chongqing from 1938 until 1945. There is a museum in the village displaying items of historic interest concerning the Southern Bureau of the Central Committee of the Chinese Communist Party. The village also served as the Chongqing office for the Eighth Route Army. For non-Chinese visitors there are many excellent photographs of the leading historic figures of the era. There are usually English-speaking guides on duty to give explanations of the items on display.

Northern Hot Springs

The Northern Hot Springs are located 33 miles north of Chongqing in the Jinyun mountain area not far from Wentang Gorge on the Jialing River. The springs are to be found in Beiwenquan, or Northern Hot Springs Park. There are pretty views in the park and interesting pavilions, the most important of which are those housing the Statue of the Giant Buddha, the Statue of the Amitabha Buddha, and the Statue of General Guan Yu famous over 1,700 years ago in the Three Kingdoms period. The springs bubble forth from the ground at a constant temperature of about 86° F (30° C).

Southern Hot Springs

The area around these springs has also been made into a park. Located 16 miles south of Chongqing, the park possesses streams that meander through the area, attractive gorges, and fine views of the surrounding mountains. The springs here are sulphurous and bubble forth at a constant temperature of 100° F (38° C).

EXCURSIONS FROM CHONGQING

Dazu Stone Carvings

Visitors with time to spare should try to visit the site of the Buddhist carvings near Dazu, about 125 miles from Chongqing by road. The carvings are over 1,100 years old and, although not as widely known as those at Dunhuang, Long Men, and Yungang, are superb works of Buddhist religious art. There are more than 50,000 statues carved at over 40 sites, the most important centers being Beishan and Baoding, both described below. Many of the sites cannot be reached by car.

CITS organizes overnight excursions to Dazu. The bus usually travels 32 miles north to **Beibei** to allow visitors the chance of visiting the **Northern Hot Springs,** located a few miles north of the town. Then the journey proceeds to the southwest 40 miles to the town of Bishan, northeast 26 miles to **Tongliang,** and finally to **Dazu,** another 32 miles to the southwest. You will pass through some beautiful scenery on the way.

Independent travelers can catch the local bus to Dazu from the northwest bus station in Chongqing. The bus leaves at 7:20 A.M. and the journey takes 5–7 hours, depending on the number of stops en route. Another way is to take the train from Chongqing to **Youtingpu,** and then a bus the remaining 23 miles to Dazu. The only problem with this approach is that the five-hour train journey from Chongqing gets you to the station late at night, and you have to wait there until the first buses early next morning.

Overnight visitors stay at the **Dazu Guest House,** which has accommodations for 140 persons. The hotel is fairly simple but comfortable, and its restaurant serves reasonable food.

Beishan

Beishan, or North Mountain, sometimes called **Dragon Mound Hill,** is about one mile north of the town of Dazu. In the ninth century it became a military base; and the general in command ordered artisans to begin work on the first Buddhist carvings. The work continued for more than 250 years, leaving the area decorated with over 10,000 figures. Many were destroyed over the ensuing centuries so that today there are only a few grottos and niches with figures worthy of inspection. On arrival at the bus terminus there is a 25-minute hike to the first grotto. The most interesting chambers are 113, 125, 136, 155, and 245.

The most celebrated carving at the site is the Wheel of Universe (cave 136) depicting the cycle of human life. The most outstanding carvings of the Guanyin, or Goddess of Mercy, are in caves 113, 125, and 136. The pagoda is about half a mile beyond the cave site.

Baoding

Baoding, which is about seven miles northeast of Dazu, represents a radical departure from the style of the statues found in Baoshan. The carvings were done in a 70-year-period between 1179 and 1249 under the direction of a monk called Zhao Zhifeng. Here the carvings are laid out along the face of a fan-shaped cliff in a manner that was "master planned," in contrast to the random approach adopted at Beishan. The most remarkable statue is the **Sleeping Buddha** which is 102 feet long and just over 16 feet high, so called because the figure is reclining in a horizontal position rather than sitting upright. There are many more sculptures at Baoding and consequently you should spend more time here than at anywhere else in the region.

There are buses for Baoding from 7 A.M. to 3 P.M., departing every 30 minutes; the last bus from Baoding to Dazu leaves at around 5 P.M. As Beishan is only about a mile north of Dazu, you can walk there in about 20 minutes. The landmark to head for is the pagoda at the site.

Jialing River Cruise

You may undertake a spectacular cruise down the Jialing River to the Yangzi River. The 19-mile journey can be made in two hours. The cruise is highly recommended, especially for those visitors who are unable to undertake the journey down the Yangzi to Wuhan or Shanghai. There is a day cruise and an evening cruise.

Journey Down the Yangzi

If you have arranged a trip down the Yangzi by ferry, you begin your journey at Chongqing; vessels depart Chaotianmen Dock at 7 A.M. every day. A bus collects passengers from their hotel around 6 A.M. (reservations at each hotel reception desk). You sail on one of the modern cruisers organized for tourists by CITS or on one of the older vessels of the Jianghan (formerly East is Red) Line with dormitory accommodation only or seats. The minimum journey time to Wuhan is three days, to Shanghai five days. Tour boats usually take five to seven days to reach Wuhan.

On the first day you will pass through hilly terrain where villages cling to the mountainsides. Your first port-of-call is **Wanxian,** where there is a bustling market. Next morning your boat will pass the town of **Fengjie** (sometimes stopping there), before arriving at the city of **Wushan.** Here passengers on tourist boats often take a six-hour excursion on smaller boats upstream along the **Daning River** through the spectacular three "little gorges"—Dragon Gate Gorge, Misty Gorge, and Green Gorge—which are often voted the highlight of the voyage. Other boats omit that section and go directly to the three **Sanxia Gorges.** On this 120-mile stretch the boat goes through the **Qutang Gorge** (five miles long), the **Wuxia Gorge** (25 miles long), and then stops at the town of **Badong.** From there the journey continues through the **Xiling Gorge** (50 miles long) where, everyone goes on deck to watch the boat pass through the locks of the enormous **Gezhouba Dam.** Shortly after the boat docks at **Yichang,** where independent travelers sometimes disembark to catch the train to Luoyang (via Xiangfan) or a plane to Xian.

Further downstream your boat passes under the bridge at **Zhicheng** before proceeding to **Shashi,** where you may disembark if you wish. The excursion to the ancient town of **Jingzhou** (also known as Jiangling) some five miles away, is worthwhile. More than 2,000 years ago it was the capital of the State of Chu, during the Spring and Autumn period (722–481 B.C.) The walls of the town, constructed under the Ming, are still standing. There are fine gates, watchtowers, and pavilions. Worthy of special note are the two temples: Yuanmiaoguan and Kaiyuanguan.

The next day is not of scenic interest because the river widens and the terrain is flat. The boat stops at **Chenglingji,** on Lake Dongting, where passengers may visit the wooden Tower of Yueyang before heading for Wuhan.

PRACTICAL INFORMATION FOR CHONGQING

FACTS AND FIGURES. Located about 1,490 miles upstream from Shanghai, and about 660 miles from Beijing, Chongqing is located at the confluence of the Yangzi and Jialing rivers in Sichuan Province. Highly industrialized, often fog-laden, and smoky, Chongqing is the largest city in Southwest China.

WHEN TO GO. The summer months, May through October, are scorching hot; they also bring the period of highest rainfall. Then from October through March, heavy fogs envelop the city. Early spring is the best time to visit.

HOW TO GET THERE. Chongqing is serviced by air from the provincial capital, Chengdu, 3 to 5 times a day depending on the day (55–60 minutes flight). There are also flights to Chongqing from Beijing (2½ hours), Shanghai (2 hours, 5 minutes), Guangzhou (1¼ hours), Guilin (1½ hours), Guiyang (1 hour 20 minutes), and Kunming (1½ hours). The new airport at Chongqing has facilitated air travel.

Train travel to Chongqing from nearby cities passes through spectacular scenery, but the journey from other tourist centers takes a long time. For example, the train journey from Chengdu takes 11–12 hours, Guiyang 11 hours, Xian 31 hours, and Kunming 32–36 hours. If you are coming from Kunming, you must change trains at Chengdu; from Guilin change at Guiyang.

HOTELS. The 21-story **Holiday Inn Yangtze** (tel. 483–3380) at Dian Zi Ping and Nan Ping Xiang in the Nan An district provides international-standard accommodations in 383 rooms. The hotel has three restaurants, coffee shop, sky lounge bar, and discotheque. Many visitors stay at the "Chinese palace" look-alike **Renmin Hotel** (tel. 351421), which stands on the south bank of the Jialing River at 175 Renmin Road, or at the renovated **Chongqing Hotel** (tel. 43233) at 41–43 Xinhua Road. Other hotels are **Chongqing Guest House** (tel. 46771) at 235 Minsheng Road, used mainly by Overseas Chinese; the **Yuzhou Guest House** (tel. 23829), 2 Youyi Road, which stands in a walled area and accommodates over 400 guests; the **Xiao Quan Hotel** near the Southern Hot Springs and about one hour's drive from Chongqing; and the **Shaping Hotel** (tel. 664196), 84 New Xiaolongtan Street in the Shaping District.

RESTAURANTS. Few restaurants outside the hotels are suitable for visitors. The best one is probably the **Weiyuan** (tel. 43592) on 37 Zhouyong Road. Then there is the **Chongqing** (tel. 43996, 43242) on Xinhua Road in the central district, the **Yuexiangcun** (tel. 41526) on Minzu Road, also in the central district, and the **Xijiao** (tel. 23106) at 1 Qianjian Zhi Road. Until the standard of restaurants in Chong-qing improves, you are probably better off eating in your hotel.

Sichuan-style food is described under *Restaurants* in the coverage of Chengdu.

TOURIST INFORMATION. CITS (tel. 51449 or 53421, ext. 435), located in the Renmin Hotel, can arrange tours around Chongqing and its surroundings, provide tickets for the 2-hour river cruise, or arrange for the more extensive journey by boat down the Yangzi. Of course, the office can also make train and air reservations for you.

CAAC/China Southwest Airlines (tel. 62970, 52813, 52643) is located at 190 Zhongshan San Road, should you wish to make air reservations yourself.

PSB (tel. 43973) is located at Linjiang Road and can be reached by taking the no. 13 bus from the Renmin Hotel.

HOW TO GET AROUND. Transport terminals, hotels, and sites are scattered around Chongqing, so sightseeing can be time consuming. Getting around on foot can be tiring in parts of the city because of the hills and the profusion of steps, while cycling is out of the question for the visitor for the same reasons. Unless you are energetic and fit, you will normally take in Chongqing's sights on CITS-organized excursions.

WHAT TO SEE. You should be certain to visit **Loquat Hill,** or Pipa Shan, which from Chaotianmen—or the **Gate to the Sky**—overlooks the confluence of the Yang-zi and Jialing rivers. From the tea-garden pavilion there is a superb view, especially at night. Another beauty spot is **Southern Hot Springs,** located about 12 miles from the city on the right bank of the Jialing River. The area has natural caves, small lakes, and pleasant gardens. So does the **Northern Hot Springs,** set in a large park overlooking the Jialing. You can also visit the **Red Crag Village,** or Hongyancun, former residence of Zhou Enlai between 1938 and 1945.

MUSEUMS. The **Sichuan Academy of Fine Arts** (tel. 23423), located in the woods at Huangtongping, is one of the foremost academies of its kind in China, serving as a center of learning for aspiring artists. In the academy you will find exhibitions of oil paintings by leading Chinese artists as well as by those who trained at the academy. A three-story gallery offers works of art for sale. Open daily 9–11:30 A.M. and 2–5:30 P.M. If you are interested in painting don't miss the academy.

The **Chongqing Museum** on Pipa Shan Road near Loquat Park has displays featuring natural, ancient, modern, and revolutionary history. Open 9–11:30 A.M. and 2–5:30 P.M.

The **Chongqing Museum of Natural History** stands in the Beibei district, some 27 miles northwest of the city, and features dinosaur bones that were found in the region in the mid-70s near Zigong and Yangchuan. Open daily 8–11:30 A.M. and 3–6:30 P.M. Worth visiting only if you happen to be going to the Northern Hot Spring Park (Beiwenquan) and Jinyun Shan (or Little Mount Emei, nearby).

Finally there is the U.S.–Chiang Kaishek **Criminal Acts Exhibition Hall** which concentrates on events that took place under the Sino-American Cooperation Organization (SACO). The hall is a reminder of the tortures that occurred under the Nationalist regime during World War II. Numerous prisons were set up in the region under SACO and various implements of torture are now on display. Unless you are a student of history, there is little of interest for you at this exhibition. Open 8:30 A.M.–5 P.M.

SHOPPING. Specialities of the province include embroidery, lacquer ware, rattan products, bamboo items, jewelery, ink-stones, and national-minority goods.

The main shopping area surrounds the Liberation Monument in the center of town (at the intersection of Minzu, Minquan, and Minsheng Streets). Food stalls and shops are scattered throughout the area. A large covered market selling mainly fruit and meat is to be found opposite the monument in Minzu Road. Some of the colorful markets off Zhongshan Road stay open until late in the evening—a rarity in China.

ENTERTAINMENT. Chongqing has resident theater and acrobatic troupes. Sichuan Opera represents an interesting variation on this unusual art form, while the city's acrobats are renowned throughout China. Your hotel or CITS can make arrangements.

LEAVING CHONGQING. By plane. Air travel times to major centers are given above (see *How To Get There*).

By boat. The Yangzi ferries can take you to Wuhan or drop you off at smaller ports along the way. They can take you all the way to Shanghai should you wish. Ferries usually leave the Chaotianmen Dock at 7 A.M., but independent travelers may board from 8 P.M. the night before. Although tickets may be purchased at the dock, it is usually preferable to make reservations and arrange tickets through CITS. Try to book at least two or three days before your intended departure date.

By bus. The long-distance bus terminal is in the northwest region of Chongqing, across the Jialing Bridge. If you have heavy luggage take a taxi, otherwise you can take bus no. 5 from the intersection of Zhongshan and Renmin roads. At the last bus stop take bus no. 10 for the short journey to the long-distance terminal.

By train. Chengdu may be reached in 11–12 hours from Chongqing. Passengers traveling to Kunming must change at Chengdu. Guiyang is an 11-hour journey. Passengers bound for Guilin must change trains there.

USEFUL ADDRESSES AND TELEPHONE NUMBERS

CITS—Renmin Hotel (tel. 51449, 53421, ext. 435).

CAAC/China Southwest Airlines—190 Zhongshan San Road (tel. 62970, 52813, 52643).

PSB—Linjiang Road (tel. 43973).

DATONG

Shanxi Province

North China

Datong, the largest town in north Shanxi, stands on a dusty, infertile plain almost 4,000 feet above sea level. It was once important as a garrison town because of its strategic position between the northern section of the Great Wall, which follows the northern boundary of Shanxi, and the southern section, about 60 miles to the south.

Datong first came into prominence in A.D. 386, when it became the capital of the Northern Wei, a non-Chinese race known as the Tobas. During that period the town prospered and the Buddhist religion flowered. Magnificent Buddhist shrines were created at Yun Gang, some nine miles west of the city. Prosperity was short-lived, however; just over a hundred years after the town became capital, the sixth emperor moved the court to Luoyang in A.D. 494, and Datong went into decline.

Toward the end of the sixth century, the empire—now reunited under the Sui—faced attack from the north and Datong resumed its importance as a garrison town. Thereafter it declined again, but in 960 the Liao overran the area and made Datong one of the secondary capitals, giving it its present name, Great Harmony.

During the twelfth and thirteenth centuries Datong retained its status as secondary capital. Then it went into decline once again. Under the Ming it was simply a fort. The walls built during that period stand today, although parts have been torn down to allow for the spread of the population.

EXPLORING DATONG

Nine Dragon Screen

Located near the center of the town, the Nine Dragon Screen, or Jiu Long Bi, was erected early in the Ming Dynasty. The screen is constructed of glazed tiles in different colors and portrays nine dragons rising out of the sea to fight among numerous suns. The screen, which is about 150 feet long, 20 feet high, and 6 feet thick, is almost 600 years old.

An ornamental pool runs the full length of the screen so that you can observe the reflection of the dragons on the surface of the water. When there is a breeze the reflections move and the dragons appear to writhe.

Upper Hua Yan Monastery

Because there are two monasteries with the same name, the Chinese describe them as "upper" and "lower" to distinguish one from the other.

A Buddhist sect known as Hua Yan was established during the Tang Dynasty, and the monasteries are named after it.

The main hall was built in A.D. 1064 and was rebuilt, after a fire had destroyed it, in 1140. It is known as the Great Temple of Powerful Treasure, or Da Xiong Bao Dian. A rare feature of the building is its orientation: it faces east rather than south, probably because it was built by the Liao.

The main temple is one of the two largest Buddhist temples currently standing in China. It has an austere style, a straight roof, bare walls except for the entrance bay which has three wooden doors, and lacks any ornamentation apart from the traditional figures at either end of the roof line. The style is quite different from that of temples built under the Song, Ming, or Qing.

When crossing the terrace to the temple entrance, note the distinctive incense burner dating from the Ming Dynasty. Above the entrance hangs a panel with characters in Chinese giving the name of the temple.

On entering you will be confronted by five large statues of the Buddha, the middle three carved in wood and the two at either end of terracotta. These and the statues around the wall all date from the middle fifteenth century (Ming). There are also a number of tablets, each supported by a giant stone tortoise.

The vivid frescoes on the rear wall date from the Qing; but note where a small section of the two-inch-thick clay covering has been chipped away to reveal Ming frescoes underneath.

Lower Hua Yan Monastery

The buildings of the lower monastery were first erected in the seventh year of the Liao Dynasty, A.D. 1038, but the present buildings date from the Ming and Qing. One of the original Laio buildings has survived, the magnificent library which houses the books in what appears to be a miniature city carved out of dark wood. The architectural style is believed to be a faithful reproduction of the two-story houses that existed in the eleventh century. These carvings have been of great value to students of ancient architecture.

The frescoes and sculptures inside this small building are said to date from the Liao and therefore form an important part of China's artistic heritage. In 1971 the building was classified as an ancient historic monument.

Shan Hua Monastery

The monastery, founded in the eighth century under the Tang, was destroyed by fire at the end of the Liao Dynasty and rebuilt under the Jin in the first half of the twelfth century. It was considerably expanded in the fifteenth century under the Ming. Now only four of the old buildings remain.

The first temple houses the four Celestial Guardians. On the right is a stele describing the restoration of the temple in 1177.

The second temple dates from the same period as the first and houses three Buddhas. Before them stand four elongated hexagonal incense burners each about three feet high. At each side of the hall are four tablets, three of which are mounted on large stone tortoises. As you come out of the building note on your left the fine reproduction in wood of a building with a double roof and circular gallery typical of Liao architecture.

The third pavilion houses five Buddhas with 12 Guardians on either side; the six-armed Guardian is a very good example of the art form. On the left-hand side note the woman with the small but rather horrible child standing beside her. Legend has it that the child used to eat babies, hence the blood on its mouth.

EXCURSIONS FROM DATONG

Three Dragon Screen

On the way to the Yun Gang Caves, about five miles out of Datong, you will come across an old temple, the Guan Yin Tang, which is in a poor state of repair. It was originally constructed in the eleventh century under the Liao; it was burned at the beginning of the Qing Dynasty and rebuilt in 1652. There is a fine Ming screen standing before the temple. It is similar in style to the Nine Dragon Screen of Datong but is smaller and depicts only three dragons in colored glazed tiles. It is thought to date from the Ming.

Mid-Air Temple

About 50 miles southeast of Datong, on the Verdant Peak in the Heng-shan ranges, the Mid-Air Temple—or the Hanging Monastery, as it is sometimes known—is one of the most extraordinary sites in China. Built halfway up the face of a cliff, the temple was first constructed more than 1,400 years ago by supporting the structure on wooden beams. Bridges and stairways link the more than 40 temples and pavilions. The buildings were renovated under the Jin, the Ming, and the Qing.

Great Wall

If you travel to Datong by train, you will catch regular glimpses of the Great Wall snaking its way along the hillsides and mountain tops. It passes Datong about 25 miles to the north, just south of the village of Fengzhen.

Wutai Shan

Wutai Mountain is one of four sacred Buddhist Mountains in China (the others are Emei, Putuo, and Jiuhua). It is 185 miles southeast of Datong as the crow flies, but it can be reached by road only by a roundabout route that trebles the distance. More than 30 temples still exist there, two of them with halls that are over 1,200 years old (the oldest wooden buildings in the world). Tourist facilities are under construction near Wutai Shan.

Pagoda at Fugong Temple

Located about 50 miles south of Datong near Ying Xian—about 1½ hours' drive—the wooden pagoda at the old temple site was constructed under the Liao in 1056. The octagonal pagoda is thus over 900 years old and is the tallest wooden pagoda of this era in China. Although it appears to be only five stories high, it has nine interior floors. Supported by six vertical beams, only five are said to be taking the load, so that you can sometimes pass a sheet of paper under the sixth.

Yun Gang Buddhist Caves

The stone carvings in the Yun Gang Caves are masterpieces of Chinese religious art, ranking with those at Mai Ji Shan and Dunhuang in Gansu Province and with those at the Long Men Caves in Henan Province. The caves are situated about 10 miles west of Datong in the north cliff face of a valley running in an east-west direction. The caves face south, and the 53 still in existence contain over 51,000 statues. The old monastery building known as the Shi Fo Gu Si forms an entrance façade to three of the largest caves.

Work on the cave temples began 1,500 years ago in the mid-period of the Northern Wei Dynasty (A.D. 386–534), under the supervision of a Buddhist monk named Tan Tao. Since most of the major caves were completed by the end of the fifth century, it is clear that the most important ones were built in as little as 40 years.

The practice of carving rock temples dedicated to the Buddha originated in India but came to China from the west. The earliest examples in China are to be found in the Dunhuang caves, which were dug out about 100 years before those at Yun Gang. However, the Dunhuang sculpture was of terra cotta, whereas the Yun Gang carvings are hewn from the rock face of the caves. They are the earliest examples of stone carvings of this type yet found in China.

The people who conquered the region in the period before the caves were built were a warlike race coming from Central Asia, although their exact origin is still obscure. They brought with them influences which had an effect on the artwork carried out at the caves. While the main style is clearly Indian, there are Iranian and Byzantine influences. Superimposed on these were the artistic interpretations of the Wei sculptors and, later, those of the Tang.

Unfortunately, the caves are located in a dry, arid area of China and have suffered a great deal from wind and soil erosion. Many of the cave faces have collapsed, leaving the interior exposed to the hostile environment. Restoration work was begun on a large scale after the State Council of the P.R.C. listed the caves among the National Ancient Monuments selected for special preservation.

A good deal of the work has been completed. Nevertheless, a large number of the statues are incomplete. Hundreds of heads of Buddhas and Bodhisattvas are missing, and a large number of bas-relief carvings were taken away and smuggled out of the country by collectors. Many of these pieces are now located in well-known museums around the world. Chinese authorities indicate that the statues pillaged or ruined amount to over 1,400. You will be shown the marks left by chisels and hammers used to free the carvings from the cave walls. A good many of the remaining carvings have been damaged by the erosive forces of nature over the 1,500 years the caves have been in existence. But despite deterioration, the caves remain a remarkable monument of Chinese religious art.

The 21 major caves may be classified according to the style and layout of the interior. For example, the five early caves have ground plans that are elliptical in shape; these caves are spacious and the main statues occupy most of the room available. The middle caves have a rectangular ground plan, and each one consists of a front and back chamber. The main statue is situated in the center and the walls and ceilings are decorated with reliefs depicting various themes of the Buddhist religion. The remaining caves are square and feature a pagoda pillar from floor to ceiling; there are carvings of Buddha and Bodhisattvas in niches all around the walls.

The caves are described in the numerical sequence given them by the museum authorities on the site. A visitor usually begins at caves 3 and 4, which are at the head of the stairs giving access to the path running by the cave entrances. Caves 1 and 2 are about a quarter of a mile from the entrance steps and are probably the least interesting of all.

Caves 1 and 2 are at the eastern end. They were hollowed out at about the same time and planned in the same style, with nearly square ground plans and carved pagoda-pillars connecting floor and ceiling. The Buddhas on the walls are weatherworn, but the Jataka story reliefs at the lower back part of the east wall in Cave 1 are still in relatively good condition.

Cave 3 is the largest of the Yun Gang Caves. The face of the cliff into which it was carved is about 80 feet high. On the central upper part are 12 rectangular holes which used to hold beams and, according to legend, the building which once stood there was known as the Monastery of the Enchanted Cliff. The cave is divided into front and back chambers. There is now only one Buddha statue and two Bodhisattvas in the west end of the back chamber. The faces of these images are full and smooth, the figures full-bodied. The sculptural style differs from that in all the other caves; it is that of later artists of the Sui (A.D. 581–618) and Tang (A.D. 618–907) dynasties.

Cave 4 has a rectangular floor plan with carved square pillar in the center. The sculptured images on the pillar and the four walls are badly worn. The only image that is still well preserved is that of a Buddha sitting cross-legged. The small adjoining cave is decorated with bas-relief carvings.

Cave 5 represents a high point in Yun Gang art. In front of the cave stands a four-story wooden hall, five bays wide, built in the eighth year of the Manchu ruler Shun Chih (1651). The presence of the monastery building has kept the cave in good condition.

The floor plan is oval. In the center is a seated 56-foot statue of Buddha, the largest sculptured image in the Yun Gang Caves and one of the largest in China. The surface of the statue was clay-plastered and repainted in the Tang Dynasty. The cave walls are filled with niches and images. The sides of the arched doorway feature two Buddhas seated facing each other under a *bodhi* (fig) tree; above are beautiful reliefs of flying asparas.

Cave 6 is another high point in Yung Gang art. Fortunately the building standing in front of the entrance has protected the cave. The ground plan is nearly square. In the center stands a two-story pagoda-pillar about 50 feet high. On its four sides are carved figures of the Buddha, and each of the four corners of its top has a small carved nine-story pagoda borne on an elephant. The walls are full of carved images of Buddhas, Bodhisattvas, Lohans (Arhats), and flying asparas. The ceiling carvings show the 33 devas in the Indra heaven and all kinds of mounts and carriages.

Especially remarkable is the Jataka, or life story, of Sakyamuni Buddha, from his birth to his attainment of Buddhahood, carved on the middle and lower parts of the east, south, and west walls as well as on the four sides of the pagoda-pillar.

Cave 7 has a three-story wooden awning forming a façade. In the center of the main wall of the back chamber is carved a Bodhisattva on a lion seat. The other three walls are full of niches and images. The Six Worshipping Bodhisattvas carved above the south-wall doorway are especially fine examples, as are the flying asparas carved on the ceiling, each soaring around a lotus-blossom motif.

Cave 8, a twin of Cave 7, was hollowed out in the same period. The statues on the four walls are badly worn. At the entrance there is a statue of Vishnu (Kumarakadeva) with five heads and six arms, riding on a peacock. On the east reveal is a statue of Siva (Mahesvara) with three heads and eight arms riding on a bull. These motifs are rather rare in the Yun Gang caves.

Cave 9 also has a front and back chamber. The pillars on both sides of the doorway of the front chamber are carved in an octagonal form. The upper parts of the east and west walls, as well as the space over the back-chamber doorway, are carved to resemble wooden houses. The other walls are full of niches with images of heavenly musicians (Gandharva Devas), dancers, and intertwining scroll-and-leaf designs.

Cave 10 was hollowed out in the same period of time as Cave 9 and also consists of front and back chambers. There are fine carved patterns on the outside and inside of the doorway arch of the back chamber. The statue of Buddha in the center is a poor clay image made during the Qing Dynasty (1644–1911).

Cave 11 has a square pagoda-pillar in its center reaching to the roof. On its four sides are carved images of Buddha, but the addition of painted clay figures in later ages has practically obliterated the original ones. The two Bodhisattvas in the front are, however, well preserved. The other walls are filled with niches and images of 1,000 Buddhas. On the upper part of the southern end of the east wall is carved an inscription giving the date of the statues—the seventh year of Tai Ho (A.D. 483).

Cave 12 is also divided into two chambers. The east and west walls of the front chamber each have a niche in the form of a building with three bays in imitation of wooden houses; these yield valuable information about the architecture of the period. Within the niches are statues. The top part of the main wall is decorated with a carved bank of celestial musicians holding different musical instruments. The statues in the back chamber are mostly clay figures or original images painted over in later ages.

Cave 13 has in its center a statue of the Buddha sitting cross-legged, about 42 feet high. Between his right arm and leg stands a four-armed *vajra,* the sole example of this figure in Yun Gang. Above the doorway arch on the south wall are the sculptured figures of seven Buddhas, very lively in expression. The shrine on the east wall is finely carved and decorated.

The front of **Cave 14** crumbled long ago, and most of the statues are badly worn. Only on the upper part of the west wall are there still some images in relief. On the east side stands a pillar with round base and square shaft.

Cave 15 is nearly square. The front wall has niches and statues. On the other walls there are more than 10,000 tiny seated Buddhas neatly arranged in rows, hence the name Cave of Ten Thousand Buddhas.

Cave 16 is one of the Five Caves of Tan Yao, the earliest to be built. Its floor plan is oval, and in the center is a giant Buddha standing on a lotus throne. On the walls there are 1,000 Buddhas and niches. The style of the cave is different from that of the rock temples of India and also from the style of the caves which evolved later at Yun Gang; in effect, it takes the form of an enlarged niche to protect the one central statue.

Cave 17 has an oval floor plan. In the center a giant cross-legged Buddha sits on a throne. A seated Buddha in a niche is carved on the east wall and a standing Buddha on the west wall. The ground level of the cave is lower than that outside. An inscription gives its date as 480. The giant Buddha and the smaller seated and standing Buddhas on either side give an impression of strength and firmness and are executed in a style different from that of the other caves in the group.

Cave 18 also has an oval ground plan. In the center stands a 50-foot Buddha, wearing a garment decorated with a thousand Buddhas and baring his right arm. On the upper part of the east wall is a skillfully carved statue of a Bodhisattva carrying a vase containing holy water. This and the other three Bodhisattvas are considered masterpieces of Chinese Buddhist art.

Cave 19 has in its center one of the largest Buddha statues (55 feet high) in Yun Gang. Outside there are two little adjunct caves hollowed out of the east and west sides. The central Buddha and sculptures on the right-hand side wall are rather severe in style, in contrast with those on the left-hand wall, which seem to point the way to the style eventually developed at Long Men when the court of the emperor was transferred to Luoyang.

The front wall of **Cave 20** has crumbled, and the 35-foot Buddha can be seen from afar. It is still relatively well preserved from the chest up. The face is full and round, with an expression of firmness and vitality; the mouth is large, the nose protruding, and the ears enormous. The Buddha has been carved in the seated position, hands in his lap. The shoulders are immense, their width being about two-thirds of the height of the seated figure. The legs are in a poor state of preservation.

The statue is probably the best known outside China; it is the most photographed of those at the site.

Cave 21 contains sculpture of a later period, possibly dating from the end of the Northern Wei. A five-story pagoda stands in the middle, each facet containing niches with Bodhisattvas within.

PRACTICAL INFORMATION FOR DATONG

FACTS AND FIGURES. Datong is at approximately the same latitude as Columbus, Ohio. It is 200 miles due west of Beijing, 8–10 hours by train.

WHEN TO GO. Datong is a hot, dusty town in summer, and in winter it is subject to below-zero temperatures and chilling winds. If possible, it is better to avoid a visit there during those seasons. In early spring dust storms are prevalent. Late spring and autumn are the best times to visit.

HOW TO GET THERE. Datong can be visited as a weekend excursion. For example, you may take the train (no. 163) from Beijing departing Friday at 5:15 P.M., arriving Datong at 1:15 on Saturday morning, an 8-hour journey. This allows you about 6½ hours' sleep before you begin your tour at 8:30 A.M. You can explore all day Saturday and until lunchtime on Sunday, then catch the 2:26 P.M. train from Datong, arriving back in Beijing at 10:45 on Sunday night.

Of course, you may want to make the journey easier for yourself by staying over an extra day at Datong. You may also prefer to take a train from Beijing that arrives at Datong at a more convenient hour. If so, discuss these requirements with CITS.

HOTELS. The **Datong Guest House** (tel. 32333), 8 Yingbin Road East, provides spartan accommodations in 150 rooms, most with private bathrooms. A CITS hotel, the **Yungang** (tel. 36202) at 21 Yingbin Road East, offers better accommodations with facilities such as a coffee shop and theater.

RESTAURANTS. There are "masses" restaurants where you may care to dine, though no restaurants outside the hotels cater especially to the foreign visitor. Three that you might care to try are: **Huayan** (tel. 32175) on West Road; **Longchi** (tel. 33279) on East Road; and the **Fengwei** (tel. 32333) on East Yingbin Road.

TOURIST INFORMATION. CITS (tel. 32607, 23215), located in the Yungang Hotel, can arrange a minibus or bus excursion to the nearby sites.

HOW TO GET AROUND. CITS arranges bus excursions to various sites.

WHAT TO SEE. The major attraction is the excursion to Yun Gang to view the man-made caves and the Buddhist stone carvings. Another popular trip is to the amazing Mid-Air temple on Hengshan (or Mount Heng).

In Datong itself you should not miss the Nine Dragon Screen or the Hua Yan Monastery established during the Tang Dynasty by the Hua Yan Buddhist sect. The library of the Lower Monastery dates from the eleventh century and is of great architectural significance.

You should also visit the Shan Hua Monastery. It was founded in the eighth century, and completely rebuilt in the twelfth, but only four halls survive. These have been restored recently.

MUSEUMS. The **Datong Museum** at the Hua Yan Monastery displays items unearthed in the district.

SHOPPING. There is no Friendship Store in Datong, but you can visit the town department store. It is also worth visiting the porcelain shop across the road, where you will find one of the specialties of the region: glazed ceramic ware. The range is limited, but there are styles that you do not see often in other parts of China.

Historical records show that glazed-tile making was first developed in Shanxi. It was in this province that roof figurines were first adopted. You now see these on roofs all over China. They take the form of lions, dragons, mythical animals, and spirits.

USEFUL ADDRESSES AND TELEPHONE NUMBERS

CITS—Yungang Hotel (tel. 32607, 36202).

DUNHUANG

Gansu Province
Northwest China

Dunhuang is one of the great centers of ancient Buddhist art in China; it stands in prestige and reputation alongside the famous sites at Yungang and Luoyang. Located near the far western border of Gansu Province, Dunhuang was once an important center of Buddhist learning on the "Silk Road," being renowned throughout China during the fifth to the twelfth centuries.

There are three groups of ancient Buddhist shrines in the Dunhuang area: the **Mogao Caves**—the most important and best known of all, located 15 miles southeast of Dunhuang; the **Elm Forest Buddhist Caves,** or Yulinsi, near the village of Tashi, not far from Anxi; and the (West) **Thousand Buddha Caves** or Qianfoya, actually 16 in number, near Nanhu or South Lake. (The site is also known as **Qianfodong**—the Thousand Buddha Caves—and is frequently shown on Chinese maps under this name.)

Most visitors prefer to stay a few days to take in the full extent of the religious art to be seen in the area, but those with a specific interest in Buddhism and its art forms would wish to stay longer.

The caves are closed during the winter period November through April. During the visitors' season not all the caves are open for viewing, a system adopted to preserve the caves from deterioration. Caves are open 8:30–11 A.M. and 2:30–5 P.M. daily.

If you take your own flashlight you will enjoy the caves more and be less dependent on the guide escorting you around the caves.

Photography is permitted at four caves only, and you must first purchase a "photography ticket." A guide will accompany you to the caves, then escort you back to the check-in point to deposit your camera before visiting the other caves.

EXPLORING DUNHUANG

Mogao Caves

The caves have been carved into the sandstone cliffs of the eastern Mingsha mountain. Behind the cliffs and sloping down on to them are the desert sands; in the valley below the oasis lies shaded by a verdant wood of poplars and willows, and fed by a mountain spring. The caves used to be connected by a rickety latticework of wooden walkways and ladders, suspended in air almost, on the face of the cliff, but these fell into ruin and have been replaced by four- and five-tiered walkways giving access to all the caves. Built into the cliff face is a nine-story pavilion, housing the giant Buddha (over 100 feet or 31 meters high).

The caves were dug into the cliffs over a period of more than 1,000 years, beginning in A.D. 366 when a monk named Yue Zun decided the place was perfect for a shrine. A legend describes how, arriving at the oasis, he saw myriad golden lights on Mount Sanwei, as though thousands of Buddhas were giving off beams of light. Inspired by this vision, he began to hew out a cave, and when this was done, he cut a statue of the Buddha. Over the succeeding centuries hundreds of caves were hewn and richly ornamented. Dunhuang became a center for the study of Buddhism from the fifth to the eleventh century and drew not only pilgrims, scholars, and artists who devoted their lives to the Buddha. The surviving caves possess a priceless collection of sculptures and murals demonstrating the evolution of Buddhist religious art in China over a period of a thousand years. They also reveal considerable detail about the way of life of the court and of the ordinary people during a period of enormous change throughout China.

There are now 492 caves in existence. Many others have been destroyed by weather and man. In 1900, a monk by the name of Wang Yuanlu, fleeing the famine in Hubei Province, happened to come to the oasis. After settling there, he had some workmen clear the sand from a cave. Murals were revealed as the sand was taken away. Because the walls sounded hollow, he had a hole broken through one of them, found a door inside the next chamber, opened that, and found a trove of ritual vessels, sutras, and documents inside another cave; there were also murals dating from the Tang. It appears that Buddhist monks, fleeing the invading Xi Xia (1038–1227), had deserted the place hurriedly and had never returned. He tried to get assistance from the Qing court in having the caves restored and the treasures preserved, but got a message back instructing him to reseal the caves.

He ignored this advice and instead went on begging pilgrimages. However, he raised no money or interest in his remarkable discovery. Nevertheless, word got out to the Western world and, in 1904, Sir Aurel Stein from England came to the site and purchased a host of treasures—29 crates in all—for a pittance. The following year, a French sinologist, Paul Pelliot, came to the Mogao caves and left with 6,000 scrolls and a collection of paintings. These were the first of many visits by foreign authorities, and collectors denuded the site of almost all of its removable treasures. Many of the objects are now housed in museums of England and France. To the Chinese, it must now seem like being able to buy the entire art collection of the Vatican for a few hundred dollars.

When you visit the site, remember cave number 16. This is the one that Wang had cleared of sand and that led to the first cave full of treasures. The characteristics of the caves are given below according to the dynastic period in which they were created.

The statues in the earlier centuries were hewn out of rock in rough form, then chiseled into fine detail. But during the late Sui period and under the Tang, only the rough outline was hewn from the rock, then a layer of clay was applied, this being shaped to provide the fine detail of the features before being painted. The wall paintings are made using water emulsions and are therefore tempera. Some are in an excellent state of preservation and display vivid colors. Only in the thirteenth century under the Yuan was the fresco technique introduced, most likely from abroad.

Northern and Western Wei (A.D. 386–557). Twenty-three caves date from this period. Wei sculpture in the caves shows Indian influences rather than Chinese, reflecting the characteristics of Buddhist art in the country of origin. These influences are evident in sculpture of the earlier Han period (206 B.C.–A.D. 220), e.g., head too large in proportion to the body; detailed head on a roughly hewn body; and generally incorrect proportions. In the Northern Wei sculpture the Indian influence is seen in the facial features: broad face with prominent cheeks; fine eyebrows; thin lips; highset nose; the body is generally slender and draped in a light clinging robe. The figures are erect, demonstrating a quality of authority, demanding respect and reverence.

Wei paintings illustrate parables, and stories (Jataka) depicting the life of the Buddha. Again, the women wear clinging robes with wide sleeves; some of the men wear tunics. The ceilings are decorated with geometric patterns, animals, and legendary figures from Chinese mythology, e.g., the royal lord of the east, the queen of the west, winged men, flying horses, dragons, tigers, phoenixes. The earlier Wei paintings feature what the Chinese call the xiao-face: the faces were highlighted with white eyeballs, and white on the bridge of the nose, while the cheekbones were outlined with a brown which subsequently oxidized and turned black. This effect renders the faces masklike resembling the Chinese character *xiao,* meaning small; hence the name attributed to the style.

The caves from the Northern Zhou dynasty (557–581) generally possess similar characteristics to those described above. In particular see caves 296 and 428.

Sui Dynasty (A.D. 589–618). Ninety-five caves date from this period of 38 years. The Sui statues reveal a distinct difference in style. Gone is the Indian influence, the statues are often shown in the sitting position, the clothing is more softly draped, and the faces show greater warmth and humanity, less majesty. The faces are fuller, too, and the ear lobes longer. The heads and torsos are generally out of proportion to the lower halves of the bodies. Statues of Ananda, a young disciple of Buddha, appear for the first time.

The Sui wall paintings reveal a richness and daring in composition and design. The theme is still the life of the Buddha, but the garments are ornately decorated, the men wearing Chinese garments, the women wearing slim robes with narrow sleeves. The ceilings are richly decorated, usually with a lotus flower at the center and at the corners, and with recurring decorative patterns. Sui artists have in some caves painted over the murals of Wei artists.

The religious art of the Sui represents an important nexus between Wei and the Tang. There has been a fusion of foreign and local influences, providing inspiration for the magnificent Tang creations of the next era.

Tang Dynasty (A.D. 618–907). Two hundred thirteen caves date from the Tang, the period of the peak artistic achievements at Dunhuang. Many of the Tang sculptors were painters as well; for the first time the names of the painters are given on their works.

The Tang statues and carvings show their subjects as people rather than as godlike figures. The Buddhas radiate a benevolence; they command respect yet possess an aura of humility; they appear to be approachable by the common man. Their clothing folds lightly, draping with exquisite softness. The facial expressions and clothing of the men and women attendants are no less perfect. Under the Tang, the wall niches have become small rooms, some having various levels. Colossal statues appeared: cave 96, protected by a nine-story pavilion of recent date, houses a statue of the Buddha just over 100 feet high; that in cave 130 is 75 feet high.

The Tang wall paintings are superb. The caves are filled with them, illustrating the life of the Buddha as well as depicting the various Bodhisattvas, the holy men in their last incarnation before attaining Buddhahood, with their floating gowns, jewels, and elaborate belts. There are also portrayals of Tang Dynasty nobles and aristocrats, both men and women, surrounded by their servants. The figures are lithe, the robes flowing; they convey a worldly sensuality. The ornamental patterns are different: geometric designs are secondary; scrolls, arabesques, and curlicues have largely taken their place. These and the often-recurring mandala reveal foreign influences, particularly those of India and Persia—not surprising in view of the extensive contact that Tang China had with the outside world. At the end of the Tang era multilimbed statues with myriad eyes began to appear.

Other Dynasties. After the Tang fell in A.D. 907, Dunhuang began to decline in importance, although some additional caves were cut during the new era and many existing caves were redecorated. There was little space left for additional caves, so the artists of the Five Dynasties period (A.D. 907–960) and those of the Song Dynasty (A.D. 960–1280) overcame the problem by enlarging some caves and completely transforming others. Many of their paintings cover paintings from an entire earlier period, particularly those of the Song, as the dynasty endured more than 300 years.

Of the caves still in existence, 33 date from the Five Dynasties period, 98 date from the Song, and 3 date from the Western Xia or Xi Xia (1038–1227). The outstanding work of these periods is a Song Dynasty wall painting in Cave 61. A landscape and figure painting, it depicts the main features of the terrain between the town of Taiyuan in Shanxi Province to Zhenzhou in neighboring Hebei Province, including representation of over a hundred structures standing at that time in the Wutai mountains, e.g., cities, towns, temples, bridges, and roads.

Generally, though, the art of these periods at Dunhuang is disappointing: it shows no evolution in composition, style, or imagination; it is repetitive yet lacks the vitality of the earlier eras—an unusual occurrence given that significant changes were taking place in art in other parts of China, particularly under the Song. One can only presume that Dunhuang had by that time become an artistic "backwater," its force spent.

Under the Yuan (1280–1368) nine new caves were cut in the north face of the cliff, the southern face being complete. They are small in size and feature a circular altar, revealing the Mongol influence, but the sculptures are disappointing. However, frescoes were introduced under the Yuan, a wall-painting technique that differs from those of the preceding periods, probably learned from artists from Nepal, or even Europe as the "Silk Road" was open again. The frescoes featuring the "Devas of Pleasure" are superb, displaying a fluidity of movement and an aura of eroticism. Many of the frescoes represent figures from the Tibetan pantheon.

The Ming (1368–1644) made no contributions to the art of Dunhaung, while the Qing (1644–1911) additions lack distinction, most of the artists' work from this period being redecoration.

Exhibition Hall. The exhibition hall stands at the foot of the cliff. It houses a collection of objects found in the caves: water pitchers, plates, jars, lamps, tools used by the artisans, but most of the portable *objets d'art* were removed by foreign collectors in the first decade of this century.

Preservation. Considerable preservation work is taking place. The Mogao Caves and the West Caves at Southlake have been declared national treasures. The Dang River has been diverted to protect the 16 West Caves and a reservoir built in 1975 to control the usual summer floods, a measure that saved them from being flooded recently. Work has been done at the Mogao Caves to strengthen the exterior walls and to prevent further deterioration from sun, wind, rain, and drifting sand. Statues have been treated with preservatives, foundations supported, humidifiers installed, and protective walls and screens built. Work is underway to remove intact some murals that have been painted over older murals, preserving both, but allowing each to be revealed in full detail. The pavilions originally built in the Tang and Song periods, but rebuilt in more recent times, have also been restored.

EXCURSIONS FROM DUNHUANG

Yulinsi

The Yulinsi or Elm Forest Buddhist Caves are located 43 miles south of Anxi, near the village of Tashi. The caves rank with the Mogao Caves and have been classified as a national treasure. There are 41 caves at the site: 3 from the Tang, 8 from the Five Dynasties, 13 from the Song, 1 from the Xi Xia, 7 from the Yuan, and 9 from the Qing. There are some magnificent works of art in the caves.

Yangguan and Hangshan Passes

The Yangguan and Hangshan mountain passes are about an hour's drive southwest of Dunhuang. The passes used to be the western gateway to China until the Mongols charged into the country on horseback and took it by force. Although the surrounding area is now desert, it was marshland under the Tang (A.D. 618–907), but was eventually submerged under the moving sand dunes from the west. The area is dotted with ruins from the Han (206 B.C.–A.D. 220) and Tang periods; many ruins have been submerged by sand. You can also visit the ruins of the Han town of Souchang where locals often dig relics such as coins, shards, and arrowheads from the encroaching sands.

Other Cave Temples

Majishan Caves. These are located southwest of Tianshui in the far south of the province, close to the border with Shaanxi Province. They are said to contain a rich and interesting collection of sculpture, in 190 caves dating from the Northern Wei, and extending through the Sui, Tang, and Song periods. The sculptures are of clay. There are also some fine wall paintings.

Matisi Monastery and Caves. The Horseshoe Monastery, as it is called, is a group of temples located near Minle, on the southwestern border of Gansu Province, about halfway between Lanzhou and Jiayuguan, and 37 miles south of Zhangye. The temples and caves are situated deep in the mountains. The caves—cut over a period dating from Northern Wei to the Ming—are in groups, each group being a few miles from the others; monasteries have been built over the cave mouths. The monasteries used to be devoted to Lamaist Buddhism, but it is not known whether they are still housing monks, nor whether the temples and caves are in good order.

Jintasi Monastery Caves. Only two caves remain, the buildings having fallen into ruins centuries ago. Located 30 miles northeast of Matisi, the caves of the Golden Pagoda Monastery, as it is known, contain no wall paintings. The statues apparently date from the Northern Wei but have suffered both damage and restoration over the centuries. The condition of the statues now is not known.

Wenwushan Temples and Caves. These caves were part of an important Buddhist center under the Northern Wei, Sui, and the Tang. The site is located 9 miles southwest of Jiuquan, a town serviced by a flight linking Lanzhou and Hami in Xinjiang. It can be reached by car, but is not yet open to tourists. Pavilions used to cover the caves, and there were many temples scattered throughout the area—both Buddhist and Taoist, most of them being rebuilt in the late nineteenth century after they were damaged during the rebellion by the Hui (Moslem) minority in the area.

Changma Caves. The Changma Caves are 38 miles southeast of Yumen, a place that was once the westernmost extremity of the Great Wall. There are several groups of caves in this location, but their condition is not known.

PRACTICAL INFORMATION FOR DUNHUANG

FACTS AND FIGURES. Dunhuang, a town over 2,100 years old, is situated on the western border of Gansu Province in northwest China. It was once an important center of the Buddhist faith as well as a settlement on the ancient "Silk Road," and is now a prosperous town in this remote area.

WHEN TO GO. Dunhuang should be visited only mid-March through mid-November; the Magao Caves are closed at other times.

HOW TO GET THERE. From Lanzhou, the provincial capital of Gansu, you can take a 4-hour flight (one stop-over) to the airport near Dunhuang. Otherwise, you can travel by train from Lanzhou to Liuyuan, a 17–18-hour journey, to connect by bus to Dunhuang, some 94 miles (and 3 hours) from the railway station. The Mogao Caves are another 15 miles southeast of Dunhuang.

HOTELS. The **Dunhuang Hotel** (tel. 2324) on Dongmenwai Street accommodates visitors in 100 rooms with basic facilities. A section of 30 older rooms just across the street is pressed into use only when there is an overflow of guests.

RESTAURANTS. There are no restaurants outside the hotels.

TOURIST INFORMATION. CITS (tel. 2325, 2497) staff are in the Dunhuang Hotel, so you will have no problem getting the benefit of their services. They also handle **CAAC** business.
PSB. If you need to visit this office, walk to the right along the street on which the hotel is located, and continue past the traffic circle. You will pass the Bank of China on your left and soon come upon the PSB building on your right. Open 7.30 A.M.–noon and 3–6.30 P.M. Closed Sunday.

HOW TO GET AROUND. The town is small so you can get around easily on foot. CITS arranges bus excursions to the sites.

WHAT TO SEE. The main reason to visit Dunhuang is to see the **Mogao Caves,** some 15 miles southeast of the town. Visitors with more time sometimes make the long excursion to **Yulinsi** or **Elm Forest Buddhist Caves,** or go to the ancient mountain passes of **Yangguan** and **Hangshan,** about 1 hour's drive from Dunhuang.

MUSEUMS. There is a museum at the site of the Mogao Caves where Chinese archaeologists work.

ENTERTAINMENT. There is no evening entertainment in Dunhuang except for documentary films that are sometimes shown at your hotel.

Useful Addresses and Telephone Numbers

CITS—Dunhuang Hotel (tel. 2325, 2497).

FUZHOU

Fujian Province

South China

Fuzhou, the "city of a sea of banyan trees," lies near the coast, 25 miles upstream from the mouth of the Min River. The capital of Fujian Province, it is known also as Sanshan because of the three hills of the town.

Early historical references suggest that the town was established at the end of the sixth century. In the time of the Five Dynasties (A.D. 907–960), it had become capital of the independent state of Minyue, and over the years it became a great trading town, selling sugar, wood, tea, fish, and tropical fruits while buying precious stones and pearls from Indian and Arab trading vessels. Marco Polo mentioned the town in his account of the journeys he made in China in the fourteenth century, referring to the presence of a Mongol garrison stationed there to keep down the local rebels, and to the presence of many merchants and craftsmen.

Fuzhou was declared an "open port" in 1842 in the first of the "unequal treaties" negotiated at Nanjing, which allowed European nations to operate trading establishments in the town. By the end of the century, it had once again become an important trading center, famous for lumber, tea, lichees, and handicrafts. Merchants continued to operate in Fuzhou until 1949 when the Communists seized power. Then trade declined, the town and the province being "sealed off" because of its strategic location opposite Taiwan, which had become the haven for the fleeing Nationalist forces under Chiang Kaishek.

Fujian Province is mountainous, only a small area being suitable for cultivation, but the rocky coastline and deep-water access makes the province ideal for fishermen. Fujian is also well known as a source of emigrants, many of whom have left to escape poverty and to make their fortune abroad. They once poured through the ports Fuzhou, Xiamen (Amoy), and Quanzhou to nearby countries, and, with their compatriots from Guangdong Province, now represent a significant economic force in Southeast Asia.

EXPLORING FUZHOU

Apart from the sights described below, there are pleasant parks and gardens and old sections of the town with quaint "match-box houses." The boat trip down the river reveals some fine scenery.

White Pagoda Monastery

The former White Pagoda Monastery stands at the foot of Mount Yu, on the western side, and is now the Yushan Library. The setting is quiet and peaceful.

Qi Jiguang Temple

East of the former monastery you will find a flight of steps leading to a fan-shaped terrace. The temple standing there was built by the people of Fuzhou to honor the memory of General Qi, who in the days of the Ming (1368–1644) defeated marauding Japanese pirates in three major battles. Other interesting sights are: Pinguan Terrace, Penglai Pavilion, and the Drunken Stone Pavilion. The whole area serves as an excellent example of the Fujian gardening style so typical of the southern regions of China.

Turtle Crown

Turtle Crown is the name given to the summit of Yushan. A road from the Qi Jiguang Temple leads there, the peak providing a fine view of the city and surrounding countryside.

White Pagoda

Originally named Ding Guang, the White Pagoda stands at the foot of Yushan. It has seven tiers, is octagonal in shape, measures 135 feet in height, and is made of brick with a lime-coated exterior. There used to be a wooden structure on the exterior of the pagoda but it was destroyed by fire over 400 years ago; now an interior wooden staircase leads to the top. On a clear day you can see the islands located just off the coast.

Ebony Pagoda

Opposite the White Pagoda stands the Ebony Pagoda, first constructed in A.D. 789. Known originally as the Pagoda of Purity, the pagoda is octagonal in shape and seven-tiered, but it is only 111 feet high. Note the base with a transposed lotus pattern and the lower tier with fine relief carvings of dragons and phoenixes.

West Lake

West Lake, in the northwest of the city, is man-made, having been first excavated more than 1,700 years ago and extended and improved over the centuries. Willows and banyans grow at the lake's edge; a small island capped by a pavilion stands offshore, a zigzag bridge pathway connecting it to the park. The building standing beside the Jade Belt Bridge is the Fujian Provincial Museum. The park is the best in the city; you can spend many an hour strolling there or rowing one of the boats on the lake.

EXCURSIONS FROM FUZHOU

Drum Hill

Nine miles east of Fuzhou, Gushan, or Drum Hill, is famous in the region for its scenery. Its name is derived from the large drum-shaped rock found at the summit. The hill is about 3,000 feet high and was once considered a "protector" of the town. The mountain boasts about 160 sites of historical or scenic interest, some of which are described below. There is also a spa in the vicinity.

Yongquan Temple

Yongquan Temple stands on the western slope of Drum Hill. Built as a Buddhist shrine in A.D. 908, famous at one time for the Buddha's tooth supposedly kept there, the temple—known as the Gushing Spring Temple—was noted for its collection of scriptures (sutras), one of which was written in the blood of a devotee. There are 25 halls and pavilions, a bell tower, and a drum tower. The most ancient edifices are the two nine-tiered octagonal pagodas standing before the Hall of the Heavenly Kings. Each is 23 feet high, faced with ceramic tiles, and more than 900 years old. There are 1,038 Buddhist figures on the sides of each pagoda and another 72 on the eaves. Note the 72 ceramic bells hung at each corner of the eaves. Some of the sutras are housed in the Sutra Pavilion where there is also a fine figure of the reclining Buddha carved in white jade. Look for the three sago palms (cycases) in the court of the meditation room; these are said to blossom annually, an extraordinary phenomenon for this plant. Legend has it that they were planted in the tenth century by Shen Yan, founder of the monastery, and Wang Shenzhi, the prince of Fujian. The architecture of the pavilions with their graceful upswept eaves is in the tradition of the southern style.

Source of Wonder Cave

The Source of Wonder Cave, located east of the Yongquan Temple, is in a 35-foot-deep ravine. On the steep cliff walls rearing up on either side, poems devoted to the beauty of the surroundings and events in the life of the poets are inscribed in a variety of calligraphy styles. The place is also known as the Fuzhou Forest of Inscriptions.

Water-Imbibing Rock

Nearby is a rock where a spring once flowed. A legend says that one day Shen Yan was discussing a point of religion with his prince, when he became irritated with the gurgling of the spring. He shouted loudly, whereupon the spring changed course and reappeared at the Bodhisattva Pavilion where it became known as the Dragon Head Spring. The water is noted for its sweetness.

Luoxing Pagoda

Luoxing Pagoda stands on the northern bank of the Ma River (Majiang), east of Drum Mountain. It is constructed of stone and red-granite clay, is octagonal in shape, and has seven tiers. According to a legend it was built by the seventh Lady of the Willow in memory of her husband who had sailed away ten years before. Whether this tale is true or not, the pagoda was once certainly used as a landmark by boats coming in from the sea.

Boat Trip Down the Min

It is possible to arrange a boat trip along the Min, through beautiful river scenery, to the sea some 25 miles downstream. You will pass Drum Hill on the way, faced on the opposite shore by Flag Hill. Another landmark is "Jingang's leg," a huge rock which according to legend is the limb of one of the Buddha's four warrior attendants. You will enjoy the variety of sailing craft that come and go along the river.

Hualin Temple

North of Yuehuang Hill, on the southern slope of Beibing Mountain stands the Hualin Temple, founded under the Tang (A.D. 608–907). It was destroyed many times over the centuries; the present buildings date only from the Qing.

PRACTICAL INFORMATION FOR FUZHOU

FACTS AND FIGURES. Fuzhou, the coastal capital of southeastern Fujian Province, lies on the Min River about midway between Shanghai and Guangzhou. Its population is 1.6 million. Quickest access is by air from Shanghai (fastest flight 2 hours) and from Guangzhou (fastest flight 2¼ hours).

WHEN TO GO. Summer is hot and humid, and spring brings coastal showers. The mild winter and the pleasant fall are the best for visiting the city.

HOW TO GET THERE. The city is connected to Shanghai by a "dog-leg" rail route (24-hour journey) and to Guangzhou by a long semi-circular rail loop. There are daily flights from Shanghai, a journey of 2 hours to 3 hours 25 minutes, according to aircraft type. There is a 6-day per week service from Guangzhou, taking from 2¼ hours up to 3 hours. CAAC (tel. 51988) is at Wuyi Zhonglu.

An interesting way to visit Fuzhou is to take the CTS air-conditioned bus from Shenzhen, departing 12 noon daily, to Shantou, Zhangzhou, and Xiamen. Then you can pick up a local bus traveling via Quanghou to Fuzhou. Alternatively, you can take a boat from Hong Kong to any of these ports, going the rest of the way by local bus; or you can take the boat direct to Mawei, a port located 45 minutes away from Fuzhou. There are also boats to Fuzhou from Shanghai.

HOTELS. The hotel with the best facilities is the **Hot Spring Hotel** (tel. 551818) on Central Wusi Road; it has 315 air-conditioned rooms with direct-dial telephone, minibar, and piped-in hot spring-water, a business center, swimming pool, tennis courts, health club, and bowling. Another new hotel is the enormous **Xihu** or **West Lake Guest House** (tel. 557008) at 150 Qianjin Road North, by the lakeside, with more than 1,000 rooms. The other major hotel is the **Overseas Chinese Mansion** (tel. 557603; cable 8008), 25 Renmin Bei Road, with 190 rooms. This should not be confused with the **Overseas Chinese Hotel** (tel. 33492) on Wusi Road. Other hotels are the 17-story **Minjiang** (tel. 557895) on Wusi Road, with 500 rooms; **Hualian Mansions** (tel. 34944) on Wuyi Road; the **Fuzhou Hotel** (tel. 33057), 36 Dongda Road; the **Fuzhou Qiaolian Mansion** (tel. 57858) at 88 Wuyi Road North in the center of the city; the **Wuyi Hotel** (tel. 32646) on Wuyi Road Central; and the **Foreign Trade Center Hotel** (tel. 550154) on Wusi Road Central.

RESTAURANTS. The **Juchunyuan Restaurant** (tel. 32338), said to be over 100 years old, is at 130 Bayiqi Bei Road. Try the jade hatchet dumplings, the 8-piece chicken, and the bee's nest bean curd. Other restaurants are: the **Huafulou** (tel. 32976) at 795 Bayiqi Zhong Road and the **Qingzhen** (tel. 33517) at 342 Bayiqi Bei Road, serving vegetarian and Muslim dishes.

TOURIST INFORMATION. CITS (tel. 55506 or 56293) is located at 44 Dongda Road.

CAAC (tel. 51988, 55113) is at Wuyi Zhong Road (May First Central Road).

PSB. To reach the PSB office, head south from the intersection of Wuyi Zhong Road and Dongda Road, turning right immediately after crossing the canal. The office is in a building on the left on the next corner.

HOW TO GET AROUND. CITS can arrange excursions for sightseeing by bus, mini-bus, or taxi. For fun, you could take a short journey in one of the pedal-rickshaws that are in use around the town. Buses are usually crammed with passengers.

WHAT TO SEE. In Fuzhou you should visit the former White Pagoda Monastery, now the **Yushan Library;** the **Qi Jiguang Temple;** the **Turtle Crown** at the summit of Yushan; the **White Pagoda;** the **Ebony Pagoda;** and the **West Lake.**
There are interesting excursions to make: the one to **Drum Hill** holds perhaps the most interest, along with the **Yongquan Temple,** the **Source of Wonder Cave,** and the **Water-Imbibing Rock.** Then there is the **Luoxing Pagoda,** and the **Hualin Temple.** The boat trip down the **Min River** is an ideal way to see the beauty of the surrounding scenery.

MUSEUMS. The **Fuzhou Provincial Museum** stands near the foot of the Jade Belt Bridge over West Lake. Many interesting historical relics are housed in the museum, the most noteworthy being a "boat coffin" of Wuyi, the Han Dynasty (206 B.C.–A.D. 220) canoe, and silk fabrics from Song Dynasty tombs.

SHOPPING. You may wish to buy some of the famous brands of Fuzhou tea, a regional specialty; Longan wood carvings, Shoushan stone carvings, and "bodiless lacquer ware" are good buys. The latter, considered one of the "three treasures" of China, is not only light in weight but strong as well. The lacquer ware is finished in an attractive range of colors. You may also choose from a wide array of arts and crafts products at the Fuzhou Branch of the **Fujian Tourist Souvenirs Production and Supply Corporation** (tel. 33491), opposite the Minjiang Hotel, all offered at most reasonable prices.

ENTERTAINMENT. Because Fuzhou is the home for many returned overseas Chinese, there are often evening cultural events to be seen. Check with your hotel or CITS.

USEFUL ADDRESSES AND TELEPHONE NUMBERS

CITS—44 Dongda Road (tel. 55506 or 56293).
CAAC—Wuyi Zhong Road (tel. 51988, 55113).

GUILIN

Guangxi Zhuangzu Autonomous Region
South China

Many people consider Guilin the number one scenic spot in China. Solitary water-scarred limestone mountains rise out of the green plain, their peaks hidden in swirling mists. Below, the caramel waters of the River Li twist away to the sea, fed by underground streams. The scenery conveys a sense of mystery; a languid brooding silence prevails. The city, situated in the northeast corner of the Guangxi Zhuangzu Autonomous Region, has been a favorite subject of painters and poets for centuries.

Guilin was founded under Qin Shi Huang Di in 214 B.C. as a small settlement on the Li Jiang. The town grew following the construction of a canal linking the river with another further north, giving a connection to the Yangzi. The emperor could thus send food and provisions by water from the Yangzi plains to the imperial armies in the far south.

The town became the provincial capital under the Ming (1368–1644) and remained so until 1914 when the capital was moved to Nanning. Guilin became capital again in 1936. During the Sino-Japanese war it became a center of resistance to the invasion but was badly damaged during the fighting. Five years after the Communists gained power the capital was once again moved to Nanning.

Numerous limestone hills within the boundaries of Guilin offer a superb view of the surrounding countryside. The many excursions to the hills outside the town allow you to explore the caves, see the rock carvings, and visit old temples.

One of the most spectacular trips you will make in China is the journey by boat downstream from Guilin. If you are particularly fortunate you may even see the Li Jiang fishermen using trained cormorants. The cormorants dive into the water, trap fish in their beaks, and bring them back to the fishermen's boat.

Warning: For many visitors Guilin has become a "tourist trap" with inadequate hotels, poor restaurants, and local hustlers. For some the Li River trip is the only worthwhile part of the visit to the city. Free-lance travelers should note that, after arriving in Guilin, it is time consuming to get bus-train-air tickets or onward reservations. Many "free-lancers" forsake a visit to Guilin altogether and go instead to Yangshuo some 50 miles to the south. The scenery is the same, but the village is peaceful.

EXPLORING GUILIN

Most visitors spend two days in Guilin, one day on the Li River tour, the other exploring the hills, caves, and parks of the town and its surround-

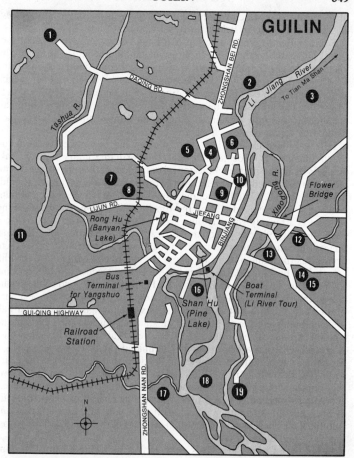

Points of Interest

Bao Ji Shan (Treasured Hoard Hill) **4**

Chen Shan (Hushan or Tiger Hill) **3**

Chuan Shan (Tunnelled Hill) **19**

Crescent Hill-Hidden Dragon Rock (Forest of Stone Carvings in the Sea of Cassia Trees) **13**

Die Cai Shan (Hill of Folded Colors)—Wind Cave (Feng Tong) **6**

Du Xiu Feng Peak (Solitary Beauty Peak) **9**

Elephant Trunk Hill (Xiang Bi Shan) **16**

Fubo Hill—Returned Pearl Cave (Huan Zhu Dong)—Thousand Buddha Cliff **10**

Hua Gai An Temple—Yin Shan Hill **8**

Laoren Shan (Old Man Mountain) **5**

Nanxi Hill—Dragon Spring Restaurant **17**

Pagoda Hill (Bao Ta Shan) **18**

Potted Landscape Area **15**

Reed Pipe Cave (Ludi Yan) **1**

Seven Star Crags (Qi Xing Shan) **12**

Western Hill (Xishan) **7**

Yu Shan Hill **2**

Zheng Yin Shan **11**

Zoo **14**

ings. The order in which you do your sightseeing is not important; however, the sequence given below is often followed.

Solitary Beauty Peak. The Du Xiu Feng rises steeply in the center of town. The climb to the top is arduous and should be undertaken only by visitors who are confident about their physical condition. There is a fine view from the summit terrace. On this peak you will see cliffs on which are engraved Chinese characters dating from as far back as the Tang (A.D. 618–907). The hill used to be surrounded by a wall enclosing a Ming palace, but all that now remains is a moat, portions of the wall, and a gate flanked by a pair of stone lions.

Hill of Folded Colors. The Die Cai Shan can be climbed without too much difficulty. It is located a little to the north of Solitary Beauty Peak, and gets its name from the limestone formations on the hill, which resemble skeins of colored silk thread. At the top, there is a small circular building known as the "Cloud Touching" Pavilion; there is a sheer drop of hundreds of feet to one side. Near the top there is a cave, known as Wind Cave: it is strangely shaped—like a gourd—big at both ends but with a neck allowing only one person at a time to pass. There are some Buddhist images and carved inscriptions on the cave walls; the strong, ever-present draft gives the name to the cave. Note the two poems carved into the cliff face: one is by Zhu De, the other by Xu Deli, a teacher of Mao Zedong.

Fuboshan. This hill is named after a Han general, a legendary hero who passed through the town on a military campaign. There used to be a temple dedicated to him, but all that remains is a bell weighing two-and-a-half tons, and a large cooking pot. The hill stands alongside the Li River and contains a famous cave called the Returned Pearl Cave (Huanzhutong). A legend tells that a pearl, which illuminated the cave, was stolen by a fisherman. He became so ashamed of his deed that he returned the pearl, so giving the cave its name. You will note a stone pillar inside the cave that comes within just a few inches of the ground. The "missing piece," according to legend, was removed with a single slash of a sword, again by the general. At another place on the hill you will see the Thousand Buddha Cliff where there are about 30 carvings of the Buddha, dating from the Tang and Song dynasties.

Seven Star Crags Park. This park derives its Chinese name, Qi Xing Shan, from the arrangement of the peaks, which resembles the pattern made by the stars of the constellation known as the Great Bear. There are six caves in the hills and many pavilions. Take bus 9, 10, or 11.

With plenty of time at your disposal, you can see all the sights in the park, but if you don't have much time, you may have to decide between seeing either the Seven Star Cave, or the Crescent Hill with its Dragon Refuge Cave. The former can take as long as two hours to see; the latter is of great historic interest. If you are to visit the Reed Pipe Cave, or have already seen it, then you are advised to select the Crescent Hill–Dragon Refuge Cave alternative.

To enter the park you must cross two bridges: the first passes over the Li River, the second—which leads straight on from the first—crosses the Xiadong River. The second bridge is known as the Flower Bridge (Huaqiao), a recent reconstruction of an elegant Song Dynasty period bridge bedecked with a gallery covered by a glazed-tile roof. The large monolith at the left-hand exit of the bridge is called the Furong Stone.

There are three alternatives on arriving in the park. On the right-hand side (downstream) there is Crescent Hill; in the middle Putuo Hill and beyond it the zoo; and to the left there is the pathway to the Seven Star Cave. We shall consider the latter first.

Turn left after crossing the bridge; ignore the first large pathway to the right (leading from the two small hump-backed bridges on the left), but take the second large pathway to the right. This leads to the Gongxing Mountain Gate, the Xuanwu Pavilion, and beyond it to the left entrance to the **Seven Star Cave.** The Bixu Pavilion stands to the left of the entrance, the Xixia Pavilion to the right. Depending on how fast you walk, the journey through the cave will take anything from one to two hours. The cave is well provided with pathways from which to view the magnificently stage-lit stalagmites (rising) and stalagtites (hanging). They are not as delicately colored as they once were, having been affected by the torch smoke of the many visitors who flocked through the cave before it was lit by electricity.

On leaving the cave you come to the Huoran Pavilion, a good place to view the Camel Rock. Below, there is a small zoo and an enclosed garden displaying hundreds of potted landscapes with miniature trees. From here you head back toward the river. The path turns to the right to reveal the Tablet Pavilion and the gate to Putuo Hill ahead, and the Putuo villa behind and above. On walking toward these pavilions you will come to the entrance to Yuanfeng Cave on the right-hand side. The path turns left near the cave entrance to lead back to the bridge.

The only remaining portion of the park to visit is that to the right after crossing the bridge (or on the left-hand side when leaving the park). This is **Crescent Hill.** Crescent Tower (Yueyalou) stands at the foot of the hill; it is a traditional-style pavilion which is now a restaurant. On the river side of Crescent Hill stands the Banyue Pavilion, the Jingjiang Pavilion, and the little Guanghan Palace. The famous **Dragon Refuge (or Longlin) Cave,** also known as the Forest of Tablets Cave, is adjacent and just a little downstream. The cave contains hundreds of inscriptions carved on the walls and ceilings, some over 1,600 years old.

Rong Hu and Song Hu. Take a stroll in the park surrounding these two lakes. If you are staying in a hotel in the middle of the city, you can do so during lunch break or after dinner. Rong Hu means Banyan Tree Lake, and Shan Hu means Pine Tree Lake. They were formed when a bridge, now called Qingdao Qiao or Green Belt Bridge, was built under the Song Dynasty, so splitting the original lake that formed part of the moat protecting the town. The area is attractive, with small pavilions, tree-lined walks, and rock gardens. You may welcome the chance to spend a few quiet moments there during your busy program.

Reed Pipe Cave. The Ludi Yan, as it is called in Chinese, is about 5 miles to the northwest of Guilin. You can see everything in this cave in about half an hour, the path through it being only a third of a mile long. The cave has been known for over a thousand years and derives its name from the reeds that grew near the cave. The large grotto inside the cave, known as the Crystal Palace, was, according to legend, the temporary palace of the Dragon King, housing his maidens, treasure, crab generals, and shrimp soldiers. The pillar in the grotto was supposedly the Dragon King's magic needle, used by the Monkey King in the famous tale *Journey to the West,* when he defeated the Dragon King's army. The stalactites and stalagmites are attractively lit with colored lights, the Lion Forest being one of the most popular grottoes. Indeed, many visitors prefer this cave to the Seven Star Cave.

Chuan Shan Park and Cave. Situated to the southeast of Guilin on the bank of the Xiaodong River, Chuan Shan Park stands opposite Pagoda Hill. The park has recently been relandscaped, and planted with more than 40,000 trees. The park is in three-sections: Chuan Shan Hill, Xiaodong Hill, and Pagoda Hill. The Chuan Shan Caves are attractively lit and can be viewed in half an hour, the pathway being only one-third of the mile long.

Yunfeng Temple. Located at the foot of Elephant Trunk Hill, the Yunfeng Temple was founded under the Tang (A.D. 618–907), but the existing temple is more recent. It used to be one of the most famous temples in the region. Inside the temple there are historic relics on display: objects from the period of the Taiping Rebellion; ceramic ware, pottery, and paintings from the Ming and Qing dynasties.

Other Temples and Pagodas

If you are particularly interested in temples and pagodas, you should note the following. At Yaoshan, about 9 miles northeast of Guilin, there is a temple known as Zhushengan close to the Dragon Pool, or Long Chi. Further up the hill there is the White Cloud Temple (Taoist), or Biayunguan; the Temple of the Buddha of Longevity, or Shoufoan (Buddhist). A further mile and a half along a path to the top of the hill stands the White Stag Temple, or Bailuan, sometimes known as the Jade Emperor Pavilion, or Yuhuang Ge. There is also the Tomb of one of the wives of the King of Jing Jiang (Ming Dynasty) on the eastern slope of the hill.

The only other temple worthy of note near the town is located in the hills west of Guilin. It is Huangian Temple, which stands at the foot of Yinshan Hill and is said to contain five Tang portraits of the Shi Liu Zun, or Sixteen Venerable Ones. There are also several caves in the hill, one with a statue of the Buddha and Lao Zi.

Many of these temples were desecrated during the Cultural Revolution, and some are under repair.

EXCURSIONS FROM GUILIN

Li River Cruise

One of the finest excursions on your tour of China will be the boat trip from Guilin along the River Li. Tour boats depart at 7:30 A.M. (or 8:30 A.M., depending on the season) from the Yangti Jetty near the Jiefang (Liberation) Bridge, adjacent to Elephant Trunk Hill, or Xiangbishan, long used as the symbol of Guilin. A little further downstream you will pass, on your left, **Baotashan** with a Ming Dynasty pagoda on top. East of its stands Chuan Shan, or the **Hill with the Hole.** Then begins a series of beautiful scenes that unfold as you glide away from Guilin on your journey south. You will spend the best part of the day on board, surrounded by scenery of indescribable beauty.

The boat journey usually takes 4–5 hours, unless the season dictates a shorter trip. Save some film for the middle part of the journey, between the towns of **Yangdi** and **Xingping.** In this region—usually during the third hour of the journey—you will be exposed to the best scenery on the river.

The standard cruise ends at the colorful market town of **Yangshuo,** some 52 miles downstream, the boat mooring at a pretty spot on the river bank. If you wish, you can climb the nearby hills and admire the scenery. A two-hour bus journey returns you to Guilin. On the way you will see something of the lush countryside of the province where tropical fruit, sugar cane, bamboo, and rice are cultivated. The journey is usually broken by a stop at the village of **Chuanyan** to see a 1,300-year-old banyan tree.

At certain times of the year—between December and February—there is sometimes insufficient depth of water to allow the passage of boats too far along the river. In those periods, you may be driven to Yangdi by bus for a boat trip downstream to Yangshuo.

Yangshuo

Yangshuo nestles at the foot of green limestone pinnacles on the west bank of the Li River, some 52 miles south of Guilin. Many visitors prefer to stay there rather than visit crowded Guilin, for its scenery is better and there are rustic villages to explore along the country lanes. The nearest hill overlooking the town is called Green Lotus Peak. To the southwest are Horse Hill and Fairy Peach Hill, to the west Crab Hill, to the north Dragon Head Hill, to the east Kitten Hill and Lion Hill, and to the southeast Dragon Back Hill and White Crane Hill. There is nothing to see in the town itself. You can get to Yangshuo by boat from Guilin, or by bus from Wuzhou (see below). Two small hotels are not far from the long-distance bus station. The best way to get around is by bicycle, which can be hired at your hotel or at a bicycle-hire stand.

When leaving Yangshuo there are buses to Guilin departing nine times each day, a journey of two hours. Alternatively, you could take a boat upstream to Yangdi, then a bus to Guilin. For those heading south, there are buses to Wuzhou.

Wuzhou

A coach service links Guilin and Wuzhou; located on the eastern border of the province, Wuzhou is about halfway to Guangzhou. On the way you pass some delightful scenery. The journey of 267 miles can be completed in one day. At Wuzhou you can connect the next day with a river ferry to take you down the Xijiang all the way to Guangzhou. A local bus from Wuzhou does the same journey.

PRACTICAL INFORMATION FOR GUILIN

FACTS AND FIGURES. Guilin is at approximately the same latitude as Miami, Florida. Elevation is 500 feet above sea level. Distances from major cities: Beijing 1,080 miles by air (1,250 miles by rail); Shanghai 810 miles (1,071 by rail); Guangzhou 225 miles by air.

The table shows the weather pattern in Guilin during the year.

Guilin Temperature Range and Average Rainfall

	Temperature High (°F)	Temperature Low (°F)	Number of Days with Rainfall	Monthly Rainfall (in inches)
January	55	41	10	1.6
April	74	59	18	9.4
July	93	76	14	8.0
October	81	62	7	2.6

WHEN TO GO. The best times to visit are fall, winter, and early spring, i.e., October through April. During these months the climate is pleasant, the rainfall modest, the visibility at its best. However, be careful of the period December through February if the main purpose of your visit is to take the boat trip down the Li River, for in these months the water level in the river is sometimes too low for the boat to pass all the way downstream. The favored period is fall, because then the osmanthus trees (acacias) are in bloom, being at their peak during the eighth moon of the lunar year.

The weather in Guilin is dominated by the pattern of rainfall, and the average level of precipitation is an enormous 74 inches per year. About 80 percent of the rainfall occurs from April through September, the worst months being May and June, when monthly averages of around 15 inches are common. You will note from the climate table that during the wet season there is rainfall more than 15 days in almost every month. And when it rains in Guilin, visibility is often reduced to a few yards.

In contrast to the wet, hot, and humid summers, spring and autumn are fairly pleasant. No pronounced winter season exists, although in midwinter the temperature occasionally drops to zero.

HOW TO GET THERE. By plane. Hong Kong is the most convenient international departure point for Guilin, but so far only charter flights for package tours depart from there. For regular flights, Guangzhou is the airport used by most travelers, as there are at least four daily flights. The fastest flight takes only 55 minutes. There are many other flights serving Guilin from provincial capitals but the frequency of the service is far less than the service from Guangzhou. Flight times vary according to aircraft type, but the following (fastest) flights to Guilin apply: Guangzhou 55 minutes; Beijing 2 hours 25 minutes; Shanghai 1 hour 55 minutes; Changsha 1 hour 20 minutes; Hangzhou 1 hour 40 minutes; Kunming 1 hour 35 minutes: Nanning 55 minutes: Chengdu $3\frac{1}{2}$ hours (including stopover at Chongqing); Chongqing 1 hour 55 minutes. Flights to and from Guilin are very heavily booked.

By train. There is no "straight-line" train service connecting Guangzhou and Guilin; there is a large range of mountains in between. So you have to take a train from Guangzhou to Hengyang (south of Changsha) and wait for the connection to Guilin. You are traveling two sides of a triangle, the first leg north-northwest (10 hours), the second southwest ($7\frac{1}{4}$ hours). The connection is a bad one, and the journey, including stopover, occupies the best part of 24 hours, so most people prefer to take the one-hour flight instead. Furthermore, trains to and from Guilin are often impossibly crowded.

By boat. Travelers who don't mind roughing it might like to try the overnight boat journey from Guangzhou (departs 12 noon) to Wuzhou (arrives 6 A.M. next day), then take the bus to Guilin, perhaps stopping off at Yangshou on the way. The boat leaves from Dashatou pier at Three Yangjian Road, in the eastern sector of Guangzhou.

By coach. Another alternative, which has considerable appeal, is the air-conditioned coach from Guangzhou. The scenic route takes you through Zhaoqing, Wuzhou, Hexian, and Yangshou. Tickets are available 3 days in advance through the ticket office at the Guangzhou Horticulture Company at 5 Zhongshan Road. The coach departs at 6:20 A.M. and the journey usually takes two days, providing an overnight stop en route.

HOTELS. The Holiday Inn Guilin (tel. 3950, cable 6333, telex 48456), 14 South Ronghu Road, has 259 international-standard guest rooms, two restaurants, a coffee shop, skylight lounge, health club, and ballroom. The 20-story **Hong Kong Hotel Guilin** (tel. 333889, cable 4359, telex 48454), 8 Xihuan Yi Road, offers first-class accommodations in 300 rooms, a revolving rooftop restaurant, a pool, two tennis courts, bowling, and a health club. The **Guishan Hotel** (tel. 443388, telex 48443) in Chuan Shan Road, another of the new deluxe hotels that line the banks of the Li River, has 610 rooms, business center, eight restaurants, pool, and tennis courts.

Other quality hotels in Guilin include the **Sheration Guilin** (tel. 225588, telex 48439), 67 Binjiang Nan Road, with an atrium lobby, "bullet" elevators, and Olympic pool, on the banks of the Li River; the **Guilin Garden Hotel** (tel. 442411 or 443611, telex 48445 GLGDN CN) in Yuang Jiang Road, with 344 rooms, a Chinese restaurant, tennis courts, and a swimming pool; the **Guilin Riverside Resort** (tel. 222291, cable 5031) overlooking the Li Jiang; and the **Guilin Osmanthus Hotel** (tel. 2261 or 5316), 451 Zhongshan South Road, whose new wing offers 400 guest rooms and a pool.

Additional hotels used by tourists include the **Rongcheng** (tel. 2311) near Seven Star Hill. At the **Lijiang** or **Li River Hotel** (tel. 2881, 3050), 1 Shanhu Road, each of its rooms offers a superb view of the surrounding hills and mountains. The **Ronghu**, or **Banyan Tree Lake Hotel** (tel. 3811), 17 Ronghu Bei Road, gets mixed reviews from guests largely depending on which of the eight buildings they stay in. Other hotels (about which, however, we hear regular complaints) are: the **Guilin Hotel** (tel. 2755, 2249), 451 Zhongshan Nan Road, the **Yinshan (or Hidden Hill) Fandian** (tel. 5484), and the **Nanxi Fandian.** More in the style of a motel, the **Jia-shan** (tel. 2986) has been subject to criticism by many guests but has been relisted here following its recent renovation.

For some inexplicable reason, the dining rooms of the older hotels in Guilin serve food that varies from bland to inedible. You may therefore wish to try one of the restaurants in Guilin.

RESTAURANTS. If you happen to be staying at one of those hotels where the food is appalling, you may be inspired to eat out. You can try the **Yueyalou** or **Crescent Tower Restaurant** (tel. 3622) in the Seven Star Park. To find the Yueyalou, cross the Flower Bridge and follow the footpath leading into the park. The restaurant, built in traditional style, is on the right; it serves wild game dishes in season. Another restaurant in the center of Guilin, is the **Donglai Guan** (tel. 3449) on Zhongshan Road, serving exotic dishes. There are many other small restaurants in Zhongshan Road.

Guilin cuisine is smiliar in style to the Cantonese, but it draws more on the indigenous animal population for inspiration. Dishes are made from scaly anteater (or pangolin), monkey, owl, bamboo-rat, giant salamander, various species of cat, and turtle. The popularity of these dishes among the locals has caused the near-extinction of some species. Most visitors usually prefer to stay with dishes that are in the Cantonese mainstream and, by coincidence, do their bit for animal preservation.

TOURIST INFORMATION. CITS (tel. 222648) is at 14 Ronghu Bei Road. Walk toward the west from the intersection of this road and Zhongshan Road (the main street) and you will come to the office on the right-hand side of the road.

CAAC (tel. 3063) is at 144 Zhongshan Road Central.

PSB (tel. 3202) is on Sandao Road, just west of the intersection of this street with Zhongshan Road. Open daily 8 A.M.–5 P.M. Closeed Sunday.

HOW TO GET AROUND. For the easily accessible parts of Guilin, bicycles are the best way to get around. There are numerous rental shops. CITS organizes bus tours and excursions, as well as trips on the Li River.

Keep in mind that visits to the peaks in and around Guilin require a lot of climbing up and down paths and steps, and that a tour of the larger caves can mean a walk of a mile or more. Although the paths are usually gentle, the steps are steep.

WHAT TO SEE. There are so many beautiful spots in and around Guilin that it is difficult to advise the visitor on those that should be given priority. There are many vantage points from the hills in and around the town where you may take in the magnificent scenery. Then there are numerous caves: some small and romantic, others enormous with strange shapes inside illuminated by colored lights. There are also Buddhist and Taoist temples to visit (although these are not always open to visitors), as well as Buddhist rock carvings, pagodas, and a *stupa*.

Most people prefer to take the full-day boat journey along the river (returning later in the day by bus or car). There is usually only a day or perhaps half a day remaining for visits to other scenic spots. This time is probably best spent visiting one or two panoramic vantage points, e.g., the Solitary Beauty Peak (very steep climb), the Hill of Folded Colors, or Die Cai Shan, or the Fubo Hill, keeping in mind that these entail some fairly arduous climbing. Then explore one or two of the major caves, e.g., the Reed Pipe (or Ludi) Cave, the Dragon Refuge (Longlin) Cave in Seven Star Park, perhaps the Seven Star Cave itself, or the Chuan Shan Cave. You can take a water cure at the Long Sheng Hot Springs.

SHOPPING. A number of regional products may interest you. Food items, such as cassia wine and tea grown locally, are worth examining. So, too, are the local bamboo products; the Zhuang-minority products such as tunics, sashes, handbags, woven articles; and the carved and hand-painted stones. The shops of interest are mainly located on Zhongshan Road Central; the **Antique Shop** (tel. 2594) is located at no. 79; **Arts and Crafts Store** (tel. 3998) at no. 108; the **Guilin Department Store** (tel. 3146, 3301); and the **Friendship Store** (tel. 2743), 119 Zhongshan Road Central. There is a covered market one block west of the Friendship Store.

USEFUL ADDRESSES AND TELEPHONE NUMBERS

International Calls: Operator, tel. 113. Information, tel. 116.
Directory Inquiries, tel. 114.
China International Travel Service, 14 Ronghu Bei Road (tel. 222648).
CAAC Ticket Office, 144 Zhongshan Road Central (tel. 2740 or 3063).
Airport: inquiries, tel. 2741.
Railway Station, tel. 3124 or 2904.
River Transport, tel. 3295, 5829, 3306, or 5878.
Taxis, tel. 2089 or 3811.
Central Bus Station, tel. 2620.
Bus Tickets, tel. 5878.

GUIYANG

Guizhou Province

Southwest China

Guiyang, the capital of Guizhou Province, is on a tributary of the Wu River in the very center of the province. Standing at an elevation of 3,000 feet, the capital is dominated by the mist-shrouded hills surrounding the Wujiang valley. The climate is mild throughout the year, but the town is very wet during the monsoonal months of April through October.

The original settlement was established under the Han about 2,000 years ago. Walls were constructed around the town under the Ming (1368–1644), and under the Qing (1644–1911) the town became provincial capital. After the revolution, industry was developed in the town, so that there is now a steel mill, as well as factories producing diesel engines, rolling stock, mining machinery, electrical equipment, and chemical fertilizers. There is also an aluminum refinery in operation. The town is also the hub of the rail network which radiates to the four surrounding provinces.

Guizhou Province is a vast plateau of hills, there being almost no level ground in the entire region. Not surprisingly, there are many watercourses, streams, and rivers, and because the rock structure of the province is largely limestone, there are underground rivers and even vast underground lakes. The elevation and rocky nature of the province have made it inaccessible. For many centuries it has been the home of a group of ethnic minorities (Bouyei, Miao, Yi, and Dong) who came under the domination of the Han Chinese relatively late in history (eighteenth century), although they paid tribute to the Chinese a long time before that. In general the minority groups inhabit the uplands of the southern, eastern, and western border areas of the province, the Han Chinese occupying the lowlands and river valley area.

The high rainfall and fertile land bring in abundant crops, even though most of the terrain requires extensive terracing. Rice and wheat are grown in the lowlands, corn and rapeseed are produced in the uplands. Livestock raising is traditional throughout the region; logging is undertaken in the forest areas. The province is rich in mineral resources: deposits of coal, silver, copper, manganese, bauxite, mercury, tungsten, and molybdenum are being mined.

EXPLORING GUIYANG

The town is not of major interest to visitors. However, if you are traveling by train from Guilin to Chongqing, or vice versa, you must change trains at Guiyang, and you may want to break up your journey. (Those on their way to China's waterfall, Huangguoshu, are better off traveling farther west and alighting at Anshun; the bus journey from there to the falls is only 90 minutes.)

EXCURSIONS FROM GUIYANG

The only excursion available to date is to China's largest waterfall, **Huangguoshu** (Yellow Fruit Tree), some 95 miles to the southwest of the town. The bus for the falls (usually no. 103) leaves Guiyang's long-distance bus station at 7 A.M., arriving four to five hours later; the return journey departs about 3 P.M. CITS organizes minibus tours, which are expensive.

PRACTICAL INFORMATION FOR GUIYANG

FACTS AND FIGURES. Guiyang stands at an elevation of 3,000 feet in the center of the Guizhou Plateau. Nearest provincial capitals are Kunming to the southwest, Chengdu to the northwest, and Changsha to the northeast.

WHEN TO GO. The Guizhou Plateau is one of China's cloudiest regions. The climate is mild all year round, average temperatures varying from 39–48° F in winter to 68–82° F in summer. The province is subject to the monsoon, so that rainfall is frequent from April to October, the winter months being dry. The best time to visit the Huangguoshu Falls is May–October, when the rains are plentiful.

HOW TO GET THERE. Air travel is the quickest, most convenient way to get to Guiyang from major Chinese cities. The most convenient point of departure for most travelers is Guangzhou—the flight takes 1¼ hours. There are also flights from Chengdu (1 hour, 20 minutes), Wuhan (1 hour, 20 minutes), Xian (1 hour, 35 minutes), Kunming (1 hour, 50 minutes), and Changsha (2 hours, 15 minutes).

HOTELS. The **Huaxi Guest House** (tel. 25973) is inconveniently located some 11 miles from the town in a pleasant setting in Huaxi Park. Other hotels are the **Yuyan Hotel** (tel. 23564) at 36 Beijing Road, not far from Qianyang Restaurant; **Jinqiao Hotel** (tel. 24872), 26 Ruijin Road, where CITS is located; **Bajiaoyan Hotel** (tel. 23662) in Beijing Road; **Guishan Hotel** in Shengfu Road; the **Guiyang Hotel** (tel. 25512) in Zhonghuazhong Road; the **Zhaoyang Zushe** on Zunyi Lu; and the 30-story **Guizhou Hotel,** offering modern accommodations in 395 rooms.

RESTAURANTS. Outside the hotel dining rooms are a few "masses" restaurants that visitors might care to try. They are: **Dongxin** (tel. 23288) in Zhongshandong Road; **Guangdong** (tel. 25593) at Dashizi for Cantonese dishes; **Pianyi** (tel. 24812) in Zhonghuanan Road; and the **Qianyang** (tel. 22451). Guizhou cuisine, similar in style to that of its northern neighbor, Sichuan, features the abundant use of spices. Regional specialities include dishes made from the endangered giant salamander.

TOURIST INFORMATION. CITS (tel. 25121 or 29693) is at 7 Yanan Road Central.
CAAC (tel. 22300, 23000) is at 170 Zunyi Road.

HOW TO GET AROUND. Buses circumnavigate the town: bus no. 1 in a counterclockwise direction, bus no. 2 in a clockwise direction. Both leave from the square opposite the railway station. The local long-distance bus terminus for the falls is located in the northwest section of town. It's easy to pick out: it looks like an old temple.

WHAT TO SEE. The **Huaxi Caves** in the park of the same name are artistically illuminated, the light and sound being triggered through photoelectric cells by your guide's flashlight. Five miles southwest of the town lies another group of caves in **Nanjiao Park.**

Ming Dynasty pavilions are to be seen in the **Hongfu Monastery** in Qianling Shan Park in the northwest sector of town. On the Qianling Mountain itself stands the **Kanzhu Pavilion,** providing views over the town.

Other sites in town are the **Jiaxiu Tower** (or First of Beauties Tower) and the **Guanfeng Terrace** (or Observe the Wind Terrace). There are pleasant parks in the city, such as the **Zhongshan Park,** the **Nanming Park,** and the **Huaxi** or **Flower Brook Park.**

USEFUL ADDRESSES AND TELEPHONE NUMBERS

CITS, 7 Yanan Road Central (tel. 25121 or 29693).
CAAC, 170 Zunyi Road (tel. 22300, 23000).

HANGZHOU

Zhejiang Province
South China

Hangzhou, the capital of Zhejiang Province, lies close to the mouth of the Qian Tang River at the western extremity of the huge estuary of the Gulf of Hangzhou.

Two thousand years ago there was nothing there but a sandbar built up by the silt carried downstream by the river. It collected between two fingers of land that jutted into the estuary. The inhabitants built a dike to reinforce the bar, and thereby created what is present-day Xi Hu, or West Lake, perhaps the most famous lake in China.

The settlement remained a small fishing village until late in the sixth century, when the extension of the Grand Canal southward from the Yangzi led to the development of a busy commercial center in the town. It prospered, especially during the tranquil early period of the Tang Dynasty, and its growth was assisted by the development of the lower Yangzi area into the nation's most important agricultural region. Over the centuries work on the dikes continued, in order to protect the town from the ravages of river and sea alike.

Hangzhou underwent dramatic development when the Song, pushed south by the conquering Jin, established their capital there. In the short space of a hundred years, the population increased to almost a million people and the town flourished as a major trading center. Even though parts of Hangzhou were destroyed during the late-thirteenth-century invasion by the Mongols, the city, when visited by Marco Polo a short time afterwards, was still impressive. He said that "it is without doubt the finest and most splendid city in the world. . . . the streets and water courses alike are very wide . . . there are said to be 12,000 bridges, mostly of stone . . . vast are the numbers of those accustomed to dainty living, to the point of eating fish and meat at one meal."

Marco Polo also observed that "these people, from childhood upwards, are used to taking cold baths all the time, a habit which they declare to be most conducive to good health." And he describes the ladies of the town as "heavily perfumed, attended by many handmaids and lodged in richly ornamented apartments. These ladies are highly proficient and accomplished in the uses of endearments and caresses . . . so that foreigners who have once enjoyed them remain utterly beside themselves and so captivated by their sweetness and charm that they can never forget them."

As for the lake, Marco Polo wrote: "On one side it skirts the city . . . and . . . commands a distant view of all its grandeur and loveliness, its temples, palaces, monasteries, and gardens with their towering trees, running down to the water's edge. On the lake itself is the endless procession of barges thronged with pleasure-seekers . . . their minds and thoughts are intent upon nothing but bodily pleasures and the delights of society."

Hangzhou continued to prosper under the Mongols, and traders flocked to the area. When the Yuan fell the town continued to flourish under the

Ming, and travelers continued to record Hangzhou's great size, enormous population, and scenic beauty of its surroundings, the majesty of its buildings, and the pleasures it offered.

Under the Qing the town was still considered one of the richest and largest in the empire.

However, Hangzhou's commercial and political importance suffered dramatically during the savage Taiping rebellion in the mid-nineteenth century, when a great part of the city was razed, monasteries, temples, and pagodas destroyed or severely damaged, and a large number of its population slaughtered. That there are so few buildings of historic interest remaining in Hangzhou is a consequence of the excesses of the rebellion.

Toward the end of the nineteenth century, following a treaty in 1895, Hangzhou was opened up to foreign (mostly Japanese) trade. Industrial development was also stimulated when Hangzhou was linked by rail to Shanghai, but the greatest impetus came after the 1949 revolution, when sizable industrial complexes were established. These now produce machine tools, iron and steel, petroleum products, and chemical fertilizers. But the main manufacturing base is still the silk-textile industry. Local craft factories also turn out chopsticks, sandalwood fans, brocades, silk tapestries, satins, and parasols.

The soil around Hangzhou is fertile. The leading agricultural product is tea, notably the famous Dragon Well brand. Areas further afield produce mandarins, oranges, sugar cane, bamboo, and timber. The main crops are rice, cotton, rape, hemp, and flax.

Even today the city is renowned for its scenic beauty, which some claim is unsurpassed in China; and although many of the historic buildings have been destroyed, the archaeological attractions that remain are still impressive. Many sections of the town have not changed for centuries, while the famous West Lake region retains its place as one of the best-known beauty spots in China, with landscaped gardens on its banks, tree-shaded walks, and, in the nearby hills, temples, pagodas, and monasteries.

If you happen to be visiting in September during the autumn equinox, you may be able to see one of the most unusual sights in the world. A tidal bore gathers momentum in the Gulf of Hangzhou, surges into the mouth of the Qiang Tang, and races up the river, reputedly at a height of 30 feet and a speed of more than 15 m.p.h. In ancient times the governors of Hangzhou used to have arrows fired at these waves in an attempt to quell their destructive force. Nowadays more effective methods are used.

EXPLORING HANGZHOU

One of the most beautiful sights you will see in China is the sun rising over West Lake. Make an effort to rise early to see the first rays touch the lake; you will not be disappointed. The sun will disappear from time to time as the slowly receding mist lifts and is carried skyward. Walk along the causeway and stand on one of the humpback bridges, and you will see emerging from the mist some of the white-walled houses on the near shores and hear the soft chatter of villagers. Nature is still, but man is beginning his day. As you stand on the bridge do not be surprised if you hear other voices coming out of the mist: a student sitting by the water's edge, reciting poetry or practicing English; from a distance, someone singing.

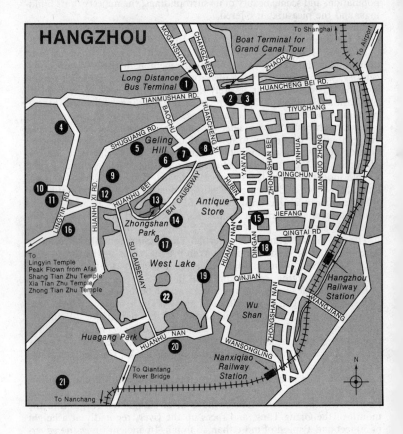

HANGZHOU

Points of Interest

Autumn Moon on the Calm
   Lake **14**
Baochu Pagoda **6**
Botanical Garden **11**
CAAC **2**
City Department Store **15**
Da Fo Si (Great Buddha
   Temple) **7**
Dragon Well Temple **21**
Exhibition Hall of Zhejiang
   Province **3**
Feng Huan Si (Mosque) **18**
Gu Shan (Solitary Hill) **13**

Hangzhou University **1**
Jade Fountain **10**
Jing Ci Temple **20**
Listening to Orioles in the
   Willows **19**
Mid-Lake Pavilion **17**
Purple Cloud Cave **9**
Three Pools Mirroring the
   Moon **22**
Tomb of Yue Fei **12**
Yellow Dragon Cave **5**
Zhao Qing Si **8**
Zhejiang Hospital **16**
Zhejiang University **4**

All around you there will be people of all ages doing *taiji quan* and other exercises, and many people will jog by. A rare sense of solitude and individual effort is here evident in a country with a reputation for group activities, and there is an atmosphere of harmony between man and nature.

As the sun rises higher and the hour moves towards seven, participants in this scene begin to stroll away, some mounting bicycles to pedal slowly to their place of work.

West Lake

West Lake, its name derived from its location west of Hangzhou city, has been famous for centuries. Indeed it has history as long as Hangzhou itself, and became famous as far back as the Han Dynasty. All around there are groves of trees which come into blossom at different times of the year: peach in spring, acacia in autumn, plum in winter. The lotus blooms on the lake during summer.

Two causeways cut the lake, the **Su Causeway,** known as Su Dong Po Dike, or Su Ti, to the west, and the **Bai Causeway,** known as Bai Ju Wi, or Bai Ti, to the north. Su Dong Po was a famous Chinese poet. The road passing along the Su Causeway crosses six bridges and this gives the causeway its other name, the **Six Bridge Dike,** or Liu Qiao Ti. The Bai Causeway is called after another famous poet who was governor of Hangzhou in the eighth century.

The causeways control the water and cut the lake into three sections: the outer section, which is the largest, the inner section to the west, and the rear lake to the north. The lake has a surface area of about 1,240 acres and an average depth of six feet. At its widest part it is approximately two miles wide by two miles long.

Three islands stand within the lake, the largest known as the **Solitary Hill,** or **Gu Shan.** You can get there from the Hangzhou Hotel by crossing a small bridge, or from the city by passing along the Bai Causeway. The Zhejiang Museum is on the island, housed in the old **Wen Lan Ge Library** founded by Emperor Qian Long. It is on the eastern side of the Sun Yatsen Garden. The library is on the western side. Other places of interest on the island are the **Pavilion of the Autumn Moon** on the Calm Lake and the **Xi Leng Seal Engravers' Society.** There are also several tombs. One is the tomb of the Song poet Lin He Qing on the north of the island; another is the tomb of Su Xiao, a legendary beauty of the fifth century. Her tomb is near the bridge linking the island at the western end to the mainland.

There is also a temple, the **Sheng Yin Si,** which after the 1912 revolution was dedicated to the memory of the Provincial Revolutionary Army.

The Louwailou Restaurant and Zhongshan Park are also located on the island.

Xi Leng Seal Engravers' Society

A group of scholars, intellectuals, and people interested in the engraving of seals often gather in a small pavilion at the top of Gu Shan. They chose a delightful spot, and the visitor will be charmed by the harmony of the surroundings. There are ornamental trees, rock pools, and a terrace providing a view of the lake. A small stone pagoda, supposedly more than 900 years old, also stands on the site.

Of great interest is a stone house, reputedly from the Han Dynasty period, with stone drums and inscribed tablets inside. One tablet of particular value is mounted in the center of the stone house. Apparently it was once sold to a collector in Japan. The members of the Seal Engravers' Society contributed money to buy back the tablet and return it to its rightful place.

The pavilion serves as the society headquarters and houses a collection of small prints depicting the style used by the Seal Engravers.

If you are interested in buying original seals, you should visit a small shop located downhill along the steep rocky path that leads from the Seal Engravers' site. There you will find a magnificent collection (not all of which originated with the Seal Society). You will also note that most are quite expensive.

Three Pools Mirroring the Moon

Three Pools Mirroring the Moon is the name given to the island in the southern part of the lake. It is said to have been formed by soil from the excavations dumped there during the building of the Su Dike. Its pleasing feature is the four small lakes; for this reason it is often known as "the island with the lakes within the island."

There are many pavilions joined by pleasant walks, some built over zig-zag bridges crossing the water. There are several varieties of trees; the willows are especially attractive. The lotus plants growing in the lake are particularly beautiful in July and August.

Offshore on the south of the island are three stone stupas, each about five feet high and containing five recesses in which candles are burned. Their reflections give rise to the island's name. They are known as the San Tan, a term from the Song Dynasty, but the stupas were built in the seventeenth century.

Tomb of Yue Fei

Yue Fei is a famous Chinese hero who lived in the twelfth century. As commander of the Song Dynasty army, he had notable successes in battle, yet he was recalled to the emperor's court and executed following accusations made by a treacherous court official. Some 20 years after his death, the emperor restored his reputation and had his corpse reburied at the present site.

A few minutes' walk west of the Hangzhou Hotel, the tomb area houses a statue of the general, wall paintings of scenes of his life, and a small pavilion sheltering the tree stump where he was beheaded.

Ling Yin Temple

It is believed that the Ling Yin Temple was first established in the fourth century by a monk known as Hui Li. It was destroyed on a number of occasions, the last time during the Taiping Rebellion, and was last rebuilt in the early part of this century. The temple fell into disrepair, but in 1956 it was carefully restored.

The temple is set at the foot of the Northern Peak in a wooded area, a stream running before it. Some of the trees in front are thought to be thousands of years old.

The front temple houses a Laughing Buddha carved in camphorwood and covered in gold with a carved gilt figure standing behind and guarding him. Both figures are set under a two-eaved wooden canopy decorated in red and gold. Ornate lamps hang on either side.

Along the two side walls of the temple are the traditional Celestial Guardians, which have been beautifully restored. Perhaps the most interesting is the one playing the pipa. One Benevolent Guardian is holding an umbrella in his right hand and a phoenix in his left, while a Malevolent Guardian holds a sword and a dragon.

The rear temple houses a 60-foot-high carved Buddha. The building itself is from the later Qing period. In the 1930s the main cross beam of the temple roof broke and crashed down, destroying some of the statues inside, but they were repaired during extensive renovations in 1956.

Built in traditional style, the temple appears to have three floors, since there are three roofs with fine upswept eaves. But inside you will find that there are no upper floor levels, the whole space being devoted to housing the enormous Buddha.

One of the most interesting sights in the temple grounds is the four Buddhist pillars installed on either side of the main door in A.D. 969 by the King of Wu Yue. These have been identified as the originals. Two octagonal stone stupas are thought to be even older than the pillars.

Northern Peak

You can travel by cable car from quite near the Ling Yin Temple (at Ling Yin Road, east of no. 7 bus terminus) to the top of Bei Feng, or Northern Peak, which towers over the surrounding area. The views from the top are splendid.

Fei Lai Feng

Facing the Ling Yin Temple over a small stream is the famous Fei Lai Feng, or "Peak Which Flew Here." The name is connected with the traditional founder of the temple, Hui Li, who saw the hill, and claimed it to be a portion of a mountain in India, which had "flown" to Hangzhou.

The hill, in the nature of a cliff, is covered with rock carvings; there are altogether 280 figures.

On the eastern side, downstream from the temple, is a hexagonal stupa dating from the sixteenth century. Behind it are two stone-carved figures representing defenders of Buddhism and dating from the thirteenth century. On the left and across the stream you will find the entrance to the first cave. The statues inside are believed to have been carved by the original adherents responsible for the introduction of Buddhism into China.

The next cave is known as the Cave That Leads to the Sky because a gap in the vault allows the light to penetrate. Another is the Thread of Light cave; here you can stand in a particular spot and see a fine thread of light coming through the roof. The walls of the caves were all carved in bas-relief under the Five Dynasties and the Song.

The rock sculptures on the cliff itself are rare examples from the thirteenth and fourteenth centuries, hewn from the rock face under the Yuan. There are few other examples of Yuan Dynasty stone carving in existence. The statues all feature Buddhist themes.

Another cave, the Jade Milk Cave, has fine stone carvings; those near the entrance are the oldest.

Bamboo Grove at Yun Qi

The beautiful and peaceful grove at Yun Qi is known in Chinese as the Abode of the Clouds. You will wander through thick stands of bamboo penetrated by shafts of hazy sunlight. It is a perfect place to relax, especially when you have been on an arduous tour program. At the top of the path there are some old buildings that appear to have once been part of a temple.

Nine Creeks and Eighteen Brooks

This is another peaceful haven. It derives its name from the nine creeks of the Yang Chia Hill, which run down to join the Qian Tang River nearby, and the 18 brooks which flow down from the Lun Chun Hill. The area is located southwest of the lake.

There are pleasant paths alongside the brooks with tea trees on either side. You will see numerous teahouses and rest homes in the area.

Dragon Well

The Dragon Well, or Longjin—famous throughout China for its tea—is worth a visit. The road leading to it from the Nine Creeks and Eighteen Brooks is in a reasonable state, even though it is overrun here and there by water making its way down the mountainside. As you pass deeper into the countryside, you will go through the delightful old village of Long Jing where you can glimpse the courtyards of old wooden houses and see the farmers going about their work. Geese, ducks, and poultry wander around the cobbled road.

The spring is located at the summit. The old temples have been converted to a restaurant and teahouse.

Jade Fountain

The Jade Fountain is also known as the Spring of Jade (Yu Quan). The water of the fountain spills into a square pool filled with enormous golden and gray carp. There is another known as the Pearl Fountain. These are located in what was once the Ching Liang Temple, which has now been converted into a teahouse for the masses. This spot is not of particular interest to the visitor and should be given a low priority if time is scarce.

Jing Ci Temple

Rebuilt during the Qing Dynasty after being razed during the Taiping Rebellion, the Jing Ci Temple, which stands on the southern shore of the lake, has been recently restored. Opposite the temple stand the remains of the Thunder Peak Pagoda, or Lei Feng Ta, first erected during the reign of one of the kings of Wue Tue. It collapsed in 1924.

Yellow Dragon Spring

The Yellow Dragon Spring is located in what was once the Taoist Monastery. The spring, known as Huang Long Dong, issues from the mouth of the stone dragon and trickles down into a series of pools below. The atmosphere is one of solitude and peace. You should follow the narrow rock path to the hill above the monastery, where you will find an unusual pavilion made entirely of bamboo. The rock formations built around the hill are interesting, and there are a number of small man-made caves to explore.

When you are leaving, be sure to visit the small garden set behind the old monastery building on your right, where you will find growing some rare examples of "square bamboo."

Bao Shu Pagoda

The Bao Shu Pagoda is a plain-brick octagonal stupa surmounted by a metal spire. There are eight "windows" on each of the seven levels, but they are purely decorative; the structure is solid and has no interior. The first stupa was built in the tenth century by a minister of the King of Wu Yue. It was destroyed and rebuilt on a number of occasions. The present structure dates from 1933.

The pagoda stands on a ridge which gives a fine view of the lake on one side and the new town on the other. There is a small open-sided pavilion on top of Bao Shi Hill where the visitor can sit and enjoy the view. The elevation is approximately 660 feet, so there are many steps to climb up to reach the top.

Liu He Pagoda

The Liu He Pagoda, otherwise known as The Pagoda of Six Harmonies, was built in A.D. 970, during the Song Dynasty. It was erected by adherents of the Buddhist religion in an attempt to protect the town from devastation by the equinoctial tides. The pagoda fell into ruin a few hundred years later and was replaced by the structure that now stands on the site. The present pagoda is thus about 800 years old.

The pagoda has 13 "roofs" but only seven floors, with a redwood exterior covering the stone interior. The "six harmonies" relate to tenets of the Buddhist religion and embrace speech, body, opinion, mind, wealth, and abstinence from temptation.

A terrace has been built around the base of the pagoda and allows the visitor a good view of the Qian Tang River and double-decker bridge nearby.

Tiger Spring

The legend suggests that the site was originally established by a monk who was impressed by the beauty and tranquility of the surroundings. However, the place had no water. One night he dreamed that two tigers clawed at the ground and water rushed forth. When he awoke next morning he went out and found the spring, thus giving the place its name.

The water has remarkable surface tension; you can easily float a great many Chinese nickel coins on it. You can also drop large numbers of the coins into a bowl of the water, and they will not cause it to overflow. The added height of the meniscus is about a quarter of an inch. Ask your guide to demonstrate the qualities. The water is also known for its fine tea-brewing qualities and its natural sweetness.

The old Hu Pao Temple has now been converted to a tearoom where you can sit admiring the view and sip the famous Long Jing tea brewed with Tiger Spring water.

Ge Ling

This hill, Ge Ling, is known as the Ge Hong Summit, after the well-known alchemist who in the fourth century supposedly tried to produce an elixir of life from cinnabar. The hill is located behind the Hangzhou Hotel, along the ridge from the hill bearing the Bao Shu Pagoda.

Purple Cloud Cave

The Ziyundong, or Purple Cloud Cave, one of five on Qixia Mountain, attracts the inhabitants of Hangzhou during summer, when they come to escape the intense heat and humidity. Apart from the view from the mountain and the display of peach blossoms in the spring, the site has no particular attractions and should be given low priority.

Zoo

Hangzhou's small zoo is well known for its giant pandas and the rare Manchurian tigers.

Other Sights

There are other sights, or their remains, that you might care to make inquiries about; some of them are under renovation and could at any time be made accessible to visitors. They include The Mosque, or Phoenix Temple, known as Feng Huang Si; the Zhao Qing Temple, now converted to a children's palace; The Great Buddha Temple, or Da Fo Si; the Three Indian Temples, or Xia, Zhong, and Shang Tian Zhu; the three caves near the Dragon Well known as the Yan Xia San Dong, which are said to be in ruins and have had their stone carvings removed.

PRACTICAL INFORMATION FOR HANGZHOU

FACTS AND FIGURES Hangzhou is at approximately the same latitude as Jacksonville, Florida. Distances: 725 miles southeast of Beijing by air, 1,035 miles southeast of Beijing by rail; 625 miles northeast of Guangzhou by air, 1025 miles northeast of Guangzhou by rail; 115 miles southwest of Shanghai. Elevation: 36 feet above sea level.

The table shows the weather pattern in Hangzhou during the year.

Hangzhou Temperature Range and Average Rainfall

	Temperature High (°F)	Temperature Low (°F)	Number of Days with Rainfall	Monthly Rainfall (in inches)
January	45	33	13	2.8
April	69	53	16	5.4
July	92	75	12	6.0
October	75	57	16	3.0

WHEN TO GO. The similarity of latitude between Hangzhou and Jacksonville can be misleading. For instance, in Hangzhou winters are cooler, varying between freezing at night to a maximum of 50° F during the day. There are about 4 days of rainfall out of 10; and the weather is often overcast. The yearly rainfall is heavy, averaging 61–62 inches, most of which falls in spring and summer. Summer is hot and very humid.

The best time to visit is in autumn, when there is little rain and the temperature is pleasant.

HOW TO GET THERE. A visit to Hangzhou is often part of a tour program beginning in Beijing, Shanghai, or Guangzhou. There are direct air services from Beijing (1 hour, 55 minutes), Shanghai (40 minutes), and Guangzhou (1¼ hours) as well as from other major centers. There are also less frequent services linking Hangzhou to Changsha (2 hours, 20 minutes), and to Guilin (1 hour, 50 minutes). There is a direct service from Hong Kong (1 hour, 50 minutes) 5 days a week.

The city is well serviced by trains from the major centers. The nearest provincial capital is Shanghai, $3\frac{1}{2}$ hours away by the fastest train; Nanchang ($12\frac{1}{2}$–13 hours); Fuzhou ($23\frac{1}{2}$ hours); Beijing ($26\frac{1}{2}$ hours); and Guilin (27 hours).

Independent travelers sometimes take the Grand Canal boat trip connecting Hangzhou and Suzhou. The voyage of 94 miles (151 km) takes 12 hours on fairly primitive local boats. Tourists seeking to travel in comfort should travel only on those Grand Canal tours arranged by CITS.

HOTELS. The best-known hotel is the **Shangri-La Hangzhou** (tel. 777951; cable 7391; telex 35005), 78 Beishan Street, on the lakeshore. The two wings and three villas have 387 rooms, business center, shopping bazaar, and swimming pool. Run by the Shangri-la group.

The newest establishment is the **Dragon Hotel** (tel. 554488; cable 1818; telex 351048) on Shuguang Road, facing the Bao Shu Pagoda. Its three towers hold 555 guest rooms, business center, tennis courts, and swimming pool. Managed by New World Hotels International.

Among other hotels are the 22-story **Friendship Hotel** (tel. 22951) at 53 Pinghai Road near West Lake and the **Xiling Guest House** (tel. 22921), just a few minutes' walk from the Shangri-La Hotel. The most exclusive place to stay is the **West Lake Guest House** (tel. 26867), 7 Xishan Road, which stands on the bank of the inner West Lake opposite Su Dike. It used to be reserved exclusively for visiting heads of state but is now used to accommodate tourists. Another hotel used frequently is the eight-story **Wanghu** (tel. 71024) at 2 West Huancheng Road, near Wushan.

Chinese expatriates usually stay at the **Overseas Chinese Hotel** (tel. 26911), 15 Hubin Road. Other hotels are the **Dahua** (tel. 23901), **Huagang** (tel. 71324), **Huajiashan** (tel. 71224), **Liulang** (tel. 21728), **Liutong** (tel. 26354), **Xinxin** (tel. 26971), and the **Zhejiang** (tel. 25601), with an indoor swimming pool.

RESTAURANTS. The major hotels mentioned above have good restaurants where you may order à la carte. There are also excellent restaurants outside the hotels. The scenic **Louwailou** (tel. 21654), 2 Waixihu, on the southeast corner of Gushan Island, is recommended for the superb fish, eel, and local seafood dishes. So, too, is the three-story **Tianxianglou** (tel. 22038), 676 Jiefang Road, where you should try the giant prawns or the Su Dongpo pork (named after the famous Chinese poet). The **Tianwaitan** (tel. 22429), 62 Lingyin Road, located near the Lingyin Temple, is also a good restaurant. Others worth trying are: the **Hangzhou Restaurant** (tel. 26414) at 52 Yanan Road (try the beggar's chicken); the **Shanwaishan** (tel. 26621); the **Kuiyuan** (tel. 25921) at 124 Jiefang Road (for breakfast); the **Ling Yin** (tel. 21433) for vegetarian dishes; and the **Zhiweiguan** (tel. 23655).

TOURIST INFORMATION. CITS (tel. 552888) is at 1 Shihan Road.

CAAC (tel. 554259 for domestic services, 552574 for international) at 160 Tiyuchang Road is open daily except Sunday 8–11:30 A.M. and 1:30–5 P.M.

PSB (tel. 22401) is located at the intersection of Huimin and Dingan roads. The office is open Monday through Saturday, 8–11.30 A.M. and 2–5 P.M.

HOW TO GET AROUND. CITS organizes tours around Hangzhou and excursions to outlying regions. Hangzhou is a good place to explore on a bike. Bikes may be hired at the Shangri-La Hotel or at the two bicycle rental shops in Beishan Lou, near the Shangri-La Hangzhou Hotel. Ask someone at the service desk of your hotel to write the Chinese characters for "bicycle hire" and then get the directions.

As for public transport, bus no. 27 is a useful one to know because it goes from the center of town to Longjing (Dragon) Well and Commune. There is a tourist shuttle bus between Longjing Temple and the zoo. Another useful bus is no. 7 from the railway station which stops at the Overseas Chinese Hotel, passes the Shangri-La Hotel as well as numerous historical and cultural sites before terminating at the Longjing Temple. From the airport, bus no. 5 connects at its last stop with no. 27, which passes near many of the town's hotels.

WHAT TO SEE. You should certainly go on the boat trip around West Lake and then visit some of the islands, particularly the curiously named Three Pools Mirroring the Moon.

You will also wish to visit Gushan Island, where there are many sites: The Zhongshan Gardens, Pavilion of the Autumn Moon, Seal Engravers' Pavilion, the Crane Pavilion, and the Zhejiang Museum. The famous tomb of Yue Fei is nearby.

The **Ling Yin Temple** should be high on your list of priorities. It was first established in the fourth century but has been destroyed and rebuilt many times since then. The setting is delightful. Across the stream is the Fei Lai Feng, or "Peak Which Flew Here," where the Buddhist carvings on the hill are more than 600 years old. The journey on the cable car from Lingyin gives a fine view of the region.

There are beautiful bamboo groves in and around Hangzhou, the best-known being the one at Yun Qi. For more relaxation you may care to visit the place called Nine Creeks and Eighteen Brooks and the Dragon Well. Another peaceful haven is the Yellow Dragon Spring. Tiger Spring is also pleasant, especially if you want to try Dragon Well tea brewed in the famous water from the spring.

If you are interested in pagodas, you should pay a visit to the 800-year-old Liu He Pagoda. Also of interest is the Bao Shu Pagoda, where you get a fine view of the West Lake and the town. The pagoda was constructed only in 1933.

MUSEUMS. Zhejiang Museum is housed in the old Wen Lan Ge buildings, which once formed part of the library founded by the Emperor Qian Long in the eighteenth century. The museum is a short walk from the Shangri-La Hangzhou Hotel.

One of the most interesting exhibits is the skeleton of a whale that was washed up on the coast in the thirteenth century; it is over 90 feet long. There is also the collection of relics unearthed in the province. Some of the more interesting items are listed below.

Relics from the Han Dynasty include iron tools, a bronze plowshare, and pieces of pottery from the tomb of a civil servant. From the Southern Dynasties up to the Yuan: a map of the Grand Canal, a map of what is now Kaifeng, a grain-storage urn, iron tools from the Song period, agricultural tools and a bronze cannon from the Yuan.

From the Ming and Qing: a model of a boat of a type once used on the Grand Canal, fine specimens of porcelain, historical paintings of the period, and samples of silk.

SHOPPING. Because of its importance as a silk center, Hangzhou offers a fine selection of silk textiles, brocades, satins, and embroideries. You can purchase good quality scarves and blouses for women, silk ties for men, and silk parasols.

Handicraft items such as engraved scissors, sandalwood fans, ivory and jade carvings are available. Local glassware is also a good buy.

Hangzhou is a good place to buy tea, especially if you like the specialties of the region, Dragon Well or Long Jing tea, famous throughout the world.

If you are looking for antiques, visit the **Hangzhou Painting and Calligraphy Shop** (tel. 22537, 24540) at 31 Hubin Road, near the Hangzhou Department Store.

LEAVING HANGZHOU By plane. Air travel times to major centers are given above (see *How To Get There*).

By boat. There are passenger boats from Hangzhou to **Suzhou,** a 12-hour journey, departing 5 A.M. or 5 P.M. Boats leave the dock in the north of Hangzhou located opposite the intersection of Changzheng and Huangcheng roads. Tickets can be purchased at the dock (5 A.M. to 6 P.M.) or at CITS.

By bus. At the long-distance bus station in Changzheng Road, just north of the boat dock, there are buses to various destinations: **Shanghai** (departures 5:50 A.M., 6 A.M., 12:30 P.M., and 12:40 P.M.); **Nanjing** (6 A.M.); **Shaoxing** (9:10 A.M., 9:20 A.M., 11:50 A.M., 12:50 P.M., and 2:50 P.M.); and **Huang Shan** (6:10 A.M., 6:40 A.M., 7:20 A.M., and 7:30 A.M.)

USEFUL ADDRESSES AND TELEPHONE NUMBERS

CITS—1 Shihan Road (tel. 552888).

CAAC—160 Tiyuchang (tel. 554259 for domestic services, 552574 for international).

PSB—Huimin and Dingan (tel. 22401).
Railway Station—Chengzhan Road (tel. 22971).
Taxis—Hangzhou Taxi Station (tel. 24697).

HARBIN

Heilongjiang Province

Northeast China

Harbin is the capital of the northernmost province of China, Heilongjiang. With a population of two million, Harbin has developed in this century into an important industrial city in northeast China, as well as a vital rail junction linking China with the Soviet Union, and the People's Republic of Mongolia.

Harbin has wide, tree-lined avenues, and European-style architecture, the buildings being painted in pastel colors, a legacy of the Russians who once populated the city. The older residential district even has Russian churches with onion domes. The houses of the suburbs possess flower and vegetable gardens quite different from those usually found throughout China. The city fronts the south bank of the Songhua River, one of China's important waterways. There is a long bridge crossing the river. After the 1933 floods which devastated Harbin, a 26-mile embankment was built to protect the city, and a promenade was laid out along it. At most times of the day, and certainly during the early hours of evening, it is a popular place to stroll. In summer, people swim in the river or sail, but in winter when the river freezes over, they skate, go ice sailing, or watch the ice-hockey games and sled competitions.

The Songhuajiang flows on from Harbin to join the Heilongjiang (Black Dragon River), which gives the province its name. The Black Dragon River, known as the Amur to the Russians, forms the northeastern frontier with the Soviet Union and has been the scene of a number of border skirmishes between the two countries over recent decades.

Harbin, a word from the Manchu dialect, means "a place for drying fishing nets in the sun," and for about 800 years it was no more than a remote village. It developed into a town in the 1890s when the Manchu contracted for the Russians to construct the Chinese Eastern Railway, a branch of the Trans-Siberian. Harbin was swelled with large numbers of "White Russians" fleeing the 1917 Revolution. They stayed on, eventually giving the town a look of a Russian settlement. Later, in an ironic twist of history, the inhabitants faced the effects of the revolution in China when the Communists took the town in 1946. The majority of the Russian settlers then accepted Stalin's offer of amnesty and returned to the Soviet Union.

Harbin was captured in 1932 by the Japanese forces invading Manchuria, and fell again to the Soviet army in 1945. When the Russians withdrew a year later, they removed most of the industrial plant and equipment of the province. The Chinese Communist armies then took the town. Since then industry has been developed. Before 1946, the town was a food-processing center only, but now it also produces machine tools, electric motors, turbines, bearings, and the "Songhua River"-brand tractors. There are also paper manufacturing plants, linen mills, and sugar refineries.

The province of Heilongjiang occupies part of the great northeastern plain—formerly known as the Manchurian Plain—a vast expanse of land that is suitable for extensive mechanized farming. Huge acreages are planted with wheat, corn, soy beans, sugar beets and sunflowers, the latter an important source of edible oil. The higher regions of the northwestern part of the province are cut for lumber. There are important sources of energy and minerals in the province: crude oil is extracted in large quantities at Daqing; and deposits of coal and gold are mined at various locations in the region.

EXPLORING HARBIN

Sun Island

Sun Island, or Taiyang, as it is called in Chinese, is well known in the region for its scenery. Located in the Songhua River, a little way upstream from the long bridge, the island has a park with pavilions, villas, pleasant walks, and fine gardens. In winter, the trees are coated with ice crystals and form a harmonious background to the intricate ice sculptures made by the townsfolk.

Stalin Park

A major recreation area for the people of Harbin, Stalin Park extends along the south bank of the river on the edge of the embankment. Visitors can arrange to take a boat excursion on the river. Along the embankment there are steps leading down to the river's edge, in summer allowing access for swimmers and small-boat sailers, in winter providing a pathway for the thousands of skaters that skim over the frozen surface. In winter, you will see a most unusual sport—ice-yachting.

Children's Park

Located not far from the center of town, near a small stream leading to the Songhua, Children's Park's major attraction is a "children's railway." The miniature train has a diesel engine and pulls seven carriages, seating 190 passengers, along a 1.2 mile rail line. There are two stations: "Harbin" and "Beijing." Take a look at it—it's fun.

Zhaolin Park

The entrance to Zhaolin Park is at 1 Senlin Street, Daoli. It is famous for the **Harbin Ice Lantern Show** (see below).

Zoo

The Harbin Zoo, on Hexing Road in the Dongli district, is set in spacious grounds and has an interesting display of animals. The prime exhibit is the rare Dongbei (Northeast) Tiger, a species that once roamed the region freely but is now almost extinct. The animal keepers at the zoo have managed to breed the tigers in captivity. Other species on display include red-crowned crane of the region, sika deer, reindeer, and the ever-popular pandas.

Ice Lantern Show

Do not miss this event if you are anywhere near Harbin at Spring Festival time. (The date varies from January to February.) The Harbin Ice Lantern Show, held in Zhaolin Park, attracts more than 30,000 visitors. The ice sculptures are in the shapes of persons, animals, flowers, trees, pavilions, and so on. The themes depict ancient legends, medieval stories, and modern historic events. Colored lights illuminate the objects at night. You will be amazed at the skill of the sculptors and beauty of the exhibits. All the other parks in Harbin feature ice sculpture as well.

Harbin Summer Music Festival

This festival is held each year in July over a 12-day period. It was banned during the Cultural Revolution but was restored to the cultural calendar of the city in 1979. The eight theaters in Harbin host the event; there is a Beijing Opera troupe in Harbin, as well as the Harbin Drama Theater and Songhuajiang Drama Group.

Heilongjiang Exhibition Center

During the year different exhibitions are held. One most interesting to visitors is the "Heilongjiang—Rich and Beautiful Land" display, shown at various times throughout the year. The center is located at 138 Xi Dazhijie Street, Nangang; tel. 35464.

Songhuajiang Art Gallery

Located at 50 Xi Shi Erdao Street, Daoli (tel. 44728), the gallery sometimes features interesting displays of art, calligraphy, poetry. Check with your CITS guide.

Other Institutes

You can sometimes arrange to visit the Science Palace, 9 Shangyou Street, Daoli (tel. 48620), the Harbin Library, 7 Yiman Street, Nangang (tel. 34469), and the Heilongjiang Library, Fendon Road, Nangang (tel. 34755).

Arts and Crafts Factory

Located at 2 Dacheng Street, Nangang (tel. 34336), the factory has artisans creating a range of items made from materials of the region. This place is usually included in the tour arranged for foreign visitors, but if it isn't and you wish to go there, ask your CITS guide.

EXCURSIONS FROM HARBIN

Daqing

One of China's major oil fields is located here: Daqing, meaning "Great Reward," is reached by taking the train to Anda, northwest of Harbin—a journey of 2½ hours—and then a bus to the oilfield. The accommodation is spartan and a visit to Daqing is only of interest to those in the oil refining industry. In the 1970s one would frequently see the slogan: "In industry learn from Daqing," the place being described as a model industrial commune where "self-reliance" is pursued and self-sacrifice is practiced by the workers. It remains an important Chinese center for the production of crude oil.

PRACTICAL INFORMATION FOR HARBIN

FACTS AND FIGURES. Harbin is the capital of Heilongjiang Province, the most northerly province in China. It is 862 miles by rail from Beijing, 1,600 miles from Shanghai, and 2,298 miles from Guangzhou. The nearest provincial capital, Changchun, is 150 miles away by rail. The flight times to Harbin by the quickest service are: from Beijing 1 hour 40 minutes; Shanghai 2 hours 40 minutes; Changchun 50 minutes; and Shenyang 1½ hours.

WHEN TO GO. Try to avoid winter: the city is bitterly cold then, average temperatures November through March being well below freezing. Spring days are often windy and overnight minimum temperatures in April and May are usually below zero. Summer is warm but not excessively hot, although the rainfall is highest at this time of the year—7.2 inches in July, 4.4 inches in August. The best period to travel in the region is August–September.

HOW TO GET THERE. The most convenient way is to take a flight from Beijing, the quickest service taking 1 hour 40 minutes. The quickest train from Beijing takes 17½ hours, one express leaving late afternoon and arriving Harbin about 9 A.M. the next day, another leaving early evening and arriving Harbin just after lunch the next day. The train from Beijing goes via Tianjin, Shenyang, and Changchun. The Trans-Siberian express, linking Beijing and Moscow, passes through Harbin.

HOTELS. The **Swan Hotel** (tel. 220201, telex 87080), 73 Zhongshan Road, about four miles from the railway station, has good accommodations for about 540 guests. The **Beifang,** or Northern Mansions (tel. 31485), on Zhonghsan Road, is well known; built in Soviet-style many years ago, it has 80 spacious rooms and a reasonable restaurant. Nearby is the **Heilongjiang Guest House** (tel. 32950) at 52 Hongjun Street, formerly the Railway Hotel, a nice old place whose dining room serves gastronomic specialties of the region. Other hotels are: **Harbin Hotel** (tel. 45846), 129 Zhongyang Street, Daoli; **Hepingcun Hotel** (tel. 32093), 109 Zhongshan Road, Daoli; **International Hotel** (tel. 31441), 124 Dazhijie Street, Nangang; **Friendship Palace** (tel. 46146), 57 Youyi Road, Daoli.

RESTAURANTS. There are good restaurants in Harbin suitable for foreign visitors, and the food served there can be both enjoyable and interesting. The region boasts numerous specialties rarely found elsewhere: bear paws, nose of the camel deer, salmon, and game. Garlic is often used and, unusual for China, potatoes are a staple in the local diet. The fish from the Songhua are tasty but full of bones. Ice cream—introduced by the Russians—is very popular. There is even a local brand of white alcohol: the Chenliang Baijiu.

You might care to try one of the following restaurants: **Beilaishun** (Moslem food), 113 Shangzhi Street, Daoli, tel. 45673, 49027; **Huamei** (Western food), 142 Zhongyang Street, Daoli, tel. 47368; **Jiangbin,** 15 Xi Shisandao Street, Daoli, tel. 44721; **Jiangnanchun,** 316 Fendou Road, Nangang, tel. 34398, 34860; **Futailou** (Peking duck dishes), 19 Xi Shisandao, tel. 47598.

TOURIST INFORMATION. CITS (tel. 221088, 52496) is located at 73 Zhongshan Road. CAAC (tel. 52334) is at 85–87 Zhongshan Road. PSB may be reached by proceeding north from the railway station along Jingwei Road and turning right into Zhongyang Dajie at the large intersection. It is a few hundred yards along on the right-hand side.

HOW TO GET AROUND. CITS organizes bus tours and excursions. Of special interest is the boat tour along the Songhua River organized by CITS.

WHAT TO SEE. There is a very attractive park on **Sun Island** in the Songhua River; the **Harbin Zoo** has an interesting collection of animals; and the **Heilongjiang Provincial Museum** has thousands of historic and animal exhibits. **Stalin Park** is a pleasant place to take a stroll or a swim; the **Children's Park** features a miniature railway run by the children themselves. You can also visit the arts and crafts factory. In July, there is the 12-day **Harbin Summer Music Festival.**

MUSEUMS. The **Heilongjiang Provincial Museum** (tel. 34151), built in 1923, has a large collection of historic and animal exhibits. Of particular interest is the display of prehistoric animals. The museum is located at 44 Hongjun Street, in the Nangang district.

SHOPPING. An excellent range of furs, some rare, may be found in Harbin. Try the **Fur Shop** of the Harbin Fur Factory, 1 Hongzhuan Street, Daoli District (tel. 42647). A good selection of antiques is available at the **Antique Shop,** 50 Hongjun Street, Nangang district (tel. 35082). Arts and crafts items may be purchased at the **Arts and Crafts Factory,** 2 Dacheng Street, Nangang district (tel. 34336); scrolls, and other artwork can be purchased at the **Beifang Calligraphy and Painting Society,** 133 Diduan Street, Daoli district (tel. 42446). If you are after books, go to the **Foreign Language Book Store,** 1 Hongzhuan Street, Daoli district (tel. 42647). Of course, there is the **Friendship Store,** 93 Dazhijie Street, Nangang district (tel. 33897) which sells a wide range of goods, and if you cannot find what you are after there, try the **Number One Department Store,** 146 Diduan Street, Daoli district (tel. 48752) or the **Songhuajiang Store,** 93 Dazhi Street, Nangang district (tel. 33115).

USEFUL ADDRESSES AND TELEPHONE NUMBERS

Long distance calls—International and domestic, tel. 03. Information, tel. 06.
Directory assistance—tel. 04.
Taxis—tel. 42728.
China International Travel Service—73 Zhongshan Road, Nangang. Tel. 221088, 52496.
CAAC Ticket Office—85 Zhongshan Road, Nangang (tel. 52334).
Baokang Pharmacy—110 Shangzhi Street, Daoli (tel. 42730).
Bank of China—90 Bei Sidao Street, Daowai (tel. 45024).
General Post Office—51 Jianshe Street, Nangang (tel. 31290).
Harbin Library—7 Yiman Street, Nangang (tel. 34469).
Songhuajiang Art Gallery—50 Xi Shierdao Street, Daoli (tel. 44728).
Harbin Zoo—Hexing Road, Dongli (tel. 34230).

HEFEI

Anhui Province

South China

Hefei, capital of Anhui Province since 1949, stands at the confluence of the north and south Fei rivers, hence its name. Although Hefei was until recently a small market town, its history goes back over 2,000 years to the Han, when the settlement was slightly to the north of the present site. However, no trace remains of the old site. The buildings of Hefei are of recent date and are of no historical or architectural interest. Indeed, Hefei being a new industrial city has few sights to attract the visitor and is not even noted for its scenery. Nevertheless, it is sometimes placed on the itinerary of package-tour groups.

The province is probably best known for its tea, the beautiful Huang-shan Mountains and its dense forests. The southeastern third of the province is cut off from the northwestern portion by the Yangzi River. Until recently, the floods from the river used to devastate large areas of Anhui, but dams have largely eliminated this destruction.

EXPLORING HEFEI

Bao Gong Temple

Bao Zheng (or Bao Xiben), an honest and fearless official of the Song Dynasty, was born in Hefei. A temple was erected in his honor at Xianghuadun, or Fragrant Flower Mound, on the Bao River, just outside the south gate of Hefei. The temple site is in the People's (Renmin) Park, formerly known as the Baohe Park.

Ming Jiao Temple

The original Ming Jiao Temple was erected in the eighth century to house an 18-foot cast-iron statue of the Buddha. The temple has recently been restored. The Terrace for Appointing Generals, built in the twelfth century, stands nearby.

Xiaoyaojin Park

A pleasant park with a lake, teahouses, and a restaurant, Xiaoyaojin Park is said to be the site of a battle that took place at the end of the Eastern Han Dynasty (A.D. 25–220). The park is located in the northeast sector of the town.

Anhui Museum

The museum has a fine collection of specimens, the most noteworthy being a reproduction of the famous jade burial suit unearthed in the province.

EXCURSIONS FROM HEFEI

Huangshan

The major excursion from Hefei is to Huangshan, a mountain in the southeast of Anhui Province that has been a source of inspiration for China's painters and poets for centuries. You can arrange a bus trip through CITS to Huangshan—the journey takes a whole day—or go by train. There are also flights to the airport at Tunxi, some 47 miles from the scenic areas.

Some visitors prefer to travel to Huangshan from Hangzhou by bus, or from Shanghai or Nanjing by air. Huangshan may also be reached by traveling upstream along the Yangzi by boat from Shanghai or Nanjing, disembarking at either Wuhu or Chizhou, then taking a bus.

Of the celebrated mountains of China, Taishan is famous for carved calligraphy, Emei for living Buddhism, and Huangshan for scenery. The three highest Huangshan peaks are the Lotus Flower (6,147 feet), the Bright Summit (6,040 feet), and the Heavenly Capital (6,000 feet).

The easy way up is by cable car, an ascent of 8 minutes to the summit; the alternative transportation is a bus from outside the CITS hotel at the "base camp" to the Yongguzhi Hostel, about halfway up. From there you will have to walk for two to three hours to reach the summit, but you will be able to rest at many vantage points. The climb all the way from the "base camp" to the peak, via the "eastern steps," takes two exhausting hours if you go all out, three to four exhausting hours when you take your time. For either climb, you will need to be fit.

You can stay overnight at the summit to view the sunrise next day. The hotel will arrange an early morning call, usually around 5 A.M., but be warned: Only rarely are you able to see the sunrise through the clouds. The two hotels at the summit are the new Xi Hai or Western Sea Hotel and the Bei Hai or Northern Sea Hotel (sea refers to the clouds that usually extend in all directions around the summit).

PRACTICAL INFORMATION FOR HEFEI

FACTS AND FIGURES. The capital of Anhui Province, Hefei is situated about 85 miles southwest of Nanjing and about 235 miles due west of Shanghai. Its population is 835,000.

WHEN TO GO. The summer, subject to monsoonal rains, is humid; winter is mild. Fall is the best time to visit the city, as spring brings showers and frequent overcast skies.

HOW TO GET THERE. Hefei is 12 hours' train journey from Shanghai and 18½ hours' journey from Beijing. You can take a flight to Hefei from Beijing, Shanghai, or Jinan, but flights are infrequent. Hefei is only slightly north of Shanghai's latitude.

Most visitors heading for Hefei travel by train from Beijing, taking in Tianjin and Jinan en route. From Jinan, the train usually goes on to Shanghai, so passengers must change trains at Bengbu. There are trains running from Shanghai to Hefei, the journey taking 11–12 hours, from Suzhou and Wuxi (11 hours), and from Nanjing (6 hours). Flight times to Hefei are: from Shanghai 1 hour; Beijing 1½ hours; Jinan 1½ hours; and Hangzhou 2¾ hours.

HOTELS. The **Hefei China** on Jinzhai Road and the **International Hotel** at Meishanloukou are the new hotels in Hefei. The **Luyang Hotel** on Shusan Road is adding tennis courts and a swimming pool. The **Wangjiang Hotel** has a new 11-story wing under construction.

The other major hotels are the **Daxianglou Guest House** (tel. 74791) at the intersection of Yanan and Dazhai roads and the **Jianghuai Hotel** (tel. 72221), 86 Changjiang Road, about eight miles from the airport.

At the summit of Huangshan, the **Xi Hai Hotel** (tel. 2223), a two-story lodgestyle, prefabricated structure, has 104 rooms and two suites, all with shower or bath, all furnished Swedish style, and two restaurants, a bar, and a dance floor. The **Bei Hai Hotel,** an older establishment, offers rudimentary accommodations and shared bath. Many visitors stay at the foot of the mountain, where the **Jade Screen (Youping Lou) Hotel** has the best views, the **Peach Brook Guest House** (tel. 2295) the most spectacular surroundings, and the **Huangshan Guest House** proximity to a hot springs area, where **CITS** (tel. 2200) is located.

RESTAURANTS. There are no restaurants suitable for foreign visitors except the dining rooms of the hotels. Area specialities include dishes made from freshwater crab, fish, and turtle from the nearby lakes.

TOURIST INFORMATION. CITS (tel. 72221/7) is located in the Jianghuai Hotel, 68 Changjiang Road.

CAAC (tel. 37398) is at 73 Changjiang Road.

HOW TO GET AROUND. CITS organizes bus tours and excursions.

WHAT TO SEE. You will wish to visit the **Bao Gong Temple** outside the city's south gate, the **Ming Jiao Temple** inside the east gate, and the **Anhui Provincial Museum.** You may also visit the East Is Red Commune, the Anhui University, and the Xiaoyaojin Park.

SHOPPING. The specialties of the city are the traditional and modern silks and brocades. These and other items of interest such as "iron pictures" can be purchased at the Hefei Department Store (tel. 3261) on Changjiang Road. There is an antique shop (tel. 5696) at 45 Huizhou Road.

USEFUL ADDRESSES AND TELEPHONE NUMBERS

China International Travel Service, tel. 72221.
Jianghuai Hotel—86 Changjiang Road (tel. 72227).
CAAC Booking Office—73 Changjiang Road (tel. 37398).
Railway Station Booking Office—Mingguang Road (tel. 3481).
Antiques Store—45 Huizhou Road (tel. 5696).
Arts and Crafts Shop—45 Huizhou Road (tel. 5625).
Hefei Department Store—corner of Changjiang Road and Huizhou Road (tel. 3261 and 2459).
Bank of China—204 Huaihe Road (tel. 2175).
Anhui Museum, tel. 3465.

INNER MONGOLIA

Nei Mongol Autonomous Region
Northern China

Inner Mongolia is a vast sweep of territory on China's northern frontier. Its proper name in the People's Republic is the Autonomous Region of Inner Mongolia, or Nei Mongol Zizhiqu. To the north of it lies the People's Republic of Mongolia and its capital, Ulan Bator. To the south lies Beijing, only about 125 miles away from the southern provincial border.

About 3,000 years ago the area was inhabited by the Huns, or Xiong Nu. Attacking bands of Huns made many attempts to take Chinese territory. Their menacing presence prompted Chinese leaders in the region to begin building the early sections of the Great Wall. Hun attacks continued, and over a period of several centuries, various clans succeeded in occupying areas of Chinese territory in the north. By 916, the Khitan, who established the Liao Dynasty in the region, became an increasing threat to China. They were eventually overthrown by the Jin, and the Jin, in turn, were overthrown by the Mongols—who established the Yuan Dynasty.

For the Chinese, the Mongols represented the greatest threat they had ever encountered from the "northern barbarians." Their fears proved to be well founded. In 1261, Kubilai Khan established the new Mongol capital at Da Du (the Great Capital) on the site of present-day Beijing and, before long, began to drive his armies south to conquer all of China. For the first time in their history, the Chinese were vanquished by foreign invaders. But the new dynasty did not last long. Within less than a century, the Mongols were driven back to their territories north of the Great Wall.

The Mongol territories came under Chinese suzerainty in the seventeenth century, the first section (Inner Mongolia) in 1635, and the remaining portion (Outer Mongolia) in 1697. These accessions to Chinese territory were made by the Manchu ruling as the Qing Dynasty. Outer Mongolia was autonomous in 1912 (after the Qing Dynasty collapsed) and became the People's Republic of Mongolia in 1924. Inner Mongolia continued under Chinese control and, in 1947, became the first autonomous region created by the Party.

Inner Mongolia is a plateau with an average altitude of 3,200 feet. The majority of the people living there are Mongols (see the section *Peoples and Languages*). But the Party policy of settling Han Chinese in frontier areas, where non-Han would normally form a majority of the population, has led to a decrease in the Mongol influence.

The Mongols live mainly by breeding and raising livestock. Although their traditional nomadic activities have been curtailed and replaced to a large extent by farming in certain areas, they still maintain vast numbers of horses, camels, sheep, and cattle on the rolling hills and green pasture lands. Many people still wear the traditional Mongol costume: a high-necked, long-sleeved tunic of mid-calf length and high leather boots. The tunic is usually tied at the middle with a colorful cloth, a matching turban being worn by the women. Often the tunic is trimmed with gold braid

380

In the smaller towns in Inner Mongolia today you will see women in such costumes riding on horseback to get their weekly provisions.

In the grasslands many Mongols still live in yurts, cylindrical shaped tents with dome roofs, the entire structures being supported inside by collapsible latticework of wood, the outsides covered with cloth and skins to keep out the cold winds. The Mongols are short, stocky people with broad, round faces; and they are superb horsemen. They sit astride small hardy horses on narrow, high-backed wooden saddles, and use short stirrups. When they are at the gallop they are practically standing upright, a tradition that has come from the days when their archery on horseback was feared throughout the length and breadth of Asia and Asia Minor. Today this riding stance is also of practical value, for when a Mongol wishes to capture a horse from the mob, he rides out carrying a long thin pole with a noose on the end.

Unlike the Han Chinese, the Mongols eat lots of mutton and beef, and their favorite drink is a wine made from fermented mare's milk.

The major towns of Inner Mongolia are Hohhot (the capital), Baotou, and Xilinhot. The towns are without a great deal of character in themselves but do possess interesting monuments and buildings from the past.

EXPLORING INNER MONGOLIA

Hohhot

Hohhot (or Huhehot, as it is sometimes spelled) means Blue Town in Mongolian. Located about 265 miles northwest of Beijing, the town has a population of half a million people. There are two wonderful things to do: watch a traditional Mongolian rodeo, where you will sit under blue domes and witness a remarkable display of horsemanship, trick riding, and shooting from horseback; and tour the **Mongolian Grasslands,** where you will visit the Mongolian tribes people, drink tea and mares' milk wine, stay in a traditional Mongolian shelter (the cylindrical tent called a yurt), and see wild horses, sheep, cattle, and herds of camel.

In the town itself you should visit **Dazhou Lamasery,** with its 400-year-old temple which is under restoration after being used as a factory during the Red Guard era. The lamasery houses a national treasure: one of the only three complete sets (108 volumes) of the Tibetan canon that exists in China. Nearby stands the **Xilitou Zhao,** a temple originally built during the reign of the Third Dalai Lama, but now dating from the late Qing. North of the temple and on the opposite side of the road stands the **Great Mosque,** still used for prayer five times a day by Hohhot's Moslem community. First built in the late seventeenth century, the mosque has a restored roofline with upswept eaves more in the style of a Chinese temple.

A half-hour ride on the suburban tram (to a site about 12 miles to the southeast) from Hohhot will bring you to the **Wanbu Hua Yanjing Pagoda,** built around 990. Although the top of the pagoda is missing, the facades of the base are considered masterpieces of Liao Dynasty sculpture. Twenty minutes to the south of Hohhot lies the 100-foot-high **Tomb of Wang Zhaojun.** In an attempt to pacify a tribe of "barbarians" (the Xiongnu) that were harassing the region, a Han Dynasty princess was married to the tribal chieftain in 33 B.C., so ushering in a period of 60 years' peace. There is a good view of the countryside from the top of her tomb.

In the old section of Hohhot is the **Wutazhou (Five-Pagoda) Temple,** dating from 1740. The temple no longer exists, and all that remains are five small pagodas decorated with fine carvings. They stand on a sutra, a 25-foot-high base possessing a curved entrance gate and carved with over 1,500 Buddhas and the four Heavenly Kings. There are inscriptions in Mongolian, Sanscrit, and Tibetan.

Baotou

Baotou, located on the upper reaches of the Huang He (Yellow River), is Inner Mongolia's largest town. There are two major sights: one—about 45 miles from the town—is the Tibetan-style **Wudang Pagoda** (Wudang-zhou) dating from the Qing; the other is the two-storied, flat-roofed, **White Pagoda or Kundulunzhou,** also in Lamaist style.

Xilinhot

Xilinhot is a small city located on the plateau almost due north of Beijing. It is open to tourists but is accessible only by plane. The major site is the Qing monastery **Beizimiao,** with its Great Hall of the Sutras. Another section of the grounds features a curious row of cylindrical mounds known as *ao bao.* These are thought to be ceremonial, perhaps sacrificial, but the origin and purpose has not yet been revealed by the texts at the temple.

PRACTICAL INFORMATION FOR
INNER MONGOLIA

FACTS AND FIGURES. Inner Mongolia is an enormous autonomous region of 456,000 square miles that extends from the border of the Soviet Union in the north almost to the Xinjiang Autonomous Region in the west. Its vast grasslands support a population of about 20 million, of whom only about 15 percent are of Mongolian origin. The capital, Hohhot, lies about 265 miles northwest of Beijing.

WHEN TO GO. Avoid winter because the plateau land is usually under snow for many months. The perfect time to go is the June–July period, when the pasture lands are at their best and the days are warm. Even so, take something warm to put on in case the wind gets up.

HOW TO GET THERE. If you have time, the best way to travel is by train, particularly if you are stopping at Datong en route. You will pass beautiful plain and mountain scenery on the way, and catch glimpses of the watchtowers and remaining sections of the Great Wall. The fast train from Beijing takes 12 hours. Some visitors come to Hohhot from Datong, a 5-hour train journey. If you have less time to spare, the quickest way to reach Hohhot, the capital of Inner Mongolia, is by direct flight from Beijing.

If you are coming from Baotou, you can take a train to Hohhot, a 3-hour journey over a distance of 70 miles. The journey from Yinchuan takes 12 hours. If you plan to arrive from Xilinhot, or Abganar Qi as it is sometimes called, you will have to fly, since there is no rail service.

HOTELS. In Hohhot the newest hotel is the 20-story **Nei Mongol Hotel** (tel. 25754) on Hulun Road South, which has air-conditioned accommodations for over 500 guests. The other major hotel is the **Xincheng** (or New City) **Guest House** (tel. 24513) on Hulun Road South, offering rooms with TV but no air-conditioning or telephones. The **Hohhot Friendship Hotel** , 7 Ying Bin Road, provides good accommodation in a building that is reminiscent of an eighteenth-century French chateau

While the appointments are far from luxurious, they are quite acceptable. The grounds are pleasant and quiet.

In Baotou, guests usually stay at the **Qingshan (or Blue Mountain) Hotel** (tel. 33355 or 33688) on Yingbin Lu, the **Baotou** (tel. 26612) on Gangtie Road, or the **Donghe,** located in the district of the same name.

RESTAURANTS. As there are no restaurants catering to foreign visitors, you will have no alternative but to dine in the restaurant in your guest house. Despite what appear to be fairly spartan kitchen facilities, the guest houses manage to turn out fairly interesting meals and banquets. Beef and lamb dishes are readily available, especially cooked barbecue-style or as a hot-pot. Local specialities include bear's paw, elk's nose, and grouse.

TOURIST INFORMATION. CITS (tel. 24494) in Hohhot has an office in the Nei Mongol Hotel at Wulanchabuxi Road. There have been rumblings from some visitors about the quality of the Grassland Tours provided by CITS, so pin them down on the itinerary and sights, and if you are trying to arrange a tour for a group *after* arriving in Hohhot, discuss carefully the price.

CAAC in Hohhot (tel. 24103, 22619) is at Xilin Beilu, Minhang Lou.

PSB in Hohhot at the intersection of the Zhongshan and Xilin roads.

The **long-distance bus station** in Hohhot is on the right after leaving the Hohhot railway station.

HOW TO GET AROUND. CITS organizes tours of the towns and excursions to outlying areas and sites. Buses are used, and on the rougher terrain, jeeps. Bicycles, which may be rented opposite the Hohhot Friendship Hotel, are an excellent means of getting around town.

WHAT TO SEE. There are four major sights in Hohhot: the **Five-Pagoda Temple** (Wutazhou); the **Dazhou Lamasery** with its irreplaceable volumes of the Tibetan canon; the **Xilitou Zhou Temple** with its "eared" dagoba; and the **Great Mosque,** center of religion for the town's 25,000 Moslems. Outside Hohhot stands the **Tomb of Wang Zhoujun,** a Han Dynasty princess who brought peace to the region; and the roofless **Wanbu Hua Yanjing Pagoda** with its superb façades.

In and around Baotou there are a few noteworthy sites, especially the **White Pagoda** and further afield the **Wudang Pagoda.**

In Xilinhot, the major sight is the Great Hall of the Sutras in the **Beizimiao Monastery.**

MUSEUMS. The **Neimongol Museum** (tel. 4924), 1 Xinhua Dajie, houses a fine collection of objects from the region. Of particular interest are Mongolian minority items: a yurt; archery equipment; saddles; craft objects; artwork; costumes. There is also the skeleton of a mammoth found by workers in a coal mine.

SHOPPING. There are opportunities to purchase Mongol handicrafts, such as brassware, hunting knives, silverware, and woodware. You can also buy Mongol tunics, accessories, and herders' leather boots—footwear traditionally worn by the men and women of the Mongol national minority group. There is an antique shop with interesting pieces for sale located just north of (and on the same side of the street as) the museum, but the major retail outlet is the **Hohhot Department Store** in Zhongshan Lu. Another source of Mongolian minority products is the shop (tel. 5379) attached to the **Hohhot Handicraft Factory.** You can purchase Mongolian-style carpets at the **Hohhot Carpet Factory** (tel. 5262).

ENTERTAINMENT. During the day, try to get to the Mongolian equivalent of the Western rodeo, an event featuring superb feats of riding, roping, acrobatics, animal-handling, and archery. Exhibitions of Mongolian wrestling are also given. Traditional tunics are worn and, on special occasions, huge Mongolian tents are erected. In the evening, there are regular cultural events featuring the song and dance of the Mongolian people. CITS can make arrangements and provide tickets for both the day excursion and the evening attractions.

USEFUL ADDRESSES AND TELEPHONE NUMBERS

Hohhot

CITS—Nei Mongol Hotel (tel. 24494).
CAAC—Xilin Beilu, Minhang Lou (tel. 24103, 22619).
PSB—Zhongshan and Xilin Roads.

Baotou

CITS—Baotou Hotel (tel. 24615).
CAAC—Donghe district (tel. 41404).

JINAN

Shandong Province

North China

Jinan is the capital of Shandong Province in the north of China. The city lies just three miles south of the Huang He (Yellow River) and a few miles north of the foothills of the Shandong mountain chain.

History

The history of Shandong Province extends back to the prehistoric era. Excavations at Longshan (northeast of Jinan) have revealed that the area was inhabited in the Neolithic period from the fourth millennium B.C. on. The tribes that lived in the area made "black" pottery and lived in a society now known as the Longshan culture. The region is also well known to archeologists for a site in the northeastern section of Jinan, which dates back to the second dynasty of Chinese history: the Shang (1766–1122 B.C.). Objects uncovered there are more than 3,000 years old.

In the next dynasty, the Zhou, Jinan was a walled town under the sovereignty of the Kingdom of Qi. It was during the Zhou that Confucius, or Kong Fu Zi ("Kong the Master"), was born (551 B.C.). His birthplace, Qufu, a small town southeast of Jinan near present-day Yanzhou, has recently been reopened to visitors. Another great philosopher Mencius, or Meng Zi ("Meng the Master"), was also born in Shandong Province in a village where Zou Xian now stands.

Jinan was an important town under the Tang and the Song. It gained prominence due to its location near the Grand Canal, which cuts through Shandong Province in the western extremity. The Grand Canal was built to link Beijing with the Chang Jiang (Yangzi River). Other towns along the canal, especially those located on canal tributaries, were once more important than Jinan. However, much later in the history of the province, Jinan became a prominent political center.

In the last years of the nineteenth century, Jinan was linked by rail to the Shandong seaport of Qingdao, and later to the industrial center, Tianjin. The Chinese government opened Jinan to foreign trade in 1906, a concession that was offered voluntarily to foreign powers for the first time in China's history. Since 1949, the town has undergone considerable industrialization.

Shandong Province is well known in Chinese literature. It was there that a famous peasant uprising occurred under the Song Dynasty, an event described in one of the best-known Chinese novels, *The Water Margin,* or *Shui Hu Zhuan.*

Visitors who follow China's politics will be interested to learn that the town of Tai An in Shandong Province is where the infamous Jiang Qing was born in 1912. She attended primary school in Jinan before she began her theatrical training in the province. Jiang Qing put her talents to good use in the fledgling film industry of Shanghai, where she acted under the name of Lan Ping (Blue Apple) in minor roles. She later joined a theatrical company that took her to Yenan in 1938. There she met Mao Zedong and became his fourth wife. Jiang Qing became very powerful in the Party during the Cultural Revolution (1966–1968) but was branded one of the Gang of Four after Mao's death (1976), when she was stripped of all posts, expelled from the Party, put on trial, and in 1981 given a suspended death sentence.

You can get to Tai Shan by traveling to the town of Tai An by rail, a 1½-hour journey; or by bus from Jinan (32 miles) or Qufu (50 miles). You can scale the mountain on foot or take a bus or mini-bus to the midway station where there is a cable car to Wangfu Peak.

EXPLORING JINAN

You may wish to visit the natural springs in Jinan: Five Dragon Spring (Wulong), Fountain Spring (Baotu Quan), Black Tiger Spring (Hei Hu Quan), and Pearl Spring (Zhenzhu). If you are traveling to Jinan especially to see the springs, choose spring or autumn rather than summer, because the dry weather then usually transforms the springs into stagnant ponds. The source of Jinan's "one hundred springs" is a lake, **Da Ming Hu** (where you can hire rowboats).

The **Thousand Buddha Mountain** (Qianfoshan) provides a fine view of the town and surrounding areas and has two temples. **Golden Ox Park** (and zoo) is a pleasant location on the outskirts of Jinan.

EXCURSIONS FROM JINAN

Liu Village

The Simenta, or **Four Gate Pagoda**, is 21 miles from Jinan, near the village of Liu. Built in the sixth century and possibly the oldest stone pagoda in China, the Simenta is at the site of the **Shentong Monastery,** first established in the fourth century. Nearby stands the **Dragon and Tiger Pagoda;** higher up is the **Thousand Buddha Cliff** with its grottoes containing over 200 carvings of the Buddha. Tour buses depart Jinan daily for these sites at 8 A.M.

Divine Rock Temple

The Divine Rock of Lingyan Temple was once the most famous of the four best-known Buddhist temples in China. First built in the Tang, but rebuilt under the Ming, its most important pavilion, the **Thousand Buddha or Qianfo Hall,** houses 40 clay statues of arhats dating from the Song (960–1279). Other important pavilions are the **Main Buddha Hall** and the **Imperial Book Hall,** or Yushu. There are two towers: the **Bell Tower** and the **Drum Tower;** one edifice: the **Pizhi Pagoda;** and various tombs.

The temple is 30 miles south of Jinan. Arrangements to visit can be made through CITS in Jinan.

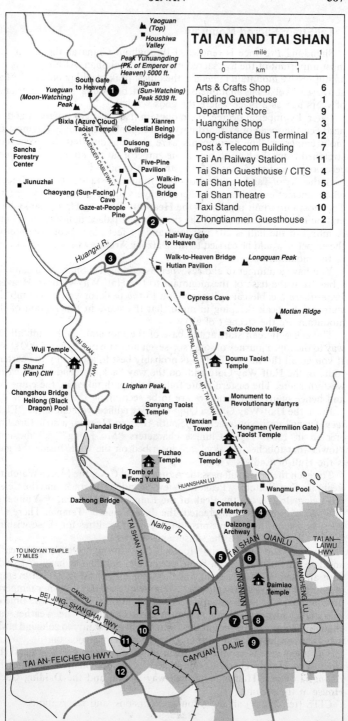

TAI AN AND TAI SHAN

Arts & Crafts Shop	6
Daiding Guesthouse	1
Department Store	9
Huangxihe Shop	3
Long-distance Bus Terminal	12
Post & Telecom Building	7
Tai An Railway Station	11
Tai Shan Guesthouse / CITS	4
Tai Shan Hotel	5
Tai Shan Theatre	8
Taxi Stand	10
Zhongtianmen Guesthouse	2

Map labels:

Yaoguan (Top)
Houshiwa Valley
Peak Yuhuangding (Pk. of Emperor of Heaven) 5000 ft.
South Gate to Heaven
Riguan (Sun-Watching) Peak 5039 ft.
Yueguan (Moon-Watching) Peak
Bixia (Azure Cloud) Taoist Temple
Xianren (Celestial Being) Bridge
Duisong Pavilion
Sancha Forestry Center
Five-Pine Pavilion
Walk-in-Cloud Bridge
Chaoyang (Sun-Facing) Cave
Gaze-at-People Pine
Jiunuzhai
PASSENGER CABLEWAY
Half-Way Gate to Heaven
Huangxi R.
Walk-to-Heaven Bridge
Hutian Pavilion
Longquan Peak
Cypress Cave
Motian Ridge
Sutra-Stone Valley
Doumu Taoist Temple
Wuji Temple
TAI SHAN HWY
Shanzi (Fan) Cliff
Linghan Peak
Monument to Revolutionary Martyrs
Changshou Bridge
Heilong (Black Dragon) Pool
Sanyang Taoist Temple
Wanxian Tower
Hongmen (Vermilion Gate) Taoist Temple
Jiandai Bridge
CENTRAL ROUTE TO MT. TAI SHAN
Puzhao Temple
Guandi Temple
Tomb of Feng Yuxiang
HUANSHAN LU
Wangmu Pool
Dazhong Bridge
Naihe R.
Cemetery of Martyrs
Daizong Archway
TAI SHAN XILU
TO LINGYAN TEMPLE 17 MILES
TAI SHAN QIANLU
TAI AN—LAIWU HWY.
HUANCHENG LU
Tai An
BEI JING- SHANGHAI HWY.
CANGKU LU
QINGNIAN
Daimiao Temple
TAI AN-FEICHENG HWY.
CAYUAN DAJIE

Tai Shan: Sacred Mountain

Shandong Province is renowned throughout China as the site of the most important of the five sacred mountains, Tai Shan. Although it is not an impressive mountain in height, the tallest peak reaching only 4,998 feet above sea level, it has an immense reputation, becoming famous thousands of years ago as a place where the gods resided.

Later, by imperial decree, the mountain itself was considered a god. It has been the scene of extraordinary processions, led by only the most famous emperors. The participants were so numerous that the procession stretched from the base to peak. The emperor, at the summit, performed ceremonies and made sacrifices to the earth and sky.

In the city of **Tai An** at the foot of the mountain stands **Daimiao Temple** where ancient emperors once offered prayers to the god of the mountain. The most important pavilion is the **Heavenly Blessing Hall** (Tiankuang), first built in 1009, and one of the three largest palace buildings in China. A mural in the hall is 203 feet long and 11 feet high. From the temple the emperor would be carried to the **Daizong Archway** to begin the ascent of the mountain.

You have a number of choices when ascending Tai Shan. You can take a bus from the base of the mountain to the **Half-Way Gate to Heaven.** From there a cable car will carry you to the peak, or you can climb the stairs to the peak (keeping in mind that the stairs in this section of the mountain are the steepest of all).

The energetic can start at the base of the mountain and climb all the way to the top, a journey of some six–seven miles up more than 7,000 steps. If you go all the way on foot, it is probably best to ascend by the eastern route to the Half-Way Gate and, on the way back, descend by the easier western route. The eastern route follows the path taken by the emperors and hence many more temples are to be seen along the way.

From the Half-Way Gate, a Qing Dynasty edifice, you climb the **"Eighteen Turns"** until you reach the **South Gate to Heaven,** a structure first erected in 1264. Three Chinese characters "Mo Kong Ge," meaning "tower that touches the sky," are inscribed on the wall. Inside the gate is the **Hall of Endless Views.**

To reach the peak, you pass the Azure Cloud Cave, the Moon-Watching Peak, the Sun-Watching Peak, the View-Shandong Terrace, and the Celestial Being Bridge. On the **Peak of the Emperor of Heaven,** or Yuhuangding, a pavilion has been erected: the **Jade Emperor Temple.** There is a guest house on the summit providing spartan facilities for those wishing to stay overnight to see the sunset and sunrise.

The best (and busiest) time to go is May through October, the early and late part of this season being preferable. Summer is hazy or cloudy with an average of only eight fine days per month. May has an average of sixteen fine days and September twenty-eight fine days. Winter temperatures are cold, some days with freezing conditions. Whatever the time of year, take adequate warm and protective clothing. The weather can change suddenly in the mountains from bright and sunny to cold and chilling. Dress in layers so that you can peel off or put back on.

The major hotels are the **Tai Shan Hotel** on Puzhao Si Road and the **Dong Yue Hotel.** There are guest houses on Tai Shan Mountain: the **Zhongtian Guest House** at the half-way station and the **Daiding Guest House** at the summit.

CITS (tel. 23259) arranges tours, excursions, and reservations.

Qufu: Birthplace of Confucius

Those interested in the life of Confucius should try to visit his birthplace at Qufu, a town 9 miles east of Yanzhou and about 65 miles from Jinan. There you will see the Temple of Confucius, the Tomb of Confucius, and a residence of the descendants of Confucius. You could spend days exploring the temples and palaces, which rival in style and grandeur those at the Forbidden City in Beijing.

The **Confucian Temple** stands in the very center of the town. It was first built in 478 B.C. in honor of Kong Fuzi (or Master Kong as Confucius was called in China) just a year before the great teacher died, almost 2,500 year ago. On the original site stood a three-room family house. Now there are 466 halls and pavilions and nine courtyards, all occupying 54 acres. The most prominent pavilion is the **Great Hall of Confucius,** or Dacheng Hall; but there are many others worthy of note, especially the **Confucian Deeds Hall,** built in 1592, which houses 120 pictures depicting various journeys of the sage.

The **Confucian Family Mansion** is also in the center of Qufu, adjacent to the temple. The mansion grew from its modest beginnings in 1038, to groups of buildings occupying 40 acres. There are nine courtyards and over 400 rooms. The western portion has been converted into a hotel.

The **Confucian Woods** occupy 495 acres about a mile to the north of Qufu. The **Tomb of Confucius** stands in the center of the woods surrounded by a red wall. The path leading to the tomb is flanked by statues of noblemen, officials, unicorns, wild beasts, and ceremonial pillars. There are numerous tombs, pavilions, and temples in the woods.

If you are traveling from Jinan, there is a three-hour train journey to Yanzhou, then a bus connection covering the nine miles to Qufu. From Tai An the train journey takes two hours. The last bus to Qufu is at 5 P.M. Local buses also run between Tai An and Qufu.

The newest place to stay is the **Quelibin Hotel,** its exterior built in classical Chinese style, but with modern facilities inside. For a trip back into the past you could stay at the old but splendid **Kong Fuzi Mansions,** the western section of the "family home."

PRACTICAL INFORMATION FOR JINAN

FACTS AND FIGURES. Jinan, the capital of Shandong Province, is 205 miles due south of Beijing by air. By rail it is 230 miles via Tianjin from Beijing.

WHEN TO GO. Autumn is the best time for traveling in Jinan. Jinan's famous springs almost dry up in summer, so avoid visiting in that season if you can. If you intend to walk to the peak of Tai Shan, you will need protective clothing because the weather can change suddenly on the mountain; even on sunny days, the breeze can be cool. Remember, the peak is over 8,000 feet high.

HOW TO GET THERE. Jinan is on the rail line connecting Beijing and Tianjin in the north, and Nanjing and Shanghai in the south. The journey by train from Beijing takes 6½ to 7½ hours, from Tianjin 4 to 5 hours, from Nanjing 7½ to 9 hours, and from Shanghai 11 to 13 hours.

Jinan is only 1¼-hour flight from Beijing. 1¼ hours from Hefei, but 3½ hours from Shanghai because of the slow aircraft used on this route.

HOTELS. Visitors usually stay at the **Qilu Hotel** (tel. 47961, cable 3906, telex

39142) on Qianfoshan Road; it has 255 rooms and tennis courts. Other hotels are the **Jinan Hotel** (tel. 35351), 372 Jingsan Road, and the **Nanjiao Hotel** (tel. 23931), 2 Ma Anshan Road. The Jinan used to be the Japanese consulate; it is small with a pleasant garden. The Nanjiao used to be reserved for China's high-ranking officials, but is now open to foreign visitors. At the edge of the town in a quiet area near tree-covered hills; it has an indoor swimming pool and air-conditioning.

RESTAURANTS. Shandong's contribution to Chinese cuisine is considerable, but only a handful of restaurants in the city cater to the foreign visitor. You might care to try the **Jufengde** (tel. 33905) at 100 Jingshan Road, the **Yanxitang** (tel. 23451) at 292 Quangcheng Road, Old Town District, or the **Daminghu** (Lake Daming) restaurant (tel. 20584) opposite the south gate of Daming Lake Park. Specialties of the town include dishes made from the lotus plant found in Jinan's lakes, monkey-head mushrooms, and duck.

TOURIST INFORMATION. CITS (tel. 45945 ext. 74) is at 26 Jingshi Road. **CAAC** (tel. 33191) is 348 Jing-2 Road and Wei-6 Road. **PSB** (tel. 35778) is at 54 Wei-5 Road, not far from the Jinan Hotel.

HOW TO GET AROUND. Tour buses go to the major sites and also undertake full-day excursions to places outside the city. CITS can provide tickets for tours and excursions. For fun, you can take a motorized three-wheeler conveyance, otherwise there are about 25 bus routes serving the town.

WHAT TO SEE. Jinan is well known for its springs, appearing in historical references more than two millennia ago as a source of fine water. The source is the Da Ming Lake in the town itself. For scenic views visit the **Thousand Buddha Mountain;** for relaxation the **Golden Ox Park.**

MUSEUMS. The **Museum of Shandong Province** (tel. 20486) on Wenhua Xi Road houses an interesting collection of objects including musical instruments, paintings, a bamboo book on the art of war written over 2,000 years ago, and rubbings from a Han Dynasty tomb. A small museum worth visiting is the one housing a collection of objects devoted to one of China's most famous poets, **Li Qingzhau.** She was born in Jinan in 1804 during the Song Dynasty. The museum is in the park located in the center of town and at the western end of Heihu Quan Road (where the source of the Fountain Spring, or Baotou Quan, is to be found).

SHOPPING. Shandong Province is well known for its handicrafts, especially those that come from Jining in the southwest of the province. Objects made of wood, bamboo, copper, and iron are the most noteworthy; also landscapes and designs made from the feathers of peacocks, pheasants, and swans. All items can be purchased at a number of shops located only a few blocks from the Jinan Hotel, e.g., **Friendship Store, Shandong Antique Store** (tel. 23446) at 321 Quancheng Road, and the **Jinan Arts and Crafts Store,** 3 Nanmen Street.

USEFUL ADDRESSES AND TELEPHONE NUMBERS

CITS—26 Jingshi Road (tel. 45945 ext. 74).
CAAC—348 Jing 2 and Wei-6 Roads (tel. 33191).
PSB—54 Wei-5 Road (tel. 35778).
Taxis—Jinan Taxi Co. (tel. 34986).

KUNMING

Yunnan Province
Southwest China

Kunming, the capital of Yunnan Province, is known as the "city of eternal spring." Located in the middle of the Yunnan plateau 6,200 feet (1,890 meters) above sea level, subtropical Kunming is encircled by mountains to the north, east, and west, while to the south lies a large lake, called Dianchi. Kunming has a temperate climate and flowers that bloom most of the year round, but its association with eternal spring can be misleading, because there are sometimes cold winds in winter, chilly days in spring, and heavy rains in summer. Generally speaking, though, the city's climate is kind to travelers most of the time.

Kunming used to be one of the most backward and isolated provincial capitals in China, with its maze of crooked lanes, rickety mud houses, unsewered streets, and marketplaces crowded with peddlers. Parts of the old city still exist, but bit by bit the old buildings are being demolished, and the narrow lanes dug up and replaced by wider roads. The old walls of the town have already been torn down. Old structures have been replaced by six-story concrete buildings; modern lighting and sewerage systems have been installed; and silver birch trees have been planted along with crabapple trees to soften the city's appearance.

The southern half of the old city is relatively uninteresting, with new commercial buildings flanking the wide streets, but the northern section is more attractive, with its institutes and parks. Unattractive dormitory and industrial suburbs surround the old city to the south, east, and west. However, throughout the year, many people visit Kunming for the flower festivals, particularly in spring and summer. Then the blossoms on the cherry, peach, plum, and apple trees adorn the city; and in the parks blooms of magnolia, camellia, and azalea dazzle the eye.

Kunming has a history spanning more than 2,000 years. It is known to have been a small settlement as early as 109 B.C., trading in salt, silver, gold, silk, and lumber. Through the eighth to the thirteenth centuries, it was the secondary capital of a small kingdom in the region, before falling to the Mongols in 1274. (A small group of Mongols still exists at Tonghai, about 75 miles due south of Kunming.) Marco Polo visited the capital a few years later and refers to the presence of both Moslems and Christians; money in the form of cowrie shells kept for safekeeping around the neck of the owner's dog; abundant fish in the large lake near the town; and the trade in salt which was largely responsible for the prosperity of the community. When the Ming routed the Mongols, Kunming also fell (in 1382), a walled town called Yunnanfu being built to the northwest of the site. Under the Qing, the town suffered various campaigns in the last half of the seventeenth century, and 200 years later was beseiged by the Sultan of Dali and badly damaged (1859–1868).

By 1910, when the French Indo-China rail line reached Kunming, the population had dwindled considerably. Although the establishment of the rail link stimulated trade and commerce, it was not until the 1930s that the town began to develop, when the settlement benefited from an influx of refugees from the east coast who were fleeing the Japanese invasion. During the 1937–1945 period, many factories were established, setting a base for the industrial development that was to follow the Communist takeover of China in 1949.

The city is now an important communications center, with rail links (currently closed) to Hanoi and Haiphong in Vietnam, a road link to Burma—the formidable Burma Road carved out of the jungle during World War II—and international air links to Rangoon and Hong Kong. Industry has been developed. There is an iron and steel mill, as well as factories producing trucks, machine tools, electrical equipment, machinery, chemicals, and textiles. A lot of industry has grown up along the southeastern shore of Dian Lake.

Yunnan Province, so named because of its location to the south of the Yun Mountains, is the home of 23 national minorities. They comprise about one quarter of the population of 28 million, living mainly in the more mountainous southern and eastern areas, whereas the Han Chinese live mainly in the east and central parts of the province. The most important national minority group by size of population is the Yi. The others are the Bai, Hani, Zhuang, Dai, Miao, Lisu, Hui, Wa, Lahu, Naxi, Jingpo, Yao, Zang, Bulang, Pumi, Achang, Nu, Benglong, Mongol, Drung, and the Jinuo. A few ethnic groups of smaller population are scattered throughout the province.

Yunnan is a plateau dotted with verdant valleys and lush river basins. The province has a well-earned reputation for the rich variety of its flora and fauna. Xishuangbanna in southwest Yunnan, for example, boasts large areas of primeval forests filled with magnificent animals such as the elephant, rhinoceros, gibbon, hornbill, and peacock—animals that are rarely associated with China in the minds of foreigners. And the province boasts scenery of astounding beauty: the rock forests of Lunan; the lakes and mountains around Dali; the majestic snow-capped peaks of Mount Yulongxue rearing to a height of over 18,000 feet. The scenery around Kunming is renowned throughout China.

Yunnan Province, known also simply as Yun or Dian, is strategically important to China, lying as it does on the border with Laos, Burma, and Vietnam. Since the Sino-Vietnamese clashes began in 1977, about 150,000 Viet refugees have settled in Yunnan province. The topography of the region varies enormously and so does the agriculture practiced in the different geographic areas. Rice, wheat, corn, and rapeseed are produced; cotton and tobacco are important cash crops; logging is carried out in the forested areas; sugar cane is grown in the lower wet regions; and livestock raising is practiced in the grasslands and foothills of the mountains. The province has rich deposits of copper and tin and good deposits of nickel and cobalt.

EXPLORING KUNMING

Old City Wall

A section of the old city wall stands in the northeastern sector of Kunming. There is a pleasant view from the tree-lined promenade on the hill which overlooks the most attractive part of the city where there are parks, gardens, and institutes.

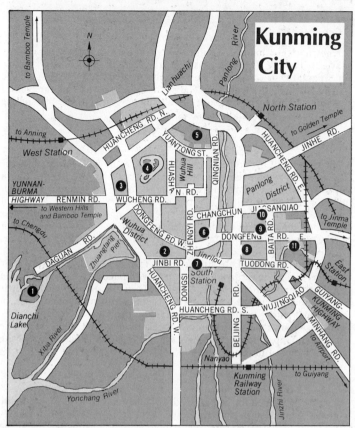

Points of Interest

Anning Hot Springs **14**
Bamboo Temple **20**
Black Dragon Pool **21**
CAAC Booking Office **10**
Caoqi Temple **13**
Chenggong Orchard **23**
Daguan Park **1**
Dongfeng Stadium **11**
Dragon Gate **16**
Exhibition Hall **3**
Golden Temple **22**
Guanyin Hill **17**
Green Lake and Park **4**
Haigeng Beach **18**
Kunming City **19**
Kunming Hotel **9**
Kunming Theater **6**
Post and Telegraph
  Bureau PSB **8**
Xiyuan Hotel **15**
Yuantong Hill and Zoo **5**
Yunnan Museum **2**
Yunnan Province No. 1
  Hospital **7**
Zheng He Park **12**

Green Lake

Known to the Chinese as Cuihu, Green Lake is located in the northwest quarter of the city. The walkways along the lake's edge are lined by willow and fragrant cassia trees and there are fine gardens, numerous pavilions, a small island, and a teahouse. The northeastern shore skirts the base of Yuantong Hill which is a blaze of color in spring from the blossoming cherry, plum, peach, and pear trees.

Yuantong Hill

Yuantong Hill overlooks Green Lake and, apart from the view at the summit, is known for the **Yuantong Monastery** standing on the southern slope. The original monastery was founded in the third century A.D. but the temples were rebuilt in the fourteenth century under the Yuan and renovated under the Ming and Qing. One of the most attractive structures is the Octagonal Pavilion, surrounded by water and reached from either side by crossing a stone bridge. However, there are many other pavilions to explore.

The slopes of the hill are studded with fruit trees and, in season, their blossoms splash the verdant surroundings with pinks, whites, yellows, and reds. In the park gardens, flower beds have been planted according to their blooming season: in the spring garden there are oriental cherry trees; in the summer garden camellias and magnolias; the autumn garden features sweet cassia; and the winter garden is resplendent with plum trees. The Yunnan and Japanese cherry trees of the spring garden show a shimmering crimson cloud of blossoms when in season.

Zoo

The zoo is located in the parklands of Yuantong Hill. There are many animals of interest in the zoo, especially the rare Yunnan hornbills (*Bucerotidae*). The even rarer white monkey of Yunnan is housed at the Kunming Institute of Zoology, but don't be disappointed—there are plenty of other fascinating species to see at the zoo itself.

Daguan Park

Daguan Park, in the southwest corner of the city, is worth a visit to see the Daguanlou, or Grand View Mansion. The mansion stands on the northern shore of Lake Dian. Built in 1690, three stories high, with galleries running around the top floors, the mansion is well known in the region for the famous "long couplet" written by the Qing Dynasty poet Sun Ranweng. The characters form two columns on either side of a beautiful folding door; those on the right praise the beauty of the town, while those on the left praise the historical sites of Yunnan.

Lake Dian

Lake Dian, or Kunming Lake, a scenic stretch of water located to the southwest of the city, occupies an area of 120 square miles (300 square kilometers) and was formed by a geological fault in the central Yunnan plateau. It has long been famous for its fish; indeed, Marco Polo praised the variety and bounty of its catch in his thirteenth-century account of his travels in the region. Now the blue lake is dotted with the white sails of long flat-decked boats that skim through the water. On the far shores the land rises gently into foothills leading farther on to gentle peaks. Nearer, the scenic Western Hills rise abruptly, providing a vantage point to view the expanse of water that stretches into the distance. Excursion boats are available to take you on a scenic tour of the lake. They depart at 8 A.M., arriving Haikou at noon; the return trip departs at 2 P.M.

EXCURSIONS FROM KUNMING

Western Hills

Known as Xishan in Chinese, the Western Hills are a 30-minute bus ride from Kunming. They are best visited in the morning when the eastern slope is bathed in sunshine and the reflected colors on Lake Dian are the most intense. You can take a boat trip on the lake from the pier. (If you plan to do this trip, ask your hotel to pack a picnic lunch to eat on board.) When you are out on the lake you will notice that the Western Hills comprise four slopes which form a contour resembling a "sleeping beauty" whose hair flows down to the water. For this reason Xishan is sometimes called Sleeping Beauty Mountain. The names of the four hills are Huating, Taihua, Taiping, and Lohan.

If you feel energetic, you can walk to the summit of the hills in about two to three hours. The wide path is steep in parts and winds its way through thick woods to emerge at a rock face. A tunnel has been cut through the rock to a Taoist temple on the peak. You pass a number of old monasteries and temples on the way to the summit and these are described in order below. The hills are usually crowded with visitors.

Temple of the Flower Pavilion

Hidden in a bamboo grove in the Western Hills, the Temple of the Flower Pavilion, or the Huatingsi, was once the country retreat of the King of Nanzhou who ruled Yunnan in the fourteenth century. The first pavilion stands before a pond, the entrance being flanked by two large Celestial Guardians. In the first hall you will see the statues of the four Heavenly Kings and the Maitreya Buddha; in the Hall of Worship stand the three large statues of the Buddha. You will also see the figures of the 500 *arhat* (disciples) and a model of the former country villa of the king who founded the site.

Great Flower Monastery

A few miles further along the path stands the Great Flower Monastery, or the Taihuasi. The original temples were built in the early fourteenth century. You will see 19 magnificent statues of the Buddha in bronze, and clay statues of the *arhat* (disciples), each sculpted with individual features. In the temple grounds there are magnificent flowering cassia trees and flowering shrubs such as camellias and magnolias.

Grave of Nie Er

Quite near the Great Flower Monastery stands the grave of Nie Er, an outstanding musician of Yunnan, who died in 1936 aged 24 years. He composed China's national anthem. Cypresses and flower beds surround the grave.

Dragon Gate

About a mile further on from the Great Flower Monastery, you will come across a path and tunnel hacked out of solid rock. This arduous task, including the carvings and other stonework was done between 1781 and 1843 by a Taoist monk, Wu Laiqing, assisted by a number of stonemasons. There are two major caves: the Cave of Compassionate Clouds (Ciyundong) and the Cave of the Splendrous Clouds (Yunhuadong). Then there is the Dragon Gate (Longmen) with its balcony jutting out from the cliff face and offering a superb view over Lake Dian below, and the Pavilion Reaching Heaven (Datiange). The last cave has many inscriptions made by students in gratitude to the god in the cave who helped those sitting for the imperial examinations.

Taoist Temple of the Three Pure Ones

The original building was once the villa of the Mongol Prince of Liang in the fourteenth century, but it later became a Taoist temple. It leans against a high cliff with a vertical drop below and commands a superb view of the lake and surrounding regions. The Temple of the Three Pure Ones is dedicated to the three main Taoist gods, hence its name in Chinese—Sanqingge.

Bamboo Temple

The Bamboo Temple stands about eight miles northwest of Kunming on a wooded slope called Jade Hill on Mount Yufeng. The original monastery, Qiongzhusi, was built in the early years of the Mongol reign (A.D. 1280–1368) but the site is thought to have been in existence well before that, under the Tang. Burned to the ground in 1419, rebuilt in 1422, the monastery was restored in 1883–1890. The centerpiece is an impressive statue of the Buddha flanked by two disciples; the wings of the main temple house innumerable statues of some of the Buddhist pantheon. However, the temple is renowned for its collection of 500 *arhat*. There are six tiers in each of the halls, each hall possessing three rows of figures which are about three feet high. They were sculpted by molding clay over a wooden model or frame. The sculptor, Li Guangxiu, was brought from Sichuan province by the abbot to do the task. With two assistants it took him seven years (1884–1891). They drew inspiration from the people of the region, using them as live models in their work. The statues are remarkably lifelike, each possessing a distinct facial expression, form of dress and posture. When completed they were treated with some contempt by the adherents of Buddhism, but now they are recognized as a superb creation of religious art.

Golden Temple

Located six miles northeast of Kunming, the Golden Temple, or Jindian, is a renowned Taoist temple that stands on the summit of a small mountain. You reach the temple by a path that leads through a pine forest, passing through three "heaven gates" and, at the top of the hill, through three *pailou*. The major point of interest is the pavilion constructed in bronze—all the walls, pillars, tiles, screens, and statues are solid bronze.

It seems that these were once ornamented with gold leaf, hence the name given to the temple.

The temple is associated with a Chinese general called Wu Sangui; his banner is still flown on the flagstaff in the grounds. His temporary alliance with the Manchu helped them win the imperial throne from the Ming. Sent by the Manchu court in 1659 to quell the rebellion against them in the province, he turned against the imperial rulers and became the warlord of the region, ruling until his death 22 years later. He used the palace as his summer home.

Black Dragon Pool

Quite near the Golden Temple, set in a park in which there are many pavilions, the Black Dragon (or Heilong) Pool is really two ponds, one clear and one muddy, which do not mix. There are pleasant tree-lined walks in the park, a teahouse well known for its sweet osmanthus brew, and the "Three Old Trees"—the Tang plum, the Song cypress, and the Ming camellia. The entrance features an ornate set of upswept eaves over a triple archway.

Hot Springs of Anning

The Anning or Tranquil Hot Springs are found 24 miles west of Kunming near a stream that eventually empties into Lake Dian. Also known as the "first hot spring under heaven," the Anningwenquan is one of the most famous in China, gushing out warm water pure enough to drink, at a rate of 1,700 tons every 24 hours. Health centers and vacation resorts are scattered throughout the surrounding terrain.

Stone Forest of Lunan

The Stone Forest of Lunan was once an ocean floor. Then about 270 million years ago it was thrust to the surface by the movement of vast subterranean plates. The hard rock that you see today was at that time covered by a 10-foot-thick layer of limestone. This layer gradually eroded leaving needle-pointed rocks and top-heavy towers jutting into the sky in a typical karstlike formation, which, from a distance resembles a forest of pines. Scattered through this strange landscape are natural pools, manmade ponds, tiny bridges, and classical pavilions. The tallest stone pillar towers 99 feet high. The most interesting sights are the Sword Peak Pool, Lotus Blossom Peak, Stone Forest Lake, and the Peak View Pavilion. There is also an interesting limestone cave to visit. The trail through the area is just over a mile in length.

If you are in Yunnan around mid-June, try to visit the Stone Forest. During June 23–25 each year, the Sani people come together for their Torch Festival. During the day they engage in archery, horseback-riding, bullfights, and other feats, while during the evening they gather around campfires to sing and dance.

You will need a full day to visit this remarkable sight. If you have sufficient time you can stay overnight at the **Shilin Hotel** (tel. Shilin 113) in order to see as much as possible of the Stone Forest. It is located 75 miles to the southeast of Kunming and the bus trip takes about three and a half hours each way. The excursion is recommended, not only to see the Stone Forest, but for the scenery that you will experience on the way.

Shilin Village

The village of Shilin stands near a pond and has pink mud-brick cottages scattered among the rock pinnacles. The villagers are of the Sani minority, a subgroup of the Yi nationality. The landscapes in the mountains surrounding Shilin are magnificent. In the evening, you will be entertained by song and dance performed by the Sani who live in the region.

XISHUANGBANNA

A trip to the region of Xishuangbanna will rank as one of the foremost excursions that you will make in China, even though getting there is not easy. Located in the deep south of Yunnan, close to the point where Burma and Laos intersect with China, the 77,000-square-mile region includes the towns of Jinghong, Menghai, and Mengla.

The Mekong (Lancang) River flows through the area. Mountains tower over subtropical rain forests, waterfalls splash into rivers and creeks, and everywhere there are hamlets with wooden houses on stilts.

The region is home to 12 minority nationalities, the most important group being the Dai, with a population numbering about 220,000 people. The other 11 ethnic minority groups collectively make up a population of similar size.

The outstanding feature of a visit to the region is the opportunity to meet and observe the customs of the Dai. They are devout Hinayana Buddhists—you will see small boys in the saffron robes of the seminary where they all undergo several years' training as novitiates—and they are culturally aligned with the same ethnic group in Burma. (There is free interchange within the groups living on opposite sides of the border.) They give expressive performances of song and dance, their Peacock Dance being especially well known. The region also has many monasteries, temples, and pagodas that are worth visiting. The local markets are especially colorful.

In deciding when to go, keep in mind that the dry season lasts from November through March, although there are often thick fogs during the winter months. The rainy monsoon season begins in May and lasts until October.

If you can get to the region in April, around the 13–15th day of the fourth lunar month, you will witness the extraordinary **Water Splashing Festival,** when many Dais get married, festivities abound, and dragon-boat races are held. Around mid-July there is a **Closing Door Festival** and in mid-October, an **Opening Door Festival,** both of which are Buddhist in origin.

Trips to Xishuangbanna are normally arranged by CITS in Kunming (or may be part of an organized package tour arranged outside of China), and independent travelers have found it difficult and time-consuming to arrange bookings (often three–four days' delay), most of the seats being reserved for the tour groups. The standard method of travel is a plane from Kunming to **Simao,** then a winding five-hour bus journey to **Jinghong,** the administrative center of the region. There is an arduous five-day trip that can be made from Kunming to Jinghong, but whether foreigners are permitted to travel there by this means is not known.

Dali

Dali stands on **Lake Erhai,** some 257 miles northwest of Kunming. It is a charming town set on the western foreshores of the lake and dominated by the snowy peaks of the **Cang Mountains.** The area is the home of the colorful Bai ethnic minority group. Although the journey to Dali is a long one, being 11 hours by bus from Kunming, the effort made is rewarded by stunning scenery along the way, and interesting sightseeing on arrival.

You may take a five-hour boat journey on Lake Erhai, visit the hot springs outside of **Xiaguan,** climb the stairs of one of the **Three Pagodas** outside Dali, and visit the **Zhong He Monastery.** The markets in the region are worth a visit, especially at **Xizhou,** about 12 miles north of Dali. There is a big regional fair held every year on the 15th–25th of the third lunar month (usually April).

Until the airport is built at Xiaguan, 10 miles south of Dali, visitors must make the rough 11-hour journey along with old Burma Road by bus. There is a daily departure at 7 A.M. from the long-distance bus station near the west gate in Kunming. Tickets and reservations must be arranged some days in advance.

The best means of travel after arrival is by bicycle. The no. 2 Hostel rents bicycles and so does the establishment next door.

PRACTICAL INFORMATION FOR KUNMING

FACTS AND FIGURES. Kunming, the capital of Yunnan Province, stands at an elevation of 6,200 feet. Located at 25°04'N and 102°41'E, it is on the same approximate latitude as the Florida Keys. The population of Kunming municipality, which encloses surrounding rural areas and satellite towns, is about 1.5 million. The city is linked by rail to Chengdu to the north, Guiyang to the east, and Hanoi; by air to major cities such as Guangzhou, Beijing, Shanghai (usually via other provincial capitals); and to international airports such as Hong Kong (2 hours direct flight) and Rangoon (½ hour).

The table shows the weather pattern in Kunming during the year.

Kunming Temperature Range and Average Rainfall

	Temperature High (°F)	Temperature Low (°F)	Number of Days with Rainfall	Monthly Rainfall (in inches)
January	61	37	2	0.4
April	76	51	5	0.8
July	77	62	19	8.8
October	70	53	12	3.0

WHEN TO GO. Kunming is one of the few Chinese cities pleasant to visit at almost any time of the year. Its winters are short, dry, and sunny; its spring delightful; its summers warm but not hot, there being late afternoon thunderstorms in July and August; and its fall is superb.

HOW TO GET THERE. From international airports, there are direct flights from Hong Kong (2¼ hours) and Rangoon, Burma (½ hour). There are local flights from Beijing (4¼–4½ hours), Shanghai (fastest flight 3 hours), Guangzhou (fastest flight 2¼ hours); and from nearby provincial capitals Chengdu (2 hours), Guiyang (1 hour 35 minutes), and Nanning (1 hour 10 minutes). A route frequently taken by visitors arriving in China via Hong Kong is Guangzhou—Guilin—Kunming, the connecting flight from Guilin to Kunming taking 1 hour 25 minutes. Kunming is also served by charter flights from Hong Kong.

Travel by rail to Kunming from Guangzhou is too long to be undertaken without breaking the journey into segments. For example, the journey from Anshun is 13 hours, Guiyang 15 hours, Mount Emei 21 hours, and Chengdu 25 hours. Some travelers with plenty of time have undertaken the long journey from the north: i.e., from Beijing to Kunming by train, stopping off at such places as Luoyang, Xian, and Chengdu en route. Others have traveled from Shanghai, stopping off at Hangzhou, Nanchang, Changsha, and Guiyang. Anyone undertaking these trips can expect to spend many days on the train.

HOTELS. The **Golden Dragon** (tel. 33104, 33015; telex 64060 GDHKM CN; cable 4456), 575 Beijing Road, Kunming's first international-standard hotel, has 302 pleasantly furnished rooms, sky lounge, disco, pool, gym, sauna, and tennis court; its three restaurants serve Cantonese, Yunan, and minority-group Dai food, and the brasserie serves Western food.

Many other hotels in Kunming accommodate tourists. Visitors often stay at the **Kunming Hotel,** 145 Dongfeng Road East (tel. 22063), where the facilities are clean, the service friendly, and the rooms comfortable. The **Xiyuan Hotel** (tel. 29969), standing in a magnificent setting on a neck of land jutting into Lake Dian at the foot of West Hill, has 30 rooms (in two villas) and a swimming pool. New hotels include the 19-story **Hua Qiao (Overseas) Chinese Hotel,** the 15-story **Kunming Tourist Hotel** with shops, restaurants, and 198 rooms, and the 17-story **Tian Kunming Hotel.**

Other hotels are the **Cuihu (Green Lake) Guest House** (tel. 22192), Cuihu Road South, the **Kunhu Hotel** (tel. 27732), Beijing Road, **Yunnan Hotel,** (tel. 25533), **Lianyunxiang Guest House, Chuncheng Hotel, Kunming Inn, Xiangyang Hotel, Dongzhan Hotel, Xizhan Hotel,** and **Lianhua Inn.** Visitors sometimes stay overnight at the **Shilin Guest House** (tel. 113), Lunan County, when visiting the famous Stone Forest.

RESTAURANTS. Kunming offers a range of restaurants that can be frequented by tourist visitors, and a series of succulent dishes that are specialties of the region. Many dishes contain a sprinkling of the area's famous herbs and plants, e.g., the Jizhong fungus (mushroom), while others feature local meats, e.g., Yunnan duck and ham, ginger chicken in a pot, and (for the iron-willed) dog-meat stew. There are beef and mutton dishes of the Hui (Chinese-speaking Moslems), such as spiced beef, beef-and-mutton chop suey, and mutton-blood noodles. At other restaurants you may care to try dishes such as Yunnan rice noodles, stewed fermented bean curd, stewed rice pancake, fried rice pancake with ham, and crisp-skin duck. In the fruit season, don't miss the apples, pears, oranges, mangoes, papaya, pineapples, and, for something a little different, the "ox-belly" fruit from Xishuangbanna.

The dining rooms of the two leading hotels are recommended. If you wish to try some of the equally good restaurants of the town, visit the **Dongfeng Restaurant** on Wucheng Road (try the chicken in a pot) and the **Yiheyuan** (formerly "Fatty Wang's House") on Zhengyi Road (try the roast duckling). For delicious snacks, don't miss Food Street One, Baoshan Street, Panlong district and Food Street Two, Daguan Street, Wuhua district.

Many restaurants specialize in the cuisine of other regions. The best Cantonese restaurant is the **Guangwei** on Jinbi Road (tel. 22970); and the best Moslem restaurant is the **Yingjianglou,** 413 Changchun Road (tel. 25198). Then there is the **Beijing Restaurant,** (tel. 23214), 77 Xinxiangyun Street (tel. 23327); Beijing Donglaishun on Xiangyun Street; and the **Shanghai Restaurant,** 77 Dongfeng Road West (tel. 22987). To explore further, try the **Chuanwei,** 35 Xiangyun Street (tel. 23171), and the **Guoqiao Mixian** Restaurant on Nantong Street, where the famous "across the bridge noodles" are a specialty. **Mr. Tong's,** at the Jinbi Road end of Xiangyun Jie, is very popular.

TOURIST INFORMATION. CITS (tel. 25922 or 24992) at the Kunming Hotel will make arrangements for tours and excursions. If you are arranging onward train reservations through them, allow 3–4 days because the visitor traffic through Kunming can be high. Plane reservations can also be a problem at times, so contact CITS early rather than late. An alternative for train travel is to go direct to the advance-ticket office or try to buy a ticket at the railway station within 24 hours of the train's departure.

CAAC (tel. 24270, 24650) is at 146 Dongfeng East Road, not far from CITS.

PSB is at 525 Beijing Road; hours are 8–11:30 A.M. and 2–5:30 P.M.

HOW TO GET AROUND. CITS arranges bus tours and excursions as well as 2-hour boat trips on the lake. If you have time and are prepared to rough it a bit, you can save yourself a lot of money by going on the excursions out of Kunming on local buses. The following services all depart from and return to the Jinri Park bus station (tel. 6243).

Destination	Departure		Service	Note
	First	Last		
Stone Forest	7 A.M.	3 P.M.	Daily	Returns same day
Golden Temple &				
Black Dragon Pool	9 A.M.	4 P.M.	Daily	Buses every ½-hour
Western Hills	9 A.M.	4 P.M.	Daily	Return journey departs from Huating Monastery
Bamboo Temple	9 A.M.	3 P.M.	Daily	Buses every ½-hour
Anning Hot				
Springs	9 A.M.	3 P.M.	Irregular	

WHAT TO SEE. Around the city itself you might care to visit the **Old City Wall, Green Lake,** and **Yuantong Hill**—all provide an interesting panorama and a glimpse of the trees and flowers in bloom. There is also a **zoo** in Yuantong Hill park. At **Daguan Park** a lovely old mansion overlooks the lake. **Lake Dian** has boat excursions to interesting places along the shores.

An excursion by bus is available to **West Hill** where you will see the **Temple of the Flower Pavilion,** the **Great Flower Monastery,** the **Dragon Gate,** and the superb view from the Taoist temple at the peak of **Xishan.** Farther afield are the **Bamboo Temple,** the **Golden Temple,** and **Black Dragon Pool.** If you have time you might spend a day relaxing at the **Hot Springs of Anning,** 1½ hours from Kunming. Do try to see the famous **Stone Forest** of Lunan, either on a one-day excursion on which you will spend a total of 6 hours on the bus or, at more leisurely pace on a 2-day excursion, spending the night at a guest house in the small village of Shilin. You will need a minimum of 3 days to see the most interesting sights of Kunming and environs, 4 if you want to see all of them, and five or more days if you wish to pursue a leisurely pace.

MUSEUMS. The **Yunnan Provincial Museum** on Dongfengxi Road (tel. 23694; or 24408 for reference room) has an interesting range of exhibits, particularly those relating to the 23 national minorities residing in the province.

SHOPPING. There are a host of colorful national minority items to buy—tunics, blouses, dresses, embroidered hats, blankets, knives, swords, satchels, sashes, necklaces, bracelets, musical instruments, and so on. Take a look at the batik materials, a rarity in China—but there are some nice lengths for sale in Kunming. Yunnan is famous for its jade which is similar in nature to Burmese jade; fine bracelets, necklaces, pendants, rings, and earrings made from this stone can be purchased. The marble of the region is also highly sought after, there being many items manufactured from this material that make excellent (but heavy) souvenirs. Jianshui pottery and Yonsheng porcelain are well known in the region and are good buys, particularly the jars. Yunnan is famous for its medicinal herbs all obtainable at the pharmacies throughout the city.

For national minority items, a good place to begin is the **Nationalities Trading Store** on Nanbing Street (tel. 25935). If it is antiques you are seeking, go to the **Kunming Antique Store,** also on Nanbing Street (tel. 26548). For arts and crafts, there are two specialty stores: **Yunnan Arts and Crafts** on Dongfengxi Road (tel. 26871) and **Kunming Arts and Crafts** on Qingnian Road (tel. 2200). For Chinese manufactured goods, try the **Kunming Department Store,** Zhengyi Road (tel. 25371), and for almost everything there is the Friendship Store.

ENTERTAINMENT. Frequent performances of song and dance by ethnic minorities are given in Kunming, and these colorful and entertaining evenings will please you. CITS or your hotel can arrange tickets. Some hotels show (on request) documentaries on the national minorities of Yunnan and these can prove to be a valuable source of information prior to a visit to the ethnic areas. Ask your hotel about these films.

If you visit the Stone Forest of Lunan and stay overnight, you will be entertained in the evening by the song and dance of the colorful Sani minority.

USEFUL ADDRESSES AND TELEPHONE NUMBERS

International calls: Operator, tel. 113. Directory assistance, tel. 116.
Directory assistance: tel. 114.
China International Travel Service: Kunming Hotel (tel. 25922 or 24992).
CAAC Booking Office: 146 Dongfeng Road East (tel. 24270).
Kunming Airport: tel. 22234.
Kunming Railway Station: Inquiries, tel. 22321. Reservations, tel. 24122.
Taxis: Headquarters, Beijing Road. Tel. 23389. Jinri Park Station, tel. 26243.
Railway Station: tel. 26042.
Tricycle taxis: tel. 23898.
Coach Station: tel. 23405.
Bank of China: 271 Huguo Road (tel. 24529).

LANZHOU

Gansu Province
Northwest China

Lanzhou, the capital of Gansu Province, lies on the Yellow River, in the Longxi basin. The settlement has existed for over two millennia. It used to be an important outpost on the caravan route known as the "Silk Road" which linked China with Central Asia and the Roman Empire.

Gansu Province has been important for over 2,000 years because of the "corridor west of the river," or hexi zoulang as it is known in China. The Gansu or hexi (pronounced "her-shee") corridor runs northwest from the Yellow River between the high Qilian Mountains on the left and the Mongolian plateau on the right, to the deserts of the north. Since the days of the Qin (206–221 B.C.) this was the route traveled by merchants and traders, their caravanserai loaded with treasures from China. This was also the way into the heart of China for the pillaging hordes from the north. To protect the corridor, the Great Wall was extended under the Han (206 B.C.–A.D. 220) as far as Yunen, located in the far northwest of Gansu. About three-quarters of a million people were sent to populate the corridor.

Lanzhou became capital of a succession of tribal states during the troubled centuries that followed the decline of the Han. It was strategically important in the series of battles that took place between the invaders and the kingdom holding the pass. But during this time of turmoil, people became attracted to ideologies that satisfied their need for hope: Taoism developed into a religion; and Buddhism became the official religion in some of the northern "barbarian" states. Buddhist religious art flourished and shrines were built in monasteries, temples, caves, and on cliffs, many of which still exist today. From the fifth to the eleventh century, Dunhuang, beyond the Yumen Gate of the Great Wall, became a center in China for the study of Buddhism, drawing scholars and pilgrims from afar. During this period, artists and artisans created magnificent works of art; their creations are still to be seen in what are among the oldest known Buddhist shrines in China, dating from as early as A.D. 366.

The province has many major shrines at various points along the Gansu corridor. These were built over a period of 500 years, from the fourth century until the Buddhist persecutions of the late Tang Dynasty. The activity at these sites was revived under the Song and continued until the Mongols overran China in the thirteenth century. Little was added under the Yuan, although a few new caves appear to have been cut and decorated. When the Ming emperor Jia Jing (1522–1567) unleashed a reign of persecution against the Buddhists, religious art in the region declined. However, some redecoration took place under the Qing.

Today, Gansu Province has become a communications center for northwest China and a region with a well-developed industrial base. It has energy resources—crude oil and coal—and mineral resources—iron ore, nickel, copper, cobalt, silver, platinum, zinc, and manganese. In agriculture, wheat, millet, oats, kaoliang, soy beans, cotton, hemp, tobacco, and fruits are produced in the loess lands of the southwest, whereas in the Gansu corridor itself, only oasis agriculture based on irrigation is possible. Stock raising and animal husbandry are carried out in the foothills of the ranges.

Lanzhou has become a rail junction linking the northwest of China to the north and northeast, and the northwest to Central China. It is the principal industrial base of the northwest, possessing large chemical and oil refineries, nitrogenous fertilizer plants, and factories producing railway equipment, oilfield machinery, machine tools, and ball bearings. There is an aluminum-reduction plant, and a uranium-enrichment facility providing nuclear fuel for China's atomic weapons. These industrial plants spread for many miles along the banks of the Yellow River, and the pollution is appalling. Being in a basin with industry stretched out on either side, Lanzhou is guaranteed to have a high pollution count every day, for whichever way the wind blows, the industrial smog is carried right into the city.

EXPLORING LANZHOU

White Pagoda Mountain

The White Pagoda Mountain, Baitashan in Chinese, is on the north bank of the Yellow River. On the crest is the seven-tiered white pagoda, constructed of brick, built by Ming Emperor Jingtai (1450–1456). There is a park with many pavilions. A terrace looks out over the river and town to the south.

Five Spring Park

Five Spring Park is in the southeastern section of the city. Known in Chinese as the Wuquan Gongyuan, the park has five freshwater springs named Hui, Taoyue, Mozi, Ganlu, and Meng. There is an interesting temple in the park, which was originally constructed in 1347, known as the Junyuan or Source of Enlightenment Temple. You can see there a number of bronze statues of attendants to the Buddha, and bronze bell known as the Great Harmony Bell. There is a small restaurant and zoo in the vicinity.

Yan Tan Park

Located in the northeastern part of the city, Yan Tan Park features an artificial lake and swimming pool. Fruits and vegetables are cultivated in the region.

EXCURSIONS FROM LANZHOU

Bilingsi

Provided the water level is high enough, you can take a 3-hour boat ride up the Yellow River to the Bilingsi Buddhist Caves, about 35 miles from Lanzhou, near a town called Yongjing. The caves date from A.D. 513

but were rediscovered only in this century, after existing for hundreds of years as one of the most important places in China celebrating the Buddhist religion. The site of the upper monastery is breathtaking, with deep ravines, and sheer cliff faces rising high to a background of craggy mountains, an inspiring setting for the giant statue of the seated Buddha, carved in the Tang period. The lower monastery stretches along a valley to the north bank of the Yellow River, and boasts some remarkable Northern Wei Dynasty statues and magnificent wall paintings from the Song and Ming. CITS and the Shengli Hotel both organize bus tours, departing 7:30 A.M. Depending on the itinerary, the round-trip can take up to 10 hours, so consider taking along food and something to drink.

Labulengsi Monastery

One of the two great monasteries outside Tibet devoted to the Lamaist yellow sect of Buddhism, Labulengsi is located at Xiahe, about 55 miles as the crow flies southwest of Lanzhou, just inside the provincial border with Qinghai. Xiahe is on a tributary of the Yellow River and further upstream from Yongjing, where the Bilingsi Monasteries are located. The road from Lanzhou passes through Linxia and the way to Xiahe.

The monastery follows the traditions of Tibetan architecture, with the buildings set against a cliff face overlooking a river or plain. The style is harmonious in the Labulengsi, even though it was built without interruption for over 200 years, from 1710 to 1949. Eventually the Labulengsi became so important in the religious life of the western regions of China that its name was sometimes used to identify all the provinces around it. It exerted authority over other religious establishments in the region. Its authority stretched into Tibet itself and was exerted as far east as Beijing. At its most powerful period, it housed more than 3,000 lamas, the number in the other monasteries under its authority being as high as 20,000.

The Labulengsi is 110 miles (as the crow flies) from the second of the two great Lamaist yellow sect monasteries outside of Tibet—the Ta Er Monastery in Lushaer village, southwest of Xining, the capital of Qinghai Province. There is no road linking the two sites, and you must travel to Xining from Lanzhou to visit the Ta Er Monastery.

GANSU PROVINCE

Gansu Province possesses an enormous number of sites of interest to the visitor. From one end of the province to the other there are caves and temples containing priceless works of Buddhist religious art. Most of the sites are located near the old oases of the caravan route known for millennia as the Silk Road. Other Buddhist monasteries are located further afield in almost inaccessible areas. Finally, some of the finest remaining sections of the Great Wall are to be seen in Gansu. The most accessible of these sites are reviewed below.

Jiayuguan

The Pass of the Pleasant Valley, to give Jiayuguan its name in English, is about 315 miles northwest of Lanzhou. It is on the Lanzhou—Ürümqi rail link and only about 18 miles from Jiuquan airport (see below, *How to Get There*). You can make a stopover at the town on your way to the Dunhuang area.

The two attractions for visitors are the Great Wall and the Ming fortress built in 1372 during the reign of Emperor Hong Wu. The Great Wall used

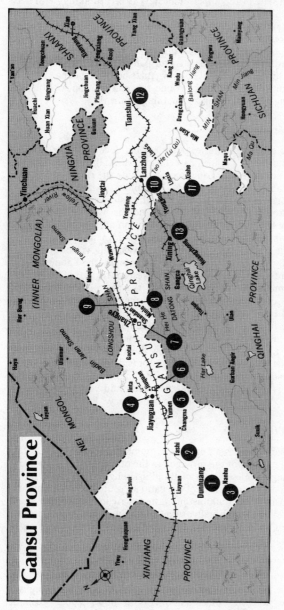

Gansu Province

Points of Interest

1) Mogao Caves
2) Yulinsi (Elm Forest) Caves
3) Qianfoya (Thousand Buddha) Caves
4) Great Wall and Ming Fortress
5) Changma Caves
6) Wenwushan Temples and Caves
7) Qingyang Caves
8) Matisi Monastery and Caves
9) Jintasi Monastery and Caves
10) Bilingsi Caves
11) Labulengsi Monastery
12) Maijishan Caves
13) Pagoda Lamasery

to end at Yumen (about 50 miles to the west of Jiayuguan) before the pass was abandoned under the Ming. The walls in the northwest region were originally constructed under the Han (206 B.C.–A.D. 220), and remains of the Han wall have been found near Dunhuang, but the portions of the wall standing at Jiayuguan (and at Yumen) date from the early Ming and are about six centuries old. There you can stand on the terrace of the gate tower and look back at the wall winding its way along the mountain ridges: to the south stand the snow-capped Qilian mountains, and to the west, the desert.

Jiayuguan once comprised an inner and outer city. The outer city is now a town with a population of about 100,000. The inner city, surrounded by a wall about 35 feet high, was a citadel housing the Chinese military commander, and was the last Chinese outpost on the Silk Road. Beyond it, travelers faced the dangers of the barbarian tribes and could not receive the protection of the Chinese state. Outside the west gate there is a stele with Chinese characters describing the Great Wall as "the greatest barrier under heaven"; it must have been a remarkable sight for travelers coming in from the desert at the end of their journey, and a moment of great anxiety for those leaving. Travelers, exiles, and disgraced officials often made inscriptions in the passage under the west gate, as they departed and left the protection of their homeland.

The Jiayuguan exhibition hall is worth visiting. There are a number of archaeological exhibits of interest, especially the objects dating from the Jin and the Wei dynasties (third to the sixth centuries A.D.), e.g., hand-painted bricks portraying scenes of everyday life in that era.

The magnificent treasures of Buddhist art located around Dunhuang have been described in the *Dunhuang* section of this book. The Dunhuang sites are situated in the far western region of Gansu Province, quite a distance from Lanzhou, and may be reached following a long train-and-bus journey (20–24 hours) from the provincial capital or by plane (4 hours).

PRACTICAL INFORMATION FOR LANZHOU

FACTS AND FIGURES. Lanzhou, capital of Gansu Province, has a population of 1.6 million, of which 1 million reside in the urban area proper of the city. It is located on approximately the same parallel of latitude as Jinan to the east, and Tokyo. Lanzhou is connected to Beijing by rail, via Yinchuan (Ningxi Hui Autonomous Region) and Hohhot (Inner Mongolia); to Chengdu and Kunming in the south; and to Ürümqi in the west. It is also connected by road to Lhasa in Tibet, through Qinghai Province. Air links are plentiful: there are flights to and from Beijing, Xian, Xining, Chengdu, Hami, Golmud, and Zhengzhou. Within Gansu Province there is an air service linking Lanzhou and Jiuquan.

WHEN TO GO. Winters are harsh and dry, January average temperatures ranging 14° F to 21° F and often falling to as low as –4° F. In the spring there are strong, dusty winds. The summer is dry but warm, average temperatures reaching 70–79° F in July. Rainfall is light throughout the year, the incidence of rain being highest in summer (9–12 days rain per month during July through September). Fall is the best time to visit, the days being pleasantly warm and the evenings cool but not cold.

HOW TO GET THERE. By plane. There are regular flights out of Beijing (fastest flight two hours); other flights service Lanzhou from Xining 1 hour 40 minutes, Yinchuan 1 hour 15 minutes, Xian 1 hour 20 minutes, Taiyuan 2½ hours, Baotou via Yinchuan 3 hours 20 minutes, Ürümqi 2 hours 25 minutes, Zhengzhou 2 hours 10 minutes, Chengdu 2 hours 15 minutes, and Golmud 2 hours. The flight to Jiuquan, the nearest airport in Gansu Province to the Dunhuang Buddhist caves takes 2 hours 15 minutes. CAAC (tel. 23432) 46 Dong-gang Xilu.

By train. The train from Beijing takes 36–37 hours, via the southern loop line that passes through Shijiazhuang, Zhengzhou, Luoyang, and Xian. Visitors usually stop over at some or all of these points along the way, spreading out the journey over 10–14 days. There is another express service by the northern loop, passing through Datong, Hohhot and Baotou in Inner Mongolia, and Yinchuan in Ningxia Hui. This journey takes just over 36 hours also. If you have plenty of time, the best course is to take the southern-loop route, stopping off along the way; then return, traveling from Lanzhou to Baotou by air before taking the train back to Beijing, stopping off *en route* at Hohhot, the capital of Inner Mongolia, and also at Datong in Shanxi Province to see the Yungang Caves. This journey could be just as easily done in the reverse direction.

From Lanzhou you can also fly or take the train to Ürümqi, capital of Xinjiang Uyger Autonomous Region. If you take the train, keep in mind that you will have the advantage of following the route of the old "Silk Road" in the comfort of your carriage. There are many sections of the Great Wall still standing along this corridor to the west, particularly between Huangyangzhen and Shandan. If you want to pass this area in daylight, you can do so by catching either the Beijing express (departs Lanzhou at 2:51 A.M.!) or the Shanghai express (departs Lanzhou 8:42 A.M.). However, on the Beijing express you pass the most interesting region between about 10:30 A.M. to 4 P.M., while on the Shanghai express you pass it between 4:30 and 10 P.M.

If you wish you can also get off at Jiayuguan to see the Great Wall and the Ming fortifications at this famous strategic pass at the western extremity of the Wall. If you plan to do this, you should perhaps avoid taking the Shanghai express from Lanzhou as it arrives at Jiayuguan at 2:28 A.M. The Beijing express arrives at 8:46 P.M.; there is a 5:30 P.M. train from Lanzhou which arrives at 12:49 P.M. next day, and this is probably the best train to take.

If you are getting off the train at Liuyuan to travel on to see the Buddhist caves, then for your own comfort, give preference to the express departing Lanzhou at 5:30 P.M. (it starts there). The other express from Zhengzhou will have been carrying passengers for over 24 hours when it departs Lanzhou at 3:30 P.M. The express from Shanghai will have been traveling 1½ days when it reaches Lanzhou to depart again at 8:42 A.M., so you can imagine what that may mean. But, all these trains can get you to Liuyuan in 24–26 hours and have you arrive at a convenient hour.

HOTELS. Visitors are lodged at the **Friendship Hotel** (tel. 30511), 14 Xijinxi Road, in the western area of Lanzhou and about a quarter of an hour bus journey from the city center. The hotel offers fairly standard rooms with big old bathrooms. The food in the dining room is only fair; both Chinese and Western dishes are served. Visitors also stay at the **Lanzhou Hotel** (tel. 22981), 204 West Donggang Road, about six miles from the railway station; it has 255 rooms and dining rooms serving Chinese, Moslem, and Western food.

Other hotels are the **Jincheng** (tel. 27931) at 363 Tianshui Road near the center of town (air-conditioned cars for hire); the **Shengli** at 133 Zhongshan Road; and the **Airport Hotel,** located 1½ hours by car from Lanzhou at the airport (50 miles from town).

RESTAURANTS. The best place to dine in Lanzhou is the **Lanzhou Canting,** a three-story restaurant on Jiuquan Road catering to foreign visitors. The food is good, certainly better than the hotel fare. Lamb and mutton is a regional specialty, and so is a fried bread called *mantou;* dishes which include petals of the lily (baihe) are favored by the locals.

TOURIST INFORMATION. CITS (tel. 49621) is next to the Lanzhou Hotel in Panxuan Road, about half a mile from the railway station. Look for the yellow CITS sign written in English. Their offices are in the building behind the bus garage (rooms 201/202). **CAAC** (tel. 23432, 23421), 46 Donggang Xilu, is a five-minute walk west of the Lanzhou Hotel. Hours are 7:30–11:30 A.M. and 3–6 P.M.

HOW TO GET AROUND. CITS arranges tours and excursions. Air-conditioned cars may be hired at the Jincheng Hotel in the center of town.

WHAT TO SEE. Parts of the old town are quaint and appeal to visitors. There are no sites of great historic interest, but visits to the **White Pagoda Mountain (Baitashan) Park** on the north bank of the Yellow River, and to the **Five Springs (Wuquan) Park** in the southern sector of the city, are worthwhile. The **Lanzhou Museum** has an interesting range of exhibits, featuring the famous "flying horse of Gansu" sculpture. Most people visit Lanzhou to make excursions. The nearest excursion is to the **Bilingsi Buddhist Caves,** about 35 miles upstream from Lanzhou and accessible by boat (3-hour journey) or by bus (two hours). Then there is the excursion to the far northwest of the province to the Dunhuang group of Buddhist caves and cliff carvings, located at 3 different sites. On the way to this group you can visit the famous pass of the Great Wall, at Jiayuguan, where a fine Ming fortress still stands. There are many other Buddhist caves and temples to visit in Gansu, including one of the 2 great Lama temples outside of Tibet.

MUSEUMS. The **Lanzhou Museum,** across the road from the Friendship Hotel, has interesting exhibits ranging from neolithic Yangshao pottery to items of recent date. The best-known exhibit is the "flying horse of Gansu," with a reproduction usually on display while the original is either being exhibited abroad or in the Imperial Palaces Museum in Beijing. There is an interesting reconstruction of a Han Dynasty (206 B.C.–A.D. 220) tomb, the skeleton of a mammoth, and fine examples of Zhou Dynasty (1122–247 B.C.) bronzes.

SHOPPING. Gansu is well known for its carpets and once had a reputation akin to that of the Ningxia Hiu region for the production of magnificent floor coverings destined for the finest palaces and houses of China. Old carpets are difficult to come across, but the new ones (not as good as those made in earlier years) are still good value. The style is similar to the Persian carpet and the colors are magnificent. Other products made from local wool, hides, and skins are good value; so too is brassware.

ENTERTAINMENT. Try to see the **Gansu Song and Dance Ensemble's** ballet *Tales of the Silk Road.* Set in Dunhuang during Tang Dynasty times, it conveys a colorful impression of what life was like along the "Silk Road" more than 1,000 years ago. In one scene the action is set in the Mogao Caves and features a female musician strumming a pipa while dancing (representing a famous Tang Dynasty mural that still exists). The theater performance will provide you with a vivid reminder of your visit to the caves.

USEFUL ADDRESSES AND TELEPHONE NUMBERS

CITS—209 Tianshui Road (tel. 26798 or 26181).
CAAC—46 Donggang Xilu (tel. 23431, 23421).

LHASA

Xizang Autonomous Region
Tibet

If Tibet is the "roof of the world," then its capital, Lhasa, is certainly the "city of the sun." Standing on a plain over 12,000 feet above sea level, surrounded by towering mountains, Lhasa is a town bathed in sunlight. In the old quarter, people go about their business as they have for centuries: farmers bring in produce for the market by donkey, vendors set up stalls, potters spread out their wares in the dust, and the crowds press into the small marketplace. Outside the temple, the devout murmur prayers, while those inside light yak butter, then prostrate themselves before a statue of the Buddha, Scriptures are chanted by holy men, and pilgrims spin their prayer wheels.

In the new quarter, life is different. So are the dwellings: barracks-like buildings replace the old stone houses of the old town, the newer buildings having been erected to house the Han Chinese who arrived in the wake of the People's Liberation Army. Now half a million Chinese live in Tibet, about one-third being troops. Tibet is a sensitive border area for the Chinese, sharing as it does a common boundary with India, Nepal, Bhutan, and Burma.

Both the old and the new quarters are dominated by the Potala standing high on Putuo Hill overlooking the town. Once the seat of the god-king of Tibetans, the Dalai Lama, today it is more a museum than a palace, as most of the lamas who once lived there have been dispersed and the Dalai Lama himself is in exile. However, it is still used for worship.

Tibet has suffered fluctuating fortunes over the centuries. Historical records reveal little about the region before the seventh century, when King Songzan Ganbu (A.D. 617–650) unified the area and introduced the Sanskrit alphabet. During the centuries that followed, Buddhism took root in Tibet, introduced from India into China by pilgrims traveling the "Silk Road" far to the north.

Buddhism was influenced by the local religion, called Bon, and developed into a form called Lamaism. By the tenth century, the religious movement began to assert political leadership as well. The monasteries were fortified, their estates grew, and the lamas began to assert total authority over their flock. Different religious sects vied for power. In 1572, a reincarnation of Zongkaba, the founder of the "yellow hat" sect devoted to religious reform, became the first Dalai Lama. The title was conferred by the leader of the Mongols who, at that time were still powerful north of the Great Wall, even though they had been driven out of China by the Ming two centuries before. The Dalai Lama in turn appointed the Panchen Lama, who ruled from Xigaze (227 miles west of Lhasa). But the sects were still in conflict and remained so until the Mongols intervened in 1641–42 to establish the authority of the fifth Dalai Lama and the yellow sect.

In the seventeenth century the Manchu invaders seized power in China and, in 1720 marched into Tibet. The seventh Dalai Lama ruled with the assistance of the Manchu garrison under the command of the viceroys from the court. Centuries later, when the Manchu rule began to weaken, the thirteenth Dalai Lama declared Tibet independent (1913). However, when the Chinese Communists took power in 1949, they reasserted the Manchu claim of sovereignty over the region, and seized Tibet by force in 1950. The Dalai Lama fled to India but returned after negotiations with the Chinese authorities.

During the 1950s, revolt simmered among the Tibetans and, in 1959, boiled over into armed rebellion. The Chinese army put down the revolt, and the Dalai Lama fled once again to India. In 1965, the Chinese established the Tibet Autonomous Region (or Xizang Zizhiqu). Many monasteries were closed, most of the lama population was dispersed, and the land distributed to the peasants and herdsmen—many of whom were still serfs. In the decade of the Cultural Revolution (1966–1976), many temples and monasteries were desecrated or destroyed. Now only a handful remain, but others are being repaired or rebuilt.

By the end of the 70s, new policies were introduced by Beijing, affecting political, economic, and religious affairs in Tibet, as part of a more relaxed administrative approach to national minorities throughout China. The authorities admitted that some excessive measures had been enforced in Tibet and other national minority territories, and attempts are being made to redress the situation. A more liberal administration has been introduced. Han cadres have been advised that greater respect is to be shown to Tibetans, that traditional ideas and practices are to be considered in the region's local code, and that restrictive policies concerned with agriculture and stockbreeding are to be changed.

In 1987 there were demonstrations by Tibetan monks and some of the people of Lhasa against Chinese rule in Tibet and, in particular, in favor of the Dalai Lama and independence. The demonstrations were put down severely by the Chinese authorities, and some monks and demonstrators were killed and others injured. Further demonstrations and deaths occurred in 1988.

Lamaism under Communism

After China took Tibet in 1950, the power of the monasteries was reduced, some monasteries were closed, and many lamas were turned over to "productive labor." The Chinese authorities say that the Tibetan ruling class was feudal and repressive, and that most of the population lived in impoverished slavery. Yet, even in 1960 there were still about 2,500 active monasteries in Tibet housing about 110,000 lamas. It was not until the period known as the Cultural Revolution that the greatest damage was inflicted upon Tibetan religious life. Temples and monasteries were pillaged, portable treasures removed, and countless sites destroyed. Only the massive logs put up to block the Potala's inner gateways saved the monastery from desecration, although the outer vestibules were severely damaged.

Chinese authorities now admit the desecration took place and are attempting to repair the damage. They have not revealed how many monasteries were destroyed, nor do they elaborate on what happened to the trove of priceless religious art, ancient manuscripts, and hoards of gold that were held in the monasteries.

Followers of the Dalai Lama say that now only 10 monasteries remain open and about 1,000 lamas practice their vocation. Followers say that they are concerned over the declining numbers of the *sangha,* or congregation of monks, one of the three jewels of Buddhism (the other two being the Buddha himself, and the *dharma,* or Buddhist law). They say that the lamas are required to study Communist doctrines in the monastery, the study and practice of Buddhism being permitted only in spare time. Only by accepting Chinese Communist policies, they say, can the lamas practice their religion at all.

On their side, the Chinese say that the former slaves are now free men; that food, clothing, housing, health services, and schooling are now available throughout Tibet, and that exploitation has ended. To emphasize the nature of the former régime, visitors are shown the torture chambers, the cells where prisoners were once eaten alive by scorpions, and the ritual objects made of human bones, all proof, the Chinese say, of the vicious nature of the theocracy.

It is hard to know just what the past means to Tibetans today. In winter, sheltering inside mud houses, warmed by a fire of brushwood, they appear to live as they have done for centuries. In spring, they emerge and are seen in the towns wearing their sheepskin coats and silver daggers. In summer, they follow the herds to higher altitudes, milking their animals and making butter in wooden churns. At days' end they take the black wool tents from the pony carts and make camp to keep out the night cold. Few observers contest that the Tibetans are materially better off; but most would question the state of their spiritual health. Followers of the Dalai Lama contend that the roots of Buddhism in Tibet are too deep and persuasive to wither. And a stroll through Lhasa provides evidence of this view: many Tibetan pilgrims praying inside and outside the temples are young. So, while the Chinese authorities continue to show greater tolerance of religious observance—as they are doing at present—Lamaist Buddhism will continue to survive in Tibet. In this situation, the major point of contention is the role of the absent Dalai Lama.

Dalai Lama

At Bylakuppe, site of the new Sera Monastery in the Mysore district of India, the fourteenth Dalai Lama of Tibet holds a religious service, sitting on a raised platform, surrounded by images of the Buddha and votive lamps, and facing hundreds of monks clothed in traditional saffron and burgundy robes. Together they offer prayers, led by a monk who chants with such a resonance that he could be calling the faithful in Lhasa, some 1,300 miles away.

Dalai is a Mongolian word meaning ocean, while *Lama* is Tibetan for man of profound wisdom. Thus, Dalai Lama literally means "a man whose wisdom is as deep as the ocean." The title was first used in 1572 and conferred by the Mongolian chieftan Altan Khan. The present Dalai Lama's seat in Dharamsala represents what is often described as a government-in-exile, although India does not recognize it as such. Yet to the 110,000 refugees who fled through the narrow mountain passes to avoid Chinese control of their homeland, it is. Most of the refugees have stayed in India, some 80,000 of them, while another 7,000 reside in Bhutan, closer to Lhasa. Others reside in Switzerland.

The Dalai Lama and many followers fled Tibet into India in 1959 through Arunchal Pradesh, then known as the North Eastern Frontier Agency. God-king to six million Tibetans living mainly in Tibet, Qinghai, Sichuan, and Yunnan provinces, the Dalai Lama escaped when the uprising against the Chinese failed. The revolt occurred just nine years after the People's Liberation Army first marched into Tibet. Contact was resumed in 1978. Then, in 1979, a fact-finding mission led by the Dalai Lama's elder brother was allowed to visit Tibet. A second and third mission followed in 1980. While the second mission was investigating conditions in their homeland, they encountered demonstrations in support of the Dalai Lama, one such demonstration being witnessed by a group of foreign journalists. Negotiations between both sides are continuing. Although Tibetans hope that the Dalai Lama will one day return to the homeland, many appear to have given up hope of an independent Tibet. In 1989 the Dalai Lama was awarded the Nobel Prize for Peace.

EXPLORING LHASA

The Potala Palace

Potala is a Sanskrit word meaning Buddha's Mountain. The Potala Palace built on this sacred mountain (Putuo Hill) is a rare piece of architecture of traditional Tibetan style. Built in the seventh century by King Songzan Ganbu—spelled Srongbtdan Sgam-po in Tibet—the palace burned down after being struck by lightning in the eighth century and a second palace was destroyed in a war during the ninth century. The Potala that stands today is really in the form of two palaces, each built in the seventeenth century by the fifth Dalai Lama (1617–1682). Construction of the White Palace was begun in 1645 and by 1653 the Dalai Lama and his court had moved in. Construction of the Red Palace began 37 years later and was completed in 1693, costing 2.1 million taels of silver. The Potala Palace comprises a series of magnificently decorated prayer rooms, sutra libraries, hallways, and antechambers; it houses priceless treasures of gold, silver and precious stones.

The Potala has 13 stories and rises 330 feet (110 meters) in height, measuring over 1,000 feet (360 meters) from east to west. Over 7,000 serfs worked daily on the construction, but many more engaged in quarrying stone and felling trees in the nearby mountains. So much mortar for the palace walls was excavated from behind the hill on which the palace stands that a huge crater was created. This was filled with water and became known as the **Dragon King Pool.** The Palace walls lean inward and the windows are lacquered in black, to create an illusion of great height. The Potala reputedly has over 1,000 rooms housing about 200,000 statues.

The front façade of the Potala faces south. Visitors are usually driven up a road at the rear of the palace to avoid any discomfort in climbing the zigzag staircase at the front. If you do enter by the front stairs, take the entrance at the eastern gate and walk to the **East Terrace,** or Deyangshar. Religious celebrations and Cham dances used to be performed here. On the eastern side of the platform is the seminary formerly housing the senior monks; on the western side stand the chanting halls and dormitories where the palace lamas lived.

White Palace. You then continue upward along a winding corridor to enter the **East Main Hall,** with its 64 pillars. This is the biggest hall in the White Palace and was the site of ceremonies for the choice of a new spiritual leader. When a Dalai Lama died, it was here that the names of infants, born at exactly the moment of his death, were placed in a gold vase. One name was withdrawn, the baby representing the Dalai Lama's reincarnation and therefore his successor. (The vase is now displayed at the Norbulingka Museum.)

The living quarters of the Dalai Lama are to be found at the top of the White Palace. Inside there are prayer halls, libraries for the Buddhist sutras, meeting rooms, sitting rooms and bedrooms. As you enter, notice the maces hanging on the gate; these used to be covered with tiger skin, a symbol of supreme authority. North of the sutra hall is the throne room where the Dalai Lama would sit while chanting holy scriptures. There you will see drums made of skin and wine vessels made from human skulls.

Red Palace. In the **West Main Hall,** you will find the Hall of Sacrifice, the largest building in the Red Palace, which contains the stupas housing the salt-dried and embalmed remains of eight of fourteen Dalai Lamas (the fifth; and the seventh to the thirteenth, inclusive). The eight stupas are of varying sizes; the largest stands almost 49 feet (15 meters) high and contains the body of the fifth Dalai Lama. According to monastery records, the gold used to coat this stupa weighs between 110,000 and 119,000 taels (about four and one-quarter tons). The jewels inlaid on it are believed to be worth even 10 times more than the gold leaf. A number of incense burners and "ever-burning" butter lamps of gold and silver, stand before the stupa along with other priceless sacrificial vessels.

The oldest building in the Potala is the **Guanyin Hall,** in the northeastern section of the Red Palace. Records suggest that it was the nuptial chamber of King Songzan Ganbu and his Tang Dynasty princess. In the highest hall of the Potala, there is a painting of Emperor Quin Long (1736–1796). A tablet stands in front of it, conveying wishes of longevity to the Emperor, written in Chinese, Tibetan, Manchu, and Mongolian scripts.

From this hall you may climb to the roof of the Red Palace and look over the steep walls. A dangerous contest used to be held here once. Leather ropes more than 300-feet (100-meters) long would be thrown over the walls. Local Tibetans used to skim down the ropes, headfirst, holding a white flag in each hand. Any man able to repeat this feat three or four times was exempted from labor in the fields. Many died during this spectacle, held on the second day of the Tibetan calendar.

Some practical advice: Take a flashlight because many of the halls are dimly lit; photography is not allowed, although it is sometimes permitted if you pay a fee (known to go as high as ¥150 per photograph!); smoking is prohibited; always walk around halls and sacred objects such as shrines in a clockwise direction to avoid offending religious sensitivities; access to the Potala is by prior arrangement to tour groups at almost all times; independent travelers can get in on Wednesdays and Saturdays, 10 A.M. to 4 P.M. (but on arrival in Lhasa check both the days of access and visiting hours).

Jokhang Temple

The temple is located in the very center of the old city. Founded more than 1,300 years ago, the Jokhang Temple, or Dazhousi in Chinese, is a mixture of Tibetan, Indian, Nepalese, and Chinese architecture. Only the great hall and the first two stories remain of the original temple, additions being made under the Yuan, Ming, and the Qing. It is one of Tibet's holiest shrines.

Above the entrance façade stand two gilded copper dagobas, between them a gilded prayer wheel supported by two gilded animals (goats). The external pillars are protected by dark wooden screens hanging from an overhead balustrade. Outside, pilgrims prostrate themselves before the temple at all times of the day.

Inside, there stands a gilded bronze statue of the Sakyamuni Buddha. Lavishly decorated it sits on a golden throne between pillars of solid silver.

It is said to have been brought to Lhasa by the Chinese princess, Wen Cheng, in the seventh century when she married the king who first unified Tibet and pushed its border into Yunnan and as far as the outskirts of the Tang Empire. Other statues of the Buddha are to be seen, as well as statues of the king (Songzan Ganbu) and his wives (one being the Tang princess, the other a Nepalese princess). There are over 200 statues in the temple, but you may not be able to see them all, because access to the other floors is sometimes restricted. A flashlight will make your visit more rewarding.

Drepung Monastery

The third famous site of Lhasa is the Drepung Monastery six miles west of Lhasa. Standing on a high cliff, its many tiers leaning into a steep mountain face, the monastery is built in traditional Tibetan style. Founded in 1416, it was one of the centers of the yellow-hat sect founded by Zongkaba, and became in its time the largest of the three great monasteries near Lhasa, housing 10,000 lamas. Only a few hundred lamas live there now. The temples of the monastery are lavishly decorated with statues of the Buddha, of Zongkaba, and others of the Buddhist pantheon. There are some superb frescoes in the Great Hall and surrounding halls. The library used to house a priceless collection of old and rare sutras; it is not known whether they are still intact. The funerary pagodas of the second, third, and fourth Dalai Lamas are housed in the monastery. The monastery is open to worshipers.

Norbulinka

The Norbulinka, in what is now the People's Park, is about two miles west of Lhasa. It used to be the summer palace of the Dalai Lama with many halls and temples, the earliest of which were constructed for the seventh Dalai Lama (1708–1757). The buildings were badly damaged by the Chinese army in 1959 and again by the Red Guards. The New Palace, constructed for the fourteenth Dalai Lama, was completed in 1956. This part of the Norbulinka has been turned into a museum. It is also possible to visit the Dalai Lama's private apartments. The Norbulinka is closed on Sundays. Visiting hours are 9–11:30 A.M. and 3:30–5 P.M. Photography is not allowed.

The Old Quarter

When you visit the Jokhang Temple, make sure you leave enough time to wander around the old quarter and the Barkhor Bazaar. The streets have grown up around the temple in an octagonal shape, hence the name given to Octagon Street itself. The old houses are built of stone, have decorated doors and windows, and almost everyone has something to sell. There is a market area where all sorts of goods are on sale: silver bowls, jewelry, traditional woven goods, rugs, woolen articles, daggers, tunics, sashes, hats, boots, and so on. Beware of the fake turquoise made from turquoise powder mixed with a binding medium.

Sky Burial Site

Tibetans dispose of the dead in four ceremonial ways: burial by fire, water, earth, and sky. In fire burial, the corpse is smeared with yak butter, laid on a pire and then set alight. Disposal by this means is reserved for temple lamas because wood is scarce and the ceremony expensive. In water burial, the body is cut up and fed to the fish. This form of disposal is reserved for beggars and those with serious diseases. (Tibetans don't eat fish.) Burial in the earth is reserved for criminals or the destitute.

In sky burial (the method used for the majority of people) the body is skinned, the bones removed and crushed, and the remains laid out at the site. Usually, several bodies are prepared at the same time. Vultures, hawks, and crows swoop down and devour the bodies, watched by the families of the deceased.

In Lhasa the sky-burial site is about three miles north of the town and a short distance south of the Sera Monastery. Access to the site has been closed to visitors following angry scenes between relatives of the deceased and overzealous photographers. Authorities are planning to build viewing towers so that foreign visitors can view the grisly ceremony without disturbing the participants. There is a fifth form—embalming—but this is practiced to preserve the remains of holy figures such as the Dalai Lama.

EXCURSIONS FROM LHASA

Sera Monastery

Sera Monastery is the second of what were once called the three great monasteries of Tibet (the others being Drepung and Ganden). Founded in 1419 by the brother of Zongkaba and located three to four miles north of Lhasa, it is built into the side of a mountain in a style different to that of the great Drepung Monastery. It houses a giant statue of the Buddha, richly decorated with gold and precious stones. There are numerous other statues of artistic merit; a number of fine frescoes—particularly the one representing Tibetan Wheel of Life (Samsara); and some ancient silk *tankas*. Tibetans still worship in the temples of the monastery.

Ganden Monastery

Ganden is the third of the former three great monasteries of Lhasa. Its partially rebuilt remains stand 37 miles east of Lhasa. Founded in 1409, and once the most powerful monastery in all Tibet, it was perched high on a mountain top, the repository of magnificent statues, frescoes, carvings, and treasures of antiquity. The original monastery was either razed by the Chinese army during the invasion of Tibet, or destroyed by the Red Guards during the Cultural Revolution. Some temples have been rebuilt to accommodate a few hundred of the 4,000 monks that once lived there. The views from Ganden are superb.

Lhasa to Kathmandu

You can make the trip from Lhasa to Kathmandu along "the international highway on top of the world" either as a three-day excursion by bus (through CITS) or by organizing a group of independent travelers and hiring a jeep, car, or minibus for what is usually a four-day tour.

The CITS tour usually stops overnight at Xigaze and also at Zhangmu on the border. A private four-day tour would probably make a two-night stop at Xigaze to allow more time for sightseeing in the region, with a third night spent at either Lhaze, Xegar, or Tingri.

The **South Route** to Xigaze is usually preferred because of the superb scenery. You cross through two passes each above 16,000 feet and between them follow the road along the northern shore of beautiful **Lake Yumzho Hum.**

The town of **Gyangze** rests in a river valley yet stands at an altitude of 12,465 feet. A ridge (with the ruins of the Dzong fort on top) divides the town. The town's **Palkhor Lamasery** is being rebuilt; it possesses a large white dagoba known as the **Kumbum,** built in 1427, which has some superb murals inside. The 130-mile trip to Gyangze takes about six hours in a four-wheel drive jeep, and about 12 hours in a bus.

The journey continues to **Xigaze** (about 62 miles farther east and a three-hour comfortable drive) for an overnight stay. The town—Tibet's second largest, with a population of about 40,000—stands at an elevation of 12,800 feet. The major sight is **Tashilumpo Monastery** (see below), religious seat of the Panchen Lamas. Fourteen miles south of Xigaze stand the remains of the **Shalu Monastery,** founded in 1040, but razed in 1966; and nine miles to the west are the remains of the **Narthang Monastery,** founded in 1153 and similarly destroyed.

From Xigaze there is a 220-mile journey westward to **Sakya Monastery,** which governed the Tibetan nation in the thirteenth century. You must take a two-hour round-trip off the main road to reach the site. The monastery is like a fortress, its walls painted red-brown on top and gray on the base. Founded in 1071, it was the foremost monastery in Tibet until eclipsed by the Tashilumpo Monastery in 1447. Only the foundations on the first monastery remain, but three halls of the thirteenth-century structure still exist.

From Sakya village, the journey proceeds to **Lhaze,** then to the Chinese checkpoint of **Xegar** (or **New Tinggri**) where there is a turn-off to the ruins of **Rongbuk Monastery,** once the highest monastery in the world (16,500 feet). The road provides magnificent views of the northeast face of Mount Everest (Qomolangma). In Xegar itself there are the ruins of the **Shining Crystal Monastery,** as well as the ruins of an old fort.

About 37 miles due west is the pretty village of **Old Tingri,** famous for its views of the Himalayas. From here there is a spectacular descent of over 10,000 feet in altitude in just 60 miles to the border post of **Zhangmu.**

Yalin Farm

Some visitors undertake the five-hour journey to the Yalin (Emancipation) Farm on the Qingzang plateau, northeast of Lhasa. The Tibetans meet you wearing their colorful national costumes, and entertain you with song and dance while you savor such delicacies as yak-milk cheese and yogurt. If travel on bumpy roads bothers you, think twice about this excursion. Although you will see some fine scenery on the way, the paved road gives way after an hour and a half to a rough track, and you will get bounced around a great deal.

Xigaze

The **Tashilumpo Monastery,** former seat of the Panchen Lama, is located at Xigaze, 227 miles west of Lhasa. You encounter superb scenery, passing on the way the beautiful **Lake Yumzho Hum,** standing at an elevation of 6,430 feet (1,960 meters) and surrounded by snow-covered mountains. The journey takes about 14 hours. The monastery, known as Zhaxilhunbu to the Chinese, was founded by the first Dalai Lama.

Once a sanctuary for 3,000 monks, there are today only about 600 in residence. The Panchen Lama, spiritual rival to the Dalai Lama, is recognized by the Chinese authorities as the political head of the Lamaist faith, a recognition not shared by the Dalai Lama and his followers.

The monastery was damaged during the Cultural Revolution but was later repaired and reopened. The monastery is the home of an enormous bronze Buddha, the largest such statue in Tibet.

PRACTICAL INFORMATION FOR LHASA

TRAVEL WARNING. Because of periodic political disturbances, tourist centers in Tibet, including Lhasa, are regularly declared off limits to freelance travelers; only organized tour groups are then permitted entry into Tibet. Independent travelers should determine whether Tibet is out of bounds before attempting to go there. Sometimes even organized tour groups are stopped.

HEALTH WARNING. Unless you are remarkably fit, the high altitude is bound to have an effect on your body. The usual symptoms are: headaches, chest pains, and brief periods of nausea. Smoking cigarettes and drinking alcohol worsen the effect. When climbing stairs you may become breathless, your heart will thump, and you will have to make frequent stops to catch your breath. Oxygen bags are usually carried in vehicles and retained in the rooms of guest houses, so that when you feel dizzy you can inhale from a bag several times to relieve the condition. There are also medicated oils to rub on your temple and around your nostrils; these appear to help.

Visitors are sometimes subjected to a medical check in China before permission is given to visit Lhasa (although this practice is in decline). If a medical test is carried out, and you are found to have a respiratory or heart condition, you will not be permitted to travel to Lhasa. High blood pressure or a common cold may also rule you out.

FACTS AND FIGURES. Lhasa, the capital of Tibet, lies only 100 miles (160 km.) to the north of the Sino-Indian border, at an altitude of 12,008 feet, or 3,660 meters. Lhasa is much closer to New Delhi than to Beijing. The city has more than 600,000 inhabitants, more than half the total number of people who live in the whole province.

Tibet, or Xizang Autonomous Region, as it is known to the Chinese, is second in area only to Xinjiang, occupying about 471,700 square miles, but with the smallest population of any province. Its southern border forms an international frontier with India, Nepal, Bhutan, and Burma. The frontier is formed by a natural boundary of huge mountains, the tallest being Mount Everest, or Qongmolangma, as it is known to the Chinese, rising to a height of 29,140 feet (8,882 meters).

The Tibetan highlands combine with those of Qinghai Province to form the highest and most extensive plateau on earth. The Qinghai-Tibet plateau's average altitude is 13,120 feet (4,000 meters) above sea level. Geologists say it is also the youngest plateau on earth, having been pushed up from the sea about 40 million years ago, a relatively recent time in geological terms.

The table shows the weather pattern in Lhasa during the year.

Lhasa Average Temperature and Rainfall

	Temperature Average (°F)	Monthly Rainfall (in inches)
January	27.8	——
February	33.4	——
March	39.7	——

	Temperature Average (°F)	Monthly Rainfall (in inches)
April	46.9	0.2
May	54.7	0.8
June	59.9	2.9
July	58.8	5.6
August	57.4	5.9
September	55.0	2.3
October	46.6	0.2
November	35.4	——
December	28.6	——

WHEN TO GO. The best time to visit Tibet is in April through August, i.e., spring and summer. In June, July, and August, the summer temperatures—tempered by the high altitude—are mild and rarely exceed the mid-80s (i.e., 30° C). They also are the months of the higher rainfall (average 3–6 inches), but the showers occur mainly during the night, leaving the days clear and sunny. Indeed Lhasa is often called "sunshine city," a reputation well earned by its average of 3,005 hours of sunshine per year. However, whenever the rain comes, it does increase the oxygen content of the air, thereby alleviating the symptoms of "mountain sickness" that many visitors develop. Warm clothing must be taken to Lhasa, because when it does rain during the day the temperature can drop quickly to around 45° F (7–8° C). Furthermore, the mornings and evenings can be chilly.

Winter is a long, dry season in Tibet with very cold temperatures dropping to lows around −12° F (−24° C). You will need plenty of warm clothing and you should adopt the local custom of dressing in layers of clothes to keep the cold out. Thick-soled shoes or boots, good gloves, and a hat that protects the ears are all essential. Some visitors take their own hot-water bottle.

HOW TO GET THERE. By plane. There are domestic air services to Gonggar airport (90 minutes by taxi/bus ride from Lhasa) from Chengdu, Golmud, and Xian. The flights from Chengdu—the usual starting point for visitors—depart daily at 7 A.M. and 12:25 P.M. Flight duration is 2 hours. The airports are about 800 miles apart; and the difference in altitude about 11,500 feet. The highest peak that you fly over is Mount Namche Barwa, its peak being 25,432 feet above sea level. The flight to Lhasa from Beijing on Sunday is sometimes direct and sometimes stops over in Chengdu.

Flights to Lhasa from Golmud depart at 9:15 A.M. Tuesdays and Saturdays, arriving at 11:25 A.M. Flights from Xian depart Tuesdays and Saturdays at 5:45 A.M., arriving at Golmud at 8:30 A.M., before leaving at 9:15 A.M. for Lhasa. Independent travelers should note that it has proven difficult in the past to get any seats on the Xian-Golmud-Lhasa flights, and also that the schedule is unreliable.

Flights are sometimes cancelled because Chinese authorities will not allow planes to take off if the weather is inclement, so your *arrival or departure* can be delayed one or more days. If your departure is delayed from Lhasa, you will probably be asked to pay for any extra days' accommodation at the guest house. You can sometimes negotiate a 50 percent cut, but rarely will you be able to stay over at no cost—unless you like camping out.

An international air link between Katmandu (in Nepal) and Lhasa operates Wednesday and Saturday until November 30; flight time is 55 minutes. The weekly service on Saturday from Hong Kong to Chengdu allows a connection from Lhasa the following day, weather permitting.

By bus. Lhasa is connected to adjacent provincial capitals by road. The Qinghai-Tibet road was completed in 1954, the Sichuan-Tibet road in the same year, the Xinjiang-Tibet road in 1957, and the Yunnan-Tibet road in 1976.

The bus journey from Golmud in Qinghai Province to Lhasa, a journey of 720 miles, is for the strong hearted. The bus takes 35–55 hours, breakdowns are frequent, and snow storms occur at the high passes at any time of the year. In Tibet, the bus makes a short stop at Amdo (about 40 miles beyond the Qinghai-Tibet border), Nagqu, about 60 miles further on, and at Damxung. Passengers must provide their own food. Modern Japanese buses make the Golmud–Lhasa trip in about 30 hours.

The **Chengdu-Lhasa** bus journey is not officially open to travelers, but has been undertaken by some hardy souls. The bus passes through beautiful scenery along dangerous mountain roads and can take anything from one to three weeks to arrive in Lhasa.

Travelers entering China from Nepal can take a bus or minibus from Kathmandu to Lhasa on a group tour. The 3-day journey is organized by CITS-authorized tour operators. The bus makes overnight stops at Zhangmu (or Kasa) on the border, and at Xigaze. The 560-mile journey is undertaken on roads that are mostly unpaved, the first 60 miles ascending about 10,000 feet in altitude, and reaching over 17,000 feet at the highest pass. Most visitors prefer to undertake this arduous journey in the reverse direction after getting used to the higher altitudes around Lhasa (12,008 feet). Sometimes the journey takes about five days because of landslides.

By train. The railway line to Lhasa is not yet complete and so trains cannot yet undertake the steep climb to the city. When finished, the Qinghai-Tibet Line as it is called, will be the highest railway route in the world, about 575 miles of it lying at an elevation of between 13,000–16,500 feet (4,000–5,000 meters). It will pass from Lhasa through Lhünzhub, Damxung, Nagqu—all in Tibet—through Golmud, Gangca, and Xining in Qinghai, and will be 1,270 miles long (2,049 kilometers). Don't expect to make reservations in the next decade.

HOTELS. The 486-room **Holiday Inn Lhasa Hotel** (tel. 22221, cable 7391, telex 68010 or 68011) at 1 Minzu Road, near the Norbulinka Palace to the west of the city, is Lhasa's first hotel of international standard with central heating, airconditioning, and TV. Each room has oxygen equipment. The hotel has two restaurants, a coffee shop, a teahouse, and a banquet hall.

At press time, foreign visitors were permitted to stay only at the Holiday Inn Lhasa. While other guest houses in Lhasa have been declared off-limits, they are listed here in the event they are reopened to foreigners in future.

The **Tibet Guest House** (tel. 23738 or 23729, telex 68013), also on Minzu Road, is under Tibetan management, its 215 rooms decorated in Tibetan style, each with bathroom, telephone, and TV. The exterior of the building bears a resemblance to the Potala Palace.

The **Lhasa Guest House** (tel. 22225, 23168) at Qu San Suo is 6 miles northwest of Lhasa. Run by CITS and often referred to as "Guest House no. 3," it has been the mainstay hotel in Lhasa for package-tour groups. While it offers good meals and is quiet, it suffers from being too far from the sights of Lhasa. **Guest House No. 1** (tel. 22184) provides spartan accommodations but is conveniently located midway between the Potala and the Jokhang Temple. One building provides dormitory accommodations and communal washrooms; the other has double rooms with cold running water and access to a hot-water bath house. **Guest House no. 2** (tel. 23196), at Yanhe Dong Lu on the eastern extremity of Lhasa, has a small but pleasant older section and a new annex with more modern facilities. Two hostels, **Snowlands** (tel. 23687) and **Banak Shol** (tel. 23829), have dormitory accommodations and rudimentary toilet facilities. The nearby **Kirey Hotel** has spartan accommodations but good showers.

RESTAURANTS. A number of restaurants have opened in Lhasa in recent years in response to the increased number of visitors. However, be warned that the "masses" restaurants outside the hotels practice dubious hygiene and have some unusual features. For example, beggars, cripples, and dogs sometimes hang around the tables waiting for leftovers. The best-known place is the **Dharkay** on Linkuo Lu near the boot factory (ownership not connected). Another place is the **Sichuan** on Xingfu Dong Lu, opposite the Banakshol hostel. Just along the street and to the west stands the **Tasty Restaurant** and, opposite, is the **Halal,** which serves Moslem dishes.

For local food, try yoghurt and cheese made from the milk of sheep, goat, or yak; noodles made from tsampa—a coarse flour made from barley; yak meat—which has a flavor and texture similar to the American bison; and chang—the gray Tibetan beer made from barley. If the beer is not to your taste, try Tibetan tea, which is brought in from neighboring Yunnan, but flavored during the brewing with yak butter. The result, more like soup than tea, is nutritious.

TOURIST INFORMATION. CITS (tel. 22980, 24406) is located at the Holiday Inn and the Lhasa Guest House. Open Monday through Saturday; 9 A.M.–noon and

3:30–6:30 P.M. Land cruisers and minibuses may be hired with a driver, but the rates—based on a per-kilometer charge—are expensive.

CAAC (tel. 22417) is at 88 Jiefang Road, opposite the eastern end of the Potala and close to the bus station.

PSB (tel. 23170) is on Zhongxue Lu, across the stream from the western end of the Potala. The office will provide an extension to your visa if required. Hours: 9 A.M.–12:30 P.M. and 4–6:30 P.M. Closed Sunday.

Nepal Consulate (tel. 22880) at 13 Norbilinka Road is just to the northeast of the Norbulinka Palace. The consulate can provide a visa for Nepal, usually within a day. You must present two passport-type photographs. An exit stamp provided by the PSB is usually not necessary (but always check). A one-month visa, valid for entry within three months, is usually granted within 24 hours.

HOW TO GET AROUND. Transportation to and from Gonggar airport is free on presentation of your plane ticket. The journey by bus takes 90 minutes and the road is paved all the way. On arrival, don't wait for your luggage; it will be delivered to your hotel (tour groups) or to the CAAC office (independent travelers). Luggage usually arrives in Lhasa 1½ hours after you do. Holiday Inn Lhasa offers its guests a shuttle bus service to and from the airport.

Bus. Travel by means of the public bus system is not a practical proposition because of the infrequent and unreliable service.

Taxis and hire cars. Apart from the hotels, there are a handful of companies offering cars, land-cruisers, and minibuses for hire. The vehicles range from new cars to battered hulks. Rates are expensive and are based on the mileage covered. All are hired with a local driver. When hiring from the companies, write out the itineraries, indicate all the stops that you wish to make en route, how long you wish to stay there, and time and date of departure and arrival. Get the company to sign it before paying a deposit, and the driver to sign it prior to departure. Pay only half the amount in advance, or less, as a deposit.

CITS arranges transport for visitors traveling in groups.

Bicycles. Touring Lhasa by bicycle is an excellent way of sightseeing, for the city and surrounding valley is mostly flat. However, be careful not to overexert yourself in the high altitudes. Bikes are rented by the no. 1 and no. 3 Guest Houses, the Snowlands Hotel, and the Banak Shol Hotel. Always check your bike carefully before riding off, especially the tires and brakes. Always lock your bike, using two locks if possible. Keep it in sight at all times, even when it is locked. Bicycle theft is common in Lhasa, and you will lose your deposit if you do not return the one you hired.

WHAT TO SEE. Everyone who goes to Tibet visits the "three sites of Lhasa." The best known landmark is the **Potala,** once the very center of Tibetan Buddhist life, formerly the seat of the Dalai Lama, and now a museum. The building and palaces comprising the Potala are known all over the world. The **Jokhang Temple** is one of Tibet's holiest shrines. There you may see Tibetan people prostrate before the edifice, murmuring prayers and fingering beads. Then there is the **Drepung Monastery,** at one time one of the largest cloisters in the world and the religious center for over 10,000 lamas. The ancient stone building dates from 1416. These three constitute the "three sites." You might also care to visit the **Norbulinka Palace,** surrounded by parks and streams; it was formerly the Dalai Lama's summer palace.

You can also journey to the grasslands of the Tibetan plateau, visit an agricultural commune, and see one of the world's highest lakes. Visits to a school and a carpet factory can also be arranged.

PHOTOGRAPHY HINTS. The atmosphere around Lhasa is dry and relatively dust free and the ultraviolet radiation high. When taking photographs in sunlight during the middle of the day, you should "shutter down," i.e., use a diaphragm level one unit smaller than your light meter shows, or else your negatives will be overexposed. An ultraviolet filter is recommended.

When you are in the lamaseries you will be asked to pay ¥ 100–150 every time you depress the shutter, a sum that usually depresses the photographer too! The charge is made to "compensate for the damage done by the photoflash."

MUSEUMS. Many of the monasteries and palaces have museums or are "living museums" and have been described. Visitors are often taken to the **Lhasa Exhibition Hall,** which features displays devoted mainly to China's "liberation" of Tibet and provides the Party rationale underlying China's occupation of this ancient land.

SHOPPING. Handicrafts are an excellent buy: colorful rugs with indigenous designs make fine souvenirs; so, too, do the crafted ornamental knives, wooden bowls, and wool aprons. Tibetan boots are popular.

Small shops and stalls sell antiques, art pieces, and decorative ware. Jewelry made from precious metals and adorned with jade, turquoise, and amethyst, is widely sought after by visitors.

You must bargain adamently (but with good humor) with individuals, with stall holders, and in the shops of the **Barkhor Bazaar.** The Tibetans enjoy bargaining and will expect you to haggle with them. However, prices are fixed at the **Friendship Store** (upstairs in the Nong Ken Ting Department Store on Renmin Road) and at the **General Department Store** (tel. 23380) on Jiefang Road. Tibetan handicrafts are on sale at the **Store for Tourist Products** on Xingfu Dong Lu, while canvas tents and awnings can be purchased or made to order at the **Lhasa Tent and Banner Factory** off Xingfu Dong Lu.

ENTERTAINMENT. Documentary films—usually devoted to Tibet, its culture, life, and geography—are shown regularly. Excellent films are screened on the ascent of mountains in the region, such as Qomolangma (Mount Everest). Dances are held at some hotels.

LEAVING LHASA. By plane. If you are taking an early morning flight, you may take the CAAC bus to Gonggar airport at 4:30 P.M. the day before. You will then have an overnight stay at the Gonggar Hotel or Gonggar Guest House. If you intend to stay at the airport overnight, you must pack an overnight bag because your other bags will be collected on the morning of your bus trip.

The other alternative—but more expensive—is to book a taxi through your hotel for an early morning dash to the airport on the day of your departure. Nevertheless you must still leave your baggage at CAAC between 9 A.M. and noon the day before the flight.

By bus. CITS arranges 3-day bus tours from Lhasa to Kathmandu (Nepal), with overnight stops at Xigaze and Zhangmu on the way.

Independent travelers going on local buses should buy their tickets a day or two in advance. There are three bus stations: one just north of the CAAC office in Jiefang Road; another near the PSB office, and a third—the new bus station—outside the city on Yanhe Xilu, just south of Norbulinka Park. Some new Japanese-made buses have been introduced on long-distance routes, so for your comfort try to get a ticket on one of them.

USEFUL ADDRESSES AND TELEPHONE NUMBERS

CITS—Holiday Inn; Lhasa Guest House (tel. 22980).
CAAC—88 Jiefang Road (tel. 22417).
PSB—Zhongxue Road (tel. 23170).
Nepal Consulate—13 Norbulinka Road (tel. 22880).
Lhasa Travel Co.—Yanhe Dong Lu (tel. 23623).
Taxi Company—Xingfu Dong Lu (tel. 23762).
Bus Station—Jiefang Road (tel. 22756).

LUOYANG

Henan Province
North China

Luoyang is in Henan Province, on the north bank of the River Luo. The town is cut by two rivers which flow into the Luo: the Jian to the west and the Chan to the east. To the north is plateau country and to the south the foothills of the Xiong Er Shan mountains, a spur of the Qinling Shan chain. The River Luo running between these mountains empties into the Huang He, or Yellow River, some 35 miles downstream. The name of the province, Henan, means "south of the river," i.e., the Yellow River.

East of Luoyang the North China Plains begin, stretching hundreds of miles eastward to the sea. Over the centuries it has been covered by silt brought downstream by the Yellow River, and because of its fertility it has always been the mainstay of Chinese agriculture. In Henan itself, which encompasses only a small area of this plain, there is little rain at all for about eight months of the year. Then in July and August the summer rains pour down. As a result, Henan has a record of disastrous floods, and a major task for rulers over the centuries has been the control of the river flow.

Henan is the heart of ancient China. As far back as the neolithic era (6,000–5,000 B.C.) the area was well populated. The capital of the bronze-age Shang Dynasty (1766–1122 B.C.) was located in the north not far from Luoyang, at present-day An Yang. Then in the eleventh century B.C. one of the Zhou kings made his temporary capital at a site outside of Luoyang called Luo Yi. Later, in 770 B.C., the eastern Zhou Dynasty set up their capital at another site in the Luoyang district.

Thus the settlements in and around Luoyang were to remain the capital on and off until A.D. 937, a period of more than 2,000 years.

Since the 1949 revolution attempts have been made to develop the industry of Luoyang, and the town now has machine-building works, chemical factories, textile plants, glass works, and a large tractor factory. This last plant, known as the East Is Red tractor factory, employs about 23,000 people and is said to produce around 26,000 tractors per year, mainly the 46-horsepower rubber-tired caterpillar type.

Thanks to water-control projects on the Yellow River and extensive irrigation, Henan has become one of the major crop-producing provinces of China. To the east of Luoyang on the plain, corn, winter wheat, and *kaoliang* are produced, and to the west, winter wheat, millet, and corn. Large acreages of cotton are planted, and in addition extensive crops of tobacco, sesame, and peanuts are grown.

Luoyang is about 70 miles west of Zhengzhou, which is now an important railway junction formed by the intersection of the north-south Beijing-Canton route and the east-west Xian-Shanghai route. It was the construction of these railway lines in the early twentieth century that pushed Henan back into importance in Chinese history, this time for economic reasons.

Luoyang and other parts of Henan Province were heavily populated during the neolithic era. However, little is known of the history of Luoyang between that period and the eleventh century B.C., when the Zhou King Wu established a temporary capital called Luo Ye near Luoyang. From the sixth century B.C. Luoyang suffered under the series of wars that took place in what was known as the Warring States period (475–221 B.C.). A period of stability was ushered in when the first ruler of the unified empire, Qin Shi Huang Di, established part of his army at Luoyang in 221 B.C..

Liu Bang, first emperor of the Han Dynasty, moved the capital to Chang An (present-day Xian) in 206 B.C., but the court moved back to Luoyang once again in A.D. 25 under the eastern Han (A.D. 25–220). The town underwent considerable development during this period; Buddhism was introduced and scholars were encouraged. The Great Imperial College drew more than 30,000 students from all over China. Considerable advances were made in astronomy, and paper was invented.

The capital continued to be an important center of learning during the Wei (220–265) and the Jin (265–316). The "chariot that pointed south," the first compass, was developed during this period.

Toward the end of the fifth century Luoyang became the capital of the Northern Wei, who had moved down from Datong in the north. Buddhism was flourishing, and one historical text refers to more than a thousand temples in the town. Work was begun on the Long Men Caves, and continued through the period of the Eastern Wei, the Western Wei, the Northern Qi, the Sui, and the Tang.

The town was totally destroyed when the Wei were overcome by the Sui. A new site for the conquering emperor was chosen near where the existing old town now stands. Only traces of the ramparts remain. During the rule of the Sui (589–618) great canal works were begun, the Southern Canal leading to Hangzhou and the Northern Canal to the outskirts of present-day Beijing. Small canals had long been in existence, making it possible to travel from the Yellow River to the Yangzi and beyond, but they were not wide or deep enough to take the large freight barges. Some of these had a capacity of 500–800 tons, a size unheard of in the West at that time. New roads were also constructed, the town flourished, and it was recorded that there were over 400 inns, many of which were used to house the large community of foreign merchants who flocked to the area. The inhabitants of Luoyang were said to number almost a million.

When the Sui fell to the Tang in 618, the capital was moved to Chang An for all but a period of about 40 of the next 289 years. However, Luoyang continued to prosper and was still a great center serving the caravans that were streaming into China from Western and Central Asia. Large sections of the town were inhabited entirely by foreigners, and it was during this time that Nestorian Christianity was established. Similar developments were taking place in Chang An. But it became increasingly difficult to supply Chang An with grain, so the capital was moved east again to Luoyang, which was more accessible to the barges bringing grain upstream from the fertile plains.

Luoyang's reign as capital was again short-lived; in 937 the Jin overran the area and established their capital at Bian Jing, present-day Kaifeng, some 100 miles downstream. Luoyang was never to be capital again and thereafter declined in significance.

EXPLORING LUOYANG

Western Han Dynasty Tomb

The Western Han Dynasty Tomb in Wang Cheng Park was removed from its original site near the railway station and reassembled in its original form. It is about 2,100 years old and is famous for its wall paintings.

A set of stairs leads down into the tomb from ground level. Above the entrance doors is a carving of a sheep's head, representing good fortune; to the right and left of the entrance are two low-ceiling rooms where pottery and other objects were found.

Inside the tomb proper, where the coffin was placed, there are paintings on the ceiling representing the sun and moon, red-and-black wavy lines indicating clouds, and red points representing the stars. The painting on the wall is drawn from mythology and represents "turning of bad fortune into good." The outlines of many animals and men are engraved into the stones of the wall, and some are painted.

Eastern Han Dynasty Tomb

A set of stairs descends from ground level to the entrance of the Eastern Han Dynasty Tomb. Note the special tongue-and-groove bricks used for the construction of the tomb. Before you stand two sets of stone doors: on the front pair a phoenix and three fishes are carved, and on the rear pair an official is shown with one vertical eye, supposedly so that he can look down on the people and up at his master. Both sets of doors have fine examples of bas-relief carvings. Also note the stone beam over the doors, which reveals three fishes carved in bas-relief.

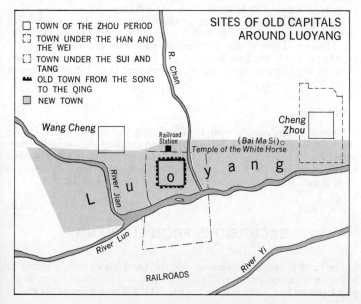

TOWN OF THE ZHOU PERIOD
TOWN UNDER THE HAN AND THE WEI
TOWN UNDER THE SUI AND TANG
OLD TOWN FROM THE SONG TO THE QING
NEW TOWN

SITES OF OLD CAPITALS AROUND LUOYANG

R. Chan

Wang Cheng

Railroad Station

Cheng Zhou

(Bai Ma Si)
Temple of the White Horse

L u o y a n g

River Jian

River Luo

River Yi

RAILROADS

Inside the chamber built to house the coffin of husband and wife is a fine vaulted ceiling supported by a vertical pillar, with engravings of a tiger and dragon to keep away evil spirits. There is a smaller chamber to the left (on entering) for the concubine. You will also see some funerary objects such as pieces of pottery as well as nails from the original coffin.

Huangcheng Park

Huangcheng Park has no great interest except that it houses the two Han tombs. To reach them you walk to the Jian River which flows through the park and either cross the suspension bridge or use the steps of the steep embankment on either side.

The doors of the tomb are finely carved; there are murals of uncertain origin in each cave and some objects that were found when the tombs were recently reopened.

The park bears the name of the old Zhou city, which translated means "Royal Town." It apparently occupies the same site.

Other Sights

The **Temple of the White Horse,** or Bai Ma Si, is five miles east of Luoyang. It is built on the site of the first Buddhist Temples ever to be erected in China under the Western Han (A.D. 68), although the present buildings are from the Ming. The name of the temple is attributed to a legend which describes the arrival of two Indian monks on a white horse bearing sutras. The temple has four halls: the first houses the Maitreya Buddha; the second the Sakyamuni Buddha covered in gilded clay (behind him a Guanyin Buddha); the third has 18 lohans (disciples) made of dry lacquer (tuotai) and dating from the Yuan; the fourth was an assembly for visiting monks. Behind the halls is a staircase leading to the Cool Terrace with cobbled courtyard and lotus pond.

The **Qigong Pagoda** is only a few minutes' walk from the temple: turn left as you leave the exit. This 13-story, 60-foot-high edifice was built at an unknown date and restored under the Song and Jin.

The **Temple of the Town Gods** (or Guandimiao) has been restored and now houses archaeological finds of the region; it used to house the Luoyang Museum. There is also the **Wenfeng Pagoda** in the southeast corner of the Old Town; the **Luzaihuiguan,** the former residence of a rich merchant of the Ming dynasty; and the **Merchants' Hall,** located southeast of the walls.

Old Town

Located in the eastern quarter of Luoyang, the Old Town is the site of the settlement under the Yuan, Ming, and the Qing. Although the ramparts have been demolished (1939), there are a few streets of white-washed houses. Beidajie is the most interesting of these; it runs north from Zongzhou Road. The no. 8 bus will carry you to the western side.

EXCURSIONS FROM LUOYANG

The most interesting excursion is to the **Long Men Caves.** Unless you have particular interest in the Buddhist religion, you would normally expect to spend half a day visiting the site. The morning is better for photo-

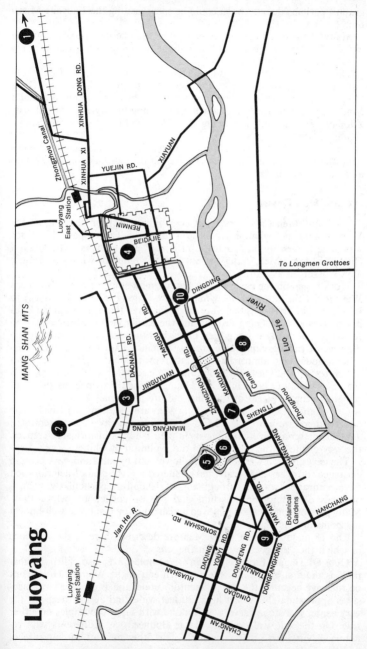

Luoyang

Points of Interest

Arts and Crafts Store **7**
Cemetery of Martyrs **2**
City Stadium **8**
Friendship Hotel **9**
Luoyang Main Station **3**

Old Town **4**
Wang Cheng Park **6**
Western & Eastern Han
  Dynasty Tombs **5**
White Horse Temple **1**
Zhougong Temple **10**

graphs; perhaps the afternoon could be spent visiting the Luoyang Museum.

Many of the excursions described below may be undertaken from the city of Zhengzhou, for the sites are about the same distance from there as they are from Luoyang.

The most interesting area is in the region of Song Shan, the Taoist holy mountain about 40 miles from Luoyang. Not far from the town of Deng Feng stand ancient monasteries and temples. The most famous is **Shaolin Monastery,** renowned as the home of the "kung fu" style of martial arts. Zhongye Temple, still practicing the Taoist faith and open to visitors, stands nearby.

An excursion to the **Three Gorges** on the Yellow River, about 12 miles from the town of Fan Men Xia, located on the rail link to Xian, would also occupy a full day.

Long Men Caves

The Long Men Caves are about eight miles south of Luoyang on the Yi River at a spot where high cliffs on either side form a pass. The place was once known as the "Gate of Yi River" and later as "The Dragon Gate" or "Long Men," after the Sui Dynasty emperor who was in those days worshiped as a dragon.

Work began on the caves in A.D. 494 when an emperor of the Northern Wei moved the capital from what is now Datong (Shanxi Province) to Luoyang. The artistry is therefore an extension of that evident in the Buddhist caves at Yun Gang just outside the earlier capital (see chapter on Datong). The work at Long Men proceeded through periods encompassing seven dynasties, and there are more than 1,300 caves, 40 small bas-relief pagodas, and almost 100,000 statues of Buddha ranging in size from 1 inch to 57 feet. These caves and the stone sculptures therein rank with the caves at Yun Gang and Dun Huang (Gansu Province) as the great remaining masterpieces of Buddhist culture in China.

One of the special features of Long Men are the many inscribed stone tablets; there are more than 3,600 of these in the caves. They represent valuable material for archaeologists in their study of historical references, the way of life of the peoples, and the evolution of Chinese script.

The caves, which were entirely hollowed out by man and have been in existence for over 1,500 years, have suffered a great deal of deterioration from natural causes and through acts of vandalism, particularly by antiquarians collecting for museums and private collections before 1949. Many precious pieces were removed and are now on display at well-known museums around the world.

The 15 major caves at Long Men are described here in the sequence in which they are encountered at the site.

Qian Qi Temple Cave: The Qian Qi Temple Cave, also called Zhaibatang, is the first big cave at the northern end of the Western Hill. Work on the cave began in the seventh century under the Tang. The cave measures approximately 30 feet high, 30 feet wide, and 30 feet deep. In the very center is a stone carving of Buddha with his two disciples on either side. On the side walls are two large Bodhisattvas (adherents who renounced Nirvana so that they might help other men attain deliverance) and two Celestial Guardians, or Kings of Heaven.

Northern Ping Yang Cave: There are two Celestial Guardians at the entrance of this cave and in the middle a large seated Buddha. On either side are Bodhisattvas. All around the walls there are niches with statues of the Buddha.

Central Ping Yang Cave: This is one of two caves built by Emperor Yuan Lo for Emperor Xiao Wen Di and Empress Dowager Wen Zhao. Work on the cave took about 25 years and, it is said, needed more than 800,000 workmen to complete. The cave features 11 large statues of the Buddha, the main statue being about 27 feet high. There are disciples and two Buddhas on either side.

The statues in the cave are typical of Northern Wei stonecarving art. The facial contours are slim and elongated, the creases of the clothes regular, and the robes fall in masterly elegance. The ceiling is particularly interesting: a large lotus flower has been carved on it along with 10 servants who are in attendance on the Heavenly Men. The magnificent adoration scenes were regrettably removed from the cave in 1935 and are now in a United States museum.

Southern Ping Yang Cave: The Buddha in this cave is carved in quite a different style from the one just described: the slim, elongated features have been replaced by a heavy-jowled, dull-eyed face. Historical records show that the work was begun under the Northern Wei and finished under the Sui (A.D. 595–616).

Jing Shan Cave: Work in this cave was done between 627 and 663. There are two Celestial Guardians keeping watch on the outside, and two Bodhisattvas on the inside on either side of the Buddha. The head of the Buddha has been damaged.

Cave of Ten Thousand Buddhas: This cave, known as the Wan Fo, was completed in 680 under the Tang. On the side walls are more than 15,000 Buddhas, while on the back wall are 54 lotus flowers, each with a Bodhisattva seated on it. The ceiling is the large lotus flower with an inscription providing the date of the cave. The Buddha is seated on a lotus seat.

Notice in particular the images at the base of the north and south walls: Dancers float gracefully, and musicians appear to be playing with a remarkable liveliness.

Lotus Flower Cave: The cave, known as Lian Hua Dong, was named for the fine carving of the lotus flower on the ceiling. The cave was dug out about 527 at the end of the Northern Wei Dynasty. The Buddha was carved in a standing position; the head and one forearm are no longer intact. Delightful carvings of clouds and flowers as well as fine geometrical designs appear all around the cave.

Wei Character Cave: There are epigraphs dating from the Wei Dynasty in this cave, which gave rise to the name Wei Zi Dong. The Buddha in this cave has been damaged.

The Tang Character Cave: Known as the Tang Zi Dong, this dates from 661. It is understood that work was begun under the Wei and continued under the Tang. The sculpture outside is in the Wei style, while that inside is Tang.

Ju Xian Temple Cave: This is one of the most important caves carved during the Tang Dynasty and certainly the largest of the caves at Long Men, measuring approximately 120 feet by 100 feet. It was completed in 675.

The central figure is a huge Buddha almost 60 feet tall; the head alone is about 15 feet high with the ears about 7 feet long. The facial expression is realistic and conveys a sense of peace and tranquility, particularly in the eyes. On either side of the Buddha stand the two disciples and two Bodhisattvas with crowns. On the side walls are a Celestial Guardian and a defender of Buddha. The Guardian on the north wall holds a pagoda in his right hand and with his left foot is trampling an evil spirit. He wears an angry expression with a deeply frowning brow.

Outside the cave you will see large square holes hollowed out to receive the supporting beams of the temple that used to stand at the entrance.

Medical Prescription Cave: Carved around the entrance are herbal recipes for about 120 remedies for diseases of the heart, liver, kidneys, and skin as well as old cures for vomiting, fever, and even madness.

Gu Yang Cave: This is one of the earliest caves, work having begun in 494 and completed under the Northern Qi in 575. It is a most important cave in the series and represents a treasure house of Northern Wei carving, rock painting, and architecture. The centerpiece is a statue of Buddha with two lions at his feet. It was restored under Guang Du, but the new face of the figure resembles Lao Zi, so it was popularly named Lao Jun and the cave itself Lao Jun Dong. Of the "twenty calligraphies" at Long Men, 19 are found in this cave.

The Cave Burnt by Fire: The cave was given this name because it was supposed to have been struck by lightening. It dates from the Northern Wei, and there are two inscriptions dated 522 and 523.

Shi Ku Temple Cave: Carved in the eighth century, this cave features various adoration scenes which are the finest at Long Men, the carvings from the Ping Yang Cave having been removed. Remarkably true to life, the scenes are a masterpiece of Buddhist stone carving.

Lu Dong Cave: The northern wall is particularly interesting; the carvings of houses with staircases provide information about the architecture of the period. On the south wall a scene depicts the Buddha's previous incarnation. Inscriptions in the cave indicate that it was completed in the sixth century under the Northern Wei.

The caves on the eastern cliff of the River Yi, directly opposite the caves you have just visited, are much larger, and all of them date from the Tang.

Neolithic Remains

An interesting excursion is to the village of **Yang Shao** some four miles north of Mian Chi, which is about 45 miles west of Luoyang. The site, discovered in 1921, was the first definite proof of the existence of a neolithic culture in China. Since then, thousands of other sites have been discovered in the northern regions. Cultures of this type are now known as Yang Shao cultures, called after the original site, and referring to the Middle Neolithic period, 6000–5000 B.C., as distinct from the later neolithic dating from 5000–4000 B.C. and known as the Long Shan culture.

The Yang Shao culture extends throughout an area covering Henan, Shanxi, Hunan, Inner Mongolia, and Hebei. The history of the Chinese nation began in the period represented by the Yang Shao culture.

Other Excursions

Another excursion is to **Sanmenxia** (or **Three Gate Gorges**) to see the nearby dam. The town, about 60 miles west of Luoyang on the railway line running to Xian, draws its name from the three gorges on the Yellow River about 12 miles downstream. The river tears through this region, the combination of rapid current and hidden reefs making the area extremely dangerous for navigation. The hazard created particular problems for the Han when they moved the capital to Chang An (now Xian) and supplies and food had to be brought upstream from the plains. The swift-flowing currents were defeated by building overhanging tow paths into the rock face so that vessels could be pulled upstream by men toiling on long bamboo cables attached to the boats in the boiling river below.

To reach the **Northern Wei Buddhist Caves** you take the train from Luoyang to Gong Xian, which is about halfway to Zhengzhou. The caves are about two miles northwest of Gong Xian, on the north bank of the river Luo. The five caves were dug out between A.D. 517–534 under the Northern Wei. Three statues of Bodhisattvas are carved into the cliff beside the cave entrances.

In other areas just outside Gong Xian you may visit the site of several iron forges established under the Han; in another location there are pottery kilns dating from the Tang period.

There is a fine excursion to the east of Luoyang to the **Song Dynasty Imperial Tombs.** These are reached by taking a train to the Yan Shi, about 18 miles away, and then proceeding by road to Song Shan, near the town of Zhi Tian Zhan.

Here you will find the tombs of the first seven emperors of the Song Dynasty; smaller tombs hold empresses and other members of the royal family. Since the tombs were built after the death of the emperor by his successor, they are less elaborate than the Tang tombs. The Sacred Way is particularly impressive, featuring elephants, lions, tigers, and horses as well as the series of statues of men representing court and military officials.

From the Song Dynasty tombs you can continue along the road a few miles to Deng Feng, which lies to the west. From this town you go another 12 miles along the road in a northwesterly direction to the **Small Forest Temple,** or **Shaolinsi.** Founded under the Northern Wei in A.D. 496, it became a great center of Chinese Buddhism. An Indian monk, Boddhidarma, known to the Chinese as Da Mo, founded the Chinese meditative Chan sect (known as Zen in Japan). Adherents reject books and doctrines and embrace only introspection. Da Mo is said to have lived for about nine years in Shaolin until his death in 535, although historical evidence concerning his visit to the area is suspect. The temple is famous for martial arts.

The center was enlarged during succeeding dynasties up to and including the Ming. Old frescoes in good condition may be seen in the main temple.

A few hundred yards from the monastery stands the Forest of Stupas, or Ta Lin, erected in memory of the leading members of the monastery through the ages.

About half a mile further on is the **Chu Zu An,** or First Ancestors Monastery, dating from the twelfth century. There are fine bas-relief carvings inside the temple, which is said to be the oldest wooden temple structure in Henan.

A number of other interesting monasteries may be visited by taking the road back to Deng Feng and then proceeding on a road leading almost due north. You will then come across the **Yong Tai Monastery** and the **Hui Shan Si,** or United Virtues Monastery.

Another monastery, the **Song Yue Si,** was founded under the Northern Wei in the sixth century. The rare 12-sided pagoda that stands there today is reputed to be the oldest in China. Located about three miles northwest of Deng Feng, it is 130 feet high and built entirely of brick. In the surrounding area is the site of what used to be **Zhongyue Miao,** or the Central Peak Temple. The original buildings, the first of which are believed to have been erected in the early part of the eighth century, were scattered over an area of about six square miles. Begun under the Tang, the structures were restored and extended under the Song, the Ming, and the Qing. The **Central Peak of the Song Shan** was believed to be a holy mountain, one of the five sacred mountains of ancient China. Emperors came here to offer sacrifices.

Two small stone buildings which used to stand on either side of a pathway leading to the temple date from 118 B.C. and contain engravings of great archaeological interest.

A monastery known as the **Bei Lou Si,** or Stele Tower Monastery, lies south of the temple. Also in the Song Shan area is the **Fa Wang Si,** or Monastery of the King of Law.

If time permits, it is well worthwhile to continue to a site nine miles southeast of Deng Feng, the **Guan Xing Tai,** an old observatory built under the Yuan in 1279. The structure is a tower made of brick, about 33 feet high, with slightly sloping sides and flights of stairs leading to the top. A flat wall runs from the bottom of the structure for a distance of almost 100 feet. Its purpose was to measure the shadow thrown by the tower, enabling observations of the sun to be made at various times of the year. It is the oldest complete astronomical observatory existing in China.

PRACTICAL INFORMATION FOR LUOYANG

FACTS AND FIGURES. Luoyang is at approximately the same latitude as Wichita Falls, Texas. Distances: 425 miles southwest of Beijing, 11½ hours' journey by train; 200 miles due east of Xian, 4½–5½ hours' journey by train.

WHEN TO GO. The best time to visit Luoyang is in October or November; the weather is pleasant then. Try to avoid the summer months, particularly July and August, when the rainfall can be particularly heavy and the humidity high. Winter is milder than in Beijing, but temperatures can be very low.

Late spring is also a convenient time to visit, but early spring often brings with it unpleasant dust storms.

HOW TO GET THERE. Luoyang now has a commercial airport, with flights from Beijing, Shanghai, Guangzhou, Xian, and Nanjing. Alternatively, you can travel all the way by train from Beijing: you will find the 6:57 A.M. express arriving Luoyang 6:26 P.M., a convenient one. This gives you an opportunity to see a good deal of the countryside and allows you to get to your hotel at a reasonable hour. There is also an 8:57 A.M. train arriving Luoyang at 9:45 P.M.

You should spend a minimum of two days in Luoyang, more if you wish to take some of the tours to the outlying areas. Then you may wish to travel by train to Xian, a 4½–5½-hour journey. If you are in a hurry, you can take the overnight train, arriving in Xian early (5:02 A.M.) the next day. If you have plenty of time, you can take a day train, get a good view of the countryside on the way, and arrive the same afternoon.

Other train services link Luoyang with nearby provincial capitals Zhengzhou (2¾ hours), Chengdu (24 hours), and Lanzhou (21½ hours).

HOTELS. You will normally be lodged at the **International Hotel** (tel. 27155) on Renmin Road, Xigong district, or at the **Friendship Hotel** (tel. 22995), 1–6 Xiyuan Road, Jianxi district, in the southwest of the town. The hotel provides good accommodations, each room with air-conditioning and color TV, a swimming pool, and Chinese and Western-style restaurants of good standard.

RESTAURANTS. Most visitors eat in their hotel dining room, but if you would like to eat out you could try the **Guangzhou Restaurant** (tel. 2170) Dongfeng Road, Jianxi district.

TOURIST INFORMATION. CITS (tel. 22200) is located at the Friendship Hotel and is open 8 A.M.–noon and 2–5 P.M.

PSB (tel. 27423) is on Kaixuan Road just north of the canal in the center of town.

The railway station (Luoyang West) serving most tourist destinations is at the northern end of Jinguyuan Road. The long-distance bus station stands opposite the railway station.

HOW TO GET AROUND. CITS organizes tours to the Long Men Caves and to other sites. Budget travelers should take bus no. 60 to the caves; it departs from the far end of the park opposite the Friendship Hotel.

WHAT TO SEE. At the top of your list will be the **Long Men Caves,** about nine miles south of Luoyang. You should try to visit the caves during the morning when the light is at its best. Allow half a day for this excursion.

In Luoyang itself you will wish to visit the **Western Han Dynasty Tomb** and the **Eastern Han Dynasty Tomb** situated in Wang Cheng Park. You should not miss a visit to the **Luoyang Museum** which has some fine exhibits.

Try to visit the **Temple of the White Horse,** about 8 miles to the east of the city. Further afield is **Song Shan,** about 40 miles from the city. A short distance from there are numerous temples and monasteries. There are similar sites near the town of **Deng Feng.** A visit to this area will require a full day.

If you are interested in neolithic remains you should try to get to the village of **Yang Shao,** about 45 miles west of Luoyang.

MUSEUMS. An archaeological museum is located in what was once the **Guan Di Miao** (temple) built during the Ming Dynasty in dedication to Guan Di, or Guan Yu, a hero from the Three Kingdoms era. There were once many temples dedicated to him throughout China.

The **Luoyang Museum** in Zhongzhon Road is divided into three sections devoted to primitive society, slave society, and feudal society. Before beginning a tour of these sections the visitor should examine the wall diagram, which illustrates how the location of the town varied according to the particular period of history. The town was once of great strategic importance and, dating from 770 B.C., nine dynasties established their capital in or near what is now Luoyang.

In the first room the huge mammoth tusks about 10 feet long are 300,000–400,000 years old, and the ostrich eggs are from the same era.

Life in the neolithic period is illustrated. The Yang Shao culture (which existed about 6,000 years ago) is called after the village about 30 miles west of Luoyang where the relics from the period were excavated. An interesting feature of this village was the red pottery made there, the color resulting from a combination of soil type and kiln temperature. Also of note are the pieces of pottery illustrating evolution from "red" to "black" forms, the latter color created by a greater kiln temperature achieved through tighter sealing of the kiln. (Black pottery is typical of the Long Shan culture, named after the site of an excavation made in the 1920s in Shangdong Province.)

Also on display are tool heads with holes bored through the stone; this technique first appeared in the Yang Shao culture and represents an important advance in tool- and implement-making.

Of the exhibits from the Xia Dynasty period (2205–1766 B.C.), the noteworthy items are shells, used for money, and the pottery, a direct development from the Long Shan culture. Items from the Shang Dynasty (1766–1122 B.C.) include a rare bronze farming tool and a beautiful set of bronze drinking vessels, one of which has handles in the form of serpents.

From the Western Zhou (1122–255 B.C.) are weapon heads in bronze, a rare bronze saw, and bronze drinking vessels with fine patterns, some featuring animal heads and serpent handles.

The extremely rare porcelains from the Western Zhou Dynasty are especially important because, until they were unearthed, experts believed that porcelain-making began in the Western Jin Dynasty, around A.D. 300. The porcelain dug up from this particular site indicates that the art may have begun 1,400 years before that date. The examples are made of special clay (kaolin), which can be treated at 1200–1300° C, as distinct from the 900° C. used for simple pottery.

Luoyang was first made capital during the spring and autumn period of the Eastern Zhou Dynasty. Swords were then worn, and there is a beautiful example of a finely worked sword sheath in ivory. Also on display are shovel-shaped coins in bronze, each about 3 to 4 inches long; a large bronze bowl about 4 feet high and

3 feet in diameter, which was made to hold water and give a perfect reflection. This was given to the daughter of one of the emperors as a wedding present.

You will also see 10 of the 13 pieces of limestone used as a stone resonator from the Spring-Autumn period. The pieces when suspended look like a row of misshapen coat hangers. The stones make a clear bell-like tone when struck; but they should not be confused with "stone chimes," which contain 14–16 pieces. Your guide may volunteer to play a short piece on the resonator, usually a patriotic refrain like "The East Is Red."

From the Han Dynasty there are various examples: grains such as hemp, rice, castor beans, glutinous millet, and two other kinds of millet; funerary objects such as a ceramic model pigsty featuring a sow with her litter; a model well; a metal clothes iron shaped like a ladle with a receptacle for hot coals.

From the Northern Wei period there is a beautiful set of figurines. First is the guard of honor, then various members of the military, then the court attendants and officials, and finally the prince in a horse-drawn covered chariot, the musicians following behind.

From the Tang Dynasty are floor stones from the palace, fine examples of Tang animal ceramics, and a glazed statue of a Persian merchant. (Traders from the Middle East appeared in China at this time via the "Silk Road.") Also on display are figurines of ladies dressed in elegant gowns and seated on horseback, two larger figures of generals, two civil officials, two fierce "devil catchers" placed before a tomb to ward off evil spirits.

From the Song Dynasty there are a fine bronze bell, celadon porcelain, and some examples of the bellows used in the manufacture of porcelain.

From the Sui Dynasty period are two stone lions, one of which is the only one of its kind yet discovered in China.

SHOPPING. Luoyang is a good place to buy reproductions of the famous tricolor Tang porcelains of creatures such as horses and camels. A number of originals are housed in the Luoyang Museum and copies are made at the arts and crafts factory in town. They may be purchased at the **Arts and Crafts Store** or at the **Friendship Store** on Huashan Road near the Friendship Hotel. Second-hand theatrical costumes are available at the **State Second-Hand Store** in the old city. Rather than buy costumes, you may want to have your photograph taken in them at the Friendship Hotel. You can also have stone seals carved with your name, Chinese or English, at a store in the Friendship Hotel.

NANCHANG

Jiangxi Province
South China

Nanchang, the capital of Jiangxi (or West River) Province, is located on the Gan River. Although it was founded under the Han (206 B.C.–A.D. 230), it was for many centuries a storage and distribution center for the famous porcelain from nearby Jingdezhen. In 1927 it became known throughout China as a revolutionary center when, on August 1, Zhou Enlai and Zhu De led 30,000 men against the troops of Chiang Kaishek and defeated them. The anniversary of the uprising is celebrated each year in China and is observed as the founding day of the Chinese People's Liberation Army.

The town is now a thriving industrial center with a population of about 700,000.

EXPLORING NANCHANG

Nanchang has been extensively rebuilt, leaving few historical or architectural sites of interest. The city is crowded, noisy, unattractive—and like a furnace in summer. If for some reason you do find yourself in Nanchang, there are a few museums to visit.

Visitors sometimes stop over in Nanchang to take excursions from the provincial capital. The excursions to Jingdezhen, Jiujiang, the Lu Mountains, and the Jinggang Mountains are described below. Otherwise, Nanchang alone is not worth a visit.

EXCURSIONS FROM NANCHANG

Jingdezhen

Those who love Chinese porcelain and ceramic ware will wish to visit this center, famous for many centuries as China's porcelain capital. Jingdezhen is about 125 miles northeast of Nanchang, on the banks of the Chang Jiang.

When we say "china" and mean "porcelain," we sometimes forget that the words became synonymous more than a thousand years ago. Porcelain was first made in China, where porcelain-making reached a perfection rarely matched anywhere else. Rulers from far-flung corners of the earth sent emissaries to procure China's porcelain. Traders risked and made fortunes shipping cargoes of porcelain to the monarchs of Europe, the czars of Russia, the sultans of the Middle East, and the Shoguns of Japan. Jingdezhen was one of the places where it all began.

Pottery (mostly earthenware and stoneware) was produced there in the first century A.D. In the seventh century, under the Tang, porcelain was developed from fine white clay known as Gao Ling Tu (kaolin), or "earth from the high hill." By firing this clay at a higher than normal temperature, the craftsmen were able to make objects that were translucent, hard, and white. The nature of the substance produced gave rise to the Chinese word for porcelain which is "ci" (pronounced something like "tzu"), meaning "an object that makes a high note when struck." Incidentally, the English word for porcelain comes from the Portuguese "pourcellana," meaning cowrie shells. Early Portuguese traders saw a distinct resemblance between the two.

The use of porcelain in China spread rapidly under the Tang. Porcelain ware was esthetically pleasing, and metal vessels were becoming scarce because copper was in short supply. At the same time, the Chinese demand for drinking vessels increased substantially because of the fast-spreading popularity of tea.

The clay sculpture produced under the Tang has remarkable beauty. Figures of people and animals, decorated with brilliant colors and preserved with translucent glazes, are now recognized round the world as foremost works of art.

The Song Dynasty porcelains (960–1280) are equally famous; they feature innovations in designs, clays, and glazes. Celadon ware, developed during this period, fulfilled the dream of every Chinese potter: to create a substance that resembled jade.

The Ming period (1368–1644) also saw the production of magnificent porcelains, especially the famous "blue and whites." They were first developed in Jingdezhen, using cobalt blue underglazes from Persia. The Ming porcelains reached a peak of perfection during the Zuan De period (1426–1435), but excellent pieces were made throughout the entire Ming era.

Under the Qing, the traditions of the previous dynasty were at first maintained by craftsmen, but later the court began to encourage extravagant and exaggerated decoration: large quantities of porcelain were produced for the West, and much of it featured discordant colors and excessive decoration. The styles that were retained by collectors within China were usually far more subdued.

As the interest in porcelain ware developed over the centuries in China, production was expanded and other centers for porcelain were developed. However, Jingdezhen remained and still remains the most important porcelain center. In the eighteenth century, the town had a population of more than a million and possessed over 500 pottery kilns. Today there are 20 porcelain factories with a collective production level of about 350 million pieces annually—almost half of China's total yearly production.

Apart from a few modern thoroughfares and a small number of modern buildings and factories, the town is probably much the same as it was under the Qing. The long narrow streets are lined by wooden houses jammed close together. Porters wheel handcarts through the congested lanes; at the river's edge, narrow boats take on cargo.

Visitors to Jingdezhen can inspect a porcelain factory but may find that the **Fine Arts Factory** is more interesting. The factory's craftsmen often spend weeks at a time hand-painting the objects. The **Jingdezhen Porcelain Museum,** or Jingdezhen Ciqi Bowuguan, has a fine range of porcelain on display and is worth a visit.

A few miles north of the town is the **Fu Liang Cheng Pagoda,** on the north bank of the Yangzi on a small hill west of the town of Fu Liang

Jiu Cheng. The pagoda was once part of the Western Pagoda Temple, believed to date from the Song Dynasty.

Jiujiang

The town and river port of Jiujiang, 75 miles north of Nanchang, may be reached from that city by train or bus, from Wuhan by boat, and from Jingdezhen by bus.

Founded under the Han, the town later became an important trading center for Jingdezhen pottery, porcelain, and tea. Although it has a long history, Jiujiang has little interest for the tourist. It is a stopover point for visitors on their way to Lushan, Guling, or Jingdezhen.

The **Yuan Tong Temple,** or Yuan Tong Si, octagonal in shape and only about 10 feet high, houses a tiny stone pagoda dating from the Song. The bas-relief carvings on the outside walls of the temple are of interest.

Lu Mountains

The mountain resort of **Guling** in the Lu Mountains (or Lu Shan) is a perfect place for a rest, even though it is often crowded with Chinese tourists. Guling is about 20 miles from Jiujiang by road. On the way, you will pass some fine mountain scenery with views of Lake Poyang, or Poyang Hu.

Guling is well known in the region because Chiang Kaishek once had a summer villa there. It is perhaps even better known for its Lushan Botanical Gardens, the first sub-alpine botanical center established in the nation. The center is in the Hanbokou Valley of Mount Lushan.

In and around Guling itself, you will see many gardens, ponds, and pavilions. One of the most celebrated subjects for Chinese painters is found there: Wu Laofeng, or Five Peaks. Also of interest are the Dragon's Head Rock, or Long Shouyan; the Round Temple, or Yuan Fo Dian; the Black Dragon Pool, or Wu Long Tan; and the Cave of the Immortals, or Xian Ren Dong.

Jinggang Mountains

The Jinggang Mountains hold a special place in modern Chinese history. It was there that Mao Zedong settled with his army of peasants, workers, and soldiers in 1927, and where the Red Army was founded in 1928. The region is considered to be the cradle of the Chinese Revolution.

Ciping, where the headquarters of the military base was located, is about 175 miles southwest of Nanchang and accessible by road. Here you may see the site of the Headquarters of the Fourth Red Army, the Jinggang Mountains Revolutionary Museum and Mao Zedong's former residence. The area is mainly of interest to students of the Chinese Revolution.

PRACTICAL INFORMATION FOR NANCHANG

FACTS AND FIGURES. Nanchang is the capital of Jiangxi Province in the south of China. By air, it is about 375 miles southwest of Shanghai, about 410 miles northeast of Guangzhou, and about 810 miles south of Beijing.

WHEN TO GO. Nanchang is in one of China's high-rainfall belts, and heavy monthly falls occur from March through July. Autumn is the best time to visit the city. At that time, the temperatures are milder and the humidity lower. Summers are extremely hot.

HOW TO GET THERE. Nanchang is closer to Shanghai and Guangzhou than to Beijing. It is linked to all three by rail; the train journey from Shanghai is about 14 hours. There are no direct services to Nanchang from Beijing or Guangzhou and you must change trains at Changsha/Zhuzhou.

There are flights to Nanchang from Beijing (2¼ hours), Fuzhou (1½ hours), Guangzhou (1¾ hours), Jingdezhen (1¼ hours), Shanghai (1¼ hours), and Wuhan (1¼ hours).

HOTELS. The 15-story **Green Mountain Lake Hotel** (tel. 64901 or 65615), 11 Wujiao Road, accommodates 525 guests and has a swimming pool. Accommodations are also available at the **Jiangxi Guest House** (tel. 64214; telex 67891), 64 Bayi Road, which has central air-conditioning, a Chinese and a Western-style restaurant, and CITS office; and the **Nanchang Hotel** (tel. 63593), 2 Zhanqian Road; and the **Jiangxi Hotel** (tel. 63624) on Changzheng Road.

RESTAURANTS. Most visitors eat in the restaurant of their hotel. Chinese-speaking visitors may care to try one of the many "masses" restaurants in the city such as the **Xingyia** or the **Fuwudalou.**

TOURIST INFORMATION. CITS (tel. 65180) is located at the Jiangxi Hotel. **CAAC** (tel. 62368, 62347) is at 26 Zhangquan Road. **PSB** is on Bayi Street, a short walk east from the Hongdu Hotel.

HOW TO GET AROUND. CITS arranges bus tours of the town and excursions to out-of-town sites. There are local buses and trains to Jingdezhen, Lu Shan, and Jiujiang.

MUSEUMS. The **Jianxi Province Museum** (tel. 64313), or Jiangxi Sheng Bo Wuguan, is on Bayi (August 1st) Street near the main square. It has a series of interesting exhibits on the neolithic era, bronzes from the Shang Dynasty, porcelains from the Song, and a model of a Ming tomb. Open Wednesday, Friday, Sunday; 8–11 A.M. and 2–5 P.M.

Another place worth visiting is the **Museum of the Nanchang Uprising,** housed in the former headquarters of the August 1st Uprising of 1927. It is located on Zhongshan Road, not far from the River Fu.

The **Revolutionary History Museum** (tel. 53884), on Bayi (August 1st) Street, has exhibits relating to the development of the revolutionary movement in the province; so does the **Memorial Hall to the Martyrs.**

The **Badrashanren Museum** is dedicated to the Zhu Da, one of the 8 great hermit (Badashanren) artists, who lived and worked in the area. The temple, Qinyunpu, where he spent 27 years, now houses some of his works. It is located a few miles south of Nanchang.

PARKS. The two pleasant parks in Nanchang are the **Bayi (August First) Park** (tel. 52864), bordering the East Lake and close to the Jiangxi Hotel, and the **People's (Renmin) Park** (tel. 64495) off Xianhu Road. The park is divided into two sections by the southern extremity of the Xianshi Lake. If you have time, both parks are worth visiting.

SHOPPING. For 2,000 years Nanchang has been a trading center for ceramics and, since the Song Dynasty, for porcelain. Because it is close to Jingdezhen, China's porcelain capital, there is no better place to buy such products.

To hunt for bargains, begin at the Nanchang Porcelainware Store, or Nanchang Ciqi Dian (tel. 52939), 12 Shengli Road. If you cannot find what you are seeking, try the **Friendship Store** (tel. 63268) in Bayi Road; porcelain is well stocked here.

If you wish to buy one of the standard products made in China, visit the **Nanchang Department Store,** or Nanchang Bai Huo Shang Chang (tel. 63849) at the intersection of Zhongshan and Bayi roads; the **August First Department Store** (tel. 52536) in Zhongshan Road, the **People's Department Store** (tel. 51523) in Jiujiang

Road; or the **Qingshan Lu Department Store** (tel. 62375) in Bayi (August 1st) Road.

LEAVING NANCHANG. In addition to the train and plane information given above (see *How To Get There*), buses leave the long-distance bus terminal for **Guling,** the lovely resort area of the Lu Mountains to the north of Nanchang. Another bus travels further north to **Jiujiang** on the Yangzi, where you can take the ferry downstream to Shanghai. You can also take a bus from Nanchang to **Jingdezhen,** in the northeast of the province.

USEFUL ADDRESSES AND TELEPHONE NUMBERS

China International Travel Service—Jiangxi Hotel (tel. 62571).
CAAC Airline—26 Zhanqian Street (tel. 62368).
Train Tickets—Shengli Road (tel. 51164).
Bus Tickets (long distance)—August First Street (Bayi Dajie) (tel. 52575).
Boat Tickets (river transport)—Yenjiang Road (tel. 52515).

NANJING

Jiangsu Province

South China

Nanjing, meaning "Southern Capital," is the capital of Jiangsu Province. It is located on the east bank of the Chang River, better known as the Yangzi. Nanjing has been national capital several times in the history of China; today it is an important national center and China's biggest inland port.

Nanjing is an attractive city with wide, tree-lined boulevards and streets. To the west is the Yangzi, to the north the large Xuanwu Lake, and to the east the Zi Jin, or Purple Mountains. Parts of the old walls of the town are still standing. They were constructed under the Ming in the late fourteenth century and were originally 35 miles in perimeter with 13 gates. A number of the gates are also standing today.

It is clear from archaeological evidence that Nanjing has been inhabited since about 4000 B.C. Indeed, cultures have existed in the province since paleolithic times.

The settlement first became significant when it was a strategic part of the border between the three warring states, Wu, Yue, and Chu, over the period 476–221 B.C. Each king in turn adopted the town as his capital during the time he controlled it. When Qin Shi Huang Di unified the country in 221 B.C. Nanjing became a command post. Later, it developed into an important center under the Three Kingdoms Dynasty. In the ensuing centuries Nanjing was the capital of the states established by the Eastern Jin, the Song, the Qi, the Liang, and the Chen, over a period of about 280 years.

During the Tang Dynasty (A.D. 618–907) Nanjing was again an important center, and when this dynasty fell it once again became the capital of a local dynasty known as the Southern Tang. Under the Southern Song the town became an advance post in the war against the invaders from the north.

During the Ming Dynasty, Nanjing developed considerably and was well known as a center for shipbuilding, metal products, timber, and pottery. It also became an important cultural center; students came from all over China to study at the Imperial College.

Under the Qing development continued, the Manchu emperors giving the city considerable attention so that commercial activities flourished. In 1842, when the first of the "unequal treaties" was signed, Nanjing was opened up to foreign traders. However, just over 11 years later the town was taken by the Taiping forces and renamed Tian Jing, or Celestial Capital. About a decade later, in 1864, it was retaken by the imperial armies and severely damaged.

The town then went into decline until the early twentieth century when some industrial expansion took place following the rail connection with Shanghai.

In 1912 Nanjing became capital of the Republic, but three months later the capital was moved to Beijing. After the 1949 revolution, considerable effort was applied to develop Nanjing, and a great deal of industrialization has taken place. The city has become an important industrial center for chemical fertilizers, machine tools, machinery, textiles, iron and steel, and cement. The main agricultural products are rice, wheat, millet, cotton, rape, tea, and fruit.

EXPLORING NANJING

Chang Jiang Bridge

The Chinese are proud of the Chang Jiang Bridge over the Yangzi at Nanjing. They have every right to be; this is the bridge that foreign experts said could not be built. It is a superb feat of engineering.

The bridge is double-decked with four vehicle lanes on the upper deck and two rail lines on the lower. It is 22,100 feet long and takes an hour to walk across. Nine giant bases, deeply imbedded into the rock beneath the river, support the 10 spans of the bridge.

The bridge has been built high enough to allow the passage of 10,000-tonners underneath (these vessels can go as far as Wuhan, about 700 miles upstream).

In the eastern tower of the bridge you can see a scale model illustrating the engineering and construction work. From the terrace of the tower you will have a fine view of the bridge and the river far below. On some days you will see on the surface objects that resemble shiny black innertubes. These are huge black fish known as "River Pigs" and said to be edible; they are river dolphins.

Drum Tower and Bell Pavilion

The Drum Tower, or Gu Lou, built under the Ming, stands at the intersection of Zhong Shan Bei and Beijing roads. It provides a good view of the town and often features exhibitions of Chinese arts and crafts. The Great Bell Pavilion, or Da Zhong Ting, stands on the eastern side of Zhong Shan Road.

The Gates of Nanjing

Many of the gates of the old wall surrounding Nanjing still survive along with sections of the wall itself. The present form of the city dates from the Ming Dynasty; the last wall was built during the final years of the fourteenth century. The bricks used were made with great precision, and on each one was engraved the name of the workman and the master brick-maker. The wall was over 35 miles long and contained 13 gates. Later a second wall was built outside the brick wall; it was made of earth and was about 70 miles around with 17 gates.

Many of the gates of the old inner wall are located in busy sections of the town where it may not be easy to stop, but there is a park surrounding Xuan Wu lake where you may quietly observe one of the 600-year-old gates.

Xuan Wu Lake

Xuan Wu lake and park lie in the north of the city outside the northern ramparts. There are five islets connected by causeways, each named after

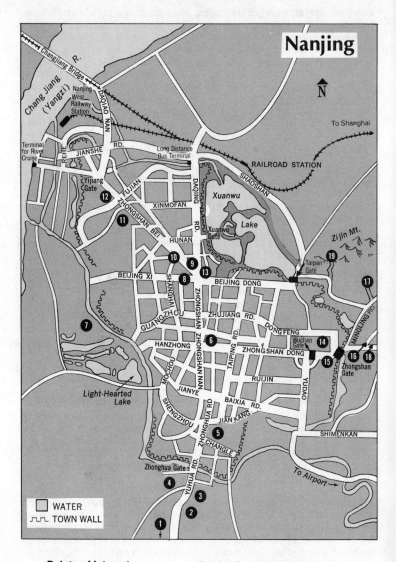

Nanjing

WATER
TOWN WALL

Points of Interest

Bell Tower **9**
Drum Tower **8**
Friendship Store **13**
King of Borneo's Tomb **4**
Linggu Temple **18**
Mausoleum of Sun Tatsen **16**
Mingxiaoling (Ming Tomb) **17**
Nanjing Hotel **11**
Nanjing & Jiangsu Museum **14**
Observatory **19**

People's Department Store **6**
Rain of Flower Terrace **3**
Remains of Ming Palace **15**
Shitoucheng (Stone City) **7**
Shuangmenlou Guest House **12**
Southern Tang Tombs and Bull's
   Head Hill **1**
Taiping Museum **5**
University of Nanjing **10**
Yuhuatai (Rain of Flowers) Terrace **2**

one of the five continents. Sections of lake have been converted into vast natural swimming areas. In summer, some of the lake is covered by acres of lotus blossoms. Whatever the season, you will see many water buffalo grazing by the edges of the lake. Ask your guide to stop your car or bus so that you can take a close look at these lovely animals. It is rare in a city that you can get close enough to photograph one.

Nanjing Zoo

A small zoo near the Xuan Wu lake is worth a visit, if only to see the famous Chinese panda, housed in a fine old pavilion with traditional Chinese roof and content behind the bars of its elegant cage.

Bull's Head Hill Pagoda

About 12 miles south of the city, Bull's Head Hill, known as Niutou Shan, was once the site of many temples, none of which now exist. However, you can see the beautiful rust-colored pagoda originally built in A.D. 774. The eight-sided, seven-story pagoda cannot be climbed because the structure inside no longer exists. In recent years two tombs of Southern Tang origin have been excavated nearby, supposedly those of the first and second Southern Tang kings, Li Bian and Li Jing.

Tomb of the King of Borneo

The existence of the tumulus west of Yu Hua Tai hill was known for a long time, but it was only recently that fragments of a stele were found bearing inscriptions indicating that the King of Po Ni died at Nanjing and was buried south of the An De Men gate, one of the gates in the old earthen wall. Apparently the king died at Nanjing in 1408 while visiting the court of Yong Le. He was 28 years old.

There is a pathway leading to the tomb with stone statues on either side. The stele with the inscription has been replaced at the site.

Remains of the Ming Palace

The site of the Ming Palace is in the eastern part of the town. Driving to the ruins, you will pass through what was once the interior of the north palace. All that remains is a huge main gate with five arches, the base of some columns, and parts of five bridges used to cross the moat. A stele commemorates the official Fang Xiaoru, who opposed the Ming emperor who had usurped the throne.

Rain of Flowers Terrace

The Yu Hua Tai, or Rain of Flowers Terrace, south of the Zhonghua Gate, derives its name from a legend about a monk who preached the tenets of Buddha so well that a rain of flowers fell upon his audience.

Throughout the centuries many temples have been built on the hill, but no trace of them remains. Several tombs have been unearthed there; there is also a modern stele erected in memory of the revolutionaries executed by the Guomindang. The terrace is covered with colored pebbles that are prized for their beauty; they can be purchased at stalls on the grounds.

Lighthearted Lake

Lighthearted lake, or Mo Chou, meaning "free of sorrow," is the name of a Chinese heroine who suffered various misfortunes in life and was later immortalized by some of China's famous poets. The lake is set in a park of the same name. There is a pavilion which dates from the Qing and several steles which refer to the legend. It is a pleasant place to take a stroll. The lake is located outside the ramparts on the western side of the town.

Nanjing University

The University of Nanjing and the former seat of the Guomindang was once the ancient palace of the Taiping Emperor Hong Xiu Quan. The western side of the university comprises the students' dormitories and living quarters; the eastern side comprises classrooms, lecture halls, and library.

Jiangsu Museum

The Jiangsu Museum is housed in a fairly modern building with a Chinese-style roof. It is on the eastern side of the town at 321 E. Zhong Shan Nan Lu (Sun Yatsen Street). Exhibits date from prehistoric times to and including the Qing period.

The exhibits feature a map of the province, objects from the Qian Lian Gang culture of about 5000 B.C., red-and-gray pottery, jewelry, bone needles, polished stone tools, fine examples of pottery with black-and-white designs from a later period, bronze objects from about 3000 B.C. unearthed near the University of Nanjing.

There are bronzes from the Shang Dynasty, models depicting the State of Wu in the Zhou era, fine examples of Han pottery, the salt trade under the Han, iron smelting, a rubbing showing a weaving loom, an old map of Nanjing, another showing the trade routes to the South Seas under the Six Dynasties, a superb set of tomb figurines from the same era, and information about the mathematician Zu Chong Zhi who made an accurate estimation of *pi*.

There are Song agricultural tools made of iron, a rubbing showing Suzhou in the thirteenth century, objects from the Southern Tang tombs unearthed south of Nanjing, early Qing scroll painting of Suzhou, examples of jade and ivory work, clocks, carved bricks, texts of works by Moslem authors, a brick with the name of the maker, a Spanish coin unearthed at Nanjing, and furniture from the house of a Qing landlord.

Taiping Museum

The Taiping Museum is in the southern part of the town, housed in buildings which once formed part of the palace of the "Eastern King" under the Taiping "Celestial Emperor" Hong Xiu Quan.

The exhibits feature a photograph of the Bridge of Jintian Guangzi province, where the first uprising occurred; a map showing how the movement spread; the declaration made by Hong Xiu Quan after taking Nanjing; his seal and that of his son; various texts relating to land taxes; coins; an address made to soldiers asking them to respect the rights of civilians; and various other texts.

There are exhibits of cannons cast during the Taiping rule; texts of civil law, one abolishing the custom of buying additional wives; passports allowing travel within the occupied region; texts indicating the suppression of the study of classics; various maps showing other uprisings; weapons and standards; and exhibits illustrating the fall of the "Celestial Capital," Tianjing (Nanjing) in 1864. The museum is located at 128 Zhanyuan Road; tel. 23024.

EXCURSIONS FROM NANJING

There are more sights of interest to the visitor outside the city than there are inside. Most are located toward the eastern hills, known to the residents of Nanjing as **Zi Jin Shan,** or the Purple and Gold Mountains.

Here you will find the tomb of the emperor who founded the Ming Dynasty, the Sun Yatsen Mausoleum, the site of the temple of the Valley of the Spirits, the Ling Gu pagoda, and the Purple and Gold hill observatory. Further to the north is the burial ground of the brothers of a Liang Dynasty emperor.

The Tomb of Emperor Hong Wu

The Mingxiaoling (Ming tomb), or Huang Ling (emperor's tomb), is the tomb of the founder of the Ming Dynasty, the "Beggar King," who died in 1398 at the age of 71. He is buried beside the empress, who died 16 years before him.

When visiting the tomb you will pass along the Sacred Way, the royal pathway that was traditional in the Ming era. First you enter through the Great Gate, passing a stele mounted on a tortoise. The path turns to the west, and you cross a bridge over a small river, after which you pass between the stone animals on either side; they are in pairs alternately standing and sitting. Then two pillars precede the court officials and the members of the military. Then you pass through the Ling Xing Men gate and follow the path until it turns into the traditional access route toward the tomb.

You pass through a gate in a wall and enter the first courtyard, which leads to a terrace and a hall housing a number of steles. A second courtyard reveals the remains of the hall. On the terrace is a pavilion (built under the Qing) leading to the third and final courtyard, which is about 500 feet long. You cross a bridge spanning a canal and follow the path to a large stone building of trapezoid shape; in it there is a wide door leading to a passage which traverses the building and rises upward to a terrace.

Before you stands the tumulus of the emperor who was the founder of one of China's most famous dynasties. It remains unexcavated.

The Mausoleum of Sun Yatsen

The mausoleum of Sun Yatsen, known as Sun Zhong Shan Ling, is on the southern slope of the Purple and Gold Mountains. Dr. Sun Yatsen, also known as Sun Zhongshan after the county near Macao where he was born, is a revered patriot who struggled to rid China of the Manchu and introduce democratic ideals to China. In 1912 Sun Yatsen became the president of the Republic of China for a short time.

You enter through a gateway with three arches, above which are to be found two Chinese characters meaning "universal love." An avenue of trees leads to the three-arched main gate, above which are inscribed the

Chinese characters meaning "the world belongs to everyone." The gate leads to a pavilion with a blue glazed roof housing a huge granite stele.

After this you climb eight sections of stairs, about 392 in all, leading to the mausoleum itself. Inside, a white marble statue of Sun Yatsen seated is mounted on a pedestal carved in bas-relief; around the walls engraved in gold letters on black marble are quotations from the first President's work and extracts from the National Charter and the 1912 Constitution of the Republic.

Behind the statue a door opens into a circular domed hall and then a gallery which overlooks the recumbent marble figure of Sun Yatsen on the tomb.

There is a fine view of the surrounding hills from the terrace in front of the mausoleum. As you gaze downward you will notice that the buildings are white with blue glazed-tile roofs, the colors being those of the Guomindang flag.

Wu Liang Dian

The Wu Liang Dian is the only building remaining on the site of the Temple of the Valley of the Spirits, or Linggu Temple. The existing name is an abbreviation of Wu Liang Shou Fo, referring to a statue of the Buddha "of immeasurable eternity" which once stood in the pavilion.

The temple was first established under a Liang emperor in the sixth century at a site about five miles east of the existing palace; it was then five stories high and constructed entirely of wood. It was destroyed and rebuilt many times over the succeeding centuries, until in the later Ming period it was dismantled and carried to the present site so that an emperor could build his own palace where the temple was standing. It was severely damaged during the Taiping Rebellion and restored in 1911 under the Guomindang and reconstructed. The building is made entirely of stone, without beams, hence its other name, "beamless hall." The interior may remind you of an ancient castle.

Linggu Pagoda

The Linggu Pagoda is of recent construction. Erected in the 1920s, it is octagonal, nine stories, or almost 200 feet, high. Each side of the pagoda has an arched doorway leading to a balcony, while inside there is a spiral staircase of stone allowing passage to the top. The internal beams are decorated with simple motifs in subdued style. The top of the pagoda is surmounted by a spire of the blue glazed tiles. The upper floors command a fine view over the surrounding countryside and look down upon the roof of the Sun Yatsen mausoleum in the distance.

Other sights in the park include the **Tomb of the Monk Bao Zhi,** who lived in the sixth century under the Liang, and a **Tang Stele** on which a poem by Li Bai is engraved.

Observatory

The trip to the observatory at Nanjing is worthwhile because you will be driven along narrow country lanes which eventually wind upward through a thick green forest to a peak of the Purple and Gold Hills.

Outside the observatory proper is a collection of magnificent bronze castings of ancient astronomical instruments. An armillary sphere is mounted on legs cast in the form of dragons. The original was made in 109 B.C. under the Han; it was reproduced over 300 years ago by the Ming, was stolen by the Germans during the Eight Power occupation of China, returned in 1921, and replaced at the Nanjing observatory in 1924.

An improved version of the armillary sphere was designed to be operated by two men. By using a graduated scale attached to the instrument, it was possible to fix the location of stars and planets. It was designed about 600 years ago under the Yuan by one of China's foremost astronomers. The reproduction of the instrument on display was taken by the French in the nineteenth century and housed in the grounds of their Embassy in Beijing; it was returned in 1905 and restored to its original position.

A sundial here is said to have been designed over 3,000 years ago. It is said that Chinese astronomers of that period had already calculated the passage of the earth around the sun as exactly 365¼ days. The instrument on display is a reproduction from the Ming cast in bronze.

It is sometimes possible to inspect the observatory facilities. You should ask your guide to call the Chinese Academy of Science office there (tel. 42700) and arrange an appointment.

Liang Dynasty Tombs

The Liang Dynasty Tombs are north of Nanjing. There is little to be seen except a few statues that have been found (A.D. 502–556). The four tombs are believed to have been those of the brothers of Emperor Wu.

There are a number of steles, some mounted on tortoises, and some interesting statues of Bi Xie mythical beasts carved from stone.

Market

Situated in the center of the city of pre-Revolution days, the market is especially worth a visit during the Lantern Festival, when families gather to show their homemade lanterns. On ordinary days there are lots of things to see: goldfish, teapot plants; homemade products, craft ware. The market is at the site of a former Confucian temple.

YANGZHOU

Yangzhou is an ancient town situated on the junction of the Grand Canal and the Yangzi River, about 45 miles east of Nanjing. First settled over 2,400 years ago, it became an important cultural and commercial center under the Sui and the Tang. It was still a great city in the thirteenth century during the time of Marco Polo; later, when the Grand Canal declined in importance, so did Yangzhou. During the Qing it has become merely a retreat for the court, and today there is little that remains as witness to its former grandeur. Nevertheless it has sites of historic and cultural interest.

Perhaps the best place to start is at **Slender West Lake,** or Shouxi Hu, in the northwest of the town. In the surrounding parklands are fine old edifices: the **Angling Pavilion,** where the famous Qing Emperor Qianlong caught fish in the eighteenth century; the **Wutang Bridge,** reputedly one of the finest ancient bridges still standing in China; and the **White Dagoba,** a copy of the one in Beijing.

Three gardens are worth visiting: the **Ge Garden,** the **He Garden,** and the **Xiaopangu Garden;** but perhaps of greater interest are the pagodas in the town. The most famous are the seven-story **Wenfang Pagoda** overlooking the Grand Canal in the south of Yangzhou, and the five-story **Wenchang Pagoda** in the grounds of the temple of the same name.

The **Daming Temple** in the northwest of the town was founded over a thousand years ago and destroyed many times over the centuries. The extant buildings date from 1934. The famous monk Jianzhen studied there and eventually became abbot; a memorable hall devoted to him stands near the temple.

The **Tomb of Puhaddin,** a sixteenth-generation descendant of Moham-med, overlooks the Grand Canal in the east of Yangzhou; and the **Xiahe Mosque,** founded in the twelfth century, stands in the center of town off Wenhe Road. Should there be time, a visit to the **History Museum** is worthwhile.

Yangzhou may be reached in two and one-half hours by bus from Nan-jing, or an hour and a half from Zhenjiang. It is also accessible by bus from Suzhou and Wuxi. There is no plane or train service direct to Yang-zhou, although it is possible to take a train to Zhenjiang, then a bus to Yangzhou.

Yangzhou-style cuisine is famous in China. People living in neighboring towns often come to Yangzhou simply to try Yangzhou's specialities. The best restaurant is in the **Yangzhou Hotel,** but others worth trying are the **Caigenxiang** (tel. 22079) at 115 Guoqing Road, and the **Yechun Restaurant** near the Xijuan Hotel.

ZHENJIANG

Zhenjiang is another ancient town on the confluence of the Yangzi and the Grand Canal, like Yangzhou, standing on the south bank of the great river, about 35 miles east of Nanjing. Compared to Yangzhou, it is a pros-perous town, due in great measure to the rail line that connects it to both Shanghai and Nanjing, but it is heavily industrialized.

The best known scenic spot in the town is at **Beigushan,** overlooking the river in the eastern suburbs. At the top of the hill is an **Iron Pagoda** dating from the Song (960–1279 A.D.) and various pavilions. Farther east, Jiaoshan or Fuyusan, the latter meaning **Floating Jade Hill,** dominates the skyline. There is an active monastery on the hillside, as well as numer-ous pavilions and steles.

A few miles northwest of the town stands **Jinshan,** well known for the two caves that are described in an ancient Chinese tale, but especially for the appealing **Jinshan Temple,** one of the oldest in the region. In the grounds stands the seven-story **Cishou Pagoda,** with its graceful upturned eaves.

PRACTICAL INFORMATION FOR NANJING

FACTS AND FIGURES. Nanjing is at approximately the same latitude as Sa-vannah, Georgia. Distances: about 560 miles southeast of Beijing by air, about 620 miles by rail; about 685 miles northeast of Guangzhou by air, no direct flight (change at Wuhan or Changsha), about 1,325 miles by rail; about 109 miles north-west of Wuxi by rail; about 140 miles northwest of Suzhou by rail; about 195 miles northwest of Shanghai by rail.

WHEN TO GO. Autumn is the best time to visit Nanjing, particularly the months of October through mid-November. In October the days are still warm, the average daily maximum being in the 70s and the average daily minimum being in the 60s. The evening temperature during that period is most pleasant. Rainfall is about twice weekly but not heavy.

Try to avoid a visit in summer. Nanjing is one of the "furnace cities" of China, with an average daily maximum in the 90s and a minimum in the high 70s. The nights are hot and it can be difficult to get a good night's rest. Humidity is very high during the day.

Winter is cold, but not excessively so as in North China. The temperature rarely goes below zero and the average daily maximum is usually in the high 40s.

Spring weather can be pleasant, with warm days, but you will often encounter drizzling rain and high humidities.

HOW TO GET THERE. The easiest and quickest way to get to Nanjing is to fly from Beijing: the daily flight takes 1 hour, 35 minutes. There is also a direct flight to Nanjing from Hong Kong, taking 1 hour, 50 minutes.

If you prefer to go by train, the most convenient departure from Beijing is at 5:50 P.M., arriving in Nanjing next day at 10:20 A.M. This is the fastest service available. Some other trains take up to an additional 8 hours.

From Nanjing you can readily embark on a tour taking in Wuxi, Suzhou, Shanghai, and Hangzhou. Wuxi is 3 hours by train, Suzhou another hour beyond that, and Shanghai another 2¼ hours beyond Suzhou. Hangzhou is 3 hours beyond Shanghai by fast train or 25 minutes by plane. One pleasant way to travel from Nanjing to Shanghai is by the river ferry. The trip takes 24 hours. Or arrive at Nanjing on the ferry that originates in Chongqing. This trip takes a few days. Boats leave daily. CITS can make the arrangements.

HOTELS. The most prestigious hotel is the luxurious **Jin Ling Hotel** (tel. 644141 or 641121; cable 6855; telex 34110) on Xinjiekou Square, a high rise towering over the city, offering 760 modern rooms and a revolving rooftop restaurant called the Sky Lounge. The Purple Mountain Ballroom is the largest pillarless function room in China seating 1,125 people. The Jin Ling is one of the foremost hotels in China. Opened more recently is the **Meiling Palace** situated near the Sun Yatsen Mausoleum. Formerly the residence of Madame Chiang Kaishek, this superb mansion will accommodate up to 15 people in luxurious style.

Many visitors are accommodated in the **Nanjing Hotel,** 259 Zhongshan Road (tel. 634131); located in quiet and pleasant grounds with neatly kept lawns and large shade trees. It is one of the most pleasant hotels in the provinces.

Other hotels are: **Dingshan,** 53 Zhenjiang Road (tel. 685931); **Shengli** or **Victory,** 75 Zhongshan Road (tel. 648181); **Shuangmenlou** or **Double Gate,** 38 Shuangmenlou/Zhongshan North Road (tel. 685965); **Renmin,** 591 Taiping Nan Road (tel. 623779); and the **Dongjiao,** 5 Zhongshanling (tel. 641700).

RESTAURANTS. There is no resident foreign community in Nanjing, apart from a few hundred students, so there are few restaurants catering to foreign visitors aside from those located in hotels. The better "masses" restaurants are:

Sichuan, 171 Taiping South Road (tel. 642243, 643651).

Jiangsu, 126 Jiankang Road (tel. 623698).

Lao Guangdong, 45 Zhongshan North Road (tel. 642482).

Dasanyuan, 38 Zhongshan North Road (tel. 641027).

Liuhuachun, 248 Shaoshan Road (tel. 652318).

Ma Xiangxing, 5 Zhongshan North Road (tel. 633807).

Beijing Yangrou, 94 Zhongshan East Road (tel. 642585).

Luliuju, 248 Taiping South Road (tel. 643644).

The Nanjing region is known for its duck dishes, local inhabitants claiming that their city prepares better roast duck than Beijing. Flat duck, duck liver, roast chicken with herbs, squirrel fish, and—in autumn—freshwater crab, are all specialties.

TOURIST INFORMATION. CITS (tel. 685921) is at 202 Zhongshan North Road. The CITS office at the Jingling Hotel handles reservations for hotel guests only, while the one at the railway office handles train bookings only.

CAAC (tel. 643378, 645482) is at 5 Rui Jin Road. Open 8–11:30 A.M. and 2:30–5 P.M.

PSB is located in a lane that runs off Zhongshan South Road. Walk south from the traffic circle at the intersection of Hanzhong Road and Zhongshan South Road. The lane is to the right (west) and the PSB is identified by a sign in English, Chinese, and Russian.

HOW TO GET AROUND. Sightseeing tours are arranged by CITS. Otherwise you may care to hire a car and driver. Budget travelers may wish to make use of the extensive bus and trolley-bus services in the city. There is also a shuttle-bus service between the Ming Tomb, the Sun Yatsen Mausoleum and the Linggu Pagoda.

WHAT TO SEE. Many visitors get most satisfaction from the sites at the eastern hills of Zi Jin Shan, or Purple and Gold Mountains. There you will see the **Ming tomb** of Emperor Hong Wu and his wife, the **Mausoleum of Sun Yatsen,** the **Wu Liang Dian temple,** and the **Ling Gu pagoda.**

The magnificent Ming reproductions, in bronze, of ancient astronomical instruments may be seen at **Nanjing Observatory** located in the hills slightly to the north of these sites.

The **Bridge over the Yangzi** will be high on your list, not only because it gives a superb view over this famous river but because it represents a remarkable feat of engineering. Next you would probably wish to visit **Xuan Wu Lake,** where you can also inspect one of the **city gates,** visit the nearby **zoo,** and then see the pagoda and the two southern **Tang tombs** at Bull's Head hill.

After this, there is still the **King of Borneo's tomb,** the remains of the **Ming Palace,** the **Liang Dynasty burial grounds** outside the city, and, if you have time, the museums and perhaps a visit to the **University of Nanjing.**

MUSEUMS. Nanjing has four museums. The best known is the **Nanjing Museum,** or Banshanyuan, at 321 Zhongshan East Road (tel. 641554) with exhibits ranging from the neolithic period to the Qing. The **Taiping Museum** at 128 Zhanyuan Road (tel. 23024) has exhibits relating to the Taiping Rebellion. Of lesser interest are the **Jiangsu Provincial Art Museum** at 266 Changjiang Road (tel. 642884) and the **Museum of Nanjing Municipality** at 4 Chaotiangong (tel. 641983).

SHOPPING. The shopping is fairly good at Nanjing. You may wish to start at the **People's Friendship Store,** 3–9 Daqing Road or the **People's Department Store,** 71 Zhongshan Nan Road. You will find an excellent range of silk fabrics available. Fine brocades and satins are also available. Tea from Nanjing is top quality. An excellent range of porcelain and ceramic ware is produced, and arts and crafts factories in the region produce excellent reproductions of centuries-old antiques; the Arts and Crafts Co. is located at 199 Zhongshan Road. Aquarium owners will be interested in the colored stones from the Yu Hua Tai (Rain of Flowers Terrace).

If you are interested in antiques, you should visit the **Antiques Shop** (tel. 644550), 7–11 Hanzhong Road.

ENTERTAINMENT. Try to see the **Nanjing Acrobatic Troupe,** one of the finest in China.

LEAVING NANJING. Departure by boat or bus present interesting alternatives to air and rail.

Two boats depart Nanjing each day for Shanghai, one at 5 P.M. (arriving noon next day), the other at 11:20 P.M. (arriving 3:20 P.M. next day). There are 2 boat services to Wuhan: the first departing 2 P.M., the second at 3.30 P.M., each arriving 40–48 hours later, depending on the strength of the current.

Buses leave Nanjing for Wuxi, Hangzhou, Huang Shan, Changzhou, and Zhenjiang.

USEFUL ADDRESSES AND TELEPHONE NUMBERS

CITS—202 Zhongshan North Road (tel. 685921).
CAAC—5 Rui Jin Road (tel. 643378, 645482).
PSB—off Zhongshan South Road.

NANNING

Guangxi Zhuangzu Autonomous Region

South China

Nanning, capital of Guangxi Zhuangzu Autonomous Region, stands on the north bank of the Yong River, about 15 miles downstream from the confluence of the You and Zuo Rivers. Nanning is only about 125 miles from the border of China and the Republic of Vietnam (and about 205 miles from Hanoi). It is the last major town in China on the rail link (closed) between Beijing and Hanoi.

Nanning is not an old town. It was founded under the Yuan and did not develop until this century. Consequently, there are few monuments, temples, or places of interest for a visitor.

The name of the province, Guangxi, means "wide west." Guangxi is an "autonomous region" by virtue of a large population of minority people known as the Zhuang; its administrative status confers upon the province a well-defined and limited degree of autonomy. The Zhuang are a Thai-speaking group of about 12 million, most of whom live in the region. Their language, closely related to Chinese, has no script of its own. Although they have some customs that resemble those of the Miao group who also live in the province, the Zhuang have become almost completely assimilated into the Han race. There are also small groups of the Yao, Dong, Shui, and Miao.

The province is best known in modern history for the development of the Taiping, or Heavenly Kingdom of Great Peace Rebellion. In 1850, in the village of Jintian, the man who was to become the leader of the rebels proclaimed himself to be the "younger brother of Jesus Christ." He established a commune that was joined eventually by tens of thousands of villagers from the region.

Edicts, designed to reform taxes, redistribute land, emancipate women, and bring about a more just and humane society, were proclaimed. The rebels formed an army and marched northward; they took Hankou (Wuhan), then Nanjing, where they set up their capital. During this period hundreds of thousands of Chinese fled their homeland and emigrated to the United States and other Pacific countries. The rebels eventually tried to take Beijing (in 1864) but, weakened by rivalry within their ranks, Taiping fell to the combined armies of the European powers and the Manchu.

EXPLORING NANNING

Nanhu

Nanhu, or South Lake, in the southeastern quarter, is a pleasant part of the city, and the gardens in the park on the lake's edge are attractive. There is a restaurant on the lakeshore. The lake's main attraction is the

Dragon Boat Festival on the fifth day of the fifth lunar month (around June 15). About a quarter of a million people participate in the festival, the highlights of which are the races between crews paddling long narrow canoes and the competition for the best decorated boats. The festival, having a tradition of 2,000 years, was stopped during the decade of the Cultural Revolution (1966–1976) but resumed in 1978.

The Old Fort

The fort in the People's (Renmin) Park was constructed by a warlord who was active in Guangxi in the early years of this century. Placed on the highest part of town, it provides an excellent view of the surrounding area, particularly the river. In the fort is a large cannon, manufactured by Krupp in 1908, one of 108 cannons purchased by the Governors of Guangzhou and Guangxi to position along the border with Vietnam in order to defend China from a possible invasion by the French who, at that time, ruled Indo-China.

White Dragon Lake

The White Dragon Lake in Renmin Park is traversed by a decorative bridge that zigzags to foil evil spirits which, according to the sages of the time, can travel only in straight lines. The bridge leads to a pavilion on the lake and to an attractive teahouse on the shore. There are a number of pavilions of Qing origin scattered through the park, as well as a herbarium displaying over 1,400 plants used in traditional Chinese medicine. Attached to each plant is a small metal plate giving the plant's name in Chinese and Latin, where it grows, the plant's medicinal use, and its physiological effects.

EXCURSIONS FROM NANNING

Yiling Cave

About 12 miles northwest of the city, close to Yiling village, Yiling Cave is in the area known as the Nanning Hills. The cave is lit with colored lights and has a path about half a mile long which allows the sights to be examined at ease. There is a small shop and restaurant at the cave entrance.

Brigade of the Two Bridges

The Zhuang production brigade of the Two Bridges is about 30 miles to the north of Nanning, near the town of Wuming. The drive provides a superb view of the countryside and, on arrival, you will be met by members of the friendly and colorful Zhuang minority. A small pagoda, built under the Qing, is only a few minutes' walk from the brigade reception center.

Rock and Cave Paintings

An interesting excursion from Nanning takes you to the area in which a series of rock and cave paintings have been found. The seven sites are within a triangular area formed by three towns: Chongzuo, Ningming, and Longzhou. All are between 60 and 80 miles southwest of Nanning.

The first rock paintings were discovered in 1957 and as yet their origin and date is uncertain. The ochre paintings, featuring people, animals, and objects, vary in height from one to 10 feet. Many are badly damaged.

The most conveniently located of the seven sites features only several figures on the walls of caves. The site is about five miles north of Ningming. The second site, with about 20 figures (most of them badly damaged), is on the right bank of the Ming River in Longxia Gorge, not far from the first site. The third site, with about 100 figures, is a few miles north of site 2. The fourth site, with more than a thousand figures, is located a few miles north of site 3 and about 15 miles north of Ningming. The fifth site has only four figures, and is north of site 1, but on the opposite side of the Ming River. The other two sites are quite a distance from the first five. The sixth site, with over four hundred figures in two caves, is about 35 miles east of Longzhou. The seventh site is due east of site 6, about 15 miles west of Chongzuo. It has only 10 figures and is in a poor state of preservation.

PRACTICAL INFORMATION FOR NANNING

FACTS AND FIGURES. Nanning, capital of the Guangxi Zhuangzu Autonomous Region (Guanxi Zhuangzu Zizhiqu), is China's southernmost city. An industrial center with a population of just over 650,000, Nanning lies on China's rail link with Vietnam. Local air and rail services link the city with the surrounding provincial capitals of Guangzhou, Changsha, Guiyang, and Kunming. The city lies on approximately the same latitude as Havana, Cuba. It is 828 miles by rail from Guangzhou, 1,281 miles from Shanghai, and 1,593 miles from Beijing.

WHEN TO GO. Nanning is reasonably pleasant all year round. The winter season (December to February) is mild and you will generally need only a light topcoat or woolen sweater. Spring ushers in showery weather, so light rainwear is normally required. Summer is warm and humid, the incidence of rainfall being greatest in this season. Fall is ideal, with warm days and crisp nights.

HOW TO GET THERE. The quickest way to go to Nanning is to take a flight from Guangzhou, a journey of 1 hour 5 minutes on the fastest aircraft on the route. You can also fly there from Guilin (55 minutes) and from Kunming (1¼ hours). Services to all other airports touch down at intermediate airports en route.

Travel by train to Nanning is time consuming. From Changsha, the journey takes 16½ hours, which in turn is 11½ hours from Guangzhou, 21½ hours from Shanghai, and 21½ hours from Beijing. Guilin to Nanning takes 9¼ hours by day train and 8 hours by night train.

There are daily bus services, some air-conditioned, to Wuzhou.

HOTELS. Visitors stay at one of four hotels: the **Mingyuan** (tel. 28923), 38 Xinmin Road; the **Yongjiang** (tel. 28123), 41 Quannan Road, overlooking the river; the gracious **Xiyuan** (tel. 29923, telex 48137), 38 Jiangnan Road, with its enormous gardens; and the **Yongzhou** (tel. 28323, telex 48145), 59 Xinmin Road, accommodating 850 in 3 buildings. The Xiyuan has a swimming pool and provides excellent accommodations—it was formerly a state guest house—while the others are of reasonable standard (although some rooms are equipped with the hard beds used commonly throughout the region). Mosquito nets are provided and are necessary at certain times of the year.

RESTAURANTS. Apart from the hotel dining rooms, a number of restaurants are worth trying. There is the **Nanhu Fish Restaurant** (tel. 2477) in South Lake

Park, specializing in fresh fish caught in the lake. The **Nanning Restaurant** (tel. 2473) in Minshen Road has many dishes to tempt the adventurous eater, such as turtle, lizard, and snake. If these tempt you try the **Snake Restaurant** (tel. 26433) in Xijiao Park. Dog is also served there. Local game dishes are prepared at the **Bailong Restaurant** in Renmin Park. Generally the cuisine of the region is similar to Guangzhou, so there are plenty of standard dishes to try, e.g., suckling pig.

TOURIST INFORMATION. CITS (tel. 22042) is at 40 Xinmin Road.

CAAC (tel. 23333) is at 64 Chaoyang Road. From the railway station walk to the first traffic circle and cross to the opposite side; continue straight ahead; it is on the left just past the corner.

The **long-distance bus terminus** is also in Chaoyang Road, on the next corner when walking south (i.e., away from the railway station) from CAAC.

HOW TO GET AROUND. Tours of the city and excursions to outlying sights can be arranged through CITS. The energetic may wish to hire a bicycle to get around the city. The two bicycle-rental shops are both difficult to find, so you will need to enlist the aid of your hotel.

WHAT TO SEE. The **Nanhu,** or **South Lake,** is worth a visit and is a "must" around June 15 when the famous Dragon Boat Festival is held. The **Old Fort,** where there is an old Krupp cannon, provides an excellent view of the surrounding area and the river. **White Dragon Lake** in Renmin Park is appealing with its zigzag bridge and teahouse. **Xijiao Park** is a pleasant place to stroll and relax; and should you feel like seeing an arts-and-crafts exhibition, the **Nanning Arts Institute** is worth a visit. For excursions, you can visit the attractive **Yiling Cave,** some 12 miles from the city, and then travel further afield to a commune known as the **Brigade of the Two Bridges.** If you have time, you should also try to visit the area south of Nanning where there are ancient rock and cave paintings of uncertain origin.

MUSEUMS. The **Guangxi Zhuang Provincial Museum** (tel. 4403) on July First Square has an interesting array of exhibits, particularly those relating to the many national minority groups living in the region. **Exhibition Hall** (tel. 4154) in Minzhu Road has periodic displays of interest to foreign visitors.

SHOPPING. Many national minority items are for sale, as well as the standard range of arts and crafts items. The plaited bamboo ware is attractive, there is a good selection of lacquerware to choose from, and carvings in wood and stone are worth inspecting. The Friendship Store (tel. 3480) in Xinmin Road is a good place to begin, then the Antiques Shop (tel. 4430) of the Nanning Museum, on July First Square, and the Arts and Crafts Store (tel. 2772) on Xinhua Street. For publications, try the Foreign Language Bookstore (tel. 7033) on Xinhua Street.

ENTERTAINMENT. The **Nanning Theater** (tel. 3515) in Jiangnan Road is a modern and attractive auditorium capable of seating 1,700 people. Built in 1975–1976, it has a large garden attached to it, with palm trees and ponds. Many concerts and plays are given at the theater, but one opera has its origins in the region: *Third Sister Liu.* This is based on a Zhuang nationality story and tells of a rebellious young woman who sides with local tea planters in a dispute with their landlord and the local authorities. After a number of misfortunes, she outwits her antagonists, then leaves to fight injustice elsewhere. In some versions a romance theme runs through the plot.

Outstanding cultural events may be witnessed throughout the year, the dates of each being based on the lunar calendar. There is the **Lantern Festival** on the fifteenth day of the first month, the **Zhuang Song Festival** on the third day of the third month, the **Dragon Boat Festival** on the fifth day of the fifth month, and the **Mid-Autumn Festival** on the fifteenth day of the eighth month.

USEFUL ADDRESSES AND TELEPHONE NUMBERS

International Calls—Operator, tel. 113. Information, tel. 116.
Directory Inquiries, tel. 114.

China International Travel Service—40 Xinmin Road (tel. 24793, 22042).
CAAC—64 Chaoyang Road (tel. 23333).
Nanning Railway Station—tel. 22468.

QINGDAO

Shandong Province
North China

Qingdao is the second largest town in Shangdong Province and an important port. The word means "green island" and derives its origin from the town's location at the tip of a promontory enclosing a large bay. Qingdao is an industrial city, known throughout China for its beer (Qingdao brand), mineral water, wine, and textiles.

The town was seized by Germany in 1897 on the pretext of punishing the Chinese for the assassination of two German missionaries. In reality, the Kaiser wished to gain a base for the German navy in the Far East. A modern town was constructed on the site of the small village that had existed there. Port installations were laid down, the town electrified, and a business section established. German troops were garrisoned. Within a few years, a railway line was built to connect Qingdao with Jinan.

The Germans held the town until the Japanese seized it in 1914. In 1922 they returned it to the Chinese. Qingdao fell to the Japanese again in 1938 during the Sino-Japanese war and was recaptured by the Chinese in 1945.

The town is well known in China as a seaside resort. The combination of sea breezes, cool water, pine forests, and white-sand beaches make it a popular vacation spot. However, by comparison with most cities in China, it offers little in the way of sightseeing; there are no ancient sites or historical monuments in the area.

EXPLORING QINGDAO

There are only a handful of places to visit in Qingdao. In the town itself, **Luxun Park** and **Zhongshan Park** are enjoyable to explore. The **Exhibition Hall of Aquatic Products** features aquariums and showcases filled with hundreds of different species of fish and other forms of marine life. There are excellent beaches for bathing near the town.

A pleasant hour or two may be spent on the scenic pier that juts into the bay. The twin-roofed **Rebounding Waves (Huilan) Pavilion** stands at the far end. You can also tour the Qingdao Brewery and sample the beer.

EXCURSIONS FROM QINGDAO

The **Laoshan** mountain range is about 28 miles east of Qingdao. The main peak is **Mount Laoding** with an altitude of 3,800 feet. There are three separate roads, the northern route leading to the Taoist **Temple of Taiping,** or Great Peace. The temple east of town was first constructed under the

Song (960–1280), but the present buildings are of more recent date. Near the palace are the scenic spots White Dragon Cave, Cuiping Grotto, Sheep Rock, Lion Crag, and Hunyuan Rock. The southern route leads to the Taoist **Temple of Taiqing,** or Supreme Purity, the largest temple complex in the region.

PRACTICAL INFORMATION FOR QINGDAO

FACTS AND FIGURES. Qingdao sits on a peninsula jutting into the Huanghai (Yellow Sea) on the east coast of Shandong Province, about 245 miles due east of the provincial capital Jinan. With a population of 1.4 million, Qingdao is an industrial center as well as a holiday resort with some fine beaches.

WHEN TO GO. The summer months are the best time to visit, as the weather is at its best, and the water—though still cool because of the cold currents sweeping down the coast—provides relief from the hot sun. In the swimming season, June through September, you will find the town filled with vacationers and the beaches crowded with bathers. June and August can bring thick sea mists of a foglike consistency. Spring and autumn are pleasant even though the sea is colder then.

HOW TO GET THERE. Qingdao may be reached by rail from Beijing (17 hours), Shenyang (26 hours), Xian (31 hours), and Shanghai (24 hours). There is a once-every-4-days boat service to Dalian (26 hours) and to Shanghai (27 hours). Boat tickets may be bought at the boat station near the Friendship Store (12 Xinjiang Lu).

HOTELS. The delightful **Zhanqiao Guest House** (tel. 83402), opposite Beach no. 6 at 31 Taiping Road, is one of the best places to stay. It has an excellent dining room. Another establishment offering good accommodations is the **Badaguan Guest House** (tel. 62800) at 15 Shanhaiguan Road. It provides rooms in the main block or in 14 villas. The **Huiquan Dynasty Hotel** (tel. 285215, telex 32178), 9 Nanhai Road, is near the 2 parks in town and overlooks Beach no. 1. Other hotels are: the **Qingdao** (tel. 26747; Qufu Road); the **Friendship** (tel. 28865; 12 Xinjiang Road); the **Yingbinguan** (tel. 26120; 45 Longshan Road); the **Haibin Hotel** (tel. 24447; Guangxi Road); the **Overseas Chinese Hotel** (tel. 86738; 72 Hunan Road); the **Longshan** at 14 Longshan Road; and the **Huanghai** (tel. 270215) at 75 Yanyi Road, with 450 rooms and a poor dining room.

RESTAURANTS. The best restaurants are located in the hotels. An exception is the **Chunhelou** (tel. 227371) on Zhongshan Road. Seafood dishes, including the slippery sea cucumber, abalone, shellfish, prawns, and scallops are specialities.

TOURIST INFORMATION. CITS (tel. 284830) is at the Huiquan Hotel, 9 Nanhai Road.
CAAC (tel. 283057) is at 29 Zhongshan Road.
The **Qingdao Harbor Passenger Terminal** is off Guanxian Road, close to the Friendship Store.

HOW TO GET AROUND. Tours and excursions are arranged by CITS. Bus no. 6 is useful for budget travelers: it runs south down Zhongshan Road, then turns east towards Beach no. 3. Three-wheeler "cabs" are available at the railway station.

WHAT TO SEE. The **Pier,** with the **Rebounding Waves Pavilion** at the far end, is one of the most prominent landmarks in Qingdao. It overlooks **Little Green Island** and the white lighthouse across the bay. Qingdao is renowned throughout China for its excellent and well-protected beaches. There are some fine parks: **Zhongshan Park** where there is a zoo, botanical gardens, and the **Zhanshan Temple; Luxun Park** overlooking no. 1 Beach; and the **Zhushuishan Park** with a "children's palace."

The **Badaguan District** is criss-crossed with streets all lined by elegant villas, and decorated with flowering plants. Here you will find the **Old German Quarter** and the villa of the former German Governor.

Other sights in the town include the **Qingdao Brewery,** the old **Catholic Church,** and the **Locomotive Factory.**

Excursions may be taken to the Laoshan region where there are a number of Taoist temples.

MUSEUMS. The two interesting museums are the **Museum of Marine Products** and the **Qingdao Museum** with its collection of paintings dating to the Yuan Dynasty.

SHOPPING. A variety of textile materials is available in Qingdao. Shell-craft mosaics and the embroidery are specialities of the region, and there is a full range of other handicrafts; the most interesting shops are in Zhongshan and Jiaozhou roads in the center of town, while the markets are in the streets near the Catholic Church.

The **Friendship Store** (tel. 27021) is in Xinjiang Road; and the **Qingdao Department Store** (tel. 24916) in Zhongshan Road. For antiques and craft products try the **Qingdao Antiques Store** (tel. 84436) at 40 Zhongshan Road, or the **Qingdao Arts and Crafts Store** (tel. 25116) at the same address.

ENTERTAINMENT. There are no specific evening events worthy of special note, but in July and August you should try to see the **Lantern Festival** in Zhongshan Park.

USEFUL ADDRESSES AND TELEPHONE NUMBERS

CITS—Huiquan Hotel (tel. 284830).
CAAC—29 Zhongshan Road (tel. 283057).
Railway Station—Tai An Road (tel. 84571).
Ferry Dock—Xinjiang Road (tel. 25001).

QUANZHOU

Fujian Province
South China

Quanzhou, the ancient seaport, was founded in A.D. 718. In the thirteenth century Marco Polo described it as one of the foremost ports in the world. Centuries before that, it was an important world center of trade, when thousands of sailing vessels would arrive to load cargo destined for Asia, India, Africa, and the Arab States. It is now a quiet town protected by the State Council as a historical monument.

Situated about 110 miles south of Fuzhou, and about 35 miles north of Xiamen, Quanzhou has many sights of interest for the visitor, even though little remains of its ancient structures.

EXPLORING QUANZHOU

The **Kaiyuan Temple** is the major sight in Quanzhou. Founded in 686, the extant buildings date from the Ming and the Qing. The main hall houses five gilded statues of the Buddha and, on the temple columns, 24 rare "flying musicians" of gilded clay. On the temple grounds stand the **Zhenguo Pagoda** to the east and the **Renshou Pagoda** to the west.

Nearby, the **Museum of Quanzhou's Overseas Trade** has a remarkable exhibit: the restored hull of a large sea-going junk that was sunk over 600 years ago. In the south of the town stands the **Mosque,** called Qingjing, constructed in 1009, the exact copy of a mosque in Damascus. Two **Moslem Tombs** outside the east gate of the city date from the Tang; about four miles east is the **Luoyang Bridge,** first built in stone in 1053 and rebuilt numerous times over the centuries.

About two miles outside the city is a **Statue of Lao Tzu,** the founder of Taoist faith.

EXCURSIONS FROM QUANZHOU

Tomb of Koxinga

Sixteen miles northwest of Quanzhou lies the tomb of Koxinga, or Zheng Chenggong, the notorious pirate-general who ruled the South China coastline as well as Taiwan in the seventeenth century.

The Ming court fled south in 1644 when their army fell to the Manchu invaders. The Ming princes enlisted the aid of Koxinga to retake the capital. His troops fought the way as far as the Grand Canal but could not get beyond it to seize Beijing. After that campaign, he led his fleet to Taiwan in 1661, to destroy the Dutch, but he never realized his dream of returning to the mainland to free China from the Manchu rule.

At the height of his power, Koxinga commanded about 800,000 pirates and soldiers, and possessed a fleet of 800 war junks. There is a museum devoted to the pirate-general in Xiamen.

PRACTICAL INFORMATION FOR QUANZHOU

FACTS AND FIGURES. The port city is located in Fujian Province in Southeast China, 122 miles southwest of the provincial capital, Fuzhou, and 61 miles northeast of Xiamen. The city stands on the north bank of the Jin River. There is no rail link to Quanzhou yet (although a spur line to Xiamen is under construction), but it is accessible by air, boat, and bus.

Quanzhou is one of the cities declared a historical monument by the Chinese State Council.

WHEN TO GO. The weather is hot and humid in summer, while the winter is mild with occasional cold spells. The rainy season extends from July through September, which is also the typhoon season. Autumn is the most pleasant season for travel.

HOW TO GET THERE. There are daily flights between Hong Kong and Xiamen, the nearest airport, 2½–3 hours away by bus. Xiamen is also served by regular flights from Beijing, Guangzhou, Shanghai, and major provincial capitals.

The long-distance bus station is in the southeastern sector of Quanzhou: services to Fuzhou (about 6 hours) begin at 6 A.M., the last bus leaving at 12:40 P.M. Eight of the 10 daily departures are between 6 A.M. and 9:50 A.M. Services to Xiamen (about 2½–3 hours) begin at 7 A.M., the last bus leaving at 3:25 P.M.

There is a daily air-conditioned bus service between Quanzhou and Shenzhen, with an overnight stopover at Shantou, and there is a service to Guangzhou.

The rail link from Guangzhou to Xiamen to the south has not been completed. Xiamen and Fuzhou are the nearest centers.

HOTELS. The **Overseas Chinese Hotel** (tel. 22192) on Beiyanqingci Road provides simple accommodations; rooms are air-conditioned and equipped with mosquito nets. Another hotel, the **Golden Fountain** (tel. 22137) on Zhongshan Road, recently opened, provides reasonable accommodations.

RESTAURANTS. Because of the abundance of seafood available, restaurants in Quanzhou specialize in fish, crab, prawns, octopus, scallops, and other shellfish. Another speciality is fried rice threads, often eaten in a soup. Restaurants mainly serve dishes in the tradition of the Fujian-Cantonese style.

Two restaurants serving regional specialities are the **Mantang** (tel. 2887) at 3–5 Zhongshan (Central) Road; and the **Furenyi** (tel. 2759) near the intersection of Zhongshan South Road and Shuimen Road.

TOURIST INFORMATION. CITS (tel. 2191, 2366) is in the Overseas Chinese Hotel on Beiyanqingci Road.

PSB is at 334 Dong Jie; from the clock tower at the intersection of Dong (East) Jie and Zhongshan Road, walk east for about 5 minutes. The office is on the left-hand side of the street.

HOW TO GET AROUND. Quanzhou is small enough to explore on foot. As there is no bus service, the only alternative to walking is to take a bicycle rickshaw that seats 2 passengers.

There are buses for destinations outside of the town; they leave from the square at the northern end of Zhongshan Road. (Long-distance buses leave from the south of town).

WHAT TO SEE. You should not miss the beautiful **Kaiyuan Temple** which was first established under the Tang (and was then known as the Lotus Temple). There are 2 Song Dynasty hexagonal stone pagodas in the temple grounds: the **Zhenguo Pagoda**, which stands 158 feet high; and the **Renshou Pagoda**, which is slightly smaller. Both are over 700 years old.

The **Qingjing Mosque** is the oldest extant mosque in China. Stone tablets on display are inscribed in both Arabic and Chinese. Two **Moslem Tombs** stand outside the east gate of the city, the final resting place of 2 missionaries of Islam. A **Statue of Lao Tzu,** the revered Taoist sage, also stands outside the city.

Fine stonework is to be seen along the **Luoyang Bridge,** first constructed over 900 years ago, and spanning the river of the same name. In the **Qingyuan Mountains** just north of the city, there are relics of old temples, rock calligraphy, caves, and springs.

MUSEUMS. The **Museum of Quanzhou's Overseas Trade** has exhibits and interesting historical references to Chinese and Arabic maritime exploits, but the major exhibit is the remains of a Chinese junk that was brought up from the bottom of Quanzhou's port in 1974. The vessel, about 80 feet long and 30 feet wide, is more than 700 years old.

SHOPPING. Some of the region's specialities are wooden puppets, wood carvings, stone carvings, laquer ware, embroidery, porcelain, artificial flowers, and woven bamboo products. Apart from the **Friendship Store** on Zhongshan Road, you can try the **Arts and Crafts Store** (tel. 2613) at 508 Zhongshan Nan Road, or the small street stalls.

SHAOSHAN

Hunan Province

South China

Shaoshan, about 80 miles southwest of the provincial capital, Changsha, is famous in China as the birthplace of Mao Zedong. A visit to the site gives you the opportunity to observe the lush scenery of rural China.

EXPLORING SHAOSHAN

The village of Shaoshan is situated in a valley surrounded by green hills. The road to the village from Changsha is paved, passing through the town of Xiang Tan before crossing the paddy fields to enter the hill country where tea plantations and orange groves abound.

The road ends at a square in front of the hotel built to provide accommodation for the people who make the pilgrimage to the site. The path leads off to the right to the white schoolhouse Mao attended, past the farm pond where he used to bathe, to the house where he was born in 1893.

According to Mao, his father was a poor peasant who joined the army in order to pay off some heavy debts he had incurred. Through frugal living the father managed to save enough money to buy back his land and, in time, became what is known in China as a "middle peasant," the family owning about 15 *mou*, or two and one-half acres, of land.

Mao recounts how he began to help his father on the farm at the age of six. At eight he entered primary school, and at age 13 he began long hours of manual labor on the farm, doing the accounts in the evening.

The farmhouse is typical of the Hunan area and is built on the slope of a hill overlooking the pond. On the other side of the pond stands a neighbor's house. Visitors pass into a courtyard, and the front door leads into a room which was once the family's altar to the ancestors. Behind there is a wash-house equipped with a stove and in the floor an open drain, then a kitchen with a large stove. The kitchen connects with the dining room, and from there the visitor passes into the bedroom of Mao's parents; this opens into Mao's room. From here you pass into the interior courtyard, around which are various sheds: tool shed, rice-storage room, cow shed, wood shed, and pigsty. There is also a guest room off the courtyard. Entering the house again, the visitor passes into a corridor; to the left is the bedroom of Mao's elder brother.

There are no organized excursions available but, if you are staying overnight, you will have time to walk along the narrow roads in the countryside surrounding the hamlet and trek into the hills. The site of a Taoist temple is to be found on the highest hill.

PRACTICAL INFORMATION FOR SHAOSHAN

FACTS AND FIGURES. Shaoshan is about 80 miles southwest of Changsha, in the hill country of Hunan Province.

WHEN TO GO. Autumn is the best time to visit, for then the hot and humid weather so typical of summer is rarely evident. Spring tends to be accompanied by showers, while winter brings cold weather, sometimes light snow.

HOW TO GET THERE. CITS arranges excursions by bus from Changsha, so inquire at their office or your hotel. Local buses depart from the Changsha long-distance bus terminal three times each morning for Shaoshan and return in the afternoon.

The train is another means of travel for many visitors, departing Changsha at 7:30 A.M. and arriving Shaoshan at 10:42 A.M. The return journey begins at 4:30 P.M. to arrive in Changsha at 8:05 P.M. For budget travelers, there is a slow bus departing at 12:45 P.M. daily from the long-distance bus terminal just north of the Changsha railway station.

HOTELS. The **Shaoshan Hotel** (tel. 2127), with accommodations for about 300 guests, provides rudimentary facilities. An alternative is the **Xiangtan Guest House** (tel. 23165) on Shaoshan Xi Road, about two miles from the railway station.

RESTAURANTS. There are no restaurants outside the hotel.

TOURIST INFORMATION. The hotel is the only source of information about sightseeing.

HOW TO GET AROUND. Everything can be covered on foot.

WHAT TO SEE. The sights are the house where Mao was born, the **Mao Zedong Museum,** and the scenery of the surrounding countryside.

Near the house a modern exhibition building has been built where memorabilia of Mao are on display. There are portraits of his wife, and also of his two brothers and his sister, all of whom died during the revolution; books he liked to read as a child; reproductions of some of his notes. Other rooms commemorate the founding of the Communist Party in Shanghai, the founding of Peasant Societies, the establishment of the First Revolutionary Base at Jinggang Shan, and records of the efforts to bring the Communist movement to the masses in the various provinces.

You may also visit the building where Mao held his first meeting on his return to Hunan in 1926–1927 to organize Peasant Societies and to spread the word of revolution. He was then 33 years old.

SHENYANG

Liaoning Province

Northeast China

Shenyang is the capital of Liaoning Province in China's Dongbei, or northeast region. The city used to be known as Mukden, a name used by the Tartar people who once ruled the area. It is an old town, its origins dating back some 2,000 years, but it did not rise to prominence until the eleventh century, when it became a busy trading post for tribes living north of the Great Wall.

When the Tartar clans were forged into a single fighting force under Nurhachi (1559–1626), Shenyang became the court of the Manchu (the "Masters" as they called themselves) and the capital of Manchuria. When the Manchu took Beijing (1644) and established the Qing Dynasty there, Mukden became their secondary capital and remained so for over 250 years.

The last decade of the twentieth century brought Shenyang tranquility to an end when China fought a disastrous war with Japan (1894–1895). The town was later involved in the Boxer Revolution (1900), then occupied during the Russian-Japanese War (1904–1905), ruled by various Chinese warlords (1916–1928), seized by the Japanese (1931–1945) following the famous "Mukden Incident," ransacked by the Russians in 1945, subjected to a 10-month siege during the Chinese Civil War (1946–1949), and finally taken by the Chinese Communist forces on November 1, 1948. Since then, Shenyang has been rebuilt, so that today it is the most important industrial center in China after Shanghai.

The province of Liaoning is the smallest of the three that make up Dongbei. It once formed part of what was known as Manchuria, a word the Chinese carefully avoid because it conveys the impression that the area is not ethnically Chinese but Manchu. Liaoning's resources are substantial: there are rich deposits of coal, iron ore, and nonferrous ore throughout the province, all contributing to the region's well-developed industrial base. On the Liao plain, crops of corn, kaoliang, and millet are cultivated; even rice is grown. Apples, cotton, and tobacco are also produced.

EXPLORING SHENYANG

The Imperial Palace

Mukden, once the heart of the old Tartar nation, became the capital of Manchuria shortly after Nurhachi founded the Qing Dynasty. At that time (1625) it had a strategic importance for the Manchu, being a short ride to the Great Wall and China, and only two days' ride from Mongolia. It was also on the land route to Korea.

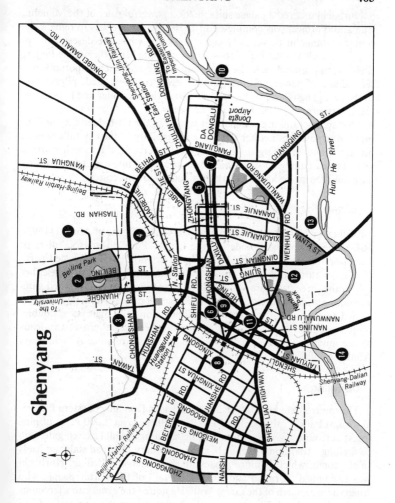

Shenyang

Points of Interest

Cemetery of Martyrs 1
China International Travel Service 11
East Pagoda 10
Friendship Store 6
Imperial Palace 7
Liaoning Exhibition Hall 12
Liaoning Guest House 9
Liaoning Mansions Hotel 3
Northern Imperial Tomb 2
North Pagoda 4
Old City 5
Shenyang Cultural Palace 14
Shenyang Railway Station 8
South Pagoda 13

Nurhachi ordered a palace suitable for a powerful ruler of the Manchu. The grand project was completed in 1636, but the site was to remain the center of Manchu power only eight years, for when the descendants of Nurhachi rode into China in 1644 and routed the Ming they made Beijing their capital instead. Yet the Shenyang palace remained important as a second seat of power, and the Qing emperors regularly made pilgrimages to the Dongling (Eastern Imperial Tomb) of their founder and to the Beiling (Northern Imperial Tomb) of his son.

The layout of the site is somewhat similar to the Forbidden City in Beijing, but it possesses neither the brooding majesty of the capital's palaces nor the grandeur, being smaller in scale. Nevertheless, it is well worth a visit. The east and west wings have been converted into a museum housing an exhibition of archaeological relics and historical objects.

Beiling

Beiling, or Northern Imperial Tomb, is the burial site of Abukai (1592–1643), the son of the founder of the Qing ("Pure") Dynasty, rulers of China between 1644 and 1911. The tomb lies in a heavily wooded park. You enter through a white stone *pailou* with four lions guarding either side of the three passageways. Next you pass through a three-arched gateway into a wide passageway. Beyond the small pavilion you enter a high-walled section with triple-roofed pavilions along the main axis; double-roofed pavilions guard the four corners of the walls. An archway leads to the inner courtyards and beyond to the burial mound. A stele bears Abukai's calligraphy.

Dongling

The tomb of Abukai's father, Nurhachi, is in Dongling (Eastern Imperial Tomb) Park on the banks of the River Shen. Over 1,000 acres of pine forest surround the site. After entering the dragon-emblazoned gate, you pass along a traditional avenue of animal statuary. A broad staircase leads to the tomb, which is more modest in scale than the Beiling. Nurhachi was the famed "Dragon and Tiger General" of the Tartar people who ruled the area north of the Great Wall. He united the clans into a ferocious fighting force that held sway from the Yellow Sea in the east, to the Gobi Desert in the west. His tribal banners streamed victoriously the length and breadth of the Manchurian plain. The rulers of Korea and Mongolia recognized him as their suzerain, but the Chinese held him and his people in contempt. To the Chinese, the Tartars were "dog people": fierce, uncivilized barbarians.

In 1616 Nurhachi proclaimed himself emperor of the "Great Pure" or Da Qing Dynasty and his domain was called Manchuria, land of the Manchu ("the masters"). He was known far and wide as Tai Zong, the Exalted Founder. He did not live to rule China—at that time under the Ming Dynasty—but his grandson did, in 1644, when the Manchu swept into the Middle Kingdom striking terror into the hearts of all those who lived south of the Great Wall. The Qing Dynasty was to rule China for over 250 years. The court became "more Chinese" than the Chinese themselves, but the Manchu were always considered by the Chinese as aliens.

EXCURSIONS FROM SHENYANG

Two major excursions may be taken from Shenyang, each involving one (or more) night's stopover. The first is to the seaside resort of **Dalian,** or Lüda as it is sometimes called; the second is to **Anshan,** a major Chinese industrial city of interest to businessmen.

Three minor excursions take you to **Qianshan Park,** some 12 miles south of Shenyang; to the village of **Xisheng,** where you may stay overnight; and to **Yixian,** about 95 miles west of Shenyang, where the **Fenggou Temple** stands, said to be the largest temple of its type in China.

Dalian or Lüda

Dalian, often called Lüda, is located near the tip of the promontory that juts from Liaoning Province into the Bo Hai Gulf. It is an important port, serving the industrial centers located in the three provinces—Liaoning, Heilongjiang, and Jilin—and a major commercial center, the focal point of the Dalian Economic and Technical Zone. Dalian is a well-known summer resort, attracting foreign tourists and locals with its excellent beaches and pleasant hotels. You can get there by taking the train from Shenyang (six and one-quarter hours), or a direct flight from Beijing (an hour and a half). The train from Beijing goes to Dalian via Shenyang. Cruise ships often call at the port.

Dalian has no monuments or ancient historic sites, but you may arrange to visit the town's schools, kindergartens, parks (e.g., Tiger Beach Park), and suburban communes. There is also an interesting zoo. Summer is the ideal time to visit; you can spend time on the beaches, have a swim, or just watch the small sailboats skimming around the bay. Spring and fall are pleasant, although the water is cooler. Winter is extremely cold. The ocean waters of Dalian never freeze.

The **Holiday Inn Dalian,** (tel. 230668; telex 86383), 18 Shengli Square, provides international standard accommodations in 226 rooms, with three restaurants, a coffee shop, and a business center. Another new hotel is the **Dalian International** (tel. 238238, telex 86363), 9 Stalin Road, a 383-room hotel of international standard situated in the heart of the city's commercial center. Other modern hotels are the **Furama Dalian** (tel. 239128; telex 86441), with 480 rooms, 4 restaurants, indoor pool, disco, and business center, and the **Dalian Regent** (tel. 238248), with 220 rooms, two restaurants, and a business center. There is a guest house complex of 10 buildings, the **Bangchui Guest House** (tel. 25131; telex 86236) on the coastal road near the beach. The **Dalian Binguan** (tel. 23111) is conveniently located at 3 Zhongshan Road in the center of town. It is an old Soviet-style building with large rooms and a magnificent dining room which was once the "Grand Ballroom." Other hotels are **Dalian Hotel** (tel. 23171, 23941) at 6 Shanghai Road; the **Friendship Guest House** (tel. 24121) at 137 Stalin Road; the **Yunshan Guest House** (tel. 25163, 26719) in Zhongshan Square; and the **Seaman's (Club) Hotel,** opposite the Friendship Store.

Dalian is famous for its seafood, particularly fish, giant prawns, and sea cucumbers. The hotel restaurants are of good standard, but if you are in Dalian for more than a few days, you might care to try one of the "masses" restaurants, such as the **Haiwei** (tel. 27067), 85 Zhongshan Road, which has an enormous menu of seafood dishes.

Anshan

Anshan is a grimy industrial town of little interest to the tourist that is often visited by foreign businessmen. Its fiery blast furnaces and belching smoke stacks dominate the skyline, offering a constant reminder to the visitor that it is one of China's major iron and steel centers. Early records show that iron was smelted at Anshan as early as 100 B.C. The industry developed over the centuries, but was closed down by the superstitious Manchu emperors who feared that their ancestral tombs far to the north would be threatened by the mining. The production of iron and steel began again in the early 1900s under the Japanese occupation of the area.

In 1945 the Soviet Army captured Anshan and immediately began to dismantle all the plants and equipment of the factories, sending it all by rail to the U.S.S.R. What little remained of Anshan's industry was destroyed during the Chinese civil war, 1946–1949, when the city changed hands 11 times in bloody fighting. Anshan has since been rebuilt and its industry restored. The town now occupies about twice the area that it did under the Japanese.

Most visitors are lodged at the **Anshan Guest House** (tel. 25993; telex 24403), 121 Shengli Road, which has 72 rooms, a Chinese and a Western-style restaurant, and a CITS office (tel. 24908 or 24403).

The most interesting sites are in **Tanggangzi Park,** about 6 miles south of the town: one is a house built by the Manchu warlord Zhang Zuolin who was the military governor of Shanyang until he was assassinated in 1928 by the Japanese, who blew up his train; the other is a house built by the last Qing emperor, Pu Yi. The hot springs and sanitarium in the park are famous, thousands traveling from all over China to enjoy the mineral baths and rest cures. There is one park in Anshan itself: **Eryijiu Park,** on the eastern edge of the city; it has three large lakes and pleasant walkways.

Two temples in the vicinity of Anshan, the Dragon Spring Temple and the Zhonghui Temple, are worth a visit.

PRACTICAL INFORMATION FOR SHENYANG

FACTS AND FIGURES. Shenyang, the capital of Liaoning Province, is about 375 miles northeast of Beijing. The journey by train from Beijing takes 10–11 hours; by air 2–2¾ hours, depending on aircraft type. Shenyang has a population of about 2½ million.

WHEN TO GO. The best times to visit are April and May, when the weather is usually warm and the rainfall light, or September and October for similar reasons. Try to avoid winter, which is severe.

HOW TO GET THERE. The train journey from Beijing takes 10–11 hours and you will pass through Tianjin, the seaside resort Beidaihe, and Shanhaiguan where the Great Wall meets the sea.

All of these places are covered in this book, and you might care to stop over at one or more towns en route. The most convenient train, if you are going all the way to Shenyang without stopovers, is the express departing Beijing at 10:13 A.M., because you will be able to take in most of the scenery in daylight. You will see the Great Wall at 5:00 P.M. before speeding on in darkness to reach Shenyang at 11:10 P.M. If you wish to save time and arrive early, take the overnight express from Beijing departing 1:13 P.M., arriving Shenyang at 6:50 A.M. next morning. By plane the journey Beijing-Shenyang takes about 2–3¼ hours, depending on the type of aircraft on the service.

HOTELS. The main hotel is the **Phoenix** (tel. 64854; telex 80045) at no. 3, section 6, Huanghe Street, in the Huanggu District. The **Liaoning Guest House** (tel. 32641), 27 Zhongshan Road, is like a trip back in time. Formerly the Mukden Hotel, it boasts a marble lobby, high ceilings, *art nouveau* stained-glass windows, and some fine slate billiard tables. It was, in the 1940s, the site of meetings for delegates from the rival political groups fighting China's civil war. A smaller guest house, the **Liaoning Mansions** (tel. 62546, 21921), at 1 Huanghe Street and adjacent to Beiling Park, provides accommodations in 500 adequate rooms. Another hotel in that area, the **Friendship Hotel** (tel. 62822, 61398), also on Huanghe Street on the western side of Beiling Park, boasts a heated indoor swimming pool.

Other hotels are: **Liaoning Dongbai** (tel. 32031) at no. 1, 7 Li 3 Duan, Taiyuan Road, suitable for budget travelers; the **Overseas Chinese (Huaqiao) Hotel** (tel. 34214) near the railway station at no. 3, section 1, Zhongshan Road.

RESTAURANTS. The best restaurants are found in the hotels mentioned above. The specialty of the region is the Mongolian Hot Pot, or Huoguo. For this dish, finely cut pieces of raw lamb, beef, and sometimes chicken, are served. A cooking pot of boiling water is brought to the table over a brazier of hot coals. You then dip each slice of meat, one at a time, into the boiling water. When the slice is cooked—usually a minute or two later—you dip it into one of the sauces prepared from sesame oil, shrimp paste, soy sauce, rice wine, chili sauce, vinegar, and scallions. Vegetables and noodles are cooked along with the meat. When the meat is finished, the water in the pot, full of juices from the meat and vegetables, is served as a broth.

Other restaurants you may care to try are the **Lumingchun** (tel. 25127) on Zhonghua Road, and the **Shenhe** (tel. 44020), Zhongjie Street. If you are after dumplings, try the **Laobian Eating House** (tel. 447941), 6 Zhongyang Road in Beishichang. You can wash them down with vodka served warm in small porcelain cups.

TOURIST INFORMATION. CITS (tel. 66037), at 3 Huanghe Street, is near the Liaoning Mansions.

CAAC/China North Airline (tel. 34089, 32396) is at 31 Zhonghua Lu, Sanduan.

HOW TO GET AROUND. Tours and excursions are organized by CITS. Bicycle hire is available from the shed next to the Liaoning Dongbei Hotel.

Budget travelers should note that bus no. 10 goes from the center of Shenyang to the Imperial Palaces, while buses no. 6 and no. 20 go from the town center to the Northern Imperial Tomb. To reach the Eastern Imperial Tomb, take bus no. 18 from the Imperial Palaces, then walk.

WHAT TO SEE. The principal historic monuments are the **Qing Dynasty Imperial Palaces,** where the Manchu rulers lived from 1625 to 1643, before they moved their capital to Beijing. There are two interesting tombs in Shenyang. The son of the founder of the Qing Dynasty is buried in one: **Beiling, or Northern Imperial Tomb,** now surrounded by a forest parkland called Beiling Park. His father is buried in **Dongling, or Eastern Imperial Tomb,** located in a park called **Dongling Park** about 5 miles from the center of Shenyang, on the Shen River.

Visitors interested in the history of the Chinese revolution may care to visit the **Cemetery of the Martyrs,** not far from Beiling Park. Anyone interested in industry should visit the **Liaoning Exhibition Hall** (tel. 82882), Nan Yijing Road, near Nanhu Park in the south of the city; the many industrial products of Shenyang and the region are on display there. The **Shenyang Cultural Palace,** located between the main railway station and Zhongshan Park, often has displays of interest.

If the **Shenyang Acrobatic Troupe** is performing at one of the theaters, do not miss the opportunity to see it. Shenyang is famous for its acrobats; you may even be able to visit one of the acrobatic schools in the city.

MUSEUMS. The east and west wings of the **Imperial Palace** (tel. 43819) house exhibitions of archaeological objects found in the province, including neolithic relics from the Xinyue site. It is one of the finest museums in China. The **Liaoning Museum** (tel. 24228) in Sanjing Road is also worth a visit. Train buffs will admire the **Shenyang Locomotives Museum.** CITS can arrange entry.

SHOPPING. Fur and feather products are specialties of the region, as are ginseng (ginger) and antler powders. Most visitors begin their shopping at the **Friendship Store** (tel. 33753) on the western side of Zhongshan Road. Those seeking antiques should check the **Antiques Shop** (tel. 34380), Taiyuan Street, while those seeking arts-and-crafts items may care to go to the **Center of Fine Arts** (tel. 35754), also on Taiyuan Street. Locally made consumer products may be purchased at the **People's Department Store** (tel. 33711) near the Liaoning Guest House.

ENTERTAINMENT. Try to see the Shenyang Acrobatic Troupe, one of the best group of acrobats in China, and well-known internationally. Check with your hotel or CITS to learn if there are any evening performances during your stay.

USEFUL ADDRESSES AND TELEPHONE NUMBERS

Hospital—Office, tel. 23784. 24-hour emergency service, tel. 21740.
Long-distance calls—Operator, tel. 03. Information, tel. 06.
Directory—Local calls, tel. 06.
Telegrams—Information, tel. 24500.
China International Travel Service—3 Huanghe Street (tel. 66037).
CAAC/China North Airline Ticket Office—31 Zhonghua Lu, Sanduan (tel. 34089, 32396).
Airport—Departure lounge (tel. 42719).
Railway Station—Information, tel. 204193. Ticket office, tel. 20161.
United States Consulate—40 Lane 4, section 5, Sanjing Street, Heping District (tel. 290038).

SHIJIAZHUANG

Hebei Province

North China

Shijiazhuang is the capital of Hebei Province in the North of China and an important railway junction. The town, sheltered on the west by the Taihang Mountains, is modern and well planned but without character.

Cotton is sown in large areas near the town and throughout Hebei Province, and Shijiazhuang has developed into one of the major textile-processing centers in China. Considerable industrialization has taken place in recent years, so that the town has numerous plants engaged in chemical production, machine building, and light industry.

Shijiazhuang itself is of little interest to tourists and is visited mainly by traders. However, several excursions of artistic, architectural, and historic interest can be made from the town.

EXPLORING SHIJIAZHUANG

You won't tire yourself when taking in the sights of Shijiazhuang, for there is not much to see. You may wish to visit the **Tomb of Dr. Norman Bethune,** who served China selflessly during the 1930s. His tomb is in the Cemetery of Martyrs located between Zhongshan Road and the Xinhua Road. There is also the Former Communist Party Headquarters for the Northern Campaign (1947–1948) and the Dongfanghong (East Is Red) **Exhibition Hall,** which mainly displays industrial products made in the region and, occasionally, holds a cultural exhibition. Other places to visit are the two parks: **Dongfanghong Park,** near the corner of Dongfanghong Road and Jianshe Street; and the People's Park off Xinhua Road.

EXCURSIONS FROM SHIJIAZHUANG

A stopover at Shijiazhuang provides an opportunity to make interesting excursions to four other centers in Hebei Province: **Zhengding, Xing Tai, Fengfeng,** and **Handan.** If you like bridges, don't miss the **Zhaozhou Bridge** at Zhaoxian, some 25 miles to the southeast. The temples, pagodas, and bridges of the **Cangyan (Green Cliff)** scenic area are worth a visit.

Zhaozhou Bridge

The graceful stone structure of the Zhaozhou Bridge, or the Anji Bridge, or the Dashi (Big Stone) Bridge, is a triumph of ancient engineering. Spanning the Jiahe River about 2 miles south of Zhaoxian County (which is 25 miles southeast of Shijiazhuang), the bridge was first constructed in 590 under the Sui. It is considered to be the first open-arched bridge ever built in the world. Of graceful proportions, it is about 150 feet long and 30 feet wide, decorated with carved balustrades of dragons and mythical beasts.

Zhengding

Zhengding is about 10 miles north of Shijiazhuang. There you will be able to visit Long Xing Si, or **Long Xing Monastery** whose temples date from the Song and the Jin, i.e., from the tenth to the thirteenth centuries. The Long Xing Si is the oldest pre-Ming monastery still standing in China.

The most famous buildings are the Da Bei Ge, or **Temple of Great Mercy,** a huge structure of magnificent proportions. It houses one of the four marvels of Hebei, a 70-foot bronze statue of Guan Yin or **Bodhisattra of Great Mercy,** with 42 arms. Molded in seven stages in 971 and now one of the tallest bronze statues extant in China, the monument represents one of the great works of bronze art from the Song period. It stands on a stone base covered with fine bas-relief carvings.

The Zhuan Lun Zang Dian, or **Pavilion of the Rotating Library,** is part of the same monastery. The pavilion, restored in the mid-1950s, is a remarkable example of Song architecture and reveals unusual innovations in architectural design. The octagonal library, constructed to hold the sutras, or holy Buddhist texts, revolves inside the pavilion.

Within the monastery grounds you will also see a number of steles, the oldest of which dates from the Sui (A.D. 589–618). In addition, there are a number of buildings constructed by the Jin during the twelfth and thirteenth centuries.

In another section of the town stands a pagoda, also built under the Jin and now classed as a historic monument. The Guang Hui Si Hua Ta, or **Flowered Tower of the Monastery of Far-Reaching Wisdom,** is built of brick on an octagonal base. Its ornate style contrasts with the austere lines of the Kai Yuan Si Zhuan Ta, or the **Pagoda of the Kai Yuan Monastery.**

Tour buses depart Shijiazhuang daily at 7:30 A.M. and 1:30 P.M. (the journey takes about 20 minutes), returning at 9:40 A.M. and 3:40 P.M. Your hotel or CITS can arrange tickets.

Xing Tai

Xing Tai, about 70 miles south of Shijiazhuang, is connected to the provincial capital by rail. You pass through the town on your way south to Zhengzhou on the Yellow River.

In the west of the town stand the two remaining temples of the Tian Ning Si, or **Monastery of Celestial Tranquility,** first built under the Tang. The present temples date from the Qing, although their style is fourteenth-century Yuan. Near the temples is a **Buddhist Chuang,** dating from the Tang, and a pagoda built under the Yuan in the early fourteenth century.

Other monuments may be seen around the site of the former Kai Yuan Si, or **Kai Yuan Monastery,** founded under the Tang in the Kai Yuan period (A.D. 713–742). There are two large Buddhist columns near an eight-roofed pagoda.

Also located nearby, northwest of the Kai Yuan Monastery, is a monument that has proved to be of great significance to China's historians— the **Dao De Jing Shi Tai,** a Taoist column with eight sides. The Dao De Jing, considered to be a sacred text by Taoists, was written in the fourth century B.C. Parts of the text are inscribed in large characters on seven of the facets. The eighth facet of the column has engravings made under the Song.

Canyang Hill

Canyang or Green Cliff Hill is a scenic area about 50 miles west of Shijiazhuang that abounds with woods, steep cliffs, temples, pagodas, and ancient bridges. One of the most famous sights is the **Hanging Palace**—a twin-roofed hall constructed on a bridge spanning a deep gorge, and said to date from the Sui (589–618). Another notable structure is the Buddhist **Fuqing Monastery** where a Sui emperor's daughter, Nanyang, once became a nun. Her tomb is nearby. There are many other sights of cultural and of historic interest in the area.

Fengfeng

Fengfeng and Handan are in the far south of Hebei Province, about 105 miles from Shijiazhuang and about midway to Zhengzhou. It is difficult to undertake this excursion without spending a night at Handan. Fengfeng, which is about 20 miles from Handan as the crow flies (about 45 miles by the rail loop), is the more interesting of the two places. However, you must go through Handan to reach Fengfeng.

At Fengfeng you will see the **Mount Xiang Tang Buddhist Carvings,** a milestone in the progress of Chinese Buddhist art and a revelation of the ultimate domination of the Chinese style over the earlier styles influenced largely by India.

There are two sets of caves about nine miles apart. The southern set is located near the village of Peng Cheng, near the Xiang Tang Si, or **Monastery of the Echoing Hall,** dating from the Qing.

Seven caves have been cut out of the rock on two levels, five above and two below. Note the fine bas-relief carvings in the rock beside the path leading from the monastery. The caves are full of statues and have basrelief carvings on the walls. Unfortunately, many of the statues are damaged.

The other group of caves is located near the village of Hu Cun near a nine-story pagoda that was once part of Chang Le Si, or the **Monastery of Eternal Joy.** Three caves in the southern group are filled with statues, carved during the Sui and early Tang periods. There are five caves on two levels in the northern group, dating from later periods.

All the caves are classified as historical monuments.

Handan

Handan is well known as the site of the former capital of the kingdom of Zhao (Warring States period, 476–221 B.C.). The remains of the old capital stand about three miles southwest of the town. The site, classified as an historical monument, is known as Zhao Wang Chang, or the **Town of the King of Zhao.**

Another feature of the area is **Cong Tai,** a large terrace built about 2,400 years ago. A pavilion of recent date now stands on the terrace, where there is a good view of the town and surrounding landscape.

Handan is also known in modern China for its large **Military Cemetery.** Many of the Party and Army members from the surrounding provinces, who died during the Chinese Communist Revolution, are buried here. A monument in the cemetery bears inscriptions by Mao Zedong and Chu

De, a former commander in chief of the Red Army and Mao's close comrade in arms.

PRACTICAL INFORMATION FOR SHIJIAZHUANG

FACTS AND FIGURES. Shijiazhuang is about 175 miles southwest of Beijing on the major rail route between Beijing and Guangzhou (Canton): 3¼–4¼ hours journey from the capital by rail.

WHEN TO GO. Autumn is the best time to travel to Shijiazhuang. Winter is cold and bleak, spring somewhat dusty, and summer hot and humid.

HOW TO GET THERE. The Beijing-Guangzhou express stops at Shijiazhuang: the 6:55 A.M. train from the capital arrives at 10:49 A.M.; the 8:55 P.M. train arrives at 12:15 A.M. Shijiazhuang is also linked by rail to Jinan and Taiyuan. CITS will provide information on connecting services. Shijiazhuang has twice-weekly air links with Beijing, Guangzhou, Shanghai, and Nanjing.

HOTELS. Visitors are lodged at the **Hebei Guest House** (tel. 48961), 23 Yucai Street. The new wing provides air-conditioned rooms with private baths, while the old wing houses rather austere facilities. Another place to stay is the **Shijiazhuang Guest House** (tel. 49986) on Changan Road West, which offers air-conditioned accommodations in the 8-story annex.

RESTAURANTS. There is no restaurant suitable for the tourist other than the one in your hotel. Chinese-speaking visitors of an adventurous spirit might care to try a meal at one of the "masses" restaurants. The new **Zhonghua Restaurant** and the **Yanchun Restaurant** are probably the best.

TOURIST INFORMATION. CITS (tel. 44766) is 22 Yucai Road.
CAAC (tel. 45084) is in Jiefang Road.

HOW TO GET AROUND. CITS arranges tours to the city sights as well as excursions to outlying areas. Ten bus lines operate within the town. Buses to sights outside the city start from the long-distance bus terminus north of Jiefang Road between Shengli and Ping An roads.

WHAT TO SEE. Shijiazhuang is of limited interest to foreign visitors and is worth a stopover more for the fine excursions available from the town rather than for the sights within the urban areas. Nevertheless the town sights include the **Tomb of Dr. Norman Bethune,** and the two city parks: **Dongfanghong Park** and **Renmin Park.**

There are fine excursions to be made, the most noteworthy being to Zhaoxian to see the famous **Zhaozhou Bridge,** to Zhending to see the **Long Xing Monastery** with its splendid temples and 70-foot bronze statue of the Buddha, and to **Xing Tai** where there are superb examples of monasteries, temples, and pagodas.

At **Cangyan Hill** you will see the marvelous **Hanging Palace** and other temples, halls, and shrines. Further afield lies **Fengfeng** in the far south of Hebei Province, center of ancient Buddhist cave art, and **Handan,** the former capital of the Kingdom of Zhao, which met its demise in 221 B.C.

MUSEUMS. Shijiazhuang has a number of museums and similar institutions of interest to visitors. First there is the **Hebei Provincial Exhibition Hall** opposite the intersection of Guang An Dajie with Chang An Road. Then there is the **Dr. Bethune Exhibition Hall,** featuring exhibits commemorating the life of this selfless Canadian medical practitioner, the **East Is Red Exhibition Hall,** and the **Former Communist Party Headquarters.**

SHOPPING. You can shop at the **People's Department Store** on Zhongshan

Road not far from Zhonghua Street. There you will find the usual array of Chinese products. Collectors of internally decorated snuff bottles will find the local products to be of interest. Porcelains from Tangshan and ceramics from Handan are of good value.

USEFUL ADDRESSES AND TELEPHONE NUMBERS

CITS—22 Yucai Road (tel. 44766).
CAAC—Jiefang Road (tel. 45084).
Taxis—4 Shifan Street (tel. 25471).

SUZHOU

Jiangsu Province

South China

Suzhou is in the south of Jiangsu Province, about 50 miles west of Shanghai and about 12 miles from Lake Tai, on the old Imperial Canal. The city has been famous for its scenic beauty for many centuries; a Chinese proverb says: "In heaven there is paradise; on earth Suzhou and Hangzhou." The city has long been noted for its beautiful women.

Suzhou is situated on the delta plain of the Yangzi River, an area dotted with lakes and ponds connected by a spider web of canals, and it is often likened to Venice. The town itself is threaded by canals, and the roadways are linked by fine old humpbacked bridges. All the canals are lined by whitewashed houses with gray-tiled roofs.

The canals of the town eventually join up with the famous local waterway known as the Grand Canal, located to the west of the city. It is believed to be the largest internal waterway in the world, originally constructed to carry tribute grain from the Yangzi plain to the capital. Marco Polo, who visited Suzhou in the thirteenth century wrote that "the great Khan . . . has made a huge canal of great width and depth from river to river and from lake to lake and made the water flow along it so that it looks like a big river . . . By this means it is possible to go . . . as far as Khan-balik" (the name for Beijing under the Yuan). Although the canal is not used for long-distance transportation now, it is still heavily frequented by a vast number of flat-bottom boats under sail and power conveying agricultural produce to nearby centers. Most communes and villages in the area have their own landing stages.

One of the oldest towns in the Yangzi basin, Suzhou was founded in the fifth century B.C., when the King of Wu, He Lu, made it the capital of his kingdom. The king is said to have been buried on Tiger Hill, a well-known landmark.

The town was given its current name in A.D. 589, under the Sui. It developed considerably under the Tang and Song. Indeed, it was under the Song, when Suzhou was about the same size as it is now but enclosed within walls, that some of the famous gardens were first established. And by then it had already become famous for silk weaving.

The city continued to develop and by the late fourteenth century was one of the most important in the Empire. Its silk and embroidery were renowned throughout the land. Marco Polo wrote that the townsfolk "have silk in great quantity and make much silken cloth for their clothing. There are merchants here of great wealth and consequence." The city is so large that it measures about 40 miles in circumference."

In the nineteenth century Suzhou was captured by the Taiping. Later, in 1896, the city was opened to foreign trade with the establishment of international concessions, a trade that was based almost entirely on the silk industry. Even today, silk spinning and weaving are the mainstay of the town's economy. However, there has been some industrial diversification, so that now there are small plants producing ferroconcrete flat-bottomed boats, chemicals, ceramics, and metal products. Handicrafts are also produced: tapestries, embroideries, velvets, and sandalwood fans.

Even so, the combination of narrow streets and canals has impeded "modernization," and the town has been relatively undisturbed by industrial development, leaving large areas just as they were centuries ago.

In the areas around Suzhou rice, wheat, and rape are the main crops; tea is also grown but as a specialty crop. The region is also well known as China's most important area for silkworm breeding; you will see large numbers of mulberry orchards. The orchards are usually located near waterways and are sometimes up to five feet above the level of adjoining crop fields because of the mud that has been dragged from the waterways and used as fertilizer.

Many sites of the famous gardens of Suzhou, known as far back as the tenth century, are intact, and some have been restored to their former beauty. A visit to these gardens will be a highlight of your visit to China.

EXPLORING SUZHOU

Suzhou is a perfect place to explore on foot. In the center of the town, people bustle along the crowded lanes, chattering, laughing, their cries pierced by the metallic ring of bicycle bells.

Turn out of the main streets and stroll down some of the small lanes, or *hutungs*. Soon you will come to narrow canals with cobblestone walks where rickety wooden houses lean against each other. Peek into the white-washed cottages as you walk by and catch a glimpse of families chatting, cooking, eating.

Long narrow boats pass along the network of canals that thread the town. On the steps to the water, women and young girls pound their washing against the stonework. Small boys swim nearby.

In summer, the evening is a good time to stroll. The street lighting is dim, and the darkness lends an anonymity rare for the foreigner in China. You will be noticed only when you pass by an open doorway into the soft glow of an oil lamp. Families sit outside in the cool air, talking quietly or chatting with their neighbors. Men smoke their pipes and children play at the edge of the inky canals.

Cold Mountain Temple

The Cold Mountain Temple, or **Han Shan Si,** will captivate you. It is located on the outskirts of town on a small canal crossed by an old hump-backed bridge called Fengqiao, or Maple Bridge. Green foliage hangs down over saffron walls. When you visit this place you will understand why many poets have been inspired by the scenery.

The temple's name comes from the hermit Han Shan, a Buddhist poet, who stayed there with another hermit known as Shi De sometime during the Tang Dynasty period. The temple was founded under the Liang (A.D. 503–557), burned down during the Taiping revolution, and rebuilt in the late Qing period. The tree standing outside the entrance is the traditional ginko tree, whose leaves are said to bring the breeze to the Buddha by fanning him. You enter through a door set into the saffron-colored walls and pass through an entrance pavilion into a courtyard. There is a tall incense burner in front of the small temple housing a statue of the Buddha

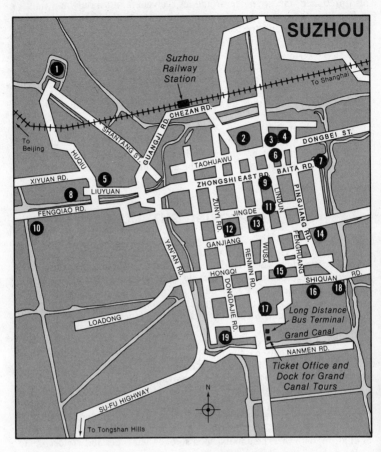

Points of Interest

Beisi (North Temple) Pagoda **2**
Canglang (Surging Wave)
  Pavilion **17**
Frienship Store **11**
Hanshan Temple **10**
Historical Museum **3**
Huqiu (Tiger Hill) **1**
Liuyuan Tarrying Garden **5**
Master of Nets Garden **16**
Nanlin Hotel **15**

Pagoda of the Temple of the
  Good Omen Light **19**
Renmin Bazaar **13**
Suzhou Hotel **18**
Shizilin (Forest of Lions Garden) **6**
Taoist Temple **9**
Twin Pagodas **14**
Xiyuan (West Garden) **8**
Yiyuan (Joyous Garden) **12**
Zhuozhengyuan (Humble
  Administrator's Garden) **4**
Zoo (East) Park **7**

and two attendants. To the right is a bell tower, built under the Qing, in which is suspended a huge bell, the original of which was taken away by Japanese pirates. The replacement bell—cast over a hundred years ago—was donated by a group of Japanese benefactors. On the eve of the Chinese New Year, you can arrange to visit the temple to hear the ringing of the bells and watch the festivities. The pavilion inside the grounds contains two steles showing the two hermit monks, along with an inscription of the poem "Mooring by Fengqiao at Night" by Zhang Ji which has immortalized the temple.

Tiger Hill

Tiger Hill, or Huqiu, a few miles northwest of the town, is very popular with visitors. It is supposedly the burial place of the King of Wu, who founded Suzhou in the sixth century B.C. and made it his capital.

Two reasons are given for the name of the hill. One is that the entrance gate resembles the mouth of a tiger and the pagoda on the top of the hill its tail. The other is that when the King of Wu was buried on top of the hill a tiger is said to have appeared there.

On arrival you will cross a small low bridge and pass through the gate into the grounds. A path leads to the top of the hill. On your left you will pass a well, and further on to your right the **Stone Where Swords Are Tried,** or Shi Jian Shi. Here you will see a thick stone apparently cut into two parts, supposedly severed by the sword of the King of Wu. A little further to the left is the **Pillow Stone,** said to have been used for that purpose by the monk Sheng Gong.

You will also pass the **Tomb of the Good Wife,** or Zhen Naing Mu, erected by the townsfolk in honor of a noble lady who committed suicide following the death of her husband, rather than become a courtesan as she would have been forced to do.

On your right you will come to a pool surrounded by large stones known as the **Thousand Stone Men,** or Qian Ren Shi. Two legends account for the existence of these stones. The first says that they were the followers of the King of Wu who were killed during his funeral rites. According to the second, the stones were so moved by a sermon of the monk Sheng Gong that they actually nodded. This legend has given the **Nodding Stone Pool** its name. There is a small pavilion dating from the Qing alongside the pool.

Next you will come to a small ravine descending into a deep pool known as the **Sword Pond,** or Jian Chi, said to be the burial place of the King of Wu, who was supposedly entombed with about 3,000 of his famous swords. The pond was drained in 1956 when the foundations of the pagoda on the hill were being reinforced, and authorities believed they had found the entrance to his tomb. However, it was decided not to undertake any excavations, since this would have endangered the pagoda even further.

Leaving the pond, you climb to cross the **Bridge with Two Wells,** so called because of the holes used by the monks to drag up water. The path leads to the top of the hill and the pagoda.

Though it is usually referred to as the **Tiger Hill Pagoda,** its correct name is Yun Yan Si Temple Pagoda. It was completed in A.D. 961, some centuries before the Leaning Tower of Pisa. A great deal was learned about the pagoda in 1956, when a workman repairing the inside removed some bricks to reveal a small stone casket hidden inside the inner wall. Other caskets and objects were found in the inner wall of other stories. Inside the caskets were scrolls of Buddhist texts, pieces of pottery, coins, a mirror, prayer beads, and two tools used in building the pagoda. Three headless stone statues of the Buddha were also found, along with an inscription on a wooden box indicating that the pagoda was finished in 961. Before this discovery its age was in doubt.

You will notice that the pagoda has a distinct lean toward the southeast. The seventh and top story was rebuilt in the seventeenth century, presumably because of damage to the structure caused by its instability; further work was done in 1956 and again in 1965 to reinforce the foundations and the internal structure in order to prevent the pagoda from falling to the ground.

The pagoda is octagonal in shape, about 150 feet high, and one of the oldest original pagodas in China. It is constructed entirely of brick and stone, and the absence of wood probably accounts for its long life. The pagoda has been declared a national monument.

Pagodas

Other pagodas are visible in Suzhou, the most conspicuous being the twin pagodas of **Two Pagoda Temple,** or Shuang Ta Si. The temple no longer exists and the site is now occupied by a school. Your guide may offer to take you to view the pagodas, which are accessible from a street called Ding Hui Si Gang.

On the outskirts of town, in the southwest, you will find the pagoda of the **Temple of Good Omen Light,** or Rui Guang Si Ta. The temple no longer exists, and only the seven-story brick pagoda remains.

The other pagoda stands beside what was once the **Temple of Gratitude,** or Pao En Si, sometimes called the Northern Temple, or Bei Si. The temple was founded in the third century A.D., rebuilt in the tenth century, destroyed in the twelfth, rebuilt again, destroyed by fire, and rebuilt under the Ming. The pagoda, thought to date from the twelfth century, provides a superb view of the town. It is well worth the climb.

West Garden Temple

Known in Chinese as the Xi Yuan Si, or Jie Chuang Lü, the West Garden Temple originally dates from the Ming but was destroyed during the Taiping rebellion and reconstructed in the early part of this century. The central pavilion, with its magnificent ceiling, houses statues of the Buddha, various disciples, and the Celestial Guardians. The **Hall of the Five Hundred Adherents** is particularly interesting; there you will see gallery after gallery of statues of the faithful.

The temple grounds are situated beside the Liu Garden, and it is convenient to visit both on the same tour.

Temple of Mystery

The Temple of Mystery, known to the Chinese as Xuan Miao Guan, is considered one of the finest in China. A sacred Taoist temple, it originates from the Jin (A.D. 265–420), but the oldest section now standing—the central San Qing Hall—dates from the Southern Song Dynasty. It has been damaged many times during its history, the last occasion being during the Taiping rebellion, and its last extensive renovation was under the Qing.

You enter through a pavilion containing statues of the four Celestial Guardians and then pass into a large courtyard with the **Hall of the Three Qing,** or San Qing Dian, facing you on the other side. It is a large double-roofed building with the eaves upturned at the corners in traditional fashion. Statues of Taoist deities, the Three Qing, are housed inside. There are a number of steles. The temple is located a short distance from the Garden of Harmony, or Yi Yuan, and it is usually convenient to combine them in the same tour.

Liu Garden

Liu or "Remaining" Garden is acknowledged as one of the four most famous gardens in China, ranking alongside the Humble Administrator's Garden in Suzhou, the Summer Palace in Beijing, and the Imperial Summer Villa in Chengde. It was one of the few gardens that escaped destruction during the Taiping rebellion, and this is symbolized in its name, the Chinese character which means "remaining." There is a play on words here: the first man to acquire the garden when it was first sold was named Liu, which in Chinese is pronounced exactly the same as the word "remaining."

The garden was first laid out during the Ming Dynasty by a civil servant who also had the West Garden, or Xi Yuan, constructed. It was in a rundown state by the middle of this century but was carefully restored and reopened in 1954.

You will find a series of small lakes linked by bridges and numerous buildings, of which the most interesting is the Hall of the Mandarin Ducks (symbols of love). Others have windows giving onto distinctive views of the landscape, and there is an artificial hill. You should take time to visit the section of the garden planted with fruit trees. Ask your guide to take you to the portion devoted to the cultivation of miniature trees. There are hundreds of them; one pomegranate tree is more than 200 years old. In this section you will see numerous trays holding miniature landscapes and rockeries. The owners and residents of the private gardens in ancient China preferred not to leave their beautiful surroundings, and therefore had miniature landscapes made to remind them of other beauty spots.

Next door to the garden is the Xi Yuan Si, or West Garden Temple, already described. It was built in a garden created by the man who built the Liu Garden.

Humble Administrator's Garden

The Humble Administrator's Garden, or Zhuo Zheng Yuan, is another of the four most famous gardens in China. Occupying an area of just over 10 acres, it is the largest in Suzhou. First recorded in history as the residence of Tang poet Lu Guimeng, it was the site of a Temple during the Yuan Dynasty, and converted into the residence and garden of the imperial censor in 1522. Upon his death the garden passed to his son, who lost it while gambling. Through the centuries it passed from hand to hand, until it was made a public garden in 1952.

Because the park was established on marshy grounds there are many lakes, some of which have small islets. Not surprisingly, three-fifths of the area is water.

The origin of the garden's name is from an old Chinese saying, "To cultivate the garden for a living is really the politics of a humble man."

Garden of Harmony

The Garden of Harmony, or Yi Yuan in Chinese, is divided into two parts by a covered way running north and south. The garden features artificial hills, some with caves, and lakes. There are numerous pavilions, one of which supposedly contains a lute belonging to the poet Su Dong Po.

The Qing official who had this garden made is said to have spent 200,000 ounces of silver on its creation. Being just over 100 years old, this garden is the most recently built in all of Suzhou, and it has adopted many of the features of the other gardens.

Master of the Nets Garden

The garden known as Wang Shi Yuan, or Master of the Nets Garden, was first created in the twelfth century by an official who called it the Fisherman's Retreat, or Yu Yin. It was restored in the eighteenth century and given its present name, which literally means "Teacher Wang's garden." It is only a short distance from the Suzhou Hotel, a little to the west, so it is a convenient place to visit on foot, perhaps after your midday meal.

The garden is small, and a great proportion of the area is occupied by buildings of various sorts. At the eastern entrance you should note the high stone step outside, which indicates that the owner was a high official; he was by tradition always carried in a sedan chair to and from his house by four bearers. Some sections of his residence still remain; they date from the Song Dynasty. There is an interesting carving in brick over the stone gate entrance.

The Dianchun Cottage is of particular interest, because an exact copy has been constructed, along with its Ming furniture, at New York's Metropolitan Museum of Art.

The garden has a number of walks alongside and through buildings, with windows opening onto bamboo and mirrors to extend the concept of space. Many walls are used to divide the area into small sections, but these again are placed to create a feeling of spaciousness.

Forest of Lions Garden

The Forest of Lions Garden, known as Shi Zi Lin, was first laid out in 1350 as part of the grounds of a temple. A number of famous artists and architects were called together to create a beautiful landscape in memory of the master of a monk who had lived previously in a region known as "the Lion Cliff." Some authorities believe it is this allusion which gives the name to the garden. Others say that the name comes from the resemblance of some of the rocks to lions.

The garden, just over an acre in area, is divided into two parts and contains four lakes. There are many small hills and rocks, bridges and caves. One lake has two islands, each with a pavilion, and there is also a stone boat. Most of the rocks were brought from Lake Taihu.

Pavilion of Rolling Waves Garden

The Pavilion of Rolling Waves Garden, or Cang Lang Ting, was first recorded during the Five Dynasties era, making it the oldest garden in Suzhou, but came into prominence in 1044 when it became the residence of the poet Su Shunqin. Under the Yuan and early Ming it was the site of a Buddhist nunnery. It then passed through many hands, was destroyed during the Taiping rebellion, and remade a short time afterward. It was opened to the public in 1954.

To enter the garden you cross a small bridge and pass into the entrance pavilion, which features a number of steles dating from the Wu to the Qing. On leaving the pavilion you pass along a covered way to an artificial hill, on top of which is the Rolling Waves or Dark Blue Pavilion. Next there is a small pond, and then to the right a small area revealing the carved bricks which are a tradition of Suzhou.

You then enter the second section of the park, which features pavilions and terraces, the path passing under a covered way to the final two pavilions next to the exit.

EXCURSIONS FROM SUZHOU

A pleasant excursion and one that will take you to the edge of the Chinese countryside, even though the site is only four miles from Suzhou, is to the **Precious Belt Bridge,** or Bao Dai Qiao, which spans the Grand Canal. The bridge derives its name from the jade ceremonial belt owned by a governor of the town under the Tang, who donated it to help meet expenses for the construction of the bridge. The existing bridge has been restored many times but is now out of use. It is about 100 yards long, with 53 arches, the three in the center being much higher than the others to allow the passage of boats. There are stone monuments at one end.

A higher modern bridge has been built alongside the old one, and this now carries all the traffic. However, the old bridge is still in a reasonable state of repair and it is possible to walk along it; it is very popular with fishermen. The bridge and the surrounding area are excellent to visit if you want to get away from town life and the crush of people or just watch the boats go by.

Another excursion worth considering is the one to the **Ling Yan Hill,** nine miles to the southwest of the town along a road leading to the Tai Hu lake. Some distance along the road on the left you will see the seven-story pagoda which stands on top of the hill.

Upon arrival at the village of Mudu, you enter a park which leads to Ling Yan Hill. You will see there many stones eroded into unusual shapes. On the way up the hill you will come to a small cave known as the Xi Shi, named after the beautiful queen of the King of Wu. On top of the hill stand the ruins of the Ling Yan Si, or **Temple of the Rock of Spirits** and a brick pagoda from the Ming period. The terrace in front of the temple provides a fine panorama of the surroundings and of Tai Hu lake. At the foot of the hill on the western side is the Tomb of Han Shizhong, a famous general of the Southern Song who was buried there in 1150.

PRACTICAL INFORMATION FOR SUZHOU

FACTS AND FIGURES. Suzhou is at approximately the same latitude as Savannah, Georgia. It lies only 52 miles by rail from Shanghai, a journey of about one hour. From Beijing it lies about 660 miles to the southeast, but there is no domestic air service available for use by foreign visitors, the nearest major airport being Shanghai, which is about two hours' flight from Beijing. Suzhou is about 940 miles by rail from Beijing, about 20 hours' journey; 715 miles northeast of Guangzhou; 1,170 miles by rail, about 36–37 hours' journey.

The table shows the weather pattern in Suzhou during the year.

Suzhou Temperature Range and Average Rainfall

	Temperature High (°F)	Temperature Low (°F)	Number of Days with Rainfall	Monthly Rainfall (in inches)
January	47	32	10	1.8
April	67	49	13	2.7
July	91	75	11	5.4
October	75	56	9	1.2

WHEN TO GO. The best time for a visit is during the fall, which lasts from October through mid-November. The days are pleasantly warm then, averaging about 70° F, and while the nights are cooler they are not disagreeably so. There will be rainfall about twice a week on average.

Probably the next best season is spring, which is relatively short—April and May. Rainfall is more frequent and the temperatures slightly higher.

The worst time to visit and the period to avoid is summer. The "Plum Rains" herald the beginning of summer in June and introduce a period of weather characterized by gray, overcast skies and constant drizzle. As summer progresses the rainfall becomes frequent and heavy and is accompanied by high temperatures and oppressive humidity.

Despite Suzhou's latitude and proximity to the coast, it can be surprisingly cold in winter, particularly in February when the cold winds sweep down from the north China plain. Then the temperatures normally drop to below freezing for periods of a few days at a time. Winter usually lasts till about late March.

HOW TO GET THERE. You will normally visit Suzhou en route to Shanghai from Beijing, or vice versa, when traveling by train. It is normally part of a tour program covering Beijing-Nanjing-Wuxi-Suzhou-Shanghai-Hangzhou. The times required for travel by train from city to city are approximately as follows: from Beijing—overnight 16 or 17 hours to Nanjing, then 3 hours to Wuxi, then ½ hour to Suzhou, then 1 hour to Shanghai. There are no flights to Suzhou.

Some organized tour groups travel between Suzhou and Wuxi, or vice versa, along the Grand Canal on luxury power-craft. There are local passenger boats plying the Grand Canal that call at Suzhou, but these are only for the hardy independent traveler. There are both overnight ferries and day-boats. They are for the most part overcrowded, uncomfortable, and dirty—with long stretches of the journey providing views only of the steep canal banks. Carry your own food. Boats from Hangzhou take about 14 hours, to Wuxi about 5–6 hours. The boats continue on to Changzhou about 4–5 hours away, and Zhenjiang 8–9 hours farther north.

HOTELS. The newest hotel is the **Bamboo Grove Hotel** or **Zhui Hui** (tel. 225601, 227601; telex 66538), overlooking the river at Zhui Hui Road. The 400 rooms have direct-dial telephone, color TV, minibar, and refrigerator; facilities include Chinese and Western restaurants, coffee shop, disco, health center, and tennis. The new **Aster Hotel** (tel. 24646), at the junction of Feng Huo and San Xiang Roads, is a tower hotel with 409 deluxe rooms, six restaurants, pool, bowling alley, and shopping arcade. Foreign visitors are also accommodated at the 320-bed **New Nanlin Hotel** (tel. 24641) at 19 Gun Xiu Lane and at the **Suzhou Hotel** (tel. 24646; cable 6333; telex 363002) at 115 Shiquan Road, which has good accommodations for 450 guests in the modern nine-story east wing or the old two-story west wing. A small stream at the rear of the hotel runs to the nearby Wang Shi Garden. The **Gusu Hotel** (tel. 25126), a 110-room establishment with air-conditioned rooms, is located in the same grounds as the Suzhou Hotel. Budget travelers should try the **Lexiang Hotel** (tel. 22890) at 18 Dajing Lane off Renmin Road, where inexpensive rooms and dormitory accommodations are available.

RESTAURANTS. Suzhou has a well-earned reputation as a place for good eating. The town's restaurants have long been the focal point for people who live in the neighborhood, and others travel even from Nanjing and Shanghai to savor the local specialties. Visits by out-of-towners usually coincide with the numerous food festivals that take place in Suzhou. Perhaps the most famous is the "Crab Feast" early in the fall, when fishermen gather at a shallow lake 5 miles to the northeast of Suzhou to capture the crabs that emerge from the rock crevices.

There are few restaurants equipped to receive foreign visitors, and you will need to speak or read some Chinese if you are to eat away from your hotel. Alternatively, you may be able to persuade your guide to accompany you. Good restaurants are: the very old **Songhelou,** 141 Guanqian Street (tel. 2066)—try their fragrant crispy duck; the **Dongting** on Renmin Road (tel. 53); the **Xinjufeng,** 657 Renmin Road (tel. 3794) and the **Yichangfu,** 1 Shi Road (tel. 2832). If you have a craving for sweets and cakes, visit Guangian Street (between nos. 35–88) where you will find a mouth-watering display of delicacies. Jasmine tea is famous in Suzhou.

TOURIST INFORMATION. CITS (tel. 224646, 222223) is in the Suzhou Hotel, 115 Shiquan Road.

CAAC (tel. 22788) is at 192 Renmin Road.

PSB (tel. 25661) is at 7 Dashitou Road.

HOW TO GET AROUND. For most of your visits to the gardens and sites of Suzhou you will travel in the car or bus arranged by CITS. However, Suzhou is one place where you should try to get about on foot to experience the charm of this old and attractive canal-lined town.

CITS arranges excursions by boat to numerous sights: from the Panmen Gates on the southeast corner of the city moat to the Precious-Belt Bridge (45 minutes); to the Western Hills across Lake Taihu (40 minutes); and to Wuxi located 28 miles away by canal (3 hours).

Budget travelers should note that bus no. 1 runs along the main North–South axis, Renmin Road, bus no. 2 circumnavigates the town, while bus no. 5 traverses the town on an East–West route. If you want to visit the Precious Belt Bridge on the Grand Canal, take bus no. 13.

WHAT TO SEE. Suzhou is famous for its **Song, Yuan, Ming,** and **Qing Dynasty Gardens.** At Tiger Hill, you will see a combination of all the best things in Suzhou: the famous leaning pagoda, fine gardens and rockeries, wells, ravines, ponds, and even a tomb. While the **Tiger Hill Pagoda** is certainly the most famous, there are others such as the **Pagoda of the Temple of Good Omen Light** and particularly the unusual twin pagodas of the **Two Pagoda Temple.** There is another pagoda standing beside what was formerly the **Temple of Gratitude.**

Gardens are here in abundance. The biggest and perhaps the best is the **Liu Garden,** but there are many others with scenery and layouts as distinctive as their names: the **"Humble Administrator's" Garden,** the **Garden of Harmony,** the **Master of the Nets Garden,** the **Garden of the Forest of Lions,** and the **Pavilion of Rolling Waves Garden.**

The most famous temple in Suzhou is the Buddhist **West Garden Temple,** adjacent to the Liu Garden and therefore convenient to visit when you are in the vicinity. By way of contrast, there is a Taoist **Temple of Mystery** which was originally founded in the third century, located near the Garden of Harmony.

One of the most delightful temples you are ever likely to see in China lies on the outskirts of Suzhou. It is the Cold Mountain or **Han Shan Temple,** founded in the sixth century but with buildings that date from the Qing. Outside the saffron walls there is a fine old humpback bridge spanning a narrow tree-lined canal that connects a few miles further south with the **Grand Canal.**

Also on the Grand Canal, 4 miles to the southeast of Suzhou, stands the **Precious Belt Bridge** with its 53 arches. A visit to this Tang Dynasty structure makes a fine excursion. Should you have time, you may wish to visit the pagodas and temples at **Ling Yan Hill,** some 10 miles west of Suzhou near the ancient village of Mudu.

MUSEUMS. The **Historical Museum** in Xi Bei Street, very close to the great pagoda of The Temple of Gratitude, features exhibits which date from the neolithic era down to and including the Qing Dynasty period.

You will see black pottery from the Liang Zhu civilization; iron ware; bronze ware; a bronze sword from the Kingdom of Wu; various maps and models; a model of the trade post beside the Han Shan temple; objects taken from the stone caskets found between the walls of the Tiger Hill Pagoda; 2 objects from the tomb of a princess buried near Suzhou; Song porcelain; silks from the Qing period; an example of the carved brickwork traditional in Suzhou; clocks; portraits; the text of steles forbidding workers' strikes under the Qing.

Another museum of interest is the **Suzhou Museum,** in Dongbei Street, a few blocks east of the pagoda near the Humble Administrator's Garden. It was once the residence of a leader of the Taiping Rebellion.

SHOPPING. You can have great fun in Suzhou wandering around the shopping district and visiting the small local shops.

However, if you wish to shop in more leisurely fashion and without the bustle of the crowds, you should go to the **Friendship Store** (tel. 4824) at 92 Guan Qian Street, where you will find the usual array of goods on sale. You might also care to visit the **People's Bazaar,** which serves as the major department store for the locals. You will enjoy strolling around Guan Qian Street in the maze of alleys that are filled with locals buying from stalls, street vendors, and eating houses. The **Antique Store** is at 334 Renmin Road (tel. 4972) and the **Arts and Crafts Store** (tel. 5513) at 274 Jingde Road.

You should keep a lookout for two of the specialties of the region. Suzhou ranks with Sichuan, Hunan, and Guangdong as the leading center for embroidery, particularly hand embroidery of the double-sided type. In this work a single thread of silk is separated into 48 filaments, and only one is used in embroidering the piece. The filament is sewn with infinite care into stretched crêpe de chine silk so that the subject can be viewed from each side. Favorite subjects are goldfish, which appear to be suspended in water, swallows, orioles, and cats. Suzhou offers bargain prices for embroidery.

There are many other types of embroidery ranging from petit point to criss-cross work, as well as tapestries featuring scenes made from woollen yarn and also from silk.

It is also worthwhile taking a close look at the local machine-made silk fabrics. They are available in a wide variety of quality, styles, and colors at most reasonable prices. Paintings are good value.

ENTERTAINMENT. There are regular evening performances of an opera peculiar to Suzhou; and also of Pingtan, a form of theater which entails storytelling and ballad singing.

USEFUL ADDRESSES AND TELEPHONE NUMBERS

CITS—Suzhou Hotel (tel. 224646, 222223).
CAAC—192 Renmin Road (tel. 22788).
PSB—7 Dashitou Road (tel. 25661).
Rail Ticket Office—203 Guanqian Street (tel. 26462).

TAIYUAN

Shanxi Province

North China

Taiyuan has probably seen more violence in its thousands of years of existence than any other city in China. It is the capital of an out-of-the-way province, Shanxi. The River Fen flows quietly by Taiyuan, and all seems peaceful and serene.

The word Shanxi means "west of the mountains." The entire province is a mountainous plateau that looks down on the vast North China Plain to the East. Taiyuan guards the northern entrance of the fertile central plain of the province, thereby giving access to the Yellow River and the North China Plain. The many invaders who came from the north had to pass Taiyuan, and for thousands of years it was a center of great strategic importance to China. The Great Wall, only 90 miles to the north, was the first barrier the invaders had to overcome; the second obstacle was Taiyuan.

The city's strategic location explains why the ruling emperor always paid great attention to its administration and fortification. Despite elaborate precautions taken to prevent invasions from the northern steppes, non-Chinese peoples took the town on a number of occasions and settled in the region. Its early name was Jinyang.

The Tobas, who formed the Wei Dynasty and took Jinyang in 396, established their capital in Datong to the north. They brought Buddhism to China and built the first Buddhist cave shrines that still exist in the region and in other parts of China.

Jinyang was also crucial to the formation of two other dynasties: the Northern Qi (550–577) and the Tang (618–907). The Tang fell only after Jinyang was taken.

The first Song emperor decided to put a stop to Jinyang's independence. In 960 he led his armies to the region with the intention of taking the town. He failed. The walls were impregnable and the defending archers too accurate and disciplined. However, when the Song armies retreated, they forced all the peasants in the surrounding areas to leave and resettle in Shandong Province, hundreds of miles away. The emperor made another attempt to take the town in 976 and failed. Once again the peasants in the region were forced to leave for Henan in the south.

The second Song emperor was even more determined to teach the small kingdom a lesson. His armies attacked the town from all sides and it fell. The emperor then ordered the town razed. Such was the emperor's determination to wipe out any trace of the town that he diverted the waters of the two rivers, the Fen and the Jin, to wash away what little remained, and had a new town built.

The town prospered, but within 150 years the inhabitants were again under siege, this time by the invading Jin. So fierce was the defense that the invaders had to build walls outside the town wall so they could fire down on the defenders. Taiyuan held out for eight months, then fell.

Taiyuan flourished as a trading post for many centuries. The Jin, and the Mongols who succeeded them, occupied areas on both sides, of the Great Wall, providing many opportunities for commerce.

Under the Ming, Taiyuan was further protected by enlarged and strengthened walls. Even so, Manchu invaders took the town in 1644. Under the Qing, the town was kept under strict control, although a number of secret societies that were distinctly anti-Manchu and antiforeign existed.

In 1911, when the revolt against the Qing broke into the open, Taiyuan and the province were among the first areas in China to rise against the emperor and his court. A military government headed by Yan Xi was then proclaimed. Yan Xi ruled the region as a dictator until the eve of the Communist takeover in 1949.

Today, Taiyuan dwellers have a more peaceful and mundane existence. The area is rich in coal and mineral deposits, particularly iron ore. The exploitation of these deposits has led to the development of modern industry in the region. At present the city is noted for its production of iron, steel, tractors, agricultural machinery, heavy machinery, cement, chemicals, and ceramic ware. The fertile farms of the province produce winter wheat, millet, corn, and fruit in great abundance. About one and a half million people now live in Taiyuan.

EXPLORING TAIYUAN

Among the interesting sights in Taiyuan are a beautiful example of an early Ming temple; another temple that was part of one of the biggest monasteries of the Song Dynasty; a collection of Buddhist sutras, or holy texts, from the Song, Yuan, and Ming periods; and a range of artistic, archeological, and historic objects on display in the Shanxi Provincial Museums.

Chongshan Temple

Chongshan Temple was once part of one of the largest Buddhist monasteries known to exist in China during the Song Dynasty (960–1280). Built on the site of an earlier temple that is thought to date from the Tang in the sixth century, it stands in the eastern section of the town. The main hall has richly decorated beams and ceilings. Behind it stands the Dabei Hall, possessing a large statue of the Goddess of Mercy with a "thousand hands and eyes." Alongside are two Bodhissatvas about 25 feet in height. All the other portions of the monastery were either destroyed or fell into ruin, except one other building, which was converted into a Confucian temple in 1882 and is now the Shanxi Provincial Museum no. 1. The main hall of the temple is described below.

Shuangta Temple

The Shuangta or Twin Pagoda Temple is part of what was once the Yongzuo Monastery. Located near the Cemetery of Martyrs in the southeast of the town, it is one of the finest examples in China of early Ming temple architecture. In front of the temple are two pagodas dating from the sixteenth century. They give the temple its name and have become the symbols of Taiyuan; they are octagonal in shape, of brick construction, and 13 stories high. The bell near the temple entrance was cast in the fifteenth century.

The temple once possessed one of the most valuable collections of sutras, or holy Buddhist texts, in China. The earliest, engraved in wood, date from the Song Dynasty (960–1280). There were also editions from the Yuan (1280–1368), Ming (1368–1644) and Qing (1644–1911); some are on display, but many of the texts have been transferred to the Shanxi Museum (see "Museums").

EXCURSIONS FROM TAIYUAN

Many interesting excursions can be made from Taiyuan to view old Buddhist temples. Religion once flourished in the region, and a great many monasteries were built. Although most of the temples have vanished, some still exist. There are also monuments, such as steles and pagodas, dating from the Tang, and tombs dating from the Han. Excursions to Wutai Shan, one of China's four "sacred" mountains, may be made from Taiyuan (see *Excursions from Datong*).

Scented Forest Monastery

About five miles southeast of Taiyuan and just north of the village of Ma Zhuang stand the remains of the Scented Forest Monastery, or Fang Lin Si. All that remains of this monastery is the gateway, the main temple, and a large pavilion, all dating from the Qing. The gate and main temple each have a roof of glazed tiles, decorated with fine *kui long zi,* or roof figurines. The original monastery dates from the Song but was almost completely destroyed under the Yuan.

White Cloud Monastery

The White Cloud Monastery, or Bai Yun Si, was founded under the reign of the second Qing emperor in the late seventeenth century. It is located to the south of Taiyuan on high ground near Hong Tu Gou. It is one of three large Buddhist monasteries established in the Taiyuan region under the Ming and the Qing.

Temple of the Jin Minister

About 3 miles northwest of the town, near a village called Lan Cun, is the Temple of the Jin Minister, or Jin Dai Fu Si. The present buildings were erected by the Yuan about the middle of the fourteenth century.

God of War Temple

To the west of Taiyuan, in the village of Xiao Wei Ying, is a temple known as Gu Guan Di Miao. It dates from the Song but was rebuilt under the Yuan in Song style. Nearby stands the temple Hou Qin Gong, housing a statue believed to be the wife of Guan Di, the God of War; it is one of about 25 statues of ladies of the court of the period.

Pagodas of the Monastery of Endless Happiness

Quite close to Taiyuan and south of the village of Hao Zhuang Cun are two pagodas, constructed under the Ming, that were once part of the Monastery of Endless Happiness, or Yong Zuo Si. The pagodas, well known in the province, appear on the Taiyuan flag.

Jin Ci

The Jin Ci Temple, at the foot of the Xuanweng Mountains some 16 miles west of Taiyuan, is one of a group of temples famous in the province. Built during the Northern Wei Dynasty (386–534) in memory of Shu Yu, the temple is surrounded by cypresses and natural springs. Two nearby tombs are believed to be those of Prince Shu Yu and his son. You can also see the remains of the walls of Jinyang, built around the new settlement after the Song destroyed the town in 979.

The Jin Ci was originally a place for worshiping ancestors, but over the centuries it became a retreat of emperors and princes and a place where they took their leisure. Fortunately, the temple and its surrounding pavilions were spared when the second emperor of the Song Dynasty razed Jinyang in the tenth century. In 1102, the Shengmu Pavilion—perhaps the best known portion of the temple—was built to house a statue of Yi Jiang, the "holy mother." The pavilion is the oldest wooden structure still standing in Taiyuan. The statues of Yi Jiang are surrounded by 43 other statues of ladies in waiting. All are prized national relics.

When you arrive at the Jin Ci, you will enter through a gateway built in this century; the old gateway is on your left. Immediately before you is the **Water Mirror Terrace,** or Shuijing Tai, with its typical Shanxi architecture. It dates from the Ming. Beyond this is the **Bridge Where the Immortals Meet** that spans a small stream.

On the other side of the bridge you will come to the **Terrace of the Metal Men,** or Jinren Tai. There you will see four statues of warriors made of iron: the one on the southwest corner was cast in 1097 and is intact; that on the northwest corner was cast a year later, but has a head dating from the Ming; the figure on the southeast corner was cast about a decade before the other two, but had the head restored earlier this century; and the statue on the northeast corner was cast in 1913.

Beyond the terrace is a gateway guarded on the left by the **Drum Tower** and on the right by the **Bell Tower,** both built in the sixteenth century under the Ming. Through the gateway stands a small temple, dating from 1168, where the faithful used to pray to the Sacred Mother. On leaving the temple you will pass over the Fei Liang, or **Flying Bridge.** Rebuilt under the Song, it has a peculiar design that makes it a rare example among China's ancient bridges. The Fei Liang leads to a stone platform built over a pool formed by the **Yuzhao Spring.**

Before you stands the **Shengmu Dian,** or Sacred Mother Hall, one of the finest examples of Song architecture still in existence. It has a double roof with slightly upturned corners and is supported by columns entwined with gilded dragons. Inside, a statue of Yi Jiang, the Sacred Mother, is surrounded by 43 life-size statues of her ladies in waiting. Each figure has a different bearing, and every face seems to convey a different mood. The statues are precious relics that reflect the life and times of the Song Court some 900 years ago.

On leaving, follow the path to the left, then turn left again through the first gateway. In a small courtyard you'll see two evergreens that are about

1,000 years old. Behind them is the **Temple of the Descendants,** or Miao Yi Tang, rebuilt under the Yuan and the Ming.

To the right of the temple you will find a long flight of steps leading to the **Cave Facing the East,** or Chao Yang Dong. There is a statue of Ling Guan holding a golden whip in his hand. To the right of it is a cave known as **Stay in the Clouds,** inhabited in the seventeenth century by Fu Shan, a well-known historic figure in the province. Fu Shan was a calligrapher, philosopher, poet, and doctor; above all he was a loyal supporter of the Ming. He became a Taoist when the Manchu overthrew the last Ming emperor. The Qing emperor offered him a post in the court on numerous occasions, but he always refused. Over the decades he became a popular folk hero, and many tales were told about his exploits and abilities.

The next place of interest is the **Tai Tai Temple** to the left of the Sacred Mother Hall. Inside the temple stands a wooden statue of Tai Tai, a legendary hero of the province, said to have made the land in the area fit for cultivation and safe from floods.

Farther to the left stands the **Water Mother Temple,** or Shui Mu Lou. Originally built under the Ming and rebuilt in 1844 under the Qing, this twin-roofed structure houses statues and frescoes of a legendary figure known as the Water Mother. The legend says that a young girl, who was forced to draw water all day for her mother-in-law, one day met a traveler and gave him water for his horse. In return for her kindness, the horseman gave her a magic whip. By waving it over her pots she was able to fill them with clear spring water. In this way, the source of the River Jin was formed, and the springs in the surrounding area became famous for their fine quality of water.

Standing in front of the temple is an octagonal pavilion that shelters the Nan Lao Quan, or **Forever Young Spring.** The spring, believed to be the major source of the River Jin, flows at a constant rate and temperature that never vary, even during drought or heavy rain. If you look past the Drum Tower and Bell Tower, you will see two octagonal pools, one large and one small. The smaller one, called the **Shan Li Quan,** is the other source of the River Jin. The large octagonal **Lotus Pool,** or Ba Jiao Lian Qi, is of later construction, dating from the Ming.

On the opposite side of the Lotus Pool is a set of steps leading to the **Temple of Prince Shu Yu of Tang,** or Tang Shu Yu Ci. As you pass into the first courtyard leading to the temple, you will see about 120 pillars on which Buddhist sutras, or holy texts, have been carved. These pillars, about 12 centuries old, originally stood at Feng Dong Li, a few miles north of Jin Ci. They were removed from the original site during the Sino-Japanese conflict, when an attempt was made by the Japanese forces to take them from China. When the local inhabitants were able to foil the attempt, the pillars were restored and placed around the first courtyard of the temple.

To reach the second courtyard, you must pass through the **Hall of Sacrifices,** or Xiang Tang; there you will see 11 poems engraved in stone: seven by Mao Zedong and four by Zhu De. At the far end of the second courtyard is **Prince Shu Yu's Temple.** The original structure, built under the Ming, was later rebuilt under the Qing; it is five bays wide and four deep.

The next place of interest is the **Tang Stele Pavilion,** or Tang Bei Ting. To reach this you must return through the two courtyards, descend the steps, and take the path to the left. The first building you reach houses the Jin Ci tablets, or steles: the one on the right was erected in 647, the replica on the left in 1773. The stele commemorates the visit of the second Tang emperor to the court of Prince Shu Yu. The engraved calligraphy records the prince's role in helping the emperor and his father overthrow the Sui Dynasty and expresses the gratitude of the Tang rulers. The stele on the left, containing the same text, was erected in the eighteenth century, when the original inscriptions were in danger of being destroyed by the weather.

Most of the interesting sights at Jin Ci have now been covered. If you have time and want to get a good overview of the palaces, go back over the first bridge you crossed on entering. Immediately to your right is a pavilion known as **Sheng Ying Lou** where, from the first floor, you will have a fine view.

Below you is the **Canal of Zhibo.** The nearest building is the **White Crane Pavilion,** or Bai He Ting. On the left of it is the **Hanging Snow Bridge**—so called because in winter ice crystals are formed from the evaporation of the warm spring water.

Upstream from the bridge is a column that rises out of the water. Legend has it that the column marks the spot where **Zhang Lang** is buried. He is said to have died when settling a dispute on the sharing of water from the stream. He had to plunge his hands into boiling water to retrieve objects and thereby determine his allocation. He won seven-tenths of the stream but died from the burns he received.

Next to the column stands a monument in the stream. Known as Bu Ji Zhou, or **Boat Not Moored,** its origin and history are not known.

Beyond the walls of the Jin Ci, you will see a tall seven-story **pagoda** that dates from the Qing but was first constructed under the Sui (589–618).

If you have time, you may visit the **Fu Shan Museum,** commemorating the scholar and artist who lived in the cave behind the Temple of the Descendants. You will see examples of his calligraphy and poetry. To reach the museum, walk toward the entrance of the Jin Ci. After passing the Water Mirror Terrace, you will note a small bridge immediately to your left. It leads to the museum, housed in a pavilion overlooking the second courtyard.

Dragon Mountain

Three miles west of Jin Ci (go via Xi Zhen village) is Dragon Mountain, or Long Shan, where the remains of the **Stone Gate Monastery** (Shi Men Si) are located. There you will see two Buddhist rock shrines that are about 13 centuries old.

The **Taoist Endless Sky Monastery,** or Hao Tian Guan, used to stand at the top of Dragon Mountain. About a mile to the south are eight cave shrines of considerable interest. The style of the carving reflects the Taoist influence on Buddhist cave art.

The Tian Long Shan, or **Celestial Dragon Mountain,** about 15 miles southwest of Jin Ci, has 25 Buddhist caves near the two peaks. The carvings are splendid examples of the Northern Qi, Sui, and Tang eras.

Twelve caves are located near the eastern peak. The remains of the summer palaces of the Northern Qi emperors are nearby. The other 13 caves are near the western peak; the large seated Buddha and the standing Buddha beneath it were carved out of the mountainside in 560 and formed part of what was once the Da Fo Ge, or Big Buddha Temple.

PRACTICAL INFORMATION FOR TAIYUAN

FACTS AND FIGURES. Taiyuan, the capital of Shanxi Province, is 260 miles southwest of Beijing by air; flight time 1 hour 20 minutes; about 285 miles by rail via Shijiazhuang, a train journey of 6 to 7 hours; about 110 miles west of Shijiazhuang by rail—about 2 to 3 hours' train journey. The town is 4,250 feet above sea level.

WHEN TO GO. Autumn is the best time to visit Taiyuan. Winter is severe, with frequent snowstorms. Spring often brings dust storms; late spring and early summer can be mild, while mid-summer is hot and dry.

HOW TO GET THERE. By direct flight from Beijing (1 hour 20 minutes), from Yanan (50 minutes), or from Xian (45 minutes); by rail from Beijing (6–7 hours), from Shijiazhuang (2–3 hours), or from Xian.

HOTELS. The newest hotel is the **Sanjin Hotel** (tel. 23216) on May 1st Square, which offers 305 rooms throughout 14 stories. Directly opposite stands the **Bingzhou** (tel. 25924), with its austere ambiance. Many visitors are lodged at the 600-bed **Yingze Hotel** (tel. 23211) at 51 Yingze Dajie just opposite Yingze Park. Guests wishing to stay near the Jin Ci Temple, should try to get rooms at the **Jin Ci Guest House** (tel. 29941), which has 8 villas set in the midst of delightful scenery. Another hotel; the **Hubin** (tel. 22644) in Yingze Street is used mainly for visiting Overseas Chinese.

RESTAURANTS. There are no restaurants outside the hotels that cater to foreign visitors. Chinese-speaking visitors may care to try one of the "masses" restaurants: the **Qingheyuan** (tel. 29160) in Qiatou Jie; the **Jinyang** (tel. 25702) on May 1st Square; and the **Jinyuanchun** located on Mao Er Hutung. The most popular dish in the province is noodles made from wheat. Dishes flavored with vinegar are a local specialty. So too is the *fen jiu,* a strong wine produced in the vineyards north of the city. A thick soup called "tounao" is famous throughout the region.

TOURIST INFORMATION. CITS (tel. 441155) is located at the Yingze Hotel.
CAAC (tel. 29903, 22402), 38 Yingze Street, is on the opposite side of the road to the Yingze Hotel and about a hundred yards to the east.
PSB may be found by walking north along the street almost opposite the Sanjin Mansion. The office is in a small cross street that runs between a department store and a church; it is easily identified by the sign written in English.

HOW TO GET AROUND. CITS organizes bus tours to sites in the town and excursions to the outlying places of interest. Budget travelers who want to go to the Jin Ci Temple by local bus (very crowded) will find the bus stop located on the large square in Yingze Street in front of the viewing platform. The journey takes 50–60 minutes.

WHAT TO SEE. In Taiyuan the two major sights are the **Chongshan Temple** with its ornate halls and statues; and the **Shuangta (Two Pagoda) Temple,** a fine example of Ming architecture.
The major excursion is to the **Jin Ci Temple** about 16 miles southwest of the town. There you will see fine halls, pools, terraces, and statues of intense archaeological interest.

MUSEUMS. The **Shanxi Provincial Museum no. 1** is definitely worth a visit. There are priceless sutras (holy Buddhist texts printed on scrolls), dating from the Jin (A.D. 265–420); stone carvings with Buddhist themes; stone and terra-cotta funerary animals about 2,000 years old (from the Han); and many objects of Han,

Tang, and Song origin. Formerly part of the Chongshan Temple complex, the museum is located in the eastern part of town just off Jianshe Bei Road.

Shanxi Provincial Museum no. 2 is one block north of Yingze Street on the western side of May 1st Square. Formerly the Chunyang Palace which was originally built towards the end of the sixteenth century and renovated under the Qing, the museum houses a fine collection of artistic and archeological items in more than 20 exhibition halls.

SHOPPING. The local specialties include copperware, brass and bronze charcoal pots, black porcelain, iron-ware reproductions, lacquer ware, and items of inlaid wood. All may be purchased at the **Friendship Store** (tel. 28731) opposite the Hubin Hotel on Yingze Street, or at the **Shanxi Arts and Crafts Store** opposite Renmin Park on Wuyi (May 1st) Street.

USEFUL ADDRESSES AND TELEPHONE NUMBERS

CITS—Yingze Hotel (tel. 441155).
CAAC—38 Yingze Street (tel. 29903, 22402).
Taxis—Yingze Hotel (tel. 23211, ext. 395).

TIANJIN

Tianjin Municipality

North China

Tianjin, China's third largest city, is at the same time a municipality, meaning that—like Beijing and Shanghai—it is under central government control. Located about 65 miles east of the nation's capital, Tianjin forms an industrial triangle with Beijing and Tangshan at the upper extremity of the North China Plain, one of the most important production centers in China.

First mentioned under the Song (A.D. 960–1280), Tianjin became important in the fourteenth century when grain, brought to the capital along the Grand Canal, was stored there. By the fifteenth century it became a garrison town completely encircled by walls. Trade flourished. The canals were thick with junks and other cargo craft, while the town filled with throngs of sailors from the China coast. A fort guarded the town, but nature also provided a defense: the entire area was surrounded by marshland that could bog down an army on foot.

Tianjin suffered during the Boxer Revolution, when the rebels dug in behind the walls of the old town. After they had been captured, European armies tore down the walls to make sure that Tianjin would never again be a sanctuary.

In the mid-nineteenth century, after China signed treaties with Britain and France at Tianjin, concessions were established in the town by the occupying powers. The area was controlled by Anglo-French forces in 1860 and, by the end of the century, concessions had also been forced upon China by the Japanese, Germans, Italians, Belgians, Austro-Hungarians, and Russians. During this time, commerce flourished and the town developed a distinctly European character.

After the fall of the Qing Dynasty in 1911, trade continued to develop. The surrounding marshland provided the base for a salt industry, which led in turn to industrialization and the production of chemicals, glass, and soap. The existing textile mills expanded their production, processing great quantities of wool and cotton brought in from far-off provinces. During that time, Tianjin developed into an international port.

The town was occupied by the Japanese in 1937, during the Sino-Japanese War. Even then, it had a strategic role as a trade and communications center. When the Communists seized power in 1949, Tianjin was marked for considerable industrial development. The chemical industry was expanded, large factories producing rubber and metallurgical products were developed, the textile industry was diversified, and consumer goods factories were established to produce a wide range of products—cigarettes, electronics, cameras, and watches among them. The new machine-making industry turned out a diversity of products including tools and precision instruments.

Tianjin also became more important in agriculture, particularly as a commercial center for produce grown in Hebei and surrounding provinces. Large quantities of wheat, corn, and rice are now handled. Alongside these warehouses, food-processing industries—particularly flour mills—have grown up. The area surrounding the city has been given over to vegetable growing, poultry raising, and dairying. Tianjin's proximity to the sea has also meant the development of the fishing industry and cold storage facilities in and around the town.

A port was constructed near the mouth of the Hai River in the 1950s. Called Xingang (literally, new port), it has been a strategic facet in the development of the town.

Tianjin has two universities: Tianjin and Nankai.

The town was damaged during the severe earthquake of 1976 and was closed to visitors for a period. Although there was some loss of life and a reduction in industrial production, Tianjin fared much better than nearby Tangshan, where an estimated 240,000 people died and the town was completely razed. The strongest shock registered 8.3 on the Richter scale—one of the most severe tremors ever recorded. The earthquake, in terms of lives lost, was the worst natural disaster to befall any country since a quake claimed the lives of over one million people in China during the seventeenth century.

EXPLORING TIANJIN

Tianjin, a manufacturing center visited mainly by business executives and industrialists, does not offer many attractions for the tourist. Some sections of town are an interesting jumble of European architecture, a visual reminder of the days when European powers ruled the region and carved up Tianjin into national concessions.

The one Buddhist edifice worth visiting is the seventeenth-century Dabei or **Grand Mercy Temple,** to the north of the town, off Tianwei Road. It is near the confluence of the **Haihe River** and the **Grand Canal,** that famous and ancient waterway (although better viewed elsewhere). The **Grand Mosque** is also in this region, located on Dafeng Road and backing onto the Grand Canal.

The best known park in Tianjin is **Shuishang** or Aquatic Park, which has a wide expanse of water criss-crossed by dykes, bridges, and pathways. There are many pavilions, the best-known being the **Garden Viewing Pavilion,** or Tiaoyuan. The park also houses the **Tianjin Zoo.**

Tianjin possesses a number of good museums and provides the opportunity for excellent shopping. **Heping Lu** in the city center is reputedly the busiest shopping center in China. In the **International Market** (10:30 A.M.– 7 P.M.) on Beijiang Road, one building has domestic and imported goods, the other Chinese products for wholesale. You can shop or stroll the **Old City** with its narrow hutungs or lanes (near the Friendship Hotel) or browse in the arts and crafts shops in Ancient Culture Street downtown. There you will find a restored **Temple of Ling Mo Niang** (the female deity who protects fishermen), a small museum, and Ming and Qing period style buildings.

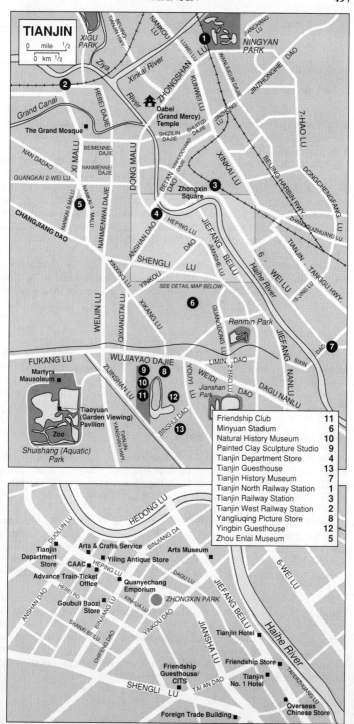

TIANJIN

0 mile 1/2
0 km 1/2

XIGU PARK

NINGYAN PARK

Grand Canal

The Grand Mosque

Dabei (Grand Mercy) Temple

Zhongxin Square

SEE DETAIL MAP BELOW

Renmin Park

Martyrs Mausoleum

Tiaoyuan (Garden Viewing) Pavilion

Zoo

Shuishang (Aquatic) Park

Jianshan Park

Friendship Club	11
Minyuan Stadium	6
Natural History Museum	10
Painted Clay Sculpture Studio	9
Tianjin Department Store	4
Tianjin Guesthouse	13
Tianjin History Museum	7
Tianjin North Railway Station	1
Tianjin Railway Station	3
Tianjin West Railway Station	2
Yangliuqing Picture Store	8
Yingbin Guesthouse	12
Zhou Enlai Museum	5

Tianjin Department Store

Arts & Crafts Service

Arts Museum

CAAC

Yiling Antique Store

Advance Train-Ticket Office

Quanyechang Emporium

ZHONGXIN PARK

Goubuli Baozi Store

Tianjin Hotel

Friendship Store

Tianjin No. 1 Hotel

Friendship Guesthouse/ CITS

Overseas Chinese Store

Foreign Trade Building

EXCURSIONS FROM TIANJIN

Temple of Solitary Joy

Visitors interested in Chinese architecture may wish to visit the Temple of Solitary Joy, or Du Le Si, at Ji Xian, about 75 miles due north of Tianjin by rail. There you will see two Buddhist temples classed as national historic monuments.

Although the monastery was probably founded under the Tang, the temples were built in 984 under the Liao. The two main buildings are the entrance hall and the **Goddess of Mercy Pavilion** or Guanyin Ge. The latter is a magnificent structure, featuring sweeping upturned eaves, two galleries, and a coffered ceiling. One of China's oldest wooden structures and erected without using a single nail, the temple has survived more than 28 earthquakes. Inside stands a 50 foot-high statue of the 11-headed Goddess of Mercy, one of the largest clay sculptures in China. This and the attendant Bodhissatvas were all molded during the Liao (916–1125). The lower walls of the temple are decorated with huge murals of the Four Heavenly Kings and the 16 disciples, painted during the Ming (1368–1644).

Mount Pan

About 7 miles to the north of Ji Xian lies Panshan, one of the foremost scenic spots in China. There used to be over 70 temples in the region but only a few remain. Poets often refer to the mountains "five peaks and three bends," the upper bend being renowned for its pines, the middle bend for its rocks, and the lower bend for its streams and waterfalls.

Eastern Qing Dynasty Tombs

The Eastern Qing Dynasty Tombs are located in Zunhua County near the Great Wall in Hebei Province. The site is 85 miles north of Tianjin and 25 east of Ji Xian. It complements the site used to inter other members of the Qing Dynasty, Yixian County, which lies 75 miles southwest of Beijing (the Western Qing Tombs).

Occupying an area within a line 80 miles north–south and 12 miles east–west, the site possesses 15 tombs, of which 5 belong to emperors. The most famous is **Xiaoling,** tomb of the first Qing Emperor; but also notable are **Jingling,** the tomb of Emperor Kangxi, and **Yuling,** the tomb of Emperor Qianlong. The most interesting tomb in terms of style is **Dingdongling,** that of Empress Dowager, Ci Xi.

You enter the area through a stone archway with five entrances, go through the Dagong Gate, pass the Robing Hall and Yingbi Hill on the right, before entering the Sacred Way lined on either side with stone statues. After passing through the Dragon-Phoenix Gate, the road branches in various directions leading to the different tombs. The tombs of emperors and empresses have yellow-glazed roof tiles, while those of lower-ranked nobility have roofs of green.

A guest reception center, a CITS office, and toilet facilities are near the Yuling Tomb.

Port of Xingang

Visitors with trade interests may wish to visit the Port of Xingang, which serves China's industrial north. The port is reached by taking a train to Tanggu, about 30 miles away, then a bus to the banks of the Hai River to a point just a few miles from where it flows into the sea.

PRACTICAL INFORMATION FOR TIANJIN

FACTS AND FIGURES. Tianjin is 75 miles southeast of Beijing—$1\frac{1}{2}$ hours' train journey from the capital (Beijing-Shenyang line) and 40 minutes by plane. The city is connected by direct air service to Hong Kong.

WHEN TO GO. Autumn is the best period to visit Tianjin and nearby areas. Although the city is close to the sea, its weather is affected more by the surrounding land mass. Spring is often dusty, when the winds sweep in from the Mongolian steppes. Summer is hot and humid, with heavy rains in June and July. Winter is cold and dry. Because most of the moisture has been removed from the air before the winds reach the area, there is little snow.

HOW TO GET THERE. Most visitors travel to Tianjin by train from Beijing. You can also stop over when traveling from the capital to the seaside resort of Beidahe, located on the Beijing-Shenyang line; or if you are traveling on the Beijing–Shanghai line. There are daily flights from Beijing (40 minutes), numerous connecting flights from provincial capitals, and daily direct flights from Hong Kong (3 hours). Tianjin is linked by boat service to Dalian (about every two days) and Yantai (once a week) through nearby Xingang port.

HOTELS. One of Tianjin's best hotels is the **Hyatt Tianjin** (tel. 318888; telex 23270 HYTJN CN), Jiefang North Road, on the west bank of the Hai River. The 20-story hotel offers accommodations in 452 rooms right in the heart of the city's commercial center. It features a 3-story glass atrium, 7 restaurants, a cafe, club bar, and lobby lounge. In the rooms there are international-dial telephones, TV, in-house movies, minibars, and 24-hour room service. The top 2 floors have executive accommodations. The hotel offers the services of its Business Center to all visiting executives. There is an airport limousine service.

The **Crystal Palace Hotel** (tel. 310567; telex 23277), at Youyi and Binshui roads, about 15 minutes by car from the center of Tianjin, offers deluxe accommodations in 346 rooms in 2 wings which overlook a small lake. There are 3 restaurants—Chinese, Japanese, and French; a coffee shop; and a banquet hall seating 250 people. Visiting executives can make use of the Business Center. The hotel operates a shuttle-bus service between Tianjin and Beijing, a 45-minute journey. In the hotel grounds are a swimming pool and tennis courts; standard indoor facilities include a health club, shops, a cocktail lounge, and club bar.

The **Sheraton Tianjin** (tel. 343388; telex 23353), on Zijingshan Road, Hexi District, is one of the newer deluxe hotels. Located about a 15-minute drive from downtown Tianjin, near the Friendship Club on the southern outskirts of the city, the 6-story hotel offers deluxe accommodations in 282 rooms. Facilities include a business center, indoor swimming pool, gymnasium, and jogging path.

Those with business in the Tianjin Economic and Technical Development Zone, located near the port, frequently use the **Victory Hotel** (tel. 985833, 984984; telex 23375), 11 Jintang Road, Tanggu District, which offers good accommodations in 350 rooms, two restaurants, coffee shop, disco, and fitness center.

The most secluded hotel is the **Tianjin Garden Hotel** (tel. 24010) at 337 Machang Road. Located just north of the Tianjin Guest House on the southern edge of the town, the hotel offers villa-style accommodations in extensive grounds.

Centrally located hotels are: the **Astor Hotel** (tel. 390013; telex 23266) at Taierzhuang Road, an old hotel recently renovated with a new 7-story wing and formerly known as the Tianjin House; and the **Friendship Hotel** (tel. 310372; telex 23264) at 94 Nanjing Road, offering accommodations for 380 people and a CITS office.

An establishment frequently used by budget travelers is the **Tianjin no. 1 Hotel** (tel. 36438) at 198 Jiefang North Road. It is located diagonally across the road from the Hyatt.

The largest of the hotels is the **Tianjin Grand Hotel** (tel. 287613; telex 23276) in the Hexi District in the south of the town on Youyi Road. It accommodates 1,065 guests; has a dining room capable of seating 1,500 people; and a 4,000-seat auditorium.

Other hotels in the city are: **The People's Hotel**, or Guomin Fandian, 52 Chi Feng Dao, tel. 23677; **Transportation Guest House**, or Jiao Teng Lu Guan, 321 Heping Street, tel. 33276; the **Hui Zhong Hotel**, 4 Hua Zhong Road, tel. 25360.

RESTAURANTS. If you wish to try a place other than your hotel restaurant, you should not miss **Food Street** in southern downtown Tianjin; it is packed with restaurants and snack bars featuring food and cooking from all over China, as well as from non-Chinese countries. There are eating places on all three levels of this arcade.

There are many other places to try: the **Dengyinglou**, 94 Binjiang Dao, tel. 23594 or 23757, for Shandong specialties; the **Quanjude**, 3 Rongji Street, tel. 20046—for Beijing cuisine; the **Tianheju,** 189 Changchun Dao, tel. 25142, for Sichuan and Jiangsu dishes; the **Yanchunlou,** 22 Rongji Street, tel. 22761—for Moslem cooking; the **Vegetarian Restaurant,** Binjiang Dao, tel. 25142; the **Hongqiao** (Red Bridge), 62 Baimenwai, tel. 50837; the **Friendship Club,** 268 Machang Dao, tel. 30329, where large banquets are frequently given; and the **Tiajin Roast Duck Restaurant,** 142 Liaoning Road, tel. 702600.

If you miss Western food, you can satisfy your craving at the **Tianjin Restaurant,** or Tianjin Fandian, at the corner of Xuzhou and Shanghai streets. Coffee and pastries are served on the ground floor, Western meals on the second floor. Also at **Ji Si Ling** (formerly Kiessling) restaurant on Zhejiang Road; and for sweet snacks, try their bakery on Jiefang North Road, two blocks from the Astor Hotel.

A food shop famous in the city for its baozi, or dumplings, is the **Tianjin Baozi Shop** at 97 Shandong Road, tel. 23277. Try the Gou bu li dumplings. In Chinese, this term means "dogs will not touch," but don't be put off, "dogs" in this sense really signifies "stupid people" or "fools."

TOURIST INFORMATION. CITS (tel. 314889) is at 20 Youyi Road.
CAAC (tel. 21224, 25888) is at 242 Heping Road.

HOW TO GET AROUND. CITS will arrange tours and excursions. The city bus service is complicated and therefore difficult to use. The underground railway system—a single line of track serving only 5 stops—is not too useful for visitors either. There appear to be no bicycle rental shops. The Sheraton Hotel provides bicycles free of charge to its guests.

MUSEUMS. The **Tianjin Arts Museum** (Yi Shu Bo Wu Guan) is about a block from the river at 77 Jie Fang Bei, tel. 31127. It contains a fine collection of Chinese paintings from the Yuan, Ming, and Qing dynasties, local handicrafts, contemporary art, and terra-cotta figurines (ni ren) inspired by Chinese literature and mythology—an art form that developed only a century ago.

The **History Museum** (tel. 41354), 4 Guanghua Road, has exhibits of painting, calligraphy, porcelain, and bronzes, as well as items of historical interest. The **Museum of Natural History** (tel. 30504) is in the south of Tainjin, near the Friendship Club, at Machang Dao, and exhibits a range of objects and fossils that have been found in the region.

The **Zhou Enlai Museum** is about 300 yards south of the intersection of the Nankai-5 Malu and Nankai-3 Malu, in the west of Nanjing. The museum exhibits items of historic interest, particularly the period 1913–1919, when Zhou Enlai was a student in the Nankai region of Nanjing.

Finally, there is the **Shuishang Park Museum** in the southwest of the city; it has a small number of paintings from the Qing and Ming, as well as some items of cultural interest.

SHOPPING. Tianjin is famous for its rugs and carpets. Styles range from classic Chinese, through additional national minority designs, to modern. Their quality is exceptional, but you must pay the retail price because factory prices are available only to foreign importers. Nevertheless, the cost is normally much less than the retail price you would pay at home. Keep in mind the freight charge, and the customs duties you may have to pay on arrival of the goods back home. The shops will arrange export to your home address.

Porcelain is another good buy. Some pieces are made in the city, but many come from the workshops of nearby Tangshan. The terra-cotta figurines of Tianjin are well known throughout China and are often purchased by foreign visitors as mementos of their visit.

The town of Yang Lin Qing, near the city, has long been famous for its "annual" posters, or nian hua, produced originally by woodblock printing. The posters are hung in homes during the Chinese New Year and replaced a year later.

There are many places to shop in the city: the Friendship Store, 229 Jie Fan Bei, tel. 392513 (only a short walk from the Tianjin Hotel); the Quanyechang Emporium, 352 Heping Road near the Binjiang intersection, tel. 703771; the Tianjin Department Store (Bai Huo Da Lou), 226 Heping Road, tel. 25916; Tianjin Arts and Crafts Store, 234 Heping Road, tel. 24516; the Yilinge Antiques Shop, 175 Liaoning Road, tel. 700308; the Overseas Chinese Store (Hua Qiao Shangdian), 29 Qu Fu Road, tel. 30339, the Painted Clay Sculpture Studio, 270 Machang Dao, tel. 36203; the Quanye Bazaar, 353 Heping Road, tel. 23771 and 20621; the Wenyuange Antiques Shop, 263 Heping Road; and the Yanglinqing Spring Festival Pictures Store, 111 Sanheli, Donglou, tel. 34843.

Another good place to shop for arts and crafts products, old books, and carpets is in Ancient Culture Street in downtown Tianjin. And don't forget the new International Market buildings on Binjiang Road, just near the Catholic church.

PARKS. Visitors who wish to relax should visit one of the many parks in the city. The main ones are: **Park on the Water,** off Fukang Road in the southwestern part of the city; **Jianshan Park** in the southeast at the southern end of Guandong Road; **Renmin (or People's) Park,** midway along Guangdong Road in the south of the city; **Zhongxin Park,** a small place in the heart of the city and just off Yingkou Road; **Zhongshan Park** in the north of the city; **Beining Park** in the northeast; and **Zigu Park,** in the northwestern sector, overlooking the **Grand Canal.**

ENTERTAINMENT. Being China's third largest city, Tianjin receives regular visits from regional theater and acrobatic troupes. The city is also home to the Tianjin-style of traditional Chinese opera. Check with your hotel or CITS for information.

USEFUL ADDRESSES AND TELEPHONE NUMBERS

Hospitals

Tianjin Chinese Medicine College Hospital, 93 Duolun Road (tel. 21798).
Tianjin Medical College Hospital—178 Anshan Road (tel. 22608).

Travel

Taxis: Main Office—383 Heping Road (tel. 35771; 35221 for charter hire).
CITS—20 Youyi Road (tel. 314889).
China Travel Service for Overseas Chinese—198 Jie Fang North (tel. 36438).
Tianjin Railway Station (East): Information, tel. 41366; Ticket Office: 284 Heping Road, Freight Office, North-East sector, tel. 54817; Sea Freight Office, 102 Tai Er Zhuang Road South, tel. 34290.
CAAC Airline: Passenger Service: 242 Heping Road, tel. 21224, 25888; Air Cargo: Zi He Chiao Bei Yan, tel. 61435.

Domestic Tourist Service, 52 Chifeng Dao (tel. 23353), for excursions from Tianjin, including Beijing and Chengde.

State Trading Corporations

China National Arts and Crafts Corp.—135 Tangshan Dao. (cable: Arts Tianjin; tel. 31539, 33865).

China National Cereals, Oils and Foodstuffs Corporation—134 Jiefang (cable: Ceroilfood Tianjin, tel. 20497, 21014).

China National Chemicals Corporation—171 Jianshe Road (cable: Sinochem Tianjin, tel. 30463, 32866).

China National Export Commodities Packaging Corporation—345 Jiefang Nau Road (cable: Chinapack Tianjin, tel. 35448).

China National Foreign Trade Transportation Corporation—80 Qufu Road (cable: Zhongwaiyun Tianjin, tel. 34651).

Tanggu Sub-Branch—44 Xingang Road, Tanggu (cable: Zhongwaiyun Tanggu).

China National Light Industrial Products Corporation—172 Liaoning Road (cable: Industry Tianjin, tel. 30191).

Arts and Crafts Branch—4 Jiefang North (cable: Arts or Porcelain or Straw Tianjin).

China National Metals and Minerals Corp.—319 Heping Street (cable: Minmetals Tianjin, tel. 22370).

China National Machinery Corporation—14 Zhangede Road (cable: Machimpex Tianjin, tel. 30283).

China National Native Produce and Animal By-Products Corporation—Animal By-Products Branch, 66 Yantai Road (cable: Byproducts Tianjin). Tianjin Native Produce Branch, 33 Harbin Road. (cable: NCNPC or Drugs Tianjin; tel. 30348, 36309, 35419).

China National Textiles Corporation—114 Dagu Road Central (cable: Chinatex Tianjin, tel. 30707).

Business Services

Bank of China —80 Jiefang North (cable: Chungkuo Tianjin, tel. 31559 or 34600).

The China Insurance Co., Ltd.—80 Jiefang North (cable: Chinsurco Tianjin).

The People's Insurance Company of China—80 Jiefang North (cable: 42001 Tianjin, tel. 31297).

Tianjin Commodity Inspection Bureau—60 Tai Er Zhuang Road, Ho Hsi District (cable: 2914 Tianjin).

Tianjin Port Affairs Bureau & Superintendent—Pan Yi Street, Tanggu (cable: Tianjin Tanggu 3263).

Shipping and Freight

China Marine Bunker Supply Co.—Xingang, Tanggu (cable: Chimbusco Xingang).

China Freight Management Corporation—Xingang, Tanggu.

China National Chartering Corporation—80 Qufu Road (cable: Zhongzu Tianjin. Tanggu Sub-Branch, 44 Xingang Road, Tanggu (cable: Zhongzu Tanggu, tel. 34651, 35232, 35055).

China Ocean Shipping Agency—23 Chongqing Dao Street (cable: Penavico Tianjin. 9 Pan Yi Street, Xingang, Tanggu (tel. 35436).

China Ocean Shipping Company—33 Zhe Jiang Road, Xingang, Tanggu (cable: Cosco Tianjin, tel. 3984, 3985).

China Ocean Shipping Tally Company—Xingang, Tanggu (cable: Costaco, Tianjin, tel. 3971, ext. 4341).

Foreign-Registered Ship Supply Corp.—Xingang, Tanggu (cable: Supco Xingang).

ÜRÜMQI

Xinjiang Uygur Autonomous Region
Northwestern China

Ürümqi, the capital of Xinjiang Uygur Autonomous Region, lies in a large flat valley near the middle of the Tianshan, or Celestial Mountains. It used to be a dust-filled town, with streets that became a quagmire in the thaw that followed the savage winter. Now it is protected from the wind by belts of trees around the outskirts, has paved roads, flower gardens at the intersections of the streets, and shade trees to protect pedestrians from the furnacelike sun. Even so, it remains an unattractive town, and the main reason for coming there is to use it as a base for excursions to the surrounding regions and for visits to the minority groups residing in the area.

Ürümqi means "beautiful grasslands," a misnomer today, for to the south stand the rugged Tianshan, forever capped in snow, and to the north the deserts of Junggor stretch out to the horizon. Only the Nanshan pastures, some 30 miles from the town can justify the description. Ürümqi has about 800,000 inhabitants belonging to 13 different nationalities. There are the Han Chinese who have swelled into the region, mostly under the direction of the state, and who are now the majority nationality. Then there are the Uygurs, a colorful Central Asian people, numbering about five million; the Kazakhs—also of Turkic origin—about half a million; and the Hui, Chinese-speaking Moslems. Other nationalities include the Khalkas, Sibo, Tajiks, Uzbeks, Mongols, Russians, Manchu, Kirgiz, and Xibe.

The Uygur people, like many of the other nationalities that live in Xinjiang, are of Islamic faith. On most days of the year, they wear the drab clothes so common throughout China, and are recognizable only by their skull caps, embroidered differently according to the region they inhabit. On feast days and holy days they dress in colorful national dress, the women in summer wearing an ornately embroidered vest over a gaily colored *quilak* with tight waist and wide sleeves, and the traditional embroidered *doba* on the head, often being covered by a colored veil. Their dress is ornamented with bright sashes, neckbands, necklaces, earrings, and bracelets of gold, silver, jade, and precious stones. In winter, the women wear a long-sleeved robe buttoned at the waist, to cover the quilak.

Most of the Uygurs live in settlements on the fringe of the Tarim Basin desert. They speak a Turkic language, many of the words used today being understood by Turkish nationals (when the Turkish Ambassador to China visits the region, he can readily converse with the Uygur people). Additional information about the Uygur nationality, as well as the Kazakhs, Kirghiz, Manchu, and Hui, is given in the "Peoples and Languages" section.

Most of the Kazakhs live a nomadic life in the northwest in the Junggar Basin, a region that borders the Soviet Union. Indeed, there are many more (seven to eight million) Kazakhs living just across the border in the

503

Soviet Union than in China, where they are better known by the Slavic term "Cossack," a word that once struck terror into the hearts of those unfortunates who happened to be living in areas subject to their on-slaughts. They are still renowned for handling horses, and if you visit the Kazakh region you will be entertained by their superb feats of horseman-ship.

The Xinjiang Uygur Autonomous Region is enormous. The largest po-litical unit in China, it occupies an area of 635,000 square miles or 1.65 million square kilometers—bigger than many countries in Europe, yet it has a population of only about 12 million people. Strategically sensitive, with international borders adjoining the Soviet Union, the People's Re-public of Mongolia, Afghanistan, Pakistan, and the Indian State of Kash-mir, it represents the northwestern "shield" for Central China. The region has long been the path of invaders threatening the nation and still is as the Chinese fear the designs of the Soviet Union—and also the path of contact with the outside world.

The ancient "Silk Road" passes through Xinjiang, one route in the north heading to Tashkent, through Central Asia to Europe, the other route in the south through Afghanistan to India. The region has been both a source of trouble and inspiration: invading armies have come through there, the Mongol hordes actually overrunning China and ruling it for al-most a century; but so did one of the great religions—Buddhism. And in the reverse direction important discoveries were passed from China to the West. In some periods, often lasting for centuries, the region was hostile and the land route was closed to merchants and travelers; but in other periods, safety of passage was guaranteed, and large caravanserai slowly plodded the paths in either direction.

Xinjiang today remains an economic backwater. The terrain being deso-late and arid, agriculture is carried out only around the oases and in some extensively irrigated areas, and the mineral deposits, while rich, are largely unexploited. Industry has barely touched the region, although there is a small iron and steel plant, some coal mines, and a few factories producing cement, chemicals, textiles, tractors, and farm equipment. Crude oil is ex-tracted near the town of Karamay, in the far northwest but known depos-its in the Tarim Basin remain untapped. Parts of Xinjiang are famous for fruit: melons (particularly the Hamimelon), grapes, apples, pears, peaches, apricots are all grown in abundance. Horse and sheep raising are impor-tant occupations.

There are many mosques in Xinjiang, serving the large population who practice the Islamic religion. Religious festival days are observed and, ever since greater toleration has been shown toward religion, i.e., since the Cul-tural Revolution ended, people have been flocking to the services held at the mosques.

Above all, the region is renowned for its song and dance, entertainments that found their way into the Middle Kingdom more than 15 centuries ago and became most popular under the Tang (A.D. 618–907). The precur-sor of Uygur music are the "twelve Mokams," consisting of more than 170 songs and 72 musical pieces that take over 20 hours to perform. The songs and dances derived from this source are performed all through the region today, the most famous being the "Grape Picking Dance."

EXPLORING ÜRÜMQI

There is not much to see or to do in Ürümqi, and most visitors spend the greater part of their time on excursions. The one site of remotely historical significance is Hongshan, or **Red Hill,** on the east bank of the Ürümqi River. The nine-tiered **Hongshan Pagoda,** built in 1788 but founded originally under the Tang, stands at the top of the cliff. There is the **People's Park** on the west bank with Chinese-style pavilions, and bridges around the shores of an artificial lake. The **Memorial Hall to the Eighth Route Army** commemorates the exploits of this famous army and is a memorial to those who lost their lives in the various campaigns. (Mao Zedong's brother, Mao Zemin, was active in Ürümqi until 1943, when he was executed by a local warlord.) The hall is located in the southern suburbs of the town in a park at a scenic spot called Yan Erwo, or Swallows Nest.

You might visit the **People's Theater** to see a cultural performance. The **Xinjiang Museum** and the **National Minorities Exhibition Hall** both have fine exhibits, as well as the **Ürümqi Museum,** displaying artifacts and models from the stone age to the age of socialism, interpreted according to Marxist canon. You can arrange a visit to a carpet factory and to a workshop making musical instruments traditional in the region, e.g., the Dongbula guitar of the Kazakh minority. For shopping, begin at the **Friendship Store,** where you will find local arts and crafts products, musical instruments, ceramics, and records featuring local song and dance. A visit to the colorful **Youhao Market** is worthwhile. However, be careful about eating at the food stalls, because their hygiene is suspect.

EXCURSIONS FROM ÜRÜMQI

Lake of Heaven

Tianchi, as the Lake of Heaven is called in Chinese, is about 30 minutes southeast of Ürümqi, at an elevation of 6,435 feet (1,950 meters). It is a beautiful lake, with blue waters that capture the reflection of the surrounding mountains. The bus journey takes 3½–4 hours and you can stay overnight, at the lakeside bungalows. A guided mountain climb can also be arranged, but it takes 10–12 hours to reach the snowline. You will see the majestic **Peak of Bodgda** reaching 17,864 feet (5,445 meters) in height and permanently capped in snow; also the famous snow lotus which grows as large as a dinner plate. If you are less energetic you can simply take a boat trip on the lake. Beyond the southern end there is an estuary leading to another lake called **Xiao Tianchi,** or **Small Lake of Heaven,** where there is a splendid waterfall. You can walk there along the lakeshore in 2½ hours.

Nanshan Grasslands

There is also a 30-mile excursion to the southern grasslands of Nanshan where, at certain times of the year, you can visit the herdsmen's yurts (dome-shaped felt tents), eat boiled mutton, and drink fermented mare's milk. Some agriculture is undertaken in the area.

Valley of the White Poplars

Three hours' drive southeast of Ürümqi is a Kazakh horse-breeding commune located in the Valley of the White Poplars, or **Baiyangge.** The Kazakhs live in yurts and move from place to place, according to the needs of the season. The tribesmen and -women will put on a horseback display that will leave you gasping in admiration; they are superb horse handlers. You may see a demonstration of *buzgashi,* where riders dash madly about trying to keep possession of a headless calf or lamb. There are also shooting competitions on horseback. Again, you can eat your fill of mutton, fermented mare's milk (which tastes better after the first few glasses!), a hard cheese called *hert,* and a deep-dried bread made from sow-milk, called *balsac.* Don't be surprised to see the eyeball of a sheep staring at you from the point of a knife. It is considered a delicacy and the guest of honor is usually asked to eat it. It is also the custom to throw the sheep's head through the central hole in the roof of the yurt. If you do this, don't stand there looking up to see if you have been successful. (Most guests of honor secretly wish that this tradition be observed *before* the eyes are offered as a delicacy.)

EXCURSIONS IN XINJIANG

Turpan

The 112-mile journey southeast from Ürümqi to the oasis of Turpan takes half a day by road. Turpan was an important town, for it once stood on the "Silk Road" where the northern and southern routes separated. The northern route skirted the northern foothills of the Tianshan mountains, and wound its way to Tashkent, through Central Asia, to Southern Europe. The southern route skirted the southern foothills on the other side of the Tianshan range, and led to Kashi, then through the Pamir ranges to India. It was along the southern route that Buddhism came, a religion that dominated the area for about 700 years, as the cave shrines in Xinjiang attest. Then in the eighth century, Islam came with the Uygurs. They ruled the area until the twelfth century, before they were in turn swept aside by the Mongols racing to conquer the east.

Turpan lies in one of the world's great land depressions, 505 feet below sea level. It is an oasis that gets all its water from an underground irrigation system called *Karez,* developed in Persia in ancient times. The tunnels begin at the foot of the mountains and rise nearer and nearer the surface as they get further from the source, finally emerging into open channels. The tunnels connect to wells at regular intervals. Fine crops and rich fruits are produced in the region by this method, Turpan grapes being particularly famous throughout China.

Turpan is known as a "furnace town," its summer temperature soaring regularly into the low 100s (40s centigrade) while the desert rocks are said to reach 170° F. It is not surprising that the people who live there dig underground shelters in their yards and go into them during the hottest part of the day. In contrast, winters are dry and cold.

The accommodations for visitors are in the **Turpan Binguan** (tel. 2301, 2907), with a new wing that has a garish interior, in contrast to the old section which has cool rooms with vaulted ceilings. However, the old section has no private baths and you must bathe at the old washstands provided, hot water being carried to your room by friendly Uygur room attendants. Outside, there is a patio separating the rows of rooms, and a pergola covered with vines to keep the sun off the walls. In winter, the rooms are heated, sometimes not very effectively. Apart from a restaurant in one of the department stores, there are no food establishments suitable for visitors. Be cautious about eating at the food stalls in the streets as you cannot be certain about their standard of hygiene. You are probably wise to eat only at your hotel. The dining room at the Turpan Binguan serves good local food: try the kebabs, rice and mutton (called *chaofan*), the tasty halvah made of honey and almonds, and the excellent fruit. If you wish to adopt the local custom and eat with your fingers, always use your right hand.

CITS (tel. 2847) has an office in the guest house.

Suliman's Minaret

Suliman's Minaret, called the Sugongta in Chinese, stands on the outskirts of Turpan. It was built around the 1700s by the Khan of Lukqun in memory of his father. The single tapering minaret, 145 feet high, is an easy landmark, should you wish to go on foot (about half an hour from the hotel).

Ruins of Gaochang

The ruins of the once thriving city of Gaochang lie to the south of Turpan. It lies, desolate and windswept, against a background of arid mountains, the remains standing like giant ant hills. The outer walls were about 39 feet thick at the base and about 35 feet high; they enclosed an inner city, an outer city, and a palace—in a layout similar to that of old Xian. Temple ruins are to be found in the southern part of the old city; shards and pieces of wall paintings have been found that provide an idea of the way of life of the inhabitants a thousand and more years ago. The place was first settled under the Han (206 B.C.-A.D. 220) as a garrison town after they had defeated the Xiongnu (Huns). By the fourth century A.D. the town had become part of a small kingdom. Under the Tang (618–907) it was a tribute-paying Central Asian province; and then it fell to the Uygur in the tenth century, becoming part of their kingdom. It was sacked by the Mongols in the thirteenth century and was eventually abandoned.

Atsana Graveyards

At the foot of the Huoyan or "Flaming" mountains stand two ancient burial grounds, one Islamic, the other Chinese, comprising over 400 underground Han tombs. A number of well-preserved bodies have been recovered, as well as ancient silks, brocades, and embroideries. Archaeologists have been able to learn a lot about everyday life in the region from the "documents" unearthed from the sands. Old discarded papers had been made up into funerary objects such as slippers and hats—a custom unknown in any other region. These have proved invaluable as historical evidence, as the papers record official business transactions, orders for essential supplies, slave purchases, details of marriages, appointment of officials, and so on. The dry conditions at the site have ensured the preservation of the documents in good condition. Only three tombs are open for inspection.

Thousand Buddha Caves

The Thousand Buddha Caves, Qianfodong in Chinese, are about 25 miles southeast of Turpan. The caves have been dug out of the cliff face in a ravine. A stream meanders along the valley floor, providing water for a little greenery on either bank. The barren lifeless mountains slope down on either side. Many of the Tang statues and wall paintings have been plundered, but some are intact and provide an indication of the state of Buddhist religious art over a thousand years ago.

The Ruins of Jiaohe

The ruins of Jiaohe, the "city between the rivers," lie about 13 miles east of Turpan. The walls, made of stamped earth, are reasonably well preserved. A citadel was constructed there under the Han, built on a precipice, with deep ravines on three sides. Being in a better state of preservation than Gaochang, the site reveals interesting details: a gate with lockout; remains of doors, windows, and corridors; old wells; remains of palaces; and the remains of rock tombs with murals, possibly those of Nestorian Christians. The city was sacked then destroyed by the Mongols as they poured into the area in the thirteenth century on their way to seize the Middle Kingdom.

Turpan Grape Farm

The Turpan grape farm produces fruit, cotton, and cereal crops on water drawn from a *karez* underground system of irrigation. Grapes are the most abundant crop, growing on high trellises, and you can walk beneath the vines and escape the sun. Old handmade carpets are usually laid out in the shade, where visitors sit and eat the succulent fruit produced at the commune.

Buddhist Cave Shrines

Over a period of hundreds of years, caves were dug out of the mountain cliffs lining the ancient "Silk Road" and decorated in the glory of Buddha. Many of them still exist—over 900 have been found in Xinjiang alone. So far, except for the group near Turpan, they have not been opened for visitors. The most important groups of caves are given below, listed in order from east to west.

Shanshan Caves, about 60 miles east of Turpan.

Thousand Buddha Caves, outside Turpan.

Yanqi Caves, near Bosten (or Bagrax) Lake southwest of Turpan and due south of Ürümqi.

Kumtura Caves, near Kuqa, due west of Bosten Lake; over 100 caves.

Baicheng Caves, due west of Kuqa; a group of 236 caves decorated between the third and the tenth centuries; this group is the most important in Xinjiang and will eventually be opened for visitors—ask your guide.

Xinhe Caves, about 25 miles southwest of Kuqa.

Wensu Caves, about 15 miles north of Aksu and southwest of the Baicheng group.

All these caves are found along the northern branch of the "Silk Road" leading to Tashkent (in the Soviet Union). The southern branch leads to Afghanistan and India.

Kashgar

Kashgar (or Kashi) lies 665 miles west of Ürümqi and 80 miles from the Soviet Union. Most visitors go there by plane, a journey of 1 hour 45 minutes from Ürümqi, while some hardy souls undertake the four-day bus journey. There is no rail link.

Apart from wanting to visit a remote settlement of nearly 200,000 inhabitants, travelers go to Kashgar to see the **Id Kah Mosque**, the **Tomb of Abakh Hoja,** the ruins of the ancient city of Shule (almost nothing remains), the Buddhist frescoes (barely visible) in the caves near the Qiakmakh River, and the large market, especially the **Sunday Bazaar.**

PRACTICAL INFORMATION FOR ÜRÜMQI

FACTS AND FIGURES. Ürümqi, the captial of Xinjiang Uygur Autonomous Region, is 2,050 miles (3,270 kilometers) from Beijing. It is linked by flight services and rail to the national capital. The fastest direct flight from Beijing takes 3 hours 20 minutes; the fastest train takes 78 hours 50 minutes, or 3 days and 7 hours.

The climatic conditions are severe. The table shows the weather pattern in Ürümqi during the year.

Ürümqi Temperature Range and Average Rainfall

	Temperature (°F)			Monthly Rainfall (in inches)	Number of Days with Rainfall
	Low	Average	High		
January	−25.6	4.6	44.6	5.4	0.22
February	−20.6	10.0	51.1	4.7	0.16
March	−10.7	33.3	40.9	10.4	0.75
April	16.0	51.4	58.2	10.3	0.90
May	33.3	66.0	96.3	11.7	1.00
June	12.8	74.1	105.6	15.7	1.16
July	51.3	78.3	104.5	18.3	0.66
August	48.2	74.8	105.3	13.6	0.76
September	31.6	63.3	98.6	9.1	0.57
October	12.9	46.8	86.4	7.0	0.69
November	−24.9	27.3	62.1	6.4	0.61
December	−25.6	10.4	54.5	5.3	0.30

WHEN TO GO. Ürümqi and other parts of Xinjiang should be avoided in winter. A glance at the above table will tell you the reason. In December and January temperatures drop to as low as −25.6° F (or −32° C)! Look at March, the temperature range can be from −23.7° C to 21.6° C, i.e., a change in one day of 45.3° C or 113.5° F! The temperature range in April is not much less. And June through August has maximums around the 104° F mark (40° C) although the averages are in the mid-to high 70s F. The best months are September and October when the maximums are bearable and the minimums are not excessive. You can forget about your umbrella at any time of the year—the rainiest month is June which averages a little over an inch.

HOW TO GET THERE. Flying is expensive. The fastest flight from Beijing takes 3 hours 20 minutes; from Shanghai 3 hours 55 minutes, and from Lanzhou 2 hours 15 minutes. The fastest train from Beijing takes 78 hours 50 minutes, or 3 days 7 hours, arriving at 7:40 P.M.; from Shanghai 82½ hours, or almost 3½ days, and even worse: it arrives at 1:40 A.M. The trains are always crowded. (Most foreign tourists usually fly to Ürümqi and part of the way back, then resume their tour by train, or vice versa.) The Beijing express takes the southern loop line through

Zhengzhou, so you may prefer to stop over at places along the way, e.g., Luoyang, Xian, and Lanzhou, rather than undertake the lengthy journey without a break. When returning you could fly back to Lanzhou, then connect with a flight to Baotou in Inner Mongolia and take the train on the northern loop to Beijing, stopping off at Hohhot (the provincial capital of Nei Mongol Autonomous Region) and at Datong in Shanxi Province. Or you could fly from Lanzhou to Chengdu and Kunming, and leave China by the South.

HOTELS. The **World Plaza Hotel** (tel. 44835; telex 79150) on Beijing Road, a new 24-story hotel, has 386 guest rooms, a revolving rooftop restaurant (one of four restaurants), coffee shop, swimming pool, tennis court, garden, and disco. Many visitors stay at the **Friendship Guest House** on Yanan Road (tel. 22940, 23991), about eight miles from the town center. The rooms are pleasant, the food adequate. The **Kunlun Hotel** (tel. 42411) on Youhao Road is about 20 minutes drive from Ürümqi railway station. The old section is austere, the new has better accommodations but the restaurant is poor.

The other hotels are: **Tianshan Mansions** (tel. 22481) 33 Donfeng Road, which is below the standard of the Kunlun; the **Xinjiang Guest House** (tel. 54002) on Changjian Road; the **State Guest House** for visiting Chinese and foreign dignitaries (at 280 Fanxiu Road, tel. 4923); the **Yingbinguan** (tel. 22233) on Yan An Road; the **Hongshan Hotel** (tel. 24761), near the corner of Guangming and Xinhua Bei roads; and the **Overseas Chinese Hotel** (tel. 23239) on Xinhua Road, formerly the Ürümqi Guest House.

RESTAURANTS. Try the local kebabs and summer fruits such as grapes and melons, which are superb, the region being famous for these delicacies. A good place to find them is the **First Moslem Restaurant** (tel. 2177) at 16 Hongmian Road, Ürümqi. You should make a reservation through your hotel or guide. You can also eat Moslem dishes in your hotel dining room; indeed it is often preferable to do so as the preparation of Chinese dishes in the hotels leave a lot to be desired.

TOURIST INFORMATION. CITS (tel. 25794) is at 72 Heping Bei Road, facing the eastern side of Renmin Square. Enter through 2 large metal gates and go to the yellow concrete building on your left. Closed Sundays.

CAAC (tel. 42942, 42351) is at 206 Youhao Road, just north of Shiyue (October) Square.

PSB is in Jiefang Bei Road, on the right-hand side and about 2 blocks north of Renmin Square when walking from Zhongshan Road.

HOW TO GET AROUND. CITS arranges tours and excursions by bus.

WHAT TO SEE. There is little to see in the town itself except for the **Hongshan Pagoda** dating from 1788. You could also visit the **People's Park** on the west bank of the Ürümqi River; a **carpet factory;** the **People's Theater;** and a factory that makes musical instruments played in the region. Fine exhibits are to be seen at the **Xinjiang Museum,** and the **National Minorities Exhibition Hall.** The Ürümqi Museum, the Memorial Hall to the Eighth Route Army, and the Ürümqi Zoo, all merit a low priority.

Most of the sightseeing is done on excursions out of the town: try not to miss **Tiachi Lake;** or the 3-hour drive to the **Kazakh Horse-Breeding Community,** where you will see demonstrations of superb horsemanship. You may care to make an excursion to **Turpan,** about 125 miles southeast of Ürümqi, staying over there to visit the **Ruins** of Gaochang, the **Ruins of Jiaohe,** and the **Turpan Grape Farm.** There are Buddhist cave shrines near Turpan; also at **Shanshan** (Piqan) about 60 miles east of Turpan.

MUSEUMS. Try to visit the **National Minorities Exhibition Hall,** opposite the Kunlun Hotel, where an interesting display is devoted to the minorities living in the region.

The **Xinjiang Museum** has many exhibits devoted to the "Silk Road," as well as items related to the life and culture of the minority groups. You will also see the preserved bodies of two men and two women who died over 3,000 years ago.

The **Ürümqi Museum** in Xibei Road is a Marxist portrayal of the history of the region and of China, from slavery to socialism.

SHOPPING. Xinjiang handmade carpets used to be world famous. The ones produced today by machine are still good value but are not of the same quality as the old handmade ones. Try to persuade your guide to take you to a second-hand carpet shop; there you may find a real bargain. Leather boots, the sort worn by the locals, are excellent. For a souvenir, you could buy an embroidered skullcap, the type adorning the heads of the Uygur men and women. Animal skins are plentiful and cheap but watch out for inferior tanning. Coats made from fur-skin (sheep, fox, wolf) are sometimes badly cut, but being inexpensive, are often worth restyling back home. The **Ürümqi Friendship Store** displays these, as well as an array of arts and crafts items.

Try to visit the **Youhao Market,** about half a mile south of the Kunlun Hotel, with its colorful display of fruit, minority foodstuffs (shish kebabs), and regional products. (Note that some visitors have had upset stomachs after eating there, so be careful.)

ENTERTAINMENT. The region has a rich heritage of song and dance, derived from the culture of the 15 or so national minorities that live there. The hotels will arrange to show films and documentaries on the Uygurs and Kazakhs—the 2 largest minority groups—and there are regular performances of minority song and dance. The music came to China along the "Silk Road" and remained part of the minority peoples' culture when they settled in these remote areas. Your hotel or CITS can provide information on these colorful evening performances.

USEFUL ADDRESSES AND TELEPHONE NUMBERS

CITS—72 Heping Bei Lu (tel. 25794).
CAAC—206 Youhao Lu (tel. 42942).
Xinjiang Mountain Climbing Association, tel. 2220.

WUHAN

Hubei Province
South China

Wuhan, the capital of Hubei Province, is roughly midway between Beijing and Guangzhou; it is traversed by the most famous river in China, the Yangzi, or Chang Jiang. Wuhan is made up of three towns that grew up along the banks of the three rivers that join there: the Yangzi, the Han, and the Xunshi. When two bridges were built to link the three towns, communications were improved, and the administration of the towns was placed under a single authority.

The town's central position on the major north–south railway, and on the major west–east water route, make it one of the most important cities in China—one that has been marked for rapid industrialization. Millions of tons of iron and steel are produced here each year, and large factories have been established to produce trucks, rail cars, agricultural machinery, and machine tools. Glass, chemicals, textiles, processed foodstuffs, bicycles, watches, and radio and electronic instruments are also produced in large quantities.

The first recorded historical reference to Wuhan was made under the Han, about 2,000 years ago. But we now know the area has a longer history. In 1974, archaeologists unearthed the remains of a richly furnished Shang Dynasty tomb of Banlong, north of present-day Wuhan. The findings indicated that the area was settled over 3,000 years ago.

Of the three towns, Wuchang is probably the oldest and was certainly more important than the other two until recent times. It stands on the right bank of the Yangzi, and was surrounded by walls until about 60 years ago. Although the walls do not exist now, the layout of the town indicates exactly where they once stood.

Wuchang was the capital of the ancient state of Wu in the third century A.D. Much later, under the Yuan (1280–1368), it was the capital of an enormous province that extended south of the sea. Under the Ming (1368–1644), it was still a major provincial capital, but with authority over an area much reduced in size.

Hanyang is directly opposite Wuchang, on the left bank of the Yangzi. It was also a walled town with a history dating back 13 centuries, but it never had the importance of Wuchang. The town walls were torn down early in this century.

The third town, Hankou, lies on the other side of the Han River, also on the left bank of the Yangzi. It was nothing more than a small fishing village until European powers established concessions there after 1861. From that date on, the town flourished. It is now much larger in area than the other two towns, and is the center for the industrial areas that have grown up in the region.

Wuhan has in this century become well known as a center of revolutionary activity. The movement that led to the overthrow of the Qing Dynasty in 1911 began there; the town's workers were in the forefront of the general strike in 1923; the Peasant Movement Institute was established in the town in 1926 and was important in bringing the Communist doctrine to peasants in the region.

EXPLORING WUHAN

Most of the sights are located in the oldest town of the three, Wuchang. To reduce traveling time to a minimum, the sights are considered not in order of interest but according to location. First, there is the bridge across the Yangzi, then the sights in the old section of Wuchang, and later the East Lake and surrounding areas. After the lake, there are the temples, lakes and monuments of Hanyang, then the sights (of minor interest only) of Hankou.

Wuhan Bridge

Built in 1957, the Wuhan Bridge was a landmark in the development of modern communications in China, as its construction allowed north and south China to be connected by rail for the first time. Perhaps better known as the Yangzi River Bridge, it is about one mile long and has two levels, one for trains, the other for cars and trucks. It is 260 feet (80 meters) high.

Snake Hill

So called because of its undulating contours, Sheshan, or Snake Hill, is the highest hill in Wuchang. It has pleasant walks and quiet pavilions where you may rest. The most interesting historical monument is the **Shengxiang Bao Ta.** The stupa has an eight-story, white circular base, decorated with bas-relief designs. On top of the stupa sits a bronze figure. The monument was erected in 1343 under the Yuan, then moved to its present site when work began on the foundations of the bridge. When the stupa was dismantled, it was found to have covered an old Buddhist pillar (chuang).

On the south slope of the hill you will find the site of the **Former Headquarters of the 1911 Revolutionary Movement** that organized the revolt in Wuhan. The revolution led to the overthrow of the Manchu Empire and the formation of the first Chinese Republic. Nearby, on the north shore of the Ziyang Lake, is the **Monument to the Martyrs** of the 1911 revolution.

Yellow Crane Tower

The old "lookout tower" known as the Huanghe or **Yellow Crane Tower** has recently been restored. One of south China's three famous towers, the 167-foot-high structure was first constructed in A.D. 223 and has been destroyed on many occasions, the last time by fire in the late Qing period. The present reconstruction is based on a design of the tower that existed between 1868 and 1884. There have been many poems written about the tower over the centuries.

Red Hill or Hongshan

A short distance away on the southern slopes of Hongshan stands the Taoist **Temple of Eternal Spring,** dating from the late nineteenth century. The original building was destroyed during the Taiping Rebellion and the present building is in almost total disrepair. On Hongshan itself there are two **pagodas:** one is the four-tiered "shadow-less" Xingfusi pagoda in stone dating from 1270; the other a seven-story octagonal pagoda dating from 1307. At the foot of the southern slope lies the **Tomb of the Revolutionary Hero,** Shi Yang.

East Lake

The East Lake of Wuchang is larger than the West Lake of Hangzhou. Its shoreline is perfect for a stroll. There are many pleasant walks along the water's edge, an abundance of shade trees, numerous pavilions, and many historic monuments. If you wish, you may hire a rowboat.

The most interesting monuments are **Xingyin,** or Strolling and Reciting Pavilion, dedicated to Qu Yuan, the famous Chinese poet; Changtian, or **Endless Sky Pavilion;** Huguang, or **Sparkling Lake Pavilion;** and the Ji-unüdun, or **Monument to the Nine Heroines** commemorating the death of nine women who drowned while fighting with the Taiping rebels against the Manchu rulers of China. In the same area you will find the **Hebei Provincial Museum,** with its fine collection of ancient objects from excavated sites and its more modern collection.

If you have plenty of time, you might care to visit the parks surrounding the Luojia Hill on the southern shores of the lake just south of **Wuhan University;** and to **Moshan Hill** (near the eastern shore of the lake), where you will be able to see the Botanical Gardens.

Site of the Peasant Movement Institute

On your way back to the bridge from East Lake, you can make a detour to visit the former site of the Peasant Movement Institute. Here, Mao Zedong prepared most of his well-known "Report on an Investigation of the Peasant Movement in Hunan,"one of the key documents in the development of the Chinese Communist Revolution.

Tortoise Hill

Tortoise Hill (Guishan, or Dabieshan, in Chinese) is the highest point in Hanyang; it is so named because of its shape. Steps lead to a terrace at the top that offers a fine view of the surrounding region and the **Lotus Lake** (Lianhua) below. To the west you can see **Moon Lake** (Yuehu), actually one large lake and two small ones. All of the lakes are worth visiting if you have sufficient time.

Guiyuan Temple

Not far from the intersection of Hanyang Road and Yingwu Road (where there is a statue of Sun Yatsen), you will find the Guiyuan Si, founded under the Qing. The most interesting part is the Hall of the Five Hundred Luohan. Here you will see row after row of statues of adherents to the Buddhist faith crafted in wood. These superb statues were supposedly done by a peasant father and son over a 10-year period. In many respects it is similar to the hall of the same name in the West Garden Temple, or Xi Yuan Si, in Suzhou. The main hall houses a huge statue of the Buddha carved from white stone and weighing just over 100 tons.

Lute Terrace

Lute Terrace, known in Chinese as Qintai or Bo Yatai, is on the southern shore of the most easterly of the three Moon Lakes near the Hanshui River. The terrace is named after a famous Qin musician who once played his lute there.

Sights in Hankou

Because Hankou is a modern town, it has much less to offer the visitor. You can relax by visiting the zoo in **Zhongshan Park** on the western extremity of the town, visit the **Monument to the Martyrs of the February 7th Strike** of 1923 (in the north of the town just off Jiefang Road), or take a stroll down Yanjiang Road along the left bank of the Yangzi to have a look at the buildings constructed by the European trading houses when they had concessions in the town. Apart from that, you might care to visit the **Arts and Crafts Building** in Zhongshan Dadao Road, or the Wuhan Exhibition Hall in Jiefang Road. A quiet hour in **Binjiang Park,** which overlooks the Yangzi, can be a satisfying experience for those who like to watch river craft.

EXCURSIONS FROM WUHAN

A number of excursions can be made from Wuhan, but they are either difficult to reach or a long way from the city.

Wudong Mountain

An excursion to the Wudong Mountains is worth making, but the journey is long. First you must travel about 255 miles to Jun Xiang, the terminal station on a line leading from Wuhan to the Shaanxi-Henan border. About 30 miles south of this town are a number of Ming temples, pavilions, and monuments set in delightful mountain scenery.

Shang Tomb at Banlong

In 1974, archaeologists excavated a Shang Dynasty tomb (1766–1122 B.C.) at Banlong, north of Wuhan. The discovery threw new light on this dynasty's sphere of influence. Previously the influence of the Shang was thought to have been confined to regions much further north. Similar tombs may be seen at Anyang in the north of Henan Province and at Yanshi between Luoyang and Zhengzhou (see *Excursions from Zhengzhou*).

PRACTICAL INFORMATION FOR WUHAN

FACTS AND FIGURES. Wuhan, the capital of Hubei Province, is located almost midway between Beijing and Guangzhou. It is on the rail link between the two cities and lies 740 (rail) miles from Beijing (18 hours' journey) and 660 miles from Guangzhou (17 hours' journey); it is also linked by air: 605 miles from Beijing (1 hour 50 minutes-flight) and 495 miles from Guangzhou (1 hour 50-minute flight).

WHEN TO GO. Autumn is the best time to visit, especially in October and November. At that time, the maximum daily temperature has dropped to reasonable levels, the cold days are still infrequent, and the rainfall is not excessive. Try to avoid summer (May–August) with its combination of high temperatures, heavy rainfall, and excessive humidity. Winter is fairly warm, although the temperatures on the coldest nights can drop as low as 10–15° F. Late winter (February) and early spring (March) are also comfortable periods for travel.

HOW TO GET THERE. You can get to Wuhan from Beijing, Shanghai, or Guangzhou by rail or by air.

The 2 daily express trains from Beijing stop at Wuhan, one at 3:17 P.M. (train no. 15: departing Beijing 10:55 P.M. the night before); and the other at 5:55 P.M. (train no. 47: departing Beijing at 10:20 P.M. the day before). The trains stop at Shijiazhuang and Zhengzhou en route.

From Guangzhou, the northbound express (train no. 16) stops at Wuhan at 2:14 P.M. (departing Guangzhou at 9:47 P.M. the night before); the other express (train 48) stops at Wuhan at 7 P.M. There is still another train from Guangzhou (no. 350), departing 9:40 P.M. which terminates at the Wuchang Station of Wuhan at 8:07 A.M. next morning; in the reverse direction the train (no. 349) departs Wuchang at 9:05 P.M. and arrives at 8:56 A.M. The train also stops at Changsha en route.

From Shanghai, the rail lines takes a long loop to the south before turning northward through Changsha to Wuhan. The journey is therefore much longer than the direct distance between the two cities would suggest. Unless you are visiting one or all of the cities of Hangzhou, Nanchang, and Changsha en route, you would be wise to consider going by air via Nanjing.

Wuhan is served by regular flights from Beijing and many provincial capitals. The fastest flights are Beijing 1¼ hours, Guangzhou 3 hours 10 minutes; Shanghai 1 hour 35 minutes; Changsha 1 hour 10 minutes; Chengdu 2 hours 15 minutes; Chongqing 3 hours; Guiyang 1 hour 40 minutes; Hefei 1 hour 20 minutes; Kunming 2 hours; and Nanjing 1 hour 50 minutes. Check the schedules with CITS or CAAC as the service varies from winter to summer.

Wuhan is also serviced by boat. Boats leave daily for Shanghai (3 days downstream) and for Chongqing, (5 days upstream). The 3-day journey from Chongqing to Wuhan (leaving daily) is popular.

HOTELS. There are a number of hotels in Wuhan, mostly in the Hankou region of the city. The most central one is the **Xuangong Hotel** (tel. 21023), 45 Jianghan Yi Road, Hankou. The **Shengli Hotel** (tel. 21241), 222 Shengli Road, Hankou, overlooks the river and has a good dining room. Built in the 1930s by the British, it has spacious air-conditioned rooms. Not far off is the **Jianghan Hotel** (tel. 23998), 245 Shengli Street, Hankou, with its European facade and renovated interior. It possesses a fine restaurant. Other hotels are **Hankou Hotel** (tel. 356941), 541 Jiefang Boulevard, Hankou; **Wuchang Hotel** (tel. 71587) on Jiefang Boulevard, Wuchang; **Aiguo Hotel** (tel. 21231) near the railway station on Zhongshan Road; and the **Wuhan Hotel** (tel. 356661) at 332 Jiefang Road. The largest hotel is the **Qingchuan** (tel. 441141; telex 40134), 1 Xima Road, between the river and Tortoise Hill. This 24-story hotel offers accommodations in 300 air-conditioned rooms; there are three dining rooms, a coffee shop, and a roof garden.

RESTAURANTS. Without doubt, the best restaurants are located in the Shengli Hotel (tel. 21023) and the Jianghan Hotel (tel. 23998). The Wuchang fish dishes are renowned in the province. Game fowl (in season) is recommended, and another regional specialty is the Three Delicious, made from prawns, egg white, and rice. The people of Hubei are fond of dumplings, so you might care to try some.

Restaurants outside hotels are: the **Wild Game (Yeweixiang) Restaurant,** 128 Yingwu Boulevard, Hanyang (tel. 443198); the **Cantonese Restaurant** (tel. 23575), 115 Jianghan Road, Hankou; and the **Wuchang** (formerly the Dazhonghua), 188 Penliuyang Road, Wuchang (tel. 72029).

For dumplings try the **Laotongcheng** (tel. 511843), 1 Dazhi Road, Hankou or the **Sijimei** (tel. 22842), 888 Zhongshan Boulevard, Hankou. For noodles try the **Noodles Canteen** (tel. 24769), 844 Zhongshan Boulevard, Hankou.

TOURIST INFORMATION. CITS (tel. 25018) is opposite the Xuangong Hotel at 48 Jianghan Yi Road and in the Xuangong Hotel (tel. 24404) at 45 Jianghan Road.

CAAC (tel. 56780, 52744) is at 209 Liji North Road, Hankou.

PSB (tel. 25129) is at 206 Shengli Road, northeast of the Jianghan Hotel and about five hundred yards south of the Shengli Hotel.

HOW TO GET AROUND. CITS organizes bus tours of the city and excursions to scenic spots in the surrounding area.

MUSEUMS. The major museum of Wuhan is the **Hubei Provincial Museum,** or *Hugei Sheng Bowuguan,* located on the shore of a tiny lake in East Park, Wuchang. There are interesting exhibits of objects excavated in the region: pottery from the neolithic site at Huang shi; ceramic ware from tombs of the Three Kingdom period (220–265); funerary objects from the tomb of Jin Zhou, the Marquis Yi. The 7,000 objects recovered from the Zhenghouyi Tomb which dates from 433 B.C. are superb. Fine examples of lacquer ware, bronzes, gold, jade, instruments, and weapons are on display. The most extraordinary items recovered were 65 bronze ritual bells which resonate over a five-octave range in 12 tones. Open 8 A.M.–noon; 2–5 P.M.; closed Monday.

The **Wuhan Arts and Crafts Building** in Zhongshan Dadao Road is worth a visit. There are displays of arts and crafts of the region.

The **Wuhan Exhibition Hall** sometimes has displays of cultural items. Ask CITS for details.

SHOPPING. There is a lot to buy in Wuhan, a center for the sale of handicrafts made in the surrounding provinces and for many of the arts and crafts products created in the city itself: wood carvings, paintings, bamboo-ware, and silk flowers.

The shopping area which is the most fun is near the railway station; here you will find street hawkers selling all kind of things. Then there are many shops to browse in. The **Friendship Store** (tel. 25781) is located on Jiefang Boulevard, Hankou; the **Antiques Shop** (tel. 21453) on Zhongshan Boulevard, Hankou; the **Arts and Crafts Store** (tel. 53478); and the **Shop for Gold and Silver Articles** (tel. 23936), both on Zhongshan Boulevard, Hankou. There are 2 department stores in Hankou: the **Wuhan Department Store** (tel. 52991), 208 Jiefang Boulevard, Hankou, and the **Central Department Store** (tel. 22354), 139 Jianghan Road, Hankou.

PARKS AND GARDENS. Wuhan has a great many parks and gardens. Some are scattered around the shores of Wuchang's East Lake. **Moshan Hill Park** has a botanical garden. **Zhongshan Park** is located in the northeast section of the city in Hankou. All have fine walks around the water's edge, attractive pavilions, groves of bamboo, and abundant shade trees.

There are also many small parks: **Hongshan Park,** near the East Lake; **Ziyang Park** off Ziyang Road in Wuchang; **Lianhua Park and Lake** at the foot of the bridge in Hanyang; and **Hanyang Park** itself.

In Hangkou, there is **Jiangshan Park,** overlooking the confluence of the Han and Yangzi rivers. Binjiang Park is not far from the Jianghan Hotel and overlooks the Yangzi River. **Jiefang Park** is located in the north of the town; Qiaokou Park is a few blocks from the Wuhan Hotel.

BOATING. A pleasant way to pass a few hours is to go boating on East Lake. Ask your guide to hire a rowboat. If you want to escape for a while, ask a desk clerk in your hotel to write the words, "East Lake" and "rowboat," take a taxi there (ask the driver to wait), go to the kiosk, then row away. You'll need to use a little sign language, but you'll have a lot of fun.

ENTERTAINMENT. The city is well known for its **Wuhan Acrobatic Troupe,** and you may be able to see their marvelous feats during your stay. Wuhan also has a resident **Song and Dance Drama** company that gives regular performances. A theater group performs **Peking opera.** The **Zhenghouyi Bells** (see "Museums") are occasionally played in public performances. Check with your hotel or CITS.

LEAVING WUHAN. Wuhan offers an alternative to the usual departure by train or plane: you can take one of the ferry boats downstream toward Shanghai or upstream toward Chongqing.

On the downstream journey there are 4 major disembarkation ports: **Jiujiang** (see Excursions from Nanchang), which is an overnight journey from Wuhan; **Wuhu** (30 hours) where you can take a bus to **Huangshan**—the famous mountain resort area in the south of Anhui Province; **Nanjing** (36 hours); and to **Shanghai** (48 hours).

Few visitors take the upstream journey to Chongqing because it takes the best part of five days.

USEFUL ADDRESSES AND TELEPHONE NUMBERS

CITS—Opposite the Xuangong Hotel, Jianghan Yi Road, Hankou (tel. 25018).
CAAC—209 Liji North Road, Hankou (tel. 56780, 52744).
PSB—206 Shengli Road (tel. 25129).
Port Terminal—Yianjiang Ave, Hankou (tel. 53875).

WUXI

Jiangsu Province
South China

Wuxi is an important town in Jiangsu Province and an attractive place to visit, with its network of canals and cobbled streets. The major attraction is Tai Lake, a few miles to the south, and the Grand Canal.

Wuxi is an old city, founded over 2,000 years ago under the Han (206 B.C.–A.D. 221). It remained a small settlement until the sixth century, when some development took place as a result of the construction of the Grand Canal. The canal passes through the center of Wuxi.

Over the centuries Wuxi remained a small country town, and it was not until the twentieth century that economic expansion took place. In the 1930s local and foreign investment led to the establishment of numerous factories producing silk, cotton, vegetable oils, and flour. It also became a central market for crops and agricultural produce destined for nearby Shanghai. Following the 1949 revolution, Wuxi was further industrialized.

Agricultural production around Wuxi is extensive. Rice and winter wheat are the predominant crops, but cotton is also important. In the areas immediately surrounding Wuxi you will note a large number of mulberry trees, a reminder that Wuxi is an important center of silkworm farming.

EXPLORING WUXI

Tai Lake

Lake Tai, or Tai Hu, is famous for its scenery and has been an inspiration to poets for over a thousand years. Tai Hu is fed by four rivers, encloses more than 100 islands, and is one of the five largest freshwater lakes in China. Its waters serve the Grand Canal, which passes between the lake and the town. The boat tour of Tai Hu is normally top priority for visitors.

The major lake excursion begins at the boat dock near Wuxi railway station. The boat passes through the center of Wuxi, cuts across the **Grand Canal,** and continues south along the **Liangxi River** until it enters **Li Lake** where it turns east toward **Liyuan Garden.** The boat then passes under Baojie Bridge towards **Dushan Hill** before turning into Lake Tai and heading for the **Turtle Head Island** and the **Three Hill Islands** with their small lighthouse.

The waters of the lake are often glasslike, and as your boat cuts its way through you will encounter mists which flatten everything out. There is no horizon; water and sky appear to be the same. Flat-sailed boats glide by.

There is a fine view of the lake and surroundings from the top of Turtle Head Island. On the foreshore there are pleasant walks among gardens and pavilions. At a point jutting out into the water two sets of characters are engraved in the rocks, one in blue, the other red. The characters in blue refer to Tai Lake's embracing two provinces: Jiangsu, which was formerly part of the Kingdom of Wu, and Zhejiang, formerly part of the Kingdom of Yue. The characters in red refer to the lake's being like "clouds between water and mountain," that is to say, encompassing Wu and Yue.

Xihui Park

Xihui Park on the eastern edge of Wuxi is home to what remains of the **Hui Shan Temple,** built in A.D. 420. The **Hui Shan Spring,** which was known as far back as the ninth century is supposedly the "second best" spring in China, long famous for the purity of its water. At the foot of the hills in the park stands **Ji Chang Garden,** which is over 400 years old and was once the private garden of a minister to the Ming court. One of the best-known gardens in south China, Ji Chang is laid out in exactly the same way as it was in the sixteenth century, and it is similar to one of the gardens in the Summer Palace at Beijing.

Dragon Light Pagoda

On top of Hui Shan, the 250-foot-high hill in Xihui Park, stands the **Dragon Light Pagoda** (Longguang). A seven-story brick and wood struc-

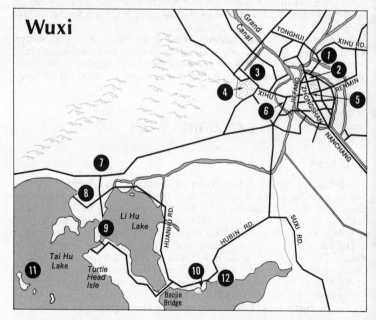

Points of Interest

Dongfanghong Market **5**
First Department Store **2**
Huishan Clay Figurine Factory **3**
Lakeside (Hubin or Lihu) Hotel **12**
Liyuan Garden **10**

Meiyuan (Plum Garden) **7**
Railroad Station **1**
Taihu Hotel **8**
Three Hills Islands **11**
Wuxi Hotel **6**
Xihui Park **4**
Zhongdushan Island **9**

ture, octagonal in cross section, it was first constructed under the Ming. The existing pagoda is of recent date. There is a fine view from the top, and also from the **Qingyun Pavilion** nearby.

Plum Garden

The Plum Garden is just off the road leading from the Tai Hu Hotel to Wuxi. The garden is famous for the thousands of plum trees that bloom in spring. There are ponds; and the **Plum Pagoda** with views of the lake. Li Yuan is reached by a road which runs along the foreshore of Li Lake. Crowded with visitors, the garden features arched bridges, covered walkways, ponds, and a miniature pagoda.

Hui Shan Figurine Factory

You may arrange to visit the Hui Shan clay figurine factory opposite Yihui Park. The figurines are not to everyone's taste, but even if you do not care for them, you will be fascinated to watch them being made.

Scenery from Wu Bridge

The Wu Bridge, or Wuqiao, crosses the **Grand Canal** in the northwest sector of the city. The road leading to the bridge is Tonghui Road from Xihui Park. From the bridge you have a fine vantage point for viewing the flotilla of river craft plying the canal. You will also look down on tiny Huangbudun Island and see an old temple.

EXCURSIONS FROM WUXI

Yixing County

Yixing County, about 40 miles from Wuxi, can be visited on a day excursion. The scenery is attractive: fertile river flats, rolling hills with tea and bamboo plantations, and mountains riddled with spectacular karst caves.

The easiest excursion is a trip to **Zhanggong Caves,** 12 miles south of the town of Yixing. Here you'll find a maze of interlocking caverns, each a different temperature. Seven miles further south lie the **Linggu Caves,** comprising five large "halls" and the spectacular white "stone curtain." Ten miles west of Zhanggong lie the **Shanjuan Caves,** inside Luoyang Mountain, with three levels as well as a water cave and an underground river that you traverse by rowboat to the exit.

In this region you may also visit the town of **Dingshu,** famous for its ceramics (especially teapots made from "purple sand"), porcelains, and figurines.

PRACTICAL INFORMATION FOR WUXI

FACTS AND FIGURES. Wuxi is at approximately the same latitude as Savannah, Georgia. Distances: 710 miles southeast of Beijing by rail, about 20 hours by fast train, 109 miles southeast of Nanjing by rail, train journey of 3 hours; 31 miles northwest of Suzhou by rail, train journey of 1 hour; 86 miles northwest of Shanghai by rail, train journey of about 1½ hours.

WHEN TO GO. The climate in Wuxi is similar to that of the southeastern states of the U.S. The best time to visit is in autumn, when there is little rainfall, the days are warm and the nights pleasant. Try to avoid summer, which is hot and humid, usually with considerable rain.

A visit during winter can be pleasant, but the days are sometimes overcast and accompanied by drizzle. The temperatures are usually cool and occasionally the thermometer can drop toward zero, particularly in January and February. Early spring is often accompanied by rain, but late spring can be very nice.

HOW TO GET THERE. Most visitors go to Wuxi as part of a tour beginning in Beijing and taking in Nanjing, Suzhou, Shanghai, and Hangzhou.

If you are in Nanjing, you may take the train to Wuxi, a journey of about 3 hours. From there it is just under 1 hour by train to Suzhou, and another 1½–2¼ hours from there to Shanghai.

Visitors traveling direct to Shanghai by international flight may consider doing the journey in reverse, i.e., proceeding Shanghai–Suzhou–Wuxi–Nanjing. Organized tour groups often travel to Wuxi from Suzhou, or vice versa, by luxury power-craft.

There is no commercial airport at Wuxi, but the military field 14 miles from Wuxi has pressed into service on Tuesdays and Fridays for flights to and from Beijing. Tickets may be obtained in Beijing at the Beijing Hotel (tel. 507766, ext. 596), or in Wuxi at the Bureau of Communications Building (tel. 29326) on Renmin Road.

HOTELS. The newest hotel, the 342-room **Wuxi Grand** (tel. 668815; telex 362055) in the heart of town, has four restaurants serving Cantonese, Sichuan, Japanese, and Western cuisines, bar, disco, gym, outdoor pool, and a business center.

Hotels located at lakeside are the **Tai Hu Hotel** (tel. 667901; telex 36212) on Meiyuan Road, overlooking Tai Lake; the **Hubin** (or Lihu or Lakeside; tel. 668812; telex 36202) on Liyuan Road, overlooking Li Lake; the **Liangxi** (tel. 26812); the **Shuixiu** (tel. 26591), east of the Lakeside Hotel.

RESTAURANTS. The cuisine at the hotels is good, and you are probably better off eating there. However, if you speak Chinese, you could visit one of the "masses" restaurants. Two restaurants worth trying, providing your expectations are suitably low, are the **China Restaurant,** Tongyun Road (tel. 5623) and the **Jiangnan,** 435 Zhongshan Road (tel. 3651).

Wherever you decide to eat, you should try the specialties of Wuxi, the best known of which are dishes made from fresh fish from Tai Lake, shrimp and crab dishes (there are a variety of these to try), crisp eel, soups based on meat stock, and spare ribs.

TOURIST INFORMATION. CITS (tel. 200416) is at 7 Xin Sheng Road, next to the Friendship Store in the southeastern part of the town.

CAAC has a reservations office in the same building as CTS (not CITS), opposite the main railway station. While no commercial airport serves Wuxi, a twice-a-week air service operates to and from Beijing using the nearby military airport.

HOW TO GET AROUND. Tours and excursions may be arranged through CITS. Especially popular are the water tours of Lake Tai and the Grand Canal, either on a replica of the Imperial Dragon Boat or on a luxury boat such as the *Taihu.*

MUSEUMS. The **Wuxi Exhibition Hall** sometimes has displays of objects unearthed in the region, art shows, and exhibits of cultural interest to visitors. Check with CITS.

SHOPPING. Since Wuxi is the center of Hui Shan figurine production, you may be interested in purchasing some during your visit. The figurines often depict characters from famous operas and plays. The clay used is taken from Hui Shan, or Hui Hill.

Another specialty of the region is Yi Xing pottery, which comes from a small village called Ding Shu, south of the town Yi Xing, and 47 miles southwest of Wuxi. This village may be visited by bus—a 2½-hour journey from Wuxi—or by boat.

Wuxi is well known for its textile production, so it is a good place to shop for silks, tapestries, and cottons. Visits to silk factories and silkworm farms can be arranged.

To begin your shopping you could start at the **Arts and Crafts Store,** 192 Renmin Road, or at the **Friendship Store,** 8 Zhongshan Road. Then there is the **Dongfanghong Bazaar** in Renmin Road or the **First Department Store,** also in the center of town. There is a good antique store known as the **Wuxi Antique and Curio Store,** at 466 Zhong Shan Road. It carries a full range of porcelain, pottery, jade, jewelry, ivory, wood carving, paintings, scrolls, and bronzes.

ENTERTAINMENT. A special event in Wuxi is the **Mid-Autumn Festival** held each year on the fifteenth day of the eighth lunar month. This is the time to try the delicious "moon cakes." During the festival try to take the evening cruise on Lake Tai. It is customary to decorate the foreshores of the lake with lanterns.

LEAVING WUXI. Apart from the train and the twice-weekly air service to the capital, there are long-distance buses west to Nanjing and east to Suzhou and Shanghai.

Being on a lake, Wuxi has frequent boat services to many destinations such as Yixing, Changzhou, and Huzhou (the latter connecting to Hangzhou).

USEFUL ADDRESSES AND TELEPHONE NUMBERS

CITS—7 Xin Sheng Road (tel. 200416).
Advance Ticket Office—24 Renmin Road (tel. 26340).

XIAMEN

Fujian Province

South China

Xiamen, 240 miles south of Fuzhou, is one of the major ports in southeast China. It has been selected for development as a Special Economic Zone. First recorded in history under the Song rulers, it became well known under the Ming during the fourteenth century, when it was established as a trading post and, centuries later, as a Ming center of resistance against the Manchu. Xiamen is also known as Amoy.

In the seventeenth century it became the base of the feared pirate-general Koxinga (also known as General Zheng Chenggong), who terrorized the coast and fought the Manchu invaders. In 1662 he forced the Dutch out of Taiwan and seized the island.

Xiamen fell to the British in 1839, and foreign concessions were obtained under the Treaty of Nanjing in 1842. Now it is a prospering port city with a number of attractions for visitors.

EXPLORING XIAMEN

Gulang Island, or Isle of the Thundering Waves, is a good place to begin. Formerly the foreign enclave, it has fine old villas in tree-lined streets, and two beaches. Some of the villas have been converted into guesthouses. In **Yanping Park** there is a hill, called **Sunlight Rock** or Riguang Yan, which provides a good view; and the **Zheng Chenggong Memorial Hall** devoted to the life and exploits of the pirate-general. Adjacent to the park lies **Suzhuang Garden,** styled after the famous garden in the classic Chinese novel *Dream of Red Mansions.*

Across the Lujiang Channel in Xiamen proper is the Buddhist **Nanputuo Temple,** founded over a thousand years ago. Although the extant buildings are only about 70 years old, they house treasures from the Song and the Ming. The **Five Elders (Wulao) Peak,** which towers over the temple, provides a good view of the Straits of Taiwan.

Jimei Island, about six miles north of the city center, is worth a brief visit. The island was the birthplace of a Chinese philanthropist who dedicated money to the education and welfare of the local population. His tomb (in **Turtle Park**) and former residence may be visited.

EXCURSIONS FROM XIAMEN

Zhangzhou

Zhangzhou lies about 37 miles to the west of Xiamen and may be reached by bus or by train. It is not on the usual tourist path, but it does offer a few attractions. There is the **Nanshan Temple** about a mile south of the town center and the **Mu Mian Hall** about nine miles outside the town. A visit to the **Arts and Crafts Factory** is worthwhile. The region is famous for its fruit, narcissus flowers, magnolia trees, and its prolific rice production.

PRACTICAL INFORMATION FOR XIAMEN

FACTS AND FIGURES. Xiamen lies near the southern border of Fujian Province in South China, about 240 miles south of the provincial capital, Fuzhou. It is actually an island (area 48 square miles) connected to the mainland by a 2-mile causeway. The island lies in the mouth of the Nine Dragon (Jiulong) River.

WHEN TO GO. Xiamen has a subtropical climate. It is hot and humid in summer, with conditions somewhat tempered by sea breezes. Winter is cool but not cold; springtime brings showers; autumn is warm, travel being most comfortable then. The rainy season is July through September. Typhoons may also occur during this period.

HOW TO GET THERE. Xiamen may be reached by air from Manila ($2\frac{1}{2}$ hours) and Hong Kong (one hour), by ship from Hong Kong (22-hour journey departing Hong Kong Tuesday and Friday), or by air-conditioned bus from Hong Kong, Shenzhen, or Guangzhou. Xiamen may also be reached by local flight from Guangzhou (1 hour), Shanghai ($1\frac{1}{2}$ hours), and Beijing ($2\frac{1}{4}$ hours).

HOTELS. The **Lujiang Hotel** (tel. 23235; telex 92423), 3 Haihou Road, is often used for tour groups, features an eighth-floor café-terrace overlooking the harbor, and has an excellent location near the ferry pier downtown. The **Jinbao** (tel. 46888; telex 93034) on Xingang Road, next to the Friendship Store, is another hotel often used by tour groups. It provides guests with a shuttle-bus service downtown.

The **Xiamen Mandarin** (tel. 43333; telex 93028), Foreigner's Residential Area, Huli, with 200 deluxe rooms and 22 "villas," provides a range of facilities including tennis courts, an outdoor swimming pool, health club; and guests may use the shuttle-bus service downtown (20 minutes) and to the airport (5 minutes). This hotel is not affiliated with the Mandarin in Hong Kong.

The **Gulangyu Guest House** (tel. 22052), 25 Huangyan Road on the south side of Gulang Island, is actually a group of converted villas. Near the beach and the International Club, it is a good place to relax, although its distance from the ferry (20–25 minutes' walk) is a disadvantage for some.

The **Overseas Chinese Mansion** (tel. 25699, 25606; telex 93029) at 70-74 Xinhua Road is in two buildings: a modern 14-story structure with 240 rooms; and an old rather dilapidated (but cheaper) annex located a few minutes' walk away.

Budget travelers may wish to try the accommodations on the old cruise ship moored in the harbor; a free passenger launch operates between ship and shore.

RESTAURANTS. Xiamen is well known for its culinary tradition, hundreds of dishes in the Cantonese-Fujian style having had their origin in the town. Many of the restaurants are clustered in the Zhongshan-Siming roads area and while not the most elegant of places, do present reasonable examples of the local fare. Seafood dishes are a speciality of the region; so also are the *dian xin* (dim sum or snacks).

You might care to try: the **Ludao** (tel. 22264) at 230 Zhongshan Road for standard Xiamen cuisine; the **Seafood Restaurant** (tel. 25561) at 1 Fengchao Shan Road opposite the Overseas Chinese Museum; or the **Xinnan Xuan** (tel. 23968) at 17–35 Siming South Road.

Specialized restaurants are the **Nanputuo Temple Restaurant** (tel. 22908) near the temple, serving only vegetarian dishes, and the **Moslem Restaurant** (tel. 24348) at 205 Zhongshan Road.

At street stalls, you might try the peanut cakes known as gongtang, or the dried longan fruit grown locally. The yupi peanuts are a local speciality.

TOURIST INFORMATION. CITS (tel. 25557; 25277) is in 7 Hai Hou Road. **CAAC** (tel. 25942, 25902 ext. 359) is at Hubin Nan Road.

PSB (tel. 22329) is near the Overseas Chinese Hotel (old building). Take the path on the right-hand side of the red brick building opposite the hotel until you come to a gate. The PSB is in the building beyond the gate.

HOW TO GET AROUND. Taxis are readily available, and there are both pedal and motor-driven rickshaws. The cheapest way to travel is by bus, but buses are always crowded.

Bus no. 1 goes from the railway station to the university; bus no. 2 from the ferry pier to the university; and bus no. 3 from the ferry to the railway station. There is an unnumbered bus which goes from the city to the Special Economic Zone (SEZ).

Minibuses ply the streets, are much faster but more expensive than buses, and you really need to know your way around before you are able to use them.

A ferry service to Gulang Island from 5 A.M. to midnight, runs every 10 minutes. The journey takes about 15 minutes, passengers usually stand, and you pay on arrival. There are usually no porters for luggage.

WHAT TO SEE. The **Nanputuo Buddhist Temple** is one of the principal sights, its sweeping roofline decorated in traditional style and its walls protecting treasures of ancient times. **Wulao** (Five Elders) **Peak** allows commanding views over the region, especially of the Straits of Taiwan.

Gulang Island is a great place to get away; there are two pleasant beaches, shaded walks, parks and gardens, an attractive hill called Sunlight Rock, and—a rarity—no cars. (While at the beach, be careful of the swift currents that sometimes run offshore.)

Another island that has some appeal is **Jimei Island,** a few miles north of Xiamen, where the main attraction is the former residence of a Chinese benefactor who once lived (and died) there.

MUSEUMS. The **Overseas Chinese Museum** is northwest of Xiamen University (which is itself on the southern tip of the island), a short distance from Nanputuo Temple. The museum features the history of the movement of Chinese people abroad, their role in the development of other nations, and their contribution to the homeland. Many of the Chinese emigrants who left their nation over recent centuries came from Fujian Province, filling ports like Xiamen on the way to their new lands. Even Imperial edicts banning their departure could not stop them.

The **Luxun Museum** on the University grounds celebrates the revered writer's stay during 1926–1927, when he taught there for a short period. There are memorabilia from his stay, along with historical references to his life and work. The items are displayed in his old room and in 5 adjoining rooms.

There is a small **Museum of Anthropology** on campus.

On Gulang Island, a permanent exhibition at the **Zheng Chenggong Memorial Hall** is devoted to the life and times of Koxinga, the fearsome pirate-general whose forces put fear into the hearts of his adversaries. He commanded a force of 800,000 pirates and a fleet of 800 vessels of war. The memorial hall is situated at 73 Yongchun Road.

SHOPPING. Xiamen has numerous bustling markets, some of them open at night, as well as a handful of shops selling antiques. Handicrafts are a speciality of the region, especially for silk figurines (known as *caiza*), vases and sculpture decorated with lacquer-thread, decorated figurines in clay and porcelain, embroidery made from glass beads, and wood ware.

As usual, a good place to start for your shopping—or at least to check the availability and price of articles—is at the **Friendship Store** (tel. 25965) at 111–117 Si Ming Bei Road or the **Overseas Chinese Store** (tel. 24163) at 7 Zhongshan Road. The **Arts and Crafts Store** is at 143 Zhongshan Road; and there is an **Antique Shop** on Gulang Island at 71 Yongchun Road.

ENTERTAINMENT. In the evening, Xiamen offers one or two night clubs in the newer hotels, as well as a few discos. Nightlife is a little more active here than in other places in China.

USEFUL ADDRESSES AND TELEPHONE NUMBERS

Xiamen Airlines and **CAAC**—Hubin Nan Road (tel. 25942, 25902).
Xiamen International Airport—Gao Qi (tel. 25902).
Hong Kong Ferries, ticket office for vessels serving Hong Kong—Dongwen Road (tel. 24458).
Gulangyu Ferry—Lujiang Road (tel. 23493/4).

XIAN

Shaanxi Province
North China

Xian is in the Wei River valley on the southern bank of the Wei River. The largest city in northeast China, it is the political, economic, and cultural center of the province of Shaanxi. To the north lies the Shaanxi Plateau, rising from about 2,500 feet above sea level to almost 4,000 feet on the northern provincial border adjoining Inner Mongolia, and, to the south, the Qinling Mountains, which are mostly over 6,000 feet with one peak, Taibai Shan, reaching 11,400 feet. The northern plateau shelters Xian from the biting northerly winds in winter, and the southern mountains protect the town from the hotter weather of the south.

Shaanxi Province should not be confused with Shanxi Province to the east. The slight difference in spelling indicates a tonal difference applied to the first syllable. You will often see Shaanxi spelled "Shensi," and Shanxi is often spelled "Shansi." These similarities can be confusing to the visitor, and there is no way around the problem other than committing the differences and locations to memory.

The name of the province means "west of the pass," referring to the pass Tong Guan about 35 miles downstream where the River Wei enters the Huang He, or Yellow River. One of the reasons Xian was preferred as the site of the ancient capital was its greater immunity from attack because of its location west of the pass. Luoyang, being about 200 miles downstream and outside the pass, was favored as a site for the ancient capital mainly for its greater accessibility to barges bringing up food from the fertile North China Plain.

The Wei Valley and middle Yellow River area of Shaanxi have been inhabited since the neolithic era and before. The regions may be considered the cradle of Chinese civilization. The first Chinese states known today from written records were later established in the area, but before then, in 1066 B.C., nomads came in from the east and founded the Zhou Dynasty. Sites in and around present-day Xian were established as the capital from this time up until the end of the Tang Dynasty, when Chang An, as the city was then called, was the most important center of Asia and the meeting point of east and west. When the Tang were eclipsed by the Song in A.D. 907, the town went into decline and emerged from obscurity again only during the Ming period.

The people of Shaanxi have struggled for thousands of years to tame the waters of the province by digging canals, making dams, and irrigating the agricultural areas. Even today water conservation projects are of great importance to the province, and there has been an upsurge in capital construction in this sector. Hillsides are being used for crop production by extensive terracing, and large-scale planting of trees and shrubs has been adopted to prevent erosion and lessen the impact of droughts, both long-time scourges of the area. One forestation program, known as the "great wall of greenness," extends some 220 miles in length.

The major agricultural crops are wheat, rice, and maize, but rape and hemp are the major cash crops. Since the south of the province, particularly the Han valley region, is subtropical, rice production accounts for about 80 percent of the total crop harvested. However, the Wei River valley around Xian raises about 90 percent of the cotton and 70 percent of the wheat produced in the province.

Shaanxi is rich in coal, and iron ore, manganese, and copper are also mined. Crude oil is extracted in the province. Since 1949 emphasis has been placed on the development of secondary industry, so that Xian now possesses factories that turn out machinery, electrical instruments, cement, chemical fertilizers, agricultural chemicals, paper, sewing machines, plastics, chemical fibers, and textiles. The motor industry is being developed.

Xian, known in former days as Chang An, or "Everlasting Peace," vied with Luoyang for recognition as the capital of succeeding dynasties for over 2,000 years. Xian was easier to defend, being "inside the pass." Luoyang, about 200 miles downstream and therefore much closer to the food-growing areas of the North China Plain, was easier to provision.

The areas surrounding Xian were populated by neolithic settlements as far back as 6000 B.C. The excavations just outside of Xian, at Ban Po village, have shown conclusive evidence of the Yang Shao culture.

Thousands of years later the Zhou kings established their capital in settlements only a few miles from the present-day city. Four tumuli, reputedly those of the four Zhou kings, have been located across the River Wei to the northwest of present-day Xian. Some doubt exists about their origin; the historical records show contradictions on this point.

Qin Shi Huang Di, the first emperor of unified China (221 B.C.), set about enlarging the settlement of Xian Yang, some 15 miles northwest of present-day Xian. This town, established under earlier Qin rulers as the capital, became heavily populated, so that in 212 B.C. Qin Shi Huang Di decided to move his court to the south bank of the River Wei. A vast palace, the A Fang, was begun. However, the work was never completed in his lifetime, and some years later (206 B.C.), when the Qin fell to the Han, this and most of the other palaces were destroyed.

The conqueror Liu Bang, first emperor of the Han, established the site of his capital a few miles north of modern Xian. Some of the older palaces were restored and new ones constructed. During the time of the Western Han, imperial tombs were built, nine in the hills running down to the north bank of the river and two in the southern hills in the fork of the Chan River.

From about A.D. 25 the town went into a decline that lasted five and a half centuries, until in 582 the Sui emperor Wen Di established his capital southeast of Chang An. The town flourished and continued its development under the Tang, so that in time it became the most important center in Asia, with a population of about a million people living in a vast, well laid out city protected by large walls and ramparts. The area occupied by the old city was greater than that of Xian today.

All but two of the Tang emperors have their tombs in the hills far back from the north bank of the Wei. There are 15 tombs along a line which extends about 100 miles in an easterly direction, the one farthest east being located near the Yellow River.

The town was extensively damaged when the Tang Dynasty fell and thereafter went into another long period of decline. It was never again capital of China.

The town did not develop again until the Ming, and even then it occupied only about one-fifth of its former area. Under the Qing it was considered one of the most beautiful towns in China; when the Qing fell in 1911 it went into another decline. Thereafter there was little development until after the 1949 revolution, when a program of industrialization was introduced and the area repopulated.

EXPLORING XIAN

The Bell Tower

The Bell Tower in Xian is often used as a symbol for the city. It stood in the center of the town during the Tang Dynasty, but subsequent alterations to the city under the Ming deprived the Tower of its position on a north-south axis. It was relocated to the center again in the sixteenth century, and the whole edifice was restored in the eighteenth century.

The present tower, built in 1384, is 117 feet high and occupies an area of over 10,000 square feet. The base is of brick and the superstructure of wood. It is typical of the Ming architectural style: no nails were used in the woodwork construction, only mortise-and-tenon joints.

The designs inside the tower are traditional, mostly dating from the Ming with a few from the Qing era. The circular design under the lamp hanging from the ceiling on the first floor is from the Qing period, and the dark wood, ivory, and pearl-inlaid furniture inside the tower is from the later Qing.

On the north side of the balcony is a fine iron bell weighing two and a half tons, made in the fifteenth century. (The original was copper and weighed six tons.) Note the double dragon head form of the fulcrum. Wind bells hang from the eaves on each of the four corners of the three roofs. From the balconies you will be close enough to examine the figures on the roof line. There is the traditional dragon at the rear; the first figure in the series is the emperor sitting on a lion-shaped seat.

The Drum Tower

The Drum Tower, or the Gu Lou, is of similar construction to the Bell Tower and was built under the Ming in 1375. It was restored in the seventeenth and eighteenth centuries and after 1949. It has a rectangular brick base, wooden superstructure, and three glazed-tile roofs.

The Ming Walls

The Xian city walls, constructed on the original Tang foundations by Ming Emperor Hong Wu between 1374 and 1378, are among the few city walls extant in China. Surrounded by a moat and built 39 feet high, 50-60 feet wide at the base, and 40-45 feet wide at the top, the walls form a rectangle with a perimeter of eight and one-half miles. It has four gateways, each topped by three towers at the middle of each wall, with watchtowers standing at each corner. The most impressive of the gates is Ximen, or **West Gate.** Six other gates have been driven through the wall since 1949 to assist the city's traffic flow. The wall, gates, towers, and moats are all being restored. You can now walk the entire 7½ miles along the top of the walls. Exit at the **South Gate** for the Shaanxi Provincial Museum.

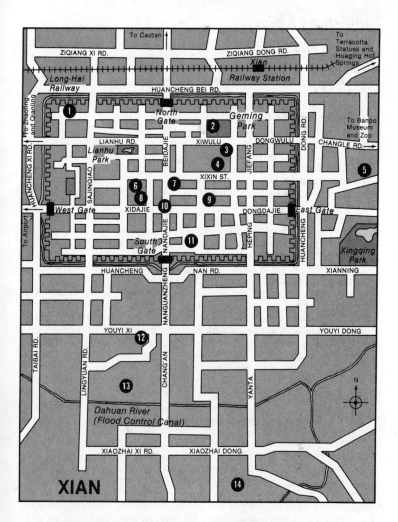

XIAN

Points of Interest

Ba Xian An (Temple of the Eight
Immortals) **5**
Bell Tower **10**
Big Goose Pagoda and Temple of
Goodwill **14**
Drum Tower **8**
Friendship Store **9**
Memorial Museum of the Eighth Route
Army—Xian Office **2**

Qing Zhen Si (Great Mosque) **6**
Renmin Hotel **4**
Renmin Theater **7**
Shaanxi Provincial Museum **11**
Shaanxi Provincial People's
Stadium **13**
Small Goose Pagoda **12**
Xian Stadium **3**
Xi Wu Tai (Five Western
Terraces) **1**

Little Goose Pagoda

The Little Goose Pagoda, or Xiao Yan Ta, stands in the area which once formed part of the famous Da Qing Fu Temple, built in A.D. 684 by the Empress Wu Ze Tian in honor of Emperor Gao Zong. Hundreds of monks once lived in the temples, the most famous of whom was Yi Jing, the pilgrim monk, who traveled to more than 30 ancient states to study Buddhism. He returned to Xian in A.D. 705 and settled in the temple to translate the Sanskrit Buddhist texts that he carried back.

At the end of the Tang Dynasty period the temple was destroyed, then rebuilt, only to be destroyed a second time. The two small temples that now exist on either side of the pagoda were constructed under the Ming. Each has the traditional roofs with upswept eaves.

The pagoda itself was built over the period A.D. 707–709 to store the Buddhist sutras. Originally 15 stories high, it was damaged during earthquakes in 1487, 1555, and 1557. During one of the earthquakes a large crack appeared in the structure and the top two stories fell to the ground. They were not replaced when the pagoda was restored. It is testimony to the building knowledge of the Tang that the pagoda has been able to withstand 70 earthquakes, 10 of which were severe, in the 1,200 years of its existence. In 1961 the State Council declared it an important historical site and in 1963 donated money for its restoration.

The entrance to the pagoda is by the southern door, as was traditional in the Ming period, in contrast to the Tang when entrance was by the northern door and exit by the south. There are Tang engravings on the stone arches of both doorways with Ming inscriptions superimposed, the latter describing the earthquakes that the pagoda was subject to over the period. The square façade with the small roof which protects the exit on the northern side is from the Qing period.

You will hear a number of unconvincing stories from your guide explaining the origin of the name given to the pagoda.

Big Goose Pagoda and Temple of Great Good Will

The first temple on this site, founded under the Sui Dynasty, had disappeared by the beginning of the seventh century. The Temple of Great Good Will, or Ba Ci En Si, was built by the third emperor of the Tang dynasty, Gao Zong, in honor of his mother, Empress Wen De. It was completed in A.D. 652. By the end of the Tang period the buildings had deteriorated, and in 1227 the temple was almost completely destroyed by fire. The temples that now stand around the pagoda are from the Ming and Qing periods.

In the first temple are three statues of the founder of Buddhism in China, with two rows of figures along both side walls; these depict the disciples. All the figures are made of clay and are poor examples.

In the next temple are a gilt bronze-cast figure of Buddha and three rubbings depicting the pilgrim monk Xuan Zang and his two disciples. Xuan Zang spent seven years in India and then returned to China to translate, over a period of 19 years, many hundreds of Buddhist texts. It was he who arranged for the Big Goose Pagoda to be built to house the precious texts. He spent 11 years in the Big Goose Pagoda temple.

The pagoda, which was then five stories high, cracked a short time after it was built. When it was restored two more stories were built, and it remains seven stories high to this day. It is approximately 225 feet in height. During reconstruction the surfaces of the bricks were ground on all six sides to allow the finest tolerance possible. Perhaps this is the reason it has been able to survive the many earthquakes that have occurred during its existence.

The base of the pagoda was rebuilt after 1949. The pagoda itself is square, and four arched doors lead to the interior from the terrace. The archway above the door reveals engravings from the Tang with Ming inscriptions superimposed. The engravings, which show Buddha and his disciples, are fine examples of Tang art.

From the eastern side of the pagoda you can see in the distance a mound that is the tomb of one of the early emperors of the Han Dynasty; the northeastern aspect reveals the tumulus of the famous emperor Qin Shi Huang Di. The northern aspect reveals a road which was once the Tang route connecting the emperor's palace to the pagoda. The higher you climb, the better the view of the town and the surrounding countryside. You can also obtain a good impression of the size and layout of the old Tang town at the time when Xian was one of the largest cities in the world.

Anqing Temple

Anqing Temple, known as the **Five Western Terraces,** or Xi Wu Tai, had original pavilions dating from the Song, but the structure remaining is of much later date. The temple is located in the northwest of Xian off Qianwei Street and is undergoing renovation.

Great Mosque of Xian

One of the largest Islamic mosques in China, the Great Mosque of Xian, or Qing Zhen Si, dates from 742 when it was founded under the Tang. Located in the **Moslem Quarter,** at Huajuegang Street, the mosque is one of four serving the thriving Hui population of Xian, estimated to number 60,000 persons. The present buildings date from the Ming and, apart from the Great Hall, have been built in Chinese rather than Islamic style. Most of the grounds are taken up by courtyards and gardens. Open daily. Visitors not of the Islamic faith are not admitted durir_ the prayer services (five times daily). Shoes must be removed on entering the mosque.

Parks

The **Xingqing Gong Park** in the western sector of the city is of interest because it was the site of a palace built for Tang Emperor Xongzong. A twin-roofed reproduction of recent date known as the **Xingqing Palace,** stands on the edge of the lake. About ¼ mile to the northeast is **Xian Zoo.** There is another interesting pavilion but again of recent date standing in **Geming Park.**

Museums

The **Xian Province Museum** has one of the finest collections of archeological treasures in China. It is also home to the magnificent **Forest of Steles.** The exhibits at both have been described extensively under the section devoted to museums in "Practical Information."

The **Museum of the Eighth Route Army** near Geming Park has items of historical interest relating to the revolutionary army's activities in the region.

EXCURSIONS FROM XIAN

There are wonderful excursions to make from Xian. The most famous is to the excavations of the subterranean vault of the first emperor of unified China, Qin Shi Huang Di. The site is one of the greatest archaeological finds in the world. On the way you can visit the hot springs of Hua Qing. Another important site is the remains of the neolithic village at Ban Po, where you will see the excavations of a society that existed more than 8,000 years ago.

Tomb of Qin Shi Huang Di

The tumulus of the first emperor of China, Qin Shi Huang, is 22 miles east of Xian near Mount Li.

After the 13-year-old boy king, Ying Zheng, inherited the throne of the Kingdom of Qin in 246 B.C., he spent 25 years in armed struggle conquering all the other kingdoms in China. Although his reign over the unified nation spanned only 10 years, he left his mark in history as a courageous soldier, a bold reformer, and a cruel tyrant.

He conscripted hundreds of thousands of peasants to complete the Great Wall, joining up the smaller lengths of wall then in existence. He standardized weights and measures, unified the system of writing, and built a network of roads. Yet he was cruel to his opponents and to those who stood in his way. He had all texts on Confucianism burned and the scholars banished or beheaded. He forced his subjects to build hundreds of palaces and elaborate gardens in the capital.

The emperor began to build his tomb at the beginning of his reign (211–209 B.C.), and hundreds of thousands of workers toiled to complete it before his death. It was finally covered with earth and planted with grass to make the tumulus resemble a hill. Traps were set inside the passageway to ensure that anyone entering would be killed. Historical records suggest that after completion of the tomb all those who had worked on the structure were entombed alive so no one could reveal its secrets. However, records suggest that the tomb was looted after the Emperor's death. We shall soon know because preliminary excavations of the site have already begun.

Qin Terra-Cotta Warriors

Just a mile east of the great tomb lies one of the greatest archaeological treasures in the world, Emperor Qin Shi Huang's vast subterranean funeral vault discovered only in 1974. Archaeologists have uncovered over 7,000 life-size figures in the vault, grouped in battle order, rank by rank, some mounted on horse-drawn chariots, others in infantry groups armed with spears, swords, and crossbows.

The artists who modeled the warriors made realistic portraits of each horseman, foot soldier, and servant in Emperor Qin Shi Huang's guard-of-honor. These legions of terra-cotta figures were interred in battle formation some 15–20 feet underground in a roofed vault measuring some 700 feet east-to-west and 200 feet north-to-south. They are lined up just as they were 2,000 years ago before marching off on a military campaign, the horses standing alert, four abreast in front of each chariot, ready to spring into action.

A hangar has been constructed over the site, allowing visitors to walk around on platforms to view the figures. Three vaults have been excavated. In **Vault no. 1** the 6,000 soldiers and charioteers are lined up facing the emperor's tomb to the east. The men vary in height from 5 feet 10 inches to 6 feet 1½ inches. The first lines comprise the crossbow men and longbow men, who are in turn supported by the soldiers in armor carrying long-shafted weapons, spears, and halberds. Amid the ranks are the 35 horse-drawn chariots, the drivers with arms extended, holding what were once leather reins. In **Vault no. 2** there are 1,430 warriors. In **Vault no. 3** another division of newly restored terra-cotta warriors is on display.

There are two bronze chariots drawn by four small horses on display. This major find was discovered in 1980 on the western side of the mausoleum.

The **Exhibition of Unearthed Weapons** displays some of the thousands of weapons that were buried with the terra-cotta warriors. The weapons, over 2,000 years old, are a remarkable find. Metal assays have revealed that a special surface coating was applied to prevent corrosion, an indication of the state of metal technology even in those ancient days of China.

Warning: The museum authorities have strict rules about photography. You have to pay a fee to take photographs of the warriors and exhibits. If you try to take photographs without making payment, your film will be confiscated. Color slides and postcards are available in the display rooms.

Huaqing Hot Springs

The excursion to the Huaqing Hot Springs 20 miles east of Xian is usually made as part of the tour to the tomb and funeral vaults of Qin Shi Huang.

This lush oasis was a favorite spot of the kings who lived at Xian, and many residences and palaces have been built there. The springs were discovered over 2,800 years ago. They are well known in China because of the love story about Tang Emperor Gao Zong and his beautiful concubine Yang Guifei. He was so entranced by her that he began to ignore the affairs of state and, when her adopted son led an uprising, the Emperor's ministers advised him that the imperial army would not fight until she was put to death. She hanged herself.

The springs and attendant buildings have been extensively restored. Pavilions, towers, and terraces have been erected in Tang-style architecture, following exactly copies of buildings that are recorded in history.

There are two front gates. Upon entering the main front gate (opposite the bus station) you will pass through the **Feishuang Hall,** then proceed along the winding corridor on your right to the **Stone Boat.** This stands in the **Nine Dragons Pond** (Jiulong), the bathing pool of the Tang Emperor Gao Zong. A pathway across the pond links the nearby **Sunset Glow Pavilion** with the **Rising Sun Pavilion** on the other side. On the southern side of the pond stands the **Longyin Pavilion** and behind it the Huaqing Hot Springs Guest House.

A short distance to the east lies the **Huaqing Hot Springs** and to its south the **Lotus Pond** (Lianhua). Here you will find the **Imperial Concubine Yang Guifei Baths.** Just south of this building is the source of the hot springs, and south of this again, the **Five-Room Pavilion.** Passing the **Wanghe Pavilion,** you cross the **Rainbow Bridge** (Feihong) towards the path leading to **Mount Li** (Lishan).

Lishan

Mount Li lies to the south of the Huaqing Hot Springs and is reached by a path from the southeastern sector of the grounds. Standing 4,100 feet high between the Wei and Ba rivers, tree-capped Mount Li offers a fine panoramic view of the region.

Of the numerous pavilions the most famous is **Zhuojiang Pavilion,** where Chiang Kaishek was captured in the "Xian Incident." The incident occurred in December 1936, when Chiang Kaishek, leader of the Chinese Nationalist Party, on hearing gunfire, fled his villa in the Hot Springs, leaving his dentures and one shoe. The pavilion marks the spot where he was arrested.

Further along the mountain path stand the **Old Master Hall** (Laojun), the **Old Mother Hall** (Laomu), and beacon towers of uncertain origin.

Neolithic Site at Ban Po

A famous neolithic site is on a hill just north of the village of Ban Po, six miles to the east of Xian. It was discovered in 1953 and excavated between 1954 and 1957. Four levels of neolithic society were uncovered, dating from 6080 to 5600 B.C. A museum housing many of the finds was built in 1958.

In an area slightly removed from the village more than 170 graves were excavated. The skeletons had their heads pointing toward the west with the faces pointing skyward. Small children were buried in large pottery vessels. Adults were buried with funerary jars, the number and type determined by their status in the clan. Some of the graves and skeletons are on display in the covered site. Only two graves were found with more than one corpse, and these were of the same sex—two men buried together and four girls buried together. Chinese anthropologists suggest this indicates a matriarchal society.

A full description of the objects unearthed at Ban Po is given below (see *Museums*).

Zhou and Han Tombs

Xian Yang was for a short time the capital of the empire of the first emperor of China. Located 12 miles to the west of Xian, it is now an industrial town lacking distinction, except for the museum described below. However, the surroundings are noted for sites of intense archaeological interest.

To the north stand the tombs of five Zhou Emperors, to the west the tombs of five Han Emperors, the best known of which is Mao Ling, the tomb of Emperor Wu (see below). Most of the 10 tombs remain unexcavated.

Xian Yang Museum

The main interest in the town itself is the Xian Yang Museum on Zhongshan Road. There you will see miniature terra-cotta statues found in the region. There are some 3,000 of them, varying in height from 15 to 24 inches, all depicting members of the court, horsemen, military men, musicians, and dancers. They represent one of the finest discoveries in the history of Chinese archaeology. Some of them are also on display at the Shaanxi Provincial Museum.

Historic Sites Near Xian

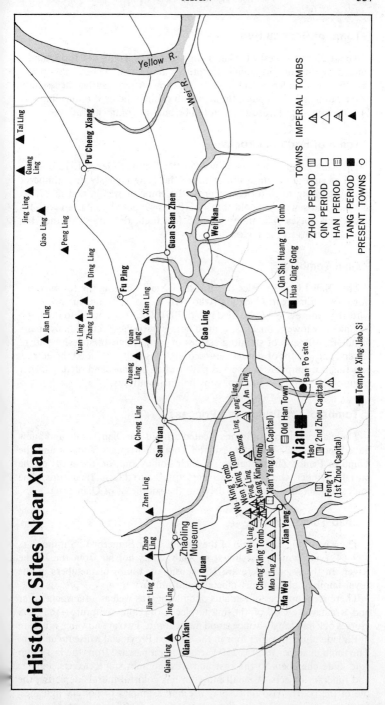

TOWNS IMPERIAL TOMBS

ZHOU PERIOD ▨ △
QIN PERIOD ☐ △
HAN PERIOD ▤ △
TANG PERIOD ■ ▲
PRESENT TOWNS ○

Tomb of General Huo

About 25 miles west of Xian Yang stands the Tomb of Huo Qubing, flanked by human and animal sculptures. In 111 B.C. he became—at age 18—the commander of Emperor Wu's army. After fighting successfully in six campaigns to repulse the Xiongnu (Huns), he died of an illness at 24. The emperor decreed that a tomb be built to commemorate his valor.

Tomb of Han Emperor Wu

The **Mao Ling,** about a mile west of the Tomb of General Huo, is the burial ground of the most illustrious of the Tang Dynasty line, Emperor Wu. According to historical records, the emperor was buried in 87 B.C. in a jade suit sewn with gold thread. He was supposedly interred with his slaves and horses. The mound is 155 feet high, the largest of the Han Dynasty tombs in the region.

Qian Tomb

The **Qian Ling,** 30 miles northwest of Xian Yang, is the tomb of the third Tang Emperor, Gaozong (who died in A.D. 683) and his notorious wife, the Empress Wu (who died in A.D. 705). The "royal way" to the tomb is flanked by towers, obelisks, winged horses, ostriches (zhu que), five pairs of horses, 10 pairs of standing statues of men, a pair of steles, a pair of towers, and groups of statues representing those who attended the emperor's funeral. Empress Wu seized power after her husband died, and her reign of 21 years was infamous for political murders.

Tombs of the Prince and Princess

There are a number of tombs located around the Qian Tomb, and a few have been opened. You can visit the Tomb of Princess Yongtai and the Tomb of Prince Zhanghuai to see their coffins and, on the walls of the burial chamber, the fine murals depicting court life in their time. The tombs are about a 10-minute drive to the southeast of Qian Ling.

Zhao Tomb

The **Zhao Ling,** the Tomb of the second Tang Emperor Li Shimin (A.D. 599–649), is 30 miles northwest of Xian Yang, not far from the Jinghe River. In the region there are 167 subsidiary tombs of members of the royal family, nobles, court officials, and military men.

There are a number of remains of buildings, as well as a sacrificial altar and a gateway. One of the masterpieces of Tang sculpture—the "Six Horses of Zhao Ling"—once stood in the tomb. Two are now in a museum in Philadelphia, the other four in the Shaanxi Provincial Museum at Xian. The tomb chamber itself is 250 yards along a passage from the last tomb gate. Side chambers to the east and west contain stone caskets, tablets, and funerary objects. A small museum has colorful murals depicting the life of the court. Also on display are fine examples of pottery figurines, featuring the famous Tang three-color glazes of different periods.

Five Temples

The temples to the south of Xian make an interesting excursion. The first, **Daxingshan Temple** is south of Chang An town, which is itself some nine miles south of Xian. Founded in the third century, the temple became well known during the Tang as a center of Buddhist learning.

Xiangji Temple, five miles to the southwest of Chang An town, is noteworthy for its 108-foot-high pagoda. The buildings date from the Qing, although the temple was founded in the eighth century. You may see many Japanese tourists there because the temple is renowned as the place where "Pure Land" Buddhism, now popular in Japan, began.

About 10 miles to the southeast of Chang An stands the **Xingjiao Temple,** famous for the activities of the monk Xuan Zang who brought Buddhist texts from India in the seventh century. He died at the temple in 664 A.D. and is buried there under a five-story pagoda. Over the centuries the temple fell into ruins and was restored on a number of occasions. The present buildings date from 1922.

Nearby is the site of the **Huayan Temple,** once the source of inspiration for the Huayan Buddhist sect, still active in Japan. Only two dagobas remain of the original temple. Many Japanese visit this site.

The Caotang Temple, or Temple of the Thatched Cottage, is 30 miles due south of Xian. Built to house the remains of the Indian monk Kumarajiva in the ninth century, the temple has been destroyed numerous times and the present buildings are of recent date. The monk supervised the translation of Indian texts into Chinese until he died in A.D. 413 There is a small stupa in the grounds, a rose garden, and a wooden statue of the monk.

Louguantai Taoist Temple

To reach the site of the Louguantai Taoist Temple, you travel west from the Caotang Temple to the town of Huxian (where you can visit the **Huxian Peasant Painting Academy**). From there it is another seven miles to Louguantai. Taoist monks are once again practicing their religion at the temple. The temple is renowned in China because the founder of Taoism, Lao Tzu, supposedly taught there. The setting is delightful.

Chariot Pit of the Western Zhou Dynasty

A number of Zhou Dynasty burial pits have been excavated in China, and the Chariot Pit is one of the most interesting. The Zhou ruled from the eleventh century B.C. to 771 B.C., so the remains of the two chariots, six horses, and one human (believed to be a slave) are at least 2,700 years old. The site is about 15 miles southwest of Xian, just north of the road to Zhouzhi.

Ruins

As one would expect from the history of Xian and its surrounding areas, there are many remains of towns, palaces, and temples. These are described here separately for the convenience of visitors with a special interest in history or archaeology. Visitors with other interests are warned that there is little to see at these sites.

Old Han Town

The old Han town, about two miles northeast of Xian, was established by Emperor Gao Zu in 206 B.C. The **Terrace of the Wei Yang Gong Palace,** which he ordered built in about 200 B.C., may be seen. Remains of the **Old Chang An City Wall** may also be seen; they surrounded the town, were 40 feet high, 10 feet wide at the top, and 15 feet wide at the base.

Palace of Brilliant Light

The remains of one of the largest palaces of the Tang town, the **Palace of Brilliant Light,** or Da Ming Gong, may be visited. It was built in A.D. 634 and for a time was a permanent residence of numerous emperors. The walls around this area once enclosed about 30 buildings as well as extensive gardens and ornamental lakes. Two buildings larger than the rest were thought to be the throne rooms; the bases of the pillars that supported the roof of these great halls have been excavated. All that can be seen at the site now are the terraces of the throne rooms and the depression in the ground that was once the ornamental lake.

Afang Palace

The remains of the Afang Palace stand in the western suburbs of Xian. Qin Shi Huang, who proclaimed himself emperor in 221 B.C. after having unified China by force, ordered the palace built in 212 B.C. near his capital, Xian Yang. Records show that the interior hall of the palace could seat 2,000 people. There was a covered way from Xian Yang across the river Wei leading toward the palace. Work had not been completed by the end of the emperor's reign (209 B.C.), and the palace was completely destroyed by the armies of Liu Bang when he overthrew the Qin in 206 B.C. and proclaimed himself first Han Emperor. All that now remains is a triangular mound about 25 feet high which is thought to have been the base of one of the buildings.

Tomb of the Yellow Emperor

About 100 miles north of Xian, near Huangling, on the road to Yan An (see below), stands the Xuan Yuan, or Tomb of the Yellow Emperor. Supposedly the "ancestor" of the Chinese people, he apparently lived over 4,000 years ago, and many legends are attributed to him. There is a temple named after the emperor, a platform that Emperor Han Wu had built over 2,000 years ago, numerous steles, and a throne room.

PRACTICAL INFORMATION FOR XIAN

FACTS AND FIGURES. Xian is at approximately the same latitude as Phoenix, Arizona. Distances: about 550 miles southwest of Beijing by air, about 625 miles by rail; about 200 miles due west of Luoyang by train.

WHEN TO GO. Autumn is the best time to visit Xian; the days are pleasantly warm and the evenings mild. The summer months should be avoided, particularly July and August, since the rainfall is always heavy then and the humidity excessively high.

In winter the mountains and plateau country to the north protect the town from the severe north winds; nevertheless, temperatures do drop quite low, particularly in January and February.

Early spring can be unpleasant if the dust-laden winds are blowing. Late spring is a little better but not as good a time to visit as autumn.

HOW TO GET THERE. Direct flights from Hong Kong twice a week take 2½ hours; daily direct flights from Beijing take 1½–2 hours, depending on type of aircraft. Xian is also connected by air services to other provincial capitals: Chengdu (2 hours), Lanzhou (1½ hours), Shanghai (2½ hours), Taiyuan (1½ hours), and Zhengzhou (1½ hours). A new airport and a highway linking it to the city are under construction.

There are regular train services connecting Xian and major cities: Beijing (18½–20 hours), Luoyang (4½–5½ hours), Lanzhou (16 hours), and Chengdu (15¼–16½ hours).

HOTELS. The stylish **New World Dynasty Hotel** (tel. 28870, 713433; telex 70156), Lianhu Road and Sajinqiao Street, forms part of the Xian Art and Cultural Center; it has 519 deluxe rooms, a nonsmokers' floor, business center, four restaurants, a "food street," indoor pool, tennis courts, fitness center, a 1,200-seat theater, airport limos and shuttle service. The massive concrete sculpture in the hotel courtyard, 45 feet high by 95 feet wide, depicts Emperor Qin Shi Huang flanked by his chief minister, Li Shi, and his general, Mon Kuo.

The **Golden Flower Hotel** (tel. 32981; telex 70145) at 8 Changle Road is an international-class deluxe hotel. Known as the Jin Hua in Chinese, it offers 215 rooms, each with color TV and 24-hour room service. There are two restaurants, one offering international cuisine, the other Chinese; piano bar on the mezzanine floor. The new second wing has 306 deluxe rooms, a heated pool, Jacuzzi, health club, and a fine cocktail lounge.

The **Jianguo Hotel** (tel. 338888; telex 700209 XAJGH CN), 20 Jinhua Road South, is the twin sister of the fine hotel of the same name in Beijing. Located at the edge of the old city, it features a scenic Chinese garden, pool, health club, and a branch of the Friendship Store in the hotel. Its 700 air-conditioned rooms have direct-dial telephone, color TV, and minibar; there are two restaurants, a coffee shop, and a cocktail lounge.

The **Holiday Inn Xian** (tel. 721822; telex 70043 COLT CN) at 8 Huang Cheng Road East, South Section, provides first-class accommodations in 358 air-conditioned rooms and suites with color TV, refrigerator, and minibar. Hotel facilities include a Chinese restaurant, coffee shop, business center, indoor pool, health club, and sauna.

The **Xian Garden Hotel** (tel. 711111, telex 70027), 4 Dong Yan Yin Lu, Da Yan Ta, stands in extensive grounds outside the Nanmen (South Gate) of the old capital and offers first-class accommodations decorated in Tang Dynasty style. A theater-restaurant and a museum are in the grounds. The **Concord Hotel** (tel. 44828; telex 70024), 12 Feng Gao Lu, has first-class accommodations, coffee shop, and bar. The new **Huashan Hotel** (tel. 725205) at Jixiang Cun has 150 guest rooms. The **Tangcheng** (tel. 54171; telex 70013), 7 South Lingyuan Road, offers accommodations for 810 guests, mainly those in tour groups. The **Bell Tower Hotel** (tel. 718767, 29203; cable 6988; telex 70124), next to the historic structure of the same name, provides first-class accommodations in 320 guest rooms. The **Xian Hotel** (tel. 711351; telex 70135) at 26 Changan Road, southeast of the Little Goose Pagoda, has reasonable accommodations in 550 rooms in its 14 stories. The **Chang An Guest House** (tel. 25031) has Chinese-style architecture. The **Renmin** (tel. 71511; telex 70176) is at 319 Dongxin Jie. Many tour groups stay at the **Scarlet Peacock** (tel. 53311; telex 70186) at 26 Xiao Zai West Road.

RESTAURANTS. Outside your hotel, there are some restaurants that you might care to try, keeping in mind that Shaanxi cuisine has a reputation for "plainness." The **Xian** (tel. 22047) at 298 Dong Dajie, serves specialties of the region such as wheat noodles, river fish, and mutton dishes. If you want to try specialties of the Wuxi-Suzhou region (Jiangsu Province), visit the **Dongya** (tel. 28410) at 45 Luomashijie; it serves local dishes as well. The **Heping** (tel. 24726), located at 88 Heping Lu, specializes in Beijing dishes, while the **Wuyi**, or **May First** (tel. 23824), at 351

Dong Dajie, serves dishes in the Huaiyang style of cuisine. Other restaurants are: the **Sichuan** (tel. 24736) at 151 Jiefang Road; and the **Minsheng** (tel. 23031), a block further south, on 75 Jiefang Road. For excellent *jiaozi* (small pastries filled with meat, seafood, or vegetables), try the **Jiaozi Restaurant** (tel. 29087) at 29 Jiefang Road.

TOURIST INFORMATION. CITS (tel. 21191 or 53201) is at 272 Jiefang Road. There is another office at the Xian Guest House (tel. 51351).

CAAC/China Northwest Airline (tel. 42264, 42362) is at 296 Xishaomen, on the southwest corner of the intersection of Xiguan Zhengjie, Fenggao Road (a continuation of the first street), and Laodong Road.

PSB (tel. 25121) is at 138 Xidajie, west of the Bell Tower.

If you are traveling by train, tickets for same-day or next-day departure are purchased at the railway station. For tickets beyond that, go to the **Advance Rail Ticket Office** (tel. 25361) on Lianhu Road. It is just west of the intersection with the main north-south avenue, Beidajie, close to the market.

HOW TO GET AROUND. You will certainly need to join a one-day or two-day coach tour to take in only a few of the places you will want to visit. This can be arranged through CITS. Local buses can be used to get to the major sites. Otherwise you will need to hire a car and driver, a costly exercise given the distances to be traveled.

WHAT TO SEE. Xian ranks as the most interesting center in China to visit after Beijing. You will need three days to see the most important sights, five days for a more complete visit.

Foremost of all the sights is the **Qin Terra-cotta Warriors,** an archaeological marvel. The **Huaqing Hot Springs** are nearby, so this ancient spa is usually visited on the same day along with **Mount Li.** A visit to the **Ban Po Neolithic Village** is usually made on the way to or returning from the Terra-cotta Warriors.

The sights in Xian itself are next in priority and a full day could be spent visiting the **Bell Tower,** the **Drum Tower** nearby, the **Big Goose Pagoda,** the **Little Goose Pagoda,** the **Shaanxi Provincial Museum,** the **Forest of Steles** within this superb museum, the **Great Mosque,** and the **Ming Walls.**

At this point you have some difficult decisions to make about the itinerary for the third day. High on your list of priorities would be the **Qian Ling,** the tomb of Tang Emperor Gao Zong and Empress Wu, flanked by a traditional "royal way." The tomb is 53 miles to the northwest of Xian. Then there is the **Zhao Ling,** or tomb of the second Tang Emperor. Located some 37 miles to the northwest of Xian, this site can be visited on the way to or from Quin Ling. While taking in these sights you would probably call in to the **Xian Yang Museum** to see its superb collection of over 3,000 miniature terra-cotta soldiers on horseback, then go to the **Tomb of Yang Guifei,** and finally visit the **Mao Ling Tomb** about 10 miles to the west.

These places can be visited by taking the road from Xian in a westerly direction to the Xian Yang Museum, then heading west to Mao Ling, then northwest toward Qian Zhou (Qian Ling Tomb), then heading west and north to the Zhao Ling Tomb. Or the route could be taken in the reverse direction. Whichever way you go the day will be a long one.

Visitors with more time still have plenty to see. To the west and south there is the **"Five Temples" Tour:** the Daxingshan, the Xiangjian, the Xiangjiao, the Huayan, and the Caotang Temples. Yet another day could be spent taking in various ruins of temples and palaces in and around Xian.

An alternative is to visit the **Louguantai Taoist Temple,** said to be where the famous Lao Tzu taught, calling in at **Huxian** town on the way to see the exhibition of paintings done by peasants in the region. During this excursion you could visit the **Chariot Pit of the Western Zhou Dynasty** to see the remains of the chariots, horses, and a slave interred there over 2,700 years ago.

MUSEUMS. The two fine museums in Xian are the Shaanxi Province Museum and the Ban Po Neolithic Museum. Try to visit them both.

Ban Po Neolithic Museum is located at the site of the neolithic village unearthed at Ban Po. The museum is divided into a number of sections depicting the life of the neolithic society of the village and illustrating with models the housing, agriculture, hunting, and handcrafts of that period.

On display are well-preserved examples of hunting implements such as arrowheads, spears, fishhooks, and a bola (smooth spherical stones connected by hemp rope and thrown at wild animals to trap their legs). But the community did not live entirely by hunting. From the evidence accumulated at the site it is clear that pigs were kept. Cattle, horses, and sheep were certainly in existence in and around the village, but were not at that stage domesticated. There is definite evidence, though, that dogs had been domesticated.

There are excellent examples of pottery made by the strip method and baked in one of the 6 kilns that were unearthed. It appears that kiln temperatures of more than 1,000° C were attained.

An excellent model of the village illustrates the different types of housing—the half-sunk form, the round form, and the square house. It is interesting that even today in North China, when people wish to construct a temporary dwelling they often adopt the half-sunk form, digging down into the earth 4–5 feet to sink the floor into the ground. Mud bricks are then used to form the walls. This construction was seen quite frequently in Beijing in 1976 when mud-brick earthquake shelters were erected quickly in the streets following the severe earthquake.

It appears that the village was built on high ground to escape the floods which are frequent in the region. In addition, the village was surrounded by a very deep moat, probably to protect the inhabitants from maurauding animals and perhaps even from other hostile tribes.

There are also on display good examples of items such as bone needles, weaving shuttles, and small-stone spinning wheels. The last are about 2 inches across and less than an inch thick with a hole in the center, and are used even today in primitive areas. There are examples of both rough and fine pottery, the former for use in cooking and storing water, the latter for ceremonial purposes. The more artistic form of pottery illustrates scenes of nature such as streams, mountains, deer, and fish. There are interesting examples of the evolution of design from pictorial to symbolic, particularly in designs of fish.

Bracelets uncovered at the site were without practical use and served merely as ornaments. Water jars with a conical base, reminiscent of Greek amphorae, were also found. When these are lowered into a stream and fill up, they flip into an upright position, proving that the culture understood the principles of center of gravity.

Shaanxi Province Museum is housed in an old Confucian temple built during the Qing Dynasty.

The first room covers the period 1122 B.C.–A.D. 221: the Zhou, Qin, and Han periods. Exhibits from these dynasties include fine examples of Zhou bronzes, particularly beautiful examples of bronze vessels dating from the Western Zhou period (many of these vessels have Chinese characters molded into their walls), and money in the form of shells.

It was a custom under the Western Zhou for the emperor to have his slaves and horses entombed alive with him after his death.

From the Warring States period there is a fine example of a bronze rhino used as a wine container, a copy of one of the 10 "stone drums" with a hunting song engraved in Chinese characters on the sides, and a diagram illustrating the "self-pointing chariot" or compass made of lodestone.

From the Han period there are models of granaries and village wells recovered from burial tombs, a copy of the bellows used to make iron implements, and a copy of an instrument which is believed to be the first known seismograph. It has 9 dragons mounted around a drum; a ball on the surface of the drum would fall into the mouth of one of the dragons according to the strength and direction of the tremor. There are also examples of 2 small gear wheels, sections of sewage pipes used in houses, and a beautiful example of a peacock lantern.

Sui and Tang dynasty exhibits include fine examples of figurines, farm tools, porcelains, and beautifully patterned silks that were a feature of the age—it was for these that the Middle Eastern merchants would travel the famous "Silk Road" from Persia, Greece, and the Arab countries to China. Also on display are gold and silver objects, beautiful examples of animals, particularly horses and camels in glazed-pottery form, and money in the form of gold and copper pieces from Middle Eastern countries, confirming the presence of foreign merchants in China.

One of the most interesting sets of exhibits is in the room housing the stone carvings. There is a magnificent life-size horse; 2 beautiful examples of Eastern Han be xie (an animal with a lion's head and a tiger's body; they were placed outside tombs to guard against evil spirits); fine examples of stone tomb gates from the Eastern Han and Tang dynasties, all carved in bas-relief; and a huge stone rhino weighing 10 tons, which was placed in front of the tomb of the first Tang emperor.

Of particular interest in this section are 4 of the 6 bas-relief carvings which covered the entrance to the tomb of Han Emperor Li Shi Min. The tomb, known as the Zhao Ling, is located on a tributary of the Wei River about 40 miles northwest of Xian. These stone chargers are considered to be masterpieces of sculpture from the Tang period. Two of the stone horses are on display in a museum in the United States, and the 4 that are on display in the museum in Shaanxi were damaged during an attempt by a private collector to have them shipped to the United States. This was during the period before 1949 when some great art treasures were stolen from China.

The fine stone Buddha is a magnificent figure, carved from a stone with green striations. The head was deliberately made too large for the body in order to correct the onlooker's visual impression when the Buddha is mounted high on a temple pedestal.

Another section of the museum is devoted to objects discovered in more recent times. There is a magnificent collection of exhibits in this hall, and the visitor is advised to allow plenty of time to see them. In particular there are fine examples of Tang dynasty glazed ceramics depicting horses, camels, and human figures. There is a magnificent set of tomb figures one to three feet high, representing members of the court and the military, some mounted on horseback, and all preceding the emperor, who is being drawn in a covered chariot. More than 3,000 of these were found in perfect condition in the tomb of a subordinate to the emperor located about two miles from the main tombs of the Tang Emperors Gao Zu and Hui. Many of them are on display at the museum at Xian Yang, to the west of Xian.

Other fine items are the life-size terra-cotta figure resting on one knee and the 2 life-size horses unearthed from the funeral vault near the tomb of the first emperor of the Qin Dynasty, Qin Shi Huang Di. With such magnificent finds from the vaults, you can imagine the anticipation of archaeologists around the world at the prospect of the major tombs being excavated.

Beautiful bronzes from the Shang and Western Zhou period are on display. Of interest is a large ding (traditional pot with handles on either side and raised on three legs).

The **Forest of Steles** in the museum grounds, the most famous collection of steles in China, was originally established in the Song Dynasty in A.D. 1090. There are more than 1,100 pieces covering the Han to Qing periods. Of great importance are 114 steles with the text of the 12 Confucian classics, comprising 560,000 characters. These date from the ninth century.

A tablet of great interest to Western visitors is one carved in A.D. 781 which records the arrival of a Nestorian priest at Chang An. The stele is mounted on a giant tortoise, and there is a crest in Chinese which reads from the top right-hand down: "Da Ching Nestorian religion popularized in China tablet," interpreted as "the tablet which records the popularization in China of the Nestorian religion originating from Da Ching" the Chinese name for ancient Rome. The original temple housing this tablet was burned down during the Tang dynasty and the tablet itself was rediscovered in 1627 toward the end of the Ming period. The full text is in Chinese with a few passages in Syriac.

Another set of 5 tablets with different kinds of handwriting engraved thereon have been of great value to scholars in studying the evolution of the early Chinese script. There is also a fine set of Song tablets, some of which are engraved with the oldest known maps of China.

From the Ming there is a tablet depicting the monk Da Mo, founder in China of the Chan ("Zen" in Japan) school of meditative or introspective Buddhism.

SHOPPING. Xian is an excellent place for shopping. To begin with there are lots of family-made items for sale at stalls outside the main tourist sights. Then there are the fine handicrafts and art reproductions produced in the city's workshops. There is also an interesting range of rubbings, an excellent item to buy because they are inexpensive, easy to carry, and attractive when framed back home.

The main shopping street of Xian is Dong Dajie, east of the Bell Tower. There are lots of shop windows, a rarity in China, and the wide range of goods are well displayed. The **Friendship Store** (tel. 21551) is located there. The **Arts and Crafts Store** (tel. 28798), 18 Nanxin Street, is almost opposite.

The **Xian Antiques Store** (tel. 27187) is at 375 Dong Dajie, next door to the **Chang An Painting and Calligraphy Shop**. The **Drum Tower Antiques Store** is, not surprisingly, located on the second floor of that historic building. Finally, there is the **Shaanxi Museum Antiques Store** in an annex to the museum.

Four workshops or factories sell ceramic reproductions, carvings, and handicrafts. You can watch craftsmen carving jade at the **Xian Jade Carving Workshop** (tel. 22570) at 173 Xi-1 Road, 2 blocks east of the Renmin Hotel; or cloisonne being made at the **Xian Special Arts and Crafts Factory** (tel. 28891) at 138 Huancheng West Road. Reproductions of the famous tricolor Tang horses and camels, as well as other objects, are made at the **Qianxian Handicraft Workshop** and the **Xian Ceramics Factory** (tel. 39942). CITS can arrange visits.

ENTERTAINMENT. Hotels often provide evening performances of local song and dance for guests. A spectacular acrobatic troupe gives regular performances, both at hotels and in the theater at Xian. Documentary films on the archaeological sites and the treasures unearthed are often shown at hotels.

The **Tang Dynasty Cultural Evening** (tel. 711633) is held at 39 Changan Road, at a dinner theater adjacent to the Xian Garden Hotel. The Chinese-style dinner usually begins at 6:30 P.M., the show at 8 P.M. (but always check). The program opens with a concert played on Tang Dynasty musical instruments, continues with a series of colorful dances, and ends with a vivid battle scene. Tickets may be purchased at the theater, at leading hotels, or through CITS.

USEFUL ADDRESSES AND TELEPHONE NUMBERS

CITS—272 Jiefang Road (tel. 53201 or 21191).
CITS—Xian Guest House (tel. 51351).
CAAC/China Northwest Airline—296 Xishaomen (tel. 42264, 42362).
PSB—138 Xidajie (tel. 25121).
Railway Station—Jiefang Road (tel. 26911).
Railway Ticket Office—Lianhu Road (tel. 25361).
Airport—Xishaomen (tel. 41989, 42225, or 42402).
Friendship Car Co.—Caochangpo (tel. 53201).
Number Two Car Co.—Xidajie (tel. 26624).
Taxi Station—12 Xidajie (tel. 23417).
Telephone Exchange—Yandian Street (tel. 24152).
Post Office—Beidajie (tel. 25413).

XINING

Qinghai Province

Northwest China

Xining, the capital of Qinghai Province, is perhaps the ugliest provincial capital in China. It is located in the far east of the province, not far from Lanzhou, the capital of Gansu Province. Xining itself holds few attractions for a visitor. It is an industrial town having an oil refinery, iron-and-steel plant, and factories producing farm tools, ball bearings, chemical fertilizers, and chemicals. The town is heavily polluted. However, there are interesting excursions to make: one to the most important Tibetan monastery outside of Tibet; another to one of China's most important Buddhist monasteries.

Qinghai Province is the source of three great rivers of Asia: the Yellow River, or Huanghe; the Yangzi, or Changjiang; and the Mekong River. With a terrain of highlands, mountains, a vast plateau, and a region of swamps and shallow salt lakes, Qinghai Province is China's third largest province by area yet one of the most sparsely populated.

The province adjoins Tibet in the south and southwest; indeed, there is a road connecting Xining and Lhasa. Groups of Tibetans are scattered throughout the province, especially around the border with Tibet, while in the north and northeastern parts of the province there are scattered groups of Mongols, Hui (Moslems), and Kazakhs.

Although most of the province suffers from harsh weather conditions most of the year—being bitterly cold in winter—it has a reputation for magnificent scenery. It also has a certain notoriety, there being many prison camps and "reform through labor" settlements scattered throughout the countryside, usually in the most inaccessible areas. Qinghai means "blue sea," a name drawn from the enormous lake not far from Xining.

EXPLORING XINING

The only place of interest to tourists in Xining is the **Dongguan Mosque** about a mile from the Xining Guest House. First established in 1380, the mosque is one of the largest in northwest China. It is still a center of religion for the local Islamic population and prayers are offered five times a day. Visitors are permitted except during periods of prayer.

Beishan Temple, which overlooks the town from the northern hills, may be reached in a 45-minute walk. Turn right (west) out of the Xining Hotel, then right again to cross the bridge over the Yangzi. Nothing much is known about the origins and history of the temple; it offers fine views over the town from the site.

EXCURSIONS FROM XINING

Ta Er Lamasery

The magnificent Ta Er Lamasery, a sacred place of the yellow-hat sect of Tibetan lamaism, is in the town of Lushaer in Huangzhong county. The lamasery is still used as a place of worship by the many Tibetans living in the region.

Worshipers gather to recite holy prayers and smear butterfat on the sacred statues. Lamas still live in the temple to attend to the spiritual needs of the faithful. The eight stupas standing in line near the entrance to the lamasery draw the eye. Behind them, the golden ornaments capping the prayer halls glint in the sun. Inside the courtyard, columns are draped with purple felt fringed at the top with a tricolored band. Stuffed animals stare down from the balconies, the skin around the eyes drawn back to convey a wild, demented look.

Lamaism took root in Tibet in the seventh century; it is a form of Buddhism that was greatly influenced by the religious beliefs that already existed in Tibet. Over the centuries that followed numerous sects developed. In the fifteenth century a well-known lama called **Zongcaba** (or Congkaba) founded a new reformed sect, the Dgelugspa (Virtuous), whose main preoccupation was the strict observance of Buddhist precepts. They were easily identified by their hats, hence the designation "yellow (hat) sect." Their influence increased to such an extent that they eventually became the ruling sect in Tibet. They were also granted the patronage of the Ming (1368–1644) and Qing (1644–1911) courts.

Zongcaba was born in Lushaer, so to honor him a number of pagodas were built. Then in 1560, a small lamasery was built to enclose them, and this was enlarged over the centuries that followed. It is today considered the most important lamasery outside of Tibet, ranking close in importance to the Dazhou Lamasery in Lhasa. And for over 400 years it has been a mecca for Tibetan, Mongolian, and Tu lamas. The lamasery encloses numerous prayer halls, palaces, and pagodas.

The focal point of the lamasery is the **Great Gold Tile Monastery,** or Dajinwa, a three-story building with the top covered in gilded bronze tiles. The building houses a 36-feet-high stupa made of silver with a niche at the top containing a statue of Zongcaba; the walls and ceilings are painted with scenes of the Buddha's life; there are many statues, lamps, and embroideries in the hall. Another important building is the **Sutra Chanting Hall,** or Dajingtang, where more than a thousand worshipers can gather. A flat-roofed structure, supported by 168 pillars draped with tapestries showing a dragon motif, the Dajingtang has a superb display of embossed Tankas in silk depicting events in the life of the Buddha. These are hung from the ceiling and run the length of the hall. There are fine murals on the veranda. The third noteworthy building is the Xiaojinwa, or **Small Gold Tile Monastery;** it is also decorated with gilded bronze tiles. Inside, the pillars are covered with animal furs. There are also stuffed animals on display (bears, horses, sheep, cattle).

There are many priceless works of art at the lamasery: old sutras, porcelains from the thirteenth century, magnificent collections of embossed embroideries, tapestries, carpets, and superb statues. Apart from the many fine statues of the Buddha and Zongcaba, one that is greatly admired is the clay sculpture of the Fairy of Miaoyin. She is sitting, legs crossed, playing a musical instrument. The statue is to be found in the **Nine-Roomed Hall.** There are also extraordinary examples of butter sculpture, particularly the one depicting the entry of Princess Wencheng into Tibet in the seventh century.

The lamasery can be reached by a 45-minute bus ride from Xining. CITS run tours there, or you can take the local bus or minibus from the Ximen (West Gate) terminus; buses leave regularly from 7 A.M. to 6 P.M. You can stay overnight in rudimentary accommodations at the lamasery.

Qutan Monastery

The Chinese authorities are said to be reopening the Buddhist Qutan Monastery to foreign visitors, so check with CITS. The monastery, one of the most famous in China, is about 12 miles south of the village of Ledu, which in turn is about 95 miles due east of Xining.

It stands within two saffron earth walls amidst beautiful scenery. The old caravan route to the western regions of China used to pass nearby. The remains date from the Ming, most of the halls having been built in the Hongwu period (1368–1399), but numerous pavilions date from later periods of the Ming. The buildings have been restored at various times over the centuries. The oldest surviving edifice is the Qutansi Dian, erected in 1394; it is decorated with fine frescoes and murals.

Qinghai Lake

Lying 10,480 feet above sea level, 140 miles from Xining, Qinghai Lake is the largest salt-water lake in China and a nature lover's delight. There you may see huge flocks of wild geese wheeling in the sky. Their favorite haunt is a small dot in the lake called **Bird Island,** where hundreds of thousands of migratory birds land.

CITS arranges bus tours from Xining to bird-watching pavilions on the lake's edge. Guests can also stay overnight at lamasery-style hostels on the lakeside. For visits to Bird Island an overnight stay is necessary because it is some 220 miles from Xining. Budget travelers can reach Bird Island (Niao Dao) by taking the local bus from Xining (opposite the main railway station) in the direction of Golmud, getting off at Heimahe, and taking another bus to Shinaihe. Bird Island is 8 miles from there. March–May, when the birds are mating, is the best time to visit; in other months you may see only scattered flocks of birds.

PRACTICAL INFORMATION FOR XINING

FACTS AND FIGURES. Xining lies at almost the same latitude as Jinan in Shandong Province (and also Tokyo). The town is connected to Beijing by rail (via provincial capitals Lanzhou, Yinchuan, and Huthot) and also to Shanghai (via provincial capitals Xian, Zhengzhou, and Nanjing). There is a rail connection to Golmud in the center of the province, and the 750-mile rail link from there to Lhasa is under construction. There are no direct flights to Xining from Beijing or Shanghai—you must fly to Lanzhou (capital of Gansu Province) and take a connecting flight. Xining is the starting point for a long highway that passes through the province and ends in Lhasa, Tibet.

WHEN TO GO. Choose carefully: it is freezing November through February; warm to hot May through August. September and early October are usually the best. For bird-watching on Qinghai Lake, March through May are the best months.

HOW TO GET THERE. You can fly in via Lanzhou from Beijing or Shanghai, or from provincial cities like Xian and Yinchuan. The flight time to Xining from Lanzhou is 45 minutes; to this you must add the quickest flight time from Beijing to Lanzhou which takes 2½ hours; or 4 hours for the quickest flight from Shanghai to Lanzhou, via Zhengzhou.

The journey by train is a long one. The express from Beijing takes 36½ hours to Lanzhou, then the connecting train (next day) takes another 4½ hours. Don't faint, but there's another train that does this last section in 7¼ hours! Or you could travel for 40½ hours to Lanzhou on the train from Shanghai, then take the connecting train for Xining next day.

HOTELS. The new hotel is the **Qinghai Hotel** (tel. 23905) at 20 Huang He (Yellow River) Road, where most visitors stay. Two guest houses are suitable for budget travelers: the **Xining Binguan** (tel. 23901) on Qiyi Road—take bus no. 9 from the railway station—and the **Xining Daxia** on Jianguo Road—take bus no. 1 from the station to the second stop.

RESTAURANTS. One restaurant you may care to try is the **Ronyuan** (tel. 54725) at 1 Xiaoqiao Street, which serves local and Sichuan-style food.

TOURIST INFORMATION. CITS (tel. 23901 ext. 700) is in the Xining Guest House on Qiyi Road.

CAAC (tel. 77434) is at 74 Xining Dong Avenue.

HOW TO GET AROUND. CITS organizes tours and excursions. Local buses and minibuses offer a less expensive alternative.

WHAT TO SEE. The major attraction in Xining is the **Dongguan Mosque,** the center of the Islamic religion in Xining. There is a temple on the outskirts of the city known as **Baishan Si,** or **North Mountain Temple,** but nothing is currently known of its history.

There are a number of excursions to make. One is to the village of Huangzhong, southwest of Xining, to visit the **Ta Er Monastery;** another takes you farther west to the vast **Lake Qinghai,** breeding ground for tens of thousands of birds, some of them rare. The Chinese authorities are said to be making arrangements to allow tourists to visit the famous **Qutan Monastery** about 107 miles due east of Xining, so check with CITS.

SHOPPING. In the small local shops in the center of town you will find minority handicrafts to buy, such as brassware, ceramics, even some Tibetan-style items.

ENTERTAINMENT. The hotels put on regular film evenings for guests, particularly documentaries about Qinghai Lake.

USEFUL ADDRESSES AND TELEPHONE NUMBERS

CITS—Xining Guest House (tel. 23901 ext. 700).
CAAC—74 Xining East Avenue (tel. 77434).

YINCHUAN

Ningxia Hui Autonomous Region

Northwest China

Yinchuan, capital of Ningxia Hui Autonomous Region, stands between two streams which are part of the Yellow River (Huanghe), in the middle of a vast plain 3,600–3,900 feet above sea level. It existed as a settlement under the Qin (221–206 B.C.) and was important for strategic reasons. It stands near the existing sections of the Great Wall that cut through the northern part of the province and flank the north bank of the Yellow River. Today, Yinchuan is a small town with some industrial development—a linen mill, a farm-tool plant, tanneries—that supports an urban population of about 360,000.

The Ningxia Hui Region is not a province but an autonomous region. These were established after 1949 to allow ethnic minorities in the territory controlled by China to maintain some degree of cultural and linguistic continuity, and a limited degree of self-government, yet pursue political and economic policies consistent with China's national goals. Many of the population are Hui, who are Moslem by faith but otherwise fully integrated into the Han Chinese way of life.

Ningxia is a small territory. It was a Chinese province from 1928 until 1954, when it was made part of Gansu Province to the west. Then in 1958, it was made an autonomous region, but in 1980, when the former boundary lines of the Nei Mongol Autonomous Region (Inner Mongolia) were restored, Ningxia had about two-thirds of its territory included in the enlarged Mongol territory.

Most of the population lives along the river flats of the Huanghe, which cuts through the northern extremity of the province. Irrigation is important for farming, indeed the whole region has a network of canals, many of which were dug as far back as the first century B.C. Some of the smaller canals use waterwheels. The population is also engaged in a constant battle against the ever-encroaching sand. Vast tracts of "green belt" have been planted in order to tame the sands' relentless movement. Dust storms are prevalent in spring, rainfall is very sparse throughout the entire year, and winter is bitterly cold.

EXPLORING YINCHUAN

The Haibao, or Sea Treasure Pagoda, standing in the northern part of the town, is an elegant brick structure nine stories high. Small bells hang on the four corners of each story. The pagoda is surrounded by pavilions enclosed within a red wall. Known also as the North Pagoda because of its location about half a mile north of the city, it was first constructed in the fifth century and rebuilt in the eighteenth century after it was destroyed by earthquake.

The Nanmen, or South Gate, has been restored and is worth a visit; it is in the southern extremity of the town, near the bus station.

The old Drum Tower that stands in the main street of the old town is worth a visit. Little is known of its origin and history.

The Chengtian Monastery Pagoda, with its octagonal glazed-tile top, is in the southwest corner of the town and is therefore known as the West Pagoda. It was built by Buddhists around 1050, when the Western Xia was at the height of its power.

The city has a large Moslem population who practice their religion at one of several mosques. The two main ones are the **Nanmen Mosque,** near the south gate, and **Zhongda Mosque.**

EXCURSIONS FROM YINCHUAN

The Great Wall

Some interesting sections of the Great Wall stand quite close to the town. To the west the wall protects the north bank of the Yellow River, following the course of the river upstream into Gansu Province, but usually located quite a few miles from the river itself. To the east, the wall snakes along just inside the boundary line with Inner Mongolia until it passes deeper into Shaanxi Province.

Qingtongxia

Qingtongxia is a small town about 40 miles south of Yinchuan near a large dam. There are 108 brick dagobas that stand on a barren hill, constructed under the Yuan (A.D. 1271–1368), but little is known of their origin or of the reason for their existence. Constructed in 12 rows to form the shape of a triangle, each dagoba stands on an octagonal base and is painted white.

Twin Pagodas of Baizikou

The Helan mountain chain runs north and west of Yinchuan. At a pass through the mountains stand the Twin Pagodas of Baizikou. Although the eastern pagoda has 13 stories and the Western one 12, they are almost equal in height. The origin and age of the pagodas is uncertain.

Western Xia Tombs

The rulers of the Xia Kingdom ruled in this region over the period A.D. 1038–1227, before the kingdom was sacked by the forces of Genghis Khan, never to recover. The tombs lie at the foot of Mount Helan, but because the historical records of the Xia are scant, little is known about the individual tombs and their exact date. Some are thought to be empty, having been built with the purpose of foiling tomb robbers.

PRACTICAL INFORMATION FOR YINCHUAN

FACTS AND FIGURES. Yinchuan, elevation 3,600 feet, is the capital of the Ningxia Hui Autonomous Region. The population is estimated at 360,000. A large proportion of the province are Hui, i.e., Chinese-speaking Moslems. Yinchuan is linked to Beijing by rail, via Baotou and Hothot in Inner Mongolia, and by air via Baotou. There are also flights connecting Yinchuan with Lanzhou and Taiyuan.

WHEN TO GO. Fall is the most pleasant time to visit the region. Winter is very cold; spring brings dust-laden winds; and summer is hot.

HOW TO GET THERE. Yinchuan is not conveniently located for the traveler. If you have reason to go there you could make it a stopover point on your train journey to Lanzhou in Gansu Province (which would be your destination only if you want to see some of the old Buddhist monasteries of that province). The train journey is a long one: about 26 hours from Beijing and, if you are coming from Hohhot, the capital of Inner Mongolia, the journey would take about 12½ hours. If you are traveling from the west, the journey by train from Lanzhou is about 10¼ hours.

Direct flights twice weekly to Yinchuan from Beijing take from 1 hour 45 minutes to 3 hours, the longer flight stopping at Baotou en route. Flight time from Lanzhou is 1 hour 20 minutes, from Xian 1 hour 45 minutes.

HOTELS. The newest hotel, the **Ningxia Binguan,** or no. 1 Guest House (tel. 24709) on Wenhua Street, provides reasonable accommodations. Other establishments are the **Oasis Hotel,** just around the corner from the Ningxi Binguan, the **Yinchuan Hotel** at 25 Jiefang West Street, and the **Zhongwei Hotel** in Zhongwei county.

RESTAURANTS. No restaurants outside those in the hotels cater specifically to foreign visitors. The **Hanmin Canting,** managed by the Yinchuan Hotel and located one block east of the Oasis Hotel, serves good food. Of the "masses" restaurants, you might care to try the **Wu Yi Restaurant** (or May First) at 204 Jiafangdong Street, which serves standard Chinese dishes; the **Yinbinlou,** on Jiefang West Street, which specializes in Moslem food; or the **Helan,** which also prepares regional fare.

TOURIST INFORMATION. CITS (tel. 24720 or 22466; telex 70191) is in the Ningxia Binguan.

CAAC (tel. 2143) is at 14 Minzu Bei Street.

HOW TO GET AROUND. Tours and excursions are arranged by CITS. Bus no. 1 runs from the train station and the old town. Local minibuses are a faster way to get around. You can hire bikes at the no. 2 Guest House.

WHAT TO SEE. There are only a few sights in the vicinity of Yinchuan. In the center of the old town there is a **Drum Tower;** at the south of the town stands the Nanmen, or **South Gate.** About half a mile north of the city stands the **Haibao Pagoda** (also known as the North Pagoda), while to the southwest stands the **Chengtian Monastery Pagoda** (or West Pagoda). West of Yinchuan at the foot of Mount Helan, there are the **Twin Pagodas of Baizikou** and the **Western Xia Tombs.**

There are excursions to the **Great Wall,** usually to the southwest, taking in Qingtongxia on the way to see the 108 **White Dagobas** of mysterious origin.

SHOPPING. The province is famous for its carpets. Many were made in the region for the imperial palaces, temples, and mansions of the rich. Old carpets are not easy to find but new ones of lesser quality are readily available.

USEFUL ADDRESSES AND TELEPHONE NUMBERS

CITS—Ningxia Binguan (tel. 24720 or 22466).
CAAC—14 Minzu North Street (tel. 2143).

ZHENGZHOU

Henan Province
North China

Zhengzhou in Henan Province is one of the oldest towns in China, yet there is little to show for it today. Now it is a "modern" town with tree-lined streets, row upon row of workers' apartment buildings, and many industrial plants, The old temples have long been replaced by factories.

Situated on the Jinshui River, about 15 miles south of the Huanghe, or Yellow River, the town is an important communications center at the intersection of two of China's important rail systems: the Beijing–Guangzhou line and the Longhai (Gansu) to-the-sea line.

In ancient times Zhengzhou had a more distinguished reputation. A large settlement occupied the site of the present town as far back as 2100 B.C. Excavations have revealed the sites of Shang Dynasty (1766–1122 B.C.) pottery kilns, bronze foundries, foundations of houses, and bone workshops. It was probably the great city of Ao, the capital of the tenth Shang ruler. Large graves in the region have revealed magnificent ritual bronze vessels, glazed pottery, and white ceramic ware so fine it was first thought to be porcelain. Also uncovered were superbly crafted jade and delicately carved ivory pieces.

The Shang were noted for burial practices that led to human sacrifices on a horrifying scale. They believed that the spirits of the dead must be comforted by the person's lifelong possessions. Members of the royal court were usually buried with their servants, guards, domestic animals, horses—and in one case, an elephant. They were dressed in the most elaborate burial costumes and surrounded by precious stones, ceramics, and paintings.

From about 1400 B.C. the town appears to have declined. Other centers, such as Luoyang, Xian, and Kaifeng, attracted the emperors of succeeding dynasties. Thereafter the town remained in obscurity for about six centuries. Then, as the industrial developments of the Western world were carried to China by the European powers, railways were built. By the early twentieth century Zhengzhou became the hub of the main arterial north-south and east-west rail systems.

After 1949 considerable industrial development took place. Zhengzhou is now the center of Henan's textile industry, known for its production of textile machinery, agricultural implements, electrical equipment, and aluminum goods. There are important coal deposits in the northwest part of the town.

The Book of Changes or Yi Jing

The province of Henan is also famous for a reason familiar to many Western visitors. In Huaiyang, southwest of Zhengzhou, there is a mound that is said to contain the **Tomb of Fu Xi,** a mythical emperor. He is supposed to have developed the eight trigrams (ba gua) that form the basis of the well-known *Book of Changes,* or *Yi Jing.* The *Yi Jing* (often spelt "I Ching" in the Wade-Giles transliteration) was first recorded in Chinese history during the twelfth century B.C. but is undoubtedly much older than that. Fu Xi is said to have taught men the art of net-making, fishing, hunting, and animal raising. Legend places his reign in the thirty-fourth century B.C.

EXPLORING ZHENGZHOU

The town itself is quite unremarkable despite its illustrious past. It now features red-brick dormitory apartment blocks and drab factories, relieved only by many trees.

The **Henan Provincial Museum** is the most interesting place in town to visit. It is filled with objects and treasures unearthed during the excavations of the many historical sites in the region. There are fine exhibits of objects over 3,000 years old (Shang Dynasty) and superb pieces from the Zhou (1122–225 B.C.) and Han (206 B.C.–A.D. 221) periods.

A modern monument, the **Monument to the February 7th Strike,** commemorates an event that took place in 1923: a strike by the town's railway workers. Over 100 strikers were killed or injured when the warlord Wu Peifu put an end to the walkout. The **February 7th Memorial Hall** displays exhibits and contains records of the history of the strike.

There are attractive parks in the town, as well as a **Horticultural Garden.** The pleasant restaurant in the People's Park is known as the **Restaurant on the Water.**

The **Yellow River Exhibition Center** is worth a visit. A trip to Mangshan (*Mount Mang*) provides a chance to look down on the Yellow River and surrounding plains; there is also a park and hydroproject in the vicinity. Some of the Yellow River levees are more than 20 feet high.

The Old Shang Town

You can't actually visit the site of the old Shang Dynasty town. All that remains of this settlement, built 2,500 years ago, are a few pottery kilns, bronze foundries, and bone workshops. The sites are scattered around Zhengzhou along the southern bank of the Xiong Er River and along the northern bank between present-day Xiangyang Road and Erligang Dadao.

If you have plenty of time and are interested in China's ancient history, you might care to visit the sections of the existing town located on the site of the old one. You won't see anything old, but here is the information you will need:

The old town stood east of the present-day Beijing-Guangzhou rail line and between the Jinshui and Xiong Er River. The geometric center of the town was where the existing February 7th Square now stands. The western wall of the old Shang town was once near present-day Shuncheng Street. The southern wall of the old town stretched along the north bank of the Xiong Er River; the eastern wall stood where Chengdong Road is now located. The northern wall ran along Jinshui Road on the north bank of the river.

EXCURSIONS FROM ZHENGZHOU

One excursion worth making is to **Anyang,** north of Zhengzhou. The remains of the Shang Dynasty capital, Yin Xu, were discovered there in 1899. Excavations provided the first definite archaeological proof that the Shang Dynasty actually existed. By the mid-1930s, over 300 graves had been uncovered, 10 of which were enormous tombs from the royal house of Shang.

If you visit Anyang and are heading north toward Beijing, you might like to visit **Handan** and **Fengfeng** just across the border in Hebei Province. The Buddhist cave carvings of Fengfeng have been discussed (see *Excursions from Shijiazhuang*). The excursion center nearest Zhengzhou is the ancient city of **Kaifeng,** about 40 miles to the east. It was the capital of China on several occasions, the first under the Wei Dynasty (220–265) during the Warring States period, then under the Five Dynasties period (907–960), and finally under the Northern Song (960–1127).

If you are thinking of taking a rest for a few days, you might arrange to visit **Ji Gong Shan,** or Mount Ji Gong, in the far south of Henan Province. Located south of Xinyang and about 185 miles from the provincial capital, the region is famous for its beautiful landscapes and agreeable climate.

Other excursions already discussed (see *Excursions from Luoyang*) may be undertaken from Zhengzhou. The place that is best known to foreign visitors is the **Shaolin Temple** of Kung Fu fame, where the monks still practice the form of martial arts that they developed there more than twelve hundred years ago. There are other magnificent sights in the **Song Shan** (Mountain) region, such as the **Song Dynasty Imperial Tombs,** and a host of historic monasteries, temples, and pagodas.

Anyang

Anyang is in the north of Henan Province near the provincial border of Hebei. It was once the site of the first capital of the Shang Dynasty (1711–1066 B.C.) and was identified by the discovery of *jia gu wen* (writing on tortoise shell and bone). For centuries, farmers in the village of Xiao Tun Cun, about a mile and a half northwest of the town, had been picking up strange bones in the fields. Some were smooth and shiny, while others had rows of notches and peculiar cracks; still others had engraved marks that resembled a primitive form of text. These were mostly sold to local herb shops, then ground up and used as an ingredient in medicines said to have restorative powers.

In 1899 one of the bones came into the hands of a noted archaeologist and scholar, who recognized the writing as a form of archaic script. He and other scholars were able to determine that the "dragon bone" had come from the vicinity of Anyang, near the banks of the River Huan. Excavations revealed thousands of fragments of bone and tortoise shell that were once used in a ritual to divine the future. Questions to be asked of the oracle were engraved on tortoise shell and the shoulder blades of oxen. The bones were then thrown into the fire and the resultant cracks in the bones were supposed to give the answers.

In 1928, the Academia Sinica began a series of extensive excavations at Anyang. Apart from more "oracle bones" with the names of 18 kings, they found bronze sacrificial vessels of a quality unequaled anywhere in the world. Tomb excavations reveal that the Shang emperors and senior members of the court were buried along with their slaves, servants, chariots, horses, and even household pets. No doubt the members of the court had good reason to keep the reigning monarch in good health for as long as possible.

The last capital of the Xia Dynasty was known as Yin. The **Yin Ruins** comprise only foundations: e.g., the emperor's palace; tombs of members of the aristocracy; workshops. Other sights include the **Wenfang Pagoda** with its dagoba-like top, and the **Tomb of Yuan Shikai,** the war lord who became President in 1913 and tried to become Emperor.

You can make excursions from Anyang to the **Temple of Yuefei,** about 15 miles from Anyang, and to the **Azure Cloud Palace** with its large statue of the Buddha, some 38 miles from Anyang.

Anyang is about 130 miles north of Zhengzhou. Zhengzhou–Beijing railway passes through the town, so the train is the most convenient way to get there. Accommodations for foreign visitors are provided at the **Anyang Guest House,** 1 Youyi Road; the **Taihang Guest House** on Dengta Dong Road; and at two establishments in the same grounds: the **Xiangzhou Hotel** and the **Xiangzhou Guest House,** both at the northern end of Huancheng Xi Road. Restaurants worth trying are the **Yingchun Garden,** which has roast duck specialities; and the **Jubinlou** in Baida Street. You can make tour and excursion arrangements through CITS (tel. 2145), located in the Anyang Guest House, 1 Youyi Road.

Kaifeng

Under the Northern Song, Kaifeng became a magnificent city with wide arcades and canals. The pomp and splendor of the period ended in 1126, when the armies of the Jin seized Kaifeng, captured the emperor and his court, and sacked the palaces. Thereafter, Kaifeng went into decline. It became the provincial capital under the Ming and Qing and has since become an industrial town.

A number of sites are worth visiting. The Long Ting, or **Dragon Pavilion,** was built in the late seventeenth century under the Qing on the site of a palace that was first erected under the Song (A.D. 960–1280). The existing building was constructed on a huge terrace. The pavilion has a double roof and is named after the large stone piece carved with dragons and housed inside the building itself.

Try to visit a number of buildings that have been erected on the site of the old **Xiang Guo Monastery** founded in 555. Rebuilt under the Tang and the Ming, it was destroyed in the devastating flood of 1644. The present structures, dating from the late eighteenth century, have been carefully restored. Of particular interest is the 20-foot-high gilded statue of the Bodhisattva, carved from the trunk of a ginko tree. It is housed inside the **Octagonal Hall with the Glazed Tiles.**

In the southeast part of the town stands the **Fan Pagoda,** or Fan Ta, dating from the Northern Song. It was built in 977, and was once nine stories high, but only three stories remain. The pagoda was erected on the site of what once was the Monastery of Celestial Purity, or Tian Qing Si.

A well-known landmark in the region is the 13-story Tie Ta, or **Iron Pagoda,** erected in 1049 during the first year of Huang Yu's reign in the Northern Song Dynasty. The brick building is octagonal in plan, and each of its 12 roofs is covered with glazed tiles. Iron bells are suspended from the eight eaves on each roof. From a distance, it looks as if it were made of iron. An internal spiral staircase leads to the top floor where you can get a fine view of Kaifeng. The pagoda, classed as a historic monument, was carefully restored following the damage it received in 1938 during the Sino-Japanese War.

You may also visit the Gu Chui Tai, or **Old Music Terrace** in the southeast sector of the town. It is so called because under the Tang leading poets were said to recite their poems and make merry there. The terrace is sometimes known as **King Yu's Terrace,** or Yuwang Tai. There are two pavilions in the park surrounding the terrace: the **Sanxian Temple** and the **Shuide Temple.**

You can either travel by train to Kaifeng from Zhengzhou or take a bus (first bus 5.30 A.M.; last bus 7 P.M.). Visitors stay at the new **Eastern Capital Hotel** (tel. 31075) on Yingbin Avenue or the **Kaifeng Guest House** (tel. 23901) at 102 Ziyou Road.

In restaurants, try the **Diyilou** (for dumplings) or the **Youyixin.**

Tours and excursions may be arranged by CITS (tel. 23737) at 64 Ziyou Road.

PRACTICAL INFORMATION FOR ZHENGZHOU

FACTS AND FIGURES. Zhengzhou is located about 405 miles south of Beijing and lies on the Beijing–Guangzhou rail link: 9–10 hours' journey from Beijing by rail; 2 hours by air.

WHEN TO GO. Zhengzhou does not have an attractive climate—as its former name, "city of sandstorms," suggests. Mid- to late autumn is probably the best time to visit; winters are severe, but without snow; spring tends to be dusty; and summer is hot and humid.

HOW TO GET THERE. The city is an important rail junction, the intersection of 2 famous rail systems in China: Beijing-Guangzhou and the "Gansu to the sea" link (Longhai). You can get to Zhengzhou by rail from Beijing (9–10 hours) or Guangzhou (21 hours); also from Shanghai and Nanjing in the East, from Xian in the West, and from Wuhan in the South.

By air, the journey from Beijing takes 2 hours; there are also flights from Guangzhou, Nanjing, and Shanghai. Flight times and services vary from summer to summer, so check with your CITS travel guide.

HOTELS. The main hotel is the **International (Guoji) Hotel** (tel. 23413; telex 46061) at 114 Jinshui Road; all rooms are air conditioned, and there is a swimming pool. The **Zhongzhou Guest House** (tel. 24255), also on Jinshui Road, is equipped with a large conference center. Visitors are also accommodated at the **Henan Hotel** (tel. 32227) on Huayuan Road, the **Henan Guest House** (tel. 22216) on Jinshui Road, the **Friendship Guest House** (tel. 25593) also on Jinshui Road, the **Zhongyuan Mansion,** opposite the railway station, or the **February 7th Hotel,** adjacent to the monument of the same name.

RESTAURANTS. You might like to try the **Restaurant on the Water** (tel. 23317) in Renmin (People's) Park. Located on the banks of the Jinshui River, it is a pleasant change from the hotel restaurants. For roast duck try the **Zhengzhou Kaoyadian** (tel. 24582). For regional dishes try the **Shaolin** (tel. 22441), a restaurant named after the temple in the province where kung-fu style of martial arts was born. It is at the corner of Jinshui and Jingsi Roads.

TOURIST INFORMATION. CITS (tel. 25396) is at 16 Jinshui Road.

CAAC (tel. 24339, 23284) is at 38 Erqi Road, one block to the north of the February 7th Memorial Tower.

PSB (tel. 25661) is at 70 Erqi Road. Closed Sundays.

HOW TO GET AROUND. CITS arranges tours of the city and excursions to Kaifeng, Dengfeng, Shaolin Monastery, and Luoyang. The last 3 sites are described in the section on Luoyang. Local buses are also available to these destinations.

WHAT TO SEE. The major sights are the **Dragon Pavilion,** an elegant structure built in the late Qing period; the **Xiang Guo Monastery** with its grand pavilions, also from the Qing; and the **Fan Pagoda.** Perhaps the best-known sight of all in Kaifeng is the **Iron Pagoda,** so called because its dark-brown tiles resemble iron from a distance.

MUSEUMS. The **Henan Province Museum** is divided broadly into two sections, one covering ancient history and the other covering the history of the revolution. In the section dealing with the dynasties, there is a fine collection of objects recovered from the many archaeological sites in Henan Province, particularly from the Shang and Zhou periods. There is also a superb collection of tomb figurines from the Han era. In the section dealing with the revolution, special emphasis is given to the Zhengzhou railwaymen's strike of 1923, and to the devastating floods of 1938 that caused the deaths of nearly half a million people. The **Yellow River Exhibition Center** is excellent.

Another place to visit is the **Provincial Cultural Palace;** sometimes there are cultural exhibits that are open to foreign visitors.

Finally, the **Zhengzhou Museum** in Laodong Park, just off Songshan Road.

SHOPPING. There are plenty of small shops in which you can buy local products, but no regional specialties. Most visitors confine purchases to goods on sale at the **Friendship Store** (tel. 26110) on Erqi Road, the **Hongqi Department Store** (tel. 26925) on Jiefang Road Central, or the **Baihuolou Emporium** (tel. 25561) on Erqi Road. There is a good antique store—the **Henan Province Antiques Shop** (tel. 26433) on Erqi Road, within walking distance of the Zhengzhou Guest House.

PARKS. There are a number of pleasant parks in the town. The **People's Park** is the most attractive, with its lake, small islands, and pavilions. Plant lovers should visit the **Horticultural Garden,** off Nongye Road in the north of the town. The only other parks of note are **Laodong Park,** containing the Zhengzhou Museum, and **Dongfanghong Park,** overlooking the river and located next to the Henan Guest House.

ENTERTAINMENT. The hotels show documentary films about the province in the evenings.

USEFUL ADDRESSES AND TELEPHONE NUMBERS

CITS—16 Jinshui Road (tel. 25396).
CAAC—38 Erqi Road (tel. 24339, 23284).
PSB—70 Erqi Road (tel. 25661).

VOCABULARY
SUPPLEMENT

INDEX

THE CHINESE LANGUAGE

TEN BASIC WORDS

While tour guides often speak excellent English, and many of the hotel staff speak some English, very few of the Chinese population speak any English at all. Every traveler knows that a few words spoken in the local language will bring smiles of appreciation and establish a friendly relationship between visitor and host. There are 10 basic Chinese words that you might care to memorize, and one tactful phrase. With just a few minutes' practice, you will be able to put them to memory, and you are sure to find the effort rewarded many times over with the approval and encouragement that you receive in return.

"Pinyin" is the official Chinese system developed to simulate the *sound* of the Chinese word, using the English alphabet (or—more correctly—the Roman alphabet). There is a later section devoted to phonetic systems, including "pinyin."

Word or Phrase	Approximate sound in English	Pinyin	Chinese
Hello (Also: How are you? How do you do? Good day)	nee how	ni hao	你好
Goodbye	dzy-jen	zàijiàn	再見
Thank you	shiay-shiay	xìe xìe	謝謝
Very good	hern-how	hen hǎo	很好
Tasty	hern-how chee	hen hao chi	很好乞
Cheers! or Your Health!	gan-bay	ganbei	十杯
Friendship	yo-yee	youyì	友谊
China	chong-gwoa	zhong guó	中国
China is wonderful	chong-gwoa ty-howla	zhong gúo tài hao le	中国太好了

You may be puzzled about the absence of the words "yes," "no," and "please." The first two don't exist in Chinese in the way they do in English and many other languages. Ask a Chinese person whether he has a bicycle and he will reply "have" or "no have." Ask if he is going to the shop and he will reply "is" or "is not." These replace "yes" and "no." On the other hand, the word "please" does exist and is greatly used, normally as the first word in a sentence, e.g., "please call a taxi," but not in the form of "yes, please." This means you will need to know a string of Chinese words to follow "please" (or "qing" as it is spelled in pinyin form) and those of you who are further advanced will find a host of examples in the list of useful expressions that follow.

If you count the "words" in the "pinyin column" above, you will note that there are only nine. The tenth is the name of your own country; and these are listed on the last two pages of the language section under "nations." Equipped with these 10 words you will be able to meet and greet people, say farewell, express appreciation, compliment their food, drink to their health, engage in a bit of international diplomacy by expressing friendship between your two nations, and tell the Chinese how much you like their country. Not bad for a 10-word vocabulary!

PRONUNCIATION OF MODERN CHINESE

It is far beyond the objectives of this book to provide the reader with more than the simplest outline of the phonetics of the modern Chinese language, "Putonghua." While good pronunciation need not correspond exactly to the pronunciation of the native speaker, it must be within an acceptable range of variation. As in all languages, best results are obtained by commencing study in early childhood. However, even when learning modern Chinese as an adult, it is possible to acquire a pronunciation acceptable to and understood by native Chinese speakers.

The basic unit of the language is considered to be a single syllable, and theoretically any syllable can have any one of four tones, or different pitches of the speaker's voice. In practice, though, some syllables have only one, two, or three tones. It is the existence of these tones that gives Chinese its characteristic singsong quality.

The tone or pitch can drastically alter the syllable's meaning. For example, there are four different Chinese characters that can represent the sound "ma." In the first tone it may mean "mother," but in the second tone it can mean "hemp" or "numb." In the third tone it may mean "horse," while in the fourth tone it means "to scold."

It is impossible to learn tones from a book, and it is therefore essential when studying Chinese to attend a class where the sounds are produced for the student to mimic, either on tape or by a teacher. The student should also realize that the levels of the tones are not absolute but relative, depending on the speaker's sex and age, as well as on the mood and circumstances under which the words are being uttered. The four tone sounds are also different in length; on the average the third tone is the longest and the fourth tone the shortest.

In the first tone the voice stays level at a fairly high pitch. The second tone starts in the middle register and rises. The third tone starts rather low and rises to middle or upper-middle level. The fourth tone falls sharply from fairly high to low. There is also a neutral tone which is a modified or weakened sound not having full phonetic value.

In the Pinyin system described below syllables are marked by symbols to indicate tonal level. Neutral tones have no symbol.

Tone Symbols

In Pinyin the tones are indicated by small marks above the word:

     —   = high level

     ╱   = high rising

     ˇ   = low dipping

     ╲   = high falling

     mā means "mother"   妈

     má means "hemp"   麻

     mǎ means "horse"   马

     mà means "to scold"   骂

mao means "cat"

máo means "ten cents"

(or is a surname, e.g., Chairman Mao)

mo means "spear"

mào means "hat"

猫
毛

矛
帽

In the last example, when using the word in a sentence you might, if you don't get your tones right, convey the message "I've dropped my spear" while groping around for your dime.

PHONETIC SYSTEMS

The student of Chinese usually has two objectives: to learn to write Chinese characters and to speak with an accurate rendition of Chinese sounds. Of course, some are content with learning to read and write, while others wish only to learn how to speak.

When a student aims to read, write, and speak, it is usually preferable to concentrate first on the sounds of Chinese and tackle the interesting but more complicated art of writing some time later. The task is then to devise a method whereby Chinese sounds may be represented in written form by the alphabet of the student's mother tongue. Fortunately, the English alphabet can be used to form sounds which very closely approximate Chinese sounds. Numerous systems have been devised over the years for representing these sounds in a comprehensible form. The best known systems in the English-speaking world are the Wade-Giles system, the Yale system, and the Pinyin system.

The Wade-Giles system was developed in the second half of the nineteenth century and is still used today, especially in dictionaries and textbooks. Many western Sinologists use the Wade-Giles system for the transcription of Chinese proper names.

In the early 1940s the Yale system was developed, reflecting the evolution of applied linguistics during the period between the 20s and the 40s. It is a system still widely used, particularly in teaching modern Chinese in the United States.

The Pinyin system is a further development of the Yale and other systems of romanization, and most experts agree it is the simplest, meeting the requirements of Chinese phonetics and the principles of contemporary linguistics. "Pinyin" comes from the expression *Han yu pinyin fang-an,* which literally translated means "Chinese Language Transcription Proposal" and refers to the official scheme put forward in 1958 for a Chinese phonetic alphabet.

The People's Republic of China announced in 1958 that Pinyin was to be adopted as the official transcription system. It was later announced that in 1976 Pinyin would be used in the P.R.C. for transcribing all place and proper nouns; but for some reason still not explained this did not happen.

Some years later, the State Council decided that Pinyin would be used from 1979 on for Chinese names and places in all English, French, Spanish, and German publications printed in China. This situation exists today.

There is another system, known as the National Romanization System, which was introduced into China in the 20s and, as its name suggests, was adopted by the Nationalist government as the official system. It is still used to some extent in the province of Taiwan.

Pinyin Spelling

The Chinese language does not possess an alphabet. Chinese words are written in "character" form with few brush strokes, each character having its own single-syllable pronunciation. The characters commonly used in newspapers, for example, number about 3,000. The Chinese are progressively reducing the number of strokes used to form characters in an attempt to simplify the Chinese script. (The Chinese characters in this book are in simplified form.)

The problem for the non-Chinese reader is to render the sound represented by each character in the reader's mother tongue. For most readers of English or European origin, this has meant simulating the sounds using the Latin alphabet, a procedure called romanization. The various phonetic systems adopted to do this were reviewed in the previous section.

Since January 1, 1979, the Pinyin system of romanization has been officially adopted by the People's Republic for names and places. From that date there has been only one standard way to write Chinese names and places in English and in European languages using the Latin alphabet. The United Nations Conference on the Standardization of Geographic Names has also adopted these standard forms.

For names: Mao Zedong is now used instead of Mao Tse-tung; Zhou Enlai instead of Chou En-lai; Deng Xiaoping instead of Teng Hsiao-ping; Jiang Qing instead of Chiang Ching, and so on. Note that the hyphen has been dropped for the "given" name.

For places: Zhongguo replaces China; Beijing replaces Peking; Guangzhou replaces Kwangchow; Chongqing replaces Chungking; Nanjing replaces Nanking; Xizang replaces Tibet, and so forth. However, it will be a long time before the familiar words China, Peking, Canton, Tibet, Hong Kong, Macao, etc. are phased out of usage outside the borders of China.

The adoption of standard Pinyin forms for names and places is the first step on the long road towards the full romanization in China of all Chinese characters. While such a development has many advantages, most scholars abhor the possibility. They claim it would impoverish the written language and actually reduce the level of communication between peoples of Chinese origin. It would also eliminate one of the existing cultural bonds between China and Japan, as the Japanese written language is derived from Chinese script.

Pronunciation—Some Examples

In the following guide to pronunciation of words written in Pinyin, especially note the pronunciation of

$$q, x, \text{ and } c$$

The sound represented by *q* may be illustrated by a word you will hear frequently: *qing,* meaning "please," "after you," etc., which is pronounced *ching* with the mouth puckered slightly. Thus *q* approximates the sound *ch.*

The sound represented by *c* is close to *ts* in English, as in the word "aunts."

The sound represented by *x* is somewhat like *sh* but more breathy. For example, the town of Wuxi is pronounced something like *Wooshee.*

The sound represented by *zh* is also frequently encountered in Chinese, for example, in the name of China's late Premier Zhou Enlai. The first word is pronounced almost like *Joe,* not "Chow" as newcomers are apt to say it. Another example occurs in the name of the old city of Canton, known in Chinese as Guangzhou and pronounced *Gwongjoe;* or in cities such as Hangzhou and Suzhou.

PRONUNCIATION TABLE

a	as in f*a* ther		c	as in aun*ts*
ai	as in l*i* ke		ch	as in *ch* ild
an	as in *an* kle		d	as in *d* aughter
ang	as in *ang* le		e	as in h*er*
ao	as in *ou* t		ei	as in *ei* ght
b	as in *b* oy		en	as in maid*en*

eng	as in *young*	r	as in *ur* ge
f	as in *f* ather	s	as in *s* on
g	as in *g* irl	sh	as in *sh* rill
h	as in *h* ome	t	as in *t* able
i	as in machi*ne*	u	as in r*u* de
ia	as in A*sia*	u	as in ph*ew*
ian	as in *yen*	ua	as in *ooa* h
ie	as in *yeah*	uai	as in *why*
in	as in k*een*	uan	as in *won* der
ing	as in s *ing*	uang	as in *Wong*
j	as in *j* eep	ue	as in *we* ar
k	as in *k* ing	ui	as in *way*
l	as in *l* amp	un	as in sw*oon*
m	as in *m* other	uo	as in *wa* r
n	as in *n* ose	w	as in *wo* ah
o	as in *o* ra	x	as in *sh* e
ong	as in s*ong*	y	as in *y* ou
ou	as in *coa*	z	as in a*dds*
p	as in *p* arty	zh	as in ur*ge*
q	as in *ch* eese		

PINYIN SPELLING OF CAPITALS, MAJOR TOWNS, AND PROVINCES

Official Hanyu Pinyin Spelling	Spelling Sometimes Adopted in English
Anhui	Anhwei
Anshan	Anshan
Aomen	Macao
Beibu Wan	Bac Bo Gulf
Beijing	Peking
Changjiang	Yangse River
Changsha	Changsha
Chengdu	Chengtu
Dalian	Dairen
Dong Hai	East China Sea
Fujian	Fukien
Fushun	Fushun
Fuzhou	Foochow
Gansu	Kansu
Guangdong	Kwangtung
Guangxi Zhuangzu Zizhiqu	Kwangsi Chuang Autonomous Region
Guangzhou	Canton
Guilin	Kweilin
Guizhou	Kweichow
Guiyang	Kweiyang
Hangzhou	Hangchow
Harbin	Harbin
Hebei	Hopei
Hefei	Hofei
Heilongjiang	Heilungkiang
Henan	Honan
Huanghai	Yellow Sea
Huanghe	Yellow River
Hubei	Hupeh
Huhhot	Huhehot
Hunan	Hunan
Jiangsu	Kiangsu
Jiangxi	Kiangsi
Jilin	Kirin
Jinan	Tsinan

Jinggang Shan	Chingkangshan
Kunming	Kunming
Lanzhou	Lanchow
Lhasa	Lhasa
Liaoning	Liaoning
Luoyang	Loyang
Nanchang	Nanchang
Nanhai	South China Sea
Nanhai Zhudao	South China Sea Islands
Nanjing	Nanking
Nanning	Nanning
Nei Mongol Zizhiqu	Inner Mongolia Autonomous Region
Ningxia Huizu Zizhiqu	Ningsia Hui Autonomous Region
Qingdao	Tsingtao
Qinghai	Chinghai
Shandong	Shantung
Shanxi	Shansi
Shaanxi	Shensi
Shanghai	Shanghai
Shaoshan	Shaoshan
Shenyang	Shenyang
Shenzhen	Shumchun
Shijiazhuang	Shihchiachuang
Sichuan	Szechuan
Suzhou	Soochow
Taibei	Taipei
Taiwan	Taiwan
Taiyuan	Taiyuan
Tangshan	Tangshan
Tianjin	Tientsin
Ürümqi	Urumchi
Wuhan	Wuhan
Wuxi	Wusih
Xian	Sian
Xianggang	Hong Kong
Xining	Sining
Xinjiang Uygur Zizhiqu	Singkiang Uighur Autonomous Region
Xizang Zizhiqu	Tibet Autonomous Region
Yan An	Yenan
Yinchuan	Yinchuan
Yunnan	Yunnan
Zhejiang	Chekiang
Zhengzhou	Chengchow

PINYIN SPELLING FOR TERMS USED IN MAPS AND ATLASES

Official Hanyu Pinyin Spelling	Meaning
Zhonghua Renmin Gongheguo Ditu	Map of the People's Republic of China (lit. "China People's Rep. Map.")
Shoudu	Capital
Sheng	Province
Zizhiqu	Autonomous region
Zhixiashi	City directly under the central authority
Shi	City
Xian	County
Zizhixian, Qi	Autonomous county, Banner
Cunzhen	Town or village

Jiang, He, Shui, Qu, Murun, Zangbo	River
Hu, Po, Chi, Nur, Co	Lake
Hai	Sea, lake
Wan	Gulf, Bay
Haixia	Strait, Channel
Yang	Ocean
Shuiku	Reservoir
Yunhe, Qu	Canal
Jing, Kuduk	Well

Official Hanyu Pinyin Spelling	**Meaning**
Quan, Bulag, Bulak	Spring
Qundao, Liedao	Archipelago, Islands
Dao, Yu	Island
Jiao	Reef
Jiao	Cape
Gang	Harbor, Port
Shan, Ling, Ul	Mountain, Range, Ridge
Shan, Feng	Mount, Peak
Shankou, Guan	Pass
Pendi	Basin
Shamo	Desert
Dong	East
Nan	South
Xi	West
Bei	North
Zhong	Central
Da	Great, Greater, Grand
Xiao	Little, Lesser
Zuo	Left
You	Right

USEFUL EXPRESSIONS FOR THE TRAVELER ON TOUR

English	**Pinyin**	**Chinese**
Please take me to the . . .	qing kai dào	请开到
airport	feijicháng	飞机场
railway station	huoche zhàn	火车站
embassy . . .	dàshíguan	大使馆
U.S.	Meiguó	美国
Canadian	Jianádà	加拿大
British	Yingguó	英国
French	Faguó	法国

English	Pinyin	Chinese
German	Déguó	德国
Wait a moment	deng yì deng	等一等
There are . . . pieces of my luggage missing	you . . . jiàn xì xìngli bú jiàn le	有……件行李 不见了!
Please call a taxi	qing tí wo jiàochuzuche	请替我叫出租车
Is there anyone who speaks English?	you méi you rén huì shuo Yingwén?	有没有人会说 英文?
Is there a car?	you méi you qì che?	有没有汽车
Please bring me . . .	qing ní gei wo	请你给我
coffee	kafei	咖啡
tea	chá	茶
a glass of water	yi bei shui	一杯水
May I take a photograph?	wo kéyi zhào xiàng ma?	我可以照相吗?

SIGNS YOU WILL SEE REGULARLY

English	Pinyin	Chinese
Entrance	rù kou	入口
Exit	chu kou	出口
Toilet	césuo	厕所
Ladies	nucè	女
Mens	náncè	男
Danger	wei xian	危险
Hospital	yiyuàn	医院
Bank	yínháng	银行
Restaurant	fànguar	饭馆（饭店）

English	Pinyin	Chinese
Railway Station	huoche zhàn	火车站
Post Office	yóu zhèng jú	邮政局
Telephone Office	diànhuà jú	电话局
Telegraph Office	diànbào jú	电报局
CAAC Airline Office	min hong jú	民航局

IN THE HOTEL

English	Pinyin	Chinese
What is my room number?	wode fángjiān ji háo?	我的房间几号?
Please write it down	qing xiexià lai	请写下来
Where is my luggage?	qing wèn, wode xíngli zài nar?	请问，我的行李在那儿?
Where is the laundry bag?	xiyidài zài nar?	洗衣袋在那儿?
Please may I have my laundry ready by . . .	qing ba wo xihao de yifù náhuilái	请把我洗好的衣服拿回来
this evening	jintian wanshàng	今天晚上
tomorrow morning	míngtian shàngwu	明天上午
midday tomorrow	míngtian zhongwu (shí èr dian zhong)	明天中午（十二点钟）
Please bring me . . .	qing gei wo	请给我
some boiled water	kai shui	开水
some tea	yìdiar chá	一点茶
some milk	yìdiar niúnai	一点牛奶
a bottle of soft drink	yi píng qì shui	一瓶汽水
some toilet paper	yi juar wèisheng zhi	一卷卫生纸（厕纸）
a towel	yi tiáo máojin	一条毛巾

English	Pinyin	Chinese
some soap	yi kuài féizào	一块肥皂
I want to rest	wo yào xiuxi	我要休息休息
I leave tomorrow	wo míngtian zou	我明天走
This is broken	zhèige huàile	这个坏了
Please send someone to re-pair . . .	qing jiào rén lái xiuli	请叫人来修理
the lavatory	cèsuo	厕所
the light	diàn deng	电灯
Please come in	qing jìnlai	请进来
After you, be my guest	qing	请
I want to make a long-distance telephone call	wo yào da chángtú diànhuà	我要打长途电话
Please call a taxi for me	qing ni ti wo jiào chuzuche lái	请你替我叫出租车
Where is the money exchange?	huàn qián chù zái nar?	换钱处在那儿
Where is the restaurant?	fànguan zài nar?	饭馆在那儿
I want to have my hair washed	wo yào xi tóu	我要洗头
I want to have my hair cut	wo yào li fà	我要理发
Not too short, please	qing, bú yào tài duan	请不要太短
Comrade (men &women)	Tungzhi	同志
Friends	Pengyou	朋友

AT THE RESTAURANT

English	Pinyin	Chinese
Please bring . . .	qing lái . . .	请来

English	Pinyin	Chinese
a bottle of beer	yi píng píjiu	一瓶啤酒
wine (grape)	pútao jiu	普通酒
Shaoxing wine	Shàoxìng jiu	绍兴酒
soft drink	qì shui	汽水
mineral water	Laoshan	崂山（矿泉水）
mao tai	máotái	茅台
glasses	boli bei	玻璃杯
fruit juice	guozi zhi	果子汁
fruit	shui guo	水果
napkins	can jin	餐巾
chopsticks	kuàizi	筷子
soy sauce	jiàng yóu	酱油
rice	mifàn	米饭
tea	chá	茶
coffee	kafei	咖啡
cigarettes	yan	烟
ice cubes	bing kuài	冰块
Tasty! Tastes good	hén hao chi	很好吃
Enough	goule	够了
Bottoms up! Cheers!	gan bei	干杯！
Friendship	youyì	友谊

SHOPPING

English	Pinyin	Chinese
I want to buy . . .	wo yào mai	我要买
a cake of soap	yi kuài féizào	一块肥皂
shaving cream	gua lian gao	刮脸膏
toothbrush	yá shuazi	牙刷子
toothpaste	yágào	牙膏

English	Pinyin	Chinese
writing paper	xie zì zhi	写字纸
notebook	benzi	本子
ballpoint pen	yuánzi bi	原子笔
pencil	qian bi	铅笔
envelopes	xìnfeng	信封
batteries	diàn chí	电池
black shoe polish	heise xié yóu	黑鞋油
brown shoe polish	kafeise xié yóu	咖啡鞋油
black-and-white film	hei bái jiaojuàn	黑白胶卷
filter cigarettes	lù zui yan	泸咀烟
nonfilter cigarettes	putong yan	普通烟
fruit	shui guo	水果
fruit juice	guozhi	果汁
mosquito coils	wén xiang	蚊香
How much is this?	zhèige duosháo qián?	这个多少钱?
I'll buy this one	wo yào mai zhèige	我要买这个
This is too large	zhèige tài dà	这个太大
This is too small	zheige tài xiao	这个太小
Please give me a receipt	qing gei wo fápiào	请给我发票

AT THE POST AND TELEGRAPH OFFICE

English	Pinyin	Chinese
I want to buy some stamps	wo yào mai yóupiào	我要买邮票
An aerogram, please	qing ní gei wo yi zhang hángkong yóujiàn	请你给我一张 航空邮件
By airmail, please	zhèi feng xìn, wo yáo jì hángkong	这封信，我要寄 航空
Where is the mailbox?	xìntong zài nar?	信桶在那儿?

English	Pinyin	Chinese
Express cable	kuài diàn	快电
Urgent cable	jí diàn	急电
Ordinary cable	putong diàn	普通电
Telex	yung hu dian	用户电报（电传）

NUMBERS

English	Pinyin	Chinese
1, 2, 3, 4, 5	yi, èr, san, sì, wu	一二三四五
6, 7, 8, 9, 10	liù, qi, ba, jiu, shí	六七八九十
20, 30, 40	èr shí, san shí, sì shí	二十，三十，四十
50, 60, 70	wu shí, liù shí, qi shí	五十，六十，七十
80, 90, 100	ba shí, jiu shí, yi bai	八十，九十．一百
101, 102	yi bai yi, yi bai èr	一百零一，一百零二
103, 104	yi bai san, yi bai sì	一百零三，一百零四

MONEY

The currency of the People's Republic of China is called Renminbi (RMB), or "People's Currency."

The unit of currency is the yuan, and the notation is ¥. There are ¥ 1 notes, ¥ 2 notes, ¥ 5 notes, ¥ 10 notes, and ¥ 100 notes. In speech, these are known as "one kuài" (pronounced "kwy"), "two kuài," and so on.

Every yuan is divided into 10 10-cent pieces written as "jiao" but pronounced "máo."

A yuan is also divided into 100 cents written "fen" and pronounced "fen."

English	Pinyin	Chinese
How much is that? (money)	duo shao qián	多少钱？
How much?	duo shao?	多少？
one dollar	yi kuài	一块

English	Pinyin	Chinese
twenty cents	liang máo	两毛
10-cent piece	yi máo	一毛
3 cents	san fen	三分
5 cents	wu fen	五分
10 cents	shí fen	十分
25 cents	liang máo wu	两毛五
50 cents	wu máo	五毛
75 cents	qi máo wu	七毛五
1 yuan	yi kuài	一块
2 yuan	èr kuài	二块
10 yuan	shí kuài	十块
50 yuan	wu shí kuài	五十块
100 yuan	yi bai kuài	一百块

TIME

English	Pinyin	Chinese
Monday	xingqi yi	星期一
Tuesday	xingqi èr	星期二
Wednesday	xingqi san	星期三
Thursday	xingqi sì	星期四
Friday	xingqi wu	星期五
Saturday	xingqi liù	星期六
Sunday	xingqi rì *or* xingqi tian	星期日　or　星期天

English	Pinyin	Chinese
morning	shàngwu	上午
afternoon	xiàwu	下午
evening	wanshàng	晚上
today	jingtian	今天
tomorrow	míngtian	明天
yesterday	zuótian	昨天
day after tomorrow	houtian	后天
7 A.M.; 8 A.M.	shàngwu qidian; shàngwu badian	上午七点；上午八点
6 P.M.; 7 P.M.	xiawu liùdian; xiàwu qidian	下午六点；下午七点
now, at present	xiànzài	现在
next week	xià xingqi	下星期

MONTHS

The months are formed by placing the numeral 1, 2, 3, etc. before the word "yuè."

English	Pinyin	Chinese
January	yi yuè	一月
February	èr yuè	二月
March	san yuè	三月
April	sì yuè	四月
May	wu yuè	五月
June	liù yuè	六月
July	qi yuè	七月

English	Pinyin	Chinese
August	ba yuè	八月
September	jiu yuè	九月
October	shí yuè	十月
November	shí yi yuè	十一月
December	shí èr yuè	十二月

NATIONS—A SELECTION

English	Pinyin	Chinese
United States	Méiguó	美国
Canada	Jianádà	加拿大
Great Britain	Yingguó	英国
Australia	Àodàliyà	澳大利亚
New Zealand	Xinxilán	新西兰
(West) Germany	Déguó	德国
France	Faguó (Falánxi)	法国（法兰西）
Switzerland	Ruìshì	瑞士
Netherlands	Hèlán	荷兰
Belgium	Bilìshì	比利时
Austria	Àodì	奥地利
Italy	Yìdàlì	意大利
Spain	Xibanyá	西班牙
Finland	Fenlán	芬兰

English	Pinyin	Chinese
Sweden	Ruìdian	瑞典
Mexico	Mòxige	墨西哥
Japan	Rìben	日本
Soviet Russia	Sulián	苏联
Norway	Nuówei	挪威
Denmark	Danmài	丹麦
Argentina	Agentíng	阿根廷
Brazil	Baxi	巴西

Index

Map pages are in **boldface**.

Fodor's Travel Guides

U.S. Guides

Alaska
Arizona
Boston
California
Cape Cod
The Carolinas & the
  Georgia Coast
The Chesapeake
  Region
Chicago
Colorado
Disney World & the
  Orlando Area

Florida
Hawaii
The Jersey Shore
Las Vegas
Los Angeles
Maui
Miami & the Keys
New England
New Mexico
New Orleans
New York City
New York City
  (Pocket Guide)

New York State
Pacific North Coast
Philadelphia
The Rockies
San Diego
San Francisco
San Francisco
  (Pocket Guide)
The South
Texas
USA
The Upper Great
  Lakes Region

Virgin Islands
Virginia & Maryland
Waikiki
Washington, D.C.

Foreign Guides

Acapulco
Amsterdam
Australia
Austria
The Bahamas
The Bahamas
  (Pocket Guide)
Baja & the Pacific
  Coast Resorts
Barbados
Belgium &
  Luxembourg
Bermuda
Brazil
Budget Europe
Canada
Canada's Atlantic
  Provinces
Cancun, Cozumel,
  Yucatan Peninsula
Caribbean
Central America
China

Eastern Europe
Egypt
Europe
Europe's Great
  Cities
France
Germany
Great Britain
Greece
The Himalayan
  Countries
Holland
Hong Kong
India
Ireland
Israel
Italy
Italy's Great Cities
Jamaica
Japan
Kenya, Tanzania,
  Seychelles
Korea

Lisbon
London
London Companion
London
  (Pocket Guide)
Madrid & Barcelona
Mexico
Mexico City
Montreal &
  Quebec City
Morocco
Munich
New Zealand
Paris
Paris (Pocket Guide)
Portugal
Puerto Rico
  (Pocket Guide)
Rio de Janeiro
Rome
Saint Martin/
  Sint Maarten
Scandinavia

Scandinavian Cities
Scotland
Singapore
South America
South Pacific
Southeast Asia
Soviet Union
Spain
Sweden
Switzerland
Sydney
Thailand
Tokyo
Toronto
Turkey
Vienna
Yugoslavia

Special-Interest Guides

Bed & Breakfast
  Guide to the Mid-
  Atlantic States

Bed & Breakfast
  Guide to New
  England
Cruises & Ports
  of Call

A Shopper's Guide
  to London
Health & Fitness
  Vacations
Shopping in Europe

Skiing in North
  America
Sunday in New York
Touring Europe